Middle East Politics Today

Florida A&M University, Tallahassee
Florida Atlantic University, Boca Raton
Florida Gulf Coast University, Ft. Myers
Florida International University, Miami
Florida State University, Tallahassee

University of Central Florida, Orlando
University of Florida, Gainesville
University of North Florida, Jacksonville
University of South Florida, Tampa
University of West Florida, Pensacola

Middle East Politics Today

Government and Civil Society

Tareq Y. Ismael

University Press of Florida
Gainesville/Tallahassee/Tampa/Boca Raton
Pensacola/Orlando/Miami/Jacksonville/Ft. Myers

Copyright 2001 by Tareq Y. Ismael
Printed in the United States of America on acid-free paper
06 05 04 03 02 01 6 5 4 3 2 1

Library of Congress Cataloging-in-Publication Data
Ismael, Tareq Y.
    Middle East politics today: government and civil society / Tareq Y. Ismael.
    p. cm.
    Includes bibliographical references and index.
    ISBN 0-8130-2098-0 (cloth: alk. paper)
    1. Middle East—Politics and government—1979– .   2. Civil society—Middle East.   I. Title.
JQ1758.A58 I86 2001
320.3'0956—dc21   2001034075

The University Press of Florida is the scholarly publishing agency for the State University System of Florida, comprising Florida A&M University, Florida Atlantic University, Florida Gulf Coast University, Florida International University, Florida State University, University of Central Florida, University of Florida, University of North Florida, University of South Florida, and University of West Florida.

University Press of Florida
15 Northwest 15th Street
Gainesville, FL 32611–2079
http://www.upf.com

To Aisha and Nadia
and wildflowers
and robins
and all the wonders of spring and summer,
the delight of their grandparents
in the autumn of their lives

Contents

Tables

Preface

*T*he approach adopted in this volume for the study of the Middle East today primarily argues that the patterns of politics over time are more important in understanding Middle Eastern politics at any given point in time than events in time. Presented as individual occurrences, political events in the region generally seem irrational or chimerical to the casual observer. Indeed, journalistic reports on the region tend to reinforce this image. However, events examined from the perspective of patterns over time are more likely to be understood in terms of their underlying dynamics rather than their sensational characteristics. Thus, the perspective adopted here is that the Middle East today is related to the Middle East of yesterday, not by events in time but by patterns through time. Events are significant as markers of patterns, rather than because of their intrinsic characteristics, no matter how interesting they may be.

In this context, *Middle East Politics Today: Government and Civil Society* addresses the interaction between government and society to examine the contemporary Middle East in the context of the patterns of its politics over time. *Civil society* denotes the politically active sector of society that can be distinguished from the state sector. Although the term first became popular in the eighteenth century, it was introduced into political theory largely as a result of social contract doctrine. It denotes the state of society in which patterns of association are accepted and endorsed by the members of a society. However, most users of the term were initially influenced by state of nature theory, seeing the individual as an atomic constituent of the civil society, which is composed by contract, consent, or submission from these self-dependent atoms. Hegel introduced a second understanding in which civil society was not formed by contract but was the sphere of contract, that is, of free association between individuals. As such, it is not a complete entity but one aspect of the political order, another aspect of which is the state. As a result of Hegel's view, many political theorists now distinguish "civil society" from that of the "state," using the first to denote forms of association that are voluntary, and in general not dependent on law, and the second to denote the legal and political institutions that protect, endorse, and bring to completion the powerful but inarticulate forces of social union.

With the beginning of the new millennium and the intense disruption to patterns of politics throughout the world brought about by the end of the cold war, what future can the people of the Middle East envision, based on their experience and current political conditions? The linkage between the discourse on civil society and the state creates a tension in Middle Eastern politics evident throughout the course of the twentieth century. Civil society exists in latent form in the modern Middle East and has a tremendous historical legacy. The state, by comparison, is the dominant force in contemporary Middle East politics, but lacks roots in the region's long and venerable history.

The organization of this volume reflects the effort to set events in the context of patterns of continuity and change. Part 1 introduces the dynamics of history and Islamic culture that have been dominant forces in shaping the patterns of Middle East politics in the twentieth century. It also examines political movements that have brought about today's oppressive state and eroded civil society. Part 2 addresses the political legacy and current political environment of each state in a comparative survey of the region.

Each chapter in part 2 attempts to clarify the patterns of political continuity and change that have evolved in the country being examined. The reader may examine each chapter individually as well as in reference to the dynamics of history, Islamic culture, and the nature of the contemporary state discussed in part 1. Each case study attempts to elucidate the patterns of political continuity and change that have evolved in the state since 1918. Thus, current events may be examined from the perspective of these patterns both within the individual state and within the region generally. The volume as a whole is an attempt to make it possible for readers to understand current events in the context of historical patterns.

Since this is meant to be a general survey, and an extensive body of basic knowledge on the subject is readily available elsewhere, the principle of parsimony should encourage readers to search bibliographic references in order to increase their understanding and enhance their further study of the region. Thus, unless the topic is controversial, or the information contentious, or there is a direct quotation, footnotes have been eliminated. With the explosion of on-line resources, we would be remiss not to encourage the use of Web-based daily and weekly newspapers from the region. Exposure to these publications may well serve as a filter against the often uniform views expressed within the mainstream western media and aid one's understanding of the region through indigenous voices.

The map of the modern Middle East is colored by arbitrary borders mostly established by the colonial powers around the end of the First World War, making a definition of the region problematic. Although it is distinguishable from Europe chiefly by religion and from the Far East by culture, the Middle East, located roughly between southwest Asia and the eastern Mediterranean, has no tangible geographic periphery. Historically, its meaning has been determined by political rather than geographic factors and therefore has changed in correspondence to the growth of western interest and involvement in the area. The very term *Middle East* is not a product of the region but a western creation. The *Near East,* although often used interchangeably with *Middle East,* is an antiquated concept, originating around the fifteenth century with the early European forays into China and India. Contemporary archaeologists often use the term to distinguish the ancient civilizations of Mesopotamia, Egypt, and Persia from those of the Far Eastern civilizations of China and Japan. Clearly, both usages have little meaning at all from an Asian or African geographic point of view. The term *Middle East* came into popular usage during the Second World War with the establishment of the British Middle East Command and the Allied Middle East Supply Center. Both organizations served the North African and Asian theaters west of India. Since then, the appellation *Middle East* has become increasingly popular while that of *Near East* has become obsolete.

The delineation of the Middle East adhered to in this volume includes the Fertile Crescent (Iraq, Syria, Lebanon, Palestine, Israel, and Jordan); the northern belt (Turkey and Iran); the Nile Valley (Egypt and Sudan); the Arabian Peninsula including both Yemen and the members of the Gulf Cooperation Council (Saudi Arabia, Qatar, Kuwait, Bahrain, Oman, and the United Arab Emirates); and North Africa, including all of the states of the Arab Maghrib Union (Morocco, Algeria, Tunisia, Mauritania, and Libya). This division, like any other, is rather arbitrary, but it takes into account the major characteristics shared by the encompassed states as well as differences they have with those states flanking the region. While the selection of case studies was restricted by space (necessitating the omission of North Africa and Sudan), the operational definition outlined above remains valid.

There are many systems of transliteration from Middle Eastern languages, and no particular standards prevail. In an effort to aid the reader's recognition of names and places, the system of transliteration used in this book follows popular usage in the media rather than a formal system. Turkish names and words are spelled in their modern Turkish form.

This endeavor would not have been possible without the contributions and encouragement, sometimes beyond the call of duty, of friends and colleagues who graciously read drafts of each chapter. All offered valuable suggestions, comments, and critical evaluations in a number of ways. However, the views expressed in this book, as well as any errors of fact or omission, are the fault of the author alone. John Sigler of Carleton University and Mehrdad Izady of Harvard were gracious enough to examine drafts of the chapter dealing with history, while William Haddad of the University of California at Fullerton kindly commented on the final version. John Strawson of the University of East London read chapter 2, on the role Islam has played in politics and the historical development of the region. Bahman Baktiari of the University of Maine and Mahdi Moslem of Oxford University were kind enough to offer comments on chapter 4 on the Islamic Republic of Iran, as was Farhad Atai of Imam Sadeq University in Iran. Chapter 5, the Republic of Turkey, was read by Seymen Atasoy of Eastern Mediterranean University (TRNC) as well as Cem C. Cakmak, of the same institution and formerly of the Middle East Technical University in Ankara, in addition to Mustafa Aydin, of Ankara University. Eberhard Kienle of the School of Oriental and African Studies, University of London, examined chapter 7—Syria and Lebanon—as did Erik Knudson of Eastern Mediterranean University and Walid Kazziha of the American University in Cairo. 'Adnan M. Hayajneh of the Hashemite University in Jordan and Kamel Abu Jabr, of the Diplomatic Institute of Jordan and the University of Jordan, reviewed chapter 8, the Hashemite Kingdom of Jordan. Chapter 9, examining the state of Israel, was reviewed by Michael Keren of Tel Aviv University and Andrej Kreutz of the University of Lodz, Poland. Mohammed 'Abdullah Al-Mahmoud, of the United Arab Emirates University, kindly examined chapter 10 on the Gulf Cooperation Council countries. I would be remiss if I did not thank Moncef Khaddar of the University of Tunis and the American University in Cairo for thoroughly and meticulously examining much of the manuscript.

I also wish to acknowledge the contributions of the University of Calgary Research Grants Committee and the Social Science and Humanities Research Council of Canada for their support of this project over the past decade. Judi Powell and Doreen Neville were invaluable during the many drafts and rewrites of the past nine years. The research assistance provided by Leben Nelson Moro in Cairo and Youssry O. Wagdy, as well as John

Measor, my graduate research assistant at the University of Calgary, particularly in tracking down the footnotes, obscure details, and help with the updating have proven a further valuable resource in the completion of this project.

PART I

Forces in
Middle East Politics

CHAPTER I

The Burden of History

From Empire to Nation-States

Although historians disagree over the exact birthplace of western civilization, they do agree that it originated either in the Nile Valley or in Mesopotamia along the Tigris and Euphrates Rivers.[1] The area was always the crossroads of migrating peoples. Successive invasions between 5000 B.C.E. and the time of Christ made the region a melting pot of races and cultures. The first of the invaders, an Asiatic variant of the Mediterranean race called the Sumerians, established a number of city-states between the Tigris and the Euphrates. The Sumerians synthesized the agricultural and urban revolutions.[2] The first work of literature, the tales of Gilgamesh, ruler of Uruk, comes from Sumeria. The maintenance and administration of canals and an irrigation system indicated an understanding of technology as well as the governmental structures required to maintain it.

The prosperity of these city-states attracted Semitic people from the surrounding areas who founded the state of Akkad along the middle Euphrates in modern-day Iraq at the beginning of the third millennium B.C.E. For 1,000 years Sumerian and Akkadian states competed. The threat of outside invasion by the non-Semitic Elamites resulted in the unification of all Mesopotamia by Hammurabi of Babylon about 1700 B.C.E. During this same period, the Hamites established in the Nile Valley a monarchical state that they were able to hold relatively undisturbed until about 500 B.C.E., when the Persians established their empire. Semitic tribes from Arabia continued to fill the area between Sumeria and the Nile, establishing communities in the area known as the Fertile Crescent.[3]

Between 1700 and 100 B.C.E., the Indo-European invasions brought successive waves of conquerors, each of whom extended the empire. By 500 B.C.E., Persians had established an empire bordered by the Indus

3

River, the Black Sea, and western Egypt. The Persian Empire, a monarchical state, was effectively controlled by the appointment of satraps to the governorship of its territorial subdivisions and by the use of spies who watched the satraps and reported directly to the emperor. The Persians also built a highway, the Royal Road, from Sardis on the Aegean Sea to their capital at Susa.

One of the major problems facing the Persian Empire was the expansionist tendency of the Greeks. Ultimately the failure to control the growth of Greek power was to have a dramatic impact on the development of the Middle East. The conquests of Alexander the Great ushered in a new age for Greece and for the Middle East. It had been Alexander's wish to blend the cultures of Greece and Persia, and before his death in 323 B.C.E. he was partially successful in Hellenizing the Middle East through his encouragement of intermarriage between his soldiers and the native women and his founding of a number of cities styled after those of Greece. After Alexander's death, the empire broke up into a series of kingdoms ruled by his generals. The Hellenizing effects of his conquest persisted, however. For the next two centuries, under the Seleucid kings (named for Seleucus, the Greek general who founded the dynasty) and the Ptolemaic dynasty in Egypt (after the general Ptolemy), the Middle East continued to enjoy intellectual and artistic achievement but to remain politically unstable.

In the first century B.C.E., the Romans began to extend their influence into the Middle East. They had already conquered North Africa from the Semitic Carthaginians and Semitic-Berber native dynasties in Numidia and Mauritania (modern Libya, Algeria, and Morocco, and source of the name of modern Mauritania). Eventually the Romans established political control over the Middle East as far eastward as Damascus and as far south as present-day Saudi Arabia, and well into the eastern portion of modern-day Turkey. What is now Iraq and Iran was controlled by Persian dynasties, first by the Parthian Empire (ca. 200 B.C.E.–220 C.E.) and then the Sassanid dynasty (220–641 C.E.). The eastern portion of the Roman Empire was tremendously influential, and centers in the East—such as Alexandria in Egypt, Antioch in Syria, and Caesarea in what is now Israel—were noted as centers of learning and commerce.

Roman control of the Middle East, however, was never tranquil. The first centuries of occupation witnessed a number of large-scale uprisings, and serious conflict with the Parthians and Sassanids was a continuing state of affairs. The furthest point of Roman expansion was under the emperor Trajan in the early second century, when Mesopotamia—modern Iraq—was briefly under Roman control. After a long period of civil war and repeated barbarian invasions, the Roman

Empire was split into two portions from the early fourth century onwards—the western empire, with its capital at Rome, and the more affluent, populous, and secure eastern empire with its capital at Constantinople (modern Istanbul). The western empire collapsed under a combination of Germanic invasion and internal dissension in the late fifth century, and the last emperor in Rome was deposed in 476 by a barbarian chieftain named Odovacar, but the eastern empire survived and prospered. Its population spoke Greek and had adopted the Christian faith, and over time the eastern Roman Empire transformed itself into the medieval Byzantine Empire.

It might be expected that the spread of Christianity throughout the Roman Empire would have brought unity, but in fact it had not. From Constantinople to North Africa, each area developed its own sect of Christianity, culture, and language, and the only link between them was that they had experienced Roman control. Christianity also developed a following outside the empire, in Parthian and Sassanid lands. These Christians, mostly of the Nestorian sect, influenced Persia from the fourth century until the Arab conquest. It has been suggested that, despite an overt attachment to the ancient Persian Zoroastrian religion, the later Sassanid Empire could best be characterized as predominantly Christian.

The Byzantine and Sassanid Empires were bitter rivals in the sixth and early seventh centuries, fighting wars from 540 to 629. Starting in 603, a Persian army under Khusro II Aparwez, ostensibly to intervene in a Byzantine dynastic struggle, marched across the Fertile Crescent, capturing the great city of Antioch in 613, Jerusalem in 614, and Egypt in 619, and placing a Persian army virtually at the gates of Constantinople in 620. The Byzantine counterstroke under the emperor Heraclius crippled both empires, impoverishing the Byzantines with its expense and pushing deep into Persian territory to loot cities, towns, and the estates of the Persian nobility. The war leveled the territories that had been fought over. Cities were left half deserted, harsh taxes stripped the wealth of the remaining people, and the Persian dynasty lost most of its armed strength. The Byzantines recaptured razed territory that produced no revenue, and they even melted down the golden ornaments of their great churches to coin gold for their mercenaries and Caucasian allies. Into this mass of political and religious strife came the Arab conquerors from the Arabian Peninsula. The Arabs had formed economic ties between the city dwellers and their own nomadic bands. Thus, as the cities allied themselves with the Arab tribes and began to seek power on the basis of their position on the east-west trade routes, western influence finally began to fall away.[4]

Islam and the Islamic Empire

By the seventh century, Mecca, midway along the trade route between Yemen and Syria, was the principal trade and cultural center of the Arabian Peninsula. It had become a wealthy and independent city, which had achieved its position of eminence through trade and financial speculation in the Red Sea and the eastern Mediterranean. The city maintained relations with the tribes in the surrounding area but carefully kept itself neutral in the conflicts between the warring Sassanid and Byzantine Empires through skillful diplomacy and leadership. The city was governed by a council of clan leaders, but each clan was independent of the council and responsible only to itself. Religion in Mecca was diverse, ranging from magic and pantheism to a clan-centered code of honor. The Arabs were steeped in idolatry, and Arabia was rife with tribal rivalry and warfare. Just as Mecca reached the height of rebelliousness, it found itself on the eve of transformation.

In this environment, in the year 610, the future prophet Muhammad, at about the age of forty, began proselytizing a religion of individual surrender to a monotheistic God. At first his movement drew a number of converts from the poor, the middle class, and a few from the wealthy elite. Although there were no religious rules or laws enacted at the time, the Meccan ruling elite proved wary of the prophetic calling of Muhammad. To submit to the will of one sovereign God meant not only divesting the elite's socioeconomic structure of privileges and power but also promising to transform society as a whole. As a result, economic sanctions were taken against the new converts, who became known as Muslims, and they were persecuted severely. The Prophet, to protect his followers, decided to send them to Ethiopia as refugees until the hostile climate could be overcome. However, in 622, a worsening of the situation forced Muhammad to regroup the Muslims and move them to Medina. Engaged in civil dispute, Medina accepted him as an arbitrator for the city's clans. From the safety of Medina he consolidated his religion and became the undisputed leader of the first Islamic city-state. This migration was called the Hijra, and so important was it to the success of Islam that it marks the first year of the Islamic calendar. Eight years of intermittent warfare with Mecca followed, until finally that city was brought to terms and Muhammad and the Muslims were able to return victorious. It was during this hostile period that Islam began to spread throughout the Arabian Peninsula and the social precepts of this new order were developed.

From the death of the prophet Muhammad in 632 until the establishment of the Umayyad dynasty at Damascus in 661, the chief men of

Mecca and Medina chose the Muslim leaders. Each of the four leaders chosen during this period—Abu Bakr, 'Umar, 'Uthman, and 'Ali—was named in his turn caliph (or successor), and he functioned as both religious and political head of the Muslim nation. During their years in power, these four men succeeded in completely entrenching Islam on the Arabian Peninsula and wresting from the Byzantine and Sassanid Empires the lands of modern Syria, Palestine, Egypt, Iraq, and Iran. The hollow shell of a Roman Empire the Byzantines had reconquered over the past century from the Germanic Vandals in North Africa and more recently in the Middle East from Persian domination simply collapsed under the Arab onslaught. Antioch in Syria fell in 637; Alexandria in Egypt in 642; and a rebuilt Carthage, in what is now Tunisia, in 698. The Muslims and Byzantines remained implacable enemies for the next eight centuries, with only Constantinople standing between Islam and Europe, often defeating Islamic armies at its very gates. The Persians fought savagely, but had nowhere to retreat after the battle of Qadesiya in 637, where the remainder of the Persian military nobility was crushed and the Sassanid Empire disappeared. Thus, the Islamic Empire expanded and rose to prominence, both religiously and politically, by the latter half of the seventh century. This remarkable conquest was viewed as liberation by the Semitic inhabitants of the Levant who viewed the Greeks and Persians as foreign occupiers.

During the reign of the third caliph, 'Uthman Ibn 'Affan (644–56), members of the Umayyad clan were given governorship over the four principal provinces, while the office of consulship was given to his cousin, Marawan Ibn al-Hakam. When 'Uthman came to office, the province of Syria was divided into four subprovinces, each having a governor selected on the basis of merit, integrity, and skill. Mu'awiyah Ibn Abu Sufian governed Damascus; Yazid Ibn Abu Sufian governed what is today Jordan; 'Abdel Rahman Ibn Alqamah (from Kinana) ruled what is presently Palestine; and 'Omyr Ibn Sa'ad al-Ansari (from Medina) ruled Homs. With the death of the last three governors, 'Uthman consolidated the whole of Syria under his cousin Mu'awiyah, a position that made him the most powerful provincial ruler.

'Uthman appointed Sa'id Ibn al-'As (an Umayyad) to rule Kufa; his cousin, 'Abdullah Ibn 'Amr Ibn Kriz, to rule over Basra; and his "brother," 'Abdullah Ibn Sa'ad Ibn Abi Sarh, to rule over Egypt. 'Abdullah was not 'Uthman's brother by birth, but he had been breast-fed by 'Uthman's mother. Only Mu'awiyah proved qualified to govern.[5] 'Uthman was a God-loving caliph and religiously impeccable, but he was also a tactless statesman and a poor judge of character. Whereas 'Uthman misinterpreted Islamic exhortation for doing goodness to family members by pursuing such appointments, the Muslim community perceived them as acts of nepotism and favoritism, which Islam had admonished.

Social unrest eventually led to 'Uthman's assassination. After the assassination of 'Ali in 661, who had been 'Uthman's successor, the Umayyad family, using today's Syria as their base, established a dynasty that was to last for nearly a century under Mu'awiyah. The Umayyads left four marks on the Islamic world: they moved the imperial capital to Damascus; they enlarged the empire to include North Africa, Spain, and parts of Asia; they reorganized and improved the imperial administration; and they replaced the elective caliphate with a hereditary monarchical system. The Umayyads at first partitioned the empire into five vice-royalties ruled by appointees, but due to the lack of qualified Arab personnel, they left the administration of each area in the hands of locals who had administered it before the conquest.

During the last half of the Umayyad reign, however, the Middle East was again torn by civil strife. Charges of corruption against the Damascene rulers aided the Abbasids, descendants of Muhammad's uncle, in their claim to the caliphate. In 750, Abu al-'Abbas overthrew the Umayyads and founded the Abbasid dynasty. The Umayyads, however, retained control of Spain, which was the furthest Islamic penetration into western Europe. The Franks under Charles Martel at Tours had stopped the Arab armies in what is now southern France in 732. The Byzantines had defeated an Arab invasion fleet in the very harbor of Constantinople in 717, halting expansion northeastward.

Following their rise to power, the Abbasids moved the capital to a new location, later named Baghdad, in what was the first planned city in history. Devising a system of viziers, they ruled their steadily dwindling dominions, marking the return of Persian influence to the Middle East. Although the Sassanids had fallen from power in Persia, the Persian language survived and became an integral part of the Abbasid court, as Persian nobility and culture formed the backbone of the governing class.[6] The disintegration of empire witnessed an independent state established in Morocco in 788, followed in 800 by a declaration of African independence. Finally, in the tenth century, the Fatimids of Egypt succeeded in establishing a western Muslim world that stretched from Syria to the Strait of Gibraltar, and in the east all the Muslim provinces in and near India fell away from Baghdad's control. In the eleventh century, the Seljuk Turks, fierce invaders from the east, seized the last of the Abbasid Empire. Concurrent with the Abbasid political decline, however, was the development of a rich culture. Notable contributions were made to philosophy and poetry, and a distinct Abbasid

style of architecture evolved, featuring tall minarets with complex geo-
metrical designs, which has had a lasting influence throughout Asia and
the Middle East. The works of Greek scholars were translated, studied,
and supplemented, and work of original and lasting value was composed in fields as diverse as medicine, astronomy, and geography.

By the eleventh century, both the Seljuk and Fatimid Empires began
to disintegrate into numerous minor states. Then, unable to present any
organized resistance, these states watched helplessly as Christian crusaders from western Europe drove a wedge of control into Syria and
Palestine during the twelfth century. The crusaders' fortunes in the
Middle East were directly related to Muslim disunity. Thus, when Salah-
al-Din Alayyubi (Saladin) was able to regroup the torn Muslim world—
starting with Egypt and proceeding on to Syria, northern Iraq, Hejaz,
Nubia, and North Africa—he extended his influence from the Nile to
the Tigris.

Upon his death, however, Arab disunity allowed the crusaders to
regain their lost territory until the Mamluks took control of Egypt.
However, as the Mamluks were driving the European crusaders from the
Middle East, there emerged a new threat. Mongol hordes under Genghis
Khan and his successors invaded from the east in a wave of destruction,
conquering as far south as Damascus, until in 1260 they were defeated
and repulsed from Syria by the Mamluk rulers of Egypt. The Mamluks,
Turkish warrior slaves of Egypt's former rulers, established feudalism as
the new social order in the region. The conquests of the Mongolian
Turks, led by Timur Leng (Tamerlane), in the last part of the fourteenth
century ended Mamluk control east of Egypt, resulted in a subdued and
diminished Ottoman state, and left Iran dismembered and weak.

The Ottoman Empire

From the time of the Seljuk invasions, the Turks had come to dominate
the Middle East, largely at the expense of the Byzantines. By the last half
of the twelfth century, the sultanate in Constantinople and the holdings
of Salah-al-Din included the greater part of Islam. The Mongol invasions, however, destroyed both. Then, about 1300, Osman, a Turkish
chieftain, began to consolidate by conquest and alliance a number of
small towns in Asia Minor, creating a small principality on the frontiers
between the Seljuk and Byzantine Empires.[7] According to Halil Inalcik
this principality

> devoted itself to *gaza* (holy war) on the frontiers of the Seljukid Sul-
> tanate in Asia Minor and the Byzantine Empire. Its initial *gazi* frontier
> character influenced the state's historical existence for six centuries: its

dynamic conquest policy, its basic military structure, and the predominance of the military class within an empire that successfully accommodated disparate religious, cultural, and ethnic elements. The society to which these elements gave rise followed in the tradition of earlier Islamic empires, but some of its most unique features were created by the Ottomans themselves.[8]

Although Osman died in 1324, the Ottoman Turks continued to expand their sphere of influence in the Middle East. In 1354, an earthquake destroyed the walls and fortifications of Gallipoli and thus enabled the Ottomans to cross the Dardanelles and gain a foothold in Europe. From there, aided by the chaos created by the Black Death, they were able to extend their dominion into the Balkans. At the same time, they pressed south and east, establishing their control over the greater part of Asia Minor. Tamerlane, however, met Ottoman expansion in the east. Tamerlane defeated Bayezid I (1389–1402) in 1402 at the Battle of Ankara and then conquered to the west as far as the Mediterranean.[9] Rather than holding Ottoman territory directly, Tamerlane divided the Ottoman conquests of Europe and the holdings of Osman and Orhan I (1324–62, Osman's son) in Asia among Bayezid's sons in exchange for an oath of allegiance.[10] Upon Tamerlane's death in 1405, the Ottoman princes asserted their independence of the Timurids, but the Ottoman state remained fragmented among Bayezid's four sons.[11] It was one of the sons of Bayezid, Mehmed I (1413–21), who reunited the Ottoman state and set it on the path of further conquest. His grandson, Mehmed II (1451–81), pushed into Hungary and southern Russia, completed the conquest of Turkey, and in 1453 captured Constantinople (renamed Istanbul), thus laying the foundation of the Ottoman Empire.

Salim I (1512–20) continued the expansion, adding Syria, Palestine, Egypt, and Algeria, until finally, in the late seventeenth century, Tunisia, the Red Sea coast of Arabia, and small holdings around the Black Sea and the Persian Gulf were brought into the empire.[12] The victory over the Mamluks in Egypt (1516–17), and occupation of the Hejaz (1517), including the holy cities of Mecca and Medina, elevated the Ottoman sultan to the formal leadership of all Muslims under the institution of the caliphate. This unification of the Ottoman concept of *gaza*, with the Islamic notion of *jihad* (holy war), gave them formal leadership over much of the Islamic world.[13]

The Ottoman Empire was ruled from the sultan's *divan* (council) in Istanbul, which met daily to make decisions on such matters as military or civil administration. The sultan was theoretically the absolute ruler of both secular state and temporal caliph of the Muslim *ummah,* but the sultan's household exercised considerable power. Also, the degree of local autonomy increased with the degree of remoteness from the administrative center at Istanbul. Because the Turks were a minority within their empire (they were a majority only in Asia Minor), administrators were drawn from any source, including nations outside the empire's borders. Officials, therefore, could be chosen on the basis of ability and loyalty to the sultan, rather than on the basis of racial or religious considerations, creating a meritocracy.[14] Indeed, the corps of Janissaries, the famed bodyguard of the sultans, was composed entirely of Islamized Christians.[15] Bribery was common in the appointment of officials, but a palace school was maintained for the education of those who would occupy the high positions of government, and thus it was ensured that the sultan and his immediate circle of deputies would be men capable of ruling.

The Ottoman Empire exercised considerable influence in European affairs, partly because of its encroachments on European territory and partly because of its control of the east-west trade routes. Particularly strong were the Ottoman ties with the Italian city-states, which represented at that time the western terminus of the Asian trade routes. But these ties were eventually weakened when in the 1490s the Portuguese discovered a new east-west passage around southern Africa.

The sixteenth century also saw the development of Istanbul as a cultural center. The city was largely rebuilt, and it is still famous for its Ottoman mosques. A canon of Turkish literature was developed, as the court retained both poets and historians. Also, Ottoman naval development in the Mediterranean led to advances in geography and cartography.[16] After the seventeenth century, however, Ottoman decline was rapid. A combination of weak sultans, civil wars, and Ottoman concessions to European states led to European expansion, driving the Ottomans first from Europe and then from North Africa. At the start of the First World War, the Ottoman Empire was reduced to Turkey, Mesopotamia, Syria, Palestine, and the fringes of Arabia.

Early European Involvement

In 1498 Vasco da Gama, a Portuguese navigator, reached India by sailing around Africa, and in the years immediately following, other Portuguese sailors retraced da Gama's route, establishing trading stations in the Persian Gulf and diverting much of the eastern trade from its earlier route through the Middle East. For a time the Portuguese enjoyed a monopoly over the Cape route. The transport costs were as much as one-third less than those of the overland route via the Middle East. And to further inhibit overland transport, the Portuguese attempted to blockade shipping on the Red Sea and Persian Gulf. Thus, Lisbon quickly replaced Venice as the European clearinghouse for Indian goods. When military efforts by the Middle Eastern and European powers failed to destroy the Portuguese monopoly, first Venice and then France and England signed trade agreements with the Turks to secure more favorable transport terms for their goods across Ottoman territory. While France and England contended for the Middle East trade, England and Holland supplanted the Portuguese in the East Indies. However, Holland, drained by its wars with the English and the French, was unable to compete with England; the Dutch withdrawal from the east left the British East India Company with a monopoly on the southern trade routes.

In the eighteenth century, European expansion became more overt. As governmental authority broke down in East Asia and the Middle East, France and England sought to secure their trade through physical supervision of the sources and routes of that trade. England seized political power in large parts of the Far East and attempted to do the same in the Middle East. France countered in 1798 with Napoleon's expedition to Egypt. The defeat of the French fleet at Aboukir Bay, however, checked French ambitions, and three years later they withdrew their army to Europe. Napoleon's fall left England the dominant power in the Middle East, but the Egyptians had been impressed by the display of military efficiency by the French expeditionary force, and Muhammad Ali and his son, Ibrahim Pasha, laid designs to build the nucleus of a modern empire. Under the leadership of these two men, Egypt rapidly expanded into the Sudan, Ethiopia, Palestine, Syria, and Arabia. British ties with the Ottomans, however, checked further expansion.

Having refused aid from Britain in modernizing their state, Muhammad 'Ali and Ibrahim Pasha turned instead to France. The French responded with trained administrators, military missions, aid in opening schools, and the training of young Egyptians in French colleges. Half of Egypt's trade, however, remained with England, and France's setback in the Franco-Prussian War left the English dominant once more throughout the Middle East.

Besides the modernization of Egypt, the French made yet another great contribution to Middle Eastern affairs. Building on a brief period of influence in the Ottoman Empire during the Crimean War, the French pressed for permission to build the Suez Canal. Granted permission by the Ottomans and supported by Russia and Austria, France was able to open the canal in 1869, thus linking Asia with the West via the Middle East. The Suez Canal was to open a new chapter of Middle Eastern relations with the West and the world at large. The incompetence and extravagance of Muhammad Ali's successors in Egypt resulted in the accumulation of an enormous national debt to the European powers. In 1879, therefore, France and England established dual political control of Egypt in an effort to secure their investments and seized control of the Suez Canal. When the Egyptians resisted this control, the British occupied the country and held all political power there from 1882 until the First World War. Although British rule was helpful in reducing the Egyptian debt, the country itself was not improved materially. Further, the use of English officials at all levels of control kept the Egyptians from developing any abilities of self-rule.

In the nineteenth century the Ottoman Empire was one of the major areas of European competition. The Roman Catholics of France engaged with the Orthodox Christians of Russia in controversies over who should control the Christian holy places in the Middle East. Russian expansionists desired to secure their entrance to the Mediterranean through the Bosphorus and to restore a Christian empire centered in Istanbul, and Austria, fearing that Russia would outflank her from the south, wanted to check Russian expansion into Ottoman territory. England, too, was apprehensive about the effect Russian expansion into the Mediterranean would have upon passage to India. In addition, both England and France were interested in Ottoman territory that lay astride the trade routes to their extensive commercial interests in the Orient. A series of small wars waged between these nations over Turkish territory kept any one of them from dominating the Ottoman Empire, now disparagingly called the "sick man" of Europe. In 1872 a serious threat to Anglo-French interests in Turkey appeared when the Ottomans brought in German investment and engineering to build the Balkan railway system. During the next thirty years, the Germans increased their influence in Turkey through extension of the railway as well as trade agreements with the Ottoman government.

The Twentieth-Century Middle East to the First World War

European intervention in the Middle East during the nineteenth century fostered nationalism. European armies, technicians, and administrators clearly demonstrated the abilities of, and the benefits accruing to, a modernized nation. Christian missionaries aided in establishing Arab schools, laying an educational foundation for modernization, and potential Muslim leaders were given the opportunity to observe and learn European methods in the academies of France and Germany. Moreover, efforts by Muhammad 'Ali and his son, Ibrahim Pasha, to unite Arabs encouraged Muslims to consider the possibilities of establishing, and the advantages of operating, a modern Arab state.

The English occupation of Egypt spurred nationalism in that state. Given that British personnel were brought in to fill administrative positions, these posts were denied to educated Egyptians. Inspired by the gains of the Young Turks, Egyptian nationalists engaged in violent agitation for self-government. Concerned for the security of the Suez Canal and their investments in Egypt, the British could not yet accede to Egyptian demands for self-government. In 1911, they reasserted their grip on Egyptian affairs with the appointment of Lord Kitchener as administrator of Egypt. Kitchener initiated programs of legislative reforms designed to break down the power of Egyptian agriculturists. Although nationalist resistance was strong, an outbreak of violence was averted by the start of the First World War. The oppression and absolutism of the Ottoman sultan and the winds of change from Europe had led to the growth of Turkish nationalism. In 1889 students at the Istanbul Military Medical College, led by Albanian student Ibrahim Temo, organized the Committee of Union and Progress (CUP), a secret society modeled after the Italian Carbonari. The movement quickly branched into the Military Academy, the Naval Academy, the Artillery and Engineering School, the Veterinary School, and the Civil College. With the blessing and support of the major ethnic and religious groups in the Ottoman Empire, the CUP led the revolution of 1908. The Young Turk Revolution, which brought in its wake a declaration of the equality of all races in the Ottoman Empire, had stirred Arab nationalism, especially in Syria and Iraq. By 1909, however, conflict within the CUP divided its members along national lines and resulted in the growth of extremism on both sides. Centralization of government and Turkification of all elements within the empire became the objectives of the Young Turks. In the Arab world rapidly growing secret societies, which at first hoped to gain autonomy within the Ottoman Empire, now advocated complete independence. Moreover, German influence had grown with Turkish nationalism. Germany's *Drang nach Osten* (drive to the east) led to German aid in Turkish modernization, development of the Berlin to Baghdad railway, and the eventual emergence of Turkey as Germany's military ally.

The first months of war saw little hostility in the Middle East, but in October 1914 the British began instigating revolt in Arabia. In the celebrated correspondence between Sharif Hussein of Mecca and Sir Henry McMahon, British high commissioner for Egypt and the Sudan, McMahon promised that an independent Arab state would be created when the war ended in return for an Arab revolt against their Turkish masters. This state was to encompass the area demarcated on the north by a line drawn eastward from Alexandretta to the Iranian frontier and thence southward to the Persian Gulf and to include the entire Arabian Peninsula with the exception of Aden. At the same time, however, the Allies were negotiating the division of both Turkish and Arab lands among themselves. The Constantinople Agreement of March 1915 gave Russia the right to annex certain areas in Asia Minor and Thrace while guaranteeing French and British interests in Turkey and Iran. The Treaty of London, signed in April 1915, gave Italy territorial claims in North Africa and Asia Minor. Finally, in May 1916, the secret Sykes-Picot Agreement was concluded defining the exact territories to be taken over by Russia, France, and Britain and recognizing the spheres of influence of France and Britain in the Arab territories. In conflict with both the McMahon promises and the Sykes-Picot Agreement, the famous Balfour Declaration surfaced on 2 November 1917. This declaration, conceived without the consultation and consent of the Arabs, stated that the British government viewed with favor the aspirations of those Jewish people who wished to establish a national home in Palestine. Although "view with favor" was not a guarantee of British support for a Jewish state, it paved the way for Zionists to claim Palestine. This declaration set the stage for a crisis in the Middle East that has lasted to this day.

Precipitated by the Young Turks' declaration of martial law in Syria, by the execution and deportation of Arab nationalists, and by the promises of an independent Arab state contained in the Hussein-McMahon correspondences, the Arab revolt of 5 June 1916 began. While hardly successful in mobilizing mass Arab support, the Arab revolt's military aspect was immensely helpful to the British in that it diverted Turkish reinforcements from facing the British advance through Palestine, ended German propaganda in Arabia, and forestalled the possibility of a German submarine base on the Red Sea.

Between Two World Wars

The Arab revolt during the First World War had been purchased with Allied promises of an independent Arab state. At the end of the war, however, each of the victorious western European powers hoped to seize a chunk of Middle Eastern territory. After two years of nearly fruitless negotiations, the Treaty of Sèvres with the Ottomans was signed on 10 August 1920. Turkey renounced all claim to Arabia, Egypt,

Mesopotamia, and Syria. Great Britain was given a protectorate in Egypt, a mandate over Palestine, and tutelage over nominally independent Mesopotamia. Syria was placed under a French mandate, and the rulers of Arabia were granted nominal independence.

The end of the war saw Allied forces in possession of much of Turkey. Greece was to occupy that state until such time as the Allies would be able to agree on its future. However, the Turks, led by Mustafa Kemal, took matters into their own hands. In 1920 the Turks raised the banner of revolt, and after two years of warfare they had forced the withdrawal of the Greek authorities as well as the occupying forces. The Turks established a new government, deposed the Ottoman sultan, and voided the legislation of his government. In 1924 they met the Allies at the Lausanne Conference to determine Turkey's future. The Lausanne Conference severed the last remnants of Ottoman rule from Turkey, leaving the Turkish Republic an independent state.

In 1923 Mustafa Kemal was elected president of the republic. A year later, he declared the official dissolution of the empire. Until his death in 1938, he directed the modernization of Turkey and encouraged the resolution of the two problems that had most concerned foreign interests: demarcation of the Iraqi-Turkish frontier in Mosul province, and foreign use of the Dardanelles and the Bosphorus. The first issue was resolved by awarding the province of Mosul to Iraq, for which Turkey received £500,000 from the Iraqi government as well as a guarantee of 10 percent of all oil royalties paid to Iraq by the concessionaire for the next twenty-five years. An international agreement allowing Turkey to fortify the Straits settled the second issue.

In the Fertile Crescent the French established a governorship in Lebanon incorporating Mount Lebanon, Beirut, and lands to the south of Beirut predominantly populated by Shi'a. They agreed, in 1936, to make Lebanon an independent state, but later refused to sign the treaties that would have granted independence. In Syria, also under French mandate, independence was again promised and later denied, and dissension arose between the French administrators and Syrian leaders over Syria's loss of Lebanon.

The British occupation of Iraq was met with fierce resistance that led to British attempts to form a stable government. In 1921 a kingdom was established, and Iraq achieved a state of nominal independence. Full independence, however, was not achieved until Iraq was admitted to the League of Nations in 1932. Oil was the great issue in Iraqi politics, both international and domestic. The Iraqis turned this problem into a source of strength by basing their economy on oil concessions. Palestine, occupied by the British, was torn by conflict between Arabs and

Jews. Each group wanted an independent Palestine for itself. According to the 1922 census, Arabs constituted approximately 90 percent of the population; the remaining 10 percent were Jews and other non-Arabs. But Jewish immigration and effective Zionist representation built up Jewish strength. With the immigration of skilled Jews and with massive financial aid from the world's Jewry, Jewish settlements in Palestine flourished. British rule was a hopeless attempt to aid the Jews while protecting Arab rights.

Egypt continued after the First World War as a British protectorate under martial law. Strong nationalist resistance, however, forced promises of eventual independence. The instability of Egyptian politics, Britain's preoccupation with other domestic and colonial matters, and allied concern for the Suez made the prospects for independence difficult. The Anglo-Egyptian Treaty of 1936 began the process of making Egypt an independent state. Elsewhere, Great Britain maintained its influence on the southern coast of the Persian Gulf, and Ibn Saud consolidated the Arabian Peninsula under his rule in 1927 and proclaimed himself king of Hejaz and Nejd.

Iran, an independent state at the start of the First World War, successfully resisted British attempts to incorporate it into the British Empire and foiled Russian attempts to secure Iranian territory. Then, in 1920 Reza Khan overthrew the Iranian government and attempted to establish a republic modeled after Mustafa Kemal's Turkey. Religious opposition, however, prevented this transformation, and in 1925 Reza Khan became shah. Reza Khan's strength was sufficient to carry out several reforms: the power of religion and of religious institutions was reduced; 15,000 miles of roads and the Trans-Iranian railway were built; efforts were made toward the improvement of irrigation and agricultural methods were advanced; and a number of industries were supported by state capital. Finally, oil concessions to Britain were reduced, and domestic control over the petroleum industry increased economic independence. In international affairs Iran sought close ties with Germany in order to protect itself from British and Russian encroachments. The Second World War, however, ended German influence and forced Iran to cooperate with Britain and reinvigorated the Soviet Union.

Initially most Middle Eastern peoples saw the Second World War as a European affair that had little effect on them. Only Turkey saw itself in the path of aggression, but since German and Russian dominance were equally repugnant, Turkey maintained careful neutrality. Iran attempted to tie itself to Germany, but England and Russia occupied the country, deposed Reza Shah, and forced Iranian cooperation. The collapse of France weakened French control in Lebanon and Syria, and attempts made by the Vichy government and France after France's liberation to reassert that control were met by strong British and indigenous opposition. Iraqi nationalists endeavored to capitalize on Britain's weakness in the early part of the war in order to stage a revolt, but they were unsuccessful. In Palestine, the Arabs were largely unconcerned with the war, but Nazi atrocities against the European Jews led to the creation of a Zionist Brigade and to dramatically increased Jewish immigration to Palestine. This massive immigration in turn led to increased hostilities between Arabs and Jews, and Palestine erupted with escalating acts of terror and ever-increasing violence. Egypt was used as a staging area for the British army, and Egyptian troops fought in the desert and in defense of Egypt in North Africa. At the end of the Second World War, Britain remained the paramount power in the Middle East, maintaining effective control over Egypt, Palestine, Transjordan, Iraq, southern Arabia, and the Persian Gulf. However, Britain also emerged from the war a weakened state unable to withstand nationalist pressures fomenting in the states under its suzerainty.[17]

The Legacy of Nationalism

Nationalism as a political ideology is a fairly recent phenomenon in the Middle East, and in 1900 it was still only nascent. However, the rapid development of nationalism has proved to be both a constructive and a destructive force in the Middle East. For example, reform and modernization have often been the first goals of the several indigenous Middle Eastern nationalist movements (Turkish, Arab, Iranian), and these efforts to reform and to modernize have contributed to the civil and social advancement of the area's peoples. However, ethnocentrism, irredentism, and national sovereignty have also been integral parts of the nationalist programs; and these aspects of nationalism have resulted in conflict and upheaval, as, for example, in the cases of Turkish versus Arab nationalism within the Ottoman Empire, Zionism versus Arab nationalism, and Turkish, Arab, and Iranian nationalism versus European colonialism. This section will deal with Arab nationalism, as the particular cases of Turkish and Iranian nationalism as well as Zionism are best examined in the context of the development of the states of Turkey, Iran, and Israel discussed in part 2.

Arab Nationalism

It is argued that the true birth of Arab nationalism took place with the rise of Islam. Islam replaced the narrow blood and tribal ties with a broader religious patriotism. The Arabs were united into one great community of the faithful, the *Ummah,* or the nation of Islam (Qur'an

3:110), and Islam was the prime originator of Arab national life and political unity on the Arabian Peninsula. As Islam and Arab power expanded, an Arab feeling of distinctness was reinforced as it expanded and came into contact with other races and cultures. This feeling, which in modern terms could be equivalent to national consciousness, was overridden by the Islamic religious paradigm of what is equivalent to a nation based on the concept of brotherhood of believers (Qur'an 49:10). Islamic nationalism thus transcends geographical and ethnic boundaries, which are the parameters of the modern western notion of nationalism. Under the Ottoman Empire, Muslim Arabs were proud of Turkish power and prestige. Consistently Arabs acquiesced to Turkish rule, as Turks were Muslims, and until later, in the nineteenth century, the Ottomans did not attempt to "Turkify" the Arabs, continuing the early Muslim administrative practice based on religion—the millet system, which respected the autonomy and integrity of each religious community. It was religion and language that sustained the national unity of Arabs, despite living under Turkish rule.

Against this backdrop, one may understand three subsequent revolts in Cairo during the French invasion of Egypt between 1798 and 1801. French occupation was seen as a sacrilege to the religious national pride of Muslims in Egypt, despite admiration for French material progress and scientific technology. Sheikh Hasan al-'Attar, a teacher in al-Azhar, was asked by the French to visit their newly established scientific laboratory; after a number of visits and through further acquaintance with French sciences, al-'Attar wrote of his experiences, urging Muslims to learn and apply new sciences and technology. Arab national consciousness of dignity and honor had survived throughout the centuries, and it was given new impetus by the educational system of Muhammad 'Ali of Egypt and his son Ibrahim Pasha, ruler of Syria, in the first half of the nineteenth century.

The activities of two Albanians, Muhammad 'Ali and his son Ibrahim, helped to kindle an Arab renaissance as they ascended to power in Egypt shortly after French withdrawal—early in the nineteenth century—making Egypt virtually independent of Istanbul. Unquestionably one of the greatest rulers of his time, 'Ali introduced important reforms in education, agriculture, industry, commerce, sanitation, and social custom. The reforms in education were of particular significance to the revitalization of Arab culture. Primary and secondary schools, preparatory schools, a medical college, and a polytechnic school staffed predominantly by Egyptians were established. Many Egyptian youth were sent to Europe for a western education, and schools were opened in Egypt for the training of civil servants.

Complementing his reforms in education, Muhammad 'Ali established a government printing press at Cairo in 1822 and thus made Cairo the intellectual center of the Arab world. The Bulaq press in Egypt printed a wide variety of Arabic books, both classical as well as translations from foreign languages. A great deal of this production was sent to Syria, Lebanon, and Palestine during the Egyptian occupation in the 1830s. Volumes discussed science, medicine, theology, mysticism, language, history, geography, and travel. Books were purchased by all of the community. By 1850 the press had printed over three hundred books in Arabic, Turkish, and Persian. It also printed newspapers in both Arabic and French that not only disseminated western ideas but also gave Arabs a vehicle through which they could regenerate their own literature.

At the same time that Muhammad 'Ali was introducing his reforms in Egypt, his son Ibrahim was encouraging modernization in Syria. Having succeeded to the governorship of Syria in 1833 as a result of his successful military campaign against Ottoman forces, Ibrahim embarked upon a program of reform similar to that of his father's in Egypt. Sydney Nettleton Fisher writes of Ibrahim's eight-year rule in Syria that "taxes were regularized, justice was more sure for people of all religions, commerce was encouraged, privileges for foreigners were less abused, education was stimulated, law and order were prevalent."[18]

Ibrahim's administration came to an end in 1840 when the British forced Muhammad 'Ali to withdraw his son from Syria. Nevertheless, Syria remained the cradle of nascent Arab nationalism. As a result of Ibrahim's edicts, Syria was opened to American Protestants and French Catholics, who were allowed to establish missionary schools. By 1860 the American missionaries had established thirty-three schools in Lebanon, Syria, and Palestine, and in 1866 the influential Syrian Protestant College in Beirut (now the American University) opened its doors. The French missionaries also founded many schools in the area, including the University of St. Joseph at Beirut in 1875. The mission of those missionary schools was to teach elements as native schools did; plus the Protestant version of the Bible. The main aim was to propagate a sectarian faith. The Syrian Protestant College did not edit or revive any of the standard Arabic texts up to the turn of the century. They instead used texts of Arabic classics edited and published in Egypt.[19]

The tremendous demand for education that resulted from the establishment of schools in Egypt and Syria was not confined to those two countries but spread in unprecedented proportions throughout the Arab world. This demand was met partially by a great increase in printed materials. Publishing houses and newspapers were established in many of the major cities, and the great volume of material printed became both a means for and a measure of the spread of nationalism throughout the Arab provinces of the Ottoman Empire.

Educational societies to facilitate inquiry into Arab history, art, and literature were also organized. The Society of Arts and Sciences was created in 1847 with the help of American missionaries, and Jesuits organized the Oriental Society in 1850. Generally, however, Muslim Arabs refused to join these groups because of their foreign Christian missionary affiliations. In 1857 the Syrian Scientific Society was established on a nonsectarian basis, and under its auspices Christians and Muslims joined to foster and develop their common Arab heritage. From this society came Arab nationalism's first rallying cry, Ibrahim Yaziji's "Ode to Patriotism," a poem appealing to the Arabs to unite and to revolt against Turkish oppression. Contemporaries, however, including the Christian Lebanese Salim Sarkis, assigned its authorship to a noted Muslim sheikh he did not name, probably, as a protective measure against the Turkish censor.[20]

The first organized response to Ibrahim Yaziji's appeal for unity and revolt came in the form of secret societies in Beirut, Damascus, Tripoli, and other cities. Their primary activity was posting placards that urged the Arabs to rebel. Such urging turned out to be premature. As a result, the secret societies proved short-lived. Nevertheless, these secret societies did serve an important purpose, for their placards contained not only statements urging the Arabs to rebellion but also specific demands that served as a model for the Arab political programs that would be formulated later. Included in these demands were the independence of Syria, in union with Lebanon, the recognition of Arabic as a national language, an end to censorship, the removal of other restrictions on the freedom of expression, and the use of only locally recruited units for local military service.[21] In the second half of the nineteenth century, and in response to large-scale Ottoman centralization, western encroachment, and a feeling of Ottoman inability to protect Arab provinces, Arab leaders called for autonomous Arab government in Arab provinces within the Ottoman Empire.

Complete independence, before 1908, was harbored only in the minds of a few Muslim extremists and primarily among the Christians of Mount Lebanon. All the literature of the period testifies to the spirit of nonseparation. Arab intelligentsia and reformers, like Jamal al-Din al-Afghani (1838–97), could not conceive of an alternative model to the Islamic paradigm. However, the proposal of ʿAbdel Rahman al-Kawakibi (1854–1909) to establish a Muslim state united under a

Qurishi-born Arab caliph captured the imagination of the Arab world and shifted the center of leadership from Christians to Muslims in the Arab national movement.

After the British occupation of Egypt in 1882, however, Egyptian leaders became preoccupied with removing the British; thus, it was in Beirut and Damascus that the search for Arab emancipation was concentrated. At the time of the Young Turk's revolt in 1908, Arab leaders hoped that the Ottoman program of the Committee of Union and Progress would bring about decentralization of the empire and give the Arabs an equal voice in the empire's government. Thus, for a time, the Arabs sought emancipation through cooperation with the Young Turks. As a measure of their sincerity, the Young Turks pressured Sultan 'Abdel Hamid into appointing Sharif Hussain as governor of the Hejaz, keeper of the holy places, and prince of Mecca. When this appointment was made in 1908, the Ottoman Arab Fraternity was created as a society for the defense of the Ottoman Constitution and the promotion of Arab welfare. In 1909, the society and other non-Turkish political groups were forced to go underground by the Young Turks' program of centralization and Turkification.

Numerous Arab societies, some clandestine and some public, came together to disseminate Arab nationalist ideas. Notable among them were the Literary Club of Istanbul, the Ottoman Decentralization Party in Cairo, al-Kahtaniya, and al-Jam'iyah al-'Arabiyah al-Fatat, of which the former two were public and the latter two underground. The Literary Club, founded in 1909 and recognized by the CUP because of its ostensible cultural rather than political objectives, played a significant role in that it "provided centres in which Arabs from all parts of the empire felt at home and talked freely in an atmosphere in which minds relaxed and the traffic of ideas could move."[22] Its membership reached thousands, and branches were established in Syria and Iraq.

The second public group, the Ottoman Decentralization Party, was founded in Cairo in 1912 for the purpose of winning equality and autonomy for the Arab provinces within the framework of the Ottoman Empire. Branches were established throughout Syria, and close contact was maintained with other Arab nationalist associations. This organization provided the Arabs with the first extensive political machinery that could coordinate their activities and maintain concerted and continuous pressure to achieve a specific political program. Al-Kahtaniya, a secret society organized in 1909, also had a well-defined program, advocating the creation of a Turko-Arab empire on the Austro-Hungarian model. But it was short-lived, and its chief contribution to the Arab nationalist movement lay in its attempt to enlist Arab officers serving in the Ottoman army into the nationalist movement.

Of these major organizations, al-Fatat, a clandestine society organized by Muslim Arab students in Paris in 1911, was the only one to reject fully the idea of collaboration with the Turks and integration into a decentralized empire. It worked for the creation of a sovereign Arab state and within a short time became an effective and widespread force. When in 1913 an interfaith Committee of Reform won public acclaim and enthusiasm for its open circulation of a plan for Arab autonomy, with the consequence that it was disbanded and many of its members arrested, al-Fatat took the initiative to convene the first Arab Congress at Paris in 1913. Representatives from most of the Arab nationalist organizations participated under the sponsorship of the Ottoman Decentralization Party. The Paris Platform that they promulgated was a moderate program calling for reform within the empire to bring the Arabs and other non-Turkish nationalities a greater amount of local autonomy. To placate Arabs, Istanbul ostensibly accepted this program, but it remained unenforced.

Partly out of this hoax was born a secret society, al-'Ahd, organized by 'Aziz 'Ali al-Misri, an Egyptian major on the Ottoman general staff who had been a founder of al-Kahtaniya. Al-'Ahd advocated essentially the same program as al-Kahtaniya, and in 1914 the Turks arrested al-Misri on a trumped-up charge of treason in the Italian campaigns in Libya and sentenced him to death. Although he subsequently was pardoned, al-Misri's arrest and trial not only outraged the Arab leaders but aroused the masses. With this act, the Turks destroyed any hope for Arab-Turkish cooperation. The Arab national movement now fully crystallized in a drive for an independent Arab state.

Although the various nationalist groups now had unanimity of purpose, unanimity of action against the Ottoman government was more difficult to achieve. However, the European powers fighting the war believed they could unhinge the region from Ottoman domination.[23] Britain, France, and Russia decided to partition the region after the war and force the diminution of Turkish influence. European intervention helped to coalesce the many factions into a united front behind the titular leadership of Sharif Hussein, who favored cooperation with the British and the Allies in return for an independent Arab state. But even though the various factions were united under Hussein, many of them still feared that cooperation with the Allies would result in European domination. They believed that a Turkish defeat would result in the dismemberment of Arab lands by the French and the British unless one or more of the Allied powers guaranteed the creation of an independent Arab state. Therefore, in 1915 the Arab revolutionists drafted the Damascus Protocol, which embodied their demands for an independent Arab state that would encompass all of the lands of western Asia that were culturally and linguistically Arabic. In return, the Arabs would revolt against the Ottoman Empire. This protocol was transmitted to Hussein, and it provided the basis for the controversial correspondence between Hussein and Sir Henry McMahon, the British high commissioner of Egypt. McMahon accepted the conditions of the Damascus Protocol on behalf of the British government, and on 5 June 1916, the Arab revolt was launched.

Thus, when the Paris Peace Conference convened in 1919, Prince Faisal attended as the representative of a people who had made a significant contribution to the Allied war effort. Armed with Allied promises of Arab independence—the Hussein-McMahon correspondence, Britain's Declaration to the Seven (a reaffirmation of Britain's pledge made to seven Arab leaders in Cairo in June 1918), President Wilson's Fourteen Points, and the Anglo-French Declaration of November 1918 (again reaffirming Allied promises)—Faisal prepared to demand the fulfillment of those promises. But Britain had made other treaties and agreements conflicting with Arab aspirations, most notably the Balfour Declaration of 1917 and the Sykes-Picot Agreement of 1916, and did not intend to fulfill its pledge to the Arabs. In an attempt to forestall British and French designs to dismember the Middle East for their own advantages, President Wilson sent the King-Crane Commission to Syria and Iraq to determine the wishes of the people regarding their future rule. Two recommendations, both directly relevant to these agreements, were strongly urged in its report to the peace conference. The first stressed that the unity of Syria (which up to that time included Palestine and Lebanon) be maintained, because "the territory concerned is too limited, the population too small, and the economic, geographical, racial, and language unity too manifest, to make the setting up of independent states within its boundaries desirable, if such division can possibly be avoided. The country is very largely Arab in language, culture, traditions, and customs."[24] The second concerned the establishment of a Jewish national home. The commission reported that the "anti-Zionist feeling in Palestine and Syria is intense and *not likely to be flouted.*"[25] It recommended that the Zionist program be greatly reduced because it could be carried out only by force of arms.

Realizing that the French and British intended to disregard Arab aspirations, and with hopes set upon the King-Crane Commission, Arab nationalist leaders in Syria organized elections and convened the first

Arab Parliament on 2 July 1919. Known as the General Syrian Congress, its resolutions may be briefly summarized:

(a) Recognition of the independence of Syria, including Palestine, as a sovereign state with the Emir Faisal as king; recognition of the independence of Iraq.

(b) Repudiation of the Sykes-Picot Agreement and the Balfour Declaration and of any plan for the partition of Syria or the creation of a Jewish Commonwealth in Palestine.

(c) Rejection of the political tutelage implied in the proposed mandatory systems but acceptance of foreign assistance for a limited period, provided it did not conflict with national independence and unity, preference being given to American or—failing American—to British assistance.

(d) Rejection of French assistance in any form.[26]

In March 1920 the congress declared the independence of Syria and Iraq and demanded the evacuation of foreign troops. However, in April the Allied Supreme Council, meeting at San Remo, disregarded the congress's decisions, Allied promises, and the King-Crane report and divided the Arab provinces into several mandates: Syria and Lebanon under France, and Palestine, Transjordan, and Iraq under Britain. Also, the Balfour Declaration, so abhorrent to the Arabs, was reaffirmed.

The effect of the mandate system on the Arab nationalist movement was most dramatic. Under the Turks the Arabs had at least enjoyed a uniform political status (except for parts of the coastal fringe of the peninsula). Now they were fragmented into a multiplicity of states, each one subjected to the political institutions of its particular mandatory power. Thus, Iraq and Transjordan, under Britain, were monarchical with parliamentary government, and Lebanon and Syria, under France, were republican. Palestine remained without any definite political character. The Arabian Peninsula alone remained independent but was itself carved into five relatively weak states, which were later unified under Ibn Sa'ud.

As a result of the mandate system, the nationalist movement fragmented and each group became preoccupied with the struggle for power and control within its own locality. Hence, a separate history began for each country. But all Arabs shared the bitter disillusionment with the results of a war that had played so piteously with their dreams of independence and had reduced them from the status of dissatisfied citizens under Ottoman hegemony to hapless subjects under colonial suzerainty. Although this sense of disillusionment was a common bond that united all Arabs in sympathy, it was not sufficiently strong to regenerate the Arab nationalist movement, and it was not until just prior to the Second World War that the nationalist movement again fused into a program of united action. The occasion for this united action was the Palestine-Arab revolt of 1936. In fact, the first violent expression of Arab feelings occurred in Palestine on Easter Sunday in April 1920. Arabs revolted again in May 1921. After a relatively quiet period, Palestinian Arabs broke out in revolt for the third time in August 1929. The major rebellion against British occupation and Zionist-sponsored immigration was carried out between 1936 and 1939. Committees for the defense of Palestine were organized throughout the Arab world, and in 1938 the various groups merged to form the World Interparliamentary Congress of Arab and Muslim Countries for the Defense of Palestine.

The Middle East after the Second World War

Four major turning points have characterized the Middle East since 1945. First, in 1948, Zionist Jews living in the British-controlled territory of Palestine declared an independent state of Israel. This ushered in strong sentiments of military-centered nationalism, and the entire region became embroiled in war. With the 1967 defeat of the Arab military forces at the hands of the Israelis, it became clear that the military nationalists had failed to provide answers to the most pressing issues of the region, including social and economic disparities, Israeli occupation of more Arab territory, and the questions of civil society. The second turning point occurred in 1978 when Egypt came to terms on a peace accord with Israel at Camp David. The next turning point was the 1982 Israeli invasion of Lebanon. The inability of any Arab government to successfully respond to the Israeli invasion led to the growth of alternative centers of power throughout the region in the various guises of radical Islam. Finally, the devastation and structural changes brought forth by the 1991 Gulf war and the subsequent Madrid and Oslo peace processes have forever altered the political landscape of the entire region.

During the Second World War, unrest continued throughout the Arab lands, resulting in the abortive coups of Rashid ʿAli al-Gilani in Iraq and General ʿAziz ʿAli al-Misri in Egypt. In recognition of this fomenting nationalist dissatisfaction, Anthony Eden, the British foreign minister, declared in May 1941 that Great Britain realized that "many Arab thinkers desire for the Arab peoples a greater degree of unity than they now enjoy. . . . His Majesty's Government for their part will give full support to any scheme that commands general approval."[27] In response to Eden's declaration, Nuri al-Saʿid, the Iraqi prime minister, circulated his own plan for the creation of a Greater Syria that was to include Syria, Lebanon, Palestine, and Transjordan, and for the formation of an Arab

League. The concept of a Greater Syria was opposed, but the idea of an Arab League gathered support, and by 1945 the Arab League pact was formalized with Iraq, Syria, Lebanon, Transjordan, Saudi Arabia, and Egypt as its members. Every Arab state subsequently joined as it achieved independence, and by 1977 the league had twenty-two members. The purpose of the Arab League was to promote cooperation among the member states in communications, health, and economics, as well as social and cultural matters. It guaranteed each member's sovereignty and could force no member to take any action. Although the league initially aroused enthusiasm, its failure to organize the Arab states effectively to oppose the Zionists during the first Palestine war discredited the organization among Arab nationalists.

When the state of Israel was established in May 1948, 750,000 Palestinians became refugees; this had greater ramifications than simply the failure of the Arab League. The Zionist victory led many youthful nationalists to condemn Arab society as a whole and to attempt, within a decade of the Palestine war, military-led nationalist revolutions in Syria, Jordan, Iraq, Lebanon, and Egypt. Today all Arab states but one have achieved national independence. British intrigue and a military victory gave Palestine to the Zionists. The UN Partition Plan in 1947 paved the way for the proclamation of the state of Israel in Palestine in May 1948.

The Militarization of Nationalism in the Arab World

The nationalist movements that came to power in the 1950s and 1960s were dedicated to the concept of Arab unity as a means of regaining control over the course and pattern of Arab development. The new nationalists were more aggressive and ideologically committed in their outlook than the old nationalists had been—pointing to the loss of Palestine as an example of the ineffectiveness of the leadership of the old guard. The new nationalists were dedicated to restructuring the regional and domestic environments. As the most technological and modern institution within Middle Eastern society, the military quickly became the principal recruiting ground for the nationalists. With the involvement of a generation of young military officers, the military was soon politicized. Unlike their predecessors, the new nationalists saw the military as the fastest, most effective, and most efficient vehicle for change available to their developing societies. This model was soon adopted throughout the region with military coups: Syria in 1949, Egypt in 1952, Iraq in 1958, Yemen in 1962, and Libya in 1969.

The most successful example and the most emulated occurred in Egypt under the Nasserist coup and popular revolution of 1952. Nasser's influence eventually extended far beyond Egypt to the greater

Arab, Muslim, and developing world. His restructuring of Egyptian society, his opposition to imperialism, and the attractiveness of his vision of a resurgent Arab world appealed to the region's youth—so much so that regimes throughout the Arab world defined and legitimized themselves largely by following his principles.

The principles that Nasser forwarded were few, and their applications varied as new situations arose, so that a firm appraisal of them is difficult. Three were notable. The first of these was anti-imperialism, the rejection of any form of foreign interference or influence in the Arab states. The second was Pan-Arabism, a major influence on Nasser's ideas and policies. He believed that Egypt was an integral part of the Arab world and the natural leader of the Arab states. The third was social democracy. Nasser's regime was not notably democratic, and this goal may seem mere propaganda to many, but that was not the case. Nasser regarded democracy as the ultimate goal of his regime. However, political democracy depended on economic and social equality, and the achievement of such equality required stern measures that might preclude the immediate establishment of democratic institutions. Furthermore, Nasser contended that Egypt's experience with parliamentary institutions under the monarchy showed that the people of Egypt were not as yet prepared for the unfettered use of democracy. Thus Nasser proposed to lead the Egyptian people forward to an indigenous democratic experience, based on the nexus of Egypt's three historical legacies (Arab, African, and Islamic), in which social justice and equality would prevail.

Nasser's status, and consequently the stature of the new nationalism, grew by leaps and bounds with his stand against imperialism—the nationalization of the Suez Canal Company, the purchase of Czechoslovakian armaments after the West's refusal to sell arms to Egypt, and Egypt's stand in the Suez crisis. Ultimately, it was not anti-imperialism but the tenet of Arab unity that was to determine the success or failure of Nasser's Arab nationalism. The most extensive attempt at Arab unity was undertaken in 1958 when the United Arab Republic (UAR)—the union between Egypt and Syria—was undertaken.

Nasser began to introduce his vision of an Arab political system through the Egyptian legislature, the National Union, as established in Egypt in 1956 and enlarged in 1958 to include Syria. As part of a completely remodeled system of government, he planned a new mass organization that would not be susceptible to subversion. The Arab Socialist Union (ASU), successor to the National Union, was designed to protect the interests of the population by requiring that half of the members of any representative body of the ASU had to be workers and peasants.

On 2 December 1962, the National Congress of Popular Forces convened to address the Nasserist experiment in general and the 1961

Syrian withdrawal from the UAR in particular. This 1,750-member body was responsible for approving the statutes of the Arab Socialist Union and was given authority over all public organizations including the press. Its leadership selected the candidates for the National Assembly and controlled the trade unions, Student Federation, and other popular organizations. It represented an effort to bring revolutionary ideals to the younger generation and provide a perpetual source of revolutionary vanguards. Its role and its position in relation to the state were more clearly defined and its powers greater than those of its predecessors, the Liberation Rally and the National Union. It provided an organization that was seen to embody the principles of social democracy and to reach down to the grassroots and serve as a mobilizing medium of the masses.

It was during the short life of the UAR that many of the illusions of the nationalists were replaced by the brutal realities of politics. The National Union proved to be unworkable for a number of reasons, most prominent of which were the incongruities between the political, economic, and social systems of the two states. The failure of the UAR proved to be a huge blow to Arab nationalists, though not a mortal one. Nasser remained firmly in control in Egypt, whereas by early 1963 the Ba'ath Arab Socialist Party controlled both Iraq and Syria, as other nationalist parties became more influential throughout the 1960s and 1970s. The movement experienced a resurgence after the 1967 and 1973 Arab-Israeli wars but lost much of its luster thereafter as a resurgent Palestinian nationalism took on a greater share of the Arab struggle in direct confrontation with Israel.

Throughout the 1970s and 1980s, the Arab states lost ground to Israel as it continued to occupy Arab lands seized in the 1967 war and the 1982 invasion of Lebanon and regularly violated the sovereignty of other Arab states. Perhaps more damaging, however, was the inability of ruling militarist-nationalist regimes to establish legitimacy and effectively rule their societies without resorting to violence and brutality, and their inability to achieve any sort of meaningful and lasting political or economic development (see chapter 3). The result of these failures is that the nationalist movement has been seriously undermined and has lost populist support. It is the contention of many that the failure of Arab nationalism and nationalist regimes has led to the resurgence of Islamic activism (see chapter 2).

After Camp David

The politicization of the military, and the rise to power of military officers since the 1950s, increased the power of the state, including its tools of oppression. In addition to the increasingly oppressive nature of domestic politics, the last quarter of the twentieth century witnessed the evolution of accommodationist policies toward the state of Israel by many states in the region, most often sponsored through western peace initiatives. The model introduced in 1978, through the Camp David accord, has been adopted in various guises throughout the region since the 1991 Gulf war, reorganizing the states of the Middle East in what we here are now identifying as the post–Camp David era.[28]

Iraq may not have invaded Kuwait in August 1990 to solve the Palestinian question, but the linkage that it insisted on establishing for political and strategic considerations highlighted the fundamental contradictions inherent in what will be called the Camp David order: the co-opting of Arab regimes into the strategic Israeli–United States axis. The international community, including Russia and France, recognized the existence of a linkage between the Iraqi occupation of Kuwait and Israeli occupation of Arab territories. The United States was virtually alone with Israel in insisting that there could be no political linkage between the two conflicts.

The identification of the Egyptian position with the American-Israeli position may be the logical consequence of a process of ideological reorientation started by President Sadat shortly after Nasser's death and completed with the signing of a separate agreement with Israel sponsored by the United States at Camp David in 1978. In accepting the logic of the Camp David accord, in effect, Egypt succumbed to American political and strategic priorities in the Middle East, abandoning its traditional role both as one of the confrontation states opposing Israel and as a leader of the Arab world.

Contrary to conventional analysis,[29] the Camp David order led inevitably to the subordination of Egypt's role in the region to Washington's two priorities: Israel's continued military domination of the region and American access to the region's natural resources and strategic facilities. It is also argued that although Sadat's successor, Hosni Mubarak, attempted to reconcile the Camp David order with a desire to regain a leading role for Egypt in the Arab world, the Gulf crisis forced these contradictions to come to the fore by placing Egypt firmly on the side of the conservative Camp David–based Mideast order.

Sadat's decisions at Camp David have their roots in an ideological reorientation, which became apparent shortly after he came to power in 1970 and unfolded more clearly shortly after the 1973 October war. This ideology was based on his personal conviction that an economic and political realignment of Egyptian policies with American policies in the Middle East would serve Egypt's interests. Sadat believed that this would induce Washington to accept Egypt as a player in its Middle East geopolitical design, which relied on Israel as its main strategic asset since the Jordanian crisis of September 1970.

Sadat was convinced that his strategy would help diminish the American special relationship with Israel, as well as increase Egypt's negotiating leverage with Israel and the Arab states, and persuade Washington to exert pressure on Israel for a settlement in the Middle East conflict. He undoubtedly understood that such a settlement would necessarily reflect the traditional American foreign policy objectives of guaranteeing Israel's security and ensuring continued access to the crucial strategic resources of the area. This strategy, however, implied more than a simple reorientation of traditional Egyptian economic and political priorities. It meant accepting the philosophical and analytical underpinning of the American foreign policy approach to the conflict. This approach held that recognizing the Palestinians' right to self-determination was not necessary to ensure access to strategic resources and guarantee Israel's security. In accepting that premise, Sadat vitiated his strategy of its stated goal of achieving a comprehensive peace based on the recognition of the Palestinians' right to self-determination. In essence, his strategy contained the seeds of a separate agreement and an implicit acceptance of the fundamental contradiction inherent in American Mideast policy: wanting to have cheap and ready access to Arab resources while helping Israel to effectively consolidate the occupation of Arab lands. In exposing this contradiction in U.S. foreign policy, the Gulf crisis forced Egypt to choose between the unstated assumptions of the Camp David order and the option of a negotiated settlement, which could have solved the Gulf crisis peacefully and allowed Iraq to remain a regional power. Washington's policy instead militated for a confrontation with Iraq and an elimination of the new order that Saddam Hussein proposed.

From Peace Process to Confrontation

As the Palestinian uprising (intifada 1987–91) challenged the Camp David assumption that the Palestinians' national aspirations need not find expression in an independent Palestinian state, the United States and Israel responded by reviving the discredited autonomy plan provided for in the Camp David accord. Egypt was the only Arab country to openly support the so-called peace process activated by Washington. Together Washington and Cairo put forward some proposals that were—in effect—drawn from the Israeli proposals. The American and Egyptian peace proposals of 1988–89 requested that Israel's own plan for elections in the West Bank and Gaza be based on the four principles of the official American policy in the Middle East: the solution must be based on UN Resolutions 242 and 338, land must be traded for peace, security must be guaranteed for all countries in the region, and Palestinian political rights must be recognized. In ignoring this demand, Israel was essentially rejecting its own plan for elections.

The Iraq-Iran War provided Egypt with an opportunity to accelerate its return to the Arab camp through its commitment to use the Egyptian military to deter the Iranian revolutionary threat to the conservative Arab states order. But the end of the Iran-Iraq War in 1988 brought into conflict the Washington-oriented Camp David order and subsequent Iraqi challenges to its dominance. Whereas, to the supporters of the Camp David order, the end of the East-West confrontation vindicated their premise that the alliance with Washington was the correct course to follow, to Saddam Hussein, the end of the cold war rivalry deprived the Arabs of their traditional Soviet support and made them even more vulnerable to the hegemonic designs of the United States. He argued that the end of the bipolar world would be replaced not by a multipolar world but rather by a unipolar world dominated by the United States. Such a world would be characterized not by interdependence but by growing economic and military inequalities. To Saddam Hussein it was imperative to ensure that Washington's quest for the extension and affirmation of its domination be challenged. And this could be achieved only if regional powers such as Iraq were able to deal with Washington from a position of strength.[30]

In its quest to reconstruct its war-ravaged country, the Iraqi regime looked to the petromonarchies for the alleviation of its crippling debt of U.S.$80 billion, half of which was owed to Saudi Arabia and Kuwait. It expected Kuwait to write off the debt in recognition of Iraq's role in stopping the threat of the Iranian Islamic revolution. Baghdad also looked forward to building on the privileged relationships it had enjoyed with Washington during the Iran-Iraq War and expected technological aid from the United States. Neither expectation materialized. The Iran-Iraq War ended Iraqi usefulness to Washington. Iraq's vision of a balance of power and its determination to rebuild its economy and modernize its military were seen as potential threats to American interests in the region. This was the argument presented by the Israelis who told Washington in early 1989 that the real threat to stability in the region did not come from their repression of the Palestinian uprising or their occupation of Arab territories but rather from Iraq's challenge to the established order.[31]

The argument coincided with a revision of American military strategy in response to a political assessment of the post–cold war era, which in essence was not unlike that made by Iraqi president Saddam Hussein. A 1988 U.S. government document entitled "Discriminate Deterrence" identified the post–cold war military challenges for the United States as coming no longer from the Soviet Union but from Third World regional powers.[32] The document recommended that the United States be prepared to militarily confront them in what was called medium-intensity warfare; medium only in that American forces would not use nuclear weapons. They would, however, strike hard and in a massive way, as became obvious from the way Washington conducted the war against Iraq.

The strategy is reminiscent of the American military doctrine of the early fifties, which became known as massive retaliation. It was supposedly designed to respond to communist aggression by retaliating massively against the territories of the communist aggressors. But when the Soviet Union mastered ballistic missile technology in the late fifties and became able to launch nuclear missiles against the territories of the United States, the strategy lost its credibility and was discarded. In the case of regional powers, a massive attack on any one of them who challenged Washington would not expose the territories of the United States to any similar response. In addition, the elimination of the Soviet Union as a rival removed the incentive for restraint. Finally, if Vietnam and mounting economic problems at home let some people predict the decline of the American empire, a massive attack against a regional power unable to retaliate against American territories would ensure the sort of victory that would restore faith in American might. It would also send a clear message to the economic giants in Europe and Japan that their economic prosperity, based on their greater need for Middle East oil, was a tributary of American power and largesse.[33]

In his first speech on national security, on 24 May 1989, President George Bush announced that the United States must challenge "the aggressive ambitions of renegade regimes." Describing a regime as renegade sets the stage for confrontation. In February 1990, Secretary of Defense Dick Cheney approved a secret document directing the American armed forces to prepare for eventual military conflicts with Third World regional powers such as Syria and Iraq.[34] By that time the North American media were full of stories about a perceived Iraqi threat and Iraqi attempts to accelerate a nuclear weapons program. In Israel, talk of imminent war with Iraq was complemented with calls for action against it. The Iraqis claimed that they learned in March 1990 that Israel was preparing another attack on Iraq similar to their 1981 strike against Iraqi nuclear facilities. As the U.S. Congress cut off Iraqi food purchase credits and as negative media stories about Iraq increased, King Hussein of Jordan told an Arab summit in Baghdad in May that there was an "unholy campaign against Iraq."[35]

Iraqi-Kuwaiti negotiations were becoming more difficult on a number of issues, such as their shared debt load as well as territorial disputes and disagreements over oil pricing policy. Syria, which sided with Iran in its eight-year war with Iraq, had shut off the oil pipeline that gave Iraqi oil access to the Mediterranean. Iran had easily been able to interdict Iraqi access to the Gulf, and Iraq's two new pipelines passed through Saudi Arabia and Turkey, both close allies of Washington. Iraq proposed to build a naval facility at the Iraqi Gulf port of Umm Qasr, linking it to the Iraqi inland port of Basra. The two uninhabited Kuwaiti islands of Bubiyan and Warba were important for the security of the new port. Kuwait reportedly proved uncooperative in the negotiations over their possession.

In addition, the Iraqis, who depend on oil sales for 95 percent of their export revenues, were antagonized by what they believed to be Kuwaiti collusion with Washington, to overproduce oil in order to drive its price down and further undermine the already drained and precarious Iraqi economy, which was devastated following its war with Iran. So when Kuwait demanded repayment of Iraqi debt with substantial interest, Baghdad claimed that Kuwait owed it $2.5 billion for oil stolen by Kuwait through slant drilling techniques into Iraq's Rumaila oil fields, which straddled the border between the two states.

Jordan, which traditionally enjoyed privileged relationships with the West, and which had been displaced by Egypt's rise as the chief supporter of a western-oriented politico-strategic alliance, saw the crisis looming. Jordanian officials expressed surprise with Kuwaiti defiance during negotiations and were told by Kuwaiti officials that Kuwait had received assurances from Washington that the United States would intervene militarily to back up the Kuwaitis in any confrontation with Iraq. (After the 2 August 1990 invasion of Kuwait, the Iraqis claimed that they had discovered in Kuwaiti government papers a 1989 memorandum describing secret Kuwaiti–CIA talks on anti-Iraqi strategies.) At the Arab Foreign Ministers' Conference in Tunis in July, the Iraqi foreign minister accused Kuwait of collusion with foreign powers to undermine the national security of Iraq. Soon thereafter Iraqi troops were moved toward the Kuwait-Iraq border.[36]

On 25 July, Saddam Hussein told the American ambassador in Baghdad, April Glaspie, that Washington must choose between friendly relations with Iraq and support for Kuwaiti economic warfare against Iraq. Glaspie replied, "We have no opinion on Arab-Arab conflicts, like your border disagreement with Kuwait."[37] During the same week, State Department officials repeated the position that the United States had no security commitments to Kuwait. Saddam Hussein must have concluded, as the *New York Times* put it, that "he had the green light" from Washington.[38]

On 31 July 1990, Kuwaiti and Iraqi delegations met in Jedda, Saudi Arabia. A second fruitless meeting was held on 1 August at which the Iraqis were reportedly angered by Kuwaiti intransigence. At 2 A.M. on 2 August, the Iraqi invasion of Kuwait began. On the same day, King Hussein spoke to Saddam Hussein, who informed him that he wanted to teach Kuwait a lesson and planned to withdraw his troops over the weekend. However, he warned that condemnations from the Arab world would complicate his withdrawal plan because it would make it appear as if he were caving in to external pressure.

That same day King Hussein flew to Alexandria to meet Hosni Mubarak. The two leaders and King Fahd of Saudi Arabia, whom they had contacted by phone, agreed to reassure Saddam Hussein and work to hold off an impending censure by the Islamic Conference Organization, which was then meeting in Cairo. They also agreed to convene a limited Arab summit in Jedda with Saddam Hussein and the emir of Kuwait to resolve the crisis peacefully. King Hussein then flew to Baghdad and obtained Saddam Hussein's approval for a negotiated settlement resulting from the planned Jedda Conference, which was scheduled for Saturday, 4 August 1990.[39]

However, the conference never took place. Mubarak informed the Egyptian Parliament five months later, on 24 January 1991, that he had called off the conference because King Hussein failed to discuss with Saddam Mubarak's condition that Iraq promise to withdraw before the negotiations began.[40] King Hussein, however, gave a different version. After returning from Baghdad, Hussein was shocked to learn that Egypt had already condemned the Iraqi invasion. Hussein phoned Mubarak in Alexandria to find out why Egypt had acted unilaterally and undermined the agreed-upon plan. Mubarak explained that he had "come under intense pressure,"[41] presumably from Washington.

On 4 August, King Fahd sent an emissary to Amman to confirm to the Jordanians that he saw no threat of an Iraqi invasion of Saudi Arabia. On Sunday, 5 August, President Bush returned from Camp David and made a statement containing the fateful description of the Iraqis as "outlaws and renegades." Discreetly but persistently, Israel and its friends in Washington lobbied for war. They argued persuasively that it was an ideal opportunity to eliminate Iraq's military capabilities and that never again would Washington be able to put together such a coalition.

Sometime between 2 and 8 August, the Iraqis notified the American embassy in Baghdad that they had no intention of entering Saudi territory. At about the same time, Secretary Cheney was persuading the Saudis to accept American troops to defend the kingdom. In King Fahd's marble palace in Jedda, Cheney told the king that without at least 200,000 American troops, Saudi Arabia, which had earlier refused to provide military facilities to the U.S. Central Command, would become another Kuwait.[42] After consulting with his advisers, Fahd accepted the American offer. Washington's position never wavered: unconditional Iraqi withdrawal from Kuwait or war. King Hussein's efforts at an Arab solution were consistently thwarted. Prince Hassan of Jordan complained, "Every time the King and other leaders said they had a package, the Americans rejected it."[43]

From the very beginning of the war it became clear that Washington's primary political goal was to eliminate Iraq as a challenge to the Camp David order in the Middle East. George Bush openly admitted as much when he said, "Whether [Saddam Hussein] gets out of Kuwait or not, Iraq must be militarily destroyed."[44] Long an Israeli strategic priority, and now without either Russian or American protection, Iraq found itself isolated even within the Arab world. According to the distinguished Egyptian political analyst Mohammad Heikal, "The destruction of the Iraqi military force was an Israeli priority in the first place, unfortunately it was transformed, . . . soon to become an Arab priority as well. Whether Arab [governments] understood the war as one to liberate Kuwait or to destroy Iraq, an alliance was created between Arab [governments] and Israel. The agreement to oppose the Iraqi invasion in such a manner made it inevitable for the two sides to formulate such an alliance, which was concluded contractually, whether they ran for it or hesitated. The Arabs went on where they were called upon, with their excuse in responding being that they were pressured by the 'new world order' that nobody can ignore or deny responding to if so ordered."[45]

CHAPTER 2

The Political Heritage of Islam

Continuity and Change

*E*xamining the role of Islam as a force of community and social justice in the Middle East may help explain to the reader why it has become such a prominent political force. The expansion of state power, often exclusionary of the people it is supposed to represent, as well as the destruction of traditional society through first colonialism and then socialism and nationalist attempts to define a "modern" and secular society, have left Islam as the sole legitimate indigenous sociopolitical force in the region for the majority of its people. The relationships between the formal doctrines of Islam and the ways in which Muslims live in the modern world will shape the future political culture of the region. Islam is not just a religious system; it is a complete way of life for the individual, society, and state. Islam does not recognize national, racial, or linguistic boundaries. It conceives of both God and his message as universal and does not permit a separation between the secular and the religious.

There are today two major schools of political-philosophical thought in Islam: the dominant Sunni school and the minority Shi'a. There is general agreement in both schools on the principal role and function of the state. In both, the establishment of a just society is possible only through the implementation of divine legislation, the Shari'ah. However, the two schools disagree over the method of selecting the head of state. While both agree that a Muslim leader should be exemplary, Sunnism emphasizes the role of a consultative council, whereas Shi'ism emphasizes that the Muslim leader should come from the house of the Prophet and his descendants. The Sunnis refer to the Muslim head of the community as a caliph, which means the successor to the Prophet who governs the Muslim community. In a legal sense, he is a de facto ruler whether he is legitimate and worthy of the post or not. The Shiites, however, use the term *imam* to refer to the legitimate ruler whether in a position of power or not; he is the de jure leader regardless. It follows that if the caliph is legitimate, he becomes de jure, and the two terms become synonymous. The term *imam* then becomes the generally acceptable reference appropriate to the function of the Muslim ruler.[1] Although Muslim politics are derived from the religious and social teachings of Islam, and although Islamic concepts of God, humanity, and the world have placed certain limitations on the development of Muslim politics, it has essentially been pragmatic.

The primary political unit in the Muslim world today is the nation-state, but the corresponding conceptual unit in Islamic law is the Ummah, the Islamic community. This community is the brotherhood of all Muslims, and it transcends national boundaries. In the past it has sometimes been a single political unit, although today it is primarily a religious and cultural one. The Ummah is held together by several basic tenets, including common belief in Tawhid (the oneness and perfect unity of God), the exemplary practice of the Prophet Muhammad, the Qur'an, the Shari'ah, and a variety of other common cultural patterns. The Ummah has functioned much like Christianity in Europe by providing a binding force that has allowed the Middle East to present a unified front to counter external interference. The Ummah has also been an underlying force in the creation and development of the Islamic Empire and in the more recent attempts at Pan-Arabism.

The community concept of the Ummah, however, is incompatible with the reality of the modern nation-state. The Middle East has rarely acted as a single political unit. Early Arab conquests led to the inclusion of diverse racial, linguistic, and cultural groups within the expanding territorial sphere of the Islamic brotherhood. The building of the Arab and Ottoman Empires led to the assimilation of a great number of people who were not Muslims. European expansion in the nineteenth century also played a major role, as it forced a potent injection of western ideas and practices into the bloodstream of the Islamic Middle East. The result of these complex historical developments has been a diversification within the Islamic world, leading to the creation of several nation-states exhibiting marked differences with one another. In 1999, fifty-four Muslim countries constituted the Islamic Conference Organization (ICO), which is a formal attempt to assert the unity of the Ummah, to overcome national borders, and to promote the unity of Muslims throughout the world. Other global organizations, like the Muslim World League, also complement the objectives of the ICO by fostering greater cohesion and unity in overcoming the economic and social problems faced by the Muslim world.

Related to the Ummah concept, and also shaping Islamic politics, is the concept of equality. There is no priesthood in Islam serving as an intermediary between man and God, and because Islam covers all aspects of Muslim life, equality before God becomes, theoretically, equality in all situations. Of course, racial, class, and gender distinctions exist in Middle Eastern states as they do elsewhere. Nonetheless, the theoretical equality of all Muslims leads to awareness that all people have certain rights. In practice, however, non-Muslims have traditionally been considered unequal to Muslims because they reject the rule of God that is enshrined in the first "pillar" of Islam.

Muhammad and the Middle East

In the seventh century, the Middle East was ravaged by constant warfare between the decaying remnants of the Byzantine and Persian Empires. The Arabian Peninsula was a disunited area where individual cities flourished on east-west trade routes. In the vast areas between cities, there were only bands of desert nomads who navigated the desert and provided an important transit and communication link across it. It was into this context that the future Prophet Muhammad, the founder of the religion of Islam, was born. The year was A.D. 569, and Muhammad was born to a noble family belonging to the tribe of the Quraysh in western Arabia. He was married at the age of twenty-five, and at forty he declared himself a messenger of God and proclaimed Islam as the religion and complete way of life ordained by Allah (God in Arabic). Persecution drove him and his small community of followers to Yathrib, now modern Medina. Muhammad established the first Islamic city-state in Medina in 622 and became the undisputed head of state and leader of the Muslim community. After consolidating power, Islam began to grow as alliances were made with the surrounding communities and tribes.

As Islam expanded from Medina, the ruling elite in Mecca began to feel threatened. Their fears were sharply accentuated by the proximity of Medina to their caravan route and the hearsay that Muslims might ambush their trade. That was sufficient for Meccan leadership to declare war against the Muslims and Muhammad. The first battle, called Badr, was the first all-out war between the Meccan chiefs and the followers of Muhammad, and the Meccan forces failed to overcome the forces of Islam. Muhammad and a small army of 317 ill-equipped men defeated the Meccan army of more than 1,000 better trained and fully equipped combatants. Two major battles followed, eventually bringing Mecca under Muhammad's power. Mecca became the center of the new religion, although the seat of government remained in Medina. Shortly after his victorious return to Mecca, Muhammad died in 632. However, by the time of his death, all Arabia had been brought under the dominion of the Islamic state.

Muhammad's contribution to the Middle East cannot be overemphasized.[2] Islam has been the greatest single factor in the development of the region, and because of Muhammad's unique position as the "Seal of the Prophets," almost all that is Islam can be traced back to his teachings. The Sunnah, or traditions of the early Islamic community, all derive from the words and actions of Muhammad. The character and exercise of authority are drawn from his practices, first in Medina and later in Mecca. Religious tolerance and the use of existing administrators in conquered territories, both of which were standard practices in the later Islamic empires, were techniques that Muhammad himself adopted while expanding the Islamic community's power.

Islamic Political Thought
in Historical and Comparative Perspective

Islam's political thought reflects some 1,400 years of philosophical and theoretical inquiry into the nature and role of government, its relationship to religious and temporal affairs, and its relationship to social change and social revolution within the Islamic world and beyond. The analysis of this theoretical and intellectual basis of Islamic government and society has been given only scant attention by western scholars in understanding the forces of change impacting on contemporary Islamic societies. Indeed, Islam has often been viewed as a "traditional" force, resisting progressive change and constituting a negative influence or barrier to social and political development. The failure to recognize the ongoing theoretical and intellectual ferment in Islamic thought, catalyzed continuously by the emergence of unique contemporary issues and problems within Islamic societies, has contributed to the image of Islam as a static rather than dynamic system of thought incapable of relevance to the complex modern issues of social and political development. A brief overview of the issues of political authority as they have emerged in Islamic thought will help place fundamentalist and indeed all Islamic political thought in a historical and comparative perspective.

The position of the Prophet Muhammad in the early Muslim community as Allah's appointed religious and temporal representative was a central factor in keeping the Muslim community united politically and religiously. The accepted infallibility of the Prophet's authority gave the community a unified outlook on life, religion, and politics. His death, however, forced Muslims to begin to look for answers to the immediate tasks suddenly facing them: Who would be his successor as leader of the community? To what form of government should they adhere? How would the Islamic community choose a successor to the Prophet? Who was best qualified to run the affairs of the community?

Because the Prophet died without leaving a clear successor, the Muslims of Medina, the Ansar or the Prophet's Partisans (early converts), held a meeting in Saqifat Bani Sa'eda to choose a successor even before his body was buried. They saw themselves as the legitimate successors because they came to help the Prophet, whereas his tribe in Mecca forced him to leave his own birthplace. But the Muhajirun— those who migrated with the Prophet from Mecca—also saw themselves as the legitimate successors, since they were the Prophet's kinsmen and the first to believe in his message. Thanks to the shrewdness and decisiveness of 'Umar Ibn al-Khattab, who nominated Abu Bakr as the first successor to the Prophet, the divisive conflict was settled. However, this led to another conflict within the camp of the Muhajirun: 'Ali Ibn Abi Taleb initially refused to accept the choice of Abu Bakr. As the Prophet's cousin and son-in-law, therefore, 'Ali saw himself as the legitimate successor.[3] Nevertheless, he did eventually accept the choice of Abu Bakr.

The question of succession, of Khilafah or Imamah (caliphate system or imamate system), and how it should be conducted has remained a source of discord. The Umayyads tried to solve this problem by having the caliph choose his own successor, usually his son. Before Abu Bakr died, he chose 'Umar as his successor. 'Umar, before his assassination, refused to choose a successor. He did not want to be responsible for such a decision in front of Allah, either while alive or after his death. Instead, he chose a consultative council, or Majlis al-Shura, to elect a worthy individual. 'Uthman was chosen as the third caliph, to the dismay of 'Ali and some other contenders. The rebellion against 'Uthman, ending in his assassination, brought 'Ali as the fourth caliph, which in turn led to the first civil war among the Muslims in the battle of al-Jamal (the Camel). 'Ali's succession led also to the second major civil war, the Battle of Siffien, between 'Ali's shi'ah supporters and the supporters of Mu'awiyah Ibn Abi Sufian, who would establish the Umayyad dynasty.[4]

These historical developments reflect the following six conclusions. First, the Qur'an did not provide a guideline on the question of succession or form of the Islamic state. Second, the Prophet neither chose a successor nor established a preference for one form of a state over another, so long as the Muslims abided by the teachings of Islam. Third, three patterns of succession emerged: limited choice (Abu Bakr), nomination by the caliph ('Umar), and Shura or consultation ('Uthman and 'Ali). Fourth, the question of succession led to internal political conflict, which turned into a religious schism within the community of Islam. The Muslim community, after the assassination of 'Uthman, was permanently divided into the Sunni and Shi'ah sects. The establishment of the Umayyad dynasty and the violent death of 'Ali's son Hussein further widened the gap between the Sunnis and the Shi'ah and consolidated their differences in religious and political matters. Fifth, the history of the Islamic caliphate, from its inception to its downfall in 1924, indicates that not one caliph was elected by the whole body of the Muslim community. Instead, a caliph was chosen for political reasons by the elite, through the doctrine of *bay'ah* (pledge of allegiance) that was contracted by *Ahl al-Hal wa al-'Aqd* (the wise people of the community).[5] Finally, a distinction between the caliph and the imam also resulted from the dispute over the question of succession. The name *Khalifah* was originally used to denote a political and religious role in the caliph's capacity to rule after the Prophet. The word *imam,* in its simplest and commonest usage, refers to the leader of the Muslims in prayer. The distinction between the two did not seem to represent a major political and religious problem in Islamic thought until the establishment of the Umayyad dynasty. Supporters of 'Ali, the Shi'ah, developed the doctrine of the Imamah, to encompass both the religious and political dimensions of a true ruler. The Sunnis, on the other hand, accepted the caliph as the temporal ruler. The caliph, particularly after the first four successors to the Prophet, did not seem to enjoy any particular religious role as far as the Islamic community itself was concerned. It is true he could still lead the Muslims in prayers, but this is a task that can be performed by any Muslim.

As Thomas Arnold aptly remarked, the caliph is "preeminently a political functionary and though he may perform religious functions, these functions do not imply the possession of any spiritual powers setting him thereby apart from the rest of the faithful."[6] The Shi'ah, however, held the view that the imamate belongs to the descendants of the Prophet and that 'Ali is the first imam. Furthermore, Shi'ah doctrine maintained that the imam must be infallible from sin.

Three Schools of Islamic Political Thought

The Sunni School

The conflict over succession led to the creation of three schools of Islamic political thought. The first is the Sunni school. As the official doctrine of state throughout Islam's history, the Sunnis sought to legitimate the rule of the first four caliphs. They argued that the role of the imam is essential, but they did not bestow on him the same mystical powers the Shi'ah attributed to Imam 'Ali and the chain of imams that followed him.[7]

The imam became the de jure ruler for the Shi'ah and the caliph became the de facto ruler for both the Sunnis and the Shi'ah.[8] Unlike the Shi'ah, the Sunnis emphasized the role of Ahl al-Hal wa al-'Aqd to justify their theory of the legitimacy of the rule of the four caliphs, but this concept was never clearly defined. How are the members to be chosen? What is their role? What is the relationship of this group with the rest of the Muslim community? These and other questions were never clearly answered, a fact which led to political turmoil throughout Islamic history. The tenuity of this concept and the ineffectiveness of the Consultative Council became obvious when the caliphate was made into a royal dynasty under the Umayyads. This was even true long before, when the Consultative Council and the wise men of the Islamic community were beset by intrigues, personal ambitions, and even class interests.[9]

Under the doctrine of Ahl al-Hal wa al-'Aqd, the Muslim community was constantly faced by a fait accompli in the issue of succession and prevented from playing an active political role in choosing the ruler. Thus dissension, factionalism, and rebellion became common. Essentially accepting the doctrine of Ahl al-Hal wa al-'Aqd as unproblematic, Sunni theorists concentrated on such problems as how many people should belong to Ahl al-Hal wa al-'Aqd, and how many constitute a legal bay'ah before the community gives its allegiance. Mohammad al-Baqelani (d. A.D. 1013), representative of this school, set down several rules: the nomination of the caliph can be done by one person, and the bay'ah can be achieved by six; the community cannot depose a caliph unless he reverts to atheism or stops praying and encourages others to do the same; the caliph is not infallible, and he has to be from the tribe of Quraysh, knowledgeable about war and protecting the community.[10] Al-Baghdadi shared al-Baqelani's views and added that the caliphate cannot be bequeathed.

The Sunni thinker Ibn Abi-Rabi'a, in his book *Suluk al-Malik fi Tadbir al-Mamalik,* emphasized that rulers are appointed by "divine laws for the organization of the people and their unity of action."[11] A ruler should be the best among all the people. One ruler should be supreme in all the land; otherwise, conflicts will arise. The duty of the Muslim is to obey the ruler.

The dominant views of Sunni religious thinkers, however, did not go uncontested. Challenges came from Muslim philosophers who were reading and commenting on Greek philosophers such as Plato and Aristotle. An example of the philosophic school was al-Farabi

(A.D. 870–950). His theory of the State, as enunciated in his book *Ahl al-Madinah al-Fadelah,* was based on "mutual renunciation of rights." This means that in a society or a state, each individual "gives up in favour of the other a part of that by which he would have overpowered him, each making it a condition that they would keep perfect peace with each other and not take away from the other anything except on certain conditions."[12]

Al-Farabi advocated the idea of Plato's philosopher king. He described his Ra'is Awwal (ruler) as the one "who by his very nature and up-bringing, does not want to be instructed by others and who has the inherent capacity for observation and of conveying his sense to others."[13] Al-Farabi listed twelve attributes of the Ra'is Awwal, but was satisfied with one who had five or six. In case there are no people with even that minimum number of attributes, then a council of two or five possessing an aggregate of ten attributes should be chosen. One of them must be a *hakim* (wiseman) to know the needs of the state and the people.

Al-Farabi listed a number of kinds of states: the ideal state run by the ideal ruler; Madinat al-Taghallub, an imperialistic state based on hegemony; Madinat al-Jahiliya, an individualistic state formed on the basis of force, patriarchal factors, and material reasons. Other such states were called the city of necessity, city of ease, and city of desires. Language and customs should provide the basis of a strong bond among the citizens. The geographical factor should also be important as a means of keeping the state together.[14]

In the ideal state, men should be organized by the ideal ruler in service departments that are in accordance with their nature, upbringing, and suitability for the job. The Ra'is Awwal would not take orders from any individual. Others would be organized hierarchically, receive orders from their superiors, and give orders to their subordinates. In al-Farabi's scheme, society should be divided into classes, with common property to which all citizens have equal rights and private property for each individual and class.[15]

Philosophic principles, however, were not to supplant religious doctrine in political theory. One of the prominent Sunni theorists was Abu al-Hassan al-Mawardi (A.D. 975–1058). He wrote a number of works on politics, the most famous of which are *Ahkam Sultaniyah, Nasihat al-Muluk,* and *Qawanin al-Wizarah.* Mawardi considered the Imamah as a "caliphate of prophethood in safeguarding religious and temporal affairs."[16] The Imamah, guided by the Shari'ah and by reason, was to follow the "right path." The imam should be characterized by justice, knowledge for the purposes of *ijtihad,* no handicaps in his physical or sense faculties, wisdom in ruling the community and running its affairs, the courage to protect Islam and fight its enemies, and finally descent from Quraysh.

The imam was to be chosen either by election by Ahl al-Hal wa al-ʿAqd or by appointment by the previous imam. He was to pledge to perform his duties, and the community was to pledge its allegiance and obedience. The role of the imam was to protect the faith, adjudicate among people, punish transgressors, appoint honest men, and lead a medium path between luxury and total dedication to prayer. The imam could be removed from his office for only two reasons: *hajr* and *qahr. Hajr* means the imam falls under the influence of one of his assistants who might act contrary to the teachings of Islam and justice, while *qahr* means that the imam falls as a prisoner in the hands of a "formidable enemy" and there is no hope of saving or freeing him.[17]

Mawardi listed two kinds of *wizara,* or ministries: wizarat Tafwidh (delegation) and wizarat Tanfith (execution). The minister of Tafwidh should have all the qualities of the imam except the condition of descent from Quraysh. He should also have an extra quality of knowledge of military affairs and tax collection. The minister of Tafwidh was not to appoint his successor and could be dismissed by the imam. The minister of Tanfith was just to be a "middle-man between the imam and his subjects and the governors."[18] Mawardi listed eight main qualities of persons occupying the position of the minister of Tanfith, but did not say they had to be Muslim.[19]

Provincial governors (emirs) were to be appointed by the imam, and this governorship (*imara*) was to be of two kinds: general and special. The general governorship was divided again into two types: *imarat istikfaʾ*, through an appointment by the imam out of his own free will, and *imarat istilaʾ*, an appointment forced on the imam if one amir controls a province by force. The "special imara" was limited to the affairs of the army, defense of the community, and safeguarding women, but could not deal with matters of justice, religious laws, or taxes.[20] Mawardi listed four main departments: Army Board, Board of Provincial Boundaries, Board of Appointment and Dismissal of Officers, and the Treasury. Justice was to be administered by an independent judge with particular qualities, including honesty and being a Muslim.[21]

Another writer, a civil servant, was Nizam al-Mulk Tusi (A.D. 1017–91), who considered "kingship and religion . . . like two brothers."[22] Nizam al-Mulk's *Siyasat-namah* is a fascinating book of practical politics. It is full of advice for the king, such as the necessity of intelligence agents, spies, diplomatic protocol and the immunity of diplomats, the army and the best way of handling its officers and weaponry, a royal guard down to its type of uniform, keeping hostages to prevent rebellions, single rather than dual appointment per person, the role of the *wazir,* and much more.

The last Sunni religious thinker we will consider is Ibn Taimiyah (A.D. 1263–1328). His *Minhaj al-Sunnah* was a book of polemics against the Shi'ah writer al-Hilli, who wrote *Minhaj al-Karamah.* To Ibn Taimiyah, the imam might reach a certain stage of perfection, but he could not be like a prophet. Ibn Taimiyah did not consider it necessary for the community to elect an imam. The bay'ah was a bilateral contract between the imam and the community. The condition of Quraysh descent for the imam was contrary to Islamic teaching of equality among Muslims. The mandate of the imam meant a victory of the divine law. Justice, the community's well-being, social stability, and safeguarding the rights of the individual were, Ibn Taimiyah maintained, the prerequisites for Allah's favorable consideration and protection of any state even though that state might not be a Muslim one. The imam was to consult the Majlis al-Shura and abide more by its decisions than had generally been practiced throughout Islamic history. The Majlis al-Shura should be representative of the religious 'ulama as well as representative of public opinion.[23] This was the closest any Sunni thinker up to that time ever came to the idea of a moderately democratic system of government. Government departments could be created in accordance with the need, the opinion of the imam, and the situation in the country at the time. There were two essential departments: the Judiciary, and the Muhtasib or the general supervisor of public morals and the executive arm of the judge.

In sum, Sunni political theory took as unproblematic the nature or origin of political power and concentrated on the issues of its implementation and administration. In part, this may be explained by the close relationship between this school and the dominant political ideology throughout the history of the Islamic state. The personal qualities of the ruler and the organization of the state were the problems to which Sunni theory addressed itself, since neither the attainment of power nor its fundamental legitimacy were at issue for the Sunni sect.

The Kharijite School

The second school of political thought is the Kharijite (renegades), which maintained that leadership of the Muslim community should be open to all Muslims, free and slave alike. A caliph who was duly elected should not abdicate or relinquish his asserted right under any circumstances. If, however, he was unjust, he should be deposed or even assassinated if the necessity arose.[24] The Kharijites went even further to assert that the caliphate and Imamah were totally unnecessary. Shahrastani, one of the Kharijites' chief thinkers, asserted, "The Imamah is not necessary according to Shari'ah. . . . It is based on people's interactions with each other. If every one of them justly deals with the others, cooperates with the others, and if each one of them fulfilled his duties and responsibilities, they do not need an imam."[25]

This school of political thought represented a radical ideology in the Islamic state. Many of its theories, however, became popularized in the nineteenth century with the advent of nationalism. Some Islamic reformers, such as Jamal al-Din al-Afghani (1838–97) and Mohammad 'Abdo (1848–1905), attempted to reconcile the ideas of western democracy with the Islamic idea of the state. However, the synthesis of the teachings of such thinkers and Kharijite theories brought into being a whole new generation of secular thinkers who wanted to completely separate religion from the state. The best representative of this school is 'Ali 'Abd al-Razeq (writing in 1925), who maintained that Islam never decided on a particular form of government and that the Muslims were never required to follow a particular system. The caliphate to him was never a religious system, and the Qur'an did not allude to it or order it. To 'Abd al-Razeq, "Islam is innocent of the caliphate because it paralysed any development in the form of government among the Muslims."[26] He even maintained that the Prophet did not have the intention of forming a government or establishing a state.[27] The caliphate in Islam, 'Abd al-Razeq contended, was "based on nothing but brutal force."[28] The goodness of the Muslims does not depend on the caliphate whether in their temporal or religious affairs. The caliphate was, and still is, "a catastrophe that hit Islam and the Muslims and is a source of evil and corruption."[29] Therefore, according to 'Abd al-Razeq, Muslims are free to choose their own form of government.

The Shi'ah School

The last school of thought, the Shi'ah, emphasized the absolute necessity of an imam without whom the community could not function and would never be able to reach happiness and the true path to goodness. Shi'ah doctrine maintained that the Imamah belonged only to the house of the Prophet and his descendants. Allah chose the imam as He chose all the prophets to guide people on the straight path. Like the Prophet Muhammad, the imam was infallible and was to be an interpreter and protector of the law.[30]

The doctrine of the occultation of the last imam and his reappearance, to rule in a just and egalitarian manner in accordance with the precepts of the Qur'an and Islamic law, has dominated Shi'ah religious and political thought. Thus, a government other than that of the imam would be unjust, a position which was reinforced in Shi'ah doctrine by the persistent harassment and oppression which the Shi'ah had to endure throughout a significant period of Islamic history.

In the face of this harassment and the expectation of the imam's return, Shi'ah theory developed the doctrine of *taqiyah,* a dissimulation of religious and political beliefs. This has been used to justify an apparent acceptance of existing governments, but has also stimulated the search for a theory of the nature of political authority during the period of the Greater Occultation of the last imam that is represented in Ayatollah Khomeini's political thought.

The contradiction posed by the usurpation of the imam's right, and the necessity of government during his absence, forced Shi'ah intellectuals to deal theoretically with the structure and functions of power in the less than ideal state. Concepts of constitutionalism and democracy were incorporated into the Shi'ah theory of government during the period of absence to deal with such problems as the nature and origins of power during the imam's absence, the limitations of the usurpation of power, and accountability in the less than ideal state. Ayatollah Khomeini's political thought was a direct product of this trend in Shi'ah theory (see chapter 4).

Islam and Politics Today

The extreme bureaucratization of the Ottoman Empire sapped the strength of medieval Islam, ended all Islamic political expansion, and initiated a period of economic, political, and cultural stagnation and decline. At the same time, western Europe was experiencing technological growth, political expansion, and the growth of liberalism. When Ottoman power was withdrawn from vast areas of the Middle East, the European powers flowed in. The European penetration not only resulted in an influx of western ideas but also contributed to the decline in the vitality of Middle Eastern culture.[31]

Islam experienced its golden age from A.D. 800 to 1100, and continued to be vibrant through the fifteenth century. Arab and Islamic scholars, under the Abbasid caliphs of Baghdad, discovered the works of the Greek philosophers, a finding which invigorated and elevated scholarship to the center of the Arab and Islamic world.[32] Building libraries to preserve and disseminate the Greek classics, Islamic scholars soon expanded their base of knowledge to include the traditions of Babylonia, Syria, Persia, India, and Chinese thought. The cultural explosion that ensued saw the building of observatories, hospitals, universities, and a number of sophisticated scientific instruments and methods. The works of scholars such as al-Razi (864–940), known in the West as Rhazes, Ibn Sina (980–1037), known in the West as Avicenna, and al-Tusi (1201–74) reached western Europe during the Renaissance and helped spark the Enlightenment.[33]

Indeed, the Islamic preservation of the works of antiquity, as well as substantial scientific endeavors in their own right, played a significant role in the flowering of European culture. The two societies, though often hostile neighbors, maintained cultural and intellectual contact through translations, pilgrimage, and the Crusades.[34] Translation centers, such as those at Salerno in Italy, which was close to Muslim Sicily, and Cremona, on the frontier of Andalus in Muslim Spain, passed on to European culture first the Greek texts and then a flood of Arab scholarship. Having discovered and preserved classical Greek philosophy and thought while Europe was suffering the intellectual malaise of medieval culture, and having elevated the role of literacy and learning while Europe was largely illiterate, the Middle East was bewildered by the increasing European technological lead and political control in the eighteenth century through the twentieth.

The political ebb of the Muslim world to European encroachment produced a strong reaction throughout the Middle East. Diverse reform movements were started, ranging from those attempting to impose a strict adherence to the letter of Qur'anic law to others seeking to change the basic doctrines of Islam itself. A particularly powerful reform *Tanzimat* movement occurred in Turkey during the first half of the nineteenth century.[35] It did not, however, have the force necessary to overthrow the Ottoman established order. It was not until the beginning of the twentieth century that the Turkish nationalist movement overthrew the Ottomans and made modernization feasible in Turkey. Since that time, the forces of nationalism and modernization have swept through the rest of the Middle East, bringing both the benefits and the problems they had brought to Turkey.

A major problem in Middle East politics today has been reconciling the western modernization process with the social values of Islam. A serious conflict occurred with the adoption of western penal codes and family law; however, a greater conflict still is the adoption and imitation of certain controversial western social values. This conflict was dealt with in Turkey by divesting the Shari'ah, the religious courts, of their secular authority, resulting in the first real separation of church and state in an Islamic society. Further, it opened the door to government control and led the government to assume the prerogative of changing the social structure whenever its needs and desires run counter to the tenets of Islam. Today this trend is being challenged somewhat by militant Turkish Muslims who advocate a return to some degree of Islamic law. While not opposed to modernization and material advancement, they are troubled by what they see as the western social evils accompanying the process of modernization.

The origin of contemporary Islamic political discourses can be traced to the Egyptian Muslim Brotherhood, which was founded in 1928 in response to the fall of the Ottoman caliphate five years earlier and the presence of colonizing powers. Its political agenda was founded on two major themes: a struggle against imperialism for the liberation of Muslims, and the establishment of a true Pan-Islamic league that would transcend the borders of those nation-states it saw as having been created by the forces of colonization. The political discourse of the Muslim Brotherhood was essentially universalistic, and it identified Israel— when it declared independence twenty years later—as the ultimate western challenge to the unity of both Muslims and Arabs. The Muslim Brotherhood movement originated at al-Azhar University in Cairo, the center of international Islamic learning in Egypt. The movement quickly spread, generating a well-organized network throughout the Arab and Muslim world in the 1940s and 1950s.

Confrontation with the new nation-states was inevitable. This led to the rapid and severe suppression of the movement and its political exclusion, beginning in the 1950s. The universalistic character of the movement collided with the relativism of the nation-states in the Middle East, which were dominated in the 1960s by strong military ruling elites, as in Egypt, Iraq, Syria, Yemen, Algeria, and Tunisia. After suffering military defeat in their 1967 and 1973 wars with Israel, the people of the Middle East had less faith in the efficacy of Pan-Arab movements and ideologies. They saw that the Arab League had lost cohesion and, instead of rallying the masses through the 1970s, had produced fragmentation and inharmonious territorial groupings,[36] to the detriment of all Muslims.

The Afghani struggle against the Soviets[37] and the Iranian Islamic Revolution in 1979 gave new impetus and a militarist dimension to the movement. This culminated in the emergence of Hizbullah in Lebanon, Jihad in the Israeli-occupied territories of Palestine, Hamas within the Palestinian community at large, the Islamic Liberation Organization in Egypt, the Jihad and the al-Da'wa Party in Iraq,[38] and an increase in Islamic militancy worldwide. The points of confrontation between all Islamic movements and the present Middle Eastern states system are numerous and sharp. In the Arab world, all the movements assert that the secular regimes have failed to bring about social justice for the masses and, instead, have fallen prey to the schemes of Zionists and the United States.

It follows, from the Islamic activist's conceptual framework, that the Middle Eastern states and their interstate organizations have become instruments for realizing the Israeli-western hegemony in the region at the expense of the Arab people (with special reference to the Palestinians) and Muslims in general. The implications of this conceptual framework are to suggest caution regarding the motives of international organizations, such as the United Nations, which are portrayed by Islamists as instruments of western domination. States in the Middle East perceive an active and independent Islam as a threat to their existence and one that must be eradicated just as the Muslim Brotherhood before them.[39] This confrontation between the secular state and Islamic activists affects the stability of the region.

The Muslim Brotherhood and Islamic Activism

Founded in Ismailia Egypt in 1928 by Hasan al-Banna, the Muslim Brotherhood possessed historical and ideological antecedents stretching back more than a century. The Brotherhood's orientation differed from contemporary and previous Islamic organizations in calling for a move toward the complete transformation of society and by distinguishing no separation between state and religion. The Brotherhood called for maximum involvement by its members in such a social transformation, and a return to the Shari'ah, which should serve as the basis for all social norms. Primarily a grassroots movement with an appeal to the lower middle class—which is the fastest growing class in the Middle East— the Brotherhood has competed with other political and social movements for popular support throughout the twentieth century.

The Brotherhood sought to achieve its goals gradually by recruiting new members, propagating its message, and initiating Islamic projects, such as building mosques, schools, and hospitals.[40] Its burgeoning popularity was aided by its much publicized support for the Palestinian struggle against the British colonial government and Zionist settlers in the 1930s. Volunteers from the Brotherhood worked for Palestinian groups through the 1948 war. Thus, the years 1945–48 were ones of considerable expansion for the Muslim Brotherhood. Their anti-British activities and their clear commitment to the Palestinian cause, as well as their social ideology, were well received by many Egyptians as well as others throughout the region. Their membership swelled to between

300,000 and 600,000 organized into some 2,000 branches. By the 1940s, members and branches existed in Syria, Lebanon, Palestine, Transjordan, Iraq, Sudan, Eritrea, Morocco, and Tunisia.

The creation of the state of Israel and the failure of the Arab states to meet the Israeli challenge intensified civil unrest in Egypt in the second half of 1948. In this context the Muslim Brotherhood's political suc-cess—coupled with their militancy and increasing use of violence—ultimately led Egyptian governments to take harsh action. On 8 December 1948, citing the Muslim Brotherhood's involvement in acts of violence and conspiracy, the Mahmoud al-Nuqurashi government issued a military order calling for the "Disbanding of the Muslim Brotherhood and their branches wherever they may be, the closing of their centres, and the seizure of their papers, documents, magazine, publications, monies and properties, and all other assets of the Association."[41] Thereafter, relations between the Brotherhood and the government rapidly deteriorated. On 28 December 1948, a member of the Muslim Brotherhood's "secret apparatus" assassinated Prime Minister al-Nuqurashi as he entered the Ministry of the Interior. As a result, al-Nuqurashi's successor, Prime Minister Ibrahim 'Abd al-Hadi Pasha, instituted a ruthless campaign of arrests and property seizure against the now outlawed organization. Al-Banna deeply regretted the assassination as well as the government reaction. He had second thoughts as to the wisdom of the Brotherhood's entrance into formal politics, and wrote that future Muslim Brotherhood activities might best be confined to education and advocation within the framework of exist-ing political parties. However, his message and any attempts at com-promise were dashed when on 12 February 1949 Hasan al-Banna—founder, director-general, and guiding force of the Muslim Brotherhood—was assassinated outside the headquarters of the Young Men's Muslim Association by members of the Egyptian secret police.

Al-Banna's death was a severe blow to the Muslim Brotherhood, as were the seven months of suppression that followed under the al-Hadi government. Eventually, however, the oppression was lessened with the coming to power of a Wafdist government under Mustapha al-Nahas. Arrested members were gradually released from prison, and the organization regained its property, published its newspapers, and became openly active in politics. Hasan Ismail al-Hudaybi, a former judge, was elected the new director-general of the movement. Nevertheless, his open condemnation of past violent acts, his dislike of the "secret apparatus," and his apparent accommodation with the palace stimulated some internal opposition to his leadership, which presaged the internecine feuding that would plague the society in the early 1950s.

Despite involvement in guerrilla warfare against the British in the Suez Canal Zone, the Brotherhood maintained a relatively low political profile until the July 1952 Egyptian revolution. Prior to the revolution, the Muslim Brotherhood had contact with the Free Officers' Movement, with several prominent members of the Free Officers later maintaining that the Brotherhood's leadership was warned of the forthcoming revolution and that it then supported the Free Officers by providing members who guarded important public buildings and mosques.[42] The Committee of Free Officers, who led the successful revolution, enacted two favorable measures that allowed the Brotherhood to rejoin the public political discussion. The first was to reopen the inquiry into the assassination of Hasan al-Banna. The second was to declare a general amnesty for political prisoners, who were disproportionately members of the Brotherhood. Moreover, in late September 1952, the Brotherhood was even invited to join the Revolutionary Cabinet formed by Muhammad Najib.

In early 1953 all political parties were dissolved and their activities banned. The Brotherhood, however, was exempted from the ban on the basis that it was a movement and not a political party. One of the Free Officers, Ahmed Hamroush, disclosed that Gamal Abdel Nasser had told the minister of the interior, Sulaiman Hafidh, that "the Brotherhood was one of the greatest supporters of the movement . . . contributed greatly to it, and still offers continuous support." In view of this, Nasser asked the minister to find a way to exempt the Brotherhood from the ban.[43] However, the distinction between religious associations and political parties—the distinction which allowed the Brotherhood to continue functioning freely under Law no. 179 of 1952—was one that the Brotherhood itself ultimately rejected, bringing it to loggerheads with the government. The explanation advanced was that the Brotherhood's religious activities were in fact political in nature. This was exemplified by their effort to have all laws scrutinized before being issued, to ensure their conformity with the Shari'ah. To one such demand, Nasser reported in an official communiqué, "I have already told the Guide [al-Hudaybi] that we will not accept guardianship. . . . I repeat the same today with determination and insistence."[44]

Late in 1953 the government created a political body, the Liberation Movement. Its declared aim was the formation of a united political organization to encompass all political groups, including the Brotherhood. The Brotherhood strongly protested, and when their pleas fell on deaf ears, the rift between the Brotherhood and the revolutionary government widened considerably. According to Egyptian historian Abd al-'Adhim Ramadhan, there were four reasons for the increasing tension. First, the Muslim Brotherhood was negotiating with the British on evacuation from the Suez Canal Zone. While these negotiations were not official, they were not clandestine either and seemed to have had the tacit approval of the Revolutionary Command Council. The rift developed when the positions of the government and the Brotherhood began to diverge over the evacuation of the British. Second, the Brotherhood was proselytizing for membership in the military and police, in effect creating a potential fifth column in the armed forces. Third, the well-armed paramilitary force of the Brotherhood continued to function, posing a serious challenge to the power of the new regime. Finally, all of the above were brought to the fore when members of the Brotherhood initiated contact with General Muhammad Najib to form an alliance against Nasser.[45] As a result, in January 1954 the Revolutionary Command Council declared the Brotherhood to be a political party and ordered its disbandment and the arrest of al-Hudaybi and some 449 other members.

In exchange for an agreement to modify political activity, the government released the arrested members of the Brotherhood and withdrew the ban on the organization. However, the Brotherhood's "secret apparatus" escalated its antigovernment activities, especially in the wake of the Anglo-Egyptian Accord on the evacuation of British troops from the Suez Canal Zone. Attempts were made to organize antigovernment demonstrations, and on 26 October 1954 a "secret apparatus" operative named Mahmud Abd al-Latif attempted to assassinate Nasser. The government struck back ruthlessly. Muslim Brotherhood properties were ransacked and seized, and thousands of members were arrested. In December al-Hudaybi was sentenced to life imprisonment, and five others involved in the plot were executed, including the would-be assassin.

The Brotherhood's experience with the revolutionary regime between 1952 and 1954 paralleled the process that had culminated in the suppression of the movement in 1948. Once again the Brotherhood had become increasingly involved in overt opposition politics, and in so doing invited the inevitable government countermeasures and organizational suppression. This process of Muslim Brotherhood politicization and confrontation would occur two more times over the next thirty years, first in the mid-1960s (in opposition to Nasser), and then with their offshoots late in the 1970s and early 1980s (amid the turmoil before and after the assassination of Anwar al-Sadat). It derives from the nature of Muslim Brotherhood ideology, which was fundamentally threatening to both the pre- and postrevolutionary governments of Egypt.

To begin with, the Muslim Brotherhood's goals of restructuring the social, political, legal, and economic order of society were in accordance with their idealization of a historically more ethical state—the Salafiyah state.[46] These inherently reactionary goals are essentially pragmatic adaptations of modern social doctrines regarding solutions to contemporary social problems. Thus, on socioeconomic and sociopolitical issues, the Muslim Brotherhood is ideologically pragmatic, focusing on the issues and solutions that have popular appeal, but these are only means to an end. Their goal is the introduction of the Shari'ah as the law of the land. The goals of this religious ideology ultimately result in opposition to any government that will not modify legal practices in accordance with the Shari'ah and alliance with any group that may further this end.

Another important dimension of Muslim Brotherhood ideology is its inherent theocratic authoritarianism. This basically derives from the fact that the moral order pursued by the Brotherhood is perceived as being dictated by God and then imposed by government. In effect, the function of the state is to maintain a moral order. By its nature, then, the government must oppose any tendency toward an increase in moral choice or moral pluralism—which can lead to levels of intolerance incompatible with contemporary civil society. These orientations have become the fundamental tenets of all modern Islamic political groupings.

The Growth of Contemporary Islamist Movements

The establishment of the Islamic state, or the advance of a consensus to achieve a wider Islamic consciousness, has not been achieved despite the efforts of the Muslim Brotherhood and the optimism engendered by the 1979 Iranian Revolution. The goal of transforming society into a purely Islamic one, modeled after the early Islamic society established by Muhammad, is at the core of the resurgence of Islamic activism. As we have seen, Islamist political groups make no distinction between religion and state because they consider the Qur'an and the *sunna* to be the basis for all aspects of social interaction within society. The failure of the modern national state in the region to respond to a vast array of social issues—especially within the areas of development, modernization, and the moral decay many see associated with the importation of western consumerism—raises enough concern to have placed Islamic activism at the forefront of new political actors. Thus far they have proved unsuccessful in overcoming the failed legacy of nationalist, liberal, socialist, and communist parties that have preceded them. Success in dealing with the poverty, unequal distribution of resources, and social decay within modern secular states will give popular credence to the validity of Islamist claims. The construction of mosques, schools, and hospitals, as well as the ability to organize a sound and workable social infrastructure, will be the path to further influence, popularity, and the prospect to govern, which will provide the opportunity to harness the power of the state in such efforts.[47]

Several factors have increased the awareness and popularity of Islamist parties and groups throughout the Middle East. First, as these activists perceive events, the failure of both the Palestine Liberation Organization and the Arab confrontation states (Lebanon, Syria, Jordan, and Egypt) to deal effectively with the Israeli occupation of Arab lands continues to challenge the Islamic disposition of Palestine and the loss of the third holiest site in the Islamic world—the Dome of the Rock in Jerusalem. Second, the inability of secular governments to successfully cope with the persistent social problems of their societies has encouraged the people of these states to examine alternatives to the militarist-nationalist and traditional leaderships. Third, networking and increased communication have allowed Islamist groups to assist one another. Fourth, various governments of the region have extended support to and for the Islamists, most notably the Islamic Republic of Iran.[48] The Iranian Revolution in 1978–79 now serves as a successful model for other Islamist groups to emulate and provides the aid only a nation-state can provide in our current international system, including moral and monetary support, training, and safe harbor from persecution. Fifth, the past efforts of Islamist groups in effecting political change—such as the assassination of Sadat in 1981 and the attacks on Israeli and American military forces in Lebanon later in the decade—have heightened their public profile. The 1990s provided even more examples, including the destruction of American barracks in Saudi Arabia in 1997 and the implication of Islamist groups in attacks against American embassies in East Africa in 1998 and the World Trade Center in New York in 1994. Sixth, American and western troops were sent to Saudi Arabia and the Gulf during the 1990–91 Gulf war and are now permanently stationed close to the holy cities of Mecca and Medina. Finally, many secular leaders who still practice Islamic rituals, especially those in the military, began their political careers in Islamic organizations such as the Muslim Brotherhood, making many tolerant of such groups. This diverse base generates sufficient interest and the membership required to translate

Islamic activist influence into concrete responses to the social questions plaguing Middle Eastern societies. The provision of an alternative to the failed policies of the western nation-state model fueled the popularity of Islamic movements throughout the Middle East.

Two models for twenty-first-century Islamic activism are those of Hamas (the Islamic Resistance Movement) in Palestine and Hizbullah (Party of God) in Lebanon. Hamas (meaning enthusiasm or zeal) was founded as the Palestinian *intifada* initiated in 1987 as an arm of the Muslim Brotherhood. Sharing much of the same leadership as the Muslim Brotherhood, it provided an Islamic and indigenous alternative during the eruption against Israeli occupation. Hamas enabled the Muslim Brotherhood to conduct organized civil disobedience throughout the occupied territories without being implicated directly, thereby sacrificing their standing within the community. Providing such an alternative to the secular Palestinian leadership, Hamas rapidly rose to a position of influence and to a level of prominence commensurate with Yasser Arafat's Fatah organization, which is the largest faction of the PLO. During the *intifada*, Hamas used a number of tactics to propel the uprising against Israeli occupation, often based out of local mosques. With mosques so prominently placed within all Muslim societies and dispersed throughout the territories, they provide a base of operations and a rallying point against which secular forces could not compete. The role of the mosque as a place of learning and political organization, as well as a center of worship, allowed Hamas to organize efficiently as well as maintain their principal goal of returning Palestine to an Islamic society. Hamas asserts that as an Islamic society, modeled on historical Islamic states, the people of Palestine—Muslim, Christian, and Jew—would live peacefully under Muslim rule. Palestine, as envisaged by Hamas, cannot be surrendered to non-Muslim authority, as no individual, association, or government has such a right before God. The Palestinian secular leadership—united under the umbrella of the Palestine Liberation Organization (PLO)—with whom Hamas disagrees, cannot negotiate away territory under the auspices of any "peace process." Rather, the Israeli forces must evacuate the occupied territories unilaterally and without guarantees of any nature, allowing for the unfettered self-determination of the Palestinian people. The seeming abandonment of a revolutionary and ideologically based position by the secular PLO in the post–Gulf war peace process has allowed for the creation of an ideological and doctrinal vacuum within Palestinian society. Hamas has filled this vacuum through its political and social activities.[49]

Hamas organized resistance against Israeli occupation in the West Bank and Gaza. The escalation of resistance against Israeli forces, including bloody reprisals against those suspected of collusion with Israeli forces in Gaza and the West Bank, gave Hamas the reputation in the West of being a brake on the peaceful intentions of the secular leadership. However, Hamas has publicly maintained that it will support any resolution to the occupation that allows for the freedom of Palestinians and their land that is democratically endorsed by the Palestinian people. The failures of the PLO leadership to establish a working democracy within the framework of the Palestinian National Authority (PNA), as well as increasing levels of political corruption and oppressive policies resulting in widespread human rights violations, continued to increase Hamas's political legitimacy.

It is the threat of a successful example that Israel and the secular and repressive governments of the region are now forced to recognize. For much of the 1990s until the Israeli withdrawal from southern Lebanon in July 2000, Hizbullah waged an almost textbook guerrilla war against both Israeli occupation forces and the Israeli sponsored South Lebanese Army. It did so within the territorial limits of Lebanon and with the express purpose of ending the Israeli occupation. When it did strike into Israel, it was in reprisal for Israeli and SLA attacks on Lebanese civilians. Such tactics earned Hizbullah the respect of the Lebanese people, even those not predisposed to support the Shiite-based militia, because it demonstrated Hizbullah's respect for the diversity of opinion in Lebanon about the extent, nature, and form that resistance to Israel's occupation should take. Most important, and unlike the PLO's guerrilla war of the 1970s and 1980s, the struggle was about freeing Lebanon's borders rather than those of another occupied Arab land such as Palestine. In the end, the resistance proved too expensive for the Israeli government in both human and material terms, forcing its withdrawal after some twenty years of engagement and occupation.

CHAPTER 3

The Oppressive State and Civil Society

*T*he purpose of this chapter is to examine the nature of the state in the Middle East by focusing on the interface between the state and society. After briefly overviewing the main parameters for the concepts of state and civil society, this chapter will examine the evolution of the oppressive state in the Middle East. This is followed by an overview of the evolution of civil society in the region. The final section focuses on human rights to examine the relationship between civil society and the state in the contemporary Middle East.

The state is a construct in social science employed to examine the exercise of power and authority in society. Historically, the state emerged from a legal fiction invented in the Treaty of Westphalia in 1648 to vest, legitimate, and perpetuate political power in territoriality. In the West, the nation-state system that evolved became entrenched in international relations, and by the mid-twentieth century it was reified in international law and practice as the paramount actor in global politics. In this context, the state represents a myth that has been imbued with power, sovereignty, and legitimacy in international politics.

As an institution, the state manifests parameters of structure and process. Embedded in a social context, these parameters serve to stabilize the control and exercise of power in an environment of economic and political change. The power of the state derives fundamentally from its monopoly over the legitimate exercise of violence, a monopoly sanctified in international law and practice. It is represented in the concept of the oppressive state, for the exercise of violence (even if only symbolically) in the service of power is oppressive by definition.

The construct of civil society relates to the interface between the state and society. It is the sphere of activity outside the political and legal authority of the state where, ideally or theoretically, citizens band together in free association to promote and pursue nonprofit objectives. Embedded in the logic of liberal capitalist society, the concept of civil society was utilized in both classical and Marxist political economy to examine the relationship between society and state, on the one hand, and economy and culture, on the other, in the context of capitalist development. The globalization of the state and capital after the Second World War universalized the context. And with the collapse of the so-called second world with the fall of the Berlin Wall in 1989, the concept of civil society gained currency to assess the adaptation of nonwestern cultures to the political culture of economic liberalism.

Conceptualized as voluntary association in the nexus between state and economy, civil society constitutes links between the social, economic, and political spheres in the social construction of everyday life. A main idea underlying the concept in liberal thought is that of a plurality of voluntary associations capable of opposing the ideological monopoly of the political order and, in Marxist thought, capable of opposing the ideological hegemony of the economic order.[1] As such, civil society outside the western capitalist core (where the hegemonic role of the state tends to be less entrenched) reflects the normative tensions within such cultural dichotomies as collective and individual, status and power, cooperation and competition, violent and nonviolent conflict. As an indicator of political culture, civil society manifests the relationship between symbolic meaning and purposeful action in substantive form. In this context, the abuse of human rights constitutes an indicator for the assessment of oppression in a society. The abuse of human rights, in other words, points to the sectors in a society where the freedom of voluntary association is restricted by the state.

Evolution of the State in the Middle East

This section examines the evolution of the state in the Middle East in terms of a periodization based on fundamental shifts in the international balance of power. Three periods are examined: the Ottoman period, the era of colonialism, and globalization in the Middle East.

The Ottoman Period

At its height, the Ottoman Empire stretched from southwest Asia to the Balkans and incorporated diverse cultures and languages. While Turkish was the official language and the language of public administration, Arabic was predominant in the cultural sphere, not only because it is the formal language of Islam but also because the Arabs constituted the largest cultural group in the empire. The Ottoman government was theoretically based on the Islamic principles embodied in both the Muslim corpus juris and the Shariʿah as administered by the religious courts under the authority of Sheikh al-Islam, the highest religious authority in the state. Separate categories of laws governed and regulated the relations of non-Muslim communities within the Ottoman Empire. As the non-Muslims could not be subjected to the Shariʿah, they were generally left to their own legal and communal arrangements and the tribunals in which their leadership chose to administer justice for each of those minority communities. They enjoyed freedom of worship, the free selection of their local representatives, the maintenance of their educational systems, and the application of their own laws in their own courts. This system of community legal autonomy was known as the millet system. Thus, from its earliest days, the Ottoman government reinforced tolerance and freedom within the empire by minimizing intercommunal contact and by removing areas of contention from intercommunal discourse. In large cities, Christians, Jews, and Muslims lived in separate quarters; children went to different schools, and the members of each community engaged in different professions and crafts.[2]

The Ottoman ruling institution was complex, for it subsumed both religious and legal governing institutions. The Ottoman sultan and his ministers were also intertwined with the administrative arm of the government. They did not act in isolation from the religious institutions, because the empire was essentially religious in character. But the sultan and the royal palace also served as a source of secular executive authority that coexisted with the principles of Islamic law. Secular royal commandments were called *qanuns,* which were issued on occasion to regulate intercommunal relations because the society was divided into such starkly defined groups. Thus, the relationship of the individual to the government was conditioned by communal affiliation as well as religious identity. The qanuns were used to refine and answer any questions regarding the obligations of individuals.

The Ottoman administrative system was largely decentralized, not only in the Middle East and North Africa but throughout the Balkans as well, while Morocco was never under Ottoman tutelage. Places like Arabia and present-day Oman were hardly under the direct control of the Ottoman government, and the holy cities of Mecca and Medina, far from paying taxes, received large sums of money from Istanbul. The emirs (princes) and the local chiefs in the Arab lands were given autonomy and charged with the internal administration of their towns and cities, particularly Damascus, Mount Lebanon, Kisirwan, and Akkad, while governors were appointed to coastal towns like Aleppo, Homs, and Tripoli.

The focus of the loose Ottoman administration up to the mid-nineteenth century was to maintain the status quo, and amelioration meant the removal of abuses. The Ottomans retained the Mamluk socioeconomic system, based on a military tax farm, which existed as a parallel hierarchy with a smaller though more formal Ottoman apparatus.

The state did not exercise economic control functions. This was left to the nonstate sector, which was primarily occupied by craft guilds as well as various other economic groupings. Consequently, the sources of social power in society, except for the military, were left diffuse, and the heads of the various minority groups, whether based on religion, the economy, ethnicity, or tribal affiliation, had the power to mediate between their communities and the state. In facing a complex pluralist society, the Ottomans adopted an essentially community-based political formula. In the provinces of the empire, local notables had direct access to the office of the ruling Turkish governor and could affect policy within the empire at large. While this proved to be a strength during the empire's expansion, it proved a major Achilles heel when faced with the aggressive economic expansion of the emerging, industrializing West. Provincial elites, who ruled either by virtue of membership in the military, in the circles of the learned, or through strong communal power bases, were able to form broad coalitions of local forces and to act as a focus of the local society to oppose the Ottoman government or oblige it to act through them.

Over time there was a tendency to increase local autonomy among intermediary groupings, especially at the periphery of the empire at the expense of Istanbul. This tendency toward decentralization of the Ottoman system engendered unintentional community-centered corporatism, especially within the various articulated modes of production that had emerged within the empire. What contributed significantly to the development of the corporatist formula in pre-capitalist Ottoman society, especially in the Arab provinces of the empire, was the fact that social links tended to be coterminous with the intermeshing of horizontal stratification (classes, elites) and vertical differentiation (tribe, sect, ethnicity). The overlapping of interclass and intraclass membership increased economic permeability and social mobility across social class strata.

Corporatist solidarity may be an important variable in explaining the rising opposition in the periphery to Ottoman attempts at centralization and administrative reform, known as the Tanzimat, which occurred between 1839 and 1876. This reform was initiated in the face of western economic and political encroachment. The centralization was, in part, a defensive attempt at modernization that borrowed heavily from the

French model and produced in its wake Turkish nationalistic solidarity. The French Revolution, with its far-reaching ideological influence, and the industrial revolution, with its destabilizing impact on local economies, initially impacted the Ottoman Empire by penetrating trade routes. European merchants used the capitulations representing a series of trade concessions made by the Ottoman state to the West to raise capital for the state as a spearhead for eventual economic domination. By the nineteenth century, the increasing European economic encroachment had culminated in the incorporation of the economy of the peripheral Ottoman provinces into developing western capitalist markets.

The Era of Colonialism

The Middle East is the only Third World region that is geographically contiguous with Europe and the only area that has been in sustained confrontation with the dominant powers in the West for over 1,400 years. European encroachment began with the Crusades. Imperialist advances were initiated with Russian forays between 1768 and 1774 that were soon followed by Napoleon's expedition into Egypt in 1798, which in turn led to Britain's military interference in 1801 to ward off Napoleonic ambitions in the region. Rivalry among the dominant powers of Europe, in other words, began to take place at the periphery of the Ottoman Empire. Involving goals of strategic communication, trade, and the pursuit of economic advantage, this rivalry eventually led to the colonization of the Ottoman periphery, which constituted the core of the Arab world and engendered the Eastern Question system.

The piecemeal sundering of the Ottoman territory resulted in the gradual but progressive establishment of various modes of imperial power throughout the empire, especially in the Arab lands. A European presence and the influence it accrued steadily increased—France in Algeria (1830), Tunisia (1881), and Morocco (1912); Italy in Libya (1911); Britain in Egypt (1882), Sudan (1898), South Arabia (1839), and in the Trucial Sheikhdoms (from late nineteenth century to 1914). At the end of the First World War, the Arab East (the Mashriq) was taken from the crumbling Ottoman Empire and parceled out: Iraq, Palestine, and Transjordan went to Britain, while Greater Syria (contemporary Syria and Lebanon) went to France. The heartland of what had been the Ottoman Empire became a Turkish republic. Unlike the Arab lands, Turkey and Iran escaped direct colonial rule. In Turkey, the military revolt of Attaturk in 1920–22 pushed out the Greek army. In Iran, popular nationalist mobilization after the First World War forced Britain to relinquish its plans for assuming a protectorate. European powers were further threatened by the revolutionary regime in Moscow and found themselves desiring a buffer zone. The Trucial Coast of the Gulf, Arabia, and North Yemen were the only Arab lands that were not subject to colonial rule. They were all ruled by conservative monarchies where tribal coalitions under strong imperial influence seized power. The discovery of oil in the region and the immense level of its potential productive capacity added a further dimension to the region's intrinsic geostrategic and political value.

Throughout the region, indigenous political movements emerged in opposition to European encroachment. In 1883, the Mahdi movement in Sudan crushed the British military force of General Gordon and was able to stay in power for ten years. There was a major protest movement against British economic influence in Iran in 1891 and an urban uprising against the shah of Iran in what came to be known as the Constitutional Revolution (1906–8). In the aftermath of the First World War, there was also a self-declared revolutionary Soviet republic in the northern Iranian province of Gilan. In 1919, a popular revolution broke out in Egypt, announcing the beginning of a national struggle against British imperialism.

In the Middle East, only the French attempted direct colonial settlement while also attempting to assimilate the indigenous populations of the Maghrib. The British attempted to rule indirectly over the local population often through pro-British indigenous allies. However, British policy met with popular rejection, which developed quickly into mass protests and the development of nationalist movements for the liberation and independence of the former Ottoman provinces. Serious uprisings in protest of colonial rule took place in Iraq (1920), Syria (1926), and Palestine (1936–39).

Imperialism and Globalization

The advocacy of imperial interests was the crux of colonial policy. The concept of globalization generally refers to the integration of local and regional economies into the international market of capitalism. While the term came into popular usage in the 1990s, in fact the process of capitalist market expansion and integration was integral to capitalist development since its inception in the eighteenth century. In the Middle East especially, the general character of the imperialist policies of western powers toward the region was the continuation and consolidation of their economic inroads. The incorporation of Middle Eastern countries into capitalist markets was an involved and prolonged process with tremendous sociopolitical consequences. Beginning with steamships in 1830, European trade and capital began to flood the region, in effect marginalizing local crafts and manufactures. A rudimentary financial system was quickly furnished to favor the importation of foreign goods and the expansion of the agricultural sector with a concentration on cash crops. Subsistence farming was marginalized in favor of cash crops. Wheat, barley, and maize—the mainstays of subsistence agriculture—had to be purchased abroad. Thus, the international market expanded. Improvements in the transportation network, such as the building of docks, roads, and railway networks and the enhancement of existing port facilities, further encouraged both imports and exports.

A change in land tenure allowed the administrative and legal system to gradually break down communal ownership of land and generated a boom in private land ownership. The population explosion and the availability of money in the form of an advance credit expanded cultivation as well as the exploitation of labor of the landless peasantry. The establishment of mortgage banks and European insurance companies allowed for the rapid emergence of minorities (Jews, Armenians, Greeks) into positions of control over the new financial sector. This also influenced foreign trade and small-scale manufacturing.

On the top of the pyramid lay the colonial authority and its European sponsors; beneath the administrative structure were the professional and commercial foreign minorities and then the emerging native landlords, who in the main allied themselves with western powers. The bulk of the population, unskilled urban labor and rural farmers, remained heterogeneous social formations whose older corporate structures were seriously eroded. Thus, as Charles Issawi noted, the importation of a middle class en bloc from abroad made it possible to exploit both the human and natural resources without developing the colony.[3] The imperial powers, in pursuit of their goals, retained the precapitalist mode of production while modernizing the agrisectors and related infrastructures, leading to lopsided and rapid socioeconomic change.

The political administrative structure of the colonial state was based mainly on the premise of a single center of authority, means of control, and security, which ushered in the development of new bureaucracies. The center of traditional authority tended to make standard rules and regulations that would apply equally to all people, and since the imported European model of the nation-state was secular, in the sense that laws were made by civil not religious authority, the historical political culture of the Middle East found itself under increasing attack. Yet, when it suited the imperial interests, the colonial authority gave special privileges and rights of self-management to some religious groups and even allocated a special place in the political arena on a communal rather than an individual basis. Seats were reserved for minorities in the legislature. The discriminatory process of special status for religious minorities was taken to the extreme in the case of Lebanon.[4] In Syria, the French played on sectarian division and employed ethnically based military forces while pitting rural areas against the urban centers. The French administered the Alawite majority–based district separately, promoted Alawite tribal leaders, and weakened the Sunni landed aristocracy through the division and redivision of Syria, which undermined indigenous governmental experience and increased factionalism.[5]

Another feature of the colonial state was the emphasis on police forces and security apparatus as the key to continued political control. The colonial expense account on security and safety averaged 60 percent of public expenditures in the 1920s and 1930s. For the same period, the amount allocated for social welfare services averaged 11.2 percent. Little was left for education and public health, and the national armies were organized to serve internal security purposes rather than national defense. The colonial power spent 28.5 percent of its budget on bureaucracy and administration.[6] Thus, the superimposed European model of the modern state within the Middle Eastern colonies was, much like the socioeconomic structure, lopsided—overdeveloped in the security and bureaucratic wing, and underdeveloped in its redistributive capacities. Furthermore, the state's ability to generate a worldview that would cement the ruler and the ruled in political consciousness did not develop because the social forces that made the modern state in Europe at a certain historical juncture did not exist in the political culture fostered under imperial encroachment in the Middle East.

The existence of an occupying power generated, in a dialectic manner, the national struggle for liberation within colonially drawn political boundaries. The emergence of national movements for independence in the interwar period as well as the concept of nationalism were fostered by colonialism—which in effect reproduced its essence (exploitation and oppression) in the newly emerging states in the so-called Third World. Thus, while the colonial state developed in opposition to the social formations of civil society, its overdeveloped capacity for applying oppressive measures was inherited by nationalism and nationalists. The state that the postindependence regimes inherited did not reflect opposing demands of dominant social classes, nor did it represent or reflect the plurality of interests in society. And certainly, according to the western notion of neoliberal capitalism, the state did not promote and defend the common interests of individual members of society.

Despite the fact that some Middle Eastern countries, such as Turkey, Iran, Saudi Arabia, Northern Yemen, and the peninsular coastal towns that were tied by treaty to Britain, never experienced direct colonial rule, they were directly impacted by imperialism, which fundamentally changed their political economies. Like the postcolonial states, they too focused on developing the security and regulatory arm of the state after independence. The West's state model was either forced on them through colonialism (as in Syria and Iraq), foisted on them through the machinations of imperialist powers (as in the sheikhdoms of the Trucial Coast), or copied by the western-oriented political elites (as in Turkey, Iran, and Egypt). Reflecting the degree of political and cultural penetration of the West into the Middle East, by whatever route the state arrived, the political elite wholeheartedly adopted the slogans of state sovereignty and authority, the paraphernalia of power it gave them access to, and the will to power it subsumed. Reflecting on the cultural impact of imperialism, Timothy Mitchell observed, "Imperialism was a global project undertaken as an enframing, and hence had the effect of representing a realm of the conceptual, conjuring up for the first time *a priori* abstractions of progress, reason, law, discipline, history, authority and order."[7]

After the Second World War, most of the colonized world gained independence, although some Middle Eastern countries had become nominally independent earlier. Fred Halliday succinctly described the general picture of the Middle Eastern state accordingly:

> The post 1945 period has seen the seizure of control by rulers of the state structures, the exploitation of economic opportunities, and consolidation of their power domestically against their subjects and regional rivals. For all the rhetoric of a national communality uniting the ruler and the ruled, the tenures of these rulers and their administrations have been marked by a persistent and often ruthless use of instruments of political and social control—repression, massacre, demagoguery, censorship, bribery, and corruption. While subjugating the socioeconomic formations to the predominant power of the state, the ruler equally concerned himself to preserve other forms of power over subject ethnic groups, such as the Kurds in Turkey, Iran or in Iraq; over confessional groups, such as in the Shiites in Lebanon and Saudi Arabia.[8]

All of the post–Second World War states in the Middle East relied too much on the instruments of oppression—a preponderant presence of the army and enhanced internal security apparatus.

Evolution of Civil Society in the Middle East

This section examines the evolution of civil society in the Middle East in terms of a periodization based on changes in political economy. The specific character of civil society changed in conjunction with changes in the political economy. These periods are examined in terms of the general character of civil society within three eras: Islamic, Ottoman, and independence.

The Islamic Era

The distinctive character of the civil society that emerged in the early centuries of the second millennium was due largely to the nature of the Islamic state. Islamic law, always held in the autonomous hands of jurists, provided a high degree of freedom to civil society. Civil society did not need to advance its interests through the state to counterbalance state power, as was the case in Europe during the Middle Ages. The strength of the Muslim bourgeoisie derived from their organization and extensive commercial and financial networks. Members of the vast array of crafts, industry, and trade organized themselves into societies or guilds that acted to advance their members' interests into the new domains of the expanding empire. From the beginning of the Abbasid period, roughly A.D. 723, until the first foreign invasion by the Buwayids in 945, city life and urban activity reached its zenith. Ellis Goldberg argues that during that period an Islamic bourgeoisie flourished and engaged in associational formations and societies that developed and sustained business and industrial activities, which were protected from state interference under Islamic law.[9]

In the Islamic Empire, markets were integral to the flourishing of urban life. They evolved into three types: *suq* (market), *qaisariyya* (caesarian), and the *khan* (caravanserai). As a rule, each trade and craft would have its own area in the market. Each industry was supplied by a great number of factories and was assigned an area in which to sell its wares. Of special interest is the khan (sometimes referred to as *funduq*). It was the storehouse of foreign traders who would then select a member to supervise the khan. Khans in major cities grew quite large, numbering up to 300 buildings, with membership reaching as high as 4,000. The khan was like a big wholesale department store whose merchandise increased in number as trade flourished. The khan also performed other mercantile functions, such as banking services whereby merchants were able to deposit their boxes of silver and gold and engage in business transactions with a monetary document called *saqq*—which was akin to a modern-day check.[10] Both Muslim and foreign business communities established quasi-agencies (*sikalat*) for the exchange of goods and services and the transfer of money. Trading activity deriving from local, regional, and international markets was free from state control, and pricing was left to market mechanisms except for consumables.[11] A clear indication of urban prosperity at the time is the dramatic increase in taxation revenues.[12]

The strength of the Muslim bourgeoisie derived from their organization and extensive commercial and financial networks. Tradesmen organized themselves into societies or guilds that maintained high standards
of professionalism and advanced the social, community, and economic
interests of their members. Those societies not only reflected solidarity
of membership but were also a medium for professional identification
and pride. The practices and ethical conventions of each society found
parajudicial legitimation and were invoked in case of legal conflicts.
The potency of socioprofessional cohesion of these societies provided
them with a political voice. "In 976 . . . they [the Buwayids] imposed a
new tax on cotton and silk textiles in Baghdad. The members of affected
societies rose in active protest until the tax was repealed. A few decades
later, members of some societies engaged in combat against Turkish military forces."[13] Social cohesion and mutual aid were integral functions
of civil society. "When any member died, the whole group cooperated in
maintaining his widow, until she remarried or passed away, and his children until they were trained in some art or occupation."[14]

The Islamic bourgeoisie established an international trade and financial network based on a credit system, which enabled them to transfer
sufficient capital without much concern about fixed assets and to build
mechanisms for capital transfer in case of serious threat to the operation
of free enterprise.[15] The trade routes (both sea and land) extended from
Baghdad to Egypt, North Africa, and Spain. They extended east to India,
China, Korea, Indonesia, Sri Lanka, and Malaysia.[16]

Internationalization of trade necessitated new forms of responsive
financial enterprises, which were formalized and legitimated under
Islamic law. A wide range of mercantile organizations developed, analogous to today's corporations. They included partnerships and limited
partnerships (shanan), limited liability (al-mufawadha), shareholders
(al-wujuh), marketing companies (al-rakkadh), and even a form of
monopoly within certain industries (al-khazan) and common agencies.
State regulatory activity of professional and economic undertakings was
minimal because of the independent religious stratum that was the
source of lawmaking and legitimation. The state engaged in assessing a
fair (almost nominal) tax regime on local industry and trade, ensured
equivalence of tariff on Muslim exports, and protected business people
from foreign impingement.

The financial houses on which the credit system was founded were
beyond the physical scope of the Islamic state. Such houses could be
found in India, China, Indonesia, Sri Lanka, and Basra. They formed networks of intermediaries that financed commercial transactions without the involvement of individual business people in each and every

agreement. Two main institutions rose above others in the network: *al-sarrafeen* (money exchange houses) and *al-jahabetha* (an equivalent to modern banks). The staunch support that the Islamic state lent to free enterprise and the middle class was epitomized by Ibn Khaldun's dictum that the state is the greatest commercial market. The Islamic urban middle class derived its independence from the sovereignty of law, independent judiciary, and integrated matrix of Islamic society.[17]

In about 945, the Buwayids invaded Baghdad and established a Turkish military government under the banner of Islam. The Buwayid period was followed by the Seljuk invasion in the eleventh century. These invasions not only undermined the political power of the Muslim Arab state in the center of the Islamic Empire; they also produced a detrimental socioeconomic restructuring of Islamic society. Both the Buwayid and Seljuk regimes were based on a militaristic hereditary form of government and were inimical to industry and trade. They favored land control in what was akin to a hereditary feudal system, establishing a form of feudalism that marginalized the farmers and prevented them from owning land. At the same time, both regimes persistently burdened craftspeople, workshops, and business ventures with heavy taxation, fraudulent minting, and confiscation.[18] This resulted in the flight of capital and skilled labor to the periphery, which had come under the rule of independent monarchies.

Succeeding periods witnessed new forms of military confrontation, such as the Crusades and the invasions of the Mongols. The Crusades began in 1096 and symbolized the arrival of conquering armies advancing in the name of religion. Foreign armies seized and occupied nearly the entire Levant coast.[19] The Crusades represented the first western attempt at imperialist penetration into the region. They established a network of trading stations to draw out resources from Islamic territories in the interior.[20]

The Mongol invasion and the rise of their empire (1258–1335) proved even more destructive than earlier invasions from the Eurasian steppe. The Mongols irreparably destroyed the delicate irrigation network, expanded the feudalistic order, and imposed heavy new taxes on the business class. The process severed Mesopotamia from the rest of the region's economic networks. As a result, interregional trade was redirected northward. Mamluk rule in Egypt (1250–1517) did little to expand economic and civil life. Land-based feudalism did not allow for the conditions required for the reemergence of urban society, resulting in further economic deterioration and widespread impoverishment.[21]

The European discovery of a sea route around the Cape of Good Hope in the late fifteenth century further eroded traditional trade routes, which had crossed the Middle East connecting European, African, and Asian civilizations. The Portuguese age of sea supremacy saw them establish military and trade stations in Aden, on the Persian Gulf, in India, and in Mombasa (today's Kenya). The Portuguese began attacking Muslim trading vessels, further disrupting regional commerce and interregional commercial networks. The five centuries following the Buwayid invasion transformed the Islamic economy and state from a predominantly urban and mercantilist economy to a rural and impoverished region.

The Ottoman Era

Following their conquest of Constantinople in 1517, the Ottoman Turks renamed the city Istanbul and established it as the capital of their empire in the Middle East. They continued to expand their empire through military conquest, and by the mid-seventeenth century it stretched from Gibraltar, across the Maghrib in North Africa and the Balkans in eastern Europe, north to the gates of Vienna, and from Yemen on the Red Sea coast westward through the Persian Gulf. The Ottoman state was founded on military feudalism, and it allowed the first trade concessions to western powers in an effort to increase the empire's revenues. These concessions (known as capitulations), first to Spain and the Dutch in the eighteenth century and to France and Britain in the nineteenth, ultimately led to the economic subordination of the region to the political economy of imperial Europe.

This increasing subordination was hastened by corruption, economic decline, and inept public policy. The economy was dominated by an increasingly awkward and costly bureaucracy. The sale of official offices and tax farming (the licensing of private agents to collect taxes for a commission) contributed to the decline of the economy, which was marked by a shrinking money supply and a steep rise in prices. The decline coincided with unfettered European access to Ottoman markets, and the increasing subordination of the Ottoman economy to western capital ensued. Major administrative reform, known as the Tanzimat, was initiated in 1839, but it failed to stem the tide of decline. Tax farming, officially abolished by the 1839 decree that initiated the Tanzimat, actually increased, symbolizing in effect the political corruption and wanton profiteering that accompanied the westernization of the Ottoman political economy.[22]

Under the classical Ottoman state (1300–1600), civil society developed in the framework of the millet system. In conjunction with the localized and fragmented political economy of the empire, voluntary associations tended to be community based and localized. In the context of a feudal system, there was little opportunity for expanded interactions or a broader consciousness of mutual interests and problems to emerge. The classical period marks the golden age of the Ottoman state. Thereafter, it began to decline, gradually at first, as it came into increasing contact with the West. In the context of expanding western economic inroads into the empire throughout the seventeenth and eighteenth centuries, the millet system offered fertile ground for the development of western-style nationalisms within the empire's diverse ethnocultural communities. The millet system not only exempted non-Muslim communities from the application of Shari'ah but also provided them with significant advantages in the new economy. Religious and educational missions from the West encouraged the development of voluntary associations, which expanded along ethnocultural lines and contributed to the emergence of ethnic nationalisms. This is exemplified in the Arab world, as demonstrated by George Antonius in his seminal book, *The Arab Awakening,* and by A. L. Tibawi in *Anglo-Arab Relations and the Question of Palestine, 1914–1921.*

The Era of Independence

In the first quarter century following the Second World War, the activities of states in the region expanded to incorporate virtually the whole public sector. In this context, autonomous civil society organizations were absorbed directly into the state structure (as in Egypt under Nasser,[23] or in Iraq under the Ba'athist regime),[24] co-opted by the state (as in Kuwait or the other oil-rich Gulf sheikhdoms),[25] and/or banned outright (as in Palestine under Israeli occupation;[26] in Turkey under the 1960–63 and 1980–83 military regimes;[27] in Syria under Hafez al-Assad; or in Iran under Ayatollah Khomeini). In this atmosphere, civil society languished and dissent was driven underground and radicalized as legitimate modes for its expression were cut off. However, the increasing withdrawal of the state from the public sphere over the last quarter of the twentieth century—an international phenomenon spearheaded in the West by Reaganomics and Thatcherism, and in the Third World by the economic restructuring policies of the International Monetary Fund and the World Bank—allowed for the rapid proliferation of civil society. According to data collected by the Ibn Khaldun Center for Developmental Studies in Cairo, for example, the number of Arab nongovernmental organizations grew from less than 20,000 in the mid-1960s to over 70,000 in the late 1980s. A large number of political parties accounted for some of the growth: 46 in Algeria, 43 in Yemen, 23 in Jordan, 19 in Morocco, 13 in Egypt, 11 in Tunisia, and so on.[28] The experience was similar in the non-Arab countries of the Middle East. In Turkey, for example, it was reported that there were about 50,000 non-governmental organizations by the early 1990s.[29] The rapid proliferation of professional syndicates is especially significant as they enjoy a high level of socioeconomic homogeneity, education, and financial independence. The professional syndicates tend to be organized on the regional level and to be networked cross-regionally and internationally. This networking provides a certain level of protection against the forces of state oppression. Furthermore, the professional syndicates are located at the heart of the economic system as well as in strategic institutions, which makes it difficult for ruling elites to effectively suppress them.

Civil formations have played a crucial role in maintaining the social fabric of society during crises. The existence of civil associations—in Lebanon during the civil war, 1975–90; in Palestine during the Intifada, 1987–90; in Kuwait during the Iraqi invasion and occupation, 1990–91; in Turkey in the aftermath of the 1999 earthquakes—and the networks of contacts they create provide material and moral support to citizens both at home and abroad.[30] However, their political role is not so clear. Strongly propagated in the West as harbingers for democratization,[31] these expectations have not been borne out in the Middle East. Optimistic analogies with the experience of Western Europe have been misleading as the overwhelming international inputs into the Middle East political system (in particular, colonialism and imperialism) have fundamentally distorted the development process in the region. Western democracy, in contrast, developed free from such foreign influences. In the Middle East generally, independence meant independent sovereign states, in most cases created directly or indirectly by western imperialist forces. In all cases, the newly independent states empowered Europeanized elites who found themselves, due to the foreign nature of their legitimacy, in opposition to indigenous political culture and the political dynamics that it legitimated indigenously.

The political elites of the post-Ottoman Middle East achieved political power through overt and/or covert cooperation with western powers in the dismantling of the Ottoman Empire. In effect, the imposition of the state system on the Middle East in the aftermath of the First World War invested anti-Ottoman, pro-western intellectual and economic elites with political authority mediated by external powers. Economically dependent on western aid to finance their regimes, and strategically dependent on western technology to modernize them, these elites tied regional political development to the global economy of the industrial world.

To maintain the compliance of an alienated public to their rule, in the era of independence, political elites in the Middle East pursued various avenues of control:

- They attempted to neutralize any potential opposition through co-optation, intimidation, or violent purge.
- They monopolized mass propaganda and mounted large-scale ideological campaigns.
- They undertook grandiose development ventures, using mega-construction projects as symbols of progress.

The constant regional tension provided by hostilities entrenched in the region by the imposition of the nation-state system (Arab-Israeli; Iraq-Iran; Kurdish uprisings in Syria, Iraq, Iran, and Turkey) provided new avenues for foreign interference in Middle East politics in the post-independence era. Reflecting the level of violence endemic in Middle East politics, between 1948 and 1991, interstate and intrastate conflicts resulted in over 2.2 million casualties in the region. More than 3 million people were displaced, and more than U.S.$1.4 trillion was spent on armaments.[32]

In addition, these tensions served to legitimate oppressive measures and human rights abuse in the region. Of the nineteen states in the Middle East, only eleven are signatories of the United Nations convention against torture, and most of those who are signatory have expressed strong reservations with Articles 21 and 22, which require the state in question to submit to examination whenever grievance petitions are filed. Furthermore, over half of the states in the region that have signed the UN declaration on human rights have not routinely responded to annual UN reports, as they are required to do under the treaty.[33]

In their quest to establish hegemony through coercive means, Middle Eastern states encroached on all aspects of civil society. In effect, throughout the region, states attempted to impose hegemony over civil society through oppressive and coercive measures administered through juridical, administrative, or security channels. In regimes that oppress and persecute political opposition, there is little room for autonomy. In their efforts to suppress dissent, Middle Eastern states increasingly restricted their populations' active participation in sociopolitical processes. Because of state dominance over modern instruments and modes of communication and articulation, avenues for effective participation in the political sphere have been severely restricted. In the sociocultural sphere, however, the withdrawal of the state from the public sphere has allowed for growth in civil society activities that can provide the sociocultural functions no longer provided by the state, particularly in such fields as social welfare, health and education, arts, and culture. Responding to the state's withdrawal from the public sector, community-based associations became active in meeting the unmet social needs. The boundary between community activism and social advocacy is a gray area, however. Because sociopolitical avenues for dissent were severely restricted, it crystallized around human rights activism and/or religious activism. In its *World Report 1999*, Human Rights Watch highlighted the fact that "Independent citizens and locally based organizations from Morocco to Iran challenged anachronistic laws and undemocratic systems of governance, monitored and publicized human rights violations, and demanded an end to impunity. There were setbacks as well as progress, but the voices of activists on the ground reached local and international audiences."[34]

As it represents the majority religion in the Middle East, Islamic activism challenges the status quo and has been resisted at the national, regional, and international levels. While Islamic activism has been variously shunned and denounced in the West, human rights activism has been enthusiastically embraced by the international civil society sector based in the West. Like Islamic activism, human rights activism represents a major challenge to the status quo in the region. However, unlike Islamic activism, high-profile advocacy groups such as Amnesty International and Human Rights Watch champion it in the West.

Human Rights and the Oppressive State

This section surveys the contemporary situation of human rights in each of the states in the Middle East as reported by the two internationally prominent human rights monitors, Amnesty International and Human Rights Watch. Human rights are defined by international law as rights that deal "with the protection of individuals and groups against violations by governments of their internationally guaranteed rights, and with the promotion of these rights."[35] The protection and promotion of human rights has been a keystone of the United Nations since its creation, and it is embodied in Article 1 of the UN Charter. While the Universal Declaration of Human Rights, adopted by the international community in 1948, is the most widely accepted standard of human rights, it is not legally binding. However, many of its provisions are contained in two covenants adopted in 1966 that are legally binding: the International Covenant on Economic, Social, and Cultural Rights and the International Covenant on Civil and Political Rights. In addition to these undertakings, the UN has promulgated a number of conventions dealing with specific types of human rights violations. These include the Convention on the Prevention and Punishment of the Crime of Genocide (1951); the International Convention on the Elimination of All Forms of Racial Discrimination (1969); the Convention on the Elimination of All Forms of Discrimination against Women (1981); the Convention against Torture and Other Cruel, Inhuman, or Degrading Treatment or Punishment (1987); the Convention on the Rights of the Child (1990); and the International Convention on the Protection of the Rights of All Migrant Workers and Members of Their Families (adopted 1990, not yet in force).

Algeria

In 1992, fearing Islamists would win a victory in national elections, the Algerian army declared a state of emergency, canceled the elections, suspended the constitution, and attempted to clamp down on the Islamists. Clearly aimed at the Islamists, an "anti-terrorist" decree was issued "relating to the struggle against subversion and terrorism," and three special courts were set up to try those charged with "terrorist activities," which were vaguely defined and could include virtually any form of political difference with the regime.[36] A brutal civil war ensued, and by 1999 it had taken much more than the 100,000 lives official sources admitted to, most of them unarmed civilians, including women and children. In addition, there were an unspecified number of "disappeared."[37] The government undertook draconian measures to suppress the Islamists, violating all the basic human rights in the process. Throughout the 1990s, human rights reports recorded the litany of human rights abuses that the Algerian government justified under the rubric of antiterrorism. The Amnesty International 1998 annual report provides a synopsis for the year 1997 that reflects the dimensions of human rights abuse from 1992 onwards:

> Thousands of civilians, including hundreds of women and children, were killed in large-scale massacres committed in rural areas by armed groups. Thousands of people were killed by the security forces and state-armed militias; hundreds were reportedly extrajudicially executed. . . . Thousands of people, including prisoners of conscience and possible prisoners of conscience, were detained during the year; hundreds were charged under the "anti-terrorist" law. Thousands of people arrested in previous years were imprisoned after unfair trials. Scores of others continued to be held without trial. Torture and ill-treatment continued to be widespread, especially during unacknowledged detention, and ill-treatment was reported in prisons. Several hundred people who "disappeared" after arrest by the security forces remained unaccounted for. Scores of people

were abducted by armed groups. Scores of death sentences were imposed, most of them in absentia, and more than 600 people were under sentence of death at the end of the year. No judicial executions were reported.

In 1999, Human Rights Watch reported that the election of a new president, 'Abdelaziz Bouteflika, on a platform of anticorruption and peace and reconciliation fueled some optimism. However, the reporter noted, "He devoted little energy to establishing safeguards against future human rights violations" and "Algeria remained the most violent country in the Middle East and North Africa."[38]

Bahrain

Fearing a democratic challenge from the marginalized and oppressed Shi'a majority, in 1975 the government dissolved the national assembly and introduced a harsh security law. Intermittent pressures for restoration of democratic rights erupted into public demonstrations in December 1994. The government responded with draconian measures of repression against the Shiite community. These measures have been sustained for almost a decade now. Shi'a religious leaders and community activists have been arrested, detained incommunicado, and/or subjected to unfair trials.[39] The Amnesty International 1999 annual report provides a synopsis for the year 1998 in its regional country index that reflects the dimensions of human rights abuse in Bahrain:

> Hundreds of people were reported to have been arrested during the year for suspected anti-government activities or in connection with anti-government protests. Hundreds of others arrested in previous years remained held without charge or trial; they included eight religious and political leaders, all prisoners of conscience, who were arrested in 1996, as well as possible prisoners of conscience. Sixteen people charged with arson and possession of "unlawful leaflets" were sentenced to prison terms after an unfair trial. Torture and ill-treatment continued to be reported. One person died in custody reportedly following torture. Three people remained under sentence of death. At least three Bahraini nationals were banned from entering the country.

In 1999, the ruling emir, Sheikh 'Isa Ibn Salman al-Khalifa, died and was succeeded by his eldest son, Hamad. Although there was a respite from the street clashes between demonstrators and security forces that were widespread between 1994 and 1997, in its *World Report 1999*, Human Rights Watch announced that "restrictions on freedom of association and expression continued to be severe," and "reports of torture and ill-treatment by security forces, arbitrary arrests and detention, and unfair trials" continued to be received.[40]

Egypt

In theory, Egypt is a constitutional democracy, with a system of checks and balances against government abuse of power and constitutional guarantees for basic human rights. In practice, however, Egypt has been in a virtually permanent state of emergency since 1952. Under this rubric, the government has assumed extraordinary powers and bypassed constitutional and judicial mechanisms to protect the citizenry from the abuse of power. The Amnesty International 1998 annual report provides a synopsis for the year 1997 in its regional country index that reflects the dimensions of human rights abuse in Egypt:

> Hundreds of opponents of a new agricultural law, including prisoners of conscience and possible prisoners of conscience, were detained without charge or trial. Scores of prisoners of conscience were held, including 58 sentenced to prison terms by the Supreme Military Court in previous years. Thousands of suspected members or sympathizers of banned Islamist groups, including possible prisoners of conscience, were held without charge or trial; others were serving sentences imposed after grossly unfair trials before military courts. Torture and ill-treatment of detainees continued to be systematic. At least 55 people were sentenced to death and at least 24 people were executed.

Egypt has two types of special courts—the Emergency Supreme State Security Courts and military courts—which deny accused the basic fair trial safeguards guaranteed in civilian courts. Military courts, in particular, follow procedures that grossly violate the rights of defendants. After investigation, Amnesty International concluded that they were "an arm of the state to silence political opponents." Since 1992, special presidential decrees have been issued ordering that military courts try groups of civilians charged with offenses related to "terrorism." The mass trials that have ensued violate the most fundamental requirements of international law. In July 1993, the UN Human Rights Committee expressed deep concern about Egypt's military courts trying civilians, concluding that "military courts should not have the faculty to try cases which do not refer to offenses committed by members of the armed forces in the course of their duties."[41]

In its *World Report 1999*, commenting on the government's enactment of legislation to decrease the independence of civil society organizations, Human Rights Watch observed that the substantial curbs on freedom of association and assembly ensured that peaceful political opposition activities remained marginalized or restricted. Furthermore, the report noted, "No steps were taken to address the grave human rights violations that had accompanied the state's pursuit of armed

Islamist militants—including torture, deaths in detention, extrajudicial executions, and 'disappearances.'" In response to such criticisms the Egyptian government established the National Council on Human Rights in the spring of 2000. The council's specific purpose is to "support and protect human rights" in Egypt. Its twenty members were selected by President Mubarak from across the political spectrum, with the express purpose of "encouraging human rights education [in Egypt] through the dispersion of information in schools and the mass media as well as representing Egypt at all international and regional meetings dealing with human rights."[42]

Iran

Once widely considered the human rights pariah of the Middle East, Iran's human rights record has steadily improved over the course of the more than twenty years since its 1979 Islamic revolution. Now Iran looks like one of the more viable democratizing governments in the region.[43] Nevertheless, there are still very serious problems in the area of human rights. Amnesty International's *Annual Report 1999* provides a synopsis for the year 1998 that reflects the dimensions of human rights abuse in Iran:

> Hundreds of political prisoners, including prisoners of conscience, were held. Some were detained without charge or trial; others continued to serve long prison sentences imposed after unfair trials. Reports of torture and ill-treatment continued to be received, and judicial punishments of flogging and stoning continued to be imposed. Reports suggested that possible "disappearances" and extrajudicial executions had occurred. Scores of people were reportedly executed, including at least one prisoner of conscience; however, the true number may have been considerably higher. An unknown number of people remained under sentence of death, some after unfair trials.

The human rights problems were brought to the fore in Iranian politics by the struggle between conservatives and reformers in February–May 2000 elections. Highlighting this, in its *World Report 1999*, Human Rights Watch noted that "human rights progress continued to be held hostage to increasingly polarized conflict within the leadership of the Islamic Republic. The conflict resulted in disturbing outbreaks of violence that threatened to quash hopes of reforms pledged by President Khatami since his election in 1997." Freedom of the press and freedom of association have been the focal point of this struggle.

Accused of persecution of religious and ethnic minorities, in 1996 Iran was cited for violation of minority rights by the UN Sub-Commission on Prevention of Discrimination and Protection of Minorities.[44]

Iran, with a population of about 65 million, is one of the most populous states in the Middle East. It contains sizable ethnic and religious minorities, including the Kurds, Baluchis, and Turkamen who are Sunni Muslims, as well as the smaller religious communities of Baha'is, Zoroastrians, Jews, and various Christian denominations. In 1997, Human Rights Watch published a report on Iran's treatment of ethnic and religious minorities. *Iran: Religious and Ethnic Minorities: Discrimination in Law and Practice* concluded, "Despite language in the constitution apparently designed to outlaw discrimination against religious and ethnic minorities, clear discrimination exists in the text of the penal and civil codes."

Iraq

The human rights situation in Iraq is unique: systematic abuse occurs not only at the national level but at the international level as well. At the national level, the human rights record of the Ba'athist government that came to power in Iraq in 1968 is the most notorious in the Middle East.[45] Islamists, communists, humanists, and intellectuals of all political shades were targeted. In a sustained campaign of terror and purge, the Ba'athist regime attempted to systematically annihilate any suspected or potential opposition to its absolute authority.[46] Following Saddam Hussein's assumption of the presidency in 1979, ethnocultural cleansing was added to the litany of the regime's human rights record. An ethnic cleansing campaign of genocide against the Kurds of northern Iraq was initiated in the 1980s in the infamous Anfal Campaign in which over 4,000 Kurdish villages were destroyed and tens of thousands of Kurds disappeared.[47] The initiation of the Iran-Iraq War in 1980 catalyzed the forced expulsion of an estimated 300,000 Iraqi Shiites of Iranian descent in an ethnic cleansing campaign against them. They were stripped of their citizenship, their property was confiscated, and they were dumped on the Iraq-Iran border. Many thousands "disappeared." In the aftermath of the 1991 Gulf war, the destruction of the marshes in southern Iraq forced the expulsion of the Marsh Arabs into Iran and destroyed their unique habitat and way of life, the oldest continuous habitat in recorded history.

The Amnesty International's *Annual Report 1999* provides a synopsis for the year 1998 that reflects the dimensions of the government's abuse of human rights in Iraq since the 1991 Gulf war:

> Suspected political opponents, including possible prisoners of conscience, continued to be arrested and tens of thousands of others arrested in previous years remained held. Scores of Kurdish families were forcibly

expelled from their homes and members of targeted families detained. Torture and ill-treatment of prisoners and detainees were widely reported. According to reports, at least six people had their hands amputated as punishment. There was no further news on the fate of thousands of people who "disappeared" in previous years. Hundreds of people, including political prisoners, were reportedly executed; some may have been extrajudicially executed. Death sentences continued to be imposed, including for nonviolent offenses.

At the international level, Iraq's population has been subject to the harshest regime of punitive international sanctions for the longest period of time (since 1991) ever imposed by the international community. The sanctions, imposed by the UN Security Council after the 1991 Gulf war for the primary purpose of ensuring the destruction of Iraq's weapons of mass destruction, banned virtually any and all international trade with Iraq. As such, the sanctions stopped not only the flow of military-related materials to Iraq but also all consumer goods, including foodstuffs and medicines, and materials needed to sustain urban life, including water purification and sanitation. During the Gulf war, the United States and its allies had specifically targeted the civil infrastructure of Iraq, destroying water treatment and sewage facilities, power stations, and transportation and communications systems. Thus, the sanctions imposed severe hardships on the civilian population of Iraq. After almost ten years of searching, destroying, and monitoring by United Nations inspectors, there is no evidence that Iraq still has weapons of mass destruction or the capacity to redevelop such weapons. Nevertheless, the sanctions regime has stayed in force, although all evidence demonstrates that their impact on the civilian population is causing a humanitarian disaster in Iraq.[48]

The Security Council's maintenance of sanctions in the face of the substantial evidence that they are causing severe suffering and death in the civilian population has resulted in increasing concern that the UN itself is violating international human rights.[49] The eminent professor of international law, Richard Falk, in a public address on 4 March 1999,[50] charged that the maintenance of sanctions in the face of the evidence that the only purpose they are serving after almost ten years is the loss of civilian life in Iraq constitutes a flagrant disregard for the human rights of Iraq's population and borders on a program of genocide. This charge was echoed in the resignations of three UN officials responsible for the implementation of the humanitarian relief program, oil-for-food, designed to reduce the impact of sanctions on the civilian population— Denis Halliday, head of the UN's humanitarian program in Iraq, resigned in 1998; Hans von Sponeck, Halliday's successor, resigned in February

2000; and Jutta Burghardt, head of the World Food Program in Iraq, resigned with von Sponeck. Each one in turn charged that the oil-for-food program fell far short of even minimal humanitarian goals and that maintenance of the sanctions was in contradiction to the moral, ethical, and legal principles of the United Nations. According to the *Economist*, Hans von Sponeck "squarely blames America and Britain for oil-for-food's failure. Their vetoes hold up contracts, he says, their carping stymies any effort at streamlining and their public statements deliberately cloud the issue by pointing the finger at Iraq."[51] Officially sounding the alarm internationally, the usually reticent International Committee of the Red Cross (ICRC), the international guardians of humanitarian law, in May 1999 issued a statement warning of the "steady deterioration of living conditions" and stressed that "humanitarian action alone can not be a substitute for the country's needs." Referring to its own water, sanitation, and health sector programs, the statement said: "While, for the ICRC, action comes first, it is also its duty, as the guardian of humanitarian law, to draw the attention of the world community to the prevailing humanitarian situation in Iraq."[52]

Israel

Since its foundation in 1948, Israel has systematically violated the human rights of Palestinians and has flagrantly disregarded humanitarian law concerning the protection of civilians in war or under occupation. Israel, in fact, has received more UN condemnations for human rights abuse than any other member state. The violations include ethnic cleansing programs, arbitrary arrest and detention without charge or trial of political detainees, the use of torture and deaths in custody after torture, unfair trials, extrajudicial executions, severe restrictions on freedom of movement of civilian populations, confiscation of land, destruction of houses, collective punishment, holding civilians as hostage in areas of armed conflict, and targeting civilians in armed conflict to cause terror and flight.[53] With the signing of the Oslo Agreement on 13 September 1993, there was widespread anticipation that a new era of respect for human rights was at hand. However, the record has dissipated this enthusiasm. Amnesty International's *Annual Report 1999* reflects the dimensions of Israel's human rights abuses in 1999:

> At least 1,200 Palestinians were arrested on security grounds and at least 270 administrative detention orders were served. Scores of administrative detainees were released early in the year. Eighty-three Palestinians remained held in administrative detention at the end of the year. Prisoners of conscience and possible prisoners of conscience included adminis-

trative detainees, conscientious objectors and sentenced prisoners. At least 40 Lebanese nationals were imprisoned in Israel; 22 of them were held without charge or trial or after expiry of their sentences. A further 140 Lebanese nationals were held without charge or trial in the part of South Lebanon occupied by Israel. Other political prisoners included more than 1,500 Palestinians sentenced after unfair trials in previous years. More than 70 Palestinian prisoners were released in the context of peace agreements. Hundreds of Palestinians were tried before military courts, whose procedures failed to comply with international fair trial standards. Torture and ill-treatment continued to be officially sanctioned and used systematically during interrogation of security detainees. Israeli security forces killed at least 20 Palestinian civilians in circumstances suggesting that they may have been extrajudicially executed or otherwise unlawfully killed. One house was destroyed as punishment.

The election of Ehud Barak as prime minister on 17 May 1999, on a peace platform, occasioned renewed optimism. The new ministers who took office on 6 July 1999 promised to address human rights issues in areas under Israeli control "including torture, prolonged administrative detention and hostage-taking, house demolitions, Jerusalem residency revocations, and discrimination against Palestinian citizens of Israel." However, little changed. The issue of Jerusalem residency revocations (which constitutes a form of ethnic cleansing of Arabs from East Jerusalem) provides a case in point. Minister of Interior Natan Sharansky announced on 17 October 1999 the termination of the policy, which inhibited the revocation of residency permits to Palestinian residents of East Jerusalem who could produce documents to prove that their "center of life" was in East Jerusalem. Between January 1996 and April 1999, 2,721 residency rights were revoked, in effect ethnically cleansing East Jerusalem of about 10,884 Arab residents. Reviewing human rights in Israel in its *World Report 1999,* Human Rights Watch concluded "widespread and systematic discrimination against ethnic and religious minorities and against women on issues such as personal status, housing, and employment continued to be a serious problem. In May the Ministry of Internal Security reported that there were more than 200,000 battered women in Israel—one in seven."

Jordan

Jordan, a constitutional monarchy in theory, had in fact been ruled by royal decree under a state of emergency since 1939. Between 1967 and 1989, 166 emergency laws were enacted by decree. In 1989, in the wake of widespread civil unrest, the first parliamentary elections since 1956

took place. The emergency laws enacted by decree were all brought to
the newly elected parliament for ratification.[54] The 1992 adoption of a
National Charter initiated reform of political and human rights, com-
mitting authorities "to protect the rights, dignity and basic freedoms of
the individual, the basis of which were laid out by Islam and confirmed
by the Universal Declaration of Human Rights and all international
covenants and treaties issued in this respect by the United Nations."[55]

In 1998, Amnesty International reviewed Jordan's progress in achieving human rights reform and identified continuing abuses in three areas:

- The use of prolonged incommunicado detention against a range
  of political suspects who are often arbitrarily arrested before being
  held without access to families and lawyers.
- The existence of laws that make possible the imprisonment of
  prisoners of conscience (those who are detained simply for
  expressing conscientiously held beliefs without using or advocating violence). . . .
- Continuing reports of torture or ill-treatment both of political and
  common law suspects. Such torture is facilitated by pre-trial
  incommunicado detention and a lack of the safeguards, which
  should ensure the thorough and prompt investigation of allegations of torture and compensation for those who have suffered
  such treatment at the hands of the security forces.[56]

While Amnesty International's reports focused on juridical issues
related to human rights, Human Rights Watch reports on Jordan in the
late 1990s highlighted concerns about freedom of the press and so-
called honor killings. Regarding freedom of the press, in May 1997,
Jordan's council of ministers amended various articles of the already
restrictive 1993 press and publications law to expand publications bans,
"imposing staggering restrictions on all forms of published information,
including news, analyses, opinions, reports, drawings, and photo-
graphs." The amended law prohibited publication of virtually any critical news, information, or analysis, explicitly banning publication of any
item that does the following:

- Offends the king or the royal family.
- Pertains to the Jordanian armed forces or security services, unless
  such material has been cleared for publication by the appropriate
  authority or the government's official spokesman.
- Disparages religions and creeds whose freedom is provided for in
  the constitution.

- Harms national unity or incites criminal action or foments hatred, discord, and disharmony among members of society.
- Offends the dignity or personal freedoms of individuals or harms their reputation.
- Involves derogatory, libellous, or abusive remarks about Arab, Islamic, or friendly heads of state, or sours the kingdom's relations with other nations.
- Promotes perversion or leads to moral corruption.
- Shakes confidence in the national currency.
- Features false news or rumors detrimental to the public interest or state agencies or their personnel.[57]

In June 1998, Jordan's chamber of deputies presented parliament with the draft of a new press and publications law. According to Human Rights Watch, the proposed law imposed "sweeping restrictions on the content of anything printed in Jordan, and gives vast powers to the information ministry to suspend newspapers, censor and ban books, and prohibit the entry of foreign publications."[58] In a letter to the Jordanian minister of higher education, Human Rights Watch criticized the draft law, charging, "The law would be a disaster for researchers and scholars in Jordan. It is hostile to the free flow of ideas and hostile to the expression of controversial viewpoints."[59]

The issue of so-called honor killings related to the legalized murder of women under the rubric of family honor. The Jordanian Penal Code treats violence against women as a lesser crime. Article 340 of the code provides for lenient sentences when men kill their female relatives in the name of "honor." Human Rights Watch reported that twenty-five to thirty women are killed in Jordan each year in the name of honor, and these constitute about a third of the annual number of homicides.[60] Women's activists in Jordan struggle against legal, administrative, and law enforcement agencies in their efforts to protect women at risk from their families. A campaign to petition the government for abolition of Article 340 of the Penal Code was launched in August 1999:

> We are a group of Jordanian citizens who have no personal, political, or racial interests, but are gathered with one unifying issue as free individuals, which is our right to a good and safe life, free from violence in a society that protects the rights of all, which abides by the rules of the Constitution which assures equality to all in front of the law in rights and duties.
>
> Through the years, our country has witnessed abhorrent crimes . . . committed in the name of honor, and those who have committed them received very soft sentences, which in turn has encouraged their

belief and that of others that the crime they committed is socially acceptable. . . .

We call for the immediate cancellation of Article 340 in its entirety, which gives reduction and exemptions to those who kill or injure in the name of honor.[61]

However, in January 2000 the Jordanian Lower House of Parliament failed for the second time in two months to abolish Article 340 of the Penal Code, even though the Upper House had agreed to its abolition in December 1999. The Upper and Lower Houses, though scheduled to address the issue, failed to amend the law in the 2000 legislative session.

Kuwait

Following Kuwait's liberation from Iraqi occupation in 1991, the Kuwaiti government unleashed a campaign of terror against the expatriate population under the pretext of rooting out those who collaborated with the Iraqi occupiers. A Human Rights Watch report observed, "Despite calls to defend human rights in rallying support for the war against Iraq, the reinstated Kuwaiti government has trampled on those rights at nearly every turn, often with the use of violence."[62] The campaign was primarily targeted at long-term Arab residents of Kuwait, who constituted a major component of Kuwait's labor force. Arab workers in Kuwait, especially those of Palestinian, Iraqi, Jordanian, and Bidun (stateless Bedouins) origin, were subjected to murder, torture, arbitrary detention, and unlawful deportation. The effective result of this campaign was the ethnic cleansing of Kuwait's labor force (which was composed primarily of foreign workers).[63]

Throughout the remainder of the 1990s, the concerns of human rights activists with regard to Kuwait focused on two population groups: the Bidun and Asian maids. The Bidun, seminomadic Arabs in origin, were residents of Kuwait for many generations, but they failed to register for citizenship in 1959 when citizenship regulations were first enacted in anticipation of independence in 1961. In 1995 Human Rights Watch observed, "After decades of treating Bedoons [Bidun] as citizens and repeatedly promising to confer formal citizenship on them, the Kuwaiti government reversed its practice and declared them illegal residents of the only country they have ever known."[64] In response to the pressures of international human rights activists, in 1996 the Kuwaiti government announced that "over 100,000 stateless people, members of the Bidun community, who claim Kuwaiti nationality, were to have their status reviewed."[65] However, a year later there was still no review, and the UN Special Rapporteur on contemporary forms of racism, racial discrimination, xenophobia, and related intolerance presented his report on Kuwait to the 53d session of the UN Commission on Human Rights. He recommended that "priority should be given to finding a definitive, humane and equitable solution to the problem of Bidun, some of whom appear to be stateless in their own country."[66] In 1999, the UN Committee on the Elimination of Racial Discrimination expressed its concern that although the status of the Bidun continued to be discussed in various committees, the Kuwaiti government "had not found a solution to the problems of the Bidun, the majority of whom remained stateless."[67]

The human rights abuse of Asian maids in Kuwait is a multifaceted problem that was highlighted in the Human Rights Watch 1995 *Global Report on Women's Human Rights* accordingly:

> Every year since the liberation of Kuwait in March 1991, nearly 2,000 women domestic workers, mainly from Sri Lanka, the Philippines, Bangladesh and India have fled the homes of abusive Kuwaiti employers and sought refuge in their embassies. The embassies of these Asian countries report a daily average of four to five runaway maids. According to L. Ariyadasa, former labor secretary at the Sri Lankan embassy in Kuwait, "Most of them are severely beaten, . . . raped or even burned." In April 1995 he said that the problem was "getting worse and worse every day."
>
> Our investigation . . . has found that . . . there exists a pattern of rape, physical assault and mistreatment of Asian maids that takes place largely with impunity. Debt bondage and illegal confinement are also common. Kuwaiti law exacerbates the problem by excluding the domestic workers from the country's labor law protections.

Amnesty International's *Annual Report 2000* highlighted the problem of the continuing stateless status of the Bidun, restrictions on freedom of expression and freedom of conscience, and the forcible return of Kuwaiti residents to their countries of origin even when they face a high risk of torture. In addition, the report provides a synopsis for the year 1999 that reflects the pattern of human rights abuse over the decade intrinsic in Kuwait's administration of justice:

> Dozens of political prisoners, including prisoners of conscience, continued to be held; they had been convicted in unfair trials since 1991. The fate of more than 70 people who "disappeared" in custody in 1991 remained unknown. At least 12 people were sentenced to death. In two separate cases the editor of the newspaper *al-Qabas* and a professor of political science were convicted on charges of insulting Islam.

Lebanon

With the end of Lebanon's protracted civil war (1975–90), the Lebanese constitution, promulgated in 1943, reassumed its role as law of the land. While the constitution enshrined the basic guarantees for human rights protection, nevertheless, in the geopolitical situation of post–civil war Lebanon, human rights abuse was the rule for the Lebanese population, though not necessarily at the hands of the government. On the one hand, Israel, in occupation of southern Lebanon from 1982 to 1985, and of the so-called security zone in the south from 1985 to June 2000, engaged in unconstrained human rights abuse in Lebanon. These abuses included the expulsion of thousands of Lebanese civilians from their villages;[68] the arbitrary detention of Lebanese civilians inside Israel without charge or trial;[69] the detention without charge and torture of prisoners in the notorious al-Khayam prison;[70] and the use of terror to effect the mass displacement of the civilian population.[71] On the other hand, Syrian military forces, deployed in Lebanon since 1976, have continued to detain Lebanese nationals incommunicado and without charge since the end of the civil war. According to Amnesty International:

> In some cases arrests were carried out directly by Syrian military personnel stationed in Lebanon, whereas in other cases detainees were reportedly handed over by Lebanese security or intelligence forces to Syrian intelligence services in Lebanon and subsequently transferred to Syria. Detainees frequently report suffering torture or ill-treatment while under interrogation by Syrian intelligence forces.[72]

In this geopolitical context, respect for the basic human rights enshrined in the Lebanese constitution and law was easily compromised in the name of state security. A report by Amnesty International in October 1997 highlighted four dimensions of human rights concern:

- waves of arbitrary arrests and detention of suspected political opponents;
- allegations of torture and ill-treatment which have not been fully investigated by the authorities;
- trials of political detainees which fail to meet fair trial standards; and
- the 1994 legislation expanding the scope of the death penalty.[73]

In the wake of Israel's announced plans in spring 2000 to withdraw unilaterally from south Lebanon in early July, Human Rights Watch raised concerns about a number of human rights issues:

- Surrender procedures for South Lebanese Army (SLA) militiamen—many of whom were forcibly conscripted into the militia and therefore have the right to protection under international humanitarian law.

- Amnesty for former combatants—a 1997 draft granting amnesty to SLA members who surrender was stalled in the Lebanese parliament and the issue was hotly debated among the public. While Human Rights Watch took no position on whether former combatants should receive amnesty for charges of treason, it did strongly caution against granting amnesty to anyone known or alleged to have committed, condoned, ordered, or authorized the commission of war crimes against humanity.

- Due process in Lebanon for former combatants—the entitlement of those not granted amnesty to legal proceedings that meet international fair trial standards.

- Civilians in the occupied zone with links with Israel—some 2,500 residents of the occupied zone worked in Israel during the occupation. Human Rights Watch noted that "no person should be subjected to any kind of reprisals for having worked in Israel. The family members of SLA militiamen should not be targeted for reprisal."

- Accountability for war crimes—the Lebanese government has a responsibility "to track down, investigate, and prosecute" all combatants in the southern Lebanon conflict who may be responsible for war crimes or other serious violations of humanitarian law.

- Palestinian refugees in Lebanon—the Lebanese government has a responsibility under international law to protect the Palestinian refugees in its territory.

- Freedom of expression in Lebanon—the Lebanese government attempted to suppress public debate about the Syrian role in Lebanon.[74]

Libya

In spite of the celebratory atmosphere surrounding the September 1999 thirtieth anniversary of the revolution that brought Colonel Mu'ammar al-Gaddafi to power, the Socialist People's Libyan Arab Jamahiriya has not developed the atmosphere required for a civil society. Human rights groups and opposition political parties are harassed and banned, and their members are prosecuted by the government, which does not tolerate independent nongovernmental organizations. Indeed, no criticism of the government is allowed under Libyan law.[75] No independent bar association exists to allow for impartial judicial review, and freedoms for the press and electronic media are nonexistent. In an attempt to curb widespread abuse, Libya was given observer status in the Euro-Mediterranean

process in 1999 and invited to accept the terms of the Barcelona
Declaration (1995), which include a commitment to human rights and
democracy.[76]

The Libyan government has used its legislative monopoly to curb freedoms, as in July 1996 when it enacted a new law that widened the scope
of the death penalty to include "speculation in food, clothes or housing
during a state of war or blockade" and "crimes relating to drugs, alcohol
and speculation in foreign currency."[77] In March 1998, a new law came
into force authorizing collective punishment for communities deemed
to have protected or helped those responsible for "terrorism," acts of
violence, unauthorized possession of weapons, or the sabotaging of
"people's power." According to the *1998 Amnesty International Annual
Report,* punitive measures against communities included government
attempts to "deprive villages or tribes of subsidized food, petrol and public services," by "cutting off water and electricity supplies" and even the
"transfer [of] development projects to other parts of the country."[78]

Citizens and foreign nationals have regularly been arrested and
detained for political activities as well as for religious beliefs and activities. Amnesty International cites a case in June and July 1998 when
"over 100 professionals, including engineers and university lecturers,
were arrested . . . and their whereabouts remained undetermined a year
later as their detention and arrest remained unacknowledged by the
Libyan government."[79] When the government acknowledged their
detention in two Tripoli prisons, it explained that their detention was
due to their "supporting or sympathizing with al-Jama'a al-Islamiya
al-Libiya, the Libyan Islamic Group."[80] This practice was not seen as
uncommon by either Amnesty International or Human Rights Watch,
as both supply reports of prisoners "held without charge or trial from as
long ago as 1973."[81] Those arrested and charged also face a justice system which conducts "grossly unfair trials [that] fail to meet basic
requirements for a fair trial as set out in international standards."[82] Both
Amnesty and Human Rights Watch have published reports that "political detainees were routinely tortured while held in incommunicado
detention,"[83] with examples of torture including "beatings, hanging
by the wrists, electric shocks, burning with cigarettes, and attacks by
aggressive dogs causing serious injuries, and sleep deprivation by the
repeated, loud and prolonged broadcast of political speeches."[84] The
UN Committee against Torture examined Libya's implementation of the
Convention against Torture and Other Cruel, Inhuman, or Degrading
Treatment or Punishment in 1999 and concluded that the Libyan
authorities had "failed to substantially address concerns and recommendations previously raised by the Committee."[85]

Furthermore, political detainees were held with convicted criminals in what were described as cruel, inhuman, or degrading conditions and "denied adequate medical care, which led to several deaths in custody."[86] Despite the attempts to coerce reforms, such as the terms stipulated in the Barcelona Declaration, Libya's commitment remains suspect as demonstrated by the comments of the Libyan representative to the UN Committee against Torture, as he stated that "the possibility of allowing external bodies to visit Libyan prisons was still being studied," after repeated calls upon the Libyan government to allow for independent monitoring.[87] The situation boiled over in July 1996 when a one-week riot and mutiny occurred at Abu Salim Prison in Tripoli. Amnesty International attributed the mutiny to "the appalling conditions in the prison, including a lack of medical care, inadequate hygiene, overcrowded cells and a poor diet." The prisoners were attempting to improve their treatment, but their mutiny led instead to several deaths when the prison was stormed by security forces that "killed inmates as well as guards who had been taken hostage."[88]

In October 1999, the UN Human Rights Committee examined Libya's implementation of the International Covenant on Civil and Political Rights and "expressed concerns about allegations of extrajudicial, arbitrary or summary executions by state agents, the systematic use of torture, and the high incidence of arbitrary arrests and detention, including prolonged detention without trial."[89] A unique aspect of Libya's systematic suppression of political opposition is its suspected extraterritorial extrajudicial actions uncovered by such investigatory mechanisms as a June 1997 inquest, held in the United Kingdom, into the murder in London of 'Ali Mohammad Abu-Zaid. A well-known Libyan opposition activist, Abu-Zaid, was found stabbed to death in his London shop in November 1995. The inquest recorded a verdict that it believed Abu-Zaid's death constituted an "unlawful killing" as it occurred "in circumstances suggesting that he may have been extrajudicially executed by agents working for, or on behalf of, the Libyan government."[90] Amnesty reported in 1997 that "two other Libyan opposition activists living abroad were killed in circumstances suggesting they were also extrajudicially executed. . . . Mohammad ben Ghali was shot dead in Los Angeles in February 1996," and " 'Amer Hisham 'Ali Mohammad was found stabbed to death in Sliema, Malta, in August 1996 . . . reports in both countries suggested individuals acting on behalf of the Libyan government were responsible for their deaths."[91] Finally, in 1993 Mansour Kikhiya, a former Libyan foreign affairs minister who went on to become a prominent opposition leader and human rights activist, "disappeared" in Egypt. Amnesty reported that "both Libyan and Egyptian authorities... deny any knowledge of his disappearance although he was allegedly executed in January 1994,"[92] and his wife was able to secure a verdict in Egypt against the Egyptian government for failing to protect her husband, although it was overturned upon appeal.[93]

Morocco

The July 1999 death of King Hassan II, who had been in power since 1961, clouded Morocco's longtime troubled human rights situation. Despite widespread abuses, King Hassan II had made public pronouncements declaring that his government would "resolve all outstanding human rights files and implement judicial reforms."[94] Following his enthronement, King Mohammed VI addressed the Moroccan people on the importance of human rights—including those of women—indicating his intention to continue and perhaps even enlarge the government's program to improve its human rights record. He subsequently began replacing government officials such as Driss Basri, who had been interior minister since 1979, as well as other security officials, raising hopes that a new era was emerging in Morocco. But disappearances continued, the UN Mission for the Referendum in Western Sahara announced that the referendum was postponed on whether Western Sahara should be independent or should be integrated into Morocco, and Moroccan authorities withdrew permission for Amnesty International to hold its international council meeting in Rabat.

Despite repeated commitments to reform the government's treatment of both its citizenry and political opposition, Morocco is still overwrought with disappearances, the violent suppression of demonstrations, unfair trials highlighting the judiciary's incapacity to meet international standards, the continued detention of political prisoners, the conditions of the Polisario camps, and finally the impunity of suspected perpetrators.[95] Early in 1999, the Conseil consultatif des droits de l'homme (Human Rights Advisory Council, CCDH) proposed that an arbitration body be established to decide on compensation claims for those connected with some of the individuals listed by the CCDH in an October 1998 report of 112 disappearance cases. In August 1999 King Mohammed VI ordered the establishment of an arbitration commission to decide on compensation for material and psychological damage suffered by the victims of disappearance and arbitrary detention and their families. Although the admission by the Moroccan government of its officials' involvement was a large step toward public recognition of past abuse, Amnesty International pointed out the limited number of those sanctified as being "disappeared." Furthermore, the families of those who were recognized still did not know when their loved ones had died or where to find their remains, and although the government seemed to be opening to the identification of Moroccan victims, it was neglecting Sahrawis as "by the end of 1999, the fate of some 450 people, the majority of them Sahrawis, who 'disappeared' between the mid-1960s and early 1990s, had not been clarified" by the government.[96]

The government's treatment of its Sahrawi citizens was amplified by the *Amnesty International 2000 Annual Report:*

> Nonviolent demonstrations continued to be dispersed with excessive force by the security forces, particularly in the form of beatings. As in previous years, it was protesters in Western Sahara who were most seriously affected. Although journalists enjoyed improved access to the territory in 1999, the human rights situation there continued to lag a long way behind that in Morocco itself, particularly with regard to freedom of expression and association.
>
> In September, a peaceful sit-in for socioeconomic demands by Sahrawi students, sacked workers, and people with disabilities in Laayoune, Western Sahara, was violently broken up by the security forces, as was a march held several days later to protest the brutal manner in which the sit-in had been dispersed. Dozens of Sahrawis were severely beaten, and many sustained serious injuries, including broken bones. Dozens were arrested and there were reports of torture and ill-treatment in custody.

The treatment of the protestors by the justice system highlighted the judiciary's incapacity to meet international standards for a fair trial. Allegations made to the courts by the accused of beatings and confessions extracted through torture[97] were not investigated. Thus, despite the efforts of both King Hassan II and King Mohammed VI, violators were allowed to carry on with impunity for their actions. The failure to achieve international standards of human rights protection was pointed out by the UN Committee against Torture and the UN Human Rights Committee when they issued periodic reports on Morocco in 1999. While recognizing the positive steps taken by the Moroccan government in the field of human rights, the Human Rights Committee urged Morocco "to intensify investigations into the whereabouts of all persons reportedly missing, to release any such persons who may still be held in detention, to provide lists of prisoners of war to independent observers, to inform families about the location of the graves of disappeared persons known to be dead, to prosecute the persons responsible for the disappearances or deaths, and to provide compensation to victims or their families where rights have been violated."[98]

Oman

As an absolute monarchy, the Omani human rights record is dominated by Sultan Qabus Ibn Sa'id. In 1998 he made it possible for women to stand for election to the Majlis al-Shura, broadening the participation of women in public affairs.[99] While only two female candidates were successful in achieving electoral success, Sultan Qabus also appointed four women to the senate, which was established in December 1998. However, accusations of the wrongful imprisonment, ill-treatment, and torture of political opposition have been detailed by Amnesty International and Human Rights Watch. Like many Gulf states, Oman's Shi'a population is targeted as a consequence of the fears that Shi'a activism heralds emulation of the Iranian Islamic Republic. Capital punishment is still practiced, including against foreign nationals, after trials that were characterized by Amnesty as unfair and to which those convicted were given no process of appeal.[100]

Palestinian Authority

The Palestinian Authority (PA) was created in May 1994 by the Agreement on the Gaza Strip and Jericho Area (also known as the Cairo Agreement) between Israel and the Palestine Liberation Organization. The Cairo Agreement gave the PA jurisdiction to administer parts of the Gaza Strip and West Bank, areas that had been occupied by the Israeli army since 1967. Subsequent agreements expanded the jurisdiction of the PA in the West Bank. In the West Bank, the PA was responsible for public order alone (which included 27 percent of the West Bank, consisting of approximately 440 West Bank villages) or public order and internal security (approximately 3 percent of the area of the West Bank, consisting of the main urban areas).

Lamentably, the human rights situation in areas under PA administration did not improve. "Political arrest and detention under the PA," noted an Amnesty International report in September 1998, "has seen the stabilization of a system of prolonged detention without charge or trial. There has been virtually no attempt by the PA to follow local laws regulating arrest and detention with regards to political prisoners." Reports of torture and ill-treatment of prisoners are also prevalent. Political prisoners include members of Islamist and leftist groups suspected of armed attacks against Israel or known for their opposition to the PA. The 1998 Amnesty International report also noted, "People who have criticized the PA, including journalists and human rights defenders, have also been detained without charge or trial."[101] In 1999, Human Rights Watch condemned the PA for the detention of eight public figures for criticizing President Yasser Arafat's policies. "The arrests are the latest in a series of attacks on free expression that have included the arrest and harassment of journalists, human rights activists, and political commentators."[102]

According to an April 1999 Amnesty International report, the prolonged detention of political prisoners "is closely linked to pressure from the international community, especially Israel and the United States." Compounding its impunity with regard to abuse of human rights, the PA undermined the rule of law by defying Palestinian High Court judgments requiring the release of specific prisoners.[103] The synopsis for the Palestinian Authority from Amnesty International's *Annual Report 2000* reflects the magnitude of abuse by the PA:

> More than 350 people were arrested during 1999 for political reasons. At least 90 were prisoners of conscience, including critics of the Palestinian leadership, journalists and members of a legal opposition Islamist party. Most were released, but at least 70 remained in detention at the end of the year. Reports of torture and ill-treatment continued to be received. More than 230 people arrested in previous years remained detained without charge or trial. . . . The High Court of Justice ordered the release of 52 detainees held without charge or trial, but only four were known to have been released as a result of these judgments by the end of the year. State security and military courts continued to sentence political detainees after unfair trials. One person was executed and four people were sentenced to death after trials before the state security or military courts. Two people were unlawfully killed during a demonstration. The Palestinian Authority (PA) failed to bring those responsible for human rights abuses to justice.[104]

Qatar

Since 1996, more than 100 people have stood trial for their alleged involvement in the failed coup attempt of February 1996 against the government headed by Emir al-Shikh Hamad Ibn Khalifa al-Thani, who had deposed his own father in a bloodless coup in 1995. Most of those held are believed to be military officers loyal to the deposed emir. The long-running trial began with some forty of the accused in absentia until a large number were forcibly returned from the UAE and Yemen.[105] Amnesty International asked the Qatari government to investigate allegations raised throughout the trial that some of the accused had been tortured while in police custody.[106] The allegations arose as the detainees began their trial and asked the presiding judge to disregard confessions as they were a result of torture that occurred immediately following arrest as well as during long-term incommunicado detention, where detainees were denied legal council until the trial began. In 1999 at least four people who were being tried in absentia were arrested as the Qatari government continued to pursue the failed coup members.

Domestic electoral reform dominated the political agenda as a central municipal council was broadened to allow for both universal suffrage and female candidates on 8 March 1999. All Qatari citizens over eighteen years old were entitled to vote, with the exception of members of the military and police. Although six female candidates ran, none succeeded in winning office. With the success of the municipal council elections, al-Shikh Hamad Ibn Khalifa al-Thani—Emir of Qatar—announced the establishment of a committee to draft the country's first permanent constitution in July 1999. When announced, the Emir stipulated that it would include provision for the establishment of a parliament that would also be elected by universal suffrage, for which the provisional constitution, adopted by his father in 1970, did not provide. Human rights observers were further encouraged by proposed initiatives from within Qatari society. Amnesty International reported in its 2000 annual report that "a group, including prominent lawyers and academics, had plans to establish two non-governmental human rights groups: an international committee for the defense of intellectual liberties and freedom of expression, and a committee for the defense of human rights."

Saudi Arabia

In its *World Report 2000* review on Saudi Arabia, Human Rights Watch succinctly outlined the human rights condition within the kingdom:

> The lack of basic freedoms of expression and association, institutionalized discrimination particularly against women and religious minorities, and the use of corporal and capital punishments to suppress and intimidate political opposition remained Saudi Arabia's most pressing human rights problems during 1999. An absolute monarchy, the state allowed no criticism of the ruling family, established religion, or the government and used the threat of arbitrary arrest, detention without trial, torture, and execution to silence criticism.[107]

Indeed, Amnesty International launched the first-ever campaign on Saudi Arabia by an international human rights organization in March 2000, which aroused the ire of the Saudi government. In the past, Saudi Arabia, like many of the Gulf states, escaped intensified scrutiny due to the closed and isolated nature of their societies; individual abuses were difficult to document. The AI report focused on the practice of arbitrary detention without charges or a subsequent trial, saying that "such conduct has become so prevalent that it has affected thousands of people over the years." The report also points out the international community's indifference in the face of proven human rights abuses in the country, which AI chalks up to Saudi Arabia's strategic position and economic might.[108] The Saudi government lashed out at the increased attention, inviting the UN Human Rights Commission's Special Rapporteur to the kingdom, and directly responding to Amnesty International on 8 October 1999 condemning the organization's "lack of objectivity" and encouraged AI to do "more thorough investigations."

The Saudi Arabian government had announced positive developments as it led a number of Gulf states in ratifying key international conventions. Saudi Arabia signed the Convention against Torture and the International Convention on the Elimination of All Forms of Racial Discrimination.[109] However, such moves did not alter the climate of abuse within the kingdom, as abuses continued under the vague Statute of Principles of Arrest, Temporary Confinement, and Preventive Detention, which was issued on 11 November 1983. Providing the guidelines for arrest and detention followed by Saudi police, security, and *mutawaeen* or religious police, it allows for arrest on almost no pretext. Human Rights Watch explained:

> Detainees had no right to judicial review, could be held for fifty-one days before their detention was reviewed by the regional governor, and could be held indefinitely if neither the governor nor the minister ordered their release or trial. Detainees had no right to legal counsel, to examine witnesses, or to call witnesses in their own defense. Saudi laws also allowed convictions on the basis of uncorroborated confessions. The minister of interior had virtually unlimited authority over suspects in "crimes involving national security," which were defined so broadly as to encompass nonviolent opposition to the government.[110]

Magnifying the arbitrary nature of arrest procedures and lack of judicial independence was the kingdom's increasing use of capital punishment, including beheadings, mutilations, and lashings.[111] Both AI and HRW confirmed more than 100 executions in 1999, a dramatic increase over the 29 executions in 1998.[112] Death sentences were imposed for such crimes as murder, rape, drug trafficking, and armed robbery, with the executions, usually beheadings, carried out in public after Friday prayers. The majority of those publicly beheaded were foreigners. Human Rights Watch pointed out that public floggings were "another type of cruel, inhuman, and degrading punishment handed down. . . . Victims included two Filipinos who were found guilty in August of performing illegal abortions and sentenced to two years and 700 lashes each."[113]

In Saudi Arabia and many of the Gulf states, women faced institutionalized discrimination, despite comments by Crown Prince ʿAbdullah bin ʿAbd al-ʿAziz—who took over the reins of power from his brother, King Fahd, after Fahd suffered a stroke in 1995—which highlighted the kingdom's economic problems, the need for a more vigorous fight against corruption, and the desire for women to play a greater role in society.[114] His comments caused an unprecedented debate in Saudi society about the role of women, even as they "continued to face institutionalized discrimination affecting their freedom of movement and association and their right to equality in employment and education. They were not allowed to drive, needed written permission from male relatives to travel, could not marry non-Muslims and their testimonies in court were equal to half those of a man. . . . [They were] compelled to cover themselves from head to toe in public, and those who did not risked beatings or detention by the *mutawaeen*."[115]

The treatment of foreign workers carries over to the entire workforce as "Saudi labor laws prohibited the right to organize and bargain collectively and gave employers extensive control over foreign workers' freedom of movement. Many foreign workers continued to suffer under oppressive working conditions and were denied legitimate claims to wages, benefits, or compensation. Labor protections did not extend to domestic workers, and labor courts rarely enforced the few protections provided by law when workers sought to have their terms of contracts honored or pursued other claims."[116]

Syria

In 1999 Hafez al-Assad died, and Syria released several of the longest held political prisoners in the region. They included Riad al-Turk, who had been detained without charge since 1980, Mustafa Tawfiq Fallah, who was arrested in 1970 and held for thirteen years beyond the expiry of his prison term, and 121 Lebanese who had been held in Syria without charge or official acknowledgment of their whereabouts.[117] However, despite the passing of Assad and the attempts to improve Syria's human rights image abroad, Human Rights Watch believed the administration of justice "remained problematic, as its legal system was not free of corruption or fully independent. Emergency or exceptional laws, which international law permitted only in extreme circumstances and for limited periods, remained in effect and circumscribed basic rights as did special security courts, whose procedures did not meet international fair-trial standards."[118]

Amnesty International agreed that civil society languished as "opposition activities remained outlawed and members of unauthorized political parties were at risk of detention." Long-standing regime actions against Islamic activism continued as members of the unauthorized Islamist groups al-Ikhwan al-Muslimun (Muslim Brotherhood) and Hizb al-Tahrir (Islamic Liberation Party) were arrested "in a wave of arrests in December 1999 when Syrian security forces raided homes of suspected members of these groups in the cities of Homs, Damascus and Aleppo." Amnesty International also reported "the work of human rights groups remained unauthorized in Syria. Five prisoners of conscience remained in detention serving up to ten years imprisonment for their involvement in the distribution of a leaflet to mark the anniversary of the Universal Declaration of Human Rights. The leaflet was produced in 1992 by an unauthorized human rights group, the Committees for the Defence of Democratic Freedoms and Human Rights in Syria (CDF). . . . Torture and ill-treatment of detainees continued to be routine, especially during the initial stage of detention and interrogation."[119] The death penalty continued to be applied, and at least two people were executed in 1999. Finally, after long-standing acknowledgment of Syria's track record of abuse and intolerance of political opposition by international organizations and the international community, the 1990s witnessed a sharp decline in condemnations by western governments. Since Syria's participation in the 1991 allied coalition against Iraq, it has been removed from the U.S. State Department list of "states who support or conduct terrorist acts" and generally has dramatically improved ties with both Europe and the United States.

Tunisia

In October 1999, presidential and legislative elections took place in Tunisia. President Zine El 'Abidine Ben 'Ali was reelected with 99.44 percent of the popular vote. Despite a poor showing, six "legal" opposition parties were allocated 34 of the 182 seats in parliament. Tunisia, like many other Middle Eastern and North African countries, has made public professions regarding its intentions to improve its human rights record. With this in mind, hundreds of political prisoners, most of them identified as "prisoners of conscience" by Amnesty International, were released in November following the elections. However, Amnesty International also noted that "human rights defenders and their families were increasingly targeted, as were other activists such as trade unionists and journalists, and government opponents and critics from across the political spectrum" and that "reports of torture and ill-treatment during secret detention and in prisons continued to be received."[120] Government repression also extended to the media with "indirect controls on the press so heavy that the private and governmental newspapers were virtually indistinguishable in their coverage of government policies. Foreign publications were plentiful on the newsstands but did not appear whenever issues contained material deemed unfavorable about Tunisia, such as the June issue of *Le Monde Diplomatique*."[121]

Human Rights Watch singled out the treatment of Islamists:

> Actual or suspected members of the outlawed al-Nahdha movement remained in prison, in exile, or at liberty but subject to harsh restrictions and the whims of the local police. They continued to comprise the majority of Tunisia's political prisoners, estimated at between 1,000 and 2,000. Most were convicted of nonviolent offenses such as membership in or attending meetings of an "unrecognized" organization. Women were barred from wearing religious headscarves in schools, government offices, and in public and were forced to remove them when visiting prisoners.[122]

Mistreatment was evidenced as "political prisoners were subjected to extreme overcrowding, beatings, and other cruel disciplinary measures, and were shuttled incessantly among institutions, forcing families to travel great distances for visits."[123] Despite legal reforms, adopted by President Zine El-'Abidine Ben 'Ali, that broadened the definition of torture and limited incommunicado detention, torture and illegal detentions remained commonplace. Magnifying matters was a complete lack of judicial independence and the "climate of impunity" that was "fostered by a judiciary that ignored evidence of torture and routinely convicted defendants on the basis of coerced confessions."[124] As noted in the Human Rights Watch *World Report 2000*, "The UN Committee against Torture in November 1998 declared itself 'disturbed by the reported widespread practice of torture' in Tunisia and 'concerned over the pressure and intimidation used by officials to prevent the victims from lodging complaints.' The committee charged that by denying these allegations, 'the authorities are in fact granting those responsible for torture immunity from punishment, thus encouraging the continuation of these abhorrent practices.'"

The Tunisian government responded by altering penal legislation as reported by Amnesty International:

> In July 1999, following recommendations made by the UN Committee against Torture in 1998, a new law was passed making torture a crime punishable by eight years' imprisonment. However, the definition of torture is more restrictive than that required by the UN Convention against Torture and Other Cruel, Inhuman or Degrading Treatment or Punishment. According to the new law, only those who torture are punishable, whereas those who give the order to torture and those who supervise it

cannot be prosecuted. The Penal Procedure Code was also modified to increase safeguards during, and reduce the length of, incommunicado detention to six days.[125]

Even sanctioned political actions were restricted by the climate of oppression in Tunisia. For example, the family code provided for greater equality between the sexes. Human Rights Watch reported that the independent Tunisian Association of Democratic Women was forced to remind the government that "women's rights included the political right to promote their cause publicly, something they were frequently blocked from doing."[126] All this despite the fact that Tunisia has been almost entirely free of political violence for several years.[127] Finally, both human rights organizations pointed out that "political trials fell far short of international standards for fairness. Examining magistrates and courts refused to investigate allegations of torture or to call defense witnesses. Lawyers were denied access to their clients' files until just before the hearing."[128]

Turkey

In December 1999, Turkey was accepted as a candidate for EU membership. Accession negotiations were to begin once certain criteria set forth by the EU were met in regards to Turkey's economy, commitment to democracy, and human rights under the Copenhagen Agreement of 1995. A monitoring of the human rights situation as well as alterations to the Turkish Penal Code accompanied the EU process. Human rights concerns in Turkey have been dominated by the government's suppression of the Kurdish minority in the southeast and the capture of PKK leader Abdullah Öcalan, who had led much of the Kurdish resistance. In the armed conflict between Turkish security forces and the Kurdish PKK, which began in 1984 in southeastern Turkey, an estimated 4,500 civilians have been killed and up to 3 million people internally displaced. For his actions, which included the use of violence to challenge government authority, Abdullah Öcalan was sentenced to death under Article 125 of the Turkish Penal Code, pending appeal. Representatives of the European Parliament, the European Union, the Parliamentary Assembly of the Council of Europe, and the United Nations High Commissioner for Human Rights monitored Öcalan's trial. When the court handed down a death sentence, the Parliamentary Assembly of the Council of Europe reminded President Demirel that Turkey had joined other states in 1997 in a pledge to abolish the death penalty.

Bülent Ecevit's center-left Democratic Left Party won general elections in April 1999 and formed a coalition government with the extreme right-wing Nationalist Action Party and the center-right Motherland Party. Human Rights Watch noted in its *World Report 2000,* "One of the first actions of Ecevit's new government was to issue a circular announcing that priority would be given to human rights and warning that police stations would be subject to impromptu checks." Giving further hope to defenders of human rights, "high-ranking judges publicly condemned the judiciary's lack of independence and the flawed constitution, which had been imposed by the military in 1982. They also criticized the prosecutions and imprisonments arising from laws that conflict with Turkey's obligations under the European Convention on Human Rights. Intense debate on human rights was stimulated when Abdullah Öcalan was brought to Turkey in February, and throughout his subsequent trial, but the limits to free expression constrained argument on the political, cultural, and language rights of the Kurdish minority." Human Rights Watch also reported:

> Political influence over the judicial process and constraints on free expression were strongly criticized by two high-ranking judges. In March, the president of the Constitutional Court, Ahmet Necdet Sezer [who was elected President of Turkey on May 16, 2000], stated that the constitution imposed unacceptable restrictions on the basic freedoms of Turkish citizens—including limits on language rights—and called for harmonization of Turkish domestic law with the European Convention. In September, at the official opening of the judicial year and in the presence of the president and prime minister, the president of the Appeal Court, Dr. Sami Selcuk, rated the legitimacy of the constitution as "almost zero" and expressed the hope that Turkey would not enter the twenty-first century under a regime which continues to "crush minds and stifle voices." Those present applauded the speech but neglected to take steps to remedy the shortcomings of the constitution or lift the legislation limiting expression.

Political freedoms were severely restricted by the state security forces. Entering the 1999 general elections, the pro-Kurdish People's Democracy Party and the Islamist Virtue Party were threatened by ban. In fact, the banishment of the Democratic Mass Party in February 1999 was the fifteenth by the Constitutional Court since Turkey returned to civilian rule in 1983. Such efforts to stifle opposition also targeted individuals such as Akin Birdal, who was then president of the Human Rights Association (IHD). He was imprisoned on 3 June 1999, only a year after barely surviving an assassination attempt. Birdal was sentenced under the draconian Penal Code Article 312(2) for speeches made in 1995 and 1996 in which he called for a peaceful resolution to the Kurdish issue. For health reasons, he was released from prison for six months in September 1999. However, his term was not commuted, and he still faced a lifetime ban from political activities and from leaving the country.[129]

The suppression of free speech was extended to "writers, publishers, trade unionists, teachers, local and national politicians, human rights defenders, and many others. . . . Those particularly targeted had expressed opinions on issues related to the Kurdish question or the role of Islam in politics. In fact, sixteen women and several journalists were indicted for 'incitement' at Istanbul State Security Court under Article 312 of the Turkish Penal Code for organizing and participating in a nationwide nonviolent demonstration against the headscarf restrictions in October 1998."[130]

State of emergency legislation remained in force in five provinces leading to widespread human rights abuses. Amnesty International reported that

> people suspected of offences under the jurisdiction of State Security Courts may be held incommunicado for up to four days, and in practice this period was often extended. Procedures laid down in the Criminal Procedure Code for the registration of detainees and for notification of families were often ignored, facilitating "disappearances" and torture. Torture methods included severe beatings, being stripped naked and blindfolded, hosing with pressurized ice-cold water, hanging by the arms or wrists bound behind the victim's back, electroshock torture, beating the soles of the feet, death threats, and sexual assaults including rape.[131]

AI campaigned against impunity for torturers in Turkey with its *Annual Report 2000,* issued in April 1999, which detailed cases in which "complaints of serious human rights violations were not pursued by the authorities. Detainees frequently could not identify their torturers because they were almost invariably blindfolded during interrogation. Medical evidence of torture was frequently suppressed. Medical officers who falsified reports have been promoted, and doctors who scrupulously carried out their duties have been put on trial or imprisoned."[132]

United Arab Emirates

Like the other Gulf monarchies, information on human rights is stifled by the closed and confined society in which the people of the Emirates live. The UAE is a federation of seven emirates: Abu Dhabi, Dubai, Sharjah, Ras al-Khaimah, Umm al-Qaiwain, 'Ajman, and Fujairah. No elections have been held and no political parties have been authorized in the thirty years of the UAE's existence. The main policy-making body is the supreme council of rulers of the seven emirates, who then appoint the individual members of the Federal National Council.

In October 1999 the president issued a new federal environment law. Amnesty International pointed out that in Article 62(2) "anyone found storing or dumping nuclear waste and polluting the environment would be subject to either the death penalty or life imprisonment, and a large fine." The AI report noted that "sentences of cruel, inhuman and degrading punishments such as flogging were reportedly passed during 1999. In October a Shari'ah court in Fujairah reportedly sentenced a number of foreign nationals to flogging for sexual offences." As a retentionist state, the UAE saw "eight people sentenced to death during 1999. Seven were foreign nationals. Six of the eight were reportedly sentenced to death on drug-related charges."[133]

Yemen

The human rights record of Yemen has come under increased scrutiny in recent years as it emerges from decades of internal civil war and internecine violence. International media attention focused on the 1999 trial of ten foreign nationals—eight Britons and two Algerians—on charges of planning terrorist attacks within Yemen. The trial "highlighted serious shortcomings in the Yemeni justice system, including arbitrary detention, torture, and unfair trials," according to Human Rights Watch.[134] Convictions resulted in prison terms of between seven months and seven years and allowed for a closer examination of the judicial system and commitment to human rights in Yemen.

On 25 September 1999, President 'Ali 'Abdullah Saleh, now entering his fifth term in office, won the first Yemeni direct presidential election. Official reports placed his support at 96.3 percent of the total vote. The only other candidate was Najib Qahtan al-Sha'bi, a member of the President's General People's Congress Party, who stood as an independent.[135] As candidates needed 10 percent of the parliamentary deputies to endorse their candidacy in order to be eligible to run, opposition candidates were unable to secure the procedural endorsement due to low representation in the national parliament.[136] After securing victory at the polls, President Saleh "pledged to fight corruption and build a modern state based on law and order. In his first act as he entered his new term he resigned his position as head of the Supreme Judicial Council, a measure that could contribute to judicial independence."[137]

Despite the end to the internal strife and the successful election of both the president and a national legislature, Yemen continued to be plagued by tribal and intercommunal violence. The new national government's inability to control such terrorist acts has undermined its own legitimacy and opened up opportunities for human rights abuses. Increasingly, foreign visitors are kidnapped and held hostage in demand of payment or concessions from the government, with the most famous incident resulting in the December 1998 deaths of four western hostages who were killed in a gun battle between kidnappers and Yemeni security forces.[138] As incidents of violence continued, including kidnappings and explosions, their political motivation became more apparent. With some twenty-two people killed and sixty injured, and the Aden-Abyan Islamic Army claiming responsibility for some bombings as well as the abduction of the hostages killed in 1998, the government felt pressure to respond. Several individuals were tried on charges related to the bombings and abductions. However, Amnesty International reported that the "trials sometimes failed to meet international standards of fairness: some failed to investigate allegations of torture; statements were issued to the press which prejudiced the defendant's right to be presumed innocent until proved guilty; there were irregularities in arrest and detention procedures, such as the use of incommunicado detention; and the defence faced obstacles such as denial of the right of lawyers to have private consultations with their clients or access to relevant documentation."[139]

In response, President Saleh announced the extension of the death penalty to cases of kidnapping in August 1999.[140] Two months later, the government in Aden established special courts to hear cases involving the abduction of foreigners, explosions targeted at oil pipelines, and other acts of sabotage. Amnesty International reported that within days of introducing the new courts, the interior minister announced that forty-six people "accused of such crimes would be immediately referred to the new courts." Furthermore, the "arrests and detentions . . . breached Yemen's own laws or international standards by which Yemen is bound, such as the International Covenant on Civil and Political Rights. Detainees were held in incommunicado detention and denied access to family and to lawyers." The death penalty continued to be imposed for both security and criminal convictions, and Amnesty International recorded thirty-five executions during 1999. "Dozens, possibly hundreds, of people were believed to have been under sentence of death or facing trial for capital offences."[141]

Human Rights Watch stated, "Many prisoners and detainees were held in unregulated detention centers operated by tribal leaders or branches of the security forces."[142] HRW also recognized that with the increasing international exposure "officials increasingly used human rights terminology even when defending proposed restrictive legislation" such as "a draft law governing demonstrations and assemblies" where Minister of Legal Affairs 'Abdallah Ahmad Ghanim cited "the democratic right to organize processions and demonstrations" in an interview with al-Sharq al-Awsat (London) published on 31 August, and noted that the proposed legislation did not "aim at confiscating or restricting the right to express opinions."[143] Media relations aside, Yemen's treatment of political and criminal prisoners was made an issue in January 1999 by the UN Committee on the Rights of the Child, which reviewed Yemen's second periodic report and "expressed concern at 'the use of physical punishment, including flogging, and torture in detention centres.'"[144]

The restriction of basic freedoms extended to the freedom of expression as reporters who published exposés on high-level government corruption faced prosecution, as did those who covered "the deepening security relationship between the Yemeni and U.S. armed forces, and the role of Yemen in the conflict between Eritrea and Ethiopia in the horn of Africa." Women were also the targets of oppression because they faced arbitrary detention if convicted of "moral" offenses and would then serve indefinite periods under the Yemeni penal code, which Human Rights Watch pointed out "violated article 15(1) of the Convention on the Elimination of All Forms of Discrimination against Women, to which Yemen was a party. The government continued to detain female prisoners beyond their sentences until they were collected by a male guardian." However, unlike many of their regional counterparts, the "Yemeni government permitted international human rights organizations to visit and local human rights groups functioned within the country," although "the freedom of local monitors was impaired by the restrictions on freedom of expression and a climate of intimidation surrounding criticism of government policy."[145]

PART II

Comparative Government and Politics

CHAPTER 4

The Islamic Republic of Iran

*I*ran, or Persia, has been the seat of eastern empires for twenty-seven centuries. The Persians are not a Semitic or Arabic people but Indo-European, who migrated to what is now Iran in the second millennia B.C.E. The Iranians appear in the historical record as the Aryans who invaded India, the Scythians and Saka of western history, and the Yueh-Chi on the northwest frontiers of China, exploding out of Central Asia from the twelfth century B.C.E. onwards. They were nomadic herders who raised horses and cattle and were renowned for their skill as mounted archers and warriors.

The early Iranians tended to establish themselves as aristocracies over indigenous peoples in areas they conquered, a pattern followed by the Achaemenids, the Parthians, and the Sassanids. The first great Persian Empire, that of the Achaemenid dynasty, was founded in the sixth century B.C.E., and at its height in the seventh century it stretched from Egypt and the Aegean to the Hindu Kush and modern north India. This was the Persian Empire, whose invasion of Greece at the beginning of the fifth century B.C.E. is related by Herodotus and which fell to the assault of Alexander of Macedon ca. 330 B.C.E. This Persian Empire also invented the term *Eranshahr,* meaning land of the Aryans, and referred to their king as Shahanshah, or King of Kings. The Iranian religion was Zoroastrianism, a dualistic system of belief of tremendous antiquity.[1]

The Macedonian invasion resulted in the creation of the Greek Seleucid dynasty, which ruled a gradually shrinking portion of what are now Iraq, Iran, and Syria until the first century B.C.E. In the eastern areas of the former Persian Empire, local Greek dynasties were quickly supplanted by the aristocracies of Iranian nomadic and seminomadic peoples concerned with control and maintenance of the trade routes between the Hellenistic and Roman West, Central Asia, India, and

China that ran through their lands. These dynasties, including the Parthian Kingdom, which was Rome's most powerful rival until the early third century C.E., were noted more for their military skills than for their administrative ones, and the largely Greek-influenced Semitic populations of the cities of the eastern Fertile Crescent were nearly autonomous under their rule.

In the early third century C.E., in what is now the Khorasan area of northeast Iran, a local dynasty arose claiming descent and inheritance from the Achaemenids. They challenged Parthian dominance in the area. After essentially eliminating the Parthian aristocracy in a series of battles (ca. 220 C.E.), this new Sassanid dynasty set about establishing a much more organized and defined Persian Zoroastrian Empire. A series of conquests extended the bounds of the empire into Central Asia in the east and to a shifting frontier with the Romans in the west. Conflict with the Byzantine (east Roman) Empire eventually resulted in the critical weakening of both the Parthians and the Byzantines and left them open to the Muslim conquest of the seventh century C.E. The last remnants of the Sassanid nobility found their way to T'ang China, where they still contemplated means by which to overthrow their Arab conquerors in the eighth century.

The high culture of the Sassanids was tremendously influential throughout Asia. Persian artistic influences reached as far afield as China and Japan, carried by Buddhists, and the courtly culture of the Sassanids became the foundation of the Abbasid dynasty although under an Islamic veneer. Persian language and literature survived and prospered even under Arabic domination, and Persian and Arabic culture enriched each other. The developments of Zoroastrian theology, and that of its sects and cults, greatly influenced both eastern Christianity and Islamic mystics. Zoroastrianism survived as a major religion in Persia and India for another millennium, and Central Asian peoples incorporated many elements of Zoroastrian ritual into their superficially Islamic rites. Nestorian Christianity was well established among the Sassanid elites, who spread it as far as China.

Following the decline of the Abbasids, the lands of Persia fell under the successive domination of Turks (who often supplanted Persian rulers who had hired them as mercenaries) and then Mongols. The Safavid dynasty (1502–1722) was founded by the Safavid family, which traced their ancestry to Shaikh Safiu'd Din, from whom the name of the empire was coined. Going further back, the ancestry of the family was also traceable to the seventh imam, Musa, a connection which closely linked them with the Prophet's family. The monarchs of this era based their legitimacy on the Shi'a school of Islam and imposed it as the state faith over the population, which had been predominantly Sunni. The Safavids, however, presided over a decline in Persian power, as the caravan routes of Central Asia were surpassed in importance by sea routes through the Indian Ocean, which linked the Mediterranean region and western Europe with China and Southeast Asia through the Middle East. This dynasty ended in 1722 when its capital, Isfahan, was overrun by the tribal army of Mahmud the Afghan, who then ruled a rapidly disintegrating Persian society. Persia entered a period of decay and anarchy from which it did not emerge until the ascendancy of the Qajar dynasty in the late eighteenth century.

The Qajar, a Persian tribe, imposed central rule through the conquest of other tribes under the leadership of Agha Mohammed Khan. The dynasty's capital was Tehran, which has since been the capital of Persia and modern Iran. In the development of a viable and modern Persia, the Qajar dynasty played a crucial role. Some of the salient features of modern Iranian history took shape at this time. Foreign interference, accompanied by Iranian xenophobia, came to play an important role in Persian development. Persia's strategic position in central Asia made it prey to invaders including Genghis Khan, Alexander the Great, and the Romans. Foreign intrigue increased instability and conflict between its people. The discovery of oil in the nineteenth century only made it more attractive to imperial powers. During the Qajar era in the nineteenth century, Iran was a prize pursued by both Great Britain and czarist Russia. British interest in the country was sustained by the determination to secure its colonial possessions in India and later to control the Persian Gulf and possible oil concessions in the region. Russian involvement was motivated by several factors, including a czarist expansionist policy, as well as the more specific strategic goals of pressuring British access to India and outflanking the Ottoman Empire. The Qajar monarchs were powerless in keeping the imperial giants from getting what they wanted; in some respects their own failings facilitated the subjugation of the country. According to Mehran Kamrava, "Needing to finance their extravagances and finding themselves caught between rival powers, the Qajar monarchs, over a period of years, granted major concessions over increasingly large tracts of territory, natural resources, and, ultimately, integral elements of their sovereignty to the rival powers of Russia and Great Britain who dominated Asia at that time; these concessions left the country in severe straits."[2]

Persia's territorial sovereignty was increasingly violated as more concessions were granted to the foreign powers, heightening xenophobia and resentment among the Persians. The Qajar monarchs maintained some measure of independence by playing one power against the other, but when the British and the Russians realized this in the late nine-teenth century, both tended to pursue a balance of power philosophy, patching up their differences when joint interests were jeopardized. This conservative desire to avoid major power struggles in Central Asia was fueled by British concerns in Africa, the rising threat of imperial Germany, and Russia's domestic weakness and involvement in several Balkan wars. The Qajar policy of exploiting the rivalry between the two countries thereafter failed to have the desired impact.

As the nineteenth century drew to a close, Persia became increasingly vulnerable to foreign pressure. The rerouting of east-west trade through the Suez Canal deprived Persia of one of its major sources of revenue. Political corruption and foreign exploitation reduced many in the country to poverty, and Persia once again fell into a state of near anarchy. The shah's control was largely limited to his capital city, and the countryside was left to tribal authority. In an effort to fill this power vacuum, the Russians organized the Persian Cossack Brigade, and it served to keep order in the capital and to protect Russian interests in Persia.

Two concessions granted to the British had an immense impact on the internal affairs of Persia: the tobacco concession of 1890 and the oil concession of 1901. In 1890 a group of British merchants obtained a fifty-year concession for the production, sale, and export of tobacco. As tobacco was a major industry in Persia, the concession aroused public outrage and triggered riots in major cities. Religious leaders issued a fatwa (judicial opinion) against the concession, and the shah was forced to have them canceled in 1892. The British government demanded compensation in the amount of £500,000 sterling for the cancellation, as had been stipulated by the agreement, and arranged for Persia to borrow this sum from the British Imperial Bank at 6 percent interest. Customs receipts of the Persian Gulf ports were used as collateral to secure the loan, and for the next forty years Persia was burdened with this debt. Thus, through the British Imperial Bank, Britain established a foothold in Persia. The oil concession was the catalyst for the emergence of the constitutional revolution of 1906, an occasion when Iranians united against the monarchy, calling for constitutional limitations on the shah's power.

The constitutional revolution, an urban-based uprising, was spearheaded by clerics, the merchants, and intellectuals with the aim of curbing the shah's powers, particularly over the economy. The economic policies of the government plus the despotic nature of the shah's rule had instigated the revolution, and these forces all shared an interest in regaining their independence from foreign domination and eliminating economic deprivation. Opposition was expressed in nonviolent ways, such as boycotts and demonstrations, and was directed not at the institution of monarchy alone but at the actions of the specific monarch in power. The shah acceded to the main demand for a constitution, which was prepared by the intelligentsia following the Belgian model. On 30 December 1906, the shah ratified the constitutional document prepared by the intelligentsia and authorized the creation of a Majlis (assembly). Accordingly, power in the state was restructured, with the legislative functions being taken over by an elected parliament; the monarchy was retained but with less power. With the involvement of the clerics and the merchants in the constitutional revolution, Islam forcefully reentered Persian politics, a phenomenon that was to recur in modern Iranian politics with the Iranian Revolution in 1978–79.

The constitutional governments that followed the new arrangement proved ineffectual, partly due to the hostile machinations of the monarchy and foreign powers. During the reign of Mohammed Ali Shah, who assumed the throne in 1907 with the backing of the Russians, attempts were made to liquidate the Majlis and the government. Steadfast opposition from the constitutionalists defeated these intrigues, and the monarch himself fled to Russia. His twelve-year-old son, Ahmad, was installed as the new shah on 16 July 1909, with Azudul-Mulk, the head of the Qajar tribe, serving as his regent. The appointment of a tribal leader to such a powerful role reflected the significance of Iran's tribal tradition. Shortly thereafter, in 1911, the Russians tried unsuccessfully to bring back the deposed shah.

It was in this period that oil was discovered in southern Persia and the Anglo-Persian Oil Company (APOC) was established. In traditional British imperial style, the British government set out to establish the company's virtual sovereignty in its areas of operation by supporting the autonomy of local leaders against the central authority of Tehran. APOC began constructing pipelines, refineries, and port facilities at Abadan, and by 1912 the first oil was exported to England. After converting the Royal Navy from coal to oil, the British became strategically concerned with APOC, and in 1914, just before the outbreak of the First World War, the British government acquired a 51 percent stake in the corporation. The British government now had formal vested interests in Persia, and these interests came to dictate its policy there.

Foreign influence in Persia intensified during the constitutional era. Realizing that their rivalry was counterproductive, the Russians and the British had signed the Anglo-Russian Treaty of 1907, which only enhanced the intrusion into the internal affairs of Iran by foreign powers. Although harmful to the country generally, the pact worked in favor of the shah and to the disadvantage of the revolutionaries and constitutionalists who opposed his rule. The Russians sided with the monarch, whereas the British favored a reform of the monarchy by lending support to revolutionary movements. However, with the signing of the treaty, the British shifted their policy to be in line with Russia's, depriving the revolutionaries of much needed support at a critical time. Consequently, the new situation bolstered the monarchy's position and contributed to the demise of the constitutional revolution.[3]

Although Persia declared its neutrality in the First World War, it could not avoid being drawn into the conflict. Its strategic location and supply of oil forced the Ottomans, Germans, Russians, and British to become involved in Persian affairs. In the end, the Russians and the British continued to be the overlords of the region, with Russia occupying the provinces of Gilan and Mazandaran in the north and Britain occupying the southern ports. As a result of the Bolshevik Revolution, Russia renounced its interest in Persia and withdrew its troops from the northern provinces in 1917, allowing the British to fill the void. With the Russian withdrawal and preoccupation with internal politics, the British promptly signed the 1919 Anglo-Persian Treaty with the pro-British government of Vosuq al-Dawleh, in effect colonizing Persia. The young and inexperienced Ahmad Shah—the last ruler of the Qajar dynasty—could not hold the country together. Centrifugal forces overwhelmed the ruling establishment. Against this background, an officer of the Persian Cossack Brigade, Reza Khan, and a journalist, Seyyed Zia el-din Tabatabaie, jointly seized power through a British-engineered coup that ousted the civilian government.

For a short period Ahmad Shah remained the titular monarch and appointed Reza Khan army commander and Seyyed Zia prime minister. Ahmad Shah soon fled for Europe, fearing his imminent removal from power. Pro-British nationalist ministers sharing his ideas controlled the cabinet, which had been formed by Seyyed Zia, a renowned pro-British nationalist. A number of reforms were initiated targeting the corrupt and illegal activities of the Qajar notables. The influence of foreign imperial powers came under pressure, and in response the new government revoked the Anglo-Persian Treaty of 1919. Attempts were made to develop closer ties with the United States. However, the change in direction only gained the government some powerful opponents. The coalition of nationalists and Reza Khan began to unravel, and Khan strengthened the military and consolidated his position in the country. Finally, when he sensed that his position had become untenable, Prime Minister Zia withdrew, leaving the door open for Khan. In 1923, Khan was made prime minister, and two years later, in October 1925, the

Majlis deposed the exiled Ahmad Shah and accepted Khan as Reza Shah, initiating the Pahlavi dynasty.

Reza Shah's rule brought a number of changes to Persia. He centralized power and ruthlessly eliminated opponents and potential contenders for power. Religious and tribal leaders came under intense pressure, and although the Majlis was allowed to exist, it was greatly emasculated. As in the Qajar dynasty, the central pillars of power were the military, the bureaucracy, and the royal court. Rapid westernization was attempted through improvements in communications and education. A number of economic and social reforms were introduced, and industrialization was adopted with a view to modernizing and diversifying the economy. Infrastructure enterprises were given priority, such as construction of roads, railways, and government-owned factories. However, little attention was paid to the agricultural base of the economy, and the burden of this policy failure fell on the populace as taxes rose.

In the social and cultural domains, the shah adopted a number of secular reforms whose aim was partly to curtail the influence of the ʿulama in the state. Men and women were compelled to adopt western dress, and from 1936 women were even forbidden to wear the traditional veil; shops were ordered not to serve veiled women, and veiled women were forbidden to appear in public or to board public transportation.[4] Some restrictions were imposed on men's traditional Islamic dress as well.

Reza Khan used his position as prime minister to consolidate Persia's military and police forces. He then used those forces to secure Persia's frontiers and to quell its restive tribes. In 1924 he attempted to establish a secular republic, although clerics managed to defeat this maneuver. In 1925, in order to meet the opposition to a secular republic, Khan took the title of shah, but his authority was limited by the British stranglehold on Iran's economy. Reza Shah attempted to negotiate better terms with the British for the Iranian oil concession, and after great effort, some improvements were grudgingly conceded by Great Britain.

Another area affected by the secularization drive was the judiciary. On 27 December 1936, the Majlis passed a law requiring all judges to obtain a degree from the University of Tehran's faculty of law, or a foreign university, and to have completed additional years of secular legal training. This legislation had a direct impact on the ʿulama, who saw their traditional hold on the judiciary fade.

However, many did not accept Reza Shah's modernization policies. The unveiling of women caused an uproar among the ʿulama, and just before the Second World War Reza Shah began establishing ties with Nazi Germany. German technicians were brought to Iran to organize government administration, agriculture, and industry; German teachers were secured for Iranian schools; many Iranian students were sent to German schools for advanced education; and commercial ties were developed between the two countries. By 1939 more than a third of Iran's trade was with Nazi Germany. Despite the opposition, nothing could alter the secularization drive during Reza Shah's time at the helm, but after he was removed from power in 1941, the implementation effort waned. The shah's removal from power came when the country was invaded by Britain and Russia, in an effort to ensure the free flow of oil for their war effort against the Germans and also to safeguard supply routes to the Russian forces who were doing most of the fighting against Germany. The shah's army quickly collapsed in the face of the joint British-Soviet action. The Allies forced Reza's abdication from the throne, and his twenty-one-year-old son, Mohammed Reza, was made shah.

On assuming the throne, the young ruler had to cultivate his own base of political and economic power, an uphill task in the turmoil both during and following the war. His immediate job was to repair Iran's severely compromised sovereignty. Russian forces continued to occupy northern Iranian territory, in violation of earlier withdrawal commitments. In the areas occupied by these forces, two autonomous republics, Azerbaijan and Kurdistan, had been established, and Tehran feared it was a prelude to their eventual incorporation into the Soviet Union. However, under intense diplomatic maneuvering from the Iranians and pressure from the United States and Britain, Iran regained these territories and Soviet forces withdrew.

Next, the government set out to capitalize on its immense oil reserves. While the Anglo-Iranian Oil Company (AIOC) secured huge revenues from its Iranian operation, only about 1 percent of its profits were staying in Iran. This inequity was a primary source of public displeasure against Britain, and in 1949 a coalition of nationalist groups formed the National Front, headed by Dr. Mohammed Mossadegh.[5] Under the banner of the National Front, Dr. Mossadegh and seven other National Front members won seats in the 1950 parliamentary elections, forming a small but vocal opposition in the Majlis. In April 1950, the government announced an agreement with AIOC that did not include concessions to Iranian interests and preserved the AIOC's near-colonial authority. Outraged at the government's seeming intransigence to negotiate better terms, a parliamentary committee demanded the nationalization of Iran's petroleum resources, throwing the government into crisis. While the shah and his cabinet, on behalf of AIOC, attempted to have the agreement passed through the Majlis, the demand for nationalization gained increasing public support. In March and April 1951, there were mass demonstrations in Tehran demanding nationalization. To pacify public demand and forestall open rebellion against the government, the shah did not bar Mohammed Mossadegh's election as prime minister in May when the National Front achieved an overwhelming majority in the Majlis. Unbowed by monarchical and foreign pressure, his first move was to enact the nationalization resolution, which was unanimously approved by the Majlis, temporarily giving the Majlis more power than it had ever possessed through popular legitimacy.

Mohammed Mossadegh's prime ministership strengthened the Majlis' as well as the nationalist cause, but only for a short period. Power in the country had alternated between the royal court and the office of the prime minister since the constitutional revolution of 1906. The Majlis' role was greatly diminished during Reza Shah Pahlavi's reign, and under his son the system of executive rule had been strengthened. The popularity of Mossadegh propelled the office of prime minister to executive power to such an extent that the shah was forced to flee the country in 1953. He was reinstated through a military coup d'état, engineered by the U.S. Central Intelligence Agency (CIA), which removed Mossadegh from office and initiated a new phase in modern Iranian politics whereby the United States emerged as the most powerful influence in the country, with the shah as willing collaborator. By the time Amir 'Abbas Hoveida, one of the shah's most trusted and loyal confidants, was made prime minister in 1965, the shah's position had been consolidated. Hoveida remained in office until 1977, as his unquestioning loyalty to the shah allowed for the further rise in executive powers held by the shah and the progressive erosion of other power centers, most notably the Majlis, leaving the shah in sole possession of political authority. Other factors also worked in favor of the shah's consolidation of power. The shah received massive military and economic assistance from the Americans because he was regarded as a valuable asset during the cold war. With American support and the relative absence of any significant opposition outside of the religious quarters of the city of Qum, the shah embarked on an extensive reform of the institutions of the state and the economy.

Occupying a central position in the shah's absolutist regime was an overwhelming bureaucracy, which planned and carried out the many government programs and initiatives aimed at modernizing the country. Government ministries maintained extensive networks of branches and offices in the remote parts of the country to implement government programs. But the ability of the bureaucracy to carry out the designated tasks was frustrated by several weaknesses of the sort endemic to most developing countries. The Iranian bureaucracy was tainted by extensive corruption and inefficiency, ills that were also rampant in the royal court itself. The court had become increasingly dissipated and sybaritic as the shah abandoned the austerity he had initially practiced. From 1953 until the time of his exit from power in 1979, the shah dramatically expanded the armed forces in line with his determination to turn the country into a regional power. In 1978 the Iranian armed forces were reported to be one of the largest military establishments in the world.[6] The rebuilding of the military greatly benefited from increased oil revenues and the Nixon-Kissinger doctrine, whose aim was to develop regional powers under American auspices. Obsessed with the Soviet threat, Iran was most willing to be promoted to a regional power under this arrangement. Thus it became one of the largest recipients of American military hardware, loans, and other assistance, second only to Israel. Iran received modern naval vessels, armored vehicles, and advanced F-14 interceptors, equipment which enabled it to survive the devastating war with Iraq during the 1980s.

Special attention was paid to the secret police, known as SAVAK. Set up in 1957 with CIA assistance, this security institution was designed to counter the activities of the guerrilla movements, foil foreign espionage activities, and monitor the bureaucracy to ensure its loyalty to the regime. In the 1960s SAVAK focused on two new two guerrilla organizations, the Islamic Mujahadeen-Khalq and the Fadaiyan-Khalq. In the 1970s, these organizations suffered immensely as several of their leaders were imprisoned and their ability to operate within Iran was crippled. However, the brutal ways in which the security agency dealt with its victims met with extensive condemnation from human rights organizations and governments around the world.

In the political arena, the shah took steps to legitimize his rule, such as in 1975 when he dissolved the two legitimate opposition parties and formed Rastakhiz (Resurgence) to act as the sole opposition. This all-embracing party was expected to solicit support for the regime in the urban areas and the countryside. Initially, the idea of a single party appealed to a number of educated and professional groups, but when the activities of the party became closely intertwined with those of the regime and at the expense of the people, attitudes quickly changed. Rastakhiz soon began suppressing the masses politically, rather than mobilizing them.[7] When revolt against the regime took shape, the Rastakhiz was a predictable target.

Cultural and social reforms started by the shah's father were continued, in spite of opposition from the 'ulama and other groups. Mohammed Reza Shah was in a less difficult position than his father, who had to initiate economic and infrastructure rebuilding from scratch without foreign assistance. Mohammed Reza Shah's package of long-term plans and reforms was called the "White Revolution." The White Revolution initially involved six elements: land reform, nationalization of forests, sale of state-owned enterprises, a workers' profit-sharing plan, female suffrage, and the creation of literacy co-ops.[8] To legitimize the reforms, in early 1963 a national referendum was organized in which the government attempted to orchestrate a resounding "affirmative vote," although the results were not those anticipated. The only reform that had a far-reaching consequence was the one relating to the reallocation of land. Opposing the land reforms were strong vested traditional landowners and foreign interests. During President Kennedy's administration, land reform in developing countries was considered a deterrent against communism, as it would theoretically placate the peasants who resented traditional landowners. Thus, the United States sponsored, and employed foreign assistance to encourage, this reform in many developing countries as a counter to the perceived Communist threat. Iran found itself compelled to adopt the reform, which benefited the shah through further American support. Domestically, the shah welcomed the measure, since it eroded the power of the landlords and gained the support of several million landless peasants. Beside the Americans and the shah, the other players in the land reform were Prime Minister Ali Amini and Minister of Agriculture Hassan Arsanjani, who was later relieved of his post by the shah when he became too popular.

In the forefront of the opposition to the shah's land reform and modernization plans were the 'ulama, whose relation to the monarchy had been cordial. In fact, some 'ulama supported the 1953 coup, which restored the monarchy. Nevertheless, there were 'ulama who had long been critical of the shah's leadership. Further modernization and land reform plans increased the tenor of opposition to the regime. A prominent cleric, Ruhollah Khomeini, emerged as one of the most outspoken voices against reform and modernization.

Khomeini, who had been born into a religious family in 1902, stood out in his opposition to the Pahlavis. After learning Arabic and the basics of Shi'ism, he went to Iraq in 1920 to study to become a mujtahid, an Islamic scholar, under Karim Hae'eri Yazdi. Khomeini became a mujtahid in 1926, the same year the Qajars were deposed by Reza Khan. As a young hojjatolislam, Khomeini witnessed the damage done to the power and fortunes of the 'ulama by Reza Shah's secularization drive. Through his writings he expressed his opposition to these measures. The repressive nature of the regime thwarted any overt action on the part of the 'ulama to halt the secular forces. Nevertheless, during Mohammed Reza Shah's rule the atmosphere gradually became conducive to the growth of opposition activities.

Khomeini would come to prominence during the events surrounding the referendum on the "White Revolution," which he heartily opposed. The regime acted sternly against those opposed to the referendum, leading to open confrontations and the deaths of several hundred people. Following these incidents, Khomeini challenged the monarchy in a speech on 3 June 1963, and shortly thereafter, he and other 'ulamas were arrested. The arrests led to increased antigovernment agitation, which forced his release after six weeks of detention. However, he was kept under house arrest in Tehran. In 1964, he was allowed to return to his home in Qum, where he received a hero's welcome. Khomeini had become a popular religious-political figure in spite of the government's actions, and his antiregime activities were increasingly hindered. In November 1965, he was forced into exile in Turkey, and from there he went to Najaf in Iraq, where he lived until 1978.

The shah's regime survived the challenge; however, a policy change by the American government following the election of Jimmy Carter would have a serious impact on the maintenance of the Pahlavi regime. Carter abandoned the Nixon-Kissinger doctrine of containment of communism at all costs, and human rights were muscled to the forefront of foreign policy issues in the United States. Although Carter sought to maintain the valuable role played by Iran in the geopolitics of the region, he also wanted the shah to improve his human rights record. Under the leverage of American aid packages and arms sales, the shah was forced to bring about some reforms in the way the country was governed. Such reforms came at a wrong time for the shah, however, as his capacity to deal with opposition was seriously compromised, contributing to his withdrawal from power.

The Iranian Revolution

The unraveling of the Pahlavi regime accelerated as the forces arrayed against it joined ranks with the 'ulama. Although Khomeini was exiled, the June uprising had transformed him into a hero. "Khomeini's themes of anti-Americanism, his fervent opposition to Zionism, his opposition to the shah's autocracy, and his emphasis on Islam attracted a large audience which cut across class distinctions and ideological persuasions."[9] It was his charismatic appeal which ultimately united the opposition. There were several groups, adhering to varying ideological persuasions, working to bring down the shah's dictatorial rule in Iran. These groups could be differentiated into the following categories: the 'ulama, secular political parties, guerrilla organizations, and the intelligentsia.

Crowning the success of their political agitation, the 'ulama, in particular Ayatollah Khomeini, led the revolution of 1978–79, placing the leadership of the country under fundamentalist Shi'ism. Unlike other lines of Shi'i thought, fundamentalist Shi'ism ultimately aims to reconstruct the society that existed under the Prophet and during the brief reign of Imam 'Ali, through the strict implementation of the Shari'ah (Islamic law).[10] According to their interpretation, other rulers of Islamic nations should be regarded as illegitimate. However, it would be some time before the fundamentalists would manage to take control of the country. Other opponents to the regime included political parties and the guerrilla movement.

Confronting the shah's dictatorship after the fall of Mossadegh in 1953 were the Tudeh Party and the National Front Party. Tudeh was founded by Communists in 1941, whereas the National Front Party, a liberal nationalist party, was formed in 1949 by a group of intellectuals and political activists led by Dr. Mohammed Mossadegh, whose opposition to the regime could be traced back to Reza Shah's reign. The Tudeh Party, which developed a monolithic organization, came to prominence due to international geopolitical factors, which also brought about its demise. The overtly pro-Soviet line of the party allowed its leadership some measure of popular support throughout the 1940s, when intense anti-British sentiment prevailed in Iran and people perceived the Soviet Union in positive terms. But when Tudeh supported the Soviet-backed secessionist movement in Azerbaijan in 1945, it lost most of its support.

The National Front was composed of a number of parties united by their strong sense of nationalism. It evolved into a major challenge to the regime and the communist Tudeh Party. Owing its success to the personal charisma of Dr. Mossadegh and its advocacy of oil nationalization, the party reached its zenith between 1951 and 1953 when Mossadegh served as prime minister. However, after the coup of 1953, the National Front and the Tudeh Party were repressed by the SAVAK. Members defected, disillusioned by their leaders' ineffectiveness. In the 1960s and 1970s, while the opposition parties only managed to exist in name, there emerged two leftist guerrilla movements. The Islamic Mujahadeen and the Fadaiyan were each founded by dissatisfied members of the two traditional opposition parties who had lost faith in the peaceful struggle against the shah. The People's Crusaders Organization of Iran (Sazmane Mujahadeen Khalq Iran) was Islamic, although it was influenced heavily by the literature of leftist armed struggle ideological orientation. In 1975, after its leadership had been imprisoned, it split into two factions:

a splinter Communist wing and a purely Islamic Mujahadeen. Another movement, the Organization of the Iranian People's Fedaiyan Guerrillas (Sazman-e Cherik-ha-ye Khalq-e Iran), was founded in February 1971, and it attacked the Pahlavi regime through urban guerrilla warfare. Both organizations had proved ineffective in the face of the tough measures adopted by the regime and its secret police agency, SAVAK, who managed to infiltrate the organizations and arrest many organizers and leaders. Another organizational weakness that both opposition movements shared was their inability to win the support of the general populace. Widespread fear of SAVAK muzzled recruitment, and subversive activities were too limited to effect change.

The last group who stood up to the shah was the intelligentsia. As in other developing countries, the intellectuals in Iran spoke out against oppressive policies. Intellectual fervor in Iran had risen as a consequence of the socioeconomic transformations started by Reza Shah, and peaked during the administration of his son, Mohammed. By the 1960s and throughout the 1970s, the main intellectual current focused on the politicization of Islam, blurring the distinction between the secular and religious opposition to the regime.[11] Before the revolution, the intellectuals and the clergy had formed a common front in opposition to the regime. Religion not only helped to bind the opposition forces; it also brought in those who had been excluded. People took pride in Shi'ism because it was uniquely Iranian and could be employed to galvanize people's support to the common cause of defeating the shah's regime.

The Role of the 'Ulama

Although many forces were now united against the shah, it was the 'ulama, relying on their extensive network of mosques to mobilize mass action, who played the largest role in toppling Pahlavi rule in Iran. The opposition political parties and the guerrilla organizations had been so ruthlessly suppressed by SAVAK that their ability to challenge the regime had been severely diminished. The intelligentsia's role was marginalized when few of them dared to speak out against the shah and their message was expressed in venues inaccessible to many Iranians.

The regime's efforts to tame the 'ulama were never successful. When Khomeini was expelled to Iraq as a result of his leadership in the antishah movement, it was believed that his deportation would curtail 'ulama-led agitation in the country. For a short time Khomeini remained inactive while in exile, but he soon resumed his antiregime activism. With Khomeini settling in Najaf, teaching jurisprudence in one of the most respected centers of Shi'a learning, he was brought into close contact with Iranian 'ulamas, who were studying in Najaf. His role as a teacher gave him the opportunity to influence younger clerics, cemented his relationship with the older religious establishment, and provided him with a wider network for communicating his political ideas. In an effort to tarnish his image, the regime began slandering his name in the state-controlled press. But this also failed, and his popularity and prestige continued to rise. In exasperation, the shah engineered his expulsion from Iraq in 1978, and Khomeini was shuttled off to France in the hope that the farther he was from Iran the less opportunity he would have to influence events. In addition, it was hoped that the exposure of his rather archaic ideas in the West would help to discredit him.

While in France, Khomeini collaborated with a growing number of intellectuals. He began to be seen as the only individual capable of overthrowing the dictatorial regime back home. Soon revolutionaries clustered around him, creating a movement that would tailor his message to suit both Iranian and world opinion, eventually directing the revolution in Iran. Within Iran itself, the political situation was approaching total collapse, as public demonstrations and antigovernment actions escalated. In 1978, the National Front and the 'ulama mobilized popular demonstrations that involved millions of people. Strikes, particularly those targeting oil production facilities, caused havoc with the economy. Guerrillas also conducted raids on military bases, further weakening an institution that was already suffering from mass desertions.

The shah tried to introduce reforms in an effort to calm the situation and maintain power, but the moves were cosmetic and only encouraged opposition forces that were nearing victory. Indecisive, the shah consulted his American allies. However, with an odd mixture of pragmatism, principle, and indecision, the Carter administration was unwilling to overtly support the teetering and internationally unpopular Pahlavi regime. Furthermore, it was unclear what course of action the American administration could adopt that could save the shah. In January 1979, the shah opted to leave the country, and a member of the National Front Party, Dr. Shapour Bakhtiar, was appointed prime minister.

Meanwhile, in Khomeini's camp a secretive council, which evolved into the Council of the Islamic Revolution (CIR), had been formed in January 1979 to coordinate the activities of the Islamic opposition against the shah's regime with the popular actions taking place in the country. The formation of the council was not well received by some within the opposition parties and organizations, as it was secret and therefore not inclusive. It was a reflection of the lack of a common viewpoint among the disparate groups opposing the status quo. There was general agreement that the shah must go but none whatsoever on what should happen next.

In effect, the existence of the CIR alongside the government of Dr. Bakhtiar created dual sovereigns in the country. Although the new government adopted a number of reforms—such as the dissolution of SAVAK, the release of many political detainees, and an unsuccessful attempt at rapprochement with Khomeini—the advancing tide of the revolution continued onward. Bakhtiar's position became more precarious after the triumphant return of Khomeini on 1 February 1979. Immediately upon his arrival, he declared the appointment of Bakhtiar to the post of prime minister "illegal." Khomeini asked Mehdi Bazargan, leader of the Iranian Freedom Movement, to form a provisional government. With the country divided, the military fractured, which led to fighting in the streets. When calm was restored, the military declared its neutrality, effectively coronating the revolutionaries because it would not move against them. Bakhtiar went into hiding, and Bazargan appointed a new chief of staff for the military, firing several of the top commanders known to be loyal to the shah. Elections to a new Majlis were held in March 1979, followed by a referendum to establish an Islamic republic, which received an approval of 98.2 percent of the national electorate. Thus the country became an Islamic republic on 11 April 1979.

The Islamic Republic

The coalition, united by hatred for the common enemy and respect for Khomeini's charisma, comprised diverse groups divided by ideological incompatibilities, generational differences, and socioeconomic and educational disparities. This made its collapse inevitable. Sharing the spoils of the victory became a main contention leading to fierce antagonism involving fundamentalists, Islamic liberal nationalists, and secular liberal nationalists. In the end, the fundamentalists won the struggle, emerging by 1981 as the dominant faction in Iranian politics. The victory, however, came at a heavy cost in human life (through rioting and guerrilla action) and national unity.

Although the revolution was drastic in getting rid of the relics of the deposed system, a key ingredient of Iranian political culture, authoritarianism, survived. The Islamist autocracy that initially replaced the shah was even more severe. Around him, Khomeini gathered a group of loyalists (the fundamentalists) who vigorously imposed their hegemony over the postrevolutionary era. To achieve this, they relied on three mechanisms: the Friday prayer meetings, the Islamic Republican Party (IRP), and the Majlis.

The Friday prayer meetings facilitated the propagation of Khomeini's ideas, while discrediting opponents or people whose loyalty was in doubt. By appointing Friday prayer imams, Khomeini brought them under his control. As for the IRP, it was founded in February 1979 by a small group of clergymen and laity purposely to consolidate the political power for the 'ulama. Under the leadership of Ayatollah Beheshti, the IRP gained prominence in government and the trust of Ayatollah Khomeini, and it came to dominate the Majlis elected in March 1980 and the Assembly of Experts elected in August 1979 to draw up the country's new constitution. The IRP was a useful tool in coalescing pro-Khomeini forces and challenging the power of other contending revolutionary forces.

Reflecting the intensity of jockeying for power and frustration over the erosion of the power of the religious-nationalist, the provisional government of Bazargan resigned on 5 November 1979, a day after the American embassy was occupied in Iran. Abolhassan Bani-Sadr, who became president after the elections of 25 January 1980, suffered a similar fate. The IRP-dominated Majlis forced the appointment of Mohammed Ali Rajai as prime minister, against Bani-Sadr's objections. Bani-Sadr was impeached by the Majlis on 10 June 1981 on the grounds of incompetence. He fled to France to form an opposition party. Mohammed Ali Rajai was elected president on 24 July 1981. Shortly after this, he was killed in a bomb blast. Beheshti, four cabinet ministers, six deputies, and a number of parliamentarians had been killed in an earlier bomb blast at IRP headquarters. Despite the elimination of some of the top leaders of the new system, the revolution survived.

After the dismissal of Bani-Sadr, pro-Khomeini forces dominated the political scene in Iran. However, differences of opinion arose as to the nature of socioeconomic policies—in other words, factions and factionalism gradually emerged. The climax of these differences was the dissolution of IRP in May 1987. When Khomeini was alive, he was able to diffuse these differences. After his death, however, factionalism reached new heights, and today factional power struggle is a distinguishing fact of Iranian politics.

The Nature of the Just Society

Intrinsic in any theory of government is the ideal of a just society. Arguing that Islam is a social system, not merely a system of worship, and that Islamic government has as its primary concern the implementation of divine social legislation, Khomeini stated:

> The Qur'an verses concerned with society's affairs are numerous compared to the verses concerned with private worship. In any of the detailed

Hadith books, you can hardly find more than three or four sections concerned with regulating man's private worship and man's relationship with God. . . . The rest is strongly related to social and economic [affairs], with human rights, with administration and with the policy of societies.[12]

Khomeini's just society is a society in which "governing is not an end in itself . . . if sought as a goal and if all means are used to attain it, then it degenerates to the level of a crime and its seekers come to be considered criminals."[13] Government has no right to arbitrarily undermine the private property of individuals.[14] It only has those rights to taxation of profits already legislated for in the Qur'an, and it is the duty of an Islamic government to ensure that this law is applied without privilege or discrimination. Therefore, the accumulation of material wealth is not proscribed. However, the taxation system and the alms system prescribed in the Qur'an guarantee that there will not be exaggerations of either wealth or poverty, and the legal system guarantees that wealth is not secured through exploitation.

The separation of economic and political power was central to Khomeini's view of society. Mechanisms ensured that political office would not result in privilege; favor or material gain required that officeholders would have to live humbly and piously.[15] Khomeini saw the accumulation of material wealth and conspicuous consumption as manifest indicators of political corruption.[16] It was not necessary for the pious executioners of political office to be religious leaders, but it was incumbent on officeholders to emulate the Prophet and pious imams in their lifestyle. The just society, then, is the society where Divine Law is implemented without privilege or discrimination—a society where both the transgressor and the transgressed are secure in their knowledge of swift, equitable application of the law.[17] It is axiomatic that God's Law is inherently just. It is man's interpretation and application of the law that leads to injustice. This must be guarded against in the structure of government during the period of absence (the last imam). In this period, the danger that "laws and rules would be changed and the heretics would add to them and the atheists would detract from them" is great.[18] The structure of civil administration emerged from Khomeini's concept of *velayat-e faqih*, the rule of the religious jurist, which has served as the central pillar of Iran's theocratic system since the revolution. By concentrating executive power in the hands of a single man, the jurists allowed the supreme leader—appointed by the Assembly of Experts—absolute authority over matters of state. Thus, as supreme leader he has final say on all matters of governance from foreign relations to domestic policy, and he is ceded control over the vehicles of authority, including the army, the security police, and the judiciary. Selected by the clerics comprising the Assembly of Experts he has always represented a conservative religious faction of Iranian society, which has allowed the religious hierarchy to maintain control. Creating a governmental system, with a sufficient structure of checks and balances to allow for the fallibility of man, was the task facing the revolutionaries in 1980. Facing such a daunting task under threat of invasion derailed the revolution as Iran became mired in ten years of struggle with Ba'athist Iraq.

The Iran-Iraq War

On 22 September 1980, Saddam Hussein sent the Iraqi army across the border into Iran. His intelligence sources led him to believe that the Iranian armed forces were opposed to the Islamic revolutionary government and that Iranian officers were ready to launch a coup if they could count on military support. He expected the Iranian defense to fall in disarray before the well-equipped Iraqi military, allowing him to install a client regime in Tehran. In the first great miscalculation of his career, Saddam was desperately wrong. The Iranian people and the Iranian army rallied behind the regime and inflicted tremendous losses on the Iraqis, aided by the sophisticated American weapons Iran had inherited from the shah. By early 1982, Iraq was on the defensive in what was to be the longest conventional war of the twentieth century.

Differences between the two states were long-standing. Their borders were disputed, especially the Shatt al-'Arab waterway that marked the southern part of their mutual frontier. Throughout the 1960s and 1970s, Iran had been an American client state, whereas the regime in Baghdad had leaned toward the Soviet Union. Iraq accused Iran of supporting Kurdish rebels in their long conflict with the Iraqi government. Finally, Iraq's substantial Shi'a population looked to Iran as its spiritual center because Khomeini had called for the overthrow of Hussein's Ba'ath regime in 1978. Hussein had oppressed millions of Shi'is, many of them ethnic Persians, in southern Iraq and executed their leaders. Hussein also had the support of the rich Gulf states, who feared the populist implications of the Iranian revolution for their authoritarian regimes.

Initially, the war was nothing short of a disaster for Iraq, as Iraqi troops proved unable to operate the sophisticated French and Soviet military equipment Hussein had spent Iraq's oil revenues on. Iran crippled the Iraqi oil industry by attacking ports and refineries. Iraq then attacked tanker vessels heading for Iranian ports. The Iranians also adopted this tactic, leading to international intervention to protect the oil supplies that the West and Japan needed to preserve their economies. Finally, the Iranians proved willing to accept horrifying losses of life in exchange for gains on the battlefield; Iraq, with perhaps one-quarter of Iran's manpower, couldn't win a war of attrition. Iranian troops carried the war to Iraqi soil, threatening Baghdad and the critical Gulf port of Basra.

The specter of a possible Iranian victory frightened most Arab states and the West. Financial and military aid flowed into Iraq, buying French and Soviet fighter jets, Italian missile boats, American helicopters, and German armament factories with Saudi and Kuwaiti money. While the international community turned a blind eye, Iraq used poisoned gas, cluster bombs, and ballistic missiles against Iran. Iran stood virtually alone. The Iranian armies showed daring, initiative, and reckless courage typified by "human wave" attacks against superior Iraqi artillery and minefields and by commando raids deep into Iraqi territory. Both sides used ballistic missiles against each other's cities; Iraq suffered more because Baghdad lay barely forty kilometers from the Iranian border and rather less from the actual battlefront. Until 1986 this was a war without negotiation, without cease-fires. The international community remained silent, supporting Iraq with money and arms.

By 1987 both sides were exhausted. Iraq was deeply in debt. Over 200,000 Iranians were dead and many more injured, and without international support Iran had little sophisticated military hardware left. In the spring of 1988, a final Iranian offensive in northern Iraq took the mostly Kurdish town of Halabja. The Iraqi ground forces retreated, to be replaced by Iraqi aircraft and artillery that dumped poison gas indiscriminately on the area. Over 5,000 Iraqi citizens were killed. This brutal, inhuman determination, and the possibility that Iraq had developed missiles capable of lifting chemical weapons to Iran, convinced the Khomeini regime to accept a UN-sponsored truce and cease-fire, which took effect in August 1988. The Iran-Iraq War was one of the most brutal and senseless in recorded history. Absolutely nothing was accomplished, except the deaths of more than 300,000 Iranians and 100,000 Iraqis, massive destruction in both states, and the plunging of Iraq into crippling debt. Hussein had only secured the Iranian regime's position because the war proved a very useful tool with which to crush internal opposition. Any criticism of Khomeini or his regime was labeled treason, and punishment was severe. Curiously, Iran's isolation during the war became its salvation—Iran financed the war effort entirely from its own reserves, which created tremendous economic hardship for its people but also a sense of unity and self-reliance, of having defeated the invader through a monumental effort that was theirs and theirs alone. It also prevented Iran from falling into a massive debt trap, as Iraq had.

The Death of Khomeini

The aging Khomeini, the *faqih* (the supreme juriconsultant), skillfully kept the system together in the face of critical difficulties. Apart from the problems caused by the actions of those who had fallen out with the regime, Khomeini had to plan the succession process and manage the factional politics within his own camp. Khomeini died without naming a successor; his earlier choice, Ayatollah Ali Montazeri, had been politically ostracized after he criticized the regime's human rights record. Nevertheless, Khomeini set the tone of the transition by allowing a constitutional revision to restructure the political system so that it should not be dependent on the charisma of the *faqih* or his religious qualifications. Accordingly, a plebiscite was held in 1989 to amend the 1979 constitution. Among the changes introduced were the redefinition of the powers of the *faqih* and the replacement of the post of the prime minister by that of a popularly elected president as the manager of state affairs. On the day after Khomeini's death in June 1989, the 86-member Council of Experts selected 'Ali Khameni, a religiously conservative cleric, to succeed Khomeini as Vaj-faqih (Supreme Leader). Rafsanjani, a hojjatolislam and Speaker of the Majlis, was elected to the presidency, while hojjatolislam Mehdi Karrubi replaced him as speaker.

Rafsanjani's administration was guided more by pragmatism than by ideological dogmatism. Keen on rebuilding the country from the ruins of the Iran-Iraq war, he favored market-oriented reforms, including privatization, made structural adjustments, and accepted foreign loans. Moreover, he introduced changes in the administration to emphasize competence and skill. Until 1993, the Left opposed Rafsanjani's economic policies, whereas the pro-*bazaaries* (merchant class) conservatives supported them. However, after 1993, the two factions reversed their positions. This led to a de facto coalition between Rafsanjani and the center-left in the Majlis election of 1996. This change in direction was not in the interest of the more conservative elements of the political system, who had turned the Majlis into a platform to voice opposition to government policies and to propagate their own views.

While Iran experienced economic growth between 1992 and 1996, this was mostly in the macro-sector, industry and international trade, and while it increased government revenues and provided basic employment, Iranians for the most part saw stabilization rather than an increase in their standard of living. There was dissatisfaction over the release of government price controls, or the raising of still-controlled prices, and over the large rural population's lack of access to basic goods and services. In urban areas, especially swelling Tehran, life was more affluent, but there was frightening pollution, poor infrastructure planning, and a penetration of western culture and influence, both in the public and private spheres, that some found disturbing. This may have been an indication of the maturity of the Iranian democracy, such as it was; the electorate had adopted the middle line, voting for the opposition when government policies displeased it, but not really voting for a massive change in established policy.

Moderate forces were given a further boost by the election of the reform-minded Mohammed Khatami (ex-minister of Islamic guidance and culture) as the new president in May 1997. Subsequently, it appeared that the Islamic Republic was moving toward a more pragmatic foreign policy and more freedom in social and political life on the internal level. The various political factions were vying for influence, but Iran's policy seemed set on continued economic expansion combined with a policy of rapprochement with the West. However, in the October 1998 election to the Assembly of Experts, Iran's conservative factions reaffirmed their control in the Assembly, in effect checkmating the forces of liberalization loosening the rigidity of the regime. Soon after the election, dissidents, journalists, intellectuals, and reformist cabinet ministers were being harassed by conservative factions and taken to the conservative-led court on charges of corruption. By late December, a wave of assassinations against liberal activists had swept the country.

Post-Khomeini National Political Institutions

The Islamic Republic of Iran has a governmental structure centered around an executive and a 270-member unicameral parliament, with several additional bodies filling roles created by the adoption of Islam as the guiding philosophy of society and state. The highest authority in the state is the Supreme Leader—based on the concept of *velayat-e faqih*—which is, in the constitution's words, "a manifestation of the integration of politics with religion." This is the position once held by the Ayatollah Ruhollah Khomeini and now held by 'Ali Khameni. On paper, the position is incredibly powerful, incorporating a general oversight of all government policy, command of the armed forces and declarations of war and peace, recognition of the president and the power to dismiss him, and regulating the relationship between the executive, the legislature, and the judiciary. The Assembly of Experts elects the Leader, while the people elect members of the Assembly for eight-year terms. The 86-member Assembly sits only once per year, as its only tasks are to appoint the Leader and deal with amendments to the constitution. All of its members are clerics.

The president is elected in a national poll, and he serves a four-year term, with a limit of two terms in office. The president is responsible for the appointment of ministers who are then accountable to the Majlis. The president, however, may only be removed by a vote of no confidence (requiring a two-thirds majority of the Majlis) in his entire government. He is also responsible for the administration of the civil service. The main legislative body is the Majlis, short for Majlis-e Shora-ye Islami (Islamic Consultative Assembly). It has 270 members, elected by direct popular vote every four years. The seats are allocated to the administrative districts of the states proportional to population, including one seat each for the small Jewish, Christian, and Zoroastrian minorities and three seats for the rather larger Armenian minority. A nonminority MP must be a practicing Muslim. The Majlis has powers similar to those in any other democratic legislature, debating all national affairs and forming committees to examine policy and table bills for discussion. The government may also table bills. The Majlis is also responsible for approving all international agreements. Above the Majlis is the Guardian Council, from which legislation approved by the Majlis is examined and evaluated, based on the principles of the constitution, Islamic law, and practice. It consists of six Islamic canonists appointed by the leader and six civil jurists elected by the Majlis from candidates forwarded by the Supreme Court. The Guardians have tended to be extremely conservative, to the point where another body, the Council for the Determination of Expediency, was formed by Khomeini in February 1988 in order to break the legislative deadlock that had arisen between the then reform-minded Majlis and the conservative Guardians. The CDE, appointed by the Leader, passes binding arbitration on disputes between the two bodies. The Iranian judiciary is led by a chief justice appointed by the Leader for a five-year term to work with the Ministry of Justice and to head the Supreme Court. The judiciary is divided into several subsections of civil and criminal courts, as well as clerical tribunals (for punishing offenses by clergy), revolutionary tribunals (for charges of terrorism and offenses against national security, such as espionage), and administrative tribunals (which deal with complaints of citizens against government organs or officials).

Dissent and Opposition

Although there is little or no organized direct opposition to the Islamic government inside Iran, it would appear a generation after the Islamic Revolution that the revolution's societal goals are finally beginning to be realized. With a population that is predominantly urban (61 percent) and incredibly young (40 percent under the age of fifteen), the conservative leadership—in place through the trials of the revolution, the war with Iraq, and constant hostility with the West—now must rely upon the system it has established to allow a new generation of Iranians to decide the shape of the society in which they wish to live. That society is vastly different from the one that ousted the shah. Literacy has escalated to 93 percent of its youth, and the number of post-secondary graduates soared in the 1990s. The treatment of minorities and the rebellious actions of the summer of 1999 seem to indicate that the regime will prove stable and that reform will come from within rather than through violence.[19] Iran seems to have achieved a modus vivendi with its Kurdish minority in the north, and Turkey has accused Iran of allowing Kurds to retreat into Iran after attacks in Turkey. Various opposition groups, some of a democratic, secular nationalist bent, and even some who favor restoration of the monarchy, do exist in exile in the West, but they are thought to have little if any influence in Iran.

Overseas, Iran has pursued its dissidents and opposition figures, both political and religious. Many are publicly harassed by Iranian students studying in the host country (mainly in Europe), and some former members of the Pahlavi regime—in exile in Europe—have been assassinated, likely by agents of the Islamic Republic. The Communist Tudeh movement has disintegrated, as have the other socialist underground groups. The army is firm in its support for the regime since the end of the war with Iraq, in which most of the pro-royal elements were purged.

On a civil scale, however, there is some popular discontent, as the revolution evolved into a theocracy during the First Republic (1979–89), human rights were ignored, and the state was consumed by a protracted war of attrition with Iraq. The Second Republic (1989–97) was forced to focus on the deeper issue of how an Iran that operates as a regional power with global economic connections will be able to retain a strict Islamic character. The social gains initiated by the First Republic, increased literacy, social services, and the development of medical clinics, television, roads, and bridges were stifled by the war with Iraq and the oppressive measures adopted during the stresses of Iran being an isolated society under constant threat from a hostile West. There are already signs that the growing middle class, and even a large proportion of the population of relatively cosmopolitan Tehran, feel constrained by the strict Islamist laws on dress and conduct and generally ignore them in private life. Women's issues are coming to the fore, with Hashemi Rafsanjani's own daughter, Fa'ezeh, a leading moderate publisher of the newspaper *Zan Daily*, elected to the Majlis in 1996 (without his public support) on what might be described as Iran's version of a feminist platform, including increased political and economic rights for women. Despite vast increases in female literacy and attempts at a larger role in public society, women still find themselves on a collision course with the agenda of the conservative political leadership. Fa'ezeh fell from the public eye as soon as she defended her father's record and the conservative judiciary shut down the *Zan Daily*.

In response to the rise in public support for an increased role for women in society, and in an effort to further Islamic teachings, parliament founded the Fatemieh Medical School for women in 1998. Its student body went on strike in late 1999 to protest the segregation of national health services.[20]

Freedom of expression is slowly gaining ground, especially in political debate, and the situation in Iran is certainly more open than that in most Arab states. The 1997 presidential elections were hailed as a new era in freedom of expression, as previously forbidden issues such as the real role of Islam in government were openly discussed and published. How the Third Republic (1997–present) deals with popular dissatisfaction, both inside and outside government, and with official corruption, which is especially pronounced in trade and smuggling activities, will serve as a guide to the potential freedoms enjoyed by the people of Iran. Civil servants are generally recognized as being poorly educated, inefficient, and desperately in need of reform, somewhat out of step with the levels of education infusing the rest of Iranian society. The clash between reform-minded students and security police in July 1999 further demonstrates the groundswell of support for the reform agenda of President Mohammed Khatami. Despite a predictable conservative backlash against reforms and those who lead and advocate them, primarily from the conservative clerical-dominated judiciary, it appears that Khatami's reforms will prove difficult to reverse due to their popular appeal. A more mature form of democracy is evidently evolving as Ayatollah Mohajerani, the minister of culture and Islamic guidance who was principally responsible for increased freedoms of the press and artistic expression, was able to stave off an impeachment proceeding in 1999. By persuading the parliament of the merits of such freedoms in an Islamic society, Mohajerani may have opened the door to future progress.[21] The underlying threat of violence remains, from reformers who feel stymied and from religious extremists who fear a reversal of the Islamic revolution, but it is increasingly tempered by events on the ground. The student clashes with security forces and hard-line activists in the summer of 1999 were reactions to the closure of an opposition newspaper, a police raid on a Tehran University dormitory—where some students were killed—and the supreme clerical control of Ayatollah 'Ali Khameni of the state security forces, army, courts, and media, rather than the backlash against the Islamic revolution itself. Student demonstrations spread beyond Tehran to at least nine other cities and towns: Yazd, Khorram, Abad, Zanjan, Mashhad, Isfahan, Urumiyeh, Shahroud, and Tabriz; this further demonstrates the widespread support for the reform movement.[22] The ability of the Khatami government to remain in power, despite the volatility of the protests, demonstrates its resilience and legitimacy.

With the struggle over the control of Iran's court system, between Khatami's vision of the "rule of law" and his clerical opponents' view of *velayat-e faqih*, four of the protesters have already been sentenced to be executed, and others face a similar fate.[23] Caught within their own crime of challenging clerical rule and the larger debate between reformers and conservative clerics, their opportunities for redress appear slim.[24] With the 2000 parliamentary elections, conservative elements in the government altered their tactics and adopted a more secular face for their own candidates responding to popular discontent with clerical rule, as well as eliminating their reform movement opponents by making them ineligible to hold office. Through the Council of Guardians, a conservative and clerically dominated panel of judges—originally established to simply run elections and now expanding its own oversight to screen candidates—several top reform candidates were excluded from the election.[25] The Islamic Participation Front and President Mohammed Khatami's reform movement were forced to encourage a large voter turnout while clearly differentiating reformist candidates from the newly secularized appeal of the conservative candidates, a difficult task because many reformist candidates were unknown commodities.[26] Khatami has come to symbolize the reform movement, melding the hope for progressive reforms within an Islamic tradition, but the movement to alter the staunchly conservative values of past clerical rule has broader support than his personal charisma alone. Khatami's clerical credentials and status as a popularly elected leader give him legitimacy as well as greater latitude in creating and implementing policy than many leaders of the reform movement.

Supporters of President Mohammed Khatami and their reformist allies won a convincing majority in Iran's 2000 parliamentary election, confirmed in his landslide second term election in June 2001, despite the obstacles placed before them. Promising specific reforms, they swept to an overwhelming majority but are bound to have nonparliamentary difficulties in carrying through some of their proposed legislation. As part of the drive for greater social freedoms, a ban on satellite dishes—originally imposed to reduce the influence of western culture—is to be lifted, a curious first act of a reformist parliament. However, despite some western media interpretations, Mohammed Reza Khatami said that all laws introduced by the reformists would be in line with the Iranian constitution.

The two parallel authorities in charge of the elections, one dependent on the interior ministry, which is under the influence of the reformists, the other reporting to the Council of Guardians, which is dominated by conservatives, had great difficulty in establishing just how large the reformist majority would be. In Tehran, where more than 3 million votes were cast and thirty seats were contested, the reformers won twenty-nine seats with conservative ex-president Rafsanjani winning the thirtieth seat with a bare margin.

Reformers promised that political development and greater freedoms would top their agenda. Changes to press and election laws are planned, especially to ensure that further conservative interference in the electoral process is curtailed. Their victory overturned the conservative domination of the parliament, which had previously blocked reforms by the moderate President Mohammed Khatami. Mohammed Reza Khatami, the president's brother and a leading reform figure in the new parliament, said his Participation Front was committed to guaranteeing personal and social rights and freedoms. The reformists believe they can now push through their plans with or without the support of other groups—after only 20 percent of the conservative-dominated outgoing parliament was reelected.[27]

The Economy

Iran has a land area of 1,648,000 sq. kilometers and a population of 65 million. It was estimated that by 1994, 58 percent of the Iranian population was urban, and the UN forecasts that 75 percent will live in urban areas by 2025. With a population of over 10 million, Tehran is the largest city in the Middle East after Cairo. The shift in population patterns has been helped by the high rate of births each year. After the revolution, the rate was put at 3.5 percent. Although the country is rich in resources, including its vast oil reserves, such a population profile could work against socioeconomic development. It is precisely for this reason that the regime in Iran backed away from its earlier policy of encouraging population growth and began embracing family planning. Iran faces a demographic crisis similar to that facing the Maghrib states. Most of its population is young. Additionally, Iran's stability and prosperity (relative to its neighbors) has resulted in massive migrations from the region—Iran is now host to 2.2 million refugees from the Soviet invasion of Afghanistan, the Gulf war, the Iraqi regime's constant savage actions against its Shi'i and Kurdish minorities, and more recently, from ethnic and civil unrest in Turkmenistan, Pakistan, and Tajikistan. Also, 1.6 million Iranians were rendered homeless during the war with Iraq, and many are not yet permanently settled or assimilated. Due to American opposition, Iran receives little aid from the International Red Cross or the United Nations in dealing with this problem.

Iran's economy has long relied on its oil sector, which facilitated the establishment of an elaborate infrastructure during the time of Mohammed Reza Shah while maintaining a high economic growth rate. Between 1960 and 1977, Iran's annual real growth rate was placed at 9.6 percent, double the average of countries in its category.[28] The regime also made a considerable investment in education and health, which greatly improved social welfare. Furthermore, the regime was able to expand and equip the military to the extent that Iran became a regional power.

It is this foundation, laid down by the shah, which enabled the postrevolutionary leaders who took over the country to weather the challenges they encountered in the early days of the revolution, including economic sanctions following the American embassy incident, the Iran-Iraq war, a fast-growing population, and external indebtedness. When Khomeini came to power, he had no clear-cut economic policies to replace the ones of the Pahlavi era, which were repudiated. It was only after the constitution of 1979 was adopted that the outlines of the regime's thinking in the economic field could be sketched out. "The document as a whole prescribes an idealistic model wherein a benevolent theocratic government controls the commanding heights of the economy—basic industry, banking, insurance, foreign trade, and public utilities; cooperatives are engaged in vital production and distribution functions; and the private sector plays an important but residual role."[29]

In line with this, all major industries were taken over by the government. Banking, insurance, and business firms were nationalized. As part of Islamizing the economy, legislation was adopted in 1982 outlawing the collection of interest. However, after the end of the war with Iraq in August 1988 and the death of Khomeini in 1989, new economic theories developed. Ideological dogma gave way to pragmatic considerations. In the wake of Rafsanjani's election to the presidency, a five-year development plan (1989/90–1993/94) was adopted which marked a shift from economic-statism to free market economy. Concern shifted to such issues as economic reform, inflation, creation of employment, joint ventures with foreign companies, and management of the country's debts. This was spurred, in part, by a public sentiment that they had "earned" some degree of prosperity, of economic and social benefit, after the terrible sacrifices they had made in the Iraqi war. Iran also continues to pursue the collection of hundreds of millions of dollars worth of Iranian assets seized by the United States following the revolution.

Although the new Islamic government deplored the overreliance on the oil sector of the deposed political system, it has done little to diversify the economy. The overall economic policies of Rafsanjani were labeled postwar Reconstruction, which opened the door for economic liberalization. Iran has had little luck in finding markets for its industrial products, and those it has—in Central Asia—are unable to pay in anything except barter. Iran's agricultural sector is slowly expanding, and Iran is reducing its dependence on imported food. Oil production in 1994 was 3.6 million barrels/day, close to the country's 3.62 million OPEC quota in 1993. This production level represents large revenues to the Iranian treasury, a large part of which go to service the country's debts, estimated at $19 billion in 1994 or 35 percent of GDP. The heavy debt repayment burden Iran faced in the 1990s led to a slowdown in the implementation of vital reforms. Iran plans to attract foreign firms to invest in its oil and other sectors. The United States has led a move to isolate Iran economically and prevent further development, but it has thus far mostly failed due to a lack of cooperation from the U.S. economic allies in the European Union and Asia, as well as Russia and the Central Asian states. This backfire of the U.S. "isolation" policy has been a major source of Iranian pride and propaganda.

Foreign Relations

Iran occupies a unique global position. It is simultaneously a Middle Eastern, a Central Asian, and a South Asian nation. History has made Iran both the seat of empires and the prized possession of them. Iran still involves itself in all these spheres. Immediately after the revolution, Iran's actions and rhetoric gave it a maverick status in the world. Its attempts to export the Iranian-Islamic revolution to other countries' support for "terrorist" groups and movements, and territorial disputes with neighbors, earned it many enemies. During the time of Khomeini, the hard-line foreign policies of those in power isolated the country so much that even the country's leaders admitted it openly and expressed their worry. Cognizant of this, the government of Rafsanjani, who was considered a pragmatist, adopted a more conciliatory foreign policy. This policy is based around forwarding Iran as a responsible, "respectable" international citizen despite the opposition of the United States to the Tehran regime. This was pursued through close involvement in international organizations; Iran is a strong supporter of the Red Crescent (the Islamic counterpart of the Red Cross) and a leader in the Islamic Conference Organization. Iran has also acted to improve relations with its neighbors and nations further abroad and hosts the highest number of refugees in the world, nearly 2 million—mainly Iraqis and Afghanis.

At the same time, Iran continues to pursue a role of leadership and, as the seat of Shi'ism, exercises tremendous influence over a significant number of the world's 1 billion Muslims, stretching from Morocco to the Philippines. Further, it has influenced the populations of both its neighbors and more distant states, is the fourth most populous Muslim nation after Indonesia, Pakistan, and Egypt, and the only one besides Sudan, Oman, and Saudi Arabia that derives its government on Islamic principles. Iran is also the most advanced and stable of the nations of Central Asia, most of whom are only now emerging from the shadow of the dismantled Soviet empire. Finally, Iran is, by a factor of four, the most populous Persian Gulf state and the one with the longest coastline. With these advantages, Iran is well placed to be a regional leader in several areas.

American Antagonism

The biggest antagonist in the foreign policy area is the United States. This is not surprising, for "the Iranian revolution, which sees itself as the vanguard of Islamic activism, thrives on its reputation as the source and centre of radical opposition to the western-dominated political system."[30] Even before the revolution, Khomeini exploited the nationalistic sentiments of the Iranian people against the United States to overthrow the shah's dictatorship. The United States was painted as the "Great Satan" bent on destroying Islam. On 4 November 1979, the American embassy was occupied by Iranians calling themselves "students following the line of imam," taking a number of the embassy staff hostage. This hostage saga, likely sanctioned by Khomeini himself, remained unresolved for 444 days, and it intensified the confrontation between Iran and the United States. Thus began one of the strangest episodes of U.S.–Iranian animosity, with the seeming inability of the

United States not to embarrass itself at every turn in dealing with Iran. During the crisis, an American military mission to rescue the hostages in Tehran ended in disaster when several of the helicopters involved crashed before reaching the targets, and American wreckage and casualties were repeatedly displayed on Iranian television, though Iran had no actual part in foiling the attempt. Despite assurances from U.S. experts that the Iranian military would collapse without American technical assistance and support, Iran has maintained much of its U.S.–built equipment, especially the F-14 Tomcat interceptors which it has continually repaired and updated, and occasionally flies in large formations for no apparent reason other than to prove their existence to American naval forces in the Gulf. Since then, Iran has developed its economy, opened close relations with Russia and Europe, and become a regional power without U.S. support. No American administration can retreat from the anti-Iran policy, as too much American machismo has been invested in the vilification of the Islamist regime there.

During the 1980–88 Iran-Iraq war, the United States threw its weight behind the Iraqis, and when Kuwaiti ships became targets of Iranian attacks, the Americans (as well as the Soviets) provided protection. In 1987, when confrontation was at its peak in the Persian Gulf, an Iranian amphibious boat planting floating mines was captured and sunk by the U.S. forces, and U.S. ships bombarded an Iranian oil platform on the Gulf. The American actions, however, cemented the supporters of the Iranian people behind their leadership, which was perceived as a victim of American imperialism. This war provided further embarrassment for the United States. Their "horse," Hussein's Iraq, was unable to defeat the isolated Iranians. Also, the United States secretly negotiated with Iran, sending small shipments of military equipment—mostly spare parts and upgrades for the U.S.–built arms they already possessed—in exchange for Iranian influence with Islamic guerrilla groups holding American hostages in Lebanon. At the same time, the Americans supplied Iraq with a massive arsenal of weapons (on a huge line of credit) that U.S. forces had to face and, more important, U.S. politicians had to justify, in the 1990–91 Gulf war. The embarrassment surrounding these issues was key to the defeat of George Bush in the 1992 U.S. presidential elections.

Under Clinton's administration, the "dual containment" policy has been adopted concentrating on Iran and including Iraq. The policy aims at demonizing Iran with a view to isolating it economically and politically. With traditionally hawkish Republicans dominating Congress, even tougher action against Iran is continually called for. In December 1995, the House of Representatives passed legislation for a secondary boycott of Iran. In addition, Newt Gingrich, the Speaker of the House, announced that the CIA should mount a U.S.$18 million covert operation to overthrow the government in Iran, an act which prompted the Iranian Majlis to retaliate by announcing, in January 1996, a U.S.$20 million fund to combat the activities of the "Great Satan."[31]

Iranian foreign policy in all spheres has been directly influenced by the American stance. The United States has placed considerable military assets in the Persian Gulf region and makes no secret that this force is directed against any provocation from Iran. In response, Iran has pursued its goals openly and publicly, in line with all international norms, in order to avoid presenting the appearance of provocation. This became critical in spring and summer 1996 when Bahraini, Israeli, and U.S. sources accused Iran of backing opposition forces in Bahrain and Palestinian guerrillas in south Lebanon. Proof of these allegations has been desperately lacking. The United States faced an election in November 1996, and some commentators suggested that some elements in the Clinton administration were trying to build a case for a military action against Iran in the leadup to the poll—the American public, especially the soft conservatives who in any other context would be called nationalists, were supportive of military action as long as U.S. casualties remained minimal. Therefore, Iran, while in no way bowing to U.S. pressure, was not taking any overt actions that could be construed as a provocation.

Iran and Europe

The American tough stance against the Iranian government, particularly economic sanctions, has not been well received by the European Union, which favors a policy of critical dialogue with Iran and strongly opposes the extraterritorial application of U.S. legislation.[32] The EU and Iran share U.S.$14 billion per year in two-way trade, mostly of petroleum products, and the EU also tends to be more pro-Palestinian and indifferent toward Israel. The American boycott has been a boon for European companies—French contractors picked up a U.S.$1 billion oil deal that the U.S. firm Conoco was forced to abandon. One outstanding issue in EU–Iranian relations is the fatwa (religious edict) of a death sentence (and the standing bounty of over U.S.$2 million offered by the Iranian 'ulama) on British author Salman Rushdie, pronounced by Iranian religious leaders who accuse him of blasphemy in portions of his novel The Satanic Verses. Rushdie has been in hiding since the fatwa was pronounced in 1989,[33] and western governments and interest groups demand that the fatwa be lifted. The Iranian government's response is that they, as Muslims, have to support the fatwa, that a fatwa cannot be lifted unless judged to be in error, and even if it was judged to be in error, the edict can only be lifted by the 'ulama, not the Iranian government. This allows the Iranian government to take minimal responsibility for the affair while maintaining its credibility in extremist Islamic circles. For this purpose they also claim that the fatwa cannot be lifted simply because of foreign pressure, as that would debase Islam. In his visit to New York in September 1995, President Khatami made clear that the "Rushdie issue" was in the past, allowing for the normalization of relations with the United Kingdom. Iran has worked to develop links with eastern European states, especially Ukraine. These, combined with Iran's influence in the Central Asian republics, would allow Iran rail access and, more important, natural gas pipelines directly to Europe. These states are also suppliers of low-cost consumer goods and military equipment.

Iran, Russia, and Central Asia

Iran has developed an extremely close relationship with the Russian Federation. The countries share mutual economic interests, especially in exploiting the mineral resources of the Caspian Sea area and preventing western penetration of the region. Russia is an immense source of technological support to Iran, as well as an oil customer and a counterbalance to the United States. They also share a mutual interest in minimizing Turkish influence in Central Asia and containing unrest in the former Soviet republics. For Russia, Iran is an important customer for high-technology industrial equipment and arms, and has symbolic importance to nationalistic Russians who view close relations with Iran as a means of cementing Russia's dominance in Asia and otherness from the West. The two countries have cooperated on developing legal regimes for resource development in the Caspian Sea.

Iran's new pragmatism is nowhere more evident than in Central Asia. In its quest to develop a "sphere of influence" for itself, Iran has abandoned the Islamist card in dealing with Central Asian states who are ruled mainly by their former Communist masters under new names. These authoritarian leaderships are deeply suspicious of political Islam, and the masses of the population, while professing Islam, are equally influenced by folk beliefs and seventy-odd years of official atheism. Iran has acted to help these states improve their economic infrastructure and provide trade opportunities in the region, as Iran provides the nearest access to the sea. This has been improved by the opening in 1996 of a rail line running through Uzbekistan, Turkmenistan, and Iran to eventually reach the Iranian port of Bandar 'Abbas. Iran has been involved in negotiations to end the ongoing civil wars in Tajikistan and Afghanistan (which have pushed numerous refugees into Iran) and has pursued the establishment of close diplomatic and cultural links with the states of Central Asia.

Iran has cultivated close ties with Pakistan. The Pakistani government and especially the military have very strong Islamist sympathies, stemming in no small part from their continuing confrontation with India. Iran and Pakistan's mutual rhetoric is based on Islamic brotherhood with a strong military implication, but at the same time Iran makes friendly overtures to India for economic purposes.

Iran and the Middle East

On the regional scene, Iran is viewed with suspicion. The Arabs are resentful of Iranian support for fundamentalist governments and groups, ranging from the pariah regime in Khartoum to armed militants bent on toppling the regimes in Egypt and Algeria. In Bahrain, Iran stands accused of fomenting Shiite opposition to the Sunni-dominated system. Also, Iraq accuses Iran of supporting Shi'a working to bring down the government. In response, the Iraqis support opposition groups fighting the Iranian regime. Moreover, Iranian relations with the UAE have been dogged by their disputed sovereignty over three small Gulf islands.

In this area as in most others, Iran has followed a pragmatic course. Iran is opposed to the peace process and opposed to Israel. Ideologically, it is viewed with suspicion by the authoritarian regimes in Egypt, Libya, Jordan, and especially Saudi Arabia, which also claims to be an Islamic leader. Among the Arab states, Iran's only close relationship is with Syria. The hard line adopted by Hafez al-Assad and Benjamin Netanyahu toward each other after the 1996 Israeli elections means that the Syro-Iranian relationship would be maintained. Toward the rest of the Gulf states, Iran's relations vary: Iran and Bahrain are at odds over Bahrain's claims that Iran supports its Shi'i dissidents. Kuwait is firmly in the western camp, but Kuwaiti and Iranian officials meet regularly and describe their relations as "very good." Relations with Qatar have become quite cordial following the latter's "family coup" in 1995, reinforced by Qatar's determination to follow a course independent from the rest of the GCC states.

Iran's threat as a regional power is often commented on. Militarily, Iran has embarked on a program of acquisitions,[34] notably several Russian-built diesel-electric submarines of the Kilo class. These vessels are limited in their reach (they have a top speed of around 20 kph over long distances) but very potent in enclosed areas such as the Persian Gulf, as they are difficult to detect. Iran has no other naval capability worth mentioning besides missile-armed patrol boats. Certainly, Iran is incapable of projecting any naval force far from its coasts. Iran has also bought MiG-29 fighter aircraft from Russia, giving it a credible air defense capability. On the ground, Iran has Chinese and Russian-built armored vehicles, as well as indigenous equipment based on American designs from the period of the shah. Much has been made of the capability of the Chinese-built surface-to-surface missiles that Iran has installed in coastal defense batteries. Iran's entire stock of SSMs, however, does not equal the firepower of one American frigate. The real "problem," from the U.S. point of view, is that Iran has learned the lessons of the Gulf war and is installing its missile launchers in underground tunnels, with camouflaged, dummy, and hidden entrances, so they are nearly invulnerable to air attack. Therefore, they pose a tremendous risk to attacking American forces.

Iran has also been accused of trying to develop a nuclear arsenal with Russian aid. Iran has contracted Russia (for approximately U.S.$800 million) to complete a nuclear reactor complex begun by the French under the shah. Iran claims the installation is to supply electric power and be used for atomic research. While the latter may be true, the former seems rather odd in a country with some of the world's largest oil and natural gas reserves. However, it is also unlikely that Iran actually intends to construct nuclear weapons. They have invited the IAEA (International Atomic Energy Agency, which monitors the transfer of nuclear equipment and the possibility for weapons proliferation) to set up a permanent office at the Bushehr complex, and the IAEA has thus far given Iran a clean bill of health. In fact, Iran has been very active in the continuing global efforts toward nuclear disarmament. There are several political reasons why Iran would want to have a nuclear reactor and associated technology. First is prestige—Iran portrays itself as the leader of the Islamic world and as the "first citizen" of Central Asia and the Persian Gulf; as a world leader, it must have the appropriate signs of technological advancement. Second is Iran's desire to be a respected member of the world community in general. By possessing nuclear technology, but not nuclear weapons, Iran joins the ranks of states such as Japan and Germany, or at a lower level Sweden or Canada, who enjoy international respect without the taint of an imperialist past. Iran would have the added "bonus" of being fiercely independent from "imperialism" on the world stage, as well as the global support of many Muslims. Third is the open provocation it presents to the United States—"Yes, we COULD build nuclear weapons . . . but we don't." If Iran were to construct a nuclear device, the U.S. military would spare no effort to crush Iran, having finally been presented with an "excuse" such as Saddam Hussein provided when he invaded Kuwait and has since provided in his refusal to cooperate fully with UN weapons inspectors.

Iran and Terrorism

The most common attack against Iran is that it supports violent Islamic fundamentalist movements in the region and internationally. In the past Iran has supported the Islamic Jihad for the Liberation of Palestine and Hizbullah in south Lebanon, groups in Afghanistan and Tajikistan, and to a lesser extent Palestinian Hamas and the Islamic regime in Sudan. It has also been accused of supporting groups in Algeria, Bahrain, Egypt, Saudi Arabia, and virtually every other state where an Islamic activist element exists.[35] Support of so-called terrorism is a complex political issue, and historically, most powerful states have supported groups whom other states refer to as "terrorists." In the past, the United States itself has supported terrorists in Nicaragua, Cuba, Indonesia and the Philippines, supported coups in Iran and Chile, and supported puppet governments in the Republic of South Vietnam and several Central American states.

To break its isolation internationally, Iran supported various liberation movements in the 1980s in order to gain leverage, being cut off from normal channels of diplomacy. In addition, it sought to implement its ideological commitment to anti-imperialism and the spreading of Islamic revolution. But despite U.S. propaganda to the contrary, Iran is neither particularly isolated nor committed to the export of the Islamic revolution. Indeed, Iran appears to accept the notion that overt support of a violent group such as Hamas, which is opposed to the western-sponsored peace process with Israel, could backfire on Iran and cause economic and political damage. Within Iran, especially since the election of Khatami as president in 1997, there has been tension between extremist religious leaders who vocally support violent Islamic groups in their actions against the United States, Israel,[36] or whatever foe they have, and more pragmatic members of the government who want Iran to be able to operate on the international stage as an accepted member of the international community.

Iran used the summit of the Islamic Conference Organization, held in Tehran in December 1997, to back away from its state-sanctioned support of terrorism while reaching out to its regional adversaries. Overtures were made to the GCC countries, the PNA and Yasser Arafat, and even Iraq, while reconciliation was couched in a strong condemnation of U.S. policy of containment and more specifically the D'Amato law, which hampers international investment in Iran. Iran, if it continues to follow its pragmatic course, appears to be almost irrevocably moving toward a position of prominence in world affairs. It is relatively stable, as the Khatami government's ability to withstand the clashes of July 1999 demonstrates. It is increasingly prosperous, and its status as a "rogue state" is more and more meaningless outside Washington. Its potential to influence regional affairs is tremendous, even without resorting to military means.

CHAPTER 5

The Republic of Turkey

*T*he migration of the Turkic people southwestward from their ancestral homeland in Central Asia, where they had lived for centuries as tribal nomads, had an immense impact on the Middle Eastern region as well as parts of Africa and Europe. In 1055, they seized the capital of the Islamic caliphate, Baghdad, and founded the Seljuk dynasty, which would rule over the entire Islamic world. By the thirteenth century, the power of the dynasty had waned, due mainly to weak leadership and defeats at the hands of Mongolian warriors. From the crumbling Seljuk Empire arose a new Turkic ruling class who would greatly expand upon the lands the Seljuks had conquered. The Ottoman Empire was the last great Islamic civilization free from foreign exploitation. Emerging in the seventeenth century, it would rule much of the Middle East until the twentieth century. However, at the close of the First World War, with the empire carved away by European powers, Turkish nationalists established the modern and secular Republic of Turkey.

The encroachment of the Turks into the Middle East had been facilitated by their superior abilities as warriors, and in the ninth century they were hired by Abbasid caliphs as mercenaries and "warriors of the faith" (*Ghazis*). However, these warriors never limited their role to the defense and expansion of the caliphate, and eventually they usurped power themselves. The Islamic caliphate, which was centered in Baghdad, was overthrown by Turgrul Bey, an Oguz Turk who proclaimed himself sultan. This led to the establishment of the Seljuk dynasty, whose influence spread over much of the Islamic world.

Modern Turks claim descent from the Oguz. These warlike tribesmen migrated from east to west up to the frontiers of the Byzantine Empire, across which they made raids into the lands of Christendom. A doomed effort was made by the Byzantines, ironically aided by Turkish mercenaries and crippled by their own internal divisions, to defeat the Muslim Turkish conquerors. In the battle of Malazgirt in eastern Turkey in 1071, Seljuk forces triumphed, as they defeated the Byzantine armies and captured the Byzantine emperor, giving them control over much of Anatolia.

In the mid-thirteenth century, the Seljuk dynasty began to decline as the invasions of the Turco-Mongol armies of Genghis Khan reached the eastern frontier. As a result of the overwhelming strength of the Mongolian invaders, the sultan of Konya was defeated and his territory occupied. The Muslim region of Asia Minor (Anatolia) was spared. With the conquest, more Turks migrated westward, drastically altering the character of Anatolia. They settled down, married local women, and converted to Islam. The indigenous Greek and Armenian populations were allowed to retain their religion.

The Mongols destroyed the central authority of the Seljuk sultan, but a number of Seljuk princes survived as independent warlords. These leaders, whose reputation and livelihood depended on the prosecution of the holy war (*jihad*) against the infidels, extended the Turkish presence up to the Anatolian coastline and irrevocably transformed its composition into that of a Turko-Muslim culture.[1] One such prince, Osman, founded the Ottoman Empire. Osman's principality was the closest to the Byzantine capital of Constantinople and well defended. Bursa, which was conquered by Osman's son, Orhan, fell to Ottoman control in 1326, serving as the capital of the Ottoman state for several decades. The Ottomans successfully expanded their empire, and in 1352, Ottoman forces crossed the Bosporus into Europe, subduing the fortifications of Gallipoli. A decade later, Sultan Murad I (1362–89) occupied Adrianople (Edirne) and made it the new capital of the empire. In 1380, Sultan Murad I succeeded in creating both in Anatolia and Rumelia an embryonic empire of vassal principalities, which was eventually transformed by Sultan Bayezid I (1389–1402) into a true empire ruled by a centralized administration.[2] Mehmed the Conqueror captured Constantinople in 1453. He renamed it Istanbul, which was a transliteration of the Greek *eis tein polein* (the City), For at its imperial heights in the ninth and tenth centuries Constantinople had been the largest city in the entire world—and was simply referred to as such. After capturing his new capital, Mehmed claimed all the lands once previously ruled by the Byzantines, establishing a mandate for later Ottoman sultans to extend the boundaries of the empire. At its zenith in the seventeenth century, the Ottoman dominion included the Balkan Peninsula, the Crimea, Iraq and the western shores of the Persian Gulf, Syria, Palestine, west and south Arabia, Egypt, Libya, Tunisia, and Algeria.[3]

The Ottoman Empire's authority in the Middle East began to recede in the eighteenth century, under a variety of pressures. Turkish administration had become highly centralized in Istanbul, with only a network of feudal overlords and governors serving as provincial governments. They were encouraged to increase their autonomy. In addition, the whole of Ottoman bureaucracy was tainted with nepotism and corruption. Also instrumental in the weakening of the empire was the penetration of European colonial powers. In the economic sphere, this had a particularly damaging impact under the system of capitulation. Capitulations were originally unilateral grants of concessions to selected western powers subject to withdrawal by the sultan. As the power balance decisively shifted in favor of the European powers, their voluntary nature changed and they became mechanisms for the exploitation of Ottoman territories.

Some historians also note that the first capitulations granted to France in 1535 were intended to support that country in its competition with the Hapsburgs, who were situated on the expansion route of the Ottomans and who sought to unify Europe under Catholic Christianity. Under the practice of capitulation, foreigners were granted special privileges as an act of goodwill and to encourage trade. They exempted foreigners from Turkish laws and taxes, and they granted the power of arrest and deportation over foreign nationals to ambassadors.[4] Under the capitulations, the region's economy was opened to western capitalism, with the direct result of stifling local industrialization of the manufacturing sector and relegating the region to the production of raw resources for European industry. This curtailed the central government's ability to raise revenues, which in turn led to borrowing from foreign banks and governments in an effort to meet any shortfalls in the budget. The first loan was contracted in 1854, and by 1877 the public debt had reached £190,997,980 sterling (plus interest of £61,803,905), forcing the Ottoman state to declare bankruptcy.[5]

With Ottoman imperial control faltering, domestic reforms were initiated. The Turkish imperial administration had been highly centralized in Istanbul, leaving a network of feudalistic overlords and governors to control the provinces of the empire. This allowed two problems to arise. First, the governors, who were increasingly autonomous because the regions they controlled were generally far removed from the administrative center, made repeated attempts to increase their individual autonomy. Second, the provinces remained predominantly non-Turkish in population and culture and eventually developed nationalist ideologies of their own.

The central government also began to decline. The sultans had long had the prerogative of appointing personal favorites to ministerial posts, quite often accepting lavish gifts in return for such favors. So long as the sultan was the only one operating in this manner, little harm resulted, but when the entire bureaucracy began following this practice, the government became paralyzed by nepotism and corruption.

European military penetration in the Middle East and later the presence of missionaries and commercial interests brought with it western culture. Many of the educated in the urban centers adopted western manner and clothing, but of far more importance was the influx of western thought. One of the fruits of this intellectual renaissance was a new literature that transformed the nationalist ideas of European liberals into local and regional political programs.

During this period of European expansion into the Middle East, Turkish leaders observed the more efficient western administrative machinery and compared it with their own institutions. This comparison made it clear to some that administrative reform was both possible and necessary. Two schools of reform emerged within the empire, both influenced by Europeans. The idealists felt that the adoption of western governmental procedures (along with the philosophy underlying those procedures) would lead to the economic and industrial development necessary to bring Turkey to equality with the western nations. The realists felt that technological development was necessary first. Such economic and technological development, they felt, would force governmental change. The Ottoman administration attempted to follow both programs, endeavoring to bring about the use of modern and predominantly western tools and techniques at all governmental levels, with direction from the top of the administrative pyramid.

The first task of the government in its effort to reform was to remove the conservative elements from the military. For this purpose a special artillery unit was devised, loyal only to the sultan. This unit surrounded the barracks of the famed Janissary Corps, the stronghold of conservatism, and annihilated them. The unit then traveled throughout the country and purged the rest of the military in a similar manner. Once the conservative elements were eliminated, a new military was created, one that supported the government in its reform attempts.[6]

Backed by its modern army, the government was able to issue two decrees (1839 *Tanzimat Fermani-Gülhane Hatt-i Sherif*, and 1856 *Islahat Fermani-Hatt-i Humayun*). Limiting its own powers, it gave non-Muslims equal protection under the law, and it reorganized corrupt governmental agencies. Although neither decree was ever fully implemented, and the pressure for reform waxed and waned periodically, these measures managed to increase governmental efficiency. Hand in hand with these reforms, government support was provided for fledgling newspapers and publishing houses, and the number of schools was increased with the express purpose of raising literacy.[7]

Finally, in 1876, Midhat Pasha, then grand vizier and last of the nineteenth-century reformers, envisioned an Ottoman state in which the citizens would be subject to only one law. He wished to overcome existing religious and ethnic differences that made the country virtually impossible to govern.[8] He succeeded in introducing a constitution and established a two-chamber parliament. However, the sultan, Abdul Hamid II, used the Russo-Turkish war of 1877–78 as a pretext to regain absolute control of the state through the emergency powers clause of the new constitution. The parliament was rendered powerless, and Midhat Pasha and the rest of the reformers were dismissed and then murdered.

With the return of the state to absolutist rule, it would be left to a later generation to realize the efforts of the nineteenth-century reformers. Their legacy was ensured, however, as many of the original reforms had focused on the military, seeking to modernize the Ottoman armed forces with the adoption of European training, tactics, equipment, and organizational structure. It was anticipated that reform ideas would gradually spill over from the military to political, economic, and cultural spheres. Many of the forces advocating for change in the reform movement would see their sentiments echoed in the Young Turks, who were trained in the now predominantly western-style military academies of the empire. Furthermore, the return to despotism was followed by the proliferation of a labyrinth of secret societies, most often centered on Turkish nationalism. These societies were divided between those that favored a continuation of central rule and those advocating decentralization. In 1907, at the Ottoman Liberal Congress in Paris, these groups were united under the Committee of Union and Progress (CUP). The committee, consisting mostly of army officers, government officials, and professional men, was dominated by the ideas of Ottomanism and centralization. The program adopted was opposed to the government of Abdul Hamid II, and in 1908 the Young Turks, who were inspired by nationalist and ethnic concerns rather than social justice,[9] led a rebellion against the sultan's government. The committee forced a return to parliamentary government and sponsored a resurgence of the programs of modernization and reform and the opening of the second constitutional period. CUP became the dominant political party in parliament during the April 1912 elections, although the Young Turk Revolutionaries declared themselves to be a political party in April 1909.[10]

However, reform efforts were constrained by a number of factors, particularly continued fighting in the Balkans, which led to the loss of the few remaining Ottoman possessions in Europe. In 1914, Turkey entered World War I on the side of the Germans. The empire collapsed four years later. The armistice agreement, signed by Turkish and British representatives, placed all Ottoman territories in the Arab and African regions as well as the Dardanelles and Black Sea fortifications under Allied control. On 2–3 November 1918, Enver, Talat, and other prominent CUP leaders fled to Berlin, while Vahdettin (known as Mehmed VI)—following the death of his brother, Sultan Mehmed V, in July 1918—assumed the throne. The new sultan was keen to accede to all demands of the Allied powers as long as his position was secured, which brought him into conflict with Turkish nationalists.

On 13 November 1918, a fleet of Allied ships anchored at Istanbul and allied forces disembarked in the city. To allay well-placed fears and suspicion, the commander of the force assured the Turks that no occupation of Ottoman territory was intended. However, in a series of secret agreements, the Allied powers had carved up the Ottoman territories among themselves. French forces landed in Istanbul on 8 February 1919, and amid an enthusiastic welcome by the non-Turkish population of the city, a great deal of resentment was evident among Turkish nationalists. It was the arrogance of the victorious powers that further spurred Turkish nationalism, and in all parts of Turkey patriotic societies sprang up, one of the earliest being the Ottoman Defense Committee of Thrace. "Weakened by years of war, despised by their former subjects, betrayed by their leaders, the Turks had suddenly begun to find themselves."[11] The nationalist spirit became militant when Greek forces, with Allied naval support, invaded Izmir on 15 February 1919. With the massacre of local Turkish inhabitants as the Greek forces pushed into the interior, an armed resistance was born. It is this militant nationalism that Mustafa Kemal Pasha came to harness while founding an independent Turkish state. For this he was given the name Atatürk ("father of the Turks") by the Turkish Grand National Assembly in the 1930s.

Turkish Nationalism

Throughout the reform period, concepts of nationalism were being developed, and during the first half of the twentieth century, the terms for fatherland and nation began to acquire specific reference in terms of the Ottoman state and Ottomanism took on increasingly patriotic overtones.[12] Thus, in 1860, Sinasi, an Ottoman journalist, was able to write an article that discussed the interests of the fatherland and spoke of an Ottoman "nation" within the Ottoman state. Namik Kemal, a gifted contemporary of Sinasi, also wrote of an Ottoman nation within the empire, but he wished that nation to be Islamic as well as Ottoman. Kemal firmly believed that Muslim values and traditions would be reconciled with his own concepts of nationalism, parliamentary democracy, and individual freedom. He was, in fact, so anxious to preserve the best of the Islamic tradition that he suggested the tie of Islamic brotherhood become the means of implementing modernization, not just in Turkey but throughout Asia and Africa.

The establishment in Geneva of secret societies that became centers of nationalist ideology, following the return to despotism and the end of the first constitutional movement, gained further momentum through adherents from all sectors of society. Many of these societies espoused Pan-Turanism, a belief that the Ottoman Turks were part of a larger Turanian race that occupied large portions of Russia, central Asia, and China. The Pan-Turanists fostered racism by concentrating on the ancient history of Turkey and the original Turkish language. Pan-Turanism, however, was countered by Ottomanism, a concept that stressed the equality of all subjects of the empire regardless of race, nationality, or religion. The secret societies were also divided between those who favored the continuation of centralism and those advocating a movement toward decentralization. The next noticeable factor in the growth of Turkish nationalism was the outstanding success of the Turkish military during and immediately after the First World War. The Turkish success in driving out the Greek army of occupation and then repelling the Allies at Gallipoli generated tremendous pride. The people began regarding themselves as Turks.

However, the complete formulation of Turkish nationalism, as it was to be expressed under the government of Atatürk, was derived from the ideas of the sociologist Ziya Gökalp.[13] From the philosophy of the French sociologist Emile Durkheim, Gökalp drew the idea of society as a reified concept. He rejected a multinational society in favor of a Turkish one, for he held that a state consisting of two or more cultures would necessarily disintegrate when the separate cultures were allowed to reassert themselves. For the same reason he made a distinction between western culture and western civilization, and he rejected the former while accepting the latter. Gökalp's program of Pan-Turkism consisted basically of two elements. The first of these was a conscious return to a pure Turkish culture. The Turkish language was to be used, particularly in prayers, and a return was to be made to the presumably superior morality of the ancient Turks in the areas of national patriotism and family relations. The second element was Gökalp's plan for the modernization of Turkey. First, he advocated that the power of the religious courts would have to be curtailed in order to deliver Turkey from theocracy and clericalism. Second, he advocated that an "economic patriotism" must be fostered, emulating the prosperity of the ancient Turks, but using the productive forces of industrialism and capitalism, with occupational unions and guilds operating as corporate persons. It was assumed that government aid would be necessary for the development of industry.

Although Atatürk adopted many of Gökalp's notions, he and the founders of the Republic rejected romantic nationalistic adventures in Central Asia, restricting their goals to the existing national boundaries. Thus, as the Ottoman Empire was on its deathbed, many intellectual and political foundations necessary for a modern Turkish state were coming clearly into existence, and on these secular and nationalistic foundations Kemal Atatürk would build the new Turkish Republic.

Mustafa Kemal, born in Salonika in 1881, was a professional soldier who progressed to the rank of pasha during the Ottoman period. In the course of the First World War, he served first as an officer in the Gallipoli campaign, where he distinguished himself as a daring and popular leader, and when given command of the Ottoman forces on the Syrian front he managed to dramatically improve morale and prevent collapse. Thus, although the war was lost, Atatürk won the admiration of many demoralized Turkish soldiers, and he emerged as a national hero. With the war over and facing the prospect of losing even those portions of the Ottoman Empire still under Turkish authority, through both independence movements and colonial ambitions, it was Mustafa Kemal who came to lead the nationalist struggle that finally won dignity and independence for the Turkish nation. The war had been waged against a number of enemies, which had both foreign and domestic constituencies within the empire: Greeks in the west, Armenians in the northeast, French in the southeast, and the British and Arab armies.

Immediately after the war, the nationalists' cause seemed hopeless given the strength of the forces arrayed against them. While the nationalists were weak and poorly organized, the Allies decided to conclude a peace treaty with the sultan's government. What came to be known as the Treaty of Sèvres, signed on 10 August 1920, if implemented, would have meant the end of the dream of an independent and united Turkish republic. This notion was clearly expressed by Atatürk: "That Treaty is a sentence of death [for Turkey], so fatal for the Turkish nation that we request that its name should not be pronounced by mouths which claim to be friends. It is impossible that Europe should be ignorant of our National Pact; perhaps it is ignorant of the text, but Europe and the whole world, seeing us spill our blood for years, must certainly reflect upon the reasons which have provoked such bloody conflicts."[14] When passed, the treaty gave impetus to the nationalist struggle.

The initial Greek advances of 1919 and 1920 were partly caused by discord in the ranks of the nationalist leaders. But as the nationalist

forces were organized under the unitary command of Atatürk, the tide
of the war turned in their favor. On 4 June 1920, the caliphate's forces
were routed and the Greeks were pushed back to Bursa on 10 January
1921, while in the east, the Armenians had been defeated. Although
relations between Armenians and Turks during the Ottoman Empire
had usually been peaceful and Armenians were often prominent in the
business, intellectual, and political life of the empire, with the appearance of an independent Armenia in the nearby Soviet Union, relations
between Christian Armenians and Muslim Turks deteriorated. The
French and the nationalists signed the Franklin-Bouillon agreement,
which brought the hostilities on the southeastern front to an end, and
when the final push against the Greeks came, on 9 September 1922, it
managed to liberate Izmir. An armistice was signed at Mudanya on
11 October 1922 in which the Allied powers conceded to all the
demands of the nationalists, and all foreign forces ended up evacuating
from Turkey. At the Lausanne peace conference, a treaty was signed on
24 July 1923, fulfilling all the conditions of Atatürk's nationalists.

Politically, the nationalists were well organized, and when the central
political institution of the nation—the Grand National Assembly
(GNA) of Turkey—held its first session on 23 April 1920, Mustafa
Kemal was elected Turkey's first president. The GNA declared the sultan
and his government captives of the Allies and therefore lacking in legitimate authority. Henceforth, the GNA was declared the true government of Turkey, and all executive powers were vested in an executive
council under the leadership of Atatürk. To cope with the security situation facing the nascent state, Atatürk was voted commander in chief of
the armed forces, a post that carried extensive powers. Finally, on
1 November 1922, the GNA voted to abolish the sultanate and formally
end the Ottoman Empire. Meanwhile, another vote on 13 October 1923
made Ankara the permanent seat of the government of the new republic, since Ankara's strategic location made it less vulnerable to foreign
incursions. The change of the seat of government symbolized a further
break with the Ottoman past, whose political center had been Istanbul
for almost five centuries. Allied forces left Istanbul on 13 October 1923,
and on 29 October a national referendum approved both the constitution of a republic and Mustafa Kemal's selection as president.

Immediately after these victories, Atatürk initiated a sweeping program of secularization and westernization, concepts that had gained
popularity among Ottoman elites. In March 1924, Atatürk pushed
through the assembly radical reforms that saw the abolition of the
caliphate and banishment from Turkey of all members of the imperial
family, closure of religious schools, the prohibition of the fez, which was

replaced by the European hat, and abolition of the ministry of holy law (Shari'ah) and of Pious Foundations. In November 1925, all Dervish orders (mostly mystics of the Sufi sect) were suppressed and Muslim shrines closed. A new penal code (and civil code, 1926) based on the Swiss civil code and legal enforcement of European styles of dress were sanctioned (1925–27). The adapted form of the Latin script replaced the Arabic alphabet as the official alphabet in 1928. These far-reaching reforms were hastily implemented, and Atatürk had no qualms about using extreme measures to force compliance. A new constitution was adopted on 24 April 1924. It provided for an elected parliament in which sovereignty was vested while Atatürk, as president, was still allowed to select the cabinet.

Political Development and Issues

System of Government

Since its foundation in 1923, modern Turkey has been a republic. Its system of government is based on the separation of powers among the three branches of government: legislative, executive, and judiciary. Over the years, the functioning of the system has been subjected to a number of strains that have contributed to its overall development. Sovereignty in the country rests in the Grand National Assembly of Turkey, whose membership stands at 550. Elections to the GNA are normally held every five years, based on a system of proportional representation. To avoid the political chaos caused by this electoral system in the 1970s, some modifications were introduced in the 1982 constitution. A party is now required to obtain a national minimum threshold of 10 percent of the popular vote in order to be represented in the GNA. Parties organized on Communist, sectarian, fascist, or theological doctrines are prohibited.

The assembly elects a president, who is the head of state, to a seven-year term. To become president, a person must not be linked to any political party, and the powers of the president have been significantly increased by the changes included in the new constitution. As some of the checks and balances introduced in the 1961 constitution were removed, the presidency gained in power at the expense of the other branches of government. The presidential purview includes calling new elections in case of a deadlock between government and parliament, appointing prime ministers and accepting the resignations of government officials relatively independent of the GNA, vetoing legislation, and declaring states of emergency. The executive branch of government is headed by the prime minister, who is the leader of the majority party in the legislature able to form a government. Most Turkish governments since the Second World War have taken the form of coalitions of several parties—a prospective prime minister must first assemble a parliamentary majority willing to support his candidacy. Approval of a new government must be sought from the GNA whose term is fixed at five years. A special branch of the judiciary known as the administrative justice (administrative courts, regional courts, and Council of State) plays an important role in checking the power of the other two branches of government, as well as administering justice in the country. All of the courts, including the Constitutional Court, are independent. Turkey is a unitary state composed of 80 provinces, the governors of which are state appointees, and about 634 districts as units to the central administration. There are mayors in the metropolitan areas and municipalities who are popularly elected, as well as village heads and councils of elders. These organs are units of local governments.

Party Politics and the Military

The military played a key role in founding and developing the Turkish Republic, and since independence it has intervened to change the government in power three times (1960–61, 1971–73, and 1980–83). The justification advanced for these actions was the reestablishment or safeguarding of democracy and/or the state.[15] According to Turkey's 1982 constitution (formulated primarily by the military), the National Security Council is an advisory body to the government. It has five civilian and five military members. The five military members include the chief of the General Staff and the chiefs of three branches of the Turkish Armed Forces as well as the head of the Gendarmerie. The president of the Republic of Turkey is the eleventh member. The National Security Council is the most powerful body of state authority and has assumed the role of the "guardian" of the state's secularism. The Armed Forces defend the nation and the Republic and perform the NATO duties outlined in international treaties. The Turkish Armed Forces have maintained a modern force with a number of weapon systems in line with NATO standards, with which the military can better defend national independence and fulfill the requirements of a collective defense system.

Even before the birth of modern Turkey, the military was an important element in Turkish society. Since their entry into the Middle East region, Turks have been known for their military prowess, a reason that led Arab Muslim monarchs to rely on their services as mercenaries. During the Ottoman era, too, the military was crucial. The slave-mercenary army known as the Janissaries—which was also composed of Christians, Kurds, Slavs, and others who could not aspire to high office themselves—occupied a special place in the hierarchy of the

Ottoman state. Although the Janissaries themselves were sometimes responsible for attempts to depose the sultan, they were more often an important source of support in the interminable intrigues surrounding the court. This setting was made possible due to the *Devshirme* (conversion) system that was adopted by the Ottomans. When the Janissaries became a stumbling block to rejuvenating the declining empire, they were disbanded. In their place there emerged a modern military force, which also continued to play an important role in the political sphere of the Ottoman state. The officer corps, which had come under the influence of reformist ideas, played an indirect role in the upheavals of the late nineteenth century before the empire finally collapsed during the First World War.

When the war ended, Mustafa Kemal relied on his military abilities to advance the political ambitions of his people. After the successful conclusion of the struggle, Kemal became the first president of Turkey, and his trusted deputy in the nationalist struggle, Ismet Inönü, was made the prime minister. Kemal took the name Atatürk (Father of Turks) in 1933. Following Atatürk's death in 1938, Inönü assumed the position of president. During Atatürk's presidency, a number of far-reaching reforms were implemented, a task that was made easier by the unwavering support of the military. Atatürk established the Republican People's Party (RPP), which won all the elections between 1923 and 1943. A committed adherent of democracy, he allowed the first opposition party to organize in 1924, and encouraged another in 1930, but both were dissolved within a few months. The emerging reactionary opponents of the regime soon became too vocal in their criticism of the policies of the state, and they were then suppressed.

The traditional republican Turkish political elite backed the regime of Atatürk and Inönü, and in return it occupied a comfortable position in the system. However, when the Democrat Party (DP), under the leadership of Celal Bayar and Adnan Menderes, emerged victorious in the multiparty elections of 1950, power slightly shifted against the military and its traditionally supportive Turkish political elite. Representation in the GNA, when broken down along occupational lines, indicated a shift in favor of lawyers, traders, and commercial and banking entrepreneurs and against the traditional Turkish political elite and civil bureaucracies.[16]

In the 1950s, the policies of the government in power further eroded the privileges and power of the Turkish political elite and civil bureaucracies, while the commercial entrepreneurs and businessmen as well as regional elites saw a rise in their political fortunes. However, the policies of the DP, particularly those involving the economy, began to cause uneasiness among much of the population. Soaring inflation wreaked havoc with personal incomes, causing deep resentment. Opposition to the DP government gained in momentum, against which it adopted a tough stance leading to the suppression of democratic freedoms. Unhappy with the authoritarian nature of the regime, nineteen deputies broke away from the DP government in February 1955 to form the Freedom Party. In the spring of 1960, a crisis point had been reached in the relations between the DP and the opposition. In February 1960 the police broke up a meeting organized by the veteran leader of the RPP, Ismet Inönü. On 10 February, the DP majority voted to convene a commission to investigate the opposition and awarded it significant powers. This move triggered riots, and the government declared martial law in Istanbul and Ankara to quell popular dissent. The military, which had stayed out of the confrontation, decided the time had come to intervene, and under the leadership of General Cemal Gürsel, a bloodless coup was staged on 27 May 1960. The DP was disbanded and its leaders, including the entire parliamentary delegation, were imprisoned pending trial, after which Menderes and two of his colleagues were hanged and a National Unity Committee (NUC) was formed to run the country.

The NUC, however, proved unwieldy as its membership included various ideological persuasions. This caused a two-way split in the ruling military junta, one including the older and more senior moderates and the other the more radical officers of junior ranks; it was resolved by the expulsion of fourteen radicals.[17] A new constitution was adopted in 1961 that sought to prevent the reemergence of an authoritarian partisan regime legitimized by a majority in the parliament.[18] A number of significant checks and balances, such as the introduction of a bicameral parliament, a presidential veto over legislation, a constitutional court, and granting of autonomy to institutions such as universities, were incorporated in the constitutional document. In effect this reduced the powers of the government while giving a strong backing to civil and social rights, resulting in advances such as a new law legalizing the right of strike action in 1963. However, the checks and balances created a stalemate in the political system that was to exert a negative impact on the political climate in the future.

When general elections were held in 1961, no party was able to achieve an electoral majority. The new Justice Party had been formed upon the return to democracy, filling the void left by the disbanded DP. Under the aging Inönü, the RPP entered into fragile coalition governments with the JP and other small parties. In the 1965 general elections, the JP won an overall majority under its young and dynamic leader, Süleyman Demirel. This heralded the return of a stable government lasting six years—after which the RPP entered into a state of turmoil.

Differences over policy occasioned a split in its ranks in 1967 when breakaway deputies formed the Reliance Party. However, in the 1969 elections, the JP increased its majority in the lower house of parliament.

In the 1970s, the JP also had problems within its own ranks, evidenced by the formation of a splinter Democratic Party in 1971. Leftist groups became more active during this time, benefiting from the liberal atmosphere created in the wake of the 1961 constitution. A polarization of politics began to take shape as violent demonstrations increased in frequency in 1971 involving extreme left- and right-wing groups. The issues under dispute were basic, revolving around standards of living, social justice, and democratic freedoms. It was this rising violence which led the military to intervene for the second time on 12 March 1971. The "coup by memorandum" forced the government to resign. A nonpartisan cabinet was then installed. Martial law was imposed, and free elections were not held again until 1973.

In 1973, the RPP and the JP emerged as the major parties in the new assembly, but there was no overall majority holder. The situation remained so throughout the 1970s, forcing the two major parties to court smaller parties in order to form coalition governments. The result was shaky governments that saw Demirel, the leader of the JP, and Bülent Ecevit, the new leader of the RPP, changing places at the head of the government according to who could forge a coalition. The rise and fall of these short-lived coalitions was based entirely on political maneuverings, with no consideration for either the actual desires of the population or the smooth transaction of governmental business. Public confidence in politicians of all parties declined steeply.

The 1970s witnessed several crises, including OPEC oil price shocks and the U.S.–Iran embargo following the Cyprus intervention, which dramatically affected the economy. Strikes and other factors, such as an inability to import oil, brought the economy to a state of stagnation. Inflation soared, unemployment rose, and basic consumer goods were often unavailable. Parallel to these economic problems were political clashes between leftists and rightists. Students, state employees, and Islamists caused society to become polarized as a result of this left-right confrontation. Street clashes and terrorist activities claimed several thousand lives a year and were the main justification the military used to legitimize its intervention into politics when on 12 September 1980, Gen. Kenan Evren intervened to restore order and a state of normalcy.

The military leaders outlawed all political parties that existed before the coup—without exception. Parliamentarians were banned from politics for five years and the leadership of many parties for up to a decade; however, these restrictions were later revoked by a national referendum.

The military men established a National Security Council (MGK) to rule the country, and a new constitution was passed in a referendum in 1982, electing Evren to a seven-year presidency. The constitution increased the powers of the president and made his cabinet responsible to the elected parliament. The military junta then encouraged the formation of only two political parties in place of the old ones. The National Democracy Party, under retired General Turgut Sunalp, was earmarked as the ruling party, and the Populist Party, under Necdet Calp, a career civil servant, was to serve as the loyal opposition. However, electoral results rebuffed the military's attempts when the Motherland Party, under Turgut Özal, won the 1983 elections by a landslide. Furthermore, in subsequent elections the old parties emerged, albeit under new names (Social Democratic Populist Party instead of the RPP and the True Path Party instead of the JP) and altered leadership.

State, Religion, and Islamic Parties

In Turkey, as in other Middle Eastern countries, religion has long played a sensitive role in politics. The relationship between Islamic political activism and domestic politics has been magnified in Turkey due to its establishment as a secular democratic republic, the only such state in the Islamic world. The success of Islamists in recent elections has triggered fears that the legacy left behind by Atatürk might soon unravel, a prospect that could invite the ever-vigilant military into the political arena once again. Tracing the role of religion in the development of the nation requires taking stock of the situation before the founding of the modern state. Since the Turks were converted to the Islamic faith, they have lived as Muslims while maintaining many of their ancestral folk traditions. For centuries the systems that governed Turkish-Ottoman society ensured the autonomy of the state from incursions by religious-based political associations.[19] It was only in the sixteenth century that the Ottoman sultan assumed the title of the caliph and accepted the responsibility of being the leader of all Muslims. In practice, there was a clear demarcation between the secular powers of the sultan and the religious domain under the tutelage of the 'ulama. The religious establishment was very successful in inculcating the Islamic tradition in the minds of the Turkish conquerors, and religion acquired a strong appeal among both urban and rural populations.

When Kemal Atatürk enacted his massive cultural, legal, and social reforms between 1923 and 1935, with the intention of turning the nation away from religion to secularism and promoting westernization, the impact on many average Turks was minimal, particularly in rural areas. After all, some of the changes ordered, such as the discouragement of Islamic styles of dress, could only be effectively implemented in the urban areas while life in the countryside continued in a traditional fashion. Consequently, Islamic traditions and appeal survived in spite of the state-sponsored drive toward secularization. Before the introduction of multiparty politics in 1945, the country was run by an authoritarian single party (RPP) whose actions thwarted the development of civil society. As a consequence, Islam became the only channel for expressing dissent.[20] Others, such as the Sufi orders, played an active role in the political arena, resulting in their increased suppression by the government.

The introduction of multiparty politics and the government's strong commitment to democracy diluted the militant secularism that threatened to dominate the government of the new republic. Aware of the strong appeal of religion among voters, especially those along the periphery, opposition politicians tailored their platforms to take advantage of the traditional and Islamic character of the electorate. In fact, even DP members (including Prime Minister Adnan Menderes himself) played on religious themes to win over voters. More politically significant, for the first time a party dedicated to the promotion of Muslim consciousness was launched in 1970 under the name of the National Order Party. Its successor, later in the 1970s, was the National Salvation Party, which was succeeded in the 1980s and 1990s by the Refah (Welfare) Party, led for three decades, in its various incarnations, by Prof. Necmettin Erbakan. Tracing the fortunes of the party over the years can give an indication of the rising Islamic trend in the country, although other factors should also be taken into account.

The turbulent political climate of the 1970s propelled the Islamists to the forefront of national politics. In 1975, Demirel included the National Salvation Party in his center-right coalition government, enabling them to push through some reforms in the realm of religious affairs, notably an increase in the number of schools based on Qur'anic teachings (*imam-hatip* schools) in which the student curriculum was mixed with religious teachings in order to train clerical personnel for mosques and other religious services, all of which are under state control.

The military coup of 1980 played a catalytic role in increasing Islamic sentiments in the country, partly through the deliberate encouragement of the leaders against the influential leftist and Communist movements, and as a response to the difficult socioeconomic conditions that developed. Free market policies, first adopted by the Demirel government, were reintroduced by the civilian government that came to power in 1983. They resulted in a lowering of living standards as inflation rose and real wages plummeted. Concurrently, the divide between the rich and the poor widened, creating a fertile ground for the activities of Islamic-based organizations.

These developments bolstered Islamic sentiments in Turkey, and in the 1970s and the 1980s there was a significant increase in the number of Islamic publications and schools. For instance, an estimate of *imam-hatip* schools under the Ministry of Education puts their number at 72 in 1970, 374 in 1980, and 467 in 1992.[21] Many of the graduates of these schools were given further education in the national universities, after which they went into the civil service and other positions of responsibility and influence. A direct beneficiary of these developments was the Refah Party, which siphoned disgruntled supporters of the parties in power. The party quickly increased its electoral support, alarming many secularists. In the 1987 elections, the party won 7.1 percent of the national vote, far short of the 10 percent minimum required for representation in the GNA. The Motherland Party, which emerged as the winner in the elections, began to suffer in public opinion due to the worsening economic situation. Local election results in both 1989 and 1994 indicated the increasing popularity of the Refah Party, while the governing parties saw a reduction in their public approval ratings.[22]

The same trend was evident in general elections. In 1991, the Refah Party and two smaller allied parties won 16.8 percent of the national vote, and in the 1995 general election the Refah Party (RP) emerged with 21 percent of the popular vote, giving them 158 seats in the GNA. The True Path Party (DYP) came second with 19 percent of the popular vote and 135 seats, while in third place was the Motherland Party (ANAP) with 20 percent of the popular vote and 132 seats. The remaining seats in the 550-member GNA were shared by two center-left parties, the Democratic Left Party (DSP) and the Republican People's Party (CHP).

Thus, for the first time since the founding of modern Turkey, an Islamist party was given the mandate to form the government; however, Refah was unable to find a coalition partner with whom to form the government. As the mantle passed to the leaders of the secular parties, Mesut Yilmaz of ANAP and Tansu Çiller of DYP, they too could not agree on the formula necessary to establish a new government. The leaders of the two center-right parties, which commanded some 40 percent of the Turkish electorate, harbored personal rivalries, which made a coalition very unlikely. In desperation Çiller attempted to work out a coalition government with the Islamist party, but she was forced to abandon such plans when rebellion erupted among her own party membership over the issue. Çiller's DYP had claimed at the outset that it would not cooperate with the Islamists, and its members were outraged at the prospect of allowing the Islamists a foothold in power. But political realities eventually dictated an agreement, and DYP announced plans to form a coalition government with Refah.

Although the Refah embraced democracy and stopped short of advocating the implementation of Shari'ah (Islamic Law), it wanted to change some of the regulations enforcing the separation of state and religion. It promised to scrap interest rates, form an Islamic common market, withdraw Turkey from NATO, and renegotiate the agreed Customs Union with the European Union.[23] These policies confirmed secularist fears as well as Turkey's western allies. It is therefore not surprising that the news of an agreement on the formation of a coalition government between the two large center-right parties was greeted with relief in many quarters. Effectively, the Islamists were denied power at the last moment.

The new agreement, reached in March 1996, entitled Yilmaz the post of prime minister for the first year, to be followed by Çiller as prime minister for the next two years, after which Yilmaz would fill the post for another year. However, the government collapsed in a series of no confidence votes in early June 1996 from internal stresses over decision-making authority in the government. The Islamist Welfare Party still held the largest number of seats but could not form a government, as no other secularist party was willing to enter a coalition with them and agree to their announced policy agenda. Çiller repeatedly failed to form a secular coalition, and in late June she attempted once again to form a coalition with the Islamists. A new coalition government was finally announced in July 1996, and Turkey, for the first time in its republican history, had an Islamic government. Necmettin Erbakan was named prime minister and Çiller became foreign minister in a shaky coalition between the DYP Party and the Islamists. Surviving its first no confidence vote only a few days into its mandate, its first major act was to deliver on promised raises to the civil service, who had seen their wages held static while high inflation pushed many into poverty. Next, Erbakan tried to defuse a worsening Kurdish situation by promising that Kurds who had been deported to other areas of the country would be allowed to return to ancestral areas in the east. Walking a fine line between resolving tensions with the Kurdish minority and being seen as too concessionary to their demands and thus abandoning Kemalist precepts—which clearly displeased the military—resulted in fears of a possible coup or military intervention. Economically, Erbakan promised to reconsider the massive westernization efforts, which were seen as having impoverished many of those who supported the Islamists. Critics charged that to withdraw after long years of modernization would damage Turkey's economy and lessen its increasing economic connection to a prosperous Europe.

The military increasingly became concerned with these developing challenges to the secular state established according to the Kemalist doctrines. As a result of the policies put into place by Turkey's first Islamic-led government, mild as they appeared, the military engineered an opposing coalition of ANAP, DSP, CHP and DTP (Democratic Turkey Party). This strong opposition against the RP-DYP coalition government developed on the grounds that as radical Islamic movements had now begun to appear around the country, they were posing a threat to the Turkish state. The Islamic supporters of the Welfare Party were threatened when a debate over compulsory eight-year elementary education was brought onto the national political agenda, with the schools' funding challenged on grounds of universality and secularism. Islamists feared this would lead to the closure of the middle sections of the *imam-hatip* school system and challenge their way of life.

With the school funding debate a clear provocation, there was wide speculation that the military was challenging the RP-DYP coalition. As a result of increased tensions and the possibility of a military coup, Erbakan resigned his post on 18 June. Completing the ascension of the new coalition, President Süleyman Demirel appointed the ANAP leader, Mesut Yilmaz, as prime minister rather than the DYP leader, Tansu Çiller. As a consequence, a new coalition government was composed of ANAP, DSP, and DTP.[24] The new coalition government (ANAP-DSP-DTP) received a vote of confidence in the GNA on 12 July 1997 including the outside support of CHP, led by Baykal leading to the appointment of a new cabinet, with Yilmaz as prime minister (ANAP) and Bülent Ecevit as deputy prime minister and minister of state (DSP).

Analysts, especially many antisecularist Islamists and minority writers, likened the military's 28 February 1997 intervention to a postmodern coup. Political Islam in Turkey was marginalized from the mainstream discourse as the military felt that their intervention was required to save the republic's secular, democratic, and nationalist character. Several events and indicators alarmed many senior military officers, including what they perceived as attacks against the legacy of Kemal Atatürk, the hesitant and grudging activities of pro-Islamist politicians in the maintenance of secular institutions, the increasing appearance of religious symbols with political overtones including wearing robes and women in headscarves, the policy plans of the RP, which wished to open a road traffic route for would-be pilgrims to Mecca (circumscribing the government quota system, which was maintained through the use of air transportation only to Mecca), some calls for Muslims to be tried not by the secular judicial system but by the Shari'ah, and finally the increase in pump-action shotgun sales, believed to indicate a commitment to violence by the Islamists.[25]

At the 28 February meeting, the military through the National Security Council outlined their concerns and issued an ultimatum to the government on the measures they felt necessary to return the country to its secular personality. The ensuing resignation of Erbakan brought the new government of Mesut Yilmaz, which then undertook major changes to satisfy the military. Bills passed in the Parliament reformed the education system and severely undermined religious education. Civil servants considered to be supportive of Islamists were dismissed, religious propaganda banned, and firearms sales restricted. Most important, the change of government and policies implemented created a sharp rise in "secular awareness" throughout Turkey.[26]

The resignation of the RP-DYP coalition and the formation of the new coalition government led analysts to debate whether the change in government constituted an "unarmed coup" by the Turkish military. The rise in political tensions, brought about by the change in government, led many MPs from the ex-coalition government, especially from the DYP, to resign in protest from the party. This altered the distribution of seats of the political parties in the Grand National Assembly, and by mid-1997 the distribution of seats was as follows: Welfare Party (RP) 150, Motherland Party (ANAP) 138, True Path Party (DYP) 93, Democratic Left Party (DSP) 67, Republican People's Party (CHP) 49, Democratic Turkey Party (DTP) 20, Great Unity Party (BBP) 8, Nationalist Movement Party (MHP) 2, independent MPs 21, and vacant seats 2. Soon after taking power, the new government tabled a bill that curbed Islamic-based education, which passed by a vote of 277–242. Finally, on 16 January 1998 the Constitutional Court ruled against the Islamist Welfare Party "because of evidence confirming its actions against the principles of the secular republic."[27] The court then banned seven party leaders, including former prime minister Erbakan, from political activities for five years, and on 22 February the Constitutional Court ordered the banishment of the Welfare Party.[28] Three days later, former Welfare parliamentarians joined the newly founded Islamic-oriented Virtue Party, in effect merely replacing the banned Welfare Party.

On 27 March 1998, in a National Security Council meeting, military leaders presented to the new government a detailed list of measures to safeguard the secular nature of the state, one of which included purging the government bureaucracy, police, and military of pro-Islamist personnel. By the end of November 1998, Yilmaz had been forced to resign over a scandalous privatization deal when the Republican People's Party (CHP), joining the Conservative True Path Party and the Islamist Virtue Party (FT), forced a no confidence vote and toppled the government. Ecevit, the deputy prime minister and leader of the DSP (Democratic Left Party), was installed as prime minister of a caretaker government in preparation for elections in 1999.[29]

The 1999 General Elections

The 18 April 1999 elections caused a major change in Turkish politics because, unlike the previous decade, a clear victor emerged. The victorious Social Democrats, under Bülent Ecevit's Democratic Left Party (DSP), and the heavy losses of the center-right parties, such as Mesut Yilmaz's Motherland Party (ANAP) or Tansu Çiller's True Path Party (DYP), cemented a rightist shift. Ecevit, a long-serving Social Democrat and confirmed Kemalist, won 22 percent of the votes cast, an increase of nine points over the previous election.[30] Yilmaz and Çiller each lost around 6 percent of the popular vote and the pro-Kurdish Democratic People's Party (HADEP) was unable to attain 10 percent, a hurdle required to attain parliamentary representation. However, as HADEP enjoyed broad support in the predominantly Kurdish areas of southeast Turkey, they managed to win several mayoral races. What was clear was that the losses for the Islamist Virtue Party (FP)[31] and landslide successes for the extreme Nationalist Movement Party (MHP), better known as the Gray Wolves, would end the factional nature of Turkey's coalition governments. The MHP not only reentered parliament but, with 18 percent of the vote, they doubled their 1995 result and became its second largest party.[32] For the first time since independence, the Republican People's Party (CHP) of Deniz Baykal is no longer represented in parliament; the CHP considers itself to be the direct successor to the party of Kemal Atatürk, which was in power from 1923 to 1950. One of Baykal's election slogans was "Don't keep the party of Atatürk out of parliament."[33]

The Islamists lost votes mainly as a result of the massive campaign of intimidation by the military. Since the 1997 ouster of the Islamists, there has been no let-up in the campaign against Islamic activism, and the army made it clear that it would not tolerate a victory by the FP in the election. For their part, the Virtue Party has constantly sworn its loyalty to the state and the official policy of secularism.

Turkey's fifty-seventh government, which emerged from the ballot boxes with a coalition 18 April 1999, has been one of the most active in Turkish history. The coalition partners—the Democratic Left Party

(DSP), the Nationalist Movement Party (MHP), and the Motherland Party (ANAP)—emerged with 350 seats in the 550-seat parliament. From 1995 to 2000, successive minority governments ruled, and little was accomplished. In its first eight months the coalition managed to pass some 113 new laws and two constitutional amendments.[34] One of its acts, on 18 July 1999, was to amend the constitution and remove the military judge of the State Security Court, forestalling foreign criticism of the Abdullah Öcalan trial. Dealing with issues as diverse as the 1999 and 2000 budgets, social security reform, and banking laws, as well as taxation laws in order to allow the government to deal with the costs of the 1999 earthquakes, the government was busy. Finally, the coalition government took steps to alleviate inflationary pressures on the economy by entering into agreements with the International Monetary Fund (IMF), further liberalizing the economy.[35] While the government debated the policy implications of the Öcalan verdict, the most pressing concern accompanied renewed hopes for entry into the European Union.[36] Improving Turkey's human rights record and normalizing relations with some form of Kurdish political leadership appear to be at the top of the government's agenda. The announcement that Turkey had been anointed "candidate status" in December 1999 in the European Union has forced the government to rapidly implement political and nonviolent responses to the Kurdish movement.[37] The new coalition has thus far worked together and will face the intertwined challenges of economic reform, Islamic activism, and regional integration.

Reforms and the general progress toward democratic and secularization was clearly motivating parliament's decision, on 5 May 2000, to elect reformist judge Ahmet Necdet Sezer as Turkey's president. It also indicated a willingness to open the political process to outsiders, as Sezer—who was a chief justice of the Constitutional Court who had never served in a political office—was unanimously supported by all of the party's leadership in parliament. As the first judge to be elected president, six out of nine of Turkey's previous presidents had been military generals; Sezer's election also signals only the third peaceful transfer of power in the republic since 1980. Sezer is on record as calling for constitutional changes to overturn alterations made during the 1980–83 period of military rule, indicating that the current constitution restricts basic rights and freedoms. His election also continues the evolution of consensus politics in Turkey's parliament, a rejection of its past feuding and plot-riddled culture. The new president has committed his administration to the continued modernization efforts driven by Turkey's pursuit of EU membership, as well as the secularization of both politics and society.[38] More so, he is committed to the rule of law and a belief that "state and society cannot be organized along the rules of religion" but rather through commitment to secularism, rule of law, democracy and a welfare state.[39] The government's election of Sezer was seen as both a commitment to the secularization process, which reaffirms the military's vision of the republic and the drive for EU membership, and a goodwill gesture that promotes support within Turkey's minority communities.[40]

Kurdish Insurgency and Human Rights

Kurds in Turkey, who number between 10 and 20 million (population figures are subject to dispute), have worked to promote their own separate nationalism through both peaceful and violent means, soliciting harsh treatment from the nationalist government. Eastern Turkey, the home of Kurds, has been embroiled in severe civil strife involving armed Kurds, government security forces, and local militia. The impact on human life and property has been devastating, and both human rights organizations and foreign governments have expressed concern about the actions of both the Turkish government and separatist guerrillas.

Among the Kurdish groups that proliferated in the 1970s, the banned Kurdish Workers' Party (PKK) evolved as the most radical and violent. The PKK, which had been led by Abdullah Öcalan, was founded in 1979 when it established itself in eastern Turkey and proclaimed an armed struggle against the Turkish government and the feudal Kurdish leaders who supported it.[41] Its program, a mix of Marxism-Leninism and extreme nationalism, is aimed at the creation of a greater independent Kurdistan incorporating Kurds in Turkey, Iraq, and Iran. Other groups, such as the Armenian Secret Army for the Liberation of Armenia (ASALA), have cooperated with the PKK to wage joint actions against the Turkish security forces. In addition, up to late 1998 PKK guerrillas found sanctuary among their kinsmen across Turkish borders in Iraq, Syria, and the Syrian-controlled areas of the Bekaa Valley in Lebanon. Turkish authorities have adopted a tough policy in dealing with the nationalist aspirations of the Kurds with the aim of assimilating the Kurds within Turkey's secular society. The view that Kurds do not have a separate identity has been persistently promoted, and at the extreme some have asserted that the Kurds are just "mountain Turks" who have lost touch with their Turkish origins. The penal code has been used to stifle Kurdish nationalism in a number of respects, including several prohibitions against political activity and the formation of public associations, which have been invoked to banish both individuals and groups.

Since 1980, the authorities have arrested and tortured many alleged separatists, actions that have raised the concerns of human rights organizations worldwide. Many Kurds have been killed or displaced from their homes in the Kurdish regions in the east of the country, and Human Rights Watch estimated that more than 13,000 people were killed between 1984 and 1994. Security forces launched a massive counterinsurgency campaign against the PKK guerrillas in eastern Turkey in 1993, and many Kurdish civilians were forced to flee their homes. The Constitutional Court outlawed the Kurdish-based Democracy Party (DEP) in June 1994 and eight parliamentarians, whose immunity had been stripped earlier in March, were charged with treason and separatism because of alleged collaboration with the banned PKK, bringing the condemnation of human rights organizations worldwide. In the parliamentary power struggle of spring 1996, the power vacuum led to outbursts of violence, such as when youth members of the Kurdish Democratic People's Party (HADEP) tore down a Turkish flag at a political convention and replaced it with the banner of the banned PKK (see below). Unidentified gunmen killed several HADEP members, and in retaliation on 1 July 1996, a Kurdish woman detonated a bomb, killing herself and nine Turkish soldiers, signaling the beginning of a new and unpredictable phase in Kurdish activism, which had previously limited itself to guerrilla operations. The human rights record of Kurdish guerrillas has been disturbing, and Human Rights Watch has accused the PKK of routinely engaging in violent acts such as summary executions, bombings, and the destruction of civilian property in order to dissuade people from cooperating with the Turkish authorities. For the civilian population, the security situation worsened when the government initiated a policy in 1986 of arming villagers to resist the guerrillas, which invited more PKK attacks against those portions of the civilian population unsympathetic to the Kurdish cause.

Since the imposition of the no-fly zones in Iraqi Kurdistan, which has provided some measure of cover to Kurdish organizations, the Turkish military has made repeated incursions into northern Iraq in pursuit of PKK guerrillas. This challenge to Iraqi sovereignty, with the temporary occupation of as many as 35,000 ground troops with tank artillery and air support, recurred several times in 1995, 1997, and 1999. The Iraqi government does not strongly protest these incursions, as much of northeastern Iraq is under the control of autonomous Kurdish authorities, which the regime in Baghdad would not be disappointed to see humbled. The lack of international outcry against this violation of Iraqi (or Kurdish) sovereignty is more the measure of a lack of western interest in the Kurds than of any special status for Turkey. Ankara has also accused Syria of supporting the PKK and has threatened to invade Syria if such (unsubstantiated) support does not cease. Tensions between

Syria and Turkey escalated sufficiently to bring the two countries to the brink of war when on 4 October 1998 Turkish troops massed on the Syrian border and Turkish president Demirel warned Syria, "I am not only warning the world. This cannot continue . . . the situation is serious. Turkey has suffered for many years and it no longer wants to suffer."[42]

This pressure led to the expulsion of the PKK from Syria in October 1998, forcing its leader, Abdullah Öcalan, to seek refuge, first in Russia, then in mid-November in Italy, as a political refugee.[43] Öcalan was apprehended by Turkish security forces in Nairobi on 15 February 1999, leading to violent Kurdish demonstrations in Turkey and throughout the world. He stood trial on the island-prison of Imrali in the south of the Marmara Sea, and was convicted of a catalog of charges for his role in leading both the PKK and its fifteen-year-old insurgency in Turkey's southeast, which has cost more than 30,000 lives. Turkish government sources reported that while Öcalan had been hiding in the Greek ambassador's residence in Nairobi, he was captured by Kenyan officials and then handed over to the Turkish government at the Nairobi airport.[44] His capture raised questions about possible U.S. or even Israeli intelligence cooperation with the Turkish authorities. While his complicity with a large number of violent acts, including those against fellow Kurds, leaves many in Turkey rejoicing his capture, many others question the nature of his punishment, trial, and possible fate as potentially creating a martyr and legitimizing his violent legacy if the death penalty is carried out after an unsuccessful appeal. His death, however, would do little to influence the cause of peace in Turkey, as he did everything possible to save himself during his trial and separated the Kurdish cause from his own fate, prompting some Kurdish leaders to disassociate themselves from him.

Further, western (predominantly European) human rights advocates have questioned both his prison conditions and the fairness of the court trying him, as a military judge was sitting on the court bench. Many observers went so far as to link the treatment he receives and the judicial process he was undergoing with Turkish acceptance into the European Union.[45] Putting the Turkish criminal justice system on trial, while it tries one of the most "wanted" terrorists in the Turkey, is a linkage Turkey could not avoid.[46] Indeed, Turkish president Süleyman Demirel announced on 11 March 1999 that he favored amending the 1980 constitution to remove military judges from courts in order to make the judicial system appear fully independent.[47] Despite the capture and trial of Öcalan, the Turkish government will still be forced to deal with the Kurdish problem in its southeastern provinces and in lieu of the military's continued crackdown against parties and members of the GNA thought sympathetic to the Kurdish cause, it would do well to promote dialogue and limit confrontational policies.

In order to meet the deadline for reforms required for accession talks leading to full membership, as set forth by the European Union, Turkey has been forced to adopt a number of institutional measures to promote human rights. Legislation, forcing all government ministries and related institutions to abide by human rights norms and standards in line with those in western Europe, is now being finalized. It will establish governmental and nongovernmental organizations (NGOs) that will be independently responsible for monitoring torture, illegal arrests, and other violations within Turkey. Under the Copenhagen criteria, Turkey has established a Human Rights High Coordination Board Secretariat that has investigated the country's police and gendarmerie for traditional human rights abuses. In May 2000, Board Secretariat staff reported to parliament that the physical state of jails and penitentiaries was generally below standard, detainees were routinely denied legal counsel, and torture was widespread and systematic.

The Board Secretariat must now expand its focus to include two sensitive issues capable of damaging Turkey's accession into the European Union: the subordination of the Turkish military to civilian authority, especially to the powerful National Security Council (MGK), and the treatment of Turkey's minorities, with special emphasis on the Kurds.[48] On paper, membership in the MGK is equally shared between military and civilian representatives. Chaired by the president, the MGK consists of the prime minister, the chief of the general staff, the defense minister, the minister of interior affairs, the minister of foreign affairs, the land forces commander, the air force commander, and the general commander of the gendarmerie.[49] The military members have increasingly dominated the Council's agenda and decision-making process, especially since the 1997 Islamic-coalition government challenged the military's vision of a secular and nationalist Turkish state. The firm assertion of civilian control over such policy creation and implementation processes is seen by the EU as a benchmark of Turkey's commitment to democracy.

It is hoped that the Board Secretariat will be successful in implementing the changes necessary to improve Turkey's human rights record. In the past, Turkey has changed the structure of the State Security Courts and lowered the custody period from fifteen days to four. However, Turkey remains a leader in the number of cases heard before the European Court of Human Rights in Strasbourg. The court is not an appeal court or a court of first instance; rather, it produces case law, which can then be adopted by the contracting state to amend legislation and promptly change its implementation of the rule of law. However, unlike other European Union members who after test cases adopt changes to their domestic legal and administrative systems, Turkey has been slow to adopt such measures and has continued to use capital punishment and systematic torture.

Freedom of speech has emerged as a considerable issue because Penal Code (TCK) Article 312 has been used to stifle dissent through the arrest of a number of prominent intellectuals, opinion makers, activists, and even politicians. Some of the most celebrated cases to date include the incarceration of former prime minister and Virtue Party (FP) leader Necmettin Erbakan; Human Rights Association (IHD) president and activist Akin Birdal; and the founder of the secular Rebirth Party (YDP), Hasan Celal Guzel, who served for over thirty years in almost all senior levels of the state hierarchy except the presidency and prime ministership. Guzel, like Erbakan and Birdal after him, was charged with "provoking hatred and enmity among people on the basis of religious and racist discrimination" as stipulated by Article 312 of the TCK, when delivering a 1997 speech entitled "Where on the road to democracy does Turkey stand?" in the central Anatolian town of Kayseri. Guzel was sentenced to one year in prison by the Ankara State Security Court and then lost his appeal to the Supreme Court. Although no acts of violence or public disorder could be attributed to Guzel's speech, he was charged and convicted under the draconian Article 312.[50]

The expansion of Turkey's understanding of democracy to include freedom of speech, thought, and expression rather than merely the competition between political parties will mark its move into the western discourse on the development of a civil society. Signaling a maturity of its appreciation of such values will be required for its full and unfettered admission to the EU. The freedom of association clauses of the Turkish constitution have often been neglected in secularization and security efforts. Indeed, notions of "public" institutions in Turkey are almost exclusively state-centered and political in nature. Such limitations must be abrogated before a true civil society can be developed.

The Turkish Economy

Aware of the need to bring about a fast improvement in living conditions, Atatürk had the leaders of the new republic convened in February 1923 in the first Economic Congress at the recently liberated town of Izmir. The gathering of some 1,100 delegates representing farmers, traders, industrialists, and laborers aimed to formulate proposals for the government in the economic sphere. Two issues were hotly debated in the conference, namely, what roles government and foreign capital would play in the economic development of the republic. This preoccupation with economic matters was indeed understandable given that in 1923 Turkey was extremely underdeveloped and heavily burdened with debts inherited from the Ottoman era as well as the costs of the recently won war for independence. Most citizens lived in poverty, and the key sector in the economy, agriculture, was backward and dominated by feudal landlords who exploited the peasantry. The ravages of war led to the flight or massacres of much of the Greek and Armenian populations, depriving the economy of professional and technical skills just as it was attempting to develop.

During the 1930s, the government adopted the etatist principle of economic development to improve production. Although theoretically vague, etatism has in practice amounted to the assumption that the state has a major responsibility for undertaking industrial development, even at the expense of private sector development.[51] Thus, within the context of this policy, the government carried out a massive program of the nationalization of foreign firms throughout the 1930s so as to address the country's balance of payment predicament. In 1933, the first development plan (to be implemented between 1934 and 1938) was outlined, and the Soviet Union, who had proposed industrial projects to be implemented in this phase, gave an interest-free loan of $8 million to finance the plan. War interrupted the second industrialization plan prepared in 1936 (for implementation between 1939 and 1943).

In the agricultural sector, government policy focused on the introduction of reforms benefiting landless farmers, and large tracts of land formerly under public ownership were divided among the landless, while big landowners continued to block land reform plans involving private property. The GNA adopted a concrete land reform bill in May 1945, but its impact on the big landowners proved marginal. Only when multiparty politics emerged was real attention paid to the peasants, as their numbers gave them newfound leverage within the democratic system.

Etatism failed to improve living standards. This opened it to criticisms from both Turkish and foreign observers who faulted the system for concentrating on heavy industrialization projects while paying little attention to the agricultural sector, which was the backbone of the economy. DP politicians won a great deal of support from the population by exposing the weaknesses of the etatist system. Not surprisingly, when they came to power in 1950, their economic policies differed from those of their predecessors. Much attention was paid to the neglected rural farming populations, and the private sector was encouraged to grow. However, the high hopes with which the DP was propelled into government dimmed in 1950 as the economy grew at a modest pace and rising inflation reduced incomes, causing widespread discontent. On the positive side, the encouragement of the private sector led to increased investment by private businessmen, which resulted in a sharp rise in industrial production.

Between 1960 and 1978, GNP grew at an encouraging average rate of 6.2 percent/year. The worldwide economic slowdown caused GNP to slump: in 1979, it fell to a meager 1.7 percent. The vigorous growth of the 1960s and early 1970s was partly accounted for by remittances from Turkish emigrants working abroad. In 1974, earnings repatriated by Turkish workers in western Europe were in excess of U.S.$1.45 billion.[52] As the 1970s came to a close, the economy slowed dramatically due to reduced remittances, a shortage of hard currency, and poor leadership from fragile and indecisive coalition governments. The difficulties facing the ordinary people worsened when the civilian government that took power from the military in 1983 continued the drive to liberalize the economy. Growth in the 1980s was limited by persistently high rates of inflation—between 60 and 100 percent per year—and by the burgeoning national debt. The gloomy economic profile continued into the 1990s, leading to the devaluation of the Turkish lira by some 28 percent in 1994.

The devaluation, as well as mounting foreign debts that have exceeded $100 billion,[53] forced the government to adopt even tougher austerity measures, a move that further alienated many citizens. Public sector salaries have remained almost stagnant in the face of worsening inflation, impoverishing many workers on fixed incomes. Unemployment ran rampant in urban areas when the events of March and April 1994, which led to the devaluation of the national currency, put some 600,000 Turks out of work, swelling the urban jobless population to 13 percent.[54] Although Tansu Çiller pressed on with the free market policies began by the late Turgut Özal, and the former government, headed by Mesut Yilmaz, had pledged to continue on the same course, the prevailing economic and political climate and the rise to power of the more isolationist Islamists led to the expectation that they would exert a negative impact on the economic liberalization drive, but they had little effect.

Turkey's economy sits at a crossroads, largely dependent on its increasing ties to the European Union. It experienced an annual growth rate in excess of 4 percent during the 1990s, but it also labored under inflation rates approaching 80 percent. Economic reality caught up with Turkey when high interest rates finally began to injure growth. The growth spurred by Özal's lifting of stringent controls on imports and capital flows—when he became finance minister in 1980, it was illegal to carry foreign currency—and the customs union with Europe, crashed under the weight of inflationary pressures that saw 1999 interest rates stand at 40 percent and inflation near 70 percent. Turkey's massive public debt has left its economy highly vulnerable to external shock, finally convincing the government to commit to proposed IMF reforms.

In exchange for some $4 billion in IMF support, the Turkish government agreed to an expansive three-year program. Reforms will make it harder to qualify for a public pension and agricultural subsidies. Government spending cuts and tax increases will be accompanied by privatization and a new and more open exchange-rate system in 2001. In spite of the hardships placed upon government spending, the increasingly competitive markets surrounding banking and capital growth, as well as the development of a number of large monopolistic moguls, Turkey's economy displayed a certain dynamism. The impossibly high cost of borrowing and the capricious nature of interest rates drove off foreign investors, but the reforms appeared to be working as inflation dropped and interest rates stabilized in 2000. In November of that year, however, a banking scandal brought Turkey to the verge of financial collapse. Turkey asked the IMF for an emergency infusion of more than $7 billion.

Foreign Relations

Turkish foreign relations at the dawn of the new millennium are centered on its role as a regional power within the Balkan–Caucasus–Middle East triangle. Making great strides in the past two years, Turkey now exudes confidence and appears ready to resolve several long-standing imbroglios. In December 1999 at the European Union's Helsinki summit, Turkey was granted candidate status, successfully concluding decades of diplomatic efforts and confirming a strong future within a secular western and Mediterranean order. Similarly, improved strategic cooperation with the United States, Israel, and the European Union, the successful conclusion of negotiations founding the Ceyhan pipeline, and improved opportunities for peaceful resolution of the long-standing and highly divisive conflicts with Greece in Cyprus and its own Kurdish population allow for considerable optimism. With the ending of the cold war, Turkey's role as the southeastern flank of the North Atlantic Treaty Organization (NATO) diminished in value. Nevertheless, its location between the democracies of western Europe, the mayhem of the Balkans and the Caucasus, and the dictatorships of the Arab region continue to sustain its central position in the geopolitical thinking of the West. Precisely, Turkey is a bridge between East and West and a pivotal player in the new world disorder.[55] Thus, the central tenets of Turkey's cold war foreign policy have largely survived, although with slight alterations in emphasis.

The country is aligned closely with the western powers, in particular the United States and the European Union. The development of this orientation can be traced to the last years of the Ottoman Empire, which by virtue of its large possessions in Europe had evolved into more of a European power than an Asiatic one. Before the empire collapsed, the Ottomans embraced reforms that introduced structures, social norms, and customs characteristic of the West. A turning point was reached when Atatürk launched a cultural revolution that secularized and westernized Turkish society following the First World War. Inherent in this quest was the determination of the republican government to integrate the country into the modern western and more precisely European world.[56] Turkish leaders who followed in the footsteps of Atatürk pressed Turkey forward down a similar secularist and pro-western development path. They included the country in NATO, the European Economic Community (as an associate member), the Organization of Economic Cooperation and Development, the Council of Europe, the Conference on Security and Cooperation in Europe, and the Western European Union (also as associate member). They also recently entered Turkey into a Customs Union with the European Union. In 1987 the country applied officially to join the European Union as a full member, provoking deep divisions in the EU, which is also planning to expand into eastern Europe.

Concerns have been expressed regarding Turkey's human rights record, the tremendous scale of economic development yet to be undertaken, and the eventual impact of having what would be the third most populous state in the European Union also being its poorest—probably provoking massive relocations of Turkish workers to more favorable economic environments in the rest of the EU. This has already occurred to some extent, and most European states—especially Germany—have steadily growing Turkish populations, who in many cases fill jobs that Europeans consider "beneath" them. These create difficult political problems, as right-wing nationalist groups in many European states campaign against immigration, and public sentiment in some circles is violently hostile to "foreigners," especially Muslims. This hostile experience remains with Turkish workers who return to Turkey after working in Europe, and fuels a certain level of anti-European sentiment. Debate also swirls around the effect of including a predominantly Muslim nation in the Union, especially one with a potentially powerful activist Islamic political force. Turkish society will be forced to entertain some fundamental alterations if it wishes to assuage European fears and guarantee entry. Constitutional amendments will need to address human rights and economic and individual freedoms of expression, enterprise, and thought.[57] Progress has been made, because the government has removed military prosecutors and judges from State Security Courts, made it more difficult to ban political parties, enacted legislation to punish the use of torture by state police and military forces, increased the freedom of the press, passed a repentance law, and increased civil servant accountability.[58]

Posing a challenge to the government's new offensive to promote human rights and individual freedoms is the issue of Kurdish language and broadcast rights. No one knows whether allowing for Kurdish language broadcasts would improve Turkish unity or promote divisiveness in Turkish society and further Kurdish independence. To meet the Copenhagen Criteria, established as a litmus test for entry to the European Union, Turkey would seem to be forced to allow for such broadcasts.[59] While human rights and personal freedoms remain a stumbling block, Turkish membership will hinge more on the positive approval of Greece. Other options, limited as they may seem, may be preferred to capitulation to Greek interests in the Aegean. If so, then the Turkish government will be forced to receive Greece's approval without abandoning its own interests in Cyprus and the Aegean.[60]

Turkey has also had a close relationship with the United States, based on the U.S. desire to maintain Turkey first as a base against the USSR and the Warsaw Pact and more recently as a tame Muslim state in the turbulent Middle East. This relationship has brought Turkey a great deal of military assistance. However, most of the equipment transferred to the Turks is fast becoming obsolete. While American strategic interest in Turkey, as in global politics, has declined with the end of the cold war, relations with the United States, regarding the Middle East, have become very significant as the United States has consistently supported Turkey in regard to issues related to the PKK, EU Customs Union membership, and oil pipelines from Azerbaijan.

Turkey's determination to become a full partner in the EU is being frustrated by its conflict with Greece, as Greece has used its seat in the EU to thwart attempts by Turkey to integrate into the European supranational institution. The long-standing belligerency over Cyprus and other territorial issues has kept alive the animosity between the two NATO members, which has also influenced relations with the United States. The dispute was brought to a head in July 1974 when the Turkish military intervened in Cyprus in the aftermath of a military coup engineered by the Greek army. Since then, the island has been divided into two communities, and talks aimed at settling the dispute have remained deadlocked. Relations were further embittered when Greece landed military forces on and claimed sovereignty of the uninhabited Kardak (Imia) Islets, which are just four nautical miles away from the Turkish coast.

The confrontation between the two countries has been a source of friction in U.S.–Turkish relations. Between 1975 and 1978, Congress attempted to force the withdrawal of Turkish forces from northern Cyprus by imposing an embargo on military assistance to its NATO ally. In retaliation, Ankara closed down U.S. bases on Turkish territory, while maintaining those belonging to NATO. However, the ban on American military aid and weapon sales was lifted in 1979 when it proved ineffectual and unprofitable. Relations have since prospered, helped recently by the support provided to the American-led 1991 Gulf war coalition. Turkish bases were opened to the use of western planes against Iraqi targets, and the country has strictly enforced the embargo imposed on Iraq by the United Nations.

While not sacrificing its long-term relations with the West, Turkey has cultivated ties with other nations in recognition of the changed climate of the post–cold war world. Recently, Turkey has actively sought to build links with some 60 million Turkic-speaking people in the former Soviet republics of Central Asia. For instance, it has proceeded with the establishment of the Baku petroleum pipeline with Azerbaijan, which both countries will highly benefit from both economically and politically. Thus far, it has met with only limited success, as some Turkish politicians and academics immediately began to discuss the prospect of a "Greater Turkish World"—an outgrowth of Turanianism—stretching into Central Asia. In March 1998, Turkey held a conference inviting all the newly independent Central Asian republics, with the notable exceptions of Russia and Iran. Some observers interpreted it as a Turkish attempt to capitalize on the existing cultural, linguistic, and historical ties shared with the Asian republics and as an opportunity for the extension of Turkish hegemony into Central Asia. Turkey, however, clearly finds its influence competing with that of Russia, Iran, and even its ally, the United States.

Relations with Russia have improved since the days of the cold war, and Turkey has even turned to Russia as a source of arms, as Moscow does not ask troublesome questions about human rights. Relations between the two states remain strained at the diplomatic level, however, due in no small part to tacit Turkish support for Chechen rebels in the Russian Caucasus in their campaign for independence, which began in 1994. There is a sizable Chechen community in Turkey, and Chechen groups have openly raised funds for the uprising in major cities as well as using Turkey as a point of transit for both arms and sympathetic volunteers from Iran and Afghanistan to enter the breakaway state. Turkish aspirations were manifested in November 1999 when Bill Clinton visited Turkey and several new agreements were reached regarding Caspian energy reserves. Kazakh oil and a pipeline with which to transport it to world markets was approved, as well as the agreement between Azerbaijan and Turkmenistan to allow for the transport of Turkmen gas through Azerbaijani territory. The Istanbul Declaration, confirming the determination of the region's six states for the construction of pipelines, and the American commitment to have energy resources transported by pipeline rather than by sea through the Turkish straits seems to isolate Russia.[61] This confirmation of the Turkish articulation of Eurasia as a political and economic unit, plus U.S. support for the states of the Caspian Basin to have control over their own energy reserves, bolster Turkey's position in central Asia.

Turkey has also tried to resume trade with the Iraqis (formerly Turkey's second largest trading partner). If successful, this is bound to bolster the already major position the country occupies in the Middle East region. The Turkish position was confirmed by its participation in the Israeli-Arab multilateral negotiations. Furthermore, Turkish-Israeli agreements on increasing trade and joint armament manufacturing, as well as initiating strategic military cooperation and intelligence sharing,[62] which were signed in February 1996, were proposed by the Turkish generals who assume supreme control over the country's foreign policy. In the absence of the Soviet threat, the generals feared the marginalization of their status and sought to find a new role within the framework of the U.S. and European strategic interests in the Middle East and the Gulf. By designating Islamic activism as the enemy "within," Turkey made itself a component of the anti-Iranian strategy; and by allying itself to Israel, Turkey could obtain sophisticated military technology while bypassing the pressure of Congress, human rights organizations, and the strong lobby of Greeks and Armenians in both the United States and Europe. In fact, Turkey, through the alliance with Israel, has succeeded in enlisting the strong support of the Israeli lobby in Congress to neutralize Greek and Armenian pressure.[63] Arab leaders at the June summit in Cairo later that year called on Turkey to reconsider the military agreements with Israel in a way to prevent any negative bearing on the security of Arab states. Turkey's military-dominated government promised to review the agreement with Israel but is likely not to change it without some commitment from Syria regarding a complete withdrawal of support for the PKK and the establishment of a commensurate source for advanced weaponry. The coalition government that came to power in 1999 (ANAP-DSP-DTP) went even further than its predecessors by signing a Military Training Cooperation Agreement with Israel.

Further complicating Turkey's relationship with Syria and Iraq is its continued development of twenty-two massive dams in southeastern Turkey, known as the Southeastern Anatolia Project (GAP). By damming the Tigris and Euphrates, Turkey hopes to create surplus hydroelectric power—which will be used to support advanced industrial development—as well as irrigation water for agriculture. However, the environmental and downstream effects throughout the Mesopotamian plain will dramatically affect the people and economies of both Iraq and Syria. Two treaties regulate the flow downstream: a 1987 protocol between Turkey and Syria guaranteeing a minimum flow of 500 cumecs (cubic meters per second) in the Euphrates at the Turkish-Syrian border, and an Iraqi-Syrian pact splitting that amount in a 58:42 ratio. All three countries need the water most during the summer, and drought in 1999 only magnified the extent to which Syria and Iraq are dependent. As it controls almost all of the water in the Euphrates and half that in the Tigris, Turkey has been able to force both Arab states to react to its own initiatives.[64] Furthermore, the destruction of Iraqi society after ten years of warfare and another ten years of draconian economic sanctions has left it in no position to affirm its rights. Syria has little leverage with which to bargain and has also to consider the water implications of its negotiations with Israel over the Golan Heights region.

Turkey has derived much of its international position up until this point from the fact that, being the only Muslim state with a moderate secular system, it offers a western-supported alternative to Islamic activism and a counterweight to first Soviet and now Iranian expansion throughout both Central Asia and the Middle East. Nevertheless, its full participation in Middle Eastern affairs is constrained by mutual suspicions among Arab states arising from its long Imperial Ottoman past, Turkey's increasingly close links with both Europe and Israel, and Turkey's disappointment at what it views as the Arab "betrayal" enveloped in the First World War and the western-sponsored "Arab revolt."

Standing at a crossroads in its history, Turkey must decide how it will respond to the European Union's "accession partnership document." Presented by the EU as a summary of the alterations required of Turkey's economic and political systems, the accession partnership document—

some 900 pages long—calls for sweeping changes centered on increasing civilian control of the Turkish state. The central role Turkey's military has thus far played in promoting the secularization and economic modernization of the country will now need to be balanced against the benefits of increased plurality and EU membership. The military's esteemed place within Turkish society, including its economic power, as well as its principal role in defending the state from foreign and internal opposition, is coming under increased scrutiny in spite of continued popular support.

The 1982 constitution established by the military following the "virtual" or "postmodern" coup of 1980, will not be sufficient to meet the criteria set forth in the Copenhagen rules, which form a major portion of the accession partnership document. In piously pursuing the twin aims of Kemalism—the indivisibility of the nation and its territory and the secularism of the republic—the military has acquired an unassailable position in Turkish politics. Their position on the National Security Council (NSC) has afforded them political primacy over civilian authorities. Furthermore, the economic privileges associated with the chief of staff's control over arms production and procurement, the amount of the annual military budget, and the tax-free status of military-controlled industries has provided them with a powerful position in Turkish society unmatched by its European contemporaries.

Challenges to continued military primacy have arisen both within Turkey as well as from the outside. Indirect pressure came in October 2000 from the International Monetary Fund (IMF), which called on the Turkish government to lower the military budget in return for some $7.5 billion in emergency financial aid.[65] Domestic challenges come in the form of President Ahmet Necdet Sezer's popularity, which in the latter half of 2000 surpassed that of the traditionally respected military high command. Finally, the army—having been accused of interfering in government business during an investigation of corruption in the state energy department—now finds itself being publicly scrutinized.

However, it would be markedly premature to assume that the cornerstone of modern Turkey—its military—would abandon its traditional role and esteemed place in Turkish society without a firm commitment to the foundational ethos on which it has based its legitimacy for eight decades. Whether a viable civil society can evolve from the basis of the Turkish state fashioned by the Kemalist legacy and robust military involvement in political life is now in question. Umit Cizre, a professor at Bilkent University in Ankara succinctly described the distressing state of civilian leadership within Turkey, as quoted by the French writer Eric Rouleau:

> Civil society has increasing latitude but no real strength; parliament contains opposition forces but has no real teeth; the judiciary operates with some independence at times but is by and large controlled politically; media can uncover dark connections of organized crime, but is itself oligopolistically owned and is prone to nationalist and populist influences.[66]

CHAPTER 6

The Republic of Iraq

*I*raq, the ancient Sumerian name meaning "country of the sun," is a relatively new state situated on an ancient land. Roughly the size of California and with a population officially estimated by the United Nations as 22.4 million in 2000, Iraq is the largest Arab state in the Middle East outside of the African continent in terms of population and second only to Saudi Arabia in geographic area. Its location at the northern end of the Arab Gulf situates it on the borders of two non-Arab states, Turkey and Iran, both of whom dwarf Iraq.

Iraq is composed of four major geographic regions: desert in the west, rolling uplands on the central plains of the upper Tigris and Euphrates Rivers, highlands in the north, and marshland in the south. The central plains are the most agriculturally productive regions because the annual deposits of silt left by the Tigris and Euphrates through many millennia have caused the soil to be rich in nutrients. Agriculture has declined in importance over the past century, as oil increasingly has become Iraq's economic lifeblood. However, the embargo against Iraqi oil and the severe sanctions and restrictions against farm imports have elevated the importance of Iraqi agriculture, but productivity has reached its lowest point.

Arabic is the official language of Iraq, although Kurdish is spoken in the northern and northeastern regions. The interplay between the dominant Arab majority and the Kurdish minority has greatly affected Iraqi history. Iraq is estimated to be 73 percent Arab and 20 percent Kurdish.[1] Arabs are evenly distributed throughout the country, but the Kurds are concentrated in the mountainous northern region. Religious diversity also has had historical and political significance. Around 95 percent of the population is Muslim, equally divided between the two major sects of Islam, Shi'a and Sunni.

Modern Iraq was admitted to the League of Nations as an independent state in 1932, but its history within the region is ancient. Mesopotamia [which means the land between the two rivers], the historical name of the lands surrounding the alluvial plain created by the Tigris and Euphrates rivers, is considered one of the cradles of civilization, where centralized government first emerged and literate culture initially flourished. At the crossroads of three continents, both agriculture and commerce prospered, fueling the constant interchange of people, products, and ideas. Numerous city-states competed for dominance and territory. Empires emerged and faded, marking the rise and fall of successive civilizations: Sumerian (2900–2350 B.C.), Akkadian (2350–2159 B.C.), Babylonian (1894–1594 B.C.), Kassite (1680–1157 B.C.), Assyrian (953–605 B.C.), Sassanid (226 B.C.–A.D. 637), and Arab (A.D. 633–1258).

Arab armies arrived in Mesopotamia in A.D. 633, and the region was one of the first conquests of the rapidly expanding Arab Empire, which was then emerging from the Arabian Desert under the banner of Islam. Following the death of the Prophet Muhammad, the center of the empire shifted from Arabia to the Fertile Crescent. In A.D. 762 the reigning caliph, Ja'far al-Mansur, founded Baghdad as the capital, and for the next five centuries, the Abbasid dynasty (750–1258) ruled. The region was integrated into the Ottoman Empire in the sixteenth century.

While this historical record constitutes the prologue to the story of modern Iraq, its influence on the contemporary government and politics of the state—while subtle—is instructive. Two interrelated historical processes have broadly determined the direct historical antecedents of the modern Iraqi state: the decline of the Ottoman Empire, and the expansion of the power of Great Britain and its successor, the United States, in the Middle East. In the early nineteenth century, Britain began chipping away at Ottoman hegemony in the region to protect, consolidate, and expand its own empire, which was centered in Asia on the Indian subcontinent.

As long as Turkey was friendly to British interests and hostile to German and Russian interests in the Middle East, Britain was unwilling to challenge Turkish rule in Mesopotamia. However, the pro-German leanings of the Young Turks and the German desire to construct a Berlin-Baghdad railway evoked ever-increasing alarm after 1908 in view of the potential threat to British transit to India. The British government became increasingly concerned about establishing a direct sphere of influence over Iraq with the outbreak of the First World War. British expeditionary forces were dispatched to Iraq in 1914, which, despite having little Arab support and suffering numerous military setbacks at the hands of Turkish forces, managed to enter Baghdad in 1917 and subdue the entire region by 1918.

Iraq was initially the administrative preserve of the India Office, which ruled with great arrogance, high-handedness, and insensitivity to local aspirations. A rigged plebiscite was held in December 1918 affirming the Iraqi people's desire for a British mandate. At San Remo, as part of the settlement of its claims to portions of the Middle East, France relinquished its claim to Mosul in September 1919 and recognized the British right to rule in the former Turkish *villayets* (provinces) of Baghdad, Basra, and Mosul, in return for a British withdrawal from Syria. The two powers reaffirmed the British ascendancy in Iraq, again at San Remo, in April 1920. However, the League of Nations never ratified the British mandate, which was submitted for approval in 1920, with Britain informing the League of Nations of its intention to govern Iraq in accordance with bilateral agreements, which had evolved during the preceding two years of occupation.

It is important to note that the territory of Iraq, as it was constituted following the First World War under British rule and later as it became independent, was not an invention of western statesmen. The boundaries resembled those established during the Early Dynastic Period, under the Sumerian king Sargon.[2] Archaeologists and historians now trace the line of Sumerian kings back before 2700 B.C. and entertain the legend of Gilgamesh, king of Uruk, taking that date as a provisional starting point for the history of ancient Iraq. Its boundaries have remained largely intact.

The Hashemite Monarchical Period (1921–1958)

In reaction to the San Remo decisions, a popular nationalist revolt erupted and engulfed the entire country. Fighting was fierce, and casualties on both sides were high. By October 1920, efforts to quell the revolt had already cost the British Exchequer £30–40 million. A new high commissioner, Sir Percy Cox, announced the British government's intention to facilitate the establishment of a national government in Mesopotamia. A truce was announced, and nationalists and other prominent Iraqis were invited to participate in creating an independent state.

Faisal Ibn al-Hussein, the former king of Syria who had been deposed by the French in 1920 and who was the son of the leader of the Arab revolt, Sharif Hussein of Mecca, was selected by a provisional council of state to rule Iraq. The council of state also proclaimed, in July 1922, that the Iraqi monarchy should be "constitutional, representative, and democratically . . . limited by law."[3] Faisal was proclaimed king on 23 August 1921, following another plebiscite in which it was claimed he drew over 98 percent of the votes cast. An Anglo-Iraqi treaty, the first of a series, in October 1922 set out the basic features of the Iraqi government and thinly disguised Britain's hegemony behind the facade of a constitutional monarchy. A great deal of effort was expended in Baghdad and London on formulating an organic law that would preserve a balance of power between the monarch and the Iraqi Constituent Assembly. The first elections were held between October 1923 and February 1924, and the Assembly convened in March 1924 to consider the draft of the organic law. The king approved the measure in March 1925.

Considerable power was vested in the hands of the king, who presided over parliament, issued writs for general elections, confirmed and enforced laws, supervised their execution, and could claim extraordinary powers under martial law. The king could pass measures intended to maintain public order with the approval of the council of ministers and authorize public expenditures not outlined in the budget. The king selected and dismissed the prime minister and appointed cabinet ministers on his recommendation. He appointed members to the senate and was also supreme head of state and commander in chief of the armed forces. The cabinet was responsible to the parliament; the prime minister was required to present his resignation to the king if parliament passed a vote of no confidence, and individual cabinet ministers had to resign if the parliament expressed a lack of confidence in them. Parliament was bicameral, consisting of the elected chamber of deputies and the numerically smaller senate appointed by the king. The chamber of deputies was modeled on the British House of Commons in all essential respects, whereas the senate, whose members were landowners and tribal chieftains, functioned like the House of Lords.

Beneath the facade of independence, the British High Commission in Baghdad retained a great deal of power, including the ability to appoint advisers to the Iraqi government. Although most of the lower-level civil servants were native Iraqis, the top administrative posts were occupied by British nationals, who assisted in training the Iraqi army; protected foreigners domiciled in Iraq in accordance with the practices of English law; advised Iraq on fiscal and monetary policy; and managed Iraq's relations abroad. A series of Anglo-Iraqi treaties ensued in January 1926, December 1927 (drafted but not ratified by the chamber of deputies), and June 1930. Under the 1930 treaty, British advisory privileges were terminated; however, British military bases and military transit privileges were maintained, and Britain continued to train and equip Iraq's army. Iraq was permitted to initiate diplomatic representation abroad and to conduct its own foreign policy independent of Britain, although regular consultations with the Foreign Office were to continue. The

treaty took effect on 3 October 1932, the date of Iraq's admission into
the League of Nations. This date is cited by many sources as the beginning of official Iraqi independence, although others cite the first Anglo-
Iraqi treaty of October 1921, which created the state organization.

Despite the inherent conflicts, King Faisal was able to maintain a precarious balance between his obligations to British imperial authority
and the demands of Iraq's domestic nationalist constituency. Upon his
sudden death in 1933, his son Ghazi succeeded him. Ghazi died in an
automobile accident in 1939, when his heir, Faisal, was only four years
old. A maternal uncle, 'Abd al-Illah, was appointed regent and crown
prince. For the next two decades, a veteran politician, Nuri al-Sa'id,
served 'Abd al-Illah in successive cabinets, heading a quarter of them
(fifteen out of sixty), and being a prominent member in more than half.
Both men were staunchly pro-British and came to symbolize British
domination in Iraq. Nuri al-Sa'id suppressed all political opposition. In
1941 anti-British, pro-Axis nationalists temporarily replaced pro-British
politicians in the Iraqi government through a bloodless coup. However,
Britain moved swiftly to reinstate its proxies and to integrate Iraq into
its war effort. Iraq was pressured to declare war against the Axis in the
fall of 1941.

In April 1946, the government officially licensed five political parties,
although the list excluded the active Communist Party of Iraq. The five
that were licensed included

• the Independence Party (al-Istiqlal), which came to represent
  conservative nationalists;
• the National Democratic Party (al-Watani al-Dimocrati), representing those with liberal and moderately socialist views similar
  to and influenced by Fabian societies and notions from
  England—primarily in social issues, although they staunchly
  maintained both an anti-imperialist and anti-British position;[4]
• the National Union (al-Itihad al-Watani);
• the left-leaning People's Party (al-Sha'ab); and
• the Liberal Party (al-Ahrar), which took the middle path between
  the National Democratic Party (NDP) and the Independence Party.

Between March 1946 and January 1948, negotiations between Baghdad
and London led to a new Anglo-Iraqi treaty to replace the unpopular
agreement of 1930. However, populist mobilization against the new
treaty—including the active participation of all five of the newly
licensed political parties through the leadership of progressive groups,
the so-called Left, and inspired by the underground Iraqi Communist
Party—prevented the treaty from ever being ratified.

The United States sought to fill the power vacuum in the Middle East left by the decline of British and French power in the region. The construction of a mutual defense alliance, the Baghdad Pact, was designed to link security arrangements in the Middle East with the North Atlantic Treaty Organization (NATO) and the South East Asia Treaty Organization (SEATO), in an effort to isolate the USSR. The Baghdad Pact's membership included Britain, Turkey, Iran, Pakistan, and Iraq. Nuri al-Saʿid led Iraq into the pact in February 1955, despite strong popular opposition, which saw it as a western strategy to stem the rising tide of Arab nationalism. Domestic opposition eventually forced Iraq to withdraw from the alliance, leading to the 1958 revolution.

Throughout the monarchical period, social conditions in Iraq, indeed, in the entire Middle East, steadily deteriorated, with widespread poverty. According to official Iraqi statistics, in 1957 the average life expectancy was a pathetically low thirty-eight to forty years. Consequently, half of the population was below the age of twenty; the cost of living had increased fivefold since independence; and on the eve of the revolution, 80 percent of the population was still illiterate, with only one doctor for every 6,000 Iraqis. Seventy-five percent of farm land was owned by less than 1 percent of the population, and 85 percent of peasants were landless.[5] Coupled with the constant internal political conflicts and the social and economic crises of Iraq was the attendant foreign domination of the country. Although Iraq gained independence before many of the other Arab states in the region, it appeared less autonomous. Consequently, the four main opposition parties, the National Democratic Party (NDP), the Iraqi Communist Party (ICP), the Independence Party, and the Baʿath Arab Socialist Party (Resurrection), all illegal parties functioning underground, coalesced to form the Patriotic Unity Front (PUF) on 9 March 1957. Their immediate objectives were declared to be:

- removing Nuri al-Saʿid from power,
- withdrawing from the Baghdad Pact,
- freeing all political prisoners,
- removing all restrictions against political parties, and
- supporting the nonaligned movement.

Military Governments and the Rise of the Baʿath

The formation of the United Arab Republic (UAR) on 1 February 1958 represented a triumph for the forces of Pan-Arab nationalism in the Middle East and posed a serious threat to the conservative monarchies of the region, particularly Iraq's. Iraq's oppressive monarchy had failed to solve socioeconomic problems. On 14 February 1958, the Iraqi government joined with the Jordanian monarchy to form the Arab Hashemite Federation. In May, the political polarization of Lebanon between Lebanese nationalists and Arab nationalists developed into a muted civil war. The Arab nationalists were supported by Syria, which was now part of the UAR, against President Chamoun and his Maronite Christian and pro-western government. Nuri al-Sa'id wished to stifle what he saw as the anti-western sentiments incorporated within the UAR and to prevent the expansion of Egyptian influence. He saw Iraq's role as guardian of western interests in general and British concerns in particular. With events in Lebanon reaching crisis proportions during the summer of 1958 and threatening to spill into Jordan, al-Sa'id argued it had become necessary for Iraq to fulfill its pledge to support its fellow monarchy. He ordered Iraqi army units to move into Jordan to support King Hussein. Instead, Col. 'Abd al-Salam 'Aref, on behalf of the clandestine Free Officers' Movement, ordered his units into Baghdad, and on the morning of 14 July 1958 'Aref led a coup against the al-Sa'id government. Jubilant Baghdad citizens poured into the streets. Scores were killed in the mob violence that ensued, including King Faisal, Crown Prince 'Abd al-Illah, and Nuri al-Sa'id. When order was restored on the evening of 16 July, a republic was proclaimed, and a new government was formed by Brig. Gen. 'Abdul Karim Kassem, the founder and chief of the secret Free Officers' Movement.

Kassem and 'Aref's first concern was to consolidate their power by cementing the coalition of broad-based political support that the revolution initially enjoyed. A council of sovereignty was established, representing Sunnis, Shi'is, and Kurds. The first cabinet was chosen so that its members would bring a broad spectrum of political opinion into the new government. The Patriotic Unity Front played a major role. Kassem became prime minister and commander in chief of the Iraqi armed forces, and 'Aref became deputy premier, minister of the interior, and deputy commander in chief. Preparations were made for a general amnesty for political crimes committed under the old regime, exiles returned from abroad, and a people's court under Col. Fadil 'Abbas al-Mahdawi tried and sentenced leading members of the old regime. There was little resistance, and it appeared that Kassem and 'Aref had unified the nation. However, the increase in political activity and the emergence of forces previously suppressed, aided by foreign pressures on the new regime, eventually led to conflict. On 26 July, Iraq was proclaimed an independent Arab republic. Its new constitution entrusted all executive and legislative power to the council of ministers, and all laws were declared to continue in force until amended or canceled.

The Struggle for Power

There arose a three-way struggle for power among the Pan-Arabists, the Iraqi nationalists, and the leftists. This struggle first manifested itself in the problem of determining the nature of UAR-Iraqi relations. 'Aref supported a union with the UAR, but the National Democrats and the leftists, including the Communists, opposed it. The leftists, supported by the Kurds, opposed any merger with Egypt and by extension Syria, primarily because of Egyptian president Gamal Abdel Nasser's opposition to communism.

Kassem initially intended to seek closer relations with the UAR than had the monarchy, but he was also determined to maintain Iraq's independence. His refusal to submerge the state into a larger political entity was to some extent a result of his desire to maintain power and his belief that he symbolized Iraq's 1958 revolution. More fundamentally, however, Kassem was cognizant of the country's heterogeneous social characteristics. Minority groups, including the Kurds and the Turkomans, were not sympathetic to an exclusively Pan-Arabist program, for it posed an implicit threat to their cultural autonomy. The large Shi'i population did not like the prospect of being further immersed in the national political life of a federation with other Arab states, which were overwhelmingly Sunni.

Therefore, in attempting to unify the country, Kassem rejected Nasser's Pan-Arab approach. A propaganda battle with the UAR ensued, as bitter as any between Nasser and the Hashemites had been, expressing itself in a power struggle between Kassem and 'Aref. On 12 September 1958, 'Aref lost his position as deputy commander in chief of the armed forces. On 30 September he was also removed from the cabinet, along with two supporters, and appointed ambassador to Germany. An uprising in his regiment was quelled on 5 October, and on 12 October he left the country. He never took up his post in Germany. When he returned to Baghdad on 4 November, he was arrested and accused of plotting against the security of the state. The Pan-Arabists were now out of power with a good number of them held in detention. In February a sentence of death was pronounced upon 'Aref and Rashid 'Ali al-Gailani, who had been a hero of the 1941 short-lived revolt against Britain. In protest, six cabinet ministers, representing the nationalists, resigned. Thus, with both the Ba'ath and the Independence Parties no longer represented in government, these two groups of the old party, along with other disenchanted Pan-Arab nationalists, formed an opposition coalition, the National Front, as a means of organizing their forces against Kassem.

To counter the growing strength of the nationalists and Nasserites, Kassem began to lean heavily on the support of the Left, including the well-organized Communist Party. As a result of Kassem's complacency, the Communists had been able to expand their influence considerably after the 1958 revolution. They created front organizations, such as the Association for the Defense of the Rights of Iraqi Women, the Partisans of Peace, and the Democratic Youth Association, and they organized labor syndicates, farmers' associations, and student unions. They infiltrated the paramilitary Popular Resistance Forces (formed immediately after the demise of the monarchy in August 1958), and they were even able to gain control over the mass media through the appointments of pro-Communists as press censors and as the head of radio-television.

In late 1958, Kassem appointed a well-known Communist sympathizer, Col. Taha Sheikh Ahmad, director of military planning in the Ministry of Defense. Ahmad was able to foster a leftist and Kassemist infiltration of the entire ministry. Furthermore, Communist-controlled committees for the defense of the republic were quickly set up in almost every department of the government, where they could function as intelligence networks to undermine political opposition. The Communists were able to bring about the removal from government and the arbitrary arrest of many Pan-Arab nationalists and Nasserites. Needless to say, these purges had a debilitating effect on government administration, removing some of the most able officials and leaving the survivors timid and cautious as well as leading to disappointment and a dampening of enthusiasm for the new republic. More fundamentally, however, Kassem and the Communists isolated political opposition to his regime from legitimate channels of protest and helped consolidate nationalist unrest.

The conflict with the nationalists came to a head in early March 1959 when Col. 'Abd al-Wahab al-Shawaf, a pro-Nasserite who opposed the growing influence of the Communists, used his Mosul-based troops to stage a revolt. The Iraqi air force bombarded Mosul, killing Shawaf and halting his poorly organized revolt. Kassem now felt that Communist distrust of the Pan-Arab nationalists was justified, and he allowed the Communists to intensify their purge. Scores of Pan-Arabs, civilian as well as military, were implicated in the attempted coup, dismissed from office, and arrested. Even Muhammad Mahdi Kubbah, head of the Independence Party and the Shi'i member of the council of sovereignty, was placed under house arrest. However, the purges would mark the peak of Communist power.

The threat of nationalist strength, especially Nasserite and Ba'athist, appeared to be effectively curbed. But in circumscribing nationalist power, Kassem had established a modus vivendi with the Communists and had allowed them considerable freedom to maneuver, and they began to demand a greater voice in policy making. In April 1959, a campaign by the Communist-friendly media demanded formal Communist participation in the government. Then the minister of the economy, Ibrahim Kubbah, an independent Marxist, and the minister of health, Dr. Muhammad 'Abd al-Malik al-Shawaf, brother of failed coup leader 'Abd al-Wahab, urged that leftists be included in the cabinet. Although Kassem voiced his disapproval of these demands, he appointed the noted Communist Dr. Naziha al-Dulaimi as minister of municipalities, making her the first female minister in Iraq's history. The delicate balance of political forces that Kassem had envisioned, and for which purpose he had suppressed the nationalists, appeared to be crumbling. But he was not a leftist sympathizer, and he had no intention of allowing their ascendance to power. His opportunity to diminish their power came on 14 July 1959, the first anniversary of the revolution, when rioting broke out in northern Iraq between Kurdish tribes and Turkoman townspeople. The Communist-controlled People's Resistance Forces aided the Kurdish demonstrators. Kassem gradually disarmed and disbanded this organization. The Communist Party, in an effort to extricate itself from the confrontation with Kassem, indulged in extensive self-criticism in July 1960. Nevertheless, further actions were taken to curtail Communist influence, including the removal of Ibrahim Kubbah and Naziha al-Dulaimi from the cabinet. Gen. Ahmad Salih al-'Abdi, military governor-general of Iraq, became the nemesis of the Communists through 1960 and 1961, during which time he further diminished their influence.

Kassem had subdued both the Communists and Pan-Arab nationalists, driving them underground, and in the process had also alienated both groups. His flirtation with the Communists, moreover, incurred the distrust of most of the nationalist elements. Thus, within a year of taking power, he had lost most of his support. On 7 October 1959, members of the Ba'ath Party made an attempt on Kassem's life; he was hospitalized until early December. Despite the alienation of many active politicians from his regime, he did establish an equilibrium of sorts, for in January 1960 he ended the six-year prohibition against political parties. Parties were allowed to operate under licenses, granted by the minister of the interior, although under certain restrictions. No military officers or government officials were allowed to join, and the organizations were not allowed to use a military or paramilitary structure. Of the first four parties to apply, three were granted licenses, including the National Democratic Party, the Democratic Party of Kurdistan, and the

Iraqi Communist Party (actually a minority splinter group of the real Communist Party paid for and supported by Kassem in an attempt to undermine and deny recognition to the majority party). Subsequently, the Iraqi Islamic Party and the Progressive National Party, the latter an offshoot of the National Democratic Party, were also granted licenses.

Two events in 1961 significantly weakened Kassem's internal and international positions. First, Kurdish leader Mullah Mustafa al-Barzani launched a rebellion against central authority and by September controlled some 250 square miles of territory in northern Iraq. The government began an offensive against the Barzani group, but the Kurds held their position. The war became protracted, and the apparent inability of government forces to bring it to a successful conclusion created dissatisfaction among many army officers. The Ba'ath, strengthened through the rise to power in Syria of Ba'ath after the fall of the UAR, capitalized on this dissatisfaction and recruited members of the army through an attraction to their more militant ideology. As a result, Kassem's hold on the military, whose loyalty was essential to the maintenance of his regime, began to wane.

On 25 June 1961, Britain terminated its protectorate over Kuwait, which had been established in 1899, and withdrew its military forces from the tiny sheikdom in preparation for Kuwaiti independence. Claiming that Kuwait had been an integral part of Iraq until British imperialism had carved it away in the late nineteenth century, General Kassem declared Iraq's annexation of Kuwait. This declaration won Iraq international condemnation, and both Britain and the Arab League sent troops to protect Kuwait.[6]

The 1963 Coup d'État

Beset by the Kurdish uprising and isolated diplomatically by the threat to Kuwaiti independence, Kassem was in a most unstable position. But opposition forces were also divided and fragmented, and he was able, albeit somewhat precariously, to maintain his hold on power until early 1963. Meanwhile, the Ba'ath organized a coalition of all nationalist and independent groups in an anti-Communist and anti-Kassem front. A group of Arab nationalists, including Ba'athists, Nasserites, and military officers, killed Kassem on 8 February 1963 and began purging leftists and Kassem supporters. Col. 'Abd al-Salam 'Aref, who had been released from prison in November 1961, was installed as president of the republic. However, the real power lay with the premier, Ahmad Hasan al-Bakr (one of the more recent military recruits to the Ba'ath Party), his cabinet (primarily Ba'ath party members), and the newly

created Revolutionary Command Council (primarily Ba'ath Party leaders). Trials and executions of Communists, pro-Kassem elements, and
others followed the coup, along with a purge of the army and civil
bureaucracies. An estimated 10,000 people were killed in the first terri-
fying month of the new regime.

The 'Aref government was nominally pro-Egyptian, and talks with
Egypt soon expanded, following the Ba'ath coup in Syria (March 1963),
in which a tripartite union between Iraq, Syria, and Egypt was pursued.
However, the successful agreement failed because of traditional rivalries
and conflicts of interest between the three Arab states. Although an
agreement for eventual union was signed on 17 April, Nasser and the
Ba'ath were soon at odds. Subsequently, on 13 May non-Ba'ath members
were forced out of the cabinet, and the Iraqi government took on a
strongly anti-Nasser disposition. Nasser declared the UAR's withdrawal
from the tripartite union pact in July 1963. On 8 October a Syro-Iraqi
military union was announced, which was expected to bring the two
Ba'ath-controlled states into closer association.

Ba'ath Dominance

Now in control of a major part of the Fertile Crescent, the Ba'ath
seemed politically preeminent; however, in Iraq there were two factors
that augured ill for the party. First, there was widespread dissatisfaction
in the military, which in Iraq had become the essential element in maintaining power. The creation of a paramilitary National Guard shortly
after the coup was the primary cause of the military's dissatisfaction.
The Ba'ath created the organization as a measure to counter potential
army dissidence and as a means of purging the population of political
opposition. The organization became quite powerful, reportedly exceeding 50,000 members, and many officers considered its existence
and activities an affront to the military and were distrustful of this con-
straint on their influence in Iraqi politics.

The second factor was an ideological split within the Ba'ath ranks.
By November 1963 two factions had emerged in an intraparty power
struggle: the radicals and the moderates. Led by Deputy Premier and
Minister of the Interior 'Ali Salih al-Sa'di, the radicals had control of the
Revolutionary Command Council, the highest authority in the land, as
well as the National Guard. The radicals demanded the immediate and
total application of socialism to Iraq, uncompromising continuance of
the fruitless and costly campaign against the Kurds, relentless opposition to Nasser, and the suppression of all internal political opposition.
The moderates were led by Hazim Jawad, minister for presidential

affairs, and Talib Hussain Shabib, minister of foreign affairs, who were supported by many among the military. The moderates were not so ideologically dogmatic and felt that accommodation and reconciliation should temper the government's overall policies.

On 4 November 1963, the moderates, in collaboration with President 'Aref, engineered a meeting of the regional command of the Ba'ath Party and elected a number of their supporters to important posts within the party leadership. Simultaneously, al-Sa'di and some of his supporters in the council were expelled from the country. Factional fighting then erupted in Baghdad within the National Guard. In an attempt to maintain party unity, Michel 'Aflaq and members of the national command of the Ba'ath Party, based in Syria, came to Baghdad and renounced the election. They proclaimed the national command the rulers of Iraq and expelled Jawad, Shabib, and others. They were unable to resolve the differences paralyzing the party, however, and on 18 November President 'Aref, supported by disaffected military elements, took advantage of the subsequent weakness of the Ba'ath administration and ousted the party from the government. 'Aflaq and his associates returned to Damascus, and civil war was averted only when the pro-Ba'athist National Guard surrendered to the army.

The 'Aref Regime

'Aref's new cabinet retained some Ba'athists, but was primarily composed of army officers and technocrats. 'Aref retained the presidency and a month later appointed his brother, Gen. 'Abd al-Rahman 'Aref, chief of staff. He assigned the premiership to his close friend and confidant, Lt. Gen. Taher Yahya, who was the former chief of staff, and he appointed Ahmad Hasan al-Bakr to the highly ceremonial job of vice president. At first, President 'Aref was strongly pro-Nasser, and he went so far as to establish a joint presidency council on 26 May 1964. On the sixth anniversary of the creation of the Republic of Iraq, 14 July 1964, the government took some momentous steps toward implementing a further union with Egypt. The first was the establishment of the Arab Socialist Union of Iraq (ASU), hailed by President 'Aref as the "threshold of the building of the unity of the Arab nation under Arab Socialism." The charter or Basic Law of the ASU of Iraq was identical in most respects to the charter of the Arab Socialist Union of the UAR. The four publicly active political groups in Iraq at the time (the Arab Nationalists, the Arab Socialists, the Socialist Unionists, and the Democratic Social Unionists) were dissolved and incorporated within the newly created structure of the Arab Socialist Union of Iraq. Also on

14 July 1964 the government nationalized all banks and some thirty large business firms with 25.5 million Iraqi dinars paid by the government to compensate private interests (I.D. 1=U.S.$2.80). An economic establishment was formed to supervise the nationalized industries. All of these measures were designed to bring Iraq closer in aims and structure to the UAR in order to make the union foreseen by the agreement of 26 May viable. The first meeting of the UAR–Iraq joint presidency council was held on 15 July 1964. However, true unity proved as elusive as ever, for although plans for union were announced on 20 December 1964, the pro-Nasser ministers resigned in protest from the Iraqi cabinet in July 1965.

On 13 April 1966, President 'Aref was killed in a helicopter crash and succeeded by his brother, 'Abd al-Rahman Mohammed 'Aref. The new president inherited the same basic socioeconomic and political problems that had thwarted all of Iraq's governments since independence. In an attempt to solve at least one problem decisively, 'Abd al-Rahman 'Aref undertook a massive spring military offensive against the Kurds, involving some 65,000 troops and aerial bombardment of Kurdish strongholds. 'Aref's prime minister, the moderate Dr. 'Abd al-Rahman Bazzaz, the first civilian premier since the 1958 revolution, then offered the Kurds significant concessions. Outraged at what it viewed as unnecessary capitulation to the Kurds, the armed forces forced Dr. Bazzaz's resignation in favor of Gen. Naji Talib, marking the return of the military to the government. By May 1967 'Aref took the office himself, while the Kurdish problem remained unresolved.

The Return of the Ba'ath

As the June 1967 Arab-Israeli war approached, Iraq moved closer to the other Arab states, but the loss of the war heightened already intense frustrations, and in July 1968 President 'Abd al-Rahman 'Aref's regime crumbled under a military coup. As a result of the coup, the Ba'ath Party again returned to power under the leadership of Ahmad Hasan al-Bakr (former premier and later briefly vice president in 1963). Saddam Hussein, a Ba'ath Party functionary and a member of al-Bakr's immediate clan from Tikrit, a small rural town northwest of Baghdad, gradually emerged as the real power behind al-Bakr in the Ba'ath Party. Affected by the 1963 experience, a power-sharing arrangement between al-Bakr and Saddam Hussein divided executive responsibilities. Saddam Hussein concentrated his efforts in the domestic security and police apparatus while al-Bakr took over the military and became nominal head of state. Under President al-Bakr, Hussein consolidated his power by assuming the posts of vice chairman of the Revolutionary Command Council, assistant secretary-general of the regional command of the Ba'ath Party, and assistant secretary-general of the national command of the Ba'ath.

The Ba'ath regime that came to power in 1968 was to become the most ruthless and oppressive yet stable of the republican era. In 1979 Ahmad Hasan al-Bakr, either by choice or through Saddam's coercion, stepped down as president of the republic after granting Saddam Hussein the military rank of general. Saddam Hussein then assumed all leadership posts: secretary-general of the Ba'ath Party (regional command), chairman of the Revolutionary Command Council, and commander in chief of the armed forces. In July 1990 Saddam Hussein was proclaimed president for life by the National Assembly of Iraq, a 250-member chamber which is a facade council without functions or powers that had been created in 1980 to legitimize and rubber stamp policies of the RCC, which in turn rubber stamps Saddam Hussein's decisions. Members of the National Assembly must have Ba'ath Party approval and are elected to four-year terms in office. The majority are Ba'ath Party members. In the election of 28 March 2000, the son of the president, Oday Hussein, was uncontested and won with 99.99 percent of the popular vote in his riding. Such election results are routine in authoritarian regimes, as in 1995 when Saddam Hussein garnered 99.96 percent of a staged national vote, formulated to appear as a presidential referendum, reaffirming his leadership.

Socialist Development under the Ba'ath, 1968–80

Between 1968 and 1980, the foreign and domestic policies of Iraq emerged fundamentally and directly from the Pan-Arab socialist ideology of the governing Ba'ath Party. The central slogans of Ba'ath ideology—unity, freedom, and socialism—were pursued in both the internal and the external arenas. However, the war with Iran, which began in September 1980 and continued to July 1988, catalyzed significant modification of Iraq's "ideological purity" in practice. In other words, as a result of the political, economic, and social exigencies produced by the war, the Ba'ath in practice veered from these principles. This was reflected in domestic policies of social development and foreign policies of regional and international relations. Furthermore, the war marked an abandonment of previous party policies regarding social development as tribal affiliations were promoted and enshrined in official activities,[7] even adjusting both civil laws and the penal code provisions, at the expense of traditional institutions of civil society developed after independence.

In the sphere of domestic development, prewar economic policies reflected the Ba'ath goal of building an independent economy with a strong socialist infrastructure. The Ba'ath government's drive for economic independence had several dimensions: the establishment of sovereignty over petroleum resources and production, economic self-reliance in the internal market, and economic diversification. Iraq's nationalization of the oil industry in 1972 was the realization of the first dimension. Economic self-reliance focused on Iraq's heavy dependence on imported goods rather than on goods made in Iraq. Instead of importing goods and services required by the existing industries, the government gave priority in industrial development to the creation of industries that would fulfill this function. Also, priority was given to industries that depended upon locally produced natural resources. In this way an industrial infrastructure independent of external suppliers was encouraged. On the third dimension, the Ba'ath government undertook large-scale development projects geared to diversify its role in the international market. For example, Iraq's rich sulfur resources were being developed with the creation of a sulfur extraction and refining industry, and Iraq's abundant phosphate resources were being developed in the framework of a fully integrated industrial project. Hence, unlike many countries rich in raw resources in the Third World, Iraq, during this period (1968–1980), was deliberately moving away from its role in the international economy as a raw resource exporter and developing a fully integrated and diversified industrial base with indigenous resources, producing finished products for market instead of exporting only its natural resources for foreign refinement.

The socialist transformation of the economy occurred in conjunction with the push for economic independence and self-reliance. While Ba'ath socialist ideology did not prohibit private enterprise, it placed such activity in a role secondary and subsidiary to state enterprise. Financed by the wealth produced by the oil sector, the socialization of industry in Iraq progressed rapidly under the Ba'ath. While there was virtually no viable socialist sector when the Ba'ath came to power in 1968, by 1978 it had become dominant. In the social sphere, Iraq's efforts to build an independent socialist economy with a self-sustaining rate of growth were complemented by social policies aimed at transforming the semitribal, semifeudal relations of production entrenched by centuries of exploitation, colonialism, and imperialism. Ideologically, the transformation of social relations from a tribal-feudal framework to a modern industrial socialist framework was the explicit objective of social development. Social policies in the areas of education, health care, labor relations, and family came to reflect these goals.

Between 1968 and 1980, the quantity and quality of all social services to Iraqi citizens improved substantially. For example, expenditures on medical services increased 40 percent between 1968 and 1974.

Unlike other Third World states committed to socialist transformation, scarce resources (and the domestic and international constraints that a lack of resources can place on government action) did not curtail Iraq's development strategies until the initiation of the Iran-Iraq war in 1980. Thus, from 1968 to 1980, Iraq pursued socialist development under conditions of capital surplus rather than under the conditions of capital shortage, which confounded development strategies in most developing world states with debt. Iraq's experience in this period represented a case of social development uncompromised and unconstrained by the contingencies of capital shortage and *realpolitik* that distort the practice of development policy.

However, the prolongation of the Iran-Iraq War drastically undermined Iraqi efforts. By 1983 the material costs of the war were estimated to be about U.S.$1 billion per month. It transformed Iraq from a capital surplus nation into a debtor nation and a foreign-aid dependent. Western economists estimated that Saudi Arabia and the Gulf emirates gave Iraq financial assistance of about U.S.$60 billion by the end of the war in 1988. (Official Iraqi sources put the figure at less than half that.) While the implementation of development projects continued throughout the war, the ideological fulcrum of development strategy—self-reliance and independence—had been dramatically checked, and the effort to sustain development during the war only increased economic and political dependence on external sources.

With the end of the war, Iraq had accumulated a foreign debt estimated at U.S.$55–80 billion. In response to pressures from lenders, Iraq undertook economic liberalization, including the privatization of some state industries, abolished socialist-inspired labor laws, and deregulated private enterprise. In the political sphere, pressures toward liberalization were also evident. Proforma parliamentary elections were held in 1984 and 1988, and Saddam Hussein promised multiparty elections in the future while also pledging to introduce a new constitution that would be accepted or rejected by popular referendum.

Republican Political Institutions and Processes: The Constitutions of 1958, 1964, and 1970

Successive constitutions were introduced with every regime change during the republican era. With each governmental change, suspension of the old constitution was declared and the new constitution adopted.

Although several Iraqi constitutions promised at least quasi-democratic institutions, powerful executives, as a close perusal of the constitutions of 1958, 1964, and 1970 will indicate, have been a fact of political life in Iraq. For example, the constitution of 26 July 1958 vested the prime minister with the central role in government. It established a figurehead presidential council (article 20) that Kassem dominated. The council of ministers (cabinet) was entrusted with the legislative function, subject to the formal approval of the presidential council (article 21). The individual ministers and the council of ministers were made collectively responsible for administrative and executive functions (article 22). In this system, Kassem, as prime minister, defense minister, and commander in chief of the armed forces, controlled the means of government, and the primary function of the constitution was simply the legitimization of his rule. Power was not diffuse.

According to the April 1964 constitution, the president was to be elected by the RCC, which itself was made up of high-ranking army officers (articles 42 and 55). This council—theoretically supreme in making policy—was to be consulted by the president and was to endorse his decision before he could declare martial law or a state of emergency, or declare war or peace (articles 48 and 49). Further, the RCC must approve presidential assumption of emergency powers (article 51). The republican council, which acts for the president in case of his absence from the country or his inability to fulfill his responsibilities, was composed of three members of the RCC (article 53). Impeachment of the president was also the province of the RCC, a two-thirds majority of that body being required for an indictment (article 60). The president was enjoined by the constitution to form a national defense council (article 50).

Despite these constitutional restrictions on presidential power, 'Abd al-Salam 'Aref still succeeded in making the presidency the most powerful office in Iraq. The 1964 provisional constitution invested the president with the powers of commander in chief of the armed forces, appointer of the prime minister, deputy prime minister, cabinet ministers, and senior civil servants, and sole retainer of executive power. The cabinet was left with primarily an administrative function. Legislative power was vested in a national assembly, which not only never met but was never elected by the populace. The vagueness of the constitutional provisions for such a body suggests that perhaps the idea was never a serious consideration. When the Ba'ath returned to power in 1968, the 1964 constitution was superseded by a new constitution in September 1968. This was supplanted by the provisional constitution of 16 July 1970, which in part was a modification of the 1968 constitution. In the late 1990s, the provisional constitution of 1970 was still the basic law of the land.

The 1970 constitution provides for a government system with three branches: executive, legislative, and judicial. The executive branch is composed of the RCC and the president, who chairs it. The RCC is the supreme body in the state (article 37), invested with the power to elect the chairman of the council, who becomes the president of the republic; select new members of the RCC from the regional command of the Ba'ath Party (article 38); promulgate laws and decrees (article 42); and conclude peace, approve the budget, and exercise many related powers (article 43). The president is the commander in chief of the armed forces, and he exercises power through a council of ministers whom he appoints (articles 57 and 58). The national assembly (articles 47–56) was not formed until 1980, when the first elections for it were held. Since that time, elections have been held every four years. The judiciary (articles 62–63) consists of civil, criminal, religious, and specific courts, and all judges are appointed by the president.

Iraqi Foreign Policy since Independence

Iraq's foreign policy has been polarized on two axes since early in the twentieth century. The first axis concerns Iraq's relations with other Arab states, chiefly Egypt and Syria. The second is the Great Power axis, first with Britain until the 1950s and then with the United States and the Soviet Union during the cold war. While the move from the thoroughly British-oriented policies of the monarchy to the nonaligned policies of the republican era represented the rejection of client state status prominent internationally in the nonaligned movement in the 1950s and 1960s, the inter-Arab and Great Power influences have remained strong just the same.

The Monarchical Period

Before the revolution of 14 July 1958, Iraq's foreign policy was tied closely to that of Britain. Nuri al-Sa'id, the guiding spirit of the government, was conservative, pro-western, and against the socialist bloc. This orientation and Nuri's concern with the prevention of rapid social revolution in Iraq placed the state in opposition to Egyptian policies. The opposition of the monarchy to Nasser's revolutionary regime and to the Pan-Arab nationalist ideology of Nasserism led to the formation of the Arab Hashemite Federation between Iraq and Jordan in 1958, when the establishment of the UAR raised the threat of Egyptian hegemony.

The Kassem Regime

After the military coup of 1958, the Kassem regime changed Iraq's foreign policy orientations. Initially Kassem appeared pro-Nasser due to his anti-imperial stance, but conflicts in two areas of policy led to a renewal of the traditional stance taken under the monarchical Iraq. First, there was conflict within the revolutionary government regarding a pro-Nasser policy orientation. This conflict ultimately led to the dismissal of 'Aref and to increased suspicion of pro-Nasserites. This pattern of a warming and then dramatic cooling of relations with Egypt repeated itself several times in the following ten years. Second, the growing friendship of the Kassem regime with the USSR led Nasser, who was at odds with the Soviets at the time, to suspect Soviet aims in the Middle East.

Kassem's most notable impact in foreign affairs was the near isolation of Iraq from its neighbors and, indeed, from the entire international community, with UAR–Iraqi relations being the first fatality. From the time of 'Abd al-Salam 'Aref's fall in September 1958, relations between the two states began to decline, and they were finally severed in March 1959. Iraq's relations with Iran also deteriorated in 1959. In a treaty of 5 July 1937, Iraq had recognized Iranian sovereignty over certain roads on the east side of the Shatt al-'Arab. In December 1959, Iraq demanded the return of these roads, Iran refused to accept these demands, and relations between the two states became strained. Jordan had broken relations with Iraq after the 1958 coup and had abandoned the Arab Federation in August of the same year. In October 1960, however, relations improved and Jordan formally recognized the Kassem regime. Road, post, and telegraph contacts were resumed between the two countries, leading to the two states restoring normal diplomatic relations in December. Iraq became even further isolated in 1961 when, in late June, Kuwait became independent and a few days later Iraq laid claim to its small oil-rich neighbor. The claim was based on Kuwait's status as part of the Ottoman *villayet* of Basra in the nineteenth century. The Kuwaitis appealed for aid from the United Kingdom when Iraq made threatening military movements, and the British responded by landing troops in Kuwait. The UN Security Council met to consider the situation, and the United States, Britain, Saudi Arabia, Iran, Jordan, and the UAR supported Kuwaiti sovereignty. On 12 July the Arab League also voted to support Kuwait with an Arab force,[8] allowing the British to begin withdrawing their troops on 19 July. When Kuwait was admitted to the Arab League on 20 July, Iraq boycotted its meetings. The Saudi Arabian, UAR, Sudanese, Jordanian, and Tunisian governments sent a token force of 3,300 troops to Kuwait two months later, which helped by symbolically deterring Iraq from pursuing any military action. In retaliation for their support and recognition of Kuwait, Iraq formally severed relations with Jordan, Japan, Iran, Lebanon, the United States, and Tunisia in 1962. Finally, the Kurdish rebellion, which began in 1960, led to Iraqi charges of Turkish complicity with the Kurds in August 1962 and the withdrawal of the Turkish ambassador on 23 August, completing Iraq's regional and international isolation.

East-West Relations

Within a few hours after the 14 July 1958 coup, Kassem announced that the new republic's foreign policy would be based on neutralism and nonalignment. Of course, the most immediate ramification of this policy concerned the Baghdad Pact. Although Iraq did not formally withdraw from the pact until 24 March 1959, it did not actually participate in the affairs of the alliance after July 1958. By August 1958, the Kassem regime had been recognized by most states, including the United States and Britain, and had, in accordance with its neutralist policy, established relations with the Soviet Union and the People's Republic of China, as well as with other Communist states. The revolution witnessed many commercial, technological, and cultural agreements with the socialist bloc. A major technical and economic cooperation agreement was signed with the USSR in March 1959. This agreement provided for the Soviet Union to extend a loan as well as the engineering and technical staff to build factories in Iraq. Despite Britain's announcement in May 1959 of its intention to provide Iraq with arms and military aircraft, Iraq withdrew from the sterling monetary bloc in June and refused offers of U.S. military aid. For the duration of the Kassem regime (July 1958–February 1963), Iraq continued to expand technical, political, economic, and cultural relations with the socialist bloc while relations with the western bloc continued to cool.

The Ba'ath Regimes

After the coup d'état of 8 February 1963, the new Ba'ath government immediately initiated a foreign policy aimed at reestablishing Iraq in the mainstream of Pan-Arab politics in accordance with Ba'ath ideology. A government spokesman announced that Iraq would seek friendlier relations with those Arab states antagonized by Kassem, and Iraq returned to the Arab League on 16 February when it attended a league meeting, the first time it had done so since 20 July 1961. A friendlier attitude was also adopted toward Kuwait, with the new government renouncing the Kassem claim to Kuwaiti territory. Nasser's government was among the first to recognize the new regime, and on 14 March President 'Aref spoke in favor of a UAR-Syria-Iraq union. A tripartite conference held in Cairo supported the idea. The official announcement of a projected union came on 17 April, and the Iraqi cabinet and Revolutionary Command Council approved the agreement. However, the Iraqi cabinet reshuffle in May, a move that ousted non-Ba'ath members from that body, once again foreshadowed serious strains in UAR-Iraqi relations.

Although the ideal of unity continued to dominate political discourse, it appeared evident that the consolidation of Ba'ath rule was being placed above the formation of a Pan-Arab union.

By late summer the two Ba'ath regimes of Syria and Iraq had moved closer together and away from the UAR. On 2 September a joint communiqué announced closer Iraqi-Syrian cooperation in several areas, especially defense, and in the following month a supreme defense council was formed by the two states. Meanwhile, relations with the UAR grew very strained, and the Arab news media in Damascus, Baghdad, and Cairo began making charges and countercharges. It is interesting to note that the Ba'ath regime's relations with the Soviet Union were also under considerable strain as a result of the Ba'ath purge of local Communists.

When 'Aref took the helm of the government November 1963, he attempted to reverse the trend established by the Ba'ath and once more restored UAR-Iraqi relations. By 26 May 1964 a joint presidency council with a secretariat in Cairo had been formed between Iraq and the UAR. On 16 October 1964, plans for a unified political command between the two countries were made known, and the following December the actual creation of such a command was announced. But the seemingly perpetual oscillation of UAR-Iraqi affairs proved to be too entrenched for even so professed a Nasserite as 'Aref. In July 1965 the inevitable pendulum began its swing back as the pro-Nasser ministers resigned from 'Aref's cabinet and relations between the two states began to deteriorate once again.

However, despite the oscillation, some improvements in Iraq's foreign affairs were made. The Kuwait question was resolved, and trade agreements with Kuwait were reached in February and again in the autumn of 1964. Relations with Iran, tense because of border conflicts and the Kurdish problem, improved with the decreased activity along the Iraq-Iran border after June 1966. Agreement was reached with Tehran on a number of issues, and a cultural and trade agreement was projected. Iraqi forces, although in scant numbers, participated in the Arab-Israeli war of June 1967, and as a direct result of the war Iraq broke diplomatic relations with the United States, relations that would not be resumed again until November 1984.

The 1968 Ba'athist Coup

Within the Ba'ath Party itself, internal splits surfaced, undermining its stated desire of creating a single Arab party under one leader. The first split in the ranks of the Ba'ath occurred in 1966 when the Syrian Ba'ath Party expelled Michel 'Aflaq, the founder of the Ba'ath Party, who subsequently fled to Iraq. In Iraq, the Ba'ath Party took power in 1968, at a time when Ba'ath unity itself was in crisis, arising from internal divisions. A few years back, 'Aref had outmaneuvered other factions in the party in an internal power struggle, essentially because of the same problem of internal splits. Clearly missing in the agenda of the Ba'ath Party was an alternative ideology to Pan-Arab nationalists, since they had rejected the classical dogmas and their propagation of Arab nationalism and Arab unity and were offering little direction in the governance of the state. Hence, the Ba'ath's main preoccupation became the extent to which they could make use of conditions to consolidate their hold on power.[9] Immediately after the overthrow of 'Abd al-Rahman 'Aref on 17 July 1968, the Ba'ath Party removed two of the four officers who had carried out the coup, Col. 'Abd al-Rahman Ibrahim al-Daud and Col. 'Abd al-Razzaq al-Naif. The all-powerful Revolutionary Command Council (RCC) was composed of five persons under the chairmanship of Ahmad Hasan al-Bakr, the president of the country as well as the secretary-general of the regional leadership (RL) of the Ba'ath Party.

The Ba'ath regime that took power in July 1968 had difficulties with inter-Arab politics, particularly with Syria and the UAR. The enmity among these governments was not overt, however, because of the desire to maintain at least a facade of unity in the face of the prevailing Arab-Israeli crisis. The new government also had some success in creating better relations with Iraq's non-Arab neighbors, Iran and Turkey. Within the international sphere, the government took a strong anti-western stand because of the Arab-Israeli crisis, although Iraqi-Soviet relations were also somewhat strained as a result of the Ba'ath regime's conflicts with both the Kurds and the Iraqi Communist Party; however, this relationship was soon to improve.

In May 1969 the most significant aspect of Iraqi-Soviet relations was initiated when Gen. Hardan al-Tikriti, Iraq's defense minister, visited Moscow. Huge military aid and arms purchases were secured in addition to the establishment of economic and technical cooperation programs culminating on 4 July 1969, when Iraq and the Soviet Union concluded new agreements. On 3 March 1970, a permanent Soviet-Iraqi committee was formed to supervise economic cooperation between the two countries. More than a dozen arrangements dealing with a variety of technical, cultural, and other matters were signed, establishing a formal framework for a strong relationship between the two states. Significant ties between Iraq and the Soviet Union continued until 1972. On 9 April 1972 Soviet premier Alexei Kosygin visited Baghdad and signed a fifteen-year Treaty of Friendship and Cooperation. The Soviet Union had traditionally supported the Kurdish leadership, but the treaty put an end to this relationship, further isolating the Kurds from international support and allowing Iraq to deal with this important domestic problem without the fear of Soviet support for the Kurdish resistance. Although Soviet-Iraqi relations were close, the Iraqis lacked any ideological commitment to the Soviet cause. For Iraq, a close relationship with the Soviets was a pragmatic policy that did not stand in the way of Iraq's desire to forge economic and trade ties with the West. Iraq pursued closer economic ties with Western Europe, but the Arab-Israeli conflict repeatedly interfered, especially in relation to any substantive ties with the United States.

The first two agreements that the European Economic Council (EEC) signed with Israel in 1964 and 1970, respectively, heightened the concern of the Arab bloc with respect to the EEC's position in the Arab-Israeli conflict. Arab states became even more critical of the EEC when a third agreement between the EEC and Israel was concluded in 1975. This agreement made Israel the first non-European state to be accepted by the EEC free-trade area as an associate member. The pro-Israeli leanings that characterized the EEC's policy on the conflict aroused Iraq's concern over the implications of dramatic increases in oil prices over a short period. Iraq believed that high oil prices would strengthen the United States' relationship with Western Europe and Japan rather than weaken them. Thus, Iraq feared that the Arab states that boycotted the West would be alienated by U.S. pressure on its allies, the EEC and Japan. As a result, Iraq pushed for a strengthening of the Euro-Arab dialogue in order to seek a European policy distinct and separate from that of the United States. Iraq argued that fostering good relations with Western Europe, coupled with a strengthening of the relationship with developing countries, would be in the best interest of the Arab world. Indeed, the rise in the amount of Arab petrodollars seemed to have propelled this expectation. An improved economic relationship with the West was characteristic of the oil boom period. Thus, in many ways, Iraq began to move closer to the West in the 1980s. However, this did not completely sever Iraq from the Soviet Union because the Soviets remained Iraq's main international supporter, weapons supplier, and commercial creditor. Not until the Iran-Iraq war and the required buildup of the Iraqi armed forces would Iraq shift its relations with the West onto friendlier ground.

As the 1970s began, all the members of the RCC were career army officers with military educations. Over time, however, systematic purges diminished the role of the military in the highest organs of the state, paving the way for a new generation of party functionaries whose main credentials were loyalty to the party apparatus. In reality, loyalty to the leader remained the fundamental criterion for filling any position. The actions of the Ba'ath Party were mostly self-serving, aiming at the further consolidation of Baʿath power. In the power hierarchy, the RCC and its chairman became predominant, and effective decisions were adopted only by the RCC executive. Even if they were allocated ministerial positions, other parties failed to significantly influence national policies, as the Baʿath Party hierarchy became predominant. Opposition groups and parties who worked with, or within, the government found themselves in the awkward situation of being accomplices in the implementation of totalitarianism and the subsequent degradation of Iraqi civil society. This was clearly the case when the Baʿath, invoking laws forbidding any activity outside the framework of the Patriotic Unity Front, forced the Communists to dissolve their youth, student, and women's organizations and transform themselves into mere party branches.[10] Even the army suffered immensely as the Baʿath Party intensified its power consolidation activities.[11] Army officers were purged if their loyalty to Saddam Hussein was questioned. The position of the military in the state was further weakened with the continued buildup of the state police and security apparatus. On 16 July 1979, President Bakr stepped down from power, allowing for the ascendancy of Saddam Hussein, who quickly followed with a large-scale purge that included many army officers and party officials for allegedly plotting to overthrow the government. The assault on the military was relentlessly pursued, increasing its subordination to the authority of the Baʿath Party. Many of the changes were implemented from outside through a party military bureau that paralleled the Defense Ministry.

The party propaganda machine had embarked on a campaign to belittle the achievements of the military since the time the Baʿath came to power. In its ninth Regional Congress, the party rewrote its own history, downplaying the role of army officers in the Baʿath coup while according more credit to the civilian Baʿath members.[12] Even when the war with Iran was being waged, the campaign prevailed, as the media highlighted the illustrious performance of some politically sanctioned officers, while the coverage of military command decisions made by professional soldiers was limited. Instead, Saddam Hussein and his loyal civilian clique in the RCC and RL, now dressed in military uniform bearing special insignia to symbolize their supremacy over the military, assumed the credit for victories in the course of the war with Iran.

Dismantling the Iraqi State: The Baʿath under Saddam Hussein

From the time the Baʿath rose to power in July 1968, they systematically set out to bolster their hold over Iraqi politics, and over time the party evolved into a one-person dictatorship. The Baʿath Party hierarchy facilitated the transformation and the unremorseful use of various repressive measures of state-sponsored terror, and repeatedly removed opposition to the government through violence. Eventually even the role of the party was greatly diminished, serving only to mobilize the public behind Saddam, who increasingly stood in clear and unassailable authority above party, state, and the people of Iraq.

Emerging during the Ba'ath coup of 1968, Saddam Hussein, who was already a powerful civilian in the hierarchy of the party, skillfully and ruthlessly consolidated his position, gradually ascending the power hierarchy to the apex of Iraqi political life. He succeeded in doing this because of his early control of the internal security apparatus of the party and his ability to expand it to become an extensive network for the suppression of any dissent to his leadership within both the party and Iraqi society. In a carefully planned shuffle of the highest institutions of the party, the RCC and the RL in November 1969, all the members of the RL were incorporated into the RCC, increasing its membership by ten. Saddam Hussein, who was by then the deputy secretary-general of the Regional Leadership, rose to the position of deputy chairman of the RCC. During this time, Saddam relentlessly tilted the balance of power in his favor through the systematic removal of his opponents from positions of power and their replacement by those loyal to him, predominantly immediate family and clan members.[13] Many opponents lost their lives at the hands of Saddam's security forces as he used the tools of party and state to ascend the state hierarchy. The most severe purge came immediately after Saddam became president, following Bakr's resignation in 1979. Five RCC members and scores of army officers and party officials were eliminated. Gradually this calculated ouster of potential rivals deprived the party of most of its veteran cadre who had led it through its rise to power. Ultimately, the members of the RCC, the highest organs of the party, and the government were Saddam's docile and trusted subordinates.[14] By 1985, virtually all major cabinet members were his relatives, and his brothers, cousins, sons, and in-laws occupied all security and high military posts. By 1979, Saddam Hussein was the president of the Republic of Iraq, chairman of the Revolutionary Command Council, secretary-general of the Regional Leadership (Command), and commander of the armed forces.

Building the Instruments of Oppression

To retain his hold on power, Saddam Hussein relied on an extensive and brutal security apparatus he personally created as his vehicle to power. Large sectors of Iraq society, the military, the opposition, and others witnessed the brutality of the secret police firsthand. Even the Ba'ath Party, with its members spread into all corners of Iraqi society, served as an instrument of control. These instruments of control and oppression spread fear among the people, which in turn sustains the one-person dictatorship. The important organizations that make up the security apparatuses of the state are Saddam's Jihaz al-Himaya al-Khas (Special Protection Apparatus), Jihaz al-Mukhabarat al-'Amma (General Intelligence Apparatus), Al-Istikhbarat al-'Askariya (Military Intelligence), Mudiriyat al-Amn al-Amma (General Security Directorate), and Maktab al-Amn al-Qawmi (Bureau for National Security). Each of these employs a vast array of informers (mu'tamanin) who infiltrate various institutions and sectors of society. Coercion, blackmail, financial inducements, and other privileges play an important part in recruiting and retaining informers. Since most of the informers arise from impoverished backgrounds, they are easily enticed by the generous privileges provided by the regime. The workings of the Jihaz al-Himaya al-Khas, Saddam's special protection force, clearly bear this out. The creation of Saddam's praetorian guard (Fidayeen Saddam) owes much of its success to the fact that "it does not rely on ideological indoctrination. Rather, it follows the same path taken by Saddam Hussein and most other influential personalities in the regime since they emerged from their impoverished home towns looking for someone to give them a humble job in Baghdad."[15]

The feeling of deep indebtedness to Saddam Hussein personally as well as the fear of losing their newfound comfortable positions created a strong bond of loyalty to the leader and his regime. Security personnel from different ethnic groups place their fate in the survival of the regime, creating comradeship. Although the recruitment of the secret agents is diverse, Saddam's close relatives head the higher echelons of the security apparatus to maintain control.

Suppression of Dissent

Saddam's repression of opposition activities has been a cause of concern not only for the Iraqi people but also for the international community. However, during Iraq's war with Iran, protests against the violation of human rights by western governments were muted. Iraq was looked upon favorably by the western powers, as it was seen as the bulwark opposing the revolutionary and fundamentalist Islamist policies of Iran. The crimes committed by the state security organs against the Iraqi people are monumental and have been extensively covered by human rights organizations the world over. Since the Ba'ath assumed power in the country, they have systematically eliminated any dissent against their rule, even brutally massacring entire communities to secure their hold on power, as was the case when poison gas was used against Kurds in 1987.

The government carries out torture, extrajudicial detention, disappearances, and murders. In their war against the Kurdish guerrillas, random attacks on civilians cause unnecessary loss of life, beyond the deliberate and indiscriminate terrorist killings of the military and security forces. Over 6,000 people, many of whom were civilian, were reported executed or killed in aerial bombings on civilian targets in northern Iraq during 1988.[16] Prohibited groups include the Shi'a Khomeini–styled al-Da'wa al-Islamiyya (Islamic Call), the Iraqi Communist Party (ICP), the Kurdish Democratic Party (KDP), the Patriotic Union of Kurdistan (PUK), the Kurdistan Socialist Party–Iraq (KSP–I), and the Kurdistan Popular Democratic Party (KPDP). All political activities that fall outside Saddam's party and any political activities that are not directed by the regime are considered subversive.

The repressive activities of Saddam's regime have only intensified during the genocidal conditions that have existed following the 1991 Gulf war. The March 1991 popular uprising (intifada) against the tyranny of Saddam Hussein was successfully crushed by government forces, despite promises of protection from the international community, which had initially encouraged the revolt. Large numbers of people retreated into the southern marshes to escape reprisal attacks by government forces. There they were encircled and subjected to constant assaults by the Iraqi army and state security forces, despite the close proximity of large western forces in Kuwait and Saudi Arabia. Under the precept of relieving the heavy bombardment of whole villages by Iraqi planes, a joint United States and British operation code-named Operation Southern Watch, imposing an indefinite no-fly zone south of the 32d parallel, was established in 1991. Also following the failed uprising against Saddam Hussein, another allied protected zone was created in the north and northeastern parts of Iraq to protect the Kurds. U.S. and British military flights enforced the ban over this area from bases on Turkish territory and from the Gulf.

Ba'ath controls extend beyond state terror and include extensive limitations upon freedom of movement. All linkages to the outside world are controlled by government agencies, including telephone, postal services, Internet connections, and even radio transmissions. Furthermore, any Iraqi citizens wishing to leave for business or personal travel must acquire exit visas, which allow the government to monitor the movement of any citizen and which have proven to be prohibitively expensive as fees amount to ten months' salary for a university professor or other members of the senior civil service. Also, Iraqi government policy has forced residents not indigenous to Baghdad to return to their ancestral homes elsewhere in Iraq in an ongoing process that amounts to the tribalization of Iraqi society.[17] In 1998 alone, some 4,000 families were forced to leave Baghdad, and laws were enacted restricting owner-ship of property in the Baghdad region to citizens born in the city and its environs, including Saddam Hussein's home village of Tikrit.[18] The Iraqi government also pursued strategies to depopulate the southern marshes through forced relocation after the 1991 *intifada*. The institu-tion of a massive drainage program has distorted the ecosystem of the marshland area, and such policies increasingly have rendered the marsh incapable of sustaining the population who has lived in the area for millennia, as water from the marshlands has been diverted to the irrigated regions east of the Tigris River.

The Iran-Iraq War (September 1980–July 1988)

The beginning of the Iran-Iraq war in 1980 led to a noticeable adjust-ment in Iraq's foreign policy on both the regional and international lev-els. Regionally, the war dramatically altered the balance of power. Before the war, Iraq's basic policy was disdainful of the area's conservative monarchies. However, because of the pressure the Iraqi regime found itself under once the war had begun, it sought the financial aid of those very same monarchies. Both Libya and Syria supported Iran in the war, further facilitating an Iraqi turn to the conservatives. For their part, the conservative regimes were more than willing to support the Iraqi effort given the effects that an Iranian victory would have had in the region. Saudi Arabia and the Gulf states fully supported Iraq logistically, finan-cially, and militarily, support which was vital to the maintenance of the Iraqi war effort. Jordan and Egypt contributed volunteer forces to Iraq despite the fact that only a few years earlier Iraq was an avowed adver-sary of both states. Even Kuwait, which had been threatened by Iraqi claims to its territories after independence and which had squabbled with Iraq over control of disputed oil fields on their common border, fully backed Iraq and was instrumental in gaining western support.

The war was caused by a wide range of interconnected factors—religion, nationalism, ideology, and geography—and it dragged on for eight years. While the *casus belli* of the conflict was control over the Shatt al-'Arab waterway, a strategically and economically important access route to the Gulf, its causes were historically rooted in age-old patterns of ethnic, religious, cultural, and territorial rivalry and ideo-logically rooted in the contemporary political dynamics between Iran's revolutionary Islamic regime and Iraq's secular Arab nationalist regime. Further, the role played by western governments and the international arms trade in building up the Iraqi war machine, in an effort to contain Iran and secure hefty profits, prolonged the conflict and became a major factor leading to the second Gulf war in 1991.[19] At the outset of the war, Iraq scored rapid military gains and occupied a large area of Iranian territory. It was only a year later, in September 1981, that Iranian forces, vastly outnumbering the Iraqis, were able to counterattack in strength and sufficiently undermine the Iraqi position. By the end of June 1982, the Iranians had forced Iraq to withdraw from Iranian territory, and by July 1982, Iranian forces were invading Iraq.

The Iranians mounted a number of offensives in southern Iraq aimed at cutting Basra (Iraq's second largest city and only port) off from Baghdad. Iranian forces were never completely successful. Iraq had superior weaponry, innovative defensive tactics, chemical weapons, and access to sophisticated American intelligence. Iraq also attempted to force Iran to accept a cease-fire or some kind of UN-sponsored settlement by attacking Iran with long-range missiles and artillery as well as its air force. Known as "the war of the cities," the heavy shelling and daily air raids on major civilian targets created a great deal of moral indignation and established a sense of bitterness and antipathy between the two adversaries. Further, Iraqi attempts at cutting Iran's economic lifeline centered around shifting the focus of the fighting away from land battles toward a maritime conflict in what came to be seen as the "tanker war"—a tactic to prevent Iran from exporting its oil through the Strait of Hormuz at the southern end of the Gulf. It quickly internationalized the war and brought the United States and the Soviet Union into the conflict, as the superpowers attempted to keep the Gulf open for international shipping. By 1988, the economic and human costs of the war became too much for both combatants to bear, and a UN-sponsored cease-fire was reached on 19 July 1988.

Little had been accomplished in the course of the war by either state. The question of sovereignty over the Shatt al-'Arab had not been settled, the Kurdish issue had been rekindled, and the levels of casualties and destruction severely undercut both combatants' socioeconomic infrastructure, hampering development programs with a decade of setbacks. Estimates put the number of war dead at 367,000 (262,000 Iranians and 105,000 Iraqi); with some 700,000 injured, many badly; casualty figures totaled over 1 million.[20] Iran officially announced figures of 123,220 dead with another 60,711 missing in action, while Baghdad claimed a higher figure of some 800,000 Iranians killed. The cost of the war is estimated to be in excess of U.S.$1 trillion.[21]

Furthermore, the unsettled nature of the peace and the instability created by such devastation caused tremendous stresses on the regional state system. This ultimately played a major role in the outbreak of the 1990 Iraqi invasion of Kuwait.

Economic Impact of the Iran-Iraq War

Between 1970 and 1980, the Iraqi economy was buoyant, with the principal economic indicators showing tremendous growth and potential.[22] Booming oil revenues resulting from increased crude prices was the primary reason for this economic performance. At the beginning of the Iran-Iraq war, Iranian bombardment destroyed Iraqi offshore oil terminals, slashing oil exports by 72 percent, from 3.281 million barrels per day to 0.926 million barrels per day.[23] This proved a severe blow to the Iraqi economy, as oil contributed 95 percent of its export earnings. In addition, the closure of the port at Basra on the Persian Gulf forced Iraq to export oil overland through pipelines across both Turkey and Jordan at an increased production cost. Complicating matters further, Syria closed the Iraqi pipeline running across its territory in 1982 in an effort to support Iran. Table 6.1 reflects the key economic indicators before the Iran-Iraq war.

As the war progressed with no end in sight, the economic condition of Iraq became more precarious. Central authorities in Baghdad sacrificed developmental spending in 1982.[24] Although the war seriously impacted Iraq's economy, the nature of the regime itself was largely

TABLE 6.1
Principal Economic Indicators for Iraq,
1970–1980

Indicators	Percentage
Growth in GDP	11.7
Government consumption	13.6
Private consumption	13.2
Gross fixed capital formation	27.0
Imports of goods and services	22.5
Industrial activity	10.2
Manufacturing	13.4
Construction	28.4
Transport and communication	19.0

Source: Abbas Alnasrawi, *The Economy of Iraq: Oil, Wars, Destruction of Development, and Prospects, 1950–2010* (Westport, Conn.: Greenwood Press, 1994), 80.

responsible for the economic devastation it caused. To create a false sense of normality while the war was raging, prestige projects were initiated; these were shelved when they became impossible to complete. Furthermore, the buildup of the Iraqi military machine, even with foreign sponsorship, consumed much of the country's resources. Arsenals of military hardware claimed a substantial proportion of the annual budget, and the maintenance of a large standing army deprived the economy of a productive labor force.[25] The agricultural sector was particularly hard hit as many rural farmers were drafted into the military or hired to fill urban jobs left vacant by those at the front.[26]

Throughout the war, Saddam Hussein relied on support from the international community. He acquired the advanced security technologies for internal repression and the advanced weapons technologies for waging war against his neighbors from Britain, France, (West) Germany, the United States, the Soviet Union/Russia, and other countries.[27] Although this support varied, depending on the unsettled sands of international diplomacy, it allowed the Iraqi dictator to acquire advanced weapons systems, training, and support for what was purported to have become the world's fourth largest military service. The military hardware and training also supported one of the most advanced state-security apparatuses, which Saddam Hussein used to further consolidate domestic power and challenge regional stability. This access to western technology extended to the acquisition of weapons of mass destruction, including the facilities with which to domestically produce the materials for nuclear, biological, and chemical agents and the delivery vehicles with which to convey its new arsenal.[28]

Iraq's pursuit of such a program was publicized in the 1980s by the mass media. This included an Israeli attack (Operation Babylon) on an Iraqi nuclear reactor at the Osirak plant in 1982; the confiscation of materials being shipped to Iraq—parts and plans for nuclear centrifuges—in September 1981 while in transit from Great Britain; and the mysterious deaths of Egyptian physicist Yahya Mashad, who was allegedly deeply involved in Iraq's nuclear program, and the Canadian engineer Gerald Bull, who allegedly designed a "supergun" for Iraq capable of launching payloads across the entire region.[29] This buildup, despite repeated public exposure, went ahead virtually unopposed by western governments.

The regime staved off the total collapse of the economy by borrowing currency from foreign lenders and through the support of the Gulf monarchies that were afraid of the menace that an Iranian victory would pose to their own survival. To augment the oil-exporting capacity of Iraq following the closure of its main port on the Persian Gulf,[30] Saudi

Arabia allowed the construction of a pipeline across its territory to the Red Sea. On 8 September 1989, the new pipeline opened, boosting the country's export capacity by 50 percent to 3.35 million barrels a day.[31] By 1991, Iraq had received loans totalling U.S.$86 billion (Arab Gulf countries, especially Saudi Arabia and Kuwait, U.S.$40 billion; western governments and banks, U.S.$35 billion; Soviet Union and other Eastern European governments, U.S.$11 billion).[32]

At the end of the war, Iraq insisted that the U.S.$40 billion owed to Arab Gulf countries was supplied as assistance to help it fight the war with Iran and not as a loan. As for western creditors, France, Italy, and West Germany rescheduled their debts in 1989, pushing forward Iraq's debt repayment.

In addition to the debt problem, the country's economy was burdened with large imports of staple and luxury consumer goods. Iraq's major trading partners—Japan, Italy, France, West Germany, and Turkey—secured a long-term loan of U.S.$20 billion for Iraq. In addition, the United Kingdom, Australia, and even the United States granted Iraq substantial agricultural credits. In 1989, "oil revenues were $15 billion—not enough to pay for $11 billion of civilian imports (including $3 billion of food), $5 billion of arms, $3 billion of debt repayment and $1 billion of transfers of foreign workers. Iraqis faced 50 percent inflation, empty pantries and a shortage of jobs for soldiers demobilized from the war with Iran. The gap between rhetoric and reality was widening, as foreign creditors balked at further loans."[33]

Indeed, Iraq's economy was left in tatters. An increase of oil revenue was the only recourse, but even this production was hampered by low prices for oil on the world market. Lack of compliance with the oil production quotas allocated by OPEC on the part of some members was partly to blame for the fall in prices. The overproducers increasingly came under fierce attacks from Iraq, particularly Kuwait and the United Arab Emirates, for the oil glut that depressed oil prices in 1990 and hampered Iraqi efforts by increasing production.[34] On a rather unsuccessful trip to some Arab Gulf countries in mid-1990, Iraqi Deputy Prime Minister Saadoun Hammadi pointed out that oil prices would rise to U.S.$18 (a barrel) if there was a cut of 1.5 million barrels (a day) by Kuwait and the Emirates.[35] Saddam Hussein claimed that Gulf countries, instigated by the United States, were conspiring to keep down prices through overproduction. The standoff between Iraq and Kuwait over production and pricing escalated, and fearing an Iraqi military onslaught, Kuwait put its armed forces on a state of alert in July 1990.[36] Attempts to resolve the disagreement diplomatically failed, and on 2 August 1990, Iraq invaded Kuwait.

The Gulf War (1990–1991)

On 2 August 1990, Iraqi forces invaded Kuwait, formally annexing it six days later on 8 August 1990 as the nineteenth province of Iraq. A few short days after the occupation of Kuwait, the United States deployed forces to Saudi Arabia, forces that were followed within the next three months by those of other countries in the American-led coalition against Iraq. Between 2 August and 28 November 1990, the Security Council passed eleven resolutions to sanction Iraq for its 2 August 1990 occupation of Kuwait. The sanctions ranged in coercive capacity from condemnation to economic embargo. Resolutions 661 and 665 were the most overtly coercive of the resolutions. UN Security Council Resolution 661 imposed stringent sanctions on all trade to and from Iraq; and 665 permitted states to use limited naval force to ensure compliance with the economic sanctions, including the right to inspect cargoes. All trading and financial dealings with Iraq were halted by UN member states. Turkey and Saudi Arabia, through which 90 percent of Iraqi oil passed for export, complied with the sanctions dictates, effectively stopping the export of Iraqi oil. Within the first month after the imposition of the oil embargo, Iraq suffered a loss of over U.S.$1.5 billion in potential oil revenues.[37] Saudi Arabia increased its oil production to compensate for the shortfall in world oil production caused by the embargo on Iraq's exports. Loans and other financial aid to Iraq were halted. Iraqi overseas assets, estimated at between U.S.$4 billion and U.S.$6 billion were frozen.[38] The toll on an economy already facing major difficulties was very high indeed.

On 29 November 1990, the Security Council passed Resolution 678, which authorized military action against Iraq. On 17 January 1991, the Gulf war, code-named Operation Desert Storm, was initiated with the air bombardment of Iraq. Coalition forces dropped some 88,000 tons of bombs on Iraq, the equivalent of one Hiroshima-size atomic bomb a week for seven successive weeks.[39] On 28 February 1991, the war ended with President Bush's order for the cessation of offensive operations. Dubbed the 1,100-hour war by the media (*Frontline*, 1998), the Gulf war was directed by the Pentagon. The U.S. Air Force, cast in the leading role, played center stage for the first 1,000 hours. Air superiority was established in the initial salvos of battle, and thereafter coalition control of the airways was unopposed. The ground war lasted for only 100 hours as Iraqi ground forces, cut off from supply lines and communications for weeks, were quickly overcome in the ground offensive initiated on 24 February 1991.

The Gulf war was dominated by high technology, and it served as a testing ground for the high-tech weaponry developed by the western powers. Table 6.2 provides an overview of the weaponry used.

The most intensive and sustained bombing campaign in history was unleashed against a population of about 23 million people. More explosives were dumped on Iraq in forty-three days than were dropped on Europe during the entire Second World War. Table 6.3 identifies selected munitions employed in Operation Desert Storm.

The destruction of Iraq's economic and social infrastructure caused by the airborne bombardment of the country resulted in the complete devastation of Iraqi society. Apart from the inevitable loss of lives in both the military and civilian sectors, bombing targets included water treatment and sanitation stations, fertilizer plants, power plants, oil facilities, hospitals, bridges, storage facilities, and industrial infrastructure. The direct human cost of the war, and the *intifada* that followed, has been estimated at between 94,000 and 281,000 dead Iraqi soldiers and 100,000 civilians.[40]

Social conditions of the populace rapidly deteriorated in the wake of, first, the imposition of the harsh and comprehensive economic sanctions and, second, the infrastructural damage caused by western bombardment. The cutting off of virtually all imports resulted in a level of scarcity unknown in Iraq, as well as an unprecedented hike in the price of basic commodities such as foodstuffs, medical supplies, and replacement parts for machinery.[41] Government-maintained ration shops, although providing insufficient nutrient and caloric levels by pre-sanction standards and UN requirements, were nonetheless successful at keeping people from starving, but little more. What portion of Iraq's infrastructure, environment, and people the 1991 six-week bombing campaign did not devastate or destroy were left at the mercy of the sanctions regime. The sanctions were exacerbated by the extensive scope of the bombing campaign. U.S. military planners had initially identified 57 sites in Iraq as strategic targets, but this number rose to more than 700 in the air campaign. This included the civilian infrastructure of Iraqi society. The postwar sanctions regime magnified the destruction, as they prevented the repair or rebuilding of facilities damaged in the allied bombing.

Originally imposed solely to affect the withdrawal of the Iraqi military from Kuwait, the sanctions were maintained in an effort to implement the terms of the cease-fire negotiated after the defeat of the Iraqi forces. This linkage to "a complex set of conditions where Iraqi compliance could be endlessly discussed, disputed and questioned" has allowed the embargo to continue, seemingly without end.[42] Sanctions have seen

TABLE 6.2

Weaponry Used during the Gulf War

Weapons	Description	Performance in Gulf War
Aircraft Systems		
AH-64 Apache	Designed for an attack role. Armed with anti-tank missiles or serial rockets	A ground-attack aircraft; tanks and fighting vehicles were its principal targets.
B-52 Stratofortress	Carries up to 60,000 pounds of bombs.	Conducted round-the-clock carpet bombing. In addition to high-explosive bombs, the B-52s saturated Iraqi positions with anti-personnel and anti-armor bombs.
E-3 AWACS	Most sophisticated airborne command post ever designed.	Formed an interlocking network of command posts able to manage the hundreds of warplanes.
F-117A Stealth	Radar-evading tactical fighter can approach targets undetected by radar and unleash HARM air-to-surface missiles and laser-guided bombs.	Logged nearly 1,300 combat sorties while the 37th Tactical Fighter Wing Provisional and its 42 stealth fighters represented just 2.5 percent of all allied fighter and attack aircraft in the Gulf. Flying 6,905 combat flying hours. Delivered over 2,000 tons of precision-guided ordinance with a hit rate of better than 80 percent.
E-8C JSTARS	Has the capability to detect, precisely locate, and track thousands of fixed and mobile targets on the ground over an area larger than 20,000 square kilometers from a stand-off distance in excess of 250 kilometers.	Used for the first time in the Gulf War for battlefield surveillance. Provided combat commanders with near real-time information on various targets, including moving targets, in all weather conditions.
Drones (RPVs)	Remote-controlled, pilotless planes act as aerial spies.	Used as long-distance eyes for battleship guns and for aerial patrols along the Saudi-Kuwait border; picked out targets for bombing runs by B-52s or F0-15s; used to collect mapping information to steer Tomahawk cruise missiles to their targets; provided TV coverage for postbombing damage assessments.

Ground Systems		
M-1A1 Abrams	World's top battle tank with armor that resists molten-metal shells and a deadly 120-mm cannon.	Principal U.S. heavy tank used in Gulf war. Fires reliably when moving at speed over rough ground, and has infrared vision that proved effective not only at night but also in the dust and smoke of the desert.
MIM-104 Patriot	Tactical Air-Defense Missile System has a radar station to pinpoint incoming rockets and a four-missile launcher.	The Army initially claimed that the Patriot achieved an 80 percent success rate in Saudi Arabia and 50 percent in Israel. Investigations in 1992 revealed that in only 9 percent of cases was there evidence that the Patriots did more than come close to the Scuds.
Munitions		
Tomahawk Missile	Computer-guided missiles fired from U.S. combat vessels carry either 1,000-lb. warheads or a cluster of 166 soda-can sized "boblets" that can be dropped over three targets en route to a fourth.	Desert Storm was the first combat test of the cruise missile system. It also marked the first coordinated Tomahawk and manned-aircraft strike in history: 197 Tomahawks were fired.
Space Systems		
Global Positioning System (GPS)	A satellite-based radio-navigation system providing precise, worldwide, three-dimensional position, velocity, and timing data.	During the Gulf war, 16 GPS satellites provided navigation and positioning data. Gulf war was the first combat use of the system. The GPS made it possible for attackers to shift their attack planes back and forth virtually up to the moment of the attack, since forces using it had no need for fixed markers on the ground.

Source: Frontline, "The Gulf War" (1998) (www.pbs.org).

TABLE 6.3

Selected Munitions Employed in Operation Desert Storm

Munitions	Air Force	Navy	Marine Corps	Total
General Purpose Bombs				
Mk-82 (500lb)	59,884	10,941	6,828	77,653
Mk-83 (1,000lb)		10,125	8,893	19,018
Mk-84 (2,000lb)	10,467	971	751	12,189
Mk-117 (B-52)	43,435			43,435
CBU-52 (fragmentation bomb)	17,831			17,831
CBU-87 (combined effects munition)	10,035			10,035
CBU-89/78 (Gator)	1,105	148	61	1,314
Mk-20 (Rockeye)	5,345	6,814	15,828	27,987
Laser Guided Bombs				
GBU-12 (laser/Mk-82)	4,086	205	202	4,493
Air-to-Surface Missiles				
AGM-114 Hellfire (Ah-64 and AH-1W)	2,876 (Army)	30	159	3,065
AGM-65 All Models (Maverick)	5,255		41	5,296

Source: Frontline, "The Gulf War" (1998) (www.pbs.org).

Note: Selected munitions includes only munitions also employed in the Kuwait theater. In the Iraq theater, other types of laser-guided bombs and air-to-surface missiles were used in addition to those identified above.

Iraqi life expectancy reduced from sixty-eight years (prewar) to forty-seven years by 1992, according to the U.S. Census Bureau.[43] One estimate suggested that in April 1994, the Iraqi government was spending about U.S.$750 million a year, a significant proportion of Iraq's meager export earnings, on providing basic rations in order to prevent mass starvation.[44]

Operation Desert Storm completely destroyed Iraq's social infrastructure but salvaged the political infrastructure of Saddam Hussein's dictatorship. In the immediate aftermath of the war, these appeared as unintended consequences. However, after more than ten years of the stringent sanctions regime imposed by the cease-fire, these appear as latent objectives because the sanctions have served to reinforce both the complex humanitarian crisis initiated by the war and the political infrastructure of the dictatorship. Latent objectives are revealed by their continual reinforcement over time. It is tenable to conclude that these outcomes are integrally related to the policy's objectives. Many have argued that the sanctions regime has constituted a policy of genocide against the Iraqi people.[45] The overt or declared objectives of the sanctions—the removal of Iraqi forces from Kuwait, and the cease-fire agreements requiring Iraq to avoid any weapons of mass destruction programs—are increasingly overwhelmed by the level of destruction, the suffering, and the hopelessness of the Iraqi people.

The combined effects of the comprehensive and long-standing sanctions regime imposed and maintained by the United Nations Security Council, and the devastating infrastructural damage incurred from coalition aerial bombardment during the Gulf war and after, has left Iraqi society far too weak for coherent indigenous opposition to Saddam's rule while he remains in possession of the state security apparatus that propelled him to power. The systematic demonization of Saddam Hussein, beginning in the summer and fall of 1990, legitimizes the persecution of the Iraqi state and, by extension, its citizens. Over 1.2 million Iraqis have died as a direct result of sanctions. This represents about 5 percent of the Iraqi population. As one observer noted, "In American equivalent terms, this would be the entire populations of Los Angeles, Boston, and Washington combined."[46]

One of the most outspoken critics of U.S. policy in Iraq, Geoff Simons, sees the Iraqi regime and its citizens as now being punished not only for the crimes of Saddam's regime but also for any potential transgressions that may be "hidden, disguised, [or] intended."[47] The measure of compliance and damage of the sanctions regime only escalated as the sanctions became dependent on weapons inspection teams. Created in April 1991 by Security Council Resolution 687, the task of the United Nations Special Commission (UNSCOM) was to ensure that Iraq's reportedly abundant chemical, nuclear, and biological weapons were destroyed. In the course of its work, writes chief UN weapons inspector Scott Ritter, UNSCOM teams "reportedly destroyed more than 38,000 chemical weapons, nearly 700 tons of chemical weapon agents, 48 SCUD missiles capable of striking neighboring states, as well as a significant biological weapons plant." Working in tandem with the International Atomic Energy Agency, UNSCOM dismantled the Iraqi nuclear weapons program. Richard Butler, the Australian who headed UNSCOM, was accused of subordinating his disarmament efforts to the CIA and being so close with Washington that he was coordinating team inspections with air strikes in March 1998.[48] In August 1998, Iraq unilaterally suspended monitoring by UNSCOM, forcing its teams to leave Iraq. After efforts to force the reinstatement of UNSCOM failed, the United States and Great Britain initiated several days of intensive bombing raids against Iraq in December 1998. Iraqi sovereignty was further undermined with the imposition of no-fly zones above 36th and below

32d parallels by the United States and Great Britain purportedly to protect the Kurdish and Shiʻa communities in the north and south, respectively, against the depredations of Iraqi air attacks, although ground attacks remain unimpeded. In the Kurdish-controlled northern area, Turkish military forces have made repeated incursions in pursuit of Kurdish Workers' Party (PKK) rebels who are fighting for an independent state in southeastern Turkey.

In spite of the precarious position of Iraq since the Gulf war, the regime of Saddam Hussein has survived. One explanation for the survival of his regime is the lack of a credible alternative. Iraqi opposition groups have for some time been under the trauma of Saddam's ruthless oppression. Repression of the leaders and members of these groups has led to the death of many and the exile of many more. Infiltration of the various groups by the state security apparatus greatly limited the capacity of these organizations to organize within the country. Nevertheless, the Gulf war provided a window of opportunity for the various groups trying to remove Saddam Hussein from power to reactivate their efforts.

The Iraqi opposition to Baʻath rule has four main strands:

1. Kurdish groups: The Kurds are the best organized, but they were weakened by the Iraqi army following the cease-fire with Iran in 1989 when their rebellion was crushed, and in the *Anfal* operation (1987–90), Iraqi forces launched attacks in which some 4,500 villages were demolished and thousands of villagers were killed. However, since the declaration of the no-fly zone in northern Iraq, they have been able to reorganize. Political parties have organized and elected government administrators in the autonomous region north of the 36th parallel.

2. Islamic activists: The Islamic fundamentalist and traditionalist groups were crushed in the 1980s when many of their leaders were executed and thousands of supporters were driven into exile. Of the many parties coming under this group, the al-Daʻwa is the largest and most organized, claiming powerful support from Iran. Also, it is thought to receive covert sympathy from approximately half of the 9 million Iraqi Shiʻi.

3. Leftist organizations: The Communists and socialists were purged almost to extinction in the 1970s and 1980s, and members are isolated, divided, and demoralized. Leftist leaders dispersed and now live in exile (concentrated predominantly in Syria and western European cities such as London, Paris, Berlin, and Stockholm).

4. Arab nationalists: Like the leftists, the Arab nationalists have mostly been driven abroad. Iraqi Ba'ath who fled Saddam Hussein have been forced to amalgamate with the Syrian wing of the party and have concentrated their efforts on propaganda against Saddam Hussein and his regime.

These groups have been trying to work out a common platform for intensifying the struggle against Saddam's rule. In August 1990, representatives from the different groups met in Damascus and agreed to join forces to overthrow Saddam Hussein, as Syria took over from Iran as the opposition's main outside supporter. The following year, a larger meeting of anti-Saddam forces met for three days in Beirut, where they agreed on three points: "Saddam must go; some form of democratic government must replace him; the Kurds must have autonomy. They discussed, but could not agree on, proposals to form a parliament-in-exile, and appoint commanders to lead rebel forces inside Iraq."[49]

With Iraq's trade with Arab countries reaching 50 percent of its total foreign trade in 1998, Trade Minister Mohammed Mehdi Saleh told the Iraqi News Agency that the Arab countries of the Gulf had netted some U.S.$400 million worth of Iraqi contracts since the oil-for-food program started in 1996.[50] Iraq was trading with all the Gulf states, except Kuwait. Under the oil-for-food deal, which Iraq accepted in 1996, Iraq was allowed to sell limited quantities of oil on the condition that proceeds are used to buy food and humanitarian goods for its people. Iraq was allowed to export up to U.S.$5.2 billion of oil every six months to buy food and medicine. Limitations on the amount of oil Iraq could export were lifted in 2000. Infrastructural damage to Iraqi oil facilities, often due to a lack of spare parts, which are not allowed to enter Iraq under the sanctions regime, severely curtailed Iraq's ability to produce crude oil. Baghdad exported only U.S.$3.9 billion worth of oil in the last six months of 1998. In addition, the sanctions regime greatly hampers the importation of so-called dual-use materials. Antibiotics, necessary to combat the spread of disease, for example, have a potential use in biological warfare; fertilizers, necessary for agriculture, have a potential use as an agent of chemical warfare.

The imposition of such vast economic sanctions against Iraq and its people has been compared to a medieval city under siege. Speaking before a UN commission examining the impact of sanctions, Warren Hamerman of the International Progress Organization surmised in 1991 that Iraq is "cut off from outside assistance; its population, deprived of adequate food, water, medical care and the means to produce for its own subsistence, is condemned to perish. It is only a matter of time."[51] Since those words were spoken, 878,856 Iraqi children have died; UNICEF indicates that 58 percent of Iraqi children under the age of five are suffering from malnutrition; cancer has increased sixfold in southern Iraq; and the UN World Food Program (WFP) estimates that 70 percent of the population have "little or no access to food."[52] In comparative terms there is no parallel to the destruction experienced by the Iraqi people; indeed, more people have died as a direct result of sanctions and the bombing campaign in Iraq since the 1990–91 Gulf war began than have been slain by all weapons of mass destruction in human history.[53]

The level of death and destruction has been criticized by Denis Halliday, who resigned from his post as UN assistant secretary-general heading the humanitarian mission in Iraq in 1998. He characterized the oil-for-food program, which he had administered, as "a continuation of the genocide that the economic embargo has placed on Iraq." He added, "I say genocide because it is an intentional programme to destroy a culture, a people, a country—economic sanctions are known to do that. [Secretary of State Madeleine] Albright herself acknowledged half a million dead children back in 1996. Yet the member states—the United States and the United Kingdom in particular—have continued the economic embargo despite their knowledge of the death rate of Iraqi children. That is genocide."[54]

The Kurdish Issue

The Kurds have long been important players in Iraqi domestic politics because of their aspirations for national autonomy, which Baghdad has consistently opposed. Throughout history, the Kurds have maintained a high degree of ethnic, linguistic, and cultural identity that has manifested itself in the desire to form a Kurdish national homeland. The spread of western ideas after the First World War for establishing nation-states and the emphasis on self-determination for all subjugated nationalities inspired the Kurds. Though spread across several of the new states (Kurdistan would encompass parts of Turkey, Syria, Iran, and northeastern Iraq as well as portions of the former Soviet Union) following the First World War, Kurds held out hope that their claims would be realized. It appeared that Kurdish demands would be met after the fall of the Ottoman Empire to the British in 1918, but the British decided instead on the direct administration of Kurdish regions through local officials. As a minority, the Kurds became a source of discomfort to all the states concerned, each of which has used different methods and tactics to suppress them.

Following the First World War, officials in Baghdad agreed to honor League of Nations recommendations that the Kurds be allowed cultural freedoms if they agreed to become part of the newly independent state of Iraq. Since 1927, the Iraqi Kurds have been in a state of revolution, on and off, calling for secession, independence, and various degrees of autonomy. Baghdad, lacking experience and tolerance, vacillated on putting any guarantees to the Kurds in writing, and elements of a Kurdish national movement, in alliance with Kurdish tribal leaders, began to appear in the 1930s, but the movement was suppressed by the central government. The movement was rekindled again in the 1940s by tribal chieftain Mustafa Barzani before he was forced by the Iraqi government to flee with his followers to the USSR via Iran. He was invited to return in 1959 after the Kassem coup. The Kurdish Democratic Party (KDP), led by Barzani, successfully articulated, for the first time, a clear program for the development of the Kurdish areas and called for increased Kurdish representation in the important educational and governmental apparatus of the young Iraqi state. Thus, when the government fell to Kassem in 1958, the Kurds and Barzani saw the opportunity to speed the pace of change by cooperating with the new regime. Kassem went further than the preceding governments in granting and recognizing certain Kurdish rights. The Iraqi provisional constitution declared that Arabs and Kurds were partners in the Iraqi nation, and the permanent constitution guaranteed the national rights of Kurds within the framework of the entity of Iraq. Furthermore, Kassem also granted a license that legalized the KDP in February 1960, and expressed a desire to improve relations through a continued open dialogue. Its platforms and program paid lip service to Marxist-Leninist principles and expressed its support for all Kurds struggling for an independent Kurdistan. The KDP continued to be directed by tribal and conservative leaders who expanded contacts with the West and kept KDP activities within the geographical boundaries of modern Iraq.[55]

Friction between Kassem and Barzani, initially of a personal nature coming soon after the legalization of the KDP, spilled over into a political confrontation over local autonomy within Iraq. Kassem responded with oppression, which met with armed Kurdish resistance in September 1961. Thus began more than a decade of escalation between Kurdish nationalists under Barzani and successive Iraqi governments. The conflict intensified with Turkish, Iranian, and even Israeli support for Kurdish elements in Iraq who aided efforts that would undermine the central government in Baghdad.

The Kurds and the Ba'ath have had a long, stormy, and often violent history. Both have intensely distrusted each other's motives and intentions; the Ba'ath distrusted the Kurds because of their particularistic demands and secessionist desires, and the Kurds were fearful of the Ba'ath's Pan-Arab ideology, especially the proposal to enter the tripartite union with the UAR and Syria after 1963. At the same time, though, the Ba'ath offered more to the Kurds than any previous regime had.

When the Ba'ath returned to power in 1968, the resolution of the conflict by peaceful means was declared a major goal of the regime, but the suspicion between the party and the Kurds outweighed any constructive efforts on either side. The Ba'ath sided with an anti-Barzani faction of the KDP, while Barzani received support from Iran, Israel, and the United States. Thus, the Kurdish problem developed important international dimensions for Baghdad. Through the late 1960s, the conflict became bloodier, more intense, and entrenched. By 1970, the squabbling within the KDP and the war-weariness of the Kurds forced Barzani to accept Ba'ath peace proposals. An agreement was drawn up in March 1970 that gave the Kurds autonomy in Kurdish areas with their own executive and legislature, as the central government began a process of rebuilding areas destroyed in the conflict. It also called for a three-year transitional period, which saw the Ba'ath stabilize their regime and establish a firm grip over the entire country, as well as a further internationalization of the Kurdish issue. By the conclusion of the transitional period, in March 1973, Baghdad, now confident of its grip on domestic politics in Iraq, attempted to expand the central government's control in Kurdish areas.

Iran, the United States, and Israel urged Barzani to demand more than the Ba'ath were prepared to give. A number of contentions developed, such as Baghdad's refusal to consider Barzani's candidate for vice president and difficulties concerning the exact boundaries of the autonomous Kurdish territory. Tensions between Barzani and Baghdad erupted, leading to Baghdad's unilateral implementation of the agreement in March 1973. By establishing the legislature and the Kurdish Executive Council, and by filling both with members who supported closer ties with the Ba'ath government, the central government forced Barzani's hand. He rejected the government's actions and retreated to his mountain strongholds to organize resistance. Full-scale conflict began in April 1974. With heavy American, Israeli, and Iranian moral, financial, and material assistance to the KDP, the conflict proved costly, with both sides taking large casualties in the two years it lasted. The Algiers Agreement of March 1975, signed by the new Iraqi vice president, Saddam Hussein, and the Shah of Iran, left the Kurds isolated with no outside help with which to face the Iraqi regime.

THE REPUBLIC OF IRAQ

The Algiers Agreement gave Baghdad the time it needed to extend its influence over northwestern Iraq. After the agreement, the Ba'ath emerged victorious, a major source of Kurdish foreign support had been destroyed, and Saddam Hussein emerged as the monopolistic new power in the Ba'ath regime. Baghdad attempted to resettle entire Kurdish communities southward into Arab areas, while moving Arabs northward in an effort to create a *cordon sanitaire* between Kurdish areas and Iraq's borders with Iran and Turkey. While the exact number of Kurds who were resettled is unknown, it is clear that tens of thousands were removed from their villages, which were subsequently destroyed. This and army actions during the war (including the use of gas and numerous human rights violations) heightened Kurdish nationalist sentiments. However, with Barzani fleeing the country in 1975, his death in the United States in 1979, and the Iranian revolution, the Kurdish leadership found itself in disarray and was unable to mount effective opposition to Iraqi government measures at the time.

The Iran-Iraq war proved to be an opportunity for the Kurds again to press Baghdad on the issue of autonomy. Kurdish military action against the Iraqi government diverted troops from the main front against Iran. At the time, the KDP had fragmented. One of its offshoots, the Patriotic Union of Kurdistan (PUK) led by Jalal Talabani, gradually emerged as the main Kurdish opponent to Iraq's centralized rule. By 1983, both the PUK and the Ba'ath were weary of fighting, and they entered into a cease-fire agreement. Baghdad agreed to some PUK demands for halting the Arabization of Kurdish areas and agreed to discuss others. However, it seems that both Talabani and Hussein viewed the agreement as nothing more than a short-term breathing space. The Kurdish nationalist movement of the late 1980s found itself full of division and internal wrangling. The loss of the charismatic leadership of Barzani and the co-opting of Kurdish elements by the Ba'ath succeeded in destroying the movement's unity and, to a certain extent, its strength. Massive Iraqi army operations, including the infamous Anfal operation of ethnic cleansing and the use of poisonous gas in 1987 and 1988, which caused a high death toll, further radicalized dissent among the Kurds and drew the opposing groups together. In May 1988, the Iraqi Kurdistan Front, a coalition of seven parties dominated by the PUK and the KDP, was formed.

The occupation of Kuwait in 1990, and the consequent relocation of men and equipment there to face the American-led coalition, relieved the Kurdish areas of the heavy military deployment that had been permanently stationed in the north. Taking advantage of this, the Kurdish guerrillas were able to remobilize and set up cell networks in the

Kurdish towns to harass Iraqi forces and reestablish a Kurdish presence in the urban areas. When the Iraq army left Kuwait in defeat and the *intifada* against Saddam's rule took shape in the south, the Kurdish guerrillas occupied several key towns and advanced on the oil-rich city of Kirkuk in the north. The pro-government Kurdish militia switched sides in an effort to support the new Kurdish coalition. The uprising, lacking outside support (except indirect help from Iran) and failing to solicit massive army defections, was a short-lived affair. Although defeated in the military confrontation against the allied forces, Iraq retained powerful assets: the multilayered secret police, armored vehicles, tanks, helicopter gun ships, and the 15,000 hand-picked members of the Presidential Guard.[56] These government forces quickly regained control of the urban areas, sending the guerrillas into the mountains bordering Turkey and Iran as well as creating several hundred thousand displaced civilians.

In response to the brutal crushing of the Iraqi *intifada,* UN Security Council Resolution 688 was adopted, on the basis of which the United States, Britain, and France imposed a no-fly zone above the 36th parallel and established a "safe haven" in Kurdish areas. The Iraqi army was forced to withdraw from Kurdish towns and much of the countryside, followed in turn by the state security and Ba'ath Party officials. Since April 1991, the Kurds have lived largely outside Saddam's control, although they are faced with the Iraqi leader's economic blockade and potential return to control in the north. In May 1992, the Iraqi Kurdistan Front organized elections for a Kurdish legislature, the results being a virtual dead heat between the two major parties leading to the formation of a coalition government. Real power, however, continued to rest with the two party leaders, Mas'ud Barzani (son of Mullah Mustafa Barzani) and Talabani, and their respective militias. Following the elections, the two leaders jointly controlled Iraq's northern Kurdish enclave. The region and their relationship proved highly unstable, however. Despite nominal support from western air forces, the Kurds had to deal with Iraqi ground forces attempting to reestablish Baghdad's sovereignty over the region, Turkish raids against PKK Turkish rebels who would slip across the border from Turkey, and communal fighting between forces allied with the two main factions. Joint administration proved tenuous and collapsed entirely in 1994 amid increased factional fighting. Disagreements centered on the distribution of KDP border revenues from an illicit diesel fuel trade with Turkey and control of the capital, Arbil, as well as the political control in developing the region economically and politically. Barzani's forces even fought with Iraqi troops at their side in order to retake the capital from Talabani forces, which had managed to capture it in August 1996. Further complicating matters, the KDP aligned itself with the Turkish forces in attacking PKK strongholds in the region. A cease-fire agreement, brokered by western diplomats and the Turkish government, allowed for negotiations between Turkey and Barzani, and Talabani forces.

A period of relative calm brought about some rather heated diplomacy. Barzani and Talabani were invited to Washington in September 1998. In an effort to reconcile the two factions, Secretary of State Madeleine Albright facilitated their signing of the Washington Agreement. This allowed them to take steps toward a joint federal administration in northern Iraq.[57] However, the secret talks in Washington did not address Turkish concerns or clearly outline the western position on the future of northern Iraq.[58]

Iraqi sovereignty was not respected, and the Turkish government was so concerned over being left out of the process that a further round of negotiations took place in Ankara. This resulted in the Joint Statement by London, Ankara, and Washington in November 1998. The statement cemented the Washington Agreement and recognized Turkey's sensitivity to the affairs of northern Iraq and the two countries' Kurdish populations. Turkey's main problems with the Washington Agreement—Turkish exclusion and the insertion of language discussing a federated Iraq in which Kurdish autonomy would be guaranteed—were addressed as the government in Ankara was centrally involved in the negotiations and American and KDP negotiators assured Ankara that such a federation would not appear on the agenda until a democratic government was in place in Iraq.[59]

With Turkish fears abated, and the weakening of the Kurdistan Workers' Party with the Turkish capture and trial of its leader, Abdullah Öcalan, in November 1998, a period of calm and reconciliation appeared at hand. The launch of KurdSat TV by Talabani in January 2000, to counter the KDP's Kurdistan TV, which began broadcasting in 1998, reflected the development of an autonomous society in northern Iraq. By the end of March 2000, both the foreign office in Ankara and the Turkish army conveyed their concerns to a visiting KDP delegation over the possible emergence of a Kurdish state in northern Iraq. Stressing the importance of Iraq's unity, the Turkish foreign ministry "reiterated that the problem of the northern Iraqi Kurds should be solved within the national territory of Iraq."[60]

CHAPTER 7

Syria and Lebanon

*F*rom ancient times until the fall of the Ottoman Empire in 1918, Syria encompassed the principal geographic area along the eastern Mediterranean between Turkey and Egypt. Under Ottoman rule from 1816 until 1915, Syria was divided into the three *vil-layets* (roughly the equivalent of administrative units, or *cantons,* in the Swiss Republic) of Aleppo, Damascus, and Beirut and the two *mutasar-rifiyyahs* (governorships) of Jerusalem and Mount Lebanon, the latter having more autonomy than any of the other four administrative units. Following the Maronite-Druze civil war in 1860, in which Napoleon III intervened with French forces, a European government for the first time imposed restrictions on local government in lands controlled by the Ottoman Empire. Under the International Protocols of 1861 and 1864, a special autonomy was guaranteed to Christian Maronites of Mount Lebanon within what was still the sovereign domain of the Ottoman Empire. Under the Ottoman millet-sectarian system, Mount Lebanon— a Druze enclave—was administered by a Christian governor. Though appointed by Istanbul, he was responsive to local input through an administrative council representative of all the various religious segments of Lebanese society. The Christian sects who made up a local majority were predominant on the council. The Young Turks would abolish the millet system half a century later, but its influence on Lebanese politics has continued to this day.

Following the First World War, the region was divided into new political entities at the Paris Peace Conference that created new territorial boundaries comprising Syria and Lebanon, the Hashemite Emirate of Transjordan, and the British Mandate in Palestine.[1] British and French forces controlled the coastal areas, and Arab forces controlled the interior. Arab forces, under the command of Sharif Faisal of Hejaz, sought to create an independent and united Arab state, beginning with Syria under the terms of the Hussein-McMahon correspondence of October and November 1915 (as discussed in chapter 2). When the Ottoman Empire collapsed, Faisal set up an Arab national government in Damascus that lasted from November 1918 until July 1920. During its tenure, the Hizb al-Istiqlal al-'Arabi (Arab Independence Party) took up the banner of nationalism from al-Fatat (a leading Arab nationalist party in Istanbul during the last years of the Ottoman Empire). Hizb al-Istiqlal al-'Arabi rallied nationalist forces around Sharif Faisal, giving the Arab national government a wide base of support. In March 1920, a Syrian General Congress was held in Damascus with eighty-five delegates drawn from throughout historically devised Syria. These delegates proclaimed Sharif Faisal of Hejaz king of Syria.

Under the guise of the League of Nations mandate system, Arab territories of the Ottoman Empire were turned over to colonial powers for administration. In essence, it was a case of the fox guarding the henhouse. The French and British had prearranged the dismemberment of the region into zones of influence in the secret Sykes-Picot Agreement of May 1916. The San Remo conference of April 1920, at which the victorious Allied powers settled the fate of the Arab provinces of the Ottoman Empire, allotted the northern half of historically devised Syria (which encompassed the territories subsequently known as Syria and Lebanon) to France and the remainder (Palestine and Jordan) to Great Britain.

In Syria, the French administration set out to squash nationalist aspirations for independence and unity. At the Battle of Maisaloun on 24 July 1920, the French routed King Faisal and his nationalist forces, then divided Syria into a number of administrative units (Aleppo, Damascus, Latakia, Jabal, and a Druze area) under military authority. The separation of Lebanon from Syria was followed by the formal establishment of the State of Greater Lebanon on 30 August 1920, which became—six years later—the Republic of Lebanon. The prewar Maronite governorship of Mount Lebanon was enlarged to incorporate all the Muslim areas it could safely dominate—almost doubling both its population and area—in spite of its inhabitants' objections. According to the Basic Law introduced by the French on 23 November 1920, the French high commissioner, stationed in Beirut, was responsible to the French foreign minister, and the French government was the intermediary between the high commissioner and the League of Nations. By 1925, the French high commissioner had ordered the promulgation of a constitution for Lebanon. It was drafted by the Representative Council of Lebanon and formally proclaimed in May 1926. The constitution was suspended in 1932, allowing the French to rule directly until 1941 when French rule fell in Syria and Lebanon to British and Free French forces with the defeat of Vichy representatives.

In 1924–25, the Druze initiated an uprising under Sultan Atrash, calling for autonomy and an end to unfair French taxation schemes. The uprising spread throughout Syria and threatened to spill over into Lebanon. The rebellion was put down in 1926, but not before Damascus was twice bombarded by the French. The rebels were unsuccessful in forcing the French to abandon their policy of separating Syria from Lebanon. In 1928 a Constituent Assembly was gathered in Damascus to formulate a Syrian constitution that was proclaimed in 1932, only to be suspended two years later in response to further nationalist agitation for Syrian independence and unity with Lebanon. In 1936, nationalist-led mass demonstrations and strikes forced the socialist "Popular Front" French government of Leon Blum to negotiate a treaty promising eventual independence. However, the Blum government soon fell, and Syria and Lebanon remained under direct military rule until 1941 when, with the defeat of the Vichy government, the French mandate came to a formal conclusion.[2]

Free French forces under Charles de Gaulle installed pro-French governments while promising independence to both Syria and Lebanon. In accordance with the plans for independence, elections were allowed to take place in 1943 in which pro-French candidates lost and nationalists came to the forefront in both Lebanon and Syria. A year later, the French handed over local government and services to the newly elected national governments, and in 1945–46 France reluctantly withdrew its troops from both Syria and Lebanon. This concluded nearly a quarter century of colonial control, under the guise of a League of Nations mandate, and both countries moved toward full independence. After the 1948 Zionist declaration of the Jewish state of Israel—in British-mandated Palestine—and the resultant first Arab-Israeli war, Palestine and Transjordan were reconstituted through force of arms into Israel and Jordan, leaving the Palestinian population occupied and scattered[3] and "greater" Syria divided into four new nation-states and the occupied territories of Palestine.

Syrian Arab Republic

With a land area of 185,180 square kilometers and a total population estimated in the mid-1990s at around 14 million, Syria has a unique position in Middle East politics. It was the epicenter of the modern Arab political awakening, the "beating heart of Arab nationalism," and it has continued to play a pivotal role in Pan-Arab nationalism.

In the historical evolution of the country, geography has played a crucial role. Historically, its strategic location sitting astride three continents has exposed it to continuous movements of diverse peoples, whose impact has been to alter the sociocultural heterogeneity of the region. Lacking any single integrating factor, such as the river systems of Egypt and Iraq, segmentation developed into a salient feature of Syrian society. Geography also has had a significant impact on another aspect of the country, namely, its economy. A complex geography of mountains, plains, and desert has produced a differentiated ecological base for economic activities. Agriculture is the main occupation in the country; other economic activities of importance are trading and nomadic pastoralism.

About half of the country's territory is considered arable land. Dry farming is constrained by scarcity of precipitation with improved irrigation and agricultural techniques creating the hope of increasing both acreage and crop yield. In addition, the government has constructed dams to replace the traditional and obsolete waterwheels, on which local people had relied for centuries. In the more arid parts of the country, nomadism is widely practiced by the Bedouin. However, the government is encouraging the settlement of these peripatetic people whose numbers have steadily declined.

Another phenomenon partly attributed to geography is the expansion of urban life. Location aside, ancient commercial routes encouraged the development of commerce in the country, and the surplus extracted from these activities contributed to the establishment of cities and towns. With the growth in cities, nationalism and politics in general became the monopoly of the urban centers, to the political detriment of the rural areas, particularly in the nationalist period of the 1930s and the early years of independence. The urban areas, in the meantime, became important centers of industry, wealth, politics, and administration while the rural population continued to be impoverished and exploited—and thus marginalized. This marginalization may help explain how these underprivileged segments of Syrian society came to feel that their only avenue for social mobility was via the military. Military education and the upward social mobility accompanying a position as a senior officer allowed them entry to Syrian politics. Control of the army by the 1960s allowed for the expansion of their influence to the economy, political culture, and society at large in the 1970s, radically restructuring Syrian life.

Independence and Nationalism

The country gained full independence in 1945, at a time when it was ill prepared to tackle the myriad problems facing it. The necessary institutional base was too weak, as the opposition to French imperial rule had exhausted the energies of the urban leadership of the country. As a consequence, independence was accompanied by a period of instability, and one government followed another in rapid succession. The military played a major role in the postindependence carousel of regimes, which was halted only after the Ba'athists came to power.

The immediate task for the politicians who took over from the French—mostly Sunni Muslims from landowning and merchant classes—was to forge unity in the face of ethnic, social, and religious discord. Syrian society has been characterized by strong sectarian divisions, as shown in table 7.1.

Whereas the Sunnis and Christians are dispersed, the Alawis, Druze, and Isma'ilis are compact communities forming regional majorities. Most of the Alawis live in the northwestern Latakia region, the Druze live in the southern province of Suwayda (also called Jabal al Druz—mountain of the Druzes), and the Isma'ilis occupy the districts of Masyaf and Salamiyah of the central province of Hama, leaving the Sunni majority to dominate the urban populations and the remaining provinces.

During the mandate era, minorities were accorded autonomous status by the French colonial authorities and were recruited in large numbers into the armed forces. Although it definitely had a role, the domination of the military by minorities in later years cannot be explained by French discriminatory recruitment practices alone. More plausible reasons include the inclination of Syrians from poorer backgrounds (where minorities dominated) to seek a career in the military for social advancement; and recruitment from minority communities would only increase

TABLE 7.1
Syrian Demographic Composition by Religion

Sunni Muslims	68.7%
Alawis	11.5%
Druze	3.0%
Isma'ilis	1.5%
Christians	14.1%

Source: Nicholas S. Hopkins and Saad Eddin Ibrahim, *Arab Society: Class, Gender, Power, and Development* (Cairo: American University in Cairo Press, 1997), pp. xv, 185–87.

as officers and soldiers would then encourage relatives to follow in their footsteps. Moreover, the postwar reformulation of the Syrian military pushed out much of the old establishment, opening a great number of positions and advancing the careers of younger officers.[4]

In the early years of independence, it was not surprising that the Sunni leaders of the country moved swiftly to break the independent power bases of the Alawites and Druze. Indeed, by 1953, communal representation in the parliament had been abolished. Nevertheless, the minority groups were successful in increasing their power and influence in both politics and the military. The emergence of the Ba'ath Party provided an excellent opportunity for many minority groups, particularly the Alawites, who would come to dominate the political life of the country a decade later. Ba'athist tactics saw the recruitment of military officers as a method of gaining national power, and the now-expanded military became not only one of the main avenues for upward social mobility open to minorities but also an avenue to political power.

While they fought for independence, the nationalists had operated under the auspices of the National Bloc. Soon afterwards, the Bloc split into the National Party, which basically represented business interests in Damascus, and the People's Party, which mainly represented business interests in Aleppo. They were now joined on the national political landscape by the Ba'ath Arab Socialist Party. Founded by Michel 'Aflaq and Salah Bitar, the party was led by a new breed of nationalists who espoused a more expansive vision of Arab nationalism as well as a clearly defined social program.

The Army in Politics

The nationalist leaders who assumed power upon independence lacked a clear vision of governance. When the first parliamentary election took place in 1947, charges of corruption and election irregularities ran rampant, and by the time of the crushing defeat of the combined Arab forces in Palestine in 1948–49, public dissatisfaction with the government was high. As a result, when the first coup by army officers occurred on 30 March 1949, led by the chief of staff, Colonel Husni al-Zaim, public support was substantial, while military support was marginal. The coup ushered in a new political era as the old nationalist centers of power, composed largely of the landed aristocracy and rich merchant families, collapsed. The political vacuum created led to a succession of coups, though none survived more than a few months.

The parliament continued to function within this environment with factions jockeying for the support of the leadership of each new coup.

The general staff of the military was able to continually counterbalance and manipulate the parliament, with the result that true power shifted from an elected body to the military. Though the parliament refused to accept this new reality, the military essentially began to appoint the head of state from within its own officer corps. Thus, by the time a new election took place in November 1949, the parliament blessed the ascension of the new chief of staff, Colonel Adib al-Shishakli, and approved the new constitution, which had been drafted by the military. While several administrations rotated through government, none were powerful enough to satisfy either the military or the parliament. On 29 November 1951, the military once again overthrew the government, dissolved the parliament, banned all political parties, and gave the military chief of staff direct legislative and executive powers to rule through military decrees.

Shishakli, who had been involved in all previous coups, now began preparing the ground for his political ascendance to the presidency, which would bring together the military and civilian leadership behind popular support. He began building a power base of support by establishing a populist organization in August 1952 known as the Arab Liberation Movement, which advanced some Arab nationalist slogans as well as progressive social and economic programs. Second, in July 1953, a new constitution was enacted ratifying Shishakli as president, while allowing some previously banned political parties to operate in preparation for new presidential elections scheduled for October.

However, new political forces had begun to acquire genuine popular support based on clear ideologies and social programs, while traditional political parties were on the wane. One of these new forces, the Syrian Social National Party (SSNP), called for a unified pro-western centralized socialist state that would unite the entire Fertile Crescent. Another, the Arab Ba'ath Socialist Party, supported a progressive semisocialist though non-Marxist program advocating the establishment of a unified Arab state that would encompass all the Arab people from the Atlantic to the Persian Gulf, while the Communist Party of Syria supported a traditional Marxist-Leninist approach. The Syrian branch of the Egyptian organization, the Muslim Brotherhood, propagated a unified Islamic world to counteract the influence of western and European imperialism, and advanced a conservative social program with an avowed antileftist and antiliberal orientation. The remnants of the traditional urban leadership of al-Kutla al-Wataniayah, the Sha'ab (People's) Party, and the Watani (National) Party, with very conservative programs and waning popular support—particularly among youth—operated especially in the urban areas. In this environment, Shishakli saw to it that his popular

Arab Liberation Movement won the election. However, amid charges of corruption, all other parties—now in open opposition to military rule—mobilized demonstrations protesting the election results leading to challenges to Shishakli even from within the military itself. The turmoil forced Shishakli to flee the country on 25 February 1954, first to Lebanon and soon after to Argentina, where he was assassinated less than two years later.

For the following seven months, the country was run by a provisional government whose mandate was to oversee a free election. The National Party and the People's Party lost seats, while the leader of the Communist Party of Syria was elected for the first time in its history. Half the seats were won by independent nationalist and progressive candidates. The Ba'athists, holding a quarter of the seats, emerged as the strongest political party and with the support of a coalition of all progressive and leftist groups, including the Communists. This gave the Ba'athists a dominant position in Syria, especially after the decline of the SSNP on charges of treason. They were implicated in the instigation of a coup—with the help of the United States—soon after the assassination in 1955 of the deputy chief of staff, a pro-Ba'athist, by an army sergeant who was a member of the SSNP. The assassination unleashed a campaign of terror, led by the Arab Nationalist head of military intelligence, Abdul Hamid al-Saraj. During the summer of 1956, the leading figures of the People's Party and the right wing of the National Party held a secret meeting to plan a strategy against the Pan-Arab and leftist elements in the government. In October, Saraj claimed that in the meeting plans were made to overthrow the government of National Unity. This led to the arrest of forty-seven prominent conservative politicians and removed right-wing leadership from the political stage.[5] The military then returned Quwatli, in August 1955, to the post of president, which he had held from Syria's independence in 1943 until his ouster in the first military coup in 1949. In July 1956, the Ba'ath gained control of the most important positions in the cabinet and the leadership of the parliament.

Union with Egypt

The popular appeal of Nasserism, particularly after the combined British, French, and Israeli invasion of the Suez in November 1956, encouraged Arab nationalists in Syria to seek political union with Egypt. The warming of ties leading up to this union began in October 1955, when Cairo and Damascus signed a military pact. The internal circumstances driving Syrian ambitions were centered on the fear of domestic communism. The dismissal of the conservative army chief of staff in the fall of 1957 and the appointment of his deputy, a Marxist general named 'Afif al-Bizri, induced all the nonleftist, conservative, and nationalist forces to unite. They feared the increasing popularity of the Soviet Union in the region, the emergence of the Syrian Communist Party as a political power (especially after the demise of the SSNP), and the growing acceptance of Khalid Bakdash, the charismatic leader of the Syrian Communist Party. They saw their salvation from civil chaos in the proposed union with Egypt and Nasser.

A marriage of ideological convenience ensued between Nasser and all nationalist groupings, including the Arab Ba'ath Socialist Party. External threats from Turkey, Israel, and Iraq as well as internal dissension from Beirut also pushed the parties together. Thus, the Ba'ath campaign for a union with Egypt became a cardinal principle of their National Front government. By 1957, the Ba'ath, bolstered by their association with Nasser, had become the most prominent force in Syrian politics.[6]

Just prior to the union, the climate within Syria was politically unstable, characterized by much jockeying for power between the various political movements, on the one hand, and the politicians and the military, on the other. The Ba'ath Party emerged as a strong political force and had joined the government of National Unity, formed in 1956. Unity with Egypt for the Ba'athists was an important step toward their grandiose goal of uniting all of the Arab peoples. Fearing the increasing popularity of the Communists and other leftist organizations, the Ba'athist leadership saw in Nasser's popularity in Syria—and the Arab world generally—the opportunity to halt the Communist ascendance and to fulfill one of the party's ideological tenets. The notion was, at that time, also popular with the military's younger officers. With the military now controlling the balance of political power, even the Marxist chief of staff, 'Afif al-Bizri, could not subdue the momentum toward unification. When a high-ranking Syrian military delegation went to Cairo in January 1958 proposing the union, the Ba'ath Party quickly endorsed it.

In the negotiations that followed, Nasser was in a strong position. The demands he made—total union, a disbanding of all political parties, the formation of a Syrian National Union modeled after its Egyptian counterpart, and the withdrawal of the military from politics—were fully accepted by the Syrians. On 1 February 1958, Nasser and Quwatli proclaimed the unity of the two countries under the name of the United Arab Republic. A referendum in the two countries endorsed the move, and Nasser was overwhelmingly elected president of the new republic. However, its constitution vested enormous powers in the presidency and generally favored Egypt. These two factors were to become the fatal flaws in the new arrangement. In the UAR cabinet, only three of the fourteen posts were held by Syrians.

During the Union era, politicized Syrian Army officers, including Ba'athists, were transferred from the Syrian region, assigned less sensitive military and police functions in Egypt, and carefully watched by the UAR intelligence agencies. In the military, party members and Ba'athist sympathizers were forced to sever their formal party connections. This prompted them to form clandestine political-social relations. In early 1960, five young, disgruntled Syrian Army officers in Egypt, most of whom were from the Alawite minority, created a secret organization known as the Military Committee. Its most active members were Capt. Hafez al-Assad, Maj. Salah Jadid, and Lt. Col. Mohammed 'Umran, who by virtue of his rank served as its de facto chair. Their professed aim was to save the Union from the corrupt cliques around Nasser, which they considered responsible for the plight of the Syrian economy through what they believed was the unnecessary sacrifice being made for development projects in Egypt.

Soon the halcyon days of the Union ended, and the underlying contradictions within the UAR increasingly became a source of discontent in Syria. Merging the unstable and fragmented multiparty Syria and the single-party and stable Egypt became problematic. Moreover, Nasser's imposition of the Egyptian system of government dissatisfied many Syrians, and the nationalization measures of July 1961 further alienated the bourgeoisie and commercial classes. Landowners resented agrarian reforms, and politicians who found themselves left out of the new system were resentful, as were army officers who had been dismissed for their political allegiances. The political insensitivity of the Egyptian military staff officers who had been based in Syria was another factor that fueled discontent. As the climate worsened, the pro-western and conservative governments of Saudi Arabia and Jordan, who were worried about the popularity of Nasserism, supported a right-wing putsch by Syrian military officers.[7] Military officers stationed outside Damascus marched into the city on 28 September 1961, declaring a military coup and ending the unity of the two countries. The Syrian Arab Republic was reborn.

The Rise of the Arab Ba'ath Socialist Party

Since its inception, the party's guiding principles have been unity, freedom, and socialism. For the minorities, the slogans were appealing, for they promised secularism and social justice. Consequently, although the party was under the direction of urban middle-class intellectuals, it had a large following among the rural minority groups, many of whom had joined the army in the 1950s to achieve upward social mobility. As middle and junior officers, many had formed cliques within the military during the period of Union, slowly gaining prominence in the military and eventually, after the September 1961 coup, in Syrian politics. However, the urban upper classes—many of them Sunnis—refrained from joining, since the party platform worked directly against the interests of many in the landed aristocracy, the merchant class, or industrialists. Consequently, the minority groups, particularly the Alawites, Druze, and Isma'ilis, came to dominate both the military and the Ba'ath Party.

Immediately after the breakup of the Union, the Ba'ath Party was in disarray, but several of its leaders denounced Nasser and blessed the secessionist movement in a published manifesto. In this environment, various military cliques struggled to assert themselves within the party. At the same time, the old civilian leadership tried to regroup and take command.

With the demise of the Union, all members of the Military Committee—except for its chairman, Mohammed 'Umran—were immediately arrested by Egyptian authorities and deported back to Syria. There they were decommissioned and given civilian assignments. However, they continued trying to recruit more junior military officers, particularly those who had Nasserite and nationalist sympathies. In March 1962, Colonel Nahlawi led a bloodless coup against the Qudsi government. However, it lasted only one month, and on 1 April 1962 Col. Jasem Alwan, supported by Syrian Nasserites, launched a coup in Aleppo that was quickly crushed by loyal factions of the military.

By the winter of 1962, secret negotiations by the trio of 'Umran, Jadid, and Assad had laid the plans for yet another coup. Assad, the youngest of the group, along with many conservative and high-ranking nationalist army officers, successfully formed a junta after staging a military coup on 3 March 1963.[8] They quickly restored some of the dismissed members of the Military Committee, but replaced over half of the previous command structure with Alawites loyal to Assad. Traditional political elites at this point were too demoralized to oppose the move, but Arab nationalist forces, particularly the Nasserites, welcomed the coup. Within a month after the new government came to power, it began moving closer to Egypt and eventually requested a trilateral union with it and its Ba'athist counterparts in Iraq—who had just come to power the month before in Baghdad. However, with the experience of the earlier union experiment still fresh in his mind, Nasser turned down this gesture at further Arab union.

With the success of the coup, Assad consolidated a base within the military officer corps that ultimately became his private "fiefdom." A twenty-man National Council for the Revolutionary Command was formed, made up of twelve Ba'athists and eight Nasserite Arab national-ists as well as some independents. Nasserites took public and often highly visible civilian jobs, while real power was concentrated in the Military Committee, forming a junta within a junta. Furthermore, the Homs Military Academy was placed under Ba'athist command and became the breeding ground for future Ba'athist officers. Those who were admitted to the academy, often including relatives of Assad and Jadid, were selected for their loyalty to the new regime. These recruits were given crash officer training courses in order to prepare them to immediately fill the vacant military posts purged for suspected disloy-alty to the junta. Hafez al-Assad emerged as the de facto chief of the air force, seen as the most powerful branch of the Syrian armed forces; Salah Jadid was promoted from lieutenant colonel to general and put in charge of the chiefs of staff and army, giving him complete control of promotions, transfers, and dismissals throughout the military.

From 28 April to 2 May, some fifty Nasserite officers were purged from the military, forcing two of the three Nasserite members of the junta to resign in protest, followed soon after by Nasserite members of the cabinet. Within four months, the Ba'athist triumvirate in the Military Committee had eliminated all opposition in the military and now controlled Syrian politics. However, writes Patrick Seale, "they were a fraction of what was itself a minority, a military splinter group of a semi-defunct party without a popular base."[9]

On 18 July 1963, the Nasserites retaliated with an attempted putsch, which resulted in heavy casualties, and soon thereafter a wholesale purge of remaining Nasserites in the army took place. On 22 July, Nasser interpreted this move as a personal attack and a betrayal, denounced the Syrian Ba'athist leadership, and formally withdrew Egypt from the Union Agreement signed just three months earlier. Thus began an era of tension between Syria and Egypt that resulted in a fur-ther purge of the remaining Nasserites from the Syrian cabinet. Fearing for their future, the Ba'athist leadership took steps ensuring that the Independents and Nationalists soon met this same fate.

With the failure of the Nasserite coup attempt, the way was paved for Jadid to become the chief of staff in August, a post he would hold until September 1965. Hafez al-Assad turned his attention to building his own political power base. He began by eliminating his rivals from power in the Military Committee, then moved into the Ba'ath Party leadership apparatus, joining the eight-man Regional Command in September 1963. According to the Ba'ath Party structure, the Regional Command was the highest party authority in Syria, although the National Command of the party theoretically directed all Regional

(Country) Commands. Furthermore, while Assad was not initially embroiled in the confrontation, which arose between Umran and Jadid, his support of Jadid proved decisive. 'Umran was accused of promoting sectarianism in the military, leading to his eventual removal and the ascendance of Jadid and Amin al-Hafiz in Syrian politics. The new clique of the Military Committee needed a high-ranking military officer to maintain political legitimacy. They chose Lt. Col. Amin al-Hafiz. A disciplined and respected Sunni, who three months after the breakup of the Union had been sent to Buenos Aires as military attaché, Hafiz had close personal ties to Committee members. Though he had never been a Ba'ath Party member, he had become acquainted with Umran while both served in Cairo as instructors in the military staff college. Hafiz was promoted to lieutenant general and minister of the interior, where he would soon distinguish himself in the eyes of the Military Committee through his brutal suppression of the May 1963 Nationalist and Nasserite riots in Aleppo and Damascus, as well as his crackdown on a rebellion in Hama in the same year. Two months later, because of his loyalty and success, he was also entrusted with the sensitive Ministry of Defense and brought into the inner circle of National Council for the Revolutionary Command to become its chairman.

In December 1964, the confrontation between Umran and Jadid reached its conclusion. Jadid, who viewed force as the primary tool to maintain power and consequently heartily supported Hafiz's bloody approach to dealing with any challenge to the junta, was able to oust 'Umran. In the course of this struggle, Hafiz became prime minister, army commander in chief, secretary of the Ba'ath Party's Regional Command, and chairman of the Presidential Council. He had no military units under his command, however, and was completely dependent on the Military Committee and the support of both Salah Jadid and Hafez al-Assad—who had now been promoted to major general and made commander of the Syrian Air Force. Being in the public eye gave Amin al-Hafiz a false sense of security, which led him to challenge both Jadid and Assad in the summer of 1965. Using disaffected Ba'ath Party members, including the traditional party leadership such as 'Aflaq—the party secretary general and party founder—Hafiz underestimated his military opponents.

Jadid, who was now the assistant secretary of the Regional Command but in reality its de facto head, seemed to have the upper hand in the struggle. However, the National Command of the Ba'ath Party, led by 'Aflaq, passed resolutions that annulled the decisions of the Regional Command. This, in effect, dissolved the Regional Command and, while seeming to remove Jadid from power, led instead to the further concentration of the Syrian political leadership in the military high command. The Ba'ath Party leadership—thinking itself free of Jadid—soon reinstated 'Umran, appointing him minister of defense and commander in chief of the armed forces. Umran began replacing key Jadid army officers. On 23 February 1966, however, forces loyal to Jadid arrested and imprisoned Hafiz, 'Umran, the civilian leaders of the Ba'ath Party, including 'Aflaq and Bitar, and their followers. Hafez al-Assad moved to support Jadid by putting the air force at his disposal. Jadid repaid Assad's loyalty by making the thirty-five-year-old air force commander his minister of defense.

A system of dual power sharing developed. Jadid controlled the party apparatus and civilian government, while Assad continued to nurture his power base in the military. These two power centers would inevitably clash as the spheres of their jurisdictions overlapped. Jadid looked upon Assad as a member of the Regional Command and even as minister of defense—only one member of the cabinet whose policies were to be controlled by the Regional Command, and namely himself, as its secretary. Thus, Jadid insisted that the Regional Command was the sole legitimate authority and Assad was bound to its dictates. However, after stopping the coup, Assad viewed his power as the reason the party was able to maintain control.

Fifteen months later, with the outbreak of the Six-Day War of 1967, Assad lost his prized air force and Syria lost the Golan Heights. The civilian authorities blamed the military and Assad. However, Assad was able to maintain both his post and his tight grip on the military. Soon after the war, the traditional leaders, imprisoned fifteen months earlier, along with purged senior army officers, were released and encouraged to leave the country. The rift between the two groups—the party's Regional Command and the cabinet on one side headed by Jadid, and the military headed by Assad on the other—developed two ideological positions for the future of Syria. Jadid favored socialism, closer cooperation with the Soviet bloc, rejection of any cooperation with the conservative regimes of the region (such as Iraq, Lebanon, Jordan, Saudi Arabia, and Egypt), and support for the Fatah faction of the Palestine Liberation Organization (PLO), led by Yasser Arafat. The Assad group, on the other hand, believed that Syria's most important mission was to liberate occupied land from Israeli control, which necessitated full coordination between all Arab countries, including the conservative ones, even if that required delaying the socialist transformation of Syria. The dissension between Assad and Jadid soon moved into a phase of confrontation between the party and the military. The issue came to a head in the party's Fourth Congress in September and October 1968, in which Assad's policies were rejected and the delegates questioned the military's prominence in Syrian Ba'ath Party affairs. The effect of this was that Assad, fearing the loss of his power, ordered his army officers to cease contact with the party, contrary to the practice up to then in which ideological indoctrination had been the prerogative of the party. In effect, Assad turned the Ba'ath into two parallel and competing structures—a military one whose allegiance was solely to Assad, and a civilian one whose loyalty was to Jadid—thus repeating the same stratagem that 'Aflaq had employed against Jadid one year earlier.

Between 1969 and 1970, power gradually shifted to the more organized camp of Assad. By September 1970, Assad had emerged as the dominant power broker in Syria. However, in an Emergency National Congress on 30 October 1970, Jadid mobilized forces loyal to him in the Regional Command in an attempt to curtail Assad's control of the military. Assad responded with what were termed "corrective measures" by taking over on 12 November 1970 and installing a fourteen-man "Provisional" Regional Command made up of his most trusted supporters. They then elected him secretary-general of the Ba'ath Party and of the Regional Command and appointed him prime minister. The Provisional Regional Command then nominated 173 members to fill the People's Assembly. Eighty-seven of those were allocated to the Syrian Ba'ath Party, thirty-six to the General Union of Peasants, and the rest to nationalists and independents.

Jadid was arrested. He died in 1994 after twenty-three years in prison. Soon after his takeover, Assad embarked on a very ambitious economic reform plan, with less commitment to classical or rhetorical socialism and more attention to feasible public policy initiatives. While touring the country, he invited old faithful party members, many of whom had been purged by Jadid, to rejoin the party. On 22 February, Assad formally assumed the presidency, and two weeks later in a plebiscite, he was confirmed as president for a seven-year term, making him the first member of a minority to hold power in Syria and initiating the longest term for a president in the Syrian Republic's history. He remained in command until his death in June 2000.

Hafez al-Assad: The New Regime

Hafez al-Assad was born to a poor peasant family in 1930, so his rise to the highest office in the country symbolized the increase in the political fortunes of minorities and the downtrodden population of Syria. Correspondingly, the majority Sunni population, particularly in Aleppo and Damascus, lost their predominant position in political affairs.

Further, as Assad's success was at the expense of the civilian wing of the Ba'ath Party, his ascension marked the complete subjugation of the party to the military and the country's entire political process to the rule of one individual.

Assad's immediate preoccupation was to break free from Syria's political isolation in the Arab world and to restore its credibility at home. On the regional level he was successful: ties with Egypt and Libya improved to the extent that, in 1972, proposals were floated for the federation of the three countries in the Tripoli Charter. However, the proposal was never seriously considered by Syria's partners. In fact, ties with these and other Arab countries later worsened. Nevertheless, the moves helped to bring Syria back into the Arab fold.

Domestically Assad tried to show that the party leadership would become more open through more cadre input. He coerced the election of party delegates to the Fifth Regional Congress in May, at which his most trusted allies managed to fill the new Regional Command. In August 1971, in preparation for the Eleventh National Congress, where the National Command was to be selected from the delegates of the National Congress, Assad managed to ensure that only those faithful to him would attend. On 3 March 1972, Assad instituted yet another layer in the centralization of his control, through what was billed as "popular input" in the Syrian political system in the elections for local councils. The formal function of these municipal councils was to aid the fourteen governors of the Syrian provinces in the administration of their duties. In the meantime, a parallel party structure was also involved in supervising both the councils and the governors, who reported to the central government and the party.

Now that he had firm control of the Ba'ath Party, Assad moved to tame the most active opposition parties, initiating a reign of terror against all other political groups and parties through arrests, assassinations, and harassment. On 7 March, he gave all opposition parties the impossible choice of either joining an umbrella organization the regime had instituted—the Progressive National Front—or facing banishment. The five most active political parties, including the Syrian Communist Party, were co-opted into the Front, ultimately causing these groups intense internal fragmentation and effectively weakening their public appeal. As a condition for joining the Front, they were prohibited from any recruitment activities, either in the military or among students, and forced into a subservient position to the Ba'ath. In effect, Assad turned these parties into instruments of the state while banning all other political parties. Driving the most activist opponents underground, Assad followed with harsh reprisals against those who refused to comply. In

March 1980, a law was instituted making membership in the Muslim Brotherhood punishable by death. At the same time, police and security agencies increased their oppression against all opponents of the official National Front members, effectively increasing the dependency of the Front membership on the regime and neutralizing all opposition to the government.

A year later, the appointed Assembly completed its mandate and drafted a permanent constitution that embodied the basic principles of the Ba'ath, provided for a republican presidential system in Syria, and stipulated that the party was the vanguard of both "state and society, as it would lead the Progressive National Front." Moreover, the constitution declared Syria to be "a democratic, popular, socialist, and sovereign state" and "an integral part of the Arab homeland." The president was to hold office for seven years, and he was to be nominated by the party and the parliament in preparation for a popular plebiscite. In effect, the president was the ultimate power, as he commanded the armed forces and held the right to appoint and dismiss the cabinet, dissolve the People's Assembly, and assume its legislative responsibility under emergency powers. The constitution was approved in a plebiscite in March 1973. It is obvious and understandable that, given these conditions, presidential plebiscites in the succeeding five elections—between 1971 and 1999—gave Assad over 99 percent of the vote. In 1974, Assad moved once more to take control of all professional associations and labor unions whose right to strike had already been revoked ten years earlier on the premise that the state represented workers and the working class.

While Assad received some semblance of legitimacy from the elections, they did nothing to increase popular participation in the running of the country. During his tenure, the presidency was transformed into the undisputed focus of power. Hafez al-Assad was state president, secretary-general of the Ba'ath Party, and the commander of the armed forces. To achieve this he relied on a close clique of kinsmen, the Alawi, to control key military, security, and intelligence positions. Nonetheless, fearing that his regime might be labeled sectarian, he appointed a number of Sunnis to visible positions in the government.

Assad's Political Legacy

Hafez al-Assad introduced a new style of leadership in the country. A realist, as opposed to being an ideologue, he pursued a pragmatic approach to running the country, something that the old guard of the party detested. His pragmatism greatly benefited Syria, as well as his family and Alawi allies, as the country rose to a prominence beyond its economic or military might. According to Christopher Dickey, Assad "never completely embrace[d] his allies, and never definitively [broke all contact] with his enemies. He [was] a master of suspense, a Hitchcock of policy" in a complex and unforgiving environment.[10] In pursuing his goals, the president was cautious but ready to use ruthless means. In Lebanon, his opponents were subjected to brutal reprisals, and at home he used harsh measures against all his political foes. For instance, when the Muslim Brotherhood in Hama staged an uprising in February 1982, 12,000 troops sealed off the city, systematically pummelled it using artillery, tanks, and helicopter gunships, and killed between 5,000 and 10,000 civilians during three weeks of bloody fighting.[11] An uprising in Aleppo met with the same fate, and other enemies of his regime were treated severely, as documented by human rights organizations worldwide. The toughness of the regime and its controversial foreign policy decisions were based on the overwhelming concern, if not obsession, Assad had with maintaining the regime.[12]

Nevertheless, the cautious and calculating nature of Hafez al-Assad's presidency enabled Syria to maneuver out of many difficult situations and to seize many opportunities to further its interests. When faced with international isolation, Assad always managed to reposition Syria, such as when faced by the loss of its main cold war ally, the Soviet Union. In the altered post–cold war international environment, Assad managed to maneuver Syria closer to the United States, the only remaining superpower.

The opportunity for increased legitimacy in the eyes of western governments presented itself when Assad's staunch enemy, Iraq, invaded Kuwait in August 1990. Syrian forces participated in the coalition counteroffensive that drove Iraq out of Kuwait (though not in the role of a combatant). Diplomatically and economically, this realignment has proved very rewarding to Syria, which has been given huge amounts of financial aid by the countries of the Gulf in payment. Meanwhile, the United States has toned down its diplomatic and media criticism of the regime. Consequently, Syria has improved its relations with the West further—for instance, by softening its policy vis-à-vis Israel. Its participation in the 1991 Madrid peace conference is testimony to the altered policy positions Syria adopted in the final years of Hafez al-Assad's rule. As Abu Khalil pointed out: "Under al-Assad a principle emerged: the more the regime feels itself isolated in the region, the more paranoid and militant its behavior becomes."[13] Nevertheless, because of Assad's leadership style, Syria became a stable nation and his personal control was secure. Syria became a regional power, without whose participation durable peace in the region would be difficult to conceive. Even his staunchest critics now appreciate that the resolution of the Arab-Israeli conflict is impossible without involving Syria, and this is reflected in the importance attached to the Israeli-Syrian track of the peace negotiations.

However, it must be understood that the stability based on Hafez al-Assad's person allowed for serious uncertainties, not the least of which arose upon his death in June 2000. The sixty-nine-year-old president had been seriously ill for some time, suffering from diabetes and liver and kidney problems, and he had not made a public appearance since his March 2000 meeting in Geneva with President Bill Clinton. Assad's poor health and advancing age made the future of his leadership undependable, and instability clouded over his succession at a time when the region—and Syria in particular—needed dynamic leadership in lieu of the "peace process" with Israel. This became increasingly evident when he suffered a heart attack in 1983 and serious rivalry surfaced among aspirants to the leadership of the country. In that case, Assad settled the matter by exiling his brother, Rifaat al-Assad, after forces loyal to him managed to defeat the plot. In recent years, Hafez al-Assad groomed his son Basil as his successor, before Basil died in a 1994 car accident in Damascus.

In 1998, Rifaat al-Assad was expelled from the Ba'ath Party's Regional Command and stripped of his title as vice president. Although the positions were largely ceremonial—Rifaat had been living in exile in France and Spain for fifteen years—it was a sign that Hafez al-Assad was attempting to stage-manage the ascension of his son Bashar to the presidency and remove any potential rivals. Another member of the National Command was expelled with Rifaat, and the head of state security was charged with economic corruption and removed from office. Hafez al-Assad had Bashar lead a public campaign against corruption in the state and party apparatus. The campaign culminated in the forced resignation of Prime Minister Mahmoud al-Zu'bi and Transportation Minister Mufeed Abdel Kareem, as well as several lower-ranking members of the bureaucracy, in March 2000. Zu'bi had been a prominent member of the Syrian ruling elite for over two decades, having served as prime minister since 1987. He was accused of amassing a great fortune through corruption. So were his vice premier for economic affairs, twenty general directors and deputy ministers, armed forces chief of staff General Hikmat al-Shihabi, and several members of their immediate families. Zu'bi committed suicide before he could be brought to trial.[14]

In the middle of March 2000, a cabinet shuffle took place and Bashar al-Assad's supporters were placed in key cabinet positions, including the post of prime minister. Two months later Bashar was selected to serve in the Ba'ath Party's Regional Command, all in an attempt to prepare him for the presidency. Observers believe that the campaign of Bashar al-Assad against corruption and for reform was to establish his power and put his stamp on Syrian politics before his father passed away. Then when Hafez al-Assad died in June 2000, the transition occurred smoothly. The key party, government, and institutional leadership, particularly the military, immediately closed ranks behind Bashar al-Assad. Despite a challenge from his uncle, Rifaat al-Assad, Bashar managed to maintain control of the coalition of family-based forces his father had developed. Most important, he was able to depend on the support of his brother-in-law, Gen. Assaf Shawkat, head of military intelligence.

Bashar al-Assad is being credited with bringing fresh blood into the government, with an emphasis on youthful ideas, economic reforms, and openness. Sixty percent of the new ministers appointed to cabinet in May 2000 were young technocrats or university professors with close connections to Bashar. This group included the ministers of foreign affairs, the interior, defense, economics and finance, planning, and agriculture.

As the only candidate in July 2000, Bashar received 97.29 percent of the votes in a public referendum. His inaugural address stressed a return of the Golan from Israel, hailed relations with Lebanon as a model for inter-Arab cooperation, and promised economic reforms to create a robust new economy.

Assad's Style of Governance and Civil Society

Hafez al-Assad controlled all aspects of Syrian politics and the life of the Syrian people. The centrality of his personality, in both military and political institutions, has been unprecedented. To attain this control, he institutionalized his power base on three levels.

First, to control the military, Assad instituted a continuous transfer of lower-ranking army officers from unit to unit as well as a policy of giving senior officers virtually empty commands. He maintained competition between Alawi and Sunni officers by placing them in parallel chains-of-command to keep watch over each other, with both reporting directly to the president on each other's activities. Further, he appointed his most trusted officers throughout the middle ranks in the military. This made it almost impossible for permanent cliques to form, which had been the primary source of all previous coups. These practices neutralized the military as an oppositional political force and linked it directly to his personal success.

Assad also ensured that the minister of defense and the chief of staff were members of the party's Regional Command. At the same time, those military personnel in the Central Committee were given parallel positions in a shadow Ba'ath Party organization he was building in the military. This, in effect, emptied the civilian party of any real content and kept it a shell, while real power became more and more concentrated in the military. This policy resulted in the building of checks and balances against a repeat of the 1970 struggle between Assad and party leaders.

In this situation, personal loyalty to Hafez al-Assad became the yardstick with which to measure party and military advancement. Personal corruption was tolerated as long as loyalty to his person was unquestioned. Thus, following Assad's rise to power, these military-political figures became economically prominent, socially powerful, and politically influential, creating a new elite that had military, economic, and political control but was always dependent for its power and privileges on the Ba'ath regime and Assad's personal approval.

Once he had complete power in the military, he moved to reconstruct the political environment. The creation of the Progressive National Front in 1972 robbed the political groupings that formed the Front of any real power and made them subservient to the Ba'ath Party, as we saw earlier. Assad was secretary-general of the party and its Syrian Regional Command. Between congresses, the Central Committee was supposed to discuss and approve, on behalf of the congress, all decisions made by the secretary-general. In the Eighth Regional Congress of January 1985, even this nominal election of the Central Committee was suspended, and Congress authorized Hafez al-Assad to appoint the Central Committee himself. The Eighth Regional Congress was the only party congress held for some fifteen years, although party bylaws called for one to be held every five years. In May 2000, the long overdue Ninth Congress was held with the express purpose of legitimizing Assad's son Bashar as his heir apparent.

The third feature of Hafez al-Assad's rule was his heavy dependence on his ethnocultural kinsmen, the Alawites, whom he placed in key positions in the military and the party. In this way he simultaneously promoted their position in Syrian society and tied their destiny to his own. For example, the Alawites hold twelve of the eighteen seats assigned to the military in the party's Central Committee, and the key positions in the military are all in their hands. Sunnis hold technical positions that have only nominal power.

In Syria, there is no civil society because no nongovernmentally controlled institutions are allowed and all legal political parties are members of the Front, which has no power to act independently. All political opposition has been banned since 1963, and all professional and labor unions have been gradually put under the direct control of the Ba'ath Party. In fact, all political activities are considered to be illegal unless they come under the banner of the Front, and special military courts were established to deal with all such "illegal" activity, leaving the executive branch—Hafez al-Assad—to make virtually all decisions for the Syrian state. For example, since March 1980, simply belonging to the Muslim Brotherhood is a crime punishable by death. Thus, opposition has been forced to go underground, and the effectiveness of Assad's policies were evident in the fact that only one opposition group, the Syrian Liberation Front, has surfaced since 1982. Representing the Muslim Brotherhood, socialist Arabs, nationalist groups, and a number of independents, it is a noncohesive umbrella organization. These groups, however, have limited local support, with the exception of the Muslim Brotherhood, which stands as the major opposition force to the regime, especially between 1979 and 1982, as the movement utilized its relationship with the mosques and imams, in the creation of a mezzo organization in an effort to penetrate the entire society of Syria. However, after the events of 1979–82, even the leftist and nationalist forces have entered into a tactical alliance with the Muslim Brotherhood against the regime. The oppression that followed the Hama massacres, in February 1982, however, has made it very difficult for the Muslim Brotherhood to have any serious impact on Syrian politics.

The Syrian Economy

Potentially Syria has the resource base to establish a prosperous economy for its citizens. Relative to many other Arab states, it is economically fortunate; it has fertile agricultural lands, oil, and other mineral resources. Moreover, it is strategically located on trade routes to the Arabian Peninsula and the Indian Ocean. Oil pipelines and road links between western and eastern Europe traverse its territory. Also, because of its dominant position in Arab politics, a legacy of Hafez al-Assad, it has benefited a great deal from aid donated by the rich countries of the Gulf.

In spite of these advantages, Syria's economic situation is dismal. Reasons for the state of the economy may well be found in some unavoidable problems as well as human failures. The country's preoccupation with security has been a major drain on its resources. The military budget consumes about 50 percent of national spending. Also, the economy is burdened by the dominance of the inefficient public sector. However, there have been moves to revitalize the private sector, albeit slowly and haphazardly. Luckily, the country has not been subjected to the rigors of International Monetary Fund structural adjustment measures.

The biggest economic problem Syria faces has been its burgeoning indebtedness, which acts to frustrate efforts to get the entire economy working again. It has been estimated that the total external national debt amounted to U.S.$16 billion, roughly equivalent to its total GDP.[15] Much of the debt is owed to Russia for trade with the former Soviet Union; the largest debt is owed to the World Bank. The inability to pay these debts has blocked the country from securing fresh loans from the World Bank and foreign investors, except from the Gulf countries.

Syria cashed in greatly on its participation in the 1991 Gulf war as a member of the U.S.–led coalition. Aid from the Arab Gulf, estimated between 1977 and 1992 at about U.S.$15 billion,[16] has continuously flowed into the Syrian treasury. Its citizens working abroad have also helped by remitting part of their earnings to the Syrian economy. The agriculture sector has also dramatically improved as a result of good weather and prudent policies. Furthermore, the government has taken steps to reform the economy at a more fundamental level. Although privatization is opposed officially, more people are setting up private businesses. Perhaps more important, the country pinned its hopes on the dividends that will accrue if comprehensive peace is achieved. In 1990 a new economic program was instituted in which subsidies previously offered to the consumer were drastically reduced. The national currency was devalued, import-export laws were altered, and in 1991 a new investment law was passed.[17] Two decrees were issued in May 2000, less than one month before Hafez al-Assad died, in which ten articles of the 1991 reforms were repealed to satisfy the criticisms of the business community. In these decrees some currency controls were lifted, and tax exemptions for investors were granted in order to stimulate the economy. The official newspaper *Tashrin* on 16 March—the day the new cabinet was sworn in—declared that the reason for economic stagnation in Syria, despite the liberalization measures of 1991, rested on the backs of investors, both foreign and domestic, as well as restrictive financial regulations. In fact, the entire investment during the eight years after 1991 did not exceed U.S.$3 billion. In addition, the country's exports decreased and the salaries of government workers were frozen. Consequently, there was virtually no improvement in the people's standard of living and no potential for consumer-driven growth.

The failure of these programs resulted in the ouster of many longtime members of the ruling elite in May 2000. Government ministers were selected on the basis of their technical expertise and their loyalty to Bashar al-Assad. With the May 2000 decrees, Bashar was seen as putting his stamp on the Syrian economy and political order before the death of his father. Decree no. 8 adjusted the penal code, allowing traders to hold foreign currency in an attempt to portray an economic openness in what had been a centrally controlled and often heavily dependent Syrian economy, which was now in need of major reform to begin opening up. Under the previous law, private citizens who used foreign currency could be prosecuted and jailed for three to ten years.

It is clear that under Bashar economic reforms have taken priority over political reforms with the promise of private banks, a free market exchange rate, and a national stock exchange being the focus of his first administration. It is hoped that by opening up the economy, foreign investment will be encouraged and some of the estimated $80 billion Syrians have invested abroad might return home. Continuing the efforts initiated in the mid-1990s by his father, Bashar has negotiated settlements with both international financial institutions and foreign governments to reschedule Syria's foreign debt. Some $1 billion has been rescheduled over the next twenty years with the German government, permitting Syria to access low-interest bank loans from the European Union. This success for Bashar follows on Hafez al-Assad's successful 1997 negotiations, which will see the World Bank return to Syria in 2002 following the repayment of past debts, and some 75 million Euros ($63.75 million) raised through a loan from the European Investment Bank (EIB) for the development of electric power. In spite of these positive steps with western financial institutions, Syria still has an outstanding debt in excess of $12 billion to its former cold war patron, Russia.

Foreign Relations

Hafez al-Assad transformed Syria into a major player in the politics of the Middle East region. His close ties with the Soviet Union during the cold war facilitated the acquisition of large amounts of advanced weaponry, magnifying Syria's position as a "confrontation state" on Israel's border. Being determined to address the military imbalance in the region, Hafez al-Assad launched a massive defense buildup. So successful was the program that—according to many analysts—Syria gained parity with Israel on defense capability, in the quantitative sense. Although Syrian units in the Gulf coalition impressed western observers with their professionalism, basic skills, and resourcefulness relative to other coalition armies, Israel's qualitative edge remains unassailable. Syrian military might was put to the test when it was drawn into the conflict in Lebanon, and ultimately Syria was able to impose its will over its neighbor through force of arms.

The Arab-Israeli conflict has dominated foreign affairs. Part of Syria's land is still under Israeli occupation. Syrian leadership sought to maintain a united Arab front in order to fight for the rights of the Arabs usurped by Israel. This proved difficult, however, due to inter-Arab squabbling, which was most evident when Egypt defected from the Arab fold to sign a separate peace deal with Israel at Camp David. By default, Syria then became the center of opposition to the Israeli occupation of Arab lands, as it was the single largest military force bordering the Jewish state. By 1996, Arab unity in confronting Israel had been almost totally shattered; Jordan normalized its relations with Israel, and even the Palestinians went ahead in signing a separate peace agreement with their former enemy in September 1993. Syria could do nothing to effectively oppose these moves. Instead, it became involved in bilateral talks with Israel, which were sponsored by the United States soon after the Oslo process began with the Palestinians. Any concrete breakthrough, however, has yet to materialize, as Syria requires complete Israeli withdrawal from the occupied Golan Heights, and Israel requires security guarantees if it removes its military forces from the strategic region. Returning to the international border that existed on 4 June 1967 (the day before the Six-Day War broke out and Israel occupied the entire Golan Heights) has been understood by the Israeli leadership to be Syria's precondition to negotiation. However, Israel has proved unwilling to unilaterally withdraw.[18]

Syria's relations with the western powers, particularly the United States, were also influenced by the conflict with Israel. During the cold war, Syrians were bitter about American support for Israel, while the United States detested Syrian leader Hafez al-Assad for his suspected close ties with the Communist world—which worked against American interests in the Arab world—and for the growing Islamic activist movement throughout the region. The U.S. State Department placed Syria on a list of states that "sponsor international terrorism."[19] British Prime Minister Margaret Thatcher cut diplomatic relations with Syria in 1986 after evidence suggested Syrian involvement in a plot to plant a bomb on an El Al jumbo jet at London's Heathrow airport. Because of the U.S. stance, the Syrian attitude against American policy hardened. In fact, Syria went so far as to endorse the actions of militant groups fighting the Israelis and Americans as well as other western powers perceived to be close to the Israelis. In Lebanon, radical groups working with full backing of the Syrians carried out devastating assaults against western and Israeli targets, destroying U.S. Secretary of State George Shultz's 1983 peace treaty between Israel and Lebanon. In retaliation, moves were made to isolate Syria in the international community.

The collapse of the Soviet Union was a serious challenge to the rulers of Syria. Militarily, diplomatically, and economically, it undermined the state. Hafez al-Assad, however, needed only the opportunity provided by the Gulf war to exercise his considerable shrewdness and bring Syria back into the ranks of international and regional political actors. Syrian forces joined the multinational forces that drove Saddam Hussein's forces from Kuwait, allowing Syria, in the aftermath of the war, to shed its pariah status in the international community. American hostility to the regime was also mollified, and Syria came to be considered a major player in the evolving regional peace process. Visits by key U.S. politicians to Syria increased, symbolizing the importance accorded to Damascus in the Madrid peace process started in 1991. Reflecting the new mood, Syria has been given a freer hand to expand its influence and protect its interests in Lebanon.

Initially, the peace process, especially after 1993, presented some difficulties for the Syrian leadership. Where other Arab states—Jordan, the Maghrib countries, and even the Gulf states—rushed to reconcile relations with Israel in order to improve their economic prospects and relations with the United States, Syria and Israel had faced each other in open hostilities as recently as 1982. The relationship between the two nations was marked by severe mistrust, and while the United States was willing to accord Syria some status due to its participation in the anti-Iraq coalition, Israel certainly was not as forgiving. Hafez al-Assad's regime was also traditionally at odds with Yasser Arafat and the PLO, removing any influence it might have had for joint negotiation with the PLO in order to facilitate a comprehensive peace agreement. Also, with both the western powers and its Arab neighbors, there was the complication of Syria's cordial relations with the Islamic Republic of Iran, which had been mostly pragmatic in nature and driven by both states' mutual enmity toward Saddam Hussein's Iraq. Assad, the secular autocrat, would certainly have no ideological reason to ally himself with the Shiite and fundamentalist forces in Tehran, especially after his own repression of all religious political activists in Syria.

Israel was quite happy to keep Syria isolated during the "successful" peace talks with Jordan and the PLO. Israel wanted to ensure its position as regional hegemony, a role that could be challenged seriously only by a coalition that included Syria. Syrian involvement in the peace process could also have resulted in U.S. acknowledgment of Syrian importance and influence, further undermining Israel's preeminence. Assad, for his part, did not seem to be in any hurry to change Syria's long-standing policies. The only leverage that could be used to alter the Syrian negotiating maneuvers, though not its bottom-line requirements for a peace deal, were economic in nature. The Syrian economy, however, while hardly booming, was not critically threatened. The flow of military equipment from the now disbanded USSR was soon replaced by smaller but well considered purchases through a 1990 Friendship Pact with Russia as well as negotiated deals with China and Iran. Syria gradually solidified its hold over Lebanon, to the point where it has become accepted by many in the international community as an annex of Syria—not in name but in deed—as all political and administrative processes have the Syrians acting as final arbiters. Hafez al-Assad seemed to have regained the confidence of long-term Middle East observers that Syria had now returned to prominence in regional politics despite the immense changes facing policymakers in Damascus.

Beginning in November 1995, with the assassination of Yitzhak Rabin, the Israeli-Palestinian peace negotiations entered a period of great difficulty. Assad refused to attend the funeral, which was exploited by many of the regional heads of state as a "photo op" for the new unilateral Middle East. Rulers who had long been at violent odds with Israel lined up with the new Israeli prime minister, Shimon Peres, for the international media. Assad's absence asserted Syria's independence and served notice that the U.S.–sponsored peace process would have to come to Damascus. By standing resolute, Assad forced the United States to regard Syria as an important regional power and to respect its position in order for peace to be achieved in the region. The Palestinian National Authority (PNA) elections in January 1996 cast more doubt on the legitimacy of the settlement, as the tactics of Yasser Arafat's Fatah faction of the PLO raised serious questions regarding the legitimacy of the PLO to be the sole representatives of the Palestinian people. When the Islamic militants of Hamas began suicide attacks against Israeli targets in February 1996, it became clear that there was indeed significant opposition to the peace process among Palestinians and other Arabs, and not all Palestinians regarded Arafat as president.

A second challenge to the unanimity of the peace negotiations came in April 1996, when Hizbullah guerrillas based in southern Lebanon began to launch rocket attacks over the border into northern Israel. Responding to Israeli attacks against Lebanese civilians and Palestinian refugees living in southern Lebanon, Hizbullah retaliated in an effort to remove Israeli occupation forces from Lebanese soil. The impact of the attacks were minor, when compared with the level of day-to-day violence of southern Lebanon or during the *intifada,* but Shimon Peres was in the middle of a difficult election campaign—facing charges from the hawkish Likud Party that he was "soft on terrorism." The response, named Operation Grapes of Wrath by the Israeli Defense Force (IDF), was a calculated move designed to trade a bit of rhetorical condemnation from the United States and its allies for potential electoral points in Israel. The military operation, driven by campaign logic, dramatically backfired when the fighter bomber, helicopter, and artillery strikes designed to flush out Hizbullah fighters killed hundreds of Lebanese civilians and Palestinian refugees. In one attack, direct artillery hits against a UN-protected refugee camp killed over 100 men, women, and children, including four Fijian soldiers serving as UN peacekeepers. The international community reacted immediately, and efforts by international organizations to secure a cease-fire quickly followed.

Due to its position in Lebanon and its links with Hizbullah, Syria suddenly possessed a great deal of leverage with the international community if it could convince Hizbullah to recognize an interim cease-fire. Assad played his cards very carefully, meeting with the Russian and French foreign ministers on their trips through regional capitals while, at one point, refusing to meet with U.S. Secretary of State Warren Christopher, who attempted in vain to visit Damascus. Syrian troops in Lebanon did not retaliate against IDF forces in Israel's occupied "security zone," but aided in the evacuation of civilians and refugees.

The cease-fire that was eventually reached had Syria acting as the representative of Hizbullah. While it only returned southern Lebanon to the pre-attack status quo—tacitly recognizing Israel's ability to strike IDF-identified "terrorist" targets in its self-declared "security zone" in southern Lebanon—it demonstrated Syria's return to status as an important Arab foil to Israel in Middle East politics. More important, it is a player that can act with the recognition of the international community, unlike Iran or Iraq, who have become isolated. As a sign of this, the United States has further retreated from its position that Syria is a major supporter of terrorism, despite Damascus's obvious links with Hizbullah, as both Israel and the United States now prefer to publicly blame the actions of Hizbullah on Iran.

Less than three months after the Oslo Agreement was signed, the United States sponsored new and secretive bilateral talks between Syria and Israel. These talks followed a summit meeting between Bill Clinton and Hafez al-Assad in January 1994, which resulted in the establishment of "a mechanism for resolving bilateral problems between Syria and the United States."[20] Syrian and Israeli diplomats began meetings a week later in the United States, establishing a framework for regular— though secret—meetings between Syrian and Israeli ambassadors in Washington, which were inaugurated on 29 July 1994. The Israeli ambassador to Washington at the time, Itimar Rabinovich, would later write that "as early as November 1994 the security issue came to dominate the talks, both in two meetings between the chiefs of staff of the Israeli and Syrian armed forces, and in our negotiations of the 'non-paper' on 'the aims and principles of the security arrangements.'"[21] The assassination of Rabin and the May 1996 election of Benjamin Netanyahu from the Likud Party as prime minister put an end to the secret negotiations."[22]

In the diplomatic tension following the May 1996 Israeli election, Syria took a hard-line negotiating stance, returning to its longtime desire for Arab unanimity against Israel. With the fall of Israel's Likud government in 1999, the United States revived peace talks between Israel and Syria. Israel's new Labor prime minister, Ehud Barak, who had been a protégé of Yitzhak Rabin and had served as IDF chief of staff in 1994 and Israel's foreign minister in 1995, met in Washington in March 2000 with Syria's foreign minister, Farouk al-Shara', in an effort to resume the stalled negotiations. With little progress since the Rabin assassination in 1996, and a loss of momentum due to the intransigent Netanyahu's Likud administration, the United States hoped to revive the process initiated in Madrid in 1991. Through U.S. intermediaries, Yitzhak Rabin had committed Israel to the basic Syrian conditions of complete Israeli withdrawal from the Golan Heights as a precondition for Syrian involvement in the talks. On 26 March 2000, Bill Clinton met with Assad in Geneva to convey the Israeli position and further encourage a resolution. However, Clinton failed to secure Syria's agreement with Israel's terms, and with Assad's death in June 2000 and the election of a conservative Republican president in November 2000, the necessary momentum for a resolution was lost.

Republic of Lebanon: Independence and Nationalism

The territory of Lebanon has been divided, occupied, and disputed for much of its modern history. At times a separate administrative unit within the Ottoman Empire, it also was under the direction of its powerful neighbor, Syria, a situation which would continue even when both countries became independent. Fractiously divided by eighteen religious and ethnic sects, it has also remained divided by the cultural influences of the Arab and Islamic worlds to which it was born and the European and secular worlds introduced with French colonialism. The creation of "Greater Lebanon," while for the Maronites a welcome fulfillment of a hard-fought dream, added fuel to Arab nationalism. The dominant Muslim Sunnis, the most vehement opponents of the border changes, felt threatened by the inevitable dwindling of their influence in the new arrangement. Druze and Greek Orthodox displeasure with the status quo arose from the fact that they were effectively cut off from the majority of their brethren in Syria. The close links within these communities, for instance, were clearly evident in 1926 when the Druze in Syria revolted against the French and their kinsmen in Lebanon came to their aid. A year later, the rebellion was contained, though resentment against the French mandate was not quelled. When a new constitution for Lebanon was drafted on 24 May 1926, it was seen as a bid to calm the situation by making the country a parliamentary democracy. On the basis of the 1932 census, representation in the parliament and the government was subject to the numerical strength of sects and was drawn from the experience of the mutassarifiate. A few years later, in November 1936, a Franco-Lebanese treaty was signed recognizing the independence of Lebanon, in the wake of a similar treaty that accorded the same status to Syria. However, events in France during the Second World War interfered with the implementation of the accord.

When British and Free French forces defeated the Nazi-supported rulers of Vichy France, Britain exerted pressure on the postwar leadership of Charles de Gaulle to grant independence to Lebanon. By this time the domestic scene was united in bringing the French Mandate to a close. De Gaulle called for elections. This brought to power a new indigenous government, headed by a Maronite Christian, Bishara Khoury, as president and a Sunni, Riad Solh, as prime minister.

The new government hastily adopted reforms that never met with French approval. In a controversial move, the French detained members of the new regime and suspended the constitution. In its place, a puppet government was installed under the leadership of Emile Edde. For the French, the move proved counterproductive, since it further united and strengthened domestic opposition to their rule. Inevitably the French had to succumb to the rising tide of discontent and withdraw in 1946. The country left behind was dominated by Maronites, but was divided as to what political orientation to pursue, pro-western or pro-Arab. Even more significantly, the dominant sectarian communities remained deeply distrustful of each other.

From the outset, independence for Lebanon was destined to be a bitter harvest. Building a single country whose past had been dogged by periods of extended acrimony from countless sectarian communities is obviously an uphill task. Although there had been ingenious attempts, such as the National Pact, to reconcile the antagonistic groups, pressures of discord proved insurmountable during certain periods of the country's independent era. Indeed, violence became a sinister and inextricable component of its political development. To shed more light on the politics of Lebanon, it is essential to have a glimpse at the social composition of the country, the religious factors as well as foreign intervention.

Marginality and Its Political Implications

Lebanon has always been a sanctuary for wandering marginals, "victims of collapsing empires, of revolutions, and struggles to integrate new nations," who "have rootlessly wandered the globe over, pathetic but fascinating in their talents at survival."[23] It is this character which gives the country its unique and, at times, traumatic experiences.

The founders of Lebanon, the Maronites, form a dominant sectarian community in the country. This Uniate Christian community escaped persecution in the second half of the seventh century in Syria and found a safe haven in Mount Lebanon. During the Crusades, they developed a strong communion with Rome. In 1861, they formed 76 percent of the population of the mountain.[24] Their numbers have grown, however, and according to the census, by 1932 they had become the single most dominant sect in Lebanon. The Maronites consider themselves a separate people, separate from the Arab world, and they look toward the West for alliances and cultural influences. French influence is indeed great within the Maronite community. For them, Lebanon is their homeland, to be defended zealously against hostile intruders, as they have been doing since the time of the Crusades.

The second largest of the Christian sects is the Greek Orthodox, who are not on good terms with the Maronite community. Contrary to the Maronites, they do not form a compact community. They are dispersed over the entire region, and many have kinsmen living in Syria. It is this factor which made them receptive to the ideas of Pan-Arabism and Pan-Syrianism. The community is known for bringing forth prominent leaders of the Arab world, such as Antun Sa'ada, the founder of the Syrian Social National Party; Michel 'Aflaq, one of the founders of the Ba'ath Arab Socialist Party, and George Habash, father of the Arab Nationalist Movement and later of the radical Popular Front for the Liberation of Palestine. Smaller Christian groups include the Roman Catholics, the Armenian (Gregorian) Orthodox, Nestorian Assyrians, as well as a few Protestants and Jews.

Among Muslims, the Sunnis are the dominant sect, and traditionally they were more prosperous and better educated than the Shiites, who remain a largely disadvantaged group in Lebanese society. There are also Alawites, or Nusayris, but most are found in Syria, where they have come to wield enormous political influence far in excess of their numerical size. The Druze are another sect in Lebanon, and while they are a closed community, they have played a crucial role in the creation of Lebanon. Historically, they are adept at organizing themselves into fierce and disciplined fighting groups.

The most recent marginal groups to flock into Lebanon in search of a safe haven were the Palestinians, arriving as refugees from the Arab-Israeli wars of 1948 and 1967 and the Jordanian civil strife of 1970. While some of the refugees have left Lebanon, most still live in the seventeen camps set up with the help of the United Nations Relief and Works Agency (UNRWA), an agency specially created to cater to the humanitarian needs of the displaced Palestinians. The total number of Palestinians in Lebanon is often unclear, but the UNRWA puts their figure at 370,000.[25] Many, particularly the Maronites, resent the Palestinian presence in Lebanon. Because they are almost entirely Sunni Muslims and only a few of them retain their refugee status, the Palestinians introduce a new demographic element that threatens the power-sharing arrangement in the country. Furthermore, their presence radically transformed Lebanon into an active front in the Arab conflict with Israel, which has cost the Lebanese dearly.

Confessional State

Lebanon is home to followers of diverse religions and sects. Christian and Muslim sects live together, forming a precarious balance. The different, and often contradictory, positions adopted by the multiple sects and communities are an ever-present menace to the balance attempted by any Lebanese coalition. Disagreements between the numerous groups often translate into political rivalry, sectarian violence, and entrenched religion into politics. Religion first played a central role in public affairs during the Ottoman mutassarifiate system of government. It was decided that the mutassarif (governor) would be a Christian from the Ottoman Empire but not of Lebanese nationality.

When independence came to Lebanon in 1943, within artificial borders arbitrarily fixed by the French colonial rulers, there were six large religious sects and about a dozen smaller ones, all with different traditions, cultures, and loyalties. The Maronites had close affiliation with France and the West, while the Sunnis, who had benefited little from the mandate, looked to the East and the emerging power of Arab nationalism.[26] It was through the wisdom and statesmanship of Bishara Khoury, the Maronite president, and Riad Solh, the Sunni prime minister, that a consensus was found. The basis of the cooperation was the unwritten National Pact, in essence a "gentlemen's agreement" that limited the ambitions of the various sects in pursuit of foreign policy desires. The Maronites, the traditional allies of the West, were not to seek full alliance with the West, and the Sunnis, who backed Pan-Arabism, were required to temper their enthusiasm in that respect. Domestically, positions were reserved for members of designated sects. Accordingly, the president, prime minister, and Assembly speaker were to come from the Maronite, Sunni, and Shiite communities, respectively. Also, ministerial and top positions in the civil service were allocated with regard to the sectarian composition of the country. In the legislature, Christian and Muslim representation was fixed by a ratio of 6 to 5. Indeed, in the beginning the Christians, particularly the Maronites, wielded enormous power over the other communities, which resulted in some resentment. This was justified by the fact that the Maronites were more numerous than other sects. However, through the establishment of "greater Lebanon" in 1920, the population balance tipped in favor of Muslims, which brought more pressure on the confessional system.

For the Shiites especially, who outnumber the Sunnis, the feeling that they are marginalized in the system is a serious and credible one indeed. Likewise, the Druze have many reasons for hating the status quo, since the agreement automatically disqualified them from the top three positions of authority in the country. These tensions contributed to the volatile political climate in the new state. The fragility of the system was put to the test in 1958 when a crisis developed between the then-president, Camille Chamoun (1952–58), who allied the country with the West within the auspices of the Eisenhower Doctrine—and Arab nationalists who were closely drawn to Nasserism. When U.S. forces were brought in to quell the crisis, the solution was found in replacing Chamoun as president with Fouad Chehab (1958–64), the Lebanese army commander who refused to use the army against the Muslim rebels. This crisis highlighted the fact that the system was not flexible enough to accommodate demands of discontented communities, a state of affairs that ultimately manifested itself in the 1975–76 crisis.[27] Over time, however, the need for reforms became paramount as civil strife exhausted the energies of the various communities and the Christian dominance of political power in the country was curtailed for the sake of peace.

Party Politics and Elections

Constitutionally, Lebanon is a parliamentary democracy, with a president whose term of office lasts six years. A prime minister is the head of government, who initially was appointed, subject to the approval of the parliament, by the president. Now the prime minister is appointed by the parliament. Although on the surface politics are conducted on the western model, in practice the situation is rather different. Politics are dominated by a closed club of elites, the Zu'ama (singular Za'im), who are the various heads of a sectarian clientele. Za'im owe their position to ancestral kinship and wield enormous power within their constituency. "The Za'im was a political leader who might not be a minister, might even not be a deputy, but whose power gave him control not only over groups of deputies but also over government ministers as well."[28] Because inheritance is a central element in the Zu'ama system, politics in the country came to be dominated by a small number of families. Some of these families owe their dominance to the wealth and power accumulated during the feudal past, while others have succeeded in business and finance. A glance at the power brokers in the country clearly illustrates the centrality of some families. For instance, the Eddie, Solh, Karami, Jumblatt, and Gemayel have provided a number of politicians; both in the parliament and government, the familiar names of the few families remain.

In the Lebanese political system, the Za'im's role is that of a mediator, an arbiter, who allocates the resources of the government to the people within his sect.[29] To maintain the loyalty of his clients or constituency, the Za'im provides a link between them and the government, allocates favors such as jobs and other benefits, and mediates disputes in times of sectarian rivalry. The Za'im forges alliances that cut across sectarian lines, in a sense bolstering the overall system, since the Za'im has a stake in its maintenance. Beyond these traditional Zu'ama, ecclesiastical hierarchy has played an important role in Lebanon. The Maronite Patriarch is a political force in Lebanon due to his large following, and Muslim clergy have also come to play a pivotal role in the politics of the country, especially due to the tendency of Shiite activists to organize into militias such as Amal and Hizbullah. Political parties, in contrast to the Zu'ama and the ecclesiastical hierarchy, are of minor importance in the political system. In fact, the sectarian parties, such as the Kataib, the Najjadah, the National Liberal Party, the Progressive Socialist Party, and the National Bloc are often mere appendages of either the za'imship or the ecclesiastical hierarchies.[30] Although some claim not to be confessional, they all lack a comprehensive platform or a nationalist ideology, which inevitably limits their appeal to specific communities. Only a few parties—the transnational parties—such as the Communists, the Ba'athists, and the Syrian Social Nationalist Party—have solicited broad support. Even the leaders of these parties are either members of the big city zu'ama or are allied with them.

Given this political environment, it is not surprising that Lebanese democracy is unique and a far cry from what is practiced in the West.

Formally, there are elections, but such exercises could never be described as free—any more than the resulting parliament could be described as representative. A candidate wishing to enter the race must attach himself to a za'im, without whose support there is no chance of electoral success. Moreover, the candidate needs large sums of money, for elections in Lebanon are expensive. Vote buying is a common practice, as is the hiring of *qabadayat* (muscle men) to disrupt the opposition and ensure that supporters toe the line.[31] This explains why deputies often come from wealthy backgrounds and why, once a candidate has made it into the parliament, he remains indebted to the za'im—for his reelection is contingent on good behavior and cooperation.

Civil Strife and the Search for National Reconciliation

Internecine conflict, in some cases catastrophic, has consumed a good portion of the country's independent era, characterized by sectarian violence, foreign intervention, and failed attempts at reconciliation. In 1958, Lebanon was engulfed in civil strife when Arab nationalists battled Camille Chamoun, who was a dedicated supporter of the western powers. When the Arab nationalists appeared to be gaining support, American forces were "invited" into Lebanon by President Dwight Eisenhower to restore the Maronite majority. In 1975, the country entered the first phase of a devastating civil war, which was followed by the invasion by the Syrian military. The Syrians became active combatants, and their diplomatic efforts to reconcile the belligerents ended in failure. Arab peacekeeping forces were sent in, but with no success. Complicating the situation further were the Israeli military incursions into Lebanese territory (1977–78) and a full-blown invasion (1982–85) that was initiated under the guise of covert military operations against enemies based on Lebanese soil. UN peacekeepers were brought in, again with little success. A sinister development was the establishment and rapid growth of sectarian militia forces, whose operations frustrated any attempts at national reconciliation. In 1989 a peace accord was agreed upon, and thus far it has held, despite isolated acts of violence and the presence of foreign forces. Lebanon has now embarked on an ambitious program of reconstruction.

Civil War

The reasons underlying the Lebanese civil war can be traced to events in the Middle East that aggravated tensions in the delicate fabric of Lebanese political society. The creation of Israel in 1948 initiated a massive exodus of displaced Palestinians seeking refuge in neighboring countries—followed by further refugees from the West Bank in 1967—

who were fleeing the hostilities of the first Arab-Israeli War and the Six-Day War. In opposition to the Israeli occupation, resistance groups sprang up. The Arab League established the Palestine Liberation Organization (PLO) in 1964 to aid the Palestinian people in the fight to regain their homeland. Initially, however, many Palestinians were skeptical of the new organization and chose to organize independently until, over time, it became the sole representative of the Palestinian people through the organization and incorporation of several armed factions, under the umbrella of the PLO and the leadership of Yasser Arafat. The armed groups began to operate from their bases in Jordan and Lebanon, which in turn invited Israeli retaliatory attacks. In Syria the guerrilla activities were placed under the control of the Syrian military, but in Lebanon, owing to its weak government, Palestinian groups were given free rein. The guerrillas could do as they pleased, launching attacks on northern Israel. This caused increased tensions in southern Lebanon, as Israeli reprisals did not discern between Palestinian and Lebanese targets. When in 1970 the Jordanians evicted the militias, all activities were shifted to Lebanon, turning it into the sole operational base of many Palestinian factions.

Some Lebanese forces, especially the Maronites, were never happy with the manner in which the Palestinian militias were turning their country into a front line with Israel. On the other hand, the Arab nationalists, who were then inspired by Nasser, were keen to see the militias allowed freedom of action in an effort to regain lost Arab lands. Under the prompting of the Maronites, the Lebanese army was ordered to take limited action against the Palestinian militias, resulting in a spiraling escalation of hostilities and the paralysis of the Lebanese government as the prime minister, Rashid Karami, resigned in protest. The government found itself isolated as many Arab states rallied behind the Palestinian guerrillas, albeit hypocritically, since they would not have allowed Palestinian militias on their own territory. In November 1969, a compromise solution was worked out in Cairo between General Bustani, the army commander, and Yasser Arafat. However, the agreement was one-sided and legitimized the Palestinian position, much to the dismay of the Maronites' political leaders. After the agreement, the animosity between the two groups only deepened, particularly as Israeli retaliation caused massive devastation in southern Lebanon. Against this background, tensions within the Lebanese body politic exploded into communal violence in 1975.

On 13 April 1975, a bus was ambushed at Ain Rummaneh, a Christian suburb of Beirut. Twenty-eight (mostly Palestinian) passengers were killed. Responsibility was claimed by Maronite Phalangists, who were acting in retaliation for a shooting at a church gathering—attended by Pierre Gemayel—attributed to Palestinian militia members. Several people had been killed, and the retaliatory cycle of violence is often identified as the trigger of the civil war. Immediately thereafter, clashes between the Maronites and the National Movement–Palestinian alliance spread across the country. Fighting paralyzed Beirut, as Maronites battled Palestinians street to street through the Lebanese capital. Politically, Rashid Solh's government collapsed, and President Suleiman Frangieh called on Nureddin Rifai to form a new cabinet. However, the National Movement and the Muslim establishment forced the new prime minister to resign, replacing him with Rashid Karami.

After several days of chaotic yet bloody fighting, a cease-fire was announced, but it was never realized, with the fighting only intensifying. The Phalange and Palestinians were both soon joined by other militias. By September 1975, the dividing line between the two groups of combatants was crystallized. On one side emerged a coalition composed of Gemayel, Chamoun, Frangieh, and Father Charbel Qassis, who called themselves the Lebanese Front. Except for Charbel Qassis, they were leaders of the LF with their own private militias. The largest militia group was that under the banner of the Phalange Party, with a force of approximately 10,000, followed by Chamoun's Tigers and Frangieh's Zghorta's Liberation Army. Opposing them were the Lebanese National Movement, nominally under the leadership of Kamal Jumblatt, the Druze leader. A loose, politically fractured grouping, it included Jumblatt's Progressive Socialist Party, two Communist parties, and some Nasserist organizations. Militarily it was weak, disorganized, and clearly not a match for the Maronite alliance. Without the Palestinian militias, they would have had little chance against the better-equipped, -trained, and -funded Maronites.

The Palestinians, still with the memories of the fate that befell them in Jordan, were divided on what course of action to follow. The radical groups appeared to have closed their minds to that sad experience and chosen to get drawn into the conflict, and Arafat and Fatah wanted to stay out of the Lebanese internal fight and to concentrate on actions against Israel. Arafat did not keep his militia out of the war for long. As Phalange militias attacked and massacred Palestinians in camps and slums around Beirut, all Palestinian groups aligned and became part of the conflict. The worst such attack occurred at Karantina on 19 January 1975, leading to the deaths of some 1,000 Palestinians and Lebanese Muslims and the expulsion of nearly 20,000 more to southern Lebanon.[32] With the intervention of the Palestinians, the balance of power shifted against the Maronites.

The Palestinians sent reinforcements to back up National Movement forces attacking Maronite coastal districts south of Beirut, made possible by the dispatch of Palestinian Liberation Army (PLA) fighters—regular PLO forces stationed in Syria under Arafat's command—by the Syrian military. The Syrian support of the National Movement and Palestinian guerrillas, which continued throughout 1975, included weapons and other supplies, and logistical support was a policy clearly aimed at escalating the fighting and weakening the Maronite factions.[33] Under the massive offensive, Damour, the "fiefdom" of Camille Chamoun, was overrun, forcing his militia to surrender, a major defeat for the Lebanese Front. Meanwhile, the Lebanese army was thrown into disorder as sectarian loyalties emerged. Lt. Ahmad Khatib (a Sunni) mutinied to form the Arab Army of Lebanon; he did this to protest the use of the air force at Damour against National Movement and Palestinian forces. This fracture in the army ranks was not the last, and by January 1976 the war had become even more sectarian, as evidenced by the movement of Christians to their sector in the east of Beirut with Muslims moving to the west.

To the alarm of the Syrians, the Christians hinted they would partition the country rather than be subjugated under a Muslim regime. Jumblatt's insistence on the elimination of the confessional system was anathema to the Maronites. Further complicating efforts to reach a compromise was Jumblatt's determination to bring the Maronite dominance to an end through the force of arms. For the Druze, who were previously barred from top positions in the government, this was a logical course of action.

Furthermore, the Syrians had to take into account the Israeli response to a total defeat of the Maronites and the establishment of a hostile Palestinian-Muslim Lebanon on its northern frontier. Through Syrian mediation, a cease-fire was arranged in January 1976 and an agreement on an outline of a peace agreement was negotiated. On 14 February, the "program of reforms," which later came to be known as the Constitutional Document, was made public in Beirut by President Suleiman Frangieh. The key elements of the reforms entailed distribution of the Assembly seats on a 50:50 basis, the election of the prime minister by parliament, and the award of civil service posts on merit, no longer in line with confession. However, the implementation of the reforms was aborted in the wake of the army's disintegration, something that the National Movement and Palestinians were thought to have had a hand in. Muslim and Maronite soldiers battled for control of garrison towns and heavy equipment. Meanwhile, Jumblatt reiterated his determination to achieve a military victory. Druze campaigns threatened the presidential palace, and President Frangieh fled to the safety of Mount Lebanon. A cease-fire was achieved only after intense Syrian pressure, including the entry of Syrian armored columns into Lebanon and the blockade of National Movement ports (Tyre, Sidon, and Tripoli) by the Syrian navy. This marked a change from a more militaristic Syrian policy in Lebanon to one committed to solving the crisis, albeit through force. The offensive targeted the alliance under Jumblatt, whom the Syrians blamed for the collapse of the Constitutional Document.

Syrian Military Involvement in Lebanon

The Syrian invasion began on 31 May 1976 and soon was bogged down by stiff resistance from the National Movement and Palestinian forces, who were helped by their high morale and knowledge of the terrain. A cease-fire went into effect on 9 June as Damascus bowed to the heavy criticism the move was receiving throughout the Arab world, vociferously led by its archenemy, Iraq. Syria became increasingly isolated and, in its next move against the Palestinians, was forced to adopt a new strategy—that of wearing down the militias' fighting capacity rather than confronting them directly. In concert with Christian forces, the Syrian army exerted gradual pressure on the Palestinian guerrillas and their leftist allies. However, although weakened, the Palestinians would not relent to Syrian pressure. Consequently, the Syrians decided to launch a full-blown military offensive between 28 September and 17 October. These offensives, carried out jointly with the Christian forces, were successful, and the Palestinians were forced to reach an accommodation with the Syrians.

The military victory greatly enhanced the Syrian position in Lebanon. The Syrians had engineered the 8 May 1975 electoral victory of their nominee, Elias Sarkis. Sarkis was to replace President Frangieh, who had become very unpopular. The succession was delayed until 23 September 1975. It became apparent that, without Syrian participation, the return of peace to the country would remain elusive. When the Riyadh mini summit of 15 October 1976 brought about a de facto cease-fire between the Palestinians and the Syrians, calling for the formation of a 30,000-man Arab Deterrent Force (ADF), it was understood that the bulk of the troops would be Syrian. Implicitly, the Syrian presence in Lebanon was legitimized.

Following the Riyadh agreement, 6,000 Syrian troops and 200 tanks, now part of the Arab Deterrent Force, took up positions in and around Beirut, while other Syrian forces entered Maronite and National Movement territories.[34] The Palestinians shifted their forces to areas in the south allocated to them under the 1969 Cairo agreement, a move intended to heighten tensions with Israel. In the first two years of the civil strife, the toll, both in terms of human lives lost and property destroyed, was immense. Officially, 50,000 people were killed, 100,000 were wounded, and 600,000 more were displaced.[35]

The Israeli Invasion of Lebanon

In its struggle against Palestinian guerrilla groups and their backers, Lebanon increasingly became an area of concern for Israeli leaders. In fact, as peace returned to Lebanese society, the Palestinians were able to turn the country into a reliable operational base and Syria was able to expand its role into north Lebanon. The threat to Israeli security coming from Lebanon only intensified. Initially, the Israelis provided support to groups allied to them, particularly the Maronites. The Israelis also supplied arms and protection to Maronite villages along the border where there was a small force under a rebel Lebanese officer, Major Saad Haddad, which was meant to fight Palestinian and National Movement militias in the south of Lebanon.

In the 1977 Israeli general elections, the Likud bloc defeated the Labour Party, bringing Menachem Begin to power. Begin, who was known for his aggressive stance toward the Palestinians, set out to liquidate the threat posed by the guerrillas operating out of Lebanon. Israeli forces entered Lebanon in 1978, followed by another massive intrusion in 1982.

The 1978 invasion—Operation Stone of Wisdom—came after the seizure of an Israeli bus on 11 March, which caused the deaths of thirty-seven Israelis and nine guerrillas in the ensuing shootout between the Israeli Defense Force and the Palestinian hijackers. A few days later, 25,000 Israeli soldiers supported by air and naval power crossed into Lebanon, occupying a southern strip up to the Litani River. The operation was aimed at eliminating the Palestinian guerrilla infrastructure in the south of Lebanon and guerrilla bases along the border. Civilian casualties were predictably high, and for the second time many Shiites had to leave their homes in the south. The guerrillas redeployed to the north, and casualties and equipment losses among the actual Palestinian fighters were minimal because the Israeli advance was slow.

On 19 March 1978, the UN Security Council met to adopt two resolutions to deal with the Israeli invasion. Resolution 425 called on Israel to withdraw its forces from Lebanese territory and authorized the establishment of a peacekeeping force. Resolution 426 outlined the mandate and composition of the peacekeeping force. Several weeks later, the force—known as the United Nations Interim Force in Lebanon (UNIFIL) and staffed by contingents from Canada, France, Iran, Norway, and Sweden—was gathered. Reinforcements from Nepal, Nigeria, and Senegal joined UNIFIL by the end of April, bringing the total personnel to 4,000. In response, Israel pulled back its force up to a line some six miles from its border—an area it called the "security belt." On 12 June 1978, Israel decided to hand this strip of territory to Haddad, whose forces would now control the area. Suddenly Haddad acquired complex military facilities and hardware, giving birth to an Israeli-sponsored militia that would come to be known as the South Lebanese Army. The SLA would subsequently be put to effective use against Israel's foes.

However, Israeli withdrawal and the deployment of the international force never calmed the situation in Lebanon. In the south, tensions were high and nothing could be done, as the government remained weak and ineffective. Haddad's militia, with tacit approval of their Israeli sponsors, continued to harass the peacekeepers and frustrate any efforts to spread government control to the south of Lebanon. In early March 1983, UN positions came under fire from Haddad's militia when government forces tried to join UNIFIL. A number of peacekeepers lost their lives, and sporadic skirmishes between rival militias occurred in other parts of the country, increasing in both intensity and frequency.

In the spring of 1981, Israel was gearing up for elections that would have profound repercussions for Lebanon. Likud's poor domestic record weakened its chances at the polls, and the party decided to contest the election on foreign policy. Attacks on Palestinian targets in southern Lebanon, Beirut, and Syrian-controlled areas took on a harsher dimension as Likud rhetoric increased Israeli fears about its northern neighbor. In addition, there were aerial confrontations between the Israeli and Syrian air forces. On 27 June 1979, five Syrian planes were shot down. In support of Christians battling Syrian forces at Zahle, Israeli planes went into action against Syrian helicopters on 28 April 1981. In this atmosphere of heightened tensions, on 29 April 1981 Syria deployed surface-to-air missiles in the Bekaa Valley, despite Israeli demands for their immediate removal. The drift toward a wider conflict was also enhanced by other events. In Israel, in the summer of 1981, a change of government brought in hard-liners Ariel Sharon (defense minister), Yitzhak Shamir (foreign minister), and Moshe Arens (United Nations ambassador). In the United States, Ronald Reagan succeeded Jimmy Carter as president in January 1981, and his new secretary of state, Alexander Haig, espoused an overtly pro-Israeli position from Washington. With the fighting in Lebanon showing no signs of abating, and believing the political support existed for action, Israeli leaders met on 5 June 1982 and approved the second invasion of Lebanon, an operation code named Peace for the Galilee. Its aims were the destruction of the Palestinian infrastructure in Lebanon, the removal of Syrian forces, and the establishment of an independent government that would sign a separate peace agreement with Israel much like that signed by Egypt.

On 6 June 1982, Israeli Defense Forces invaded Lebanon from their positions in the occupied "security belt." Palestinian positions were subjected to attacks from land, air, and sea, and UNIFIL forces were easily pushed aside as the IDF swept past. Clashes in the Bekaa Valley were minimal, although the Syrian air force took high losses. This was so because both Syria and Israel tried to avoid a wider war. Nevertheless, there were grave incidents that nearly did exactly that. On 9 June, Israeli air strikes destroyed the missiles planted by the Syrians in the Bekaa. Diplomatic measures intensified to contain the escalating development of events. A cease-fire was agreed to on 11 June, ending further conflict between Syria and Israel. The main Israeli moves shifted from the Bekaa to the Beirut-Damascus highway that the IDF later occupied (12–26 June) and the laying of a siege around Beirut (from 26 June to 1 September). The Israelis announced a general cease-fire on 25 June. Massive bombardments by air and artillery were brought to bear on the Palestinian guerrillas and Syrian forces trapped in Beirut so as to force them to leave. One of Israel's objectives was met when, in August, American envoys received word of Palestinian and Syrian acceptance of the evacuation demand. The withdrawal was to be supervised by a multinational force in which the United States would take part. On 21 August 1982, the first of about 8,000 Palestinians left by sea. The whole exercise came to a close on 31 August, by which time about 6,000 Syrian soldiers and PLO brigades had evacuated Beirut, and the multinational force, including units from Italy, France, and the United States, left 10–12 September, after its task had been completed.

Seemingly, the Israelis had achieved all of their objectives: The Palestinians had been resoundingly defeated and forced to retreat to Tunisia, leaving behind over 500,000 refugees; the pro-Israeli Bashir Gemayel was elected president on 23 August 1982, only to be assassinated three weeks after taking office and replaced by his brother Amin a week later. Amin signed the American-brokered Lebanese-Israeli agreement of 17 May 1983. For the Syrians, these symbolized serious defeats and were quickly opposed. Unable to launch direct attacks on its own, the Syrians relied on proxies to carry out their plans including the militias of Walid Jumblatt (Druze), Amal and Hizbullah (Shiites), the Syrian Social Nationalist Party (Greek Orthodox and Druze), the Syrian Ba'ath

Party, and supporters of Suleiman Frangieh (Maronite) and Rashid Karami (Sunni). Through acts of violence and armed resistance, these groups pressured the Israelis and guaranteed that Lebanon was not pacified nor was Israel's northern border secure. The Syrians, who were well schooled in the use of guerrilla and underground violence,[36] depended on the actions of these groups to eliminate their mutual Lebanese opponents and undermine Israeli allies and occupation forces. The 17 May agreement was abrogated, and the multinational forces were forced to leave due to the increasing violence, making Syria once again the foremost power in Lebanon.

The Syrian ascendancy was made possible by the rising popularity and sophisticated development of Islamic fundamentalist militias— such as Hamas and Hizbullah—who made devastating suicide attacks against the Israelis and their local allies (see chapter 2). The pro-Khomeini groups that sprang up in the course of the war established a strong foothold among the Shiite community of south Lebanon, threatening the influence of Amal. Playing an important role in the transformation of these groups were the 1,500 or so "revolutionary guards" who, during the war, reached Baalbek. The Islamic groups strove to set up an Islamic republic on the Iranian model. Although incompatible with the Syrian model, strong mutual interests between the Syrians and the backers of these groups gave them freedom of action. In the summer of 1983, these groups carried out a number of suicide operations against the Israeli occupation forces and western targets. For example, a suicide attack on the American embassy left sixty-three Americans dead, and on 4 November 1983, another suicide attack killed twenty-eight Israelis at Tyre. In February 1984, the Americans withdrew their military forces from Beirut following an October 1983 suicide bombing that killed 241 Marines. The Israelis faced international outrage when Israeli and Israeli-supported Lebanese soldiers massacred hundreds of Palestinians in the Sabra and Shatila refugee camps in Beirut. Threatened with a general uprising of the Shiite community, the Israelis were forced to withdraw—first to the Awwali River on 4 September 1983, and then to the sanctity of their "security zone" at the end of May 1985. All these withdrawals proved to be diplomatic successes for the Syrians, who with minimal involvement and cost were now controlling much of Lebanon.[37]

To capitalize on this opportunity, the Syrians launched a peace initiative that resulted in the 28 December 1985 Tripartite Agreement signed in Damascus by three major militias: Amal, the Lebanese Forces, and Druze Socialist Progressive Party. However, this agreement soon hit thorny ground when the leader of the Lebanese Forces, Eli Hobeika (who had been instrumental in the construction of the agreement), was deposed by Samir Jaja. Sporadic communal violence and assassinations never halted, and Amin Gemayel's government was too fragile to do anything to rectify matters.

With the expiry of Amin's term in office, yet another crisis loomed. The Syrians used their influence to sway the presidential election in favor of a candidate of their choosing, causing confusion. The result was that a power vacuum developed, and on 22 September 1988, Amin appointed Michel 'Aoun, commander in chief of the Lebanese army, as the prime minister in spite of the fact that the Syrians refused to recognize him. The Syrians' candidate, Salim al-Hoss, a rival claimant of the position, allowed two governments to emerge. Aoun was a dynamic personality who cultivated considerable support within the Christian camp. His crusade against the Syrians caused further destruction in Beirut. Although he had some initial success against overwhelming odds, he soon was locked into a conflict between the Lebanese army loyal to him and the Lebanese Front militia of Samir Jaja. He made further enemies when he attempted to close down illegal ports on which many guerrilla groups had come to rely for supplies. Aoun declared a war of liberation from Syrian occupation on 14 March 1989. The fighting between the Christians and Syrians that ensued attracted more Arab and international pressure, forcing Syria to seek a peaceful solution. The heads of state of Algeria, Morocco, and Saudi Arabia (at the behest of the Arab League) developed a framework for talks between the Lebanese factions, at Ta'if in Saudi Arabia, which was endorsed by the United States, the USSR, and the European Community. After months of difficult negotiations, the result was the Ta'if Accord of October 1989.

The Ta'if Accord

Arab countries were jolted into action when the conflict between Aoun and the Syrians took a dangerous turn, threatening to degenerate into a wider regional conflict. Iraqi military support for Aoun, it was feared, would bring Damascus and Baghdad into a head-on collision. In the Casablanca Summit of May 1989, the Arab League decided to create the Tripartite High Commission, consisting of leaders of Algeria, Saudi Arabia, and Morocco, to resolve the conflict. Under the auspices of this committee, sixty-two members of the Lebanese parliament met in Ta'if from 30 September to 22 October 1989. The parliamentarians were split evenly between Christian and Muslim factions, and from this meeting emerged the Document of National Understanding, which did not depart drastically from stipulations of previous reform efforts. In

essence, the document upheld the central features of the National Pact
of 1943, and conceded the futility of ridding the country of political sectarianism. The UN backed the accord on 31 October 1989. In Lebanon,
the Chamber of Deputies approved constitutional reforms based on the
accord forming Lebanon's de facto constitution. The key reform was the
loss of the Maronite monopoly over presidential powers, which were
transferred to the prime minister. The speaker of the Assembly, who
would be elected to a four-year term, and the nomination of the prime
minister, a Sunni, would be carried out by the president in consultation
with the speaker. The cabinet would be the executive authority, and the
position of the prime minister would now be the single most important
in the Lebanese political system. Distribution of the 128 seats in the
Assembly would be on the principle of Christian-Muslim parity.
According to David Gordon, "There is no question that the Maronites
were the big losers in the Ta'if Accord, and that the Shi'a Muslims had
the most gains. The political predominance of the Maronites, symbolized notably in the prerogatives of the president, became history."[38]

Aoun delayed implementation of the accord on the grounds that the
accord was vague as to when Syrian forces must withdraw from
Lebanon. Under the terms of the accord, Syrian forces were to be redeployed to the Bekaa Valley in less than three years, but no timetable for
a complete withdrawal was established. By mid-1989, it was estimated
that more than 1 million people had fled Beirut due to the exchange of
artillery fire between the eastern and western sectors of the city, and
more than 800 people had been killed.[39]

The Syrians engineered the November presidential election of Rene
Mu'awad, but seventeen days later he was assassinated, and once again
the Lebanese parliament was forced to meet in order to fill the vacant
post of president. Elias Hrawi was chosen, although he had no power
base of his own, relying strictly on his close links with the Syrians.
However, he soon won the support of the Arab countries and the world
in general. Prime Minister al-Hoss's government was recognized, and it
was decided that the Syrians would remove 'Aoun from the Ba'abda
Palace by force. Under the cover of the 1990–91 Gulf crisis, the Syrians
made a decisive move against 'Aoun in the fall of 1990, leading to his
defeat on 13 October. Taking refuge in the French embassy, 'Aoun later
would find exile in France.

Implementation of the Ta'if Accords was now free to proceed. Karami
formed a government of national unity on 24 December 1990, and
the first postwar cabinet was composed of militia leaders, with some
thirty members split equally between Christians and Muslims. The various militias withdrew from Beirut by the end of December, allowing

parliament to declare the dissolution of all militias with the exception of Hizbullah. The army expanded its deployment to much of Lebanon, and in September 1992 elections brought Rafiq al-Hariri to power as prime minister and Nabih Berri as speaker of the Assembly. The process of reconciliation and reconstruction was soon consolidated. Syrian influence remains overwhelming: Syria has disregarded the agreement that its troops would withdraw to the Bekaa region by 1992, and the 1995 presidential election was canceled when Hafez al-Assad indicated he wanted Elias Hrawi to remain in power and he had the parliament extend Hrawi's term by three years, despite its unconstitutionality. Eventually, parliament approved a constitutional amendment extending his term, further legitimizing the Syrian intervention.

Lebanon and the Palestinians

Lebanon's most difficult obstacle remains the presence of hundreds of thousands of Palestinians who live in refugee camps in the south of Lebanon. They draw Lebanon ever further into the Arab-Israeli conflict, constantly destabilizing the country. Such impacts were most evident in the "Battle of the Camps" in May 1988, when new fighting erupted in which Syria's proxy forces expelled pro-Arafat fighters from Sabra and Shatila refugee camps, and once again in April 1996, when Israeli strikes against Hizbullah guerrillas near refugee camps killed hundreds of Lebanese citizens and Palestinian refugees. Lebanon had not been extensively involved in the peace negotiations, which have been going on since 1991, as most of its foreign policy is controlled by Damascus. The resolution of the Israeli-Hizbullah conflict indicated the central government's lack of influence and even legitimacy in the south, despite the fact that the conflict took place entirely on Lebanese soil. Negotiations were undertaken between Syria and Israel.

The Lebanese Economy

Lebanon, before the war, was more prosperous than most other developing countries. Its per capita income was higher than all of the countries in the Asian region except for Japan, Singapore, Israel, and Kuwait. The prosperity was powered mainly by the private sector, contrary to the situation in many Arab countries. In particular, trade and banking were the key areas driving the economy, overshadowing industry and agriculture. The strategic position of the Levant coast between east and west has been conducive to commercial pursuits for millennia. Moreover, the growth of oil production in the Middle East and the associated expansion of links with markets in Europe added more importance to the Levant's role as mediator. The region also has been a tourist attraction.

Prewar social conditions also pointed to a high level of development. Malaria and smallpox had been eliminated, and 80 percent of the country's people were literate. Nevertheless, the country was plagued by serious ills that factionalism left unaddressed. The wide division between the rich and the poor was a grave matter and may have contributed to the tensions that led to the civil war. In the outskirts of Beirut, where the affluent led luxurious lives, were a majority of people living in the misery of poverty. The numbers of the disadvantaged swelled as migrants from the countryside came to take advantage of the robust economy or security from Syrian and Israeli occupation forces.

The generally positive economic profile of the country was destroyed when the civil war swallowed Lebanese society. The sixteen years of death and destruction took a toll on the economy and social infrastructure. The cost for the country's nightmare has been estimated at U.S.$25 billion and over 150,000 deaths as many Lebanese were forced to desert their homeland.[40] The conflict is over, however, and the Lebanese are devoting their energies to the restoration and revival of their country to its previous cultural and financial preeminence in the region. The government of Prime Minister Rafiq al-Hariri spearheaded efforts to reconstruct Lebanon from the ruins of conflict instituting a ten-year program, dubbed "Horizon 2000." It devoted the expenditure of U.S.$11.7 billion for rebuilding damaged or destroyed infrastructure, rehabilitating institutions, and rejuvenating the private sector.[41] Furthermore, the international political and investment community was encouraged to contribute to the reconstruction efforts. When the program is finally over, Beirut will be reborn as a modern city, with a strong commitment to the preservation of whatever architectural glories managed to survive the civil war.

As the rebuilding process continues, agricultural yield is poor and grossly neglected by the state, exports are low, and imports are high. Most important, the Arab sheikhs, on whose investments and spending the Lebanese government has staked much of its reconstruction plan, have not returned. Yet the currency is stable, and inflation is under control. Figures provided by the Central Bank and international agencies present a bleak picture of the economy and the state's neglect of its structural requirements. The informal sector—to which belong, among others, all the Palestinians in various camps who are forbidden to work in Lebanon—represents as much as 70 percent of the economy. Taxes on profit dropped from 37 percent in 1974–75 to nearly 10 percent in 2000; indirect taxes account for 80 percent of government revenues.

The agricultural sector suffers from neglect and the stranglehold of large landowners. Only 3–4 percent of Lebanese families own 70 percent of all cultivable land. Independent farmers are so starved for credit that nearly all borrow from suppliers, paying as much as 100 percent interest. As a result, agriculture accounts for only 10–12 percent of GDP, even though the land is fertile. Lebanon has a sophisticated food-processing industry and a made-to-order clientele among Arab immigrants abroad. Manufacturing contributes 20–35 percent of GDP, while the service sector yields some 55–70 percent of GDP. Exports make up barely 10–15 percent of Lebanon's import costs; hence the country suffers chronically from balance of trade deficits. Despite skewed distributive patterns, people's living standards are distinctly superior to those in Arab countries that do not produce oil. While unemployment is not low, thousands of Syrian, Sri Lankan, and Filipino workers are in Lebanon because they work for lower wages and employers do not have to pay toward their pensions and social security funds.

What seems to stabilize Lebanon's economy are expatriates, many of whom left Lebanon during the civil war and have settled abroad, integrating themselves into their host economies. About 8 million people, double the current domestic population, are believed to be "active" expatriates—those who still support families and/or invest in Lebanon, mostly through bank deposits. Since foreign remittances are frequently made through private channels, no reliable figure exists of its actual size. But it is largely due to expatriate investment that bank deposits equal 150–200 percent of Lebanon's GDP, and a large share of it ends up in government hands. Lebanese expatriates also constitute the backbone of Lebanon's tourist trade. A stable currency promotes confidence, tourism, and investment, as do low inflation rates, steady at 4–5 percent; finally the interest offered on treasury bills is 17 percent, making investment in Lebanon attractive to expatriates and foreign investors alike. Such stability, while impressive, has come at the expense of increasing the national debt, which stands in excess of $17 billion, $3.5 billion of which is in foreign hands.

Postwar Governments and Reconstruction

When he came to power in 1992, Hrawi devoted great energy to meeting the objectives of the Horizon 2000 plan in spite of exaggerated expectations. The Lebanese pound was stabilized, inflation was lowered from 131 percent to 10 percent annually, and Beirut's infrastructure was steadily repaired.[42] Development was slow to materialize, however, and although Hrawi's presidential tenure was extended—through the Hafez al-Assad–inspired constitutional alteration—Lebanon needed new leadership in 1998. Although multiple suitors announced their candidacy, the choice—with the strong backing of Damascus—was Lebanon's top military commander, Emile Lahoud, a Maronite Christian. Obstacles quickly surfaced because, under Article 49 of Lebanon's constitution, senior civil servants such as General Lahoud are obligated to resign their posts two years before announcing their candidacy. After finessing the amendment to have Elias Hrawi's term extended by three years in 1995, such a change, when supported by Damascus, was merely a formality, however. Hrawi, also a Maronite Christian, had lost support within his own constituency, as reforms were slow and development had stagnated. General Lahoud's considerable stature within the Maronite Christian community as well as in the international community—American and French officials were impressed with his reform and professionalization of the Lebanese Army after the end of the civil war—afforded him much more leeway.

Lahoud's new regime did face obstacles to rebuilding Lebanon's wartorn infrastructure, including Syrian controls over policy, the increased role and power of the prime minister, the need for foreign investment for the rebuilding of Lebanese society, the absorption of over 1 million Lebanese who fled the country during the civil war as well as the ideas and societal expectations with which they returned, the continued growth of Hizbullah, Israeli occupation, and the concomitant problems of having large numbers of Palestinian refugees living in Lebanon. The limitations of having Syrian oversight—to which Lahoud was firmly committed—centered on the continued rejection of the Palestinian-Israeli peace process, although such rejection hinders the amount of reconstruction financing available from Arab states who have largely signed on and recognized Israel as well as the process's western and economically preponderant sponsors. Furthermore, by not being represented at the negotiation table, Lebanon has been unable to have a voice in the future resolution of the final status of Palestinians' right to return.

However, for the first time since the end of the fifteen-year civil war, the unanimous support Lahoud received from the entire Lebanese parliament, as the country's new president, bolstered his standing and gave his administration considerable momentum. Lahoud, who won the hearts of most Lebanese voters by promising a new era of political and economic reforms and an iron fist against corruption, started his term by showing the strength of his new office. He refused to bow to pressure from former Lebanese prime minister Rafiq al-Hariri and immediately appointed veteran Lebanese politician Salim al-Hoss to be his successor as prime minister. The beginning of 1999 saw the swift implementation of many of Lahoud's promises for administrative and political reform, starting with a crackdown on corruption. In this framework, the judiciary investigated a number of cases relating to the affairs of the former government. The most spectacular of these came in March, when the former oil minister, Shahe Barsoumian, was detained on suspicion of having approved deals that had stripped the Treasury of more than $800 million. The first minister in the country's history to have been detained on corruption charges, Barsoumian remains in custody. At last count, his requests for bail had been refused twenty-two times.

As Lahoud's administration took shape, Lebanon also witnessed its first mayoral and municipal elections in thirty-five years, with voter turnout often exceeding 80 percent in most districts. The elections' outcome, with an equal number of Christian and Muslim candidates, was hailed as a victory for national coexistence and harmony, as well as for democracy, and further added to the feeling of positive momentum building in the country. Large gains were registered by Hizbullah and opposition Christian candidates. An alliance between civil war rivals Walid Jumblatt, leader of the Druze, and Dory Chamoun of the right-wing National Liberal Party, in an effort to maintain sectarian balance in the Mount Lebanon region, seemingly pointed toward a new era of electoral politics and an end to violent confrontations. Even exiled Michel 'Aoun supported a slate of candidates under former deputy Albert Mokhbaier, despite opposition to continued Syrian domination. Such alliances maintained sectarian balance in elections that for the first time in Lebanese history were not governed by confessional restrictions. The government's support for "consensus" candidates, in an effort to dilute the growing influence of Hizbullah in the south and Beirut's southern suburbs, was the only blemish on elections that were seen as fair and proper by international monitors.

The Lebanese National Elections of 2000

The August–October 2000 national elections in Lebanon sent a stinging blow to the Lahoud-backed government of Salim al-Hoss as Rafiq al-Hariri returned at the helm of an election landside for opposition candidates. Returning to the prime ministership he had been ousted from in 1998, al-Hariri again promoted himself as the man capable of pulling Lebanon out of its acute economic crisis—with the national debt surpassing $25 billion—at a time of great tension in the region. With international attention again focused on Palestinian civil uprisings against Israeli occupation, Lebanon elected a 128-member parliament equally divided between Christian and Muslim sects. Hariri had the backing of

92 candidates in his quest to again form the government. His 30-member cabinet did not include members from any Christian party though it had representation from nearly all Muslim and leftist parties. Tense relations between Hariri and Lahoud, the Israeli withdrawal and concomitant rise of Hizbullah, relations with Syria, and the staggering economic burden of reconstruction will be prominent issues in Lebanese politics leading to the presidential elections of 2004 and general elections of 2005. The specter of the Syrian presence has been alleviated by the economic and civil reforms of Bashar al-Assad in Syria as well as the loss of Syrian justifications for a continued military presence with the retreat of the IDF.

One Muslim party that increased representation in the elections but was not included in Hariri's cabinet was Hizbullah (party of God). Despite the protestations of its leader—Sayed Hassan Nassrallah—that the "Party of God" would not use its military presence in southern Lebanon to challenge central authority, it remains to be seen what role it will take in the future of Lebanese politics. Its October 2000 capture of three IDF soldiers from the Lebanese-Israeli border, followed one week later by its "capture" of IDF colonel Elhanan Tennenbaum, continues to exacerbate Lebanese relations with Israel.

Foreign Relations

Foreign policy in Lebanon is a contentious matter, principally because of the identity problem that the country has faced in coming to terms with its own fractious politics and the longtime occupation by Syrian and Israeli forces. While some communities have been keen to be fully integrated into the Arab world, others were resentful and preferred relations with the West. After the civil strife resulting from one president's attempt to move the country closer to the West, leaders have attempted to find a balance between relations with the Arab world and with the West. Since Hafez al-Assad, the Syrian leader, assumed the role of "godfather" to Lebanon, the country has never adopted positions contrary to Syrian policy. It is difficult to speak of an independent foreign policy in Lebanon as long as this condition remains. This situation was most clearly demonstrated in the Operation Grapes of Wrath crisis in April 1996, when Lebanon's responsibility in the resolution process was assumed by Syrian representatives.

CHAPTER 8

The Hashemite Kingdom of Jordan

*T*he territory of Jordan (formerly Transjordan) has a long historical legacy, although the same is not true of its existence as a nation-state. Accounts from the Bible and other sources point to the rich past of the territory, strategically located between Arabia and Syria. For most of the time, it was incorporated into powerful ancient kingdoms and empires. Until the beginning of the sixteenth century when it was absorbed into the Ottoman *villayet* (administrative district) of Damascus, it had been for centuries a part of Syria, governed from Egypt. During the Ottoman rule, the area was neglected and remained in a state of stagnation. However, this was to change with the advent of the First World War.

At the end of the war, the Arab armies under Prince Faisal, one of the sons of King Hussein of Hejaz, controlled the area. The Arab revolt of 1916 against the Ottoman rule was carried out with the understanding that at the end of the war the Arabs would be allowed to establish their own independent state. Faisal attended the February 1919 Paris Peace Conference and demanded independence for the Arabs in accordance with the British promises. However, as was discussed in chapter 1, the victorious Europeans had never been prepared to honor their commitments. The British and the French had plans of their own for the liberated Ottoman provinces. A secret agreement, named for its negotiators, Sir Mark Sykes and François Georges Picot, had been concluded in May 1916 between the British and French governments to partition the Arab part of the Ottoman Empire. Adding a further complication to Arab demands was the Balfour Declaration of 1917, which committed Britain to the establishment of a Jewish homeland in Palestine.

Failing to convince the British to honor their prewar promise, Faisal formed an Arab government in Damascus. In March 1920, the General

Syrian Congress in Damascus declared independence for Syria under Faisal's leadership. At the same conference, the Iraqi delegates also declared the independence of their kingdom under the leadership of Faisal's older brother, Abdullah. However, Abdullah could not claim the throne in Iraq, because the British authorities were well entrenched. His father, King Hussein, longed to be the uncontested leader of the Arab government he established at the conclusion of the war. In response to Faisal, the British and French denounced the Damascus declaration. Meanwhile, a conference of the victorious Allies at San Remo in April 1920 sanctioned British and French mandatory rule in the region. Accordingly, Palestine became a British mandate, and Syria and Lebanon were placed under French mandatory rule. Soon French forces were deployed against those of Faisal, and in the ensuing confrontation, Faisal lost and had to flee to Europe, where he remained until his enthronement as king of Iraq in 1921. The Transjordan region, although formally included in the Palestine mandate, was left in a chaotic state.

Meanwhile, in a significant move in October 1920, Emir (Prince) Abdullah left his father's kingdom at the head of an army of 2,000 men to restore Faisal to the Syrian throne. The emir's arrival in Ma'an, then part of the Hashemite Kingdom of Hejaz, was well received. Abdullah, an experienced politician and a veteran of many wars, called upon all Syrians to join him in the liberation of the fatherland from the imperialist occupation. From Ma'an he resumed his journey, reaching Amman on 2 March 1921, where the Arab tribal chiefs of the area welcomed him. In effect he set himself up as the leader of Transjordan, something the British readily accepted, since his actions resolved the problem of what to do with this part of the Palestine mandate and also accorded the opportunity to repair the wrongs done to Arabs and the Hashemites in particular.[1] However, Abdullah's hold on the territory would be contingent on his abiding by some conditions set out in a meeting in Jerusalem on 28 March 1921 between him and Winston Churchill, British colonial secretary, Herbert Samuel, British high commissioner for mandated territories, and T. E. Lawrence, Churchill's adviser on Arab matters. The emir was required to renounce his claim over the whole of Syria and to leave the Iraqi throne to his brother Faisal. He was also told that he could not extend his claim over the rest of Palestine, since the British had other plans for these areas. Abdullah conceded to these demands.

The British proceeded to make legal arrangements to exclude Transjordan from the area earmarked for the Jewish homeland. The final draft of the Palestine mandate passed by the League of Nations in July 1922 included a clause giving much leeway to the mandatory power in the administration of the areas east of the Jordan River. Based on this, a memorandum was approved expressly excluding Transjordan from the clause relating to the establishment of a future Jewish national homeland, much against the interests of the Zionists.

From then on, nothing could stop Abdullah from forming his own state. On 11 April 1921, the first government was organized in Amman, composed of eight consultants, only one of whom came from Transjordan. Reflecting the emir's Pan-Arab nationalist orientation, the other members of the government were drawn from different parts of the Arab world: one from Mount Lebanon, another from Palestine, two from the Hijaz, and three from Syria. The same spirit was followed in forming the security apparatus. Kamal Salibi notes, "Clearly what Abdullah had in mind at the time was not a Transjordanian administration but a nuclear Pan-Arab government for the whole of Syria based in the available territory of Jordan, with elements representing the central Arab government of [his father] King Hussein in the Hijaz."[2]

The British, however, had their own interests, which went contrary to those of the emir, and they possessed the means to enforce them. Lacking any stable source of finance, the emir had to ask for British support, which initially amounted to £5,000 sterling per month for a six-month trial period, after which it was regularized at £150,000 sterling annually. This was obviously a significant means of control for the British.

In May 1923, the British recognized an "independent" government in Transjordan with Abdullah as its emir; however, the country was still referred to as a mintaqa (region). This changed in February 1928, when a new Anglo-Transjordanian agreement went into effect. The country became a full imara (emirate), and its position internationally was thus clarified. Throughout the 1920s, Abdullah's administration was greatly subordinated to, although not part of, the Palestinian mandate.[3] The most important government positions were held by British officials responsible to Abdullah but in practice working closely with British residents Sir Henry Cox, 1927–39, and Sir Kirbride, 1939–51. Meanwhile, under the command of Frederick Peake, the British organized an efficient security force called the Arab Legion. The competence of this force was put to the test when it was deployed against enemies of the British who had usurped power in Iraq during the war. During the summer of 1941, the Arab Legion was sent to Syria to help the war efforts of British and Free French forces against Vichy forces. Abdullah, to whom the British were grateful, expected a lot from his support of the British at this critical time: He expected to be rewarded with the leadership of Greater Syria, an idea that would never have been supported by the Syrians and Lebanese. The formation of the Arab League in Cairo in

May 1945, whose founding charter emphasized the individual sovereignty of member states, was in fact a rebuke to the Greater Syria notion. The British could not afford to antagonize the Lebanese and Syrians further by endorsing Abdullah's scheme at a time when they were trying to win the support of the same people. Subsequently, the decision was reached to reward Abdullah with the independence of the territory he ruled.

After the end of the Second World War, Abdullah was invited to London to negotiate a new deal with the British. The mandate was terminated and the Anglo-Transjordanian Treaty of Alliance was signed on 22 March 1946, granting the territory its independence. On 15 May 1946, the Transjordanian cabinet resolved to change Abdullah's title from emir to king. The decision was approved in a parliamentary session on 22 May 1946, and Transjordan became Jordan. On 25 March 1946, the emir was crowned king of the Hashemite Kingdom of Jordan, which immediately met with the recognition of other Arab states. The United States and the Soviet Union refused to recognize the new state in 1948; in fact, the Soviets tried to block its admission to the United Nations. The reasons behind their decisions were different, however. The United States bowed to the pressure of the Zionist lobby, which opposed the independence of Jordan because the Zionists viewed Transjordan as part of a Jewish national homeland. The Soviets took offense at the military terms in the Anglo-Jordanian treaty, contending that the treaty made Jordan a permanent British base.

At this point, Jordan encompassed areas to the south and east of the Jordan River extending to Ma'an and Aqaba, which had been incorporated into Transjordan in June 1925 when Ali, eldest son of King Hussein, was pushed out of Hejaz in the face of his imminent defeat by Ibn Sa'ud's forces. The new state adopted a constitution on 1 February 1947, providing for the formation of two houses of parliament, made up of a Chamber of Deputies and a Council of Notables (Majlis al-Ayan). The former, elected for five years by male suffrage, was to have twenty members, the majority of whom represented Muslims, but provision was made for representation from the Bedouin tribes and the Christian, Chechen, and Circassian communities. Thus proportional representation became the hallmark of the constitution. On the other hand, the Council of Notables was to have ten members chosen by the king.

The first election was held on 20 October 1947. The seats in the first parliament were contested by independents and government-sponsored candidates. On 1 January 1950, the first parliament was dissolved to make way for the election of a new parliament following the Union of

Transjordan and the West Bank. Developments in Jordan were soon greatly influenced by events in Palestine, which the British had evacuated on 15 May 1948. The area was plunged into a state of turmoil. Immediately, the Zionists who had long prepared for this occasion, proclaimed the establishment of their state to coincide with the termination of the British mandate. Arab reaction to this maneuver was to wage war. However, the Arab military effort was poorly organized and ill equipped, and it ended in disaster. The Jordanian Arab Legion nonetheless performed well and managed to occupy the West Bank of the Jordan River (including the Old City of Jerusalem), areas designated for the projected Arab state in the UN partition plan of 29 November 1947. An armistice agreement was reached between Israel and Jordan on 3 April 1949.

Abdullah, who had always been keen to expand his territory, was given an opportunity to do so, albeit not to the Greater Syria extent he had long been advocating. On 1 April 1949, he annexed the West Bank. The decision, only endorsed by Britain and Pakistan, solicited a hostile response from the Arab League. Arab leaders threatened to expel Jordan from the organization, but a compromise was worked out whereby the West Bank was to be held temporarily by Jordan in trust. The league was forced to accept the annexation in exchange for Abdullah's desisting from going through with his plan of signing a nonleague deal with Israel, the draft of which had been negotiated in February 1950.[4]

The decision to unite the two banks of the Jordan River and extend Jordanian citizenship to all residents of the West Bank along with Palestinian refugees from the 1948 war on the newly expanded territory had a significant impact on Jordan. Suddenly, to the country's modest population of 400,000 were added about 400,000 Palestinians who lived on the West Bank and 40,000 or 50,000 refugees fleeing the newly founded Jewish state.[5] Economically, socially, and politically, Jordan was greatly affected. In the administrative and political life of the country, the Palestinians came to play an important role, partly because of their relatively superior educational status. The king made it a point to include Palestinians in the cabinet and other leadership positions.[6]

However, many Palestinians resented Abdullah's actions. In fact, among the Palestinian notables, the king's staunchest opponent was Hajj Amin al-Hursaini, the Grand Mufti of Jerusalem, the leader and founder of the Palestine National Movement for three decades, and later the president of the Arab Executive Council. This religious luminary and incorruptible nationalist wanted to remove Abdullah from the Palestinian picture.

Given this hostile atmosphere among the Palestinians, it was not surprising that Abdullah was assassinated by a young Palestinian on 20 July 1951 as he was entering Aqsa Mosque in Jerusalem. The forty-one-year-old crown prince, Talal, automatically ascended the throne. However, his mental illness made it impossible for him to rule. So the decision was reached for Hussein, then yet a minor, to take over. According to the constitution, the king's designate was too young to assume the royal office. Consequently, during this time a regency council, appointed by the cabinet, performed the duties of the royal office. Ultimately, on 2 May 1953, the young king began his active reign. The smooth transfer of power, an indicator of the stability of the establishment, was spearheaded by the competent veteran statesman Tawfig Abul-Huda, who had served as the prime minister during the interim period. Elections were called in 1951, and a liberal constitution was adopted on 8 December 1952. This constitution was unique in that—for the first time—the government was made responsible to parliament.

Early Challenges to the Monarchy

While Hussein was being prepared for the monarchy, he attended the Sandhurst Royal Military Academy in Berkshire as an officer cadet, where he became friends with the Jordanian ambassador to Britain, Fawzi al-Mulqi. Fawzi was a believer in liberal politics as practiced in Britain and other western countries. When Hussein appointed him prime minister in May 1953, Fawzi immediately put his ideals into practice. The country enjoyed unprecedented freedom of speech and press.

The liberal atmosphere came to an abrupt halt, however, when opposition groups used this opportunity to criticize and insult the ruling establishment. This period was characterized by revolutionary ideas and ambitions. Several nationalist and other groups worked for aims that ran contrary to the official policies of the monarchy. In fact, some groups were entirely ambivalent about the whole idea of Jordan being ruled by a monarch. Arab military officers resented being commanded by British officers. These desperate groups used the freedom of speech to create havoc. So extreme was the agitation that the king was forced to act. Abul-Huda formed a government replacing that of Mulqi, parliament was dissolved, fresh elections were called, and a clampdown on the press was declared as a warning to the radical opponents of the regime. However, the agitation continued unabated, reaching a peak on 16 October 1954, the date scheduled for the elections. The Arab Legion was brought out onto the streets in Amman to disperse rioting mobs, and ten civilians were killed.[7] Thus from a small and vibrant new nation, the country was transformed virtually into a police state.

King Hussein's domestic predicament had an external dimension. Arab nationalists outside the country, and their supporters within it, were bitter because of Jordan's relationship with Britain, and they used this in their propaganda to discredit the Jordanian leadership. When the charismatic Nasser established himself as the unrivalled leader of Pan-Arabism, Hussein's position was made even more difficult. While Egypt and Syria worked closely to align the Arab world with the socialist bloc, Britain was striving to form a security alliance with Arab countries, referred to as the Baghdad Pact, to counter the influence of the Soviet Union. Being a small and weak country, Jordan was forced to make a difficult choice.

King Hussein decided to distance himself from the British and mend fences with Nasser, whose appeal to the Arab masses was indeed immense. The first step was to Jordanize the army. The command of the Arab Legion by British officers was a liability in that it caused resentment among Arabs and was a point exploited by nationalists abroad to foment troubles among local peoples. On 1 March 1956, Lt. Gen. John Glubb, the British commander of the army, was dismissed. Furthermore, in the aftermath of the October-November Suez Canal crisis when Israel, Britain, and France invaded Egypt in what became known in the Arab world as the tripartite aggression, the king allowed the nationalists and leftists to downgrade ties between Jordan and Britain. The nationalist-socialist bloc won the 1956 election, gained the majority in parliament, and forced the king to appoint Sulaiman al-Nabulsi to form the government. During the election, this bloc campaigned vigorously against the Anglo-Jordanian Treaties and for closer ties with Egypt. Thus, the controversial Anglo-Jordanian Treaty of 1946 was annulled on 14 March 1957. A few weeks earlier, on 19 January 1957, Jordan had entered into the Arab Solidarity Treaty with Egypt, Syria, and Saudi Arabia, which would replace British financial subsidies with contributions from these three countries.

However, the rapprochement was soon checked by differences that developed between the king and government over policy. The nationalist and leftist-dominated legislature and executive wanted the recognition of the Soviet Union and Communist China, which the king rejected. The showdown came when the king wanted to align the country with the United States in what was known as the Eisenhower doctrine of January 1957, which the government rejected. The impasse was solved when the government of Sulaiman al-Nabulsi resigned.

Meanwhile, in the hope of exploiting the chaos in the country, an abortive military coup was staged in April 1957. General 'Ali Abu Nuwar, the chief of staff, and his fellow conspirators then fled the country. There were massive political demonstrations in major towns organized by the nationalists and leftists. Martial law was imposed, political parties were banned, and their leaders were arrested. The crackdowns were ferociously denounced by both Syria and Egypt, while Saudi Arabia was supportive. Diplomatic relations between Egypt and Jordan were suspended in June 1957, and all cooperation agreements with Egypt were severed.

On 1 February 1958, Egypt and Syria united at a time when propaganda against Jordan was at its peak. Nasser became president of the new United Arab Republic. King Hussein immediately turned to his cousins in Iraq for a union, which came to be called the Hashemite Arab Federation. However, the Hashemite regime in Iraq was violently overthrown in a military coup on 14 July 1958. To the masses of the Arab world, this was viewed as a step toward Arab unity under Nasser. The Jordanian monarchy, long considered one of the impediments in this march toward unity, was expected to collapse. However, Hussein's regime was not as precarious as it appeared. The king was charismatic and charming. Behind him was a dynastic heritage, which had tempered his manners in ways beneficial to his continued leadership. Perhaps more important was the loyalty of the civilian establishment and the military to the regime. The army's allegiance had been put to the test when a coup was attempted.

In spite of this, the monarchy was still exposed to conspiracies, whose negative impact could not be minimized. Hostile propaganda and assassination plots were a constant threat, to which the king had to be vigilant. Nasserism continued to be a strong force that won over army officers. In fact, on 15 March 1959, another coup was attempted while King Hussein was visiting the United States. General Sharaa, the alleged coup leader, was sentenced to death, but later Hussein commuted the sentence to life imprisonment. The king escaped several assassination plots, one of which ended in the death of his loyal prime minister, Hazza al-Majali, on 29 August 1960.

In 1961, the regime in Amman received a respite from the danger posed by Nasserism. Egypt's union with Syria ended, and Nasser's popularity plummeted. A year later, Nasser made a major miscalculation when he committed Egyptian forces to a civil war in Yemen. This alienated many conservative Arabs, including the Gulf leaders. Moreover, an attempt by the new Ba'athist regimes in Iraq and Syria to establish a union in 1963 of Egypt, Syria, and Iraq never really took hold. In the face of these setbacks, Nasser tried to restore his image by turning his attention completely to the issue of Palestine, a development that had a special impact on Jordan in particular and the Arab region in general.

Palestinian Guerrillas and Stability in Jordan

In January 1964, Nasser invited Arab leaders to Cairo for a summit meeting. The outcome was the establishment of the Palestine Liberation Organization (PLO) under the umbrella of the Arab League. The organization was eventually to be entrusted to Ahmed Shukairy, a Palestinian who was then working in the diplomatic service of Saudi Arabia. The sole purpose of the organization was to preserve Palestinian national identity and to provide political and military mechanisms to regain national rights lost to the Israelis.[8] King Hussein accepted the establishment of the organization on the condition that it would function in cooperation with Jordan, which was concerned with the implications of such an organization on its own national security, given its vulnerability to Israeli offensive actions. Nevertheless, the organization set up its offices in Jordan.

As the organization was being formed, young Palestinians working in Kuwait, under the sponsorship of King Faisal of Saudi Arabia, organized another Palestinian group. The leading figure in this group, called Fatah (conquest), was Muhammad Abdul-Rauf al-Qudwa, who chose the nom de guerre Yasser Arafat. This group was bent on organizing raids into Israel, which meant that it had to find an operational base close to Israel's borders. Jordan came to provide such a base. However, the price the country had to pay soon became a matter of serious concern.[9] Israeli retaliatory attacks undermined the image of Jordan's leadership. Thus, the king decided to contain the activities of the PLO and Fatah, drawing protests and intensifying the antiregime propaganda. In 1965, the PLO offices were closed in Jordan, and personnel of the PLO and Fatah who conducted activities deemed contrary to the security of the state were threatened with arrest.

However, the king had to back down from the hard stance he had taken toward the Palestinian guerrillas in the face of intense propaganda from the rest of the Arab world, which was reflected in the tense climate in the country itself whose population was more than half Palestinian. Palestinian armed incursions continued to attract massive Israeli punitive responses. In one of the reprisal attacks by Israelis, Jordanian soldiers were killed. A large demonstration ensued, only to be put down by the Jordanian military. Ironically, the Jordanians were seen by the Israelis as not having done enough to curb Palestinian activities.

In the mid-1960s, when the atmosphere in the Arab region was tending toward war, Jordan decided to align itself more closely with Egypt. Unexpectedly, on 16 May 1967, Nasser asked for the withdrawal of the UN forces from the Sinai, a request that was complied with in two days.

On 22 May, Egypt ordered a closure of the straits of Tiran. All these moves were expected to lead to war. The expected Israeli attack commenced on 5 June with a fatal attack on Egyptian air bases. In response, Jordanian troops were ordered to attack positions inside Israel. However, a swift counterattack on the Jordanian front led to the Israeli capture of the entire West Bank, including Jerusalem, by 7 June. On the Syrian front, Arab forces were driven back up to the outskirts of Damascus; on 11 June the Six-Day War came to an end with a UN-imposed cease-fire. The Arab defeat was total, leaving Israel in control of the Sinai, the Gaza Strip, the West Bank, and the Golan Heights.

For Jordan, the war was disastrous. Symbolically it lost the Old City of Jerusalem, a holy site for adherents of Islam. In material terms, the country lost the relatively developed West Bank, a lucrative tourist destination because of its important biblical sites. The influx of refugees from the Israeli-occupied territories was a major strain on an economy already faced with numerous ills. In addition, it soon became apparent that it would be difficult to recover the occupied territories from the Israelis, who also had a strong religious attachment to these areas, particularly the city of Jerusalem.

The UN adopted Resolution 242 on 22 November 1967, demanding withdrawal from the territories as a precondition for peace. Israel, Jordan, Egypt, and Lebanon accepted it, while Syria refused. King Faisal, who sided with Syria, increased Saudi Arabia's support of the Fedayeen fighters. Other countries joined in, creating or supporting other groups of guerrillas amenable to their political direction, resulting in a proliferation of the Fedayeen. At this time, support for the Palestinian fighters was solid in the Arab world. Only the Popular Front for the Liberation of Palestine, led by the leader of the Arab Nationalist Movement, Dr. George Habash, was independent of the area's regimes.[10]

In 1968, most of these groups joined the PLO, and in the following year the organization was taken over by Yasser Arafat. In time, many of the Fedayeen relocated to Jordan, where over half of the population was already Palestinian. Differences between these groups and the leadership in Amman soon pushed the country into a state of turmoil. The Fedayeen acted as a state within a state, gravely threatening the already precarious position of the Jordanian monarchy. Some groups, like the PFLP and DPFLP, even called openly for the overthrow of the monarchy. This continued in spite of calls by Arafat for restraint on the part of Palestinian armed groups. The acrimonious relationship ultimately led to open warfare in 1970. King Hussein became a target of assassination attempts, which prompted the military to shell refugee camps in the outskirts of the capital. In September 1970, three planes were hijacked, the town of Irbid was taken over by the Fedayeen, and the Palestinians declared a "people's government" by the PFLP. The king responded by decreeing military rule and appointing a military government in preparation for war. The conflict that ensued claimed many casualties. Several cease-fires were negotiated, but they never held for long. The Jordanian air force virtually destroyed the Syrian force of 200 tanks that came to the aid of the encircled Palestinians. Warnings from Israel forced the Syrians not to get further involved in the Jordanian crisis.

In a final assault by government troops on the Fedayeen, 13–18 July 1971, the armed rebellion was put down. Many civilians were killed, and some guerrillas who surrendered were allowed to relocate to other countries. As of 19 July 1971, the guerrilla movement, including the PLO, ceased to exist in Jordan. Many Palestinians working in Jordan left, and those working for the Jordanian government were dismissed. The monarchy survived this crisis, and many "old" Transjordanians remained loyal to the king during those critical times, in a way exacerbating the already existing divisions between the Jordanian and Palestinian populations of the country, making the split a much more evident and permanent feature of Jordanian society and politics.[11] Consequently, subsidies from various Arab countries ceased, as Jordan's commitment to Arab unity and support of the Palestinians seemed to be in question.

Political Liberalization and Regime Survival

As in the other Arab countries, opening up the political process has been fraught with difficulties and fears. The maintenance of a delicate balance between people's participation in the politics of the country and the survival of the system is an important preoccupation for each government. The monarchies in the Arab region are known for their suspicion of any calls or moves to enhance the people's participation in governance. Jordan's experience in democracy clearly reflected the link between the regime's survival and attempts to liberalize its politics. When King Hussein ascended the throne, he tried to open up the political process. As we have already seen, by 1957, a coup had brought the experiment to an abrupt end, martial law had been imposed, and political parties were banned. The parliament elected in 1958, like the others that followed, had its powers drastically reduced. Another serious setback to democratization occurred in the aftermath of the 1967 Arab-Israeli war. Martial law was reimposed, and parliament was suspended on the grounds that as part of the kingdom was under occupation by Israel, any elections would be invalid. Moreover, the conflict of September 1970 with the Palestinian Fedayeen led to further curtailment of freedoms.

The 1970s witnessed increased financial remittances from abroad, mainly from Palestinians working in Arab oil-producing countries as a consequence of high oil prices, and the attention of the people was focused once again on exploiting the available economic opportunities for self-improvement. At the same time, political agitation was minimal, perhaps because of the forceful reaction by the state and an implicit deal between the regime and the developing (largely Palestinian) bourgeoisie, which entailed acceptance of the lack of opportunities for political expression and participation, in exchange for economic freedom in financial activities.[12]

In the 1980s the situation was changing. A growing middle class emerged, the populace was becoming politically more aware, and alterations in the external arena were taking place. Egypt and Israel had reached a peace deal, Israel had invaded Lebanon in 1982, and the PLO had experienced a serious fracture within its ranks. All these events worked for the opening up of the political process, as people strove to join the debate on issues crucial to the Arab nation.

The government response was the dissolution of the National Consultative Council formed in 1978 and a call for parliamentary elections in 1984. Meanwhile, in the occupied territories, an uprising began among Palestinians in 1987 against continued Israeli occupation. In response, the king renounced all claims over these territories the following year. Even more important at this time was the decline in the country's economy, as the dinar dropped in value to an all-time low in mid-1988. Sowing the seeds of trouble, the package imposed by the International Monetary Fund (IMF) to turn the economy around involved cutbacks in subsidies. These had terrible consequences for the people, especially the poor, and resulted in serious riots, which began in the south and eventually engulfed the entire country. Most alarming to the king, these riots began in areas like Ma'an, traditionally considered loyal to the throne. This crisis resulted in a call for a restoration of the Jordanian constitution, which had been suspended since 1957, after which the country— off and on—had been under martial law. King Hussein responded with promises to ease the tension and restore the constitution.

A transitional government was appointed to replace the outgoing one, and it immediately announced plans for elections. The November 1989 elections were conducted in a relatively free atmosphere. Censorship was lifted, and although parties were still illegal, many had formed. Islamists (the Muslim Brotherhood and independents) took one-third of the seats in parliament. In spite of this success, the Islamists were not able to translate their parliamentary victory into real political clout or to win other elections in the country.[13] In 1990, measures to ease internal security were implemented. Travel restrictions were lifted, all political prisoners were released, and those who had been dismissed from government jobs as well as universities—often for political reasons—were reinstated. By 1992 the antiquitated anticommunist laws of 1952 were annulled, martial law was abolished, political party laws were enacted, more than twenty political parties were licensed before the 1993 elections, and more liberal press laws were passed. Furthermore, the parliament was active in dealing with corruption and political abuse. On 9 April 1990, a Royal Committee was struck, composed of sixty leading personalities representing the wide political spectrum within the country, for the purpose of drafting a national charter, which would then be presented to a general congress. When King Hussein convened the congress on 9 June 1990, it endorsed the respect for the rule of law as well as democracy, the "social contract" between the people and the monarchy embraced, and the congress renewed its allegiance to the king.[14]

In July 1992, the National Assembly adopted legislation sanctioning the formation of political parties, in preparation for the first official multiparty elections since 1956, and a royal decree approved the legislation in August. In March 1993, the government had formally approved nine political parties. Elections to a multiparty Assembly were held on 8 November 1993. The exercise of democracy was smooth and peaceful, with 534 candidates running for eighty seats. Half of the twenty registered parties fielded candidates, although many ran as independents. Except for the Islamic Action Front, the parties were not well established. The IAF, an alliance between the Muslim Brotherhood and other Islamic groups, won sixteen seats, the largest among the parties that took part. However, their win was six seats lower than that in the 1989 elections. Leftist and Arab nationalist parties came in second with eight seats. For the first time, a woman gained a seat in the Assembly.

The powerful Palestinian politician Taher al-Masri was elected as speaker of the Assembly on 23 November 1993. Dr. Abd as-Salam al-Majali's government received a vote of confidence on 8 December 1993, but it was dismissed in early 1995 and replaced by that of Sharif Zaid Ibn Shaker, whose government was replaced by that of Abdul Karim al-Kabariti in 1996.

Economy

Jordan is a small country, situated between powerful neighbors. Its land area is only 97,740 square kilometers, and its population numbered 4.94 million in 1994. Its encirclement by powerful countries in a volatile region has made Jordan highly sensitive to crises, whether political or economic, regional or international. Hence, to survive it had to lean on a powerful nation. In its pre-independence time and during early years of independence, Britain maintained Jordan's economic and political security. When this relationship proved a liability, Jordan turned to economic subsidies from rich Arab countries. However, this aid was strained by vested interests of the donors and could be withheld any time when Jordan adopted "wrong" policies. Also, American aid came to play an important role in the country's well-being. As recent events in the Gulf have shown, the aid is also sensitive to politics and may be used to influence the policy options of the country.

Up to 1948, the country's economy was dominated by agriculture, and productivity was greatly determined by the availability of water. In the highlands, there is sufficient precipitation to support the growth of grains and other crops requiring less water. In the irrigated areas, citrus fruits and vegetables are grown, while in the desert fringes animals are raised. The dominance of agriculture in the economy was replaced by the service sector after 1948.

The economic profile of the country changed greatly after the 1948 Arab-Israeli war. Refugees entered the East Bank, and the West Bank became a part of the country. Services provided by the government and the United Nations Relief and Works Agency helped to meet the needs of refugees. Moreover, Palestinians with capital and entrepreneurial skills flocked into Amman, boosting the private sector. Rapid economic growth occurred between 1954 and 1967. GNP growth was placed at 11 percent.[15]

Between 1967 and 1973, however, the economy suffered a setback. This was the time when the economically rich West Bank was lost to the Israelis and Jordan experienced a massive influx of refugees. Besides, Palestinian incursions into Israel in 1968, 1969, and 1970 invited severe retaliations from Israeli forces, which greatly affected productive activities in the Jordan River valley. Another important matter was the civil war of 1970 and 1971 involving government forces and Palestinian guerrilla groups. Some economic sectors were virtually shut down, and a number of Arab countries withheld subsidies. The GNP growth recovered in 1975 to the pre-1967 level.

The economy grew rapidly after the 1973 Arab-Israeli war due to a dramatic rise in oil prices. Citizens working in the rich Gulf countries brought in a lot of remittances. By 1983, around 272,000 Jordanians were working abroad out of a total labor force of 430,000 workers, and remittances in that year were put at 412.1 million dinars.[16] Moreover, more foreigners invested in the economy, particularly during the Lebanese civil war.

In the 1980s, the economy experienced a downturn under the pressure of heavy defense spending, reduced remittances, low aid commitments, and debt problems. About 43 percent of government spending went for defense. At the end of 1993, the country's debt was still placed at U.S.$6.5 billion, or equivalent to 120 percent of GDP,[17] in spite of measures taken to alleviate the problem. The Arab countries and the United States have reduced their aid commitment to Jordan, particularly in the aftermath of the 1991 Gulf war. U.S. aid recently has been used to force Jordan to comply with the peace process and with the embargo imposed on Iraq. When it seems that Jordan is not moving in the right direction, the aid weapon is employed. Stephen Zunes notes, "From 1986 to 1990, aid averaged slightly under U.S.$60 million in economic support funds and $47 million in military assistance. These totals were reduced by half in 1991 and half again in 1993."[18]

To come out of the economic mess, the country turned to the IMF, which as usual imposed conditions that paid little attention to the social dimension. Cuts in subsidies and other austerity measures led to serious riots in 1989. Nevertheless, the adoption of the IMF programs opened the doors for aid from the international donor institutions and enabled it to reschedule its debts. In May 1994, the United States extended $187 million to support the programs, augmented in September by $37 million.[19] The United States also rescheduled debts worth $1.2 billion at the Paris Club. The measures seem to be working. GDP growth met the 5.5 percent target for 1994, and inflation remained at 5 percent.

The country's economic future is expected to improve rapidly as peace moves advance in the region. Currently, it is cashing in on the benefits of its October 1994 peace deal with Israel. The economic benefits of the deal include the commitment to wipe out Jordan's $700 million official debts to the United States and write off debts worth $90 million and $5 million owed to the United Kingdom and France, respectively.[20] The United States wrote off $220 million of its debts to Jordan during the 1994 fiscal year, partly reducing total foreign debts to $5 billion in 1995 from $8 billion in 1989.[21] However, the Republican-dominated U.S. Congress was less forthcoming in slashing the remaining debts.

Nevertheless, in September 1995 the United States canceled a further $420 million of Jordan's outstanding debts.

In spite of these actions to reduce debt obligations and positive movements in some economic sectors, the hopes for rapid improvement in living standards immediately after the signing of the peace deal have proven exaggerated. With an estimated 30 percent of its adult population unemployed, the Jordanian government has to do more.[22]

Foreign Relations

Jordan is a small country, situated in a volatile region. Its neighbors are powerful and not always friendly. In its infant state, King Abdullah realized its vulnerability. Thus he aligned closely with Britain. The relationship ensured not only Jordan's economic viability but also its security from hostile powers. In the regional context, the Arab-Israeli conflict exhausted many of Jordan's resources. Major wars with Israel in 1948 and 1967 had far-reaching territorial consequences. Indeed, Jordan's leaders were very alarmed since some Israeli leaders expressed claims to Jordanian territory, which they considered part of biblical Jewish lands.

However, in spite of these events, contacts between Jordan and Israel continued, particularly with the moderate Labour Party leaders. In fact, before the 1948 war broke out, secret contacts between King Abdullah and Jewish leaders had yielded an agreement to partition Palestine between them. The contacts came to a halt when Abdullah was killed. During King Hussein's time, contacts with Israelis produced functional agreements in areas such as border crossings. Jordan had been keen to resolve the Arab-Israeli conflict but within the context of a comprehensive agreement based on UN Resolutions 242 and 338. However, with the break in the Arab ranks occasioned by the Camp David accord of 1978, the notion of a comprehensive peace agreement at one time was broken. Nevertheless, attempts were made for the Arabs to present a joint negotiating position with Israel. But this also failed when the Palestinians reached a separate deal in Oslo, Norway, in 1993. Then Jordan decided that the time was right to transform the secret contacts into a full agreement. This came on 26 October 1994. The Jordan-Israeli treaty covered a broad spectrum including economic, environmental, and security issues. Crucially, it settled water and border issues.

With the other powerful neighbors, relations have never been smooth. Syria conducted overt and covert offensive actions against the country in the past. Recently, it criticized Jordan for what it saw as an unfair peace deal with Israel. Likewise, Jordanian-Iraqi relations have been far from smooth. When the Hashemite leadership in Iraq was overthrown, relationships reached an all-time low. However, under Saddam Hussein, much rapprochement occurred. The main catalyst behind the thawing of relations was economic. Iraq loaned Jordan money and became an important trading partner. The port of Aqaba boosted its revenues between 1979 and 1988, as it became a major transit point for Iraqi cargo. Iraq's share in Jordan's total foreign trade surpassed that of any country in 1988, and in 1990 nearly three-fourths of Jordan's industry was producing for the Iraqi market.[23] So it is not surprising that when the 1991 Gulf Crisis started, Jordan sided with Iraq.

This alliance, however, cost Jordan dearly in terms of lost revenues and strained diplomatic support from the powerful countries of the world. Actually, Jordan became a pariah state. Its losses in the Gulf Crisis included blockade of its only port at Aqaba by the United States, return of 500,000 expatriate workers, the loss of remittances from the Gulf states, and loss of its aid.[24] However, Jordan's image has been rehabilitated since it made peace with Israel and distanced itself from Iraq, further cementing its traditionally strong pro-western posture.

Jordan has openly cooperated with groups opposed to the regime in Iraq. King Hussein invited the opposition to set up offices in his country. In late 1995, the country hosted two prominent Iraqi defectors, General Hussein Kamel and his brother, Saddam Kamel al Majeed, both cousins and sons-in-law to Saddam Hussein. Both left Jordan on 20 February 1996. They were assassinated shortly after they returned to Iraq, and the government in Jordan denounced their murders. King Hussein also cooperated with American plans to destabilize the regime in Baghdad, further endearing Jordan to the United States and its allies.

In general, the anti-Saddam policy has helped the country in its efforts to win back friends in the Gulf region. In spite of some animosity between the royal houses, ties with Saudi Arabia have improved. The ban on granting permits to dependents of Jordanians and Palestinians working in Saudi Arabia was partly revoked in March 1995. The same warming of ties has also occurred with the Kuwaitis. A senior Jordanian diplomat visited Kuwait in September 1994, and later it was announced that the country's embassy in Kuwait would reopen. Also, Kuwait agreed to readmit thousands of Jordanian workers expelled in 1991.

As the complexity of the Arab-Israeli peace process increased in late 1995 with the assassination of Yitzhak Rabin, King Hussein chose to move Jordan closer to Israel. His reasons were pragmatic, as Israel controls almost all of Jordan's water supplies and is Jordan's only reasonably prosperous neighbor. Saudi Arabia and Syria have little to offer as trading partners, though for different reasons, and Iraq is an isolated ruin. Jordan and Syria are at odds, as Jordan accused Assad's government of sending saboteurs across its borders. Also, there is little doubt about Jordan's fate in the event of actual hostilities between the larger Arab states and Israel. King Hussein allied himself to Hosni Mubarak of Egypt and lesser players, such as Tunisia and Morocco, in a moderate Arab camp that was willing to consider the sterner measures proposed by the right-wing Likud government in Tel Aviv. Domestic opposition to the pro-Israel policy forced King Hussein to put a cap on political reforms to quell internal dissent.

Jordan after King Hussein

On 7 February 1999, King Hussein lost his long battle with cancer. He had gained wide acclaim for moving Jordan and its Arab neighbors toward peace with Israel. He will be remembered as one of the most remarkable leaders and statesmen of the second half of the twentieth century. He was a survivor who had transcended mere survival, blending it with a large degree of statesmanship, maintaining the monarchy for forty-six years in the murky waters of the Arab-Israeli conflict, and overcoming challenges to the monarchy by Arab nationalism, aggressive neighbors, and the populist threat of Islamic activism.

He should be remembered not because he reached out to Israel—Egypt's Anwar Sadat had already done that—but because he infused humanity and substance into the making of peace, which elevated not only his own standing but that of his country in the international community. He played a critical role in the whole context of Arab-Israeli peacemaking and in terms of the Arab-Israeli conflict itself, both in war and peace. He was a leader in regional politics in terms of regional security and stability. He had to fend off many forces that were targeted against his regime, bringing moderation and a stabilizing influence to the region.

He transformed Jordan into a "real" country, a country that will survive his passing because he balanced the nation's reliance on the West with an accommodation with both Arab public opinion and the twin domestic constituencies of Palestinian and Jordanian public opinion, in an effort to further the viability of the monarchy. He was able to do so because he recognized that Hashemite Jordan was different from the radical Arab regimes around it—Nasser's Egypt, Saddam Hussein's Iraq, Ba'athist Syria. He knew that for Hashemite Jordan to survive, his conservative ruling elite had to have alliances with the West and a strategic understanding with Israel—never as allies but because they had common interests, a fear of radicalism, and a fear of Palestinian irredentism.

King Hussein surprised everyone by naming his eldest son, 'Abdullah, crown prince, in spite of the fact that his brother, Hassan, had held that position since 1965. Just hours after announcing the switch, Hussein flew back to the Mayo Clinic in Minnesota for cancer treatments; he died a few days later. The thirty-seven-year-old 'Abdullah was seen as a political novice with little experience in international affairs, but he spent his first days as crown prince meeting world leaders, including many past and present heads of state, first at his father's state funeral and then in a whirlwind global tour. 'Abdullah inherited a realm that is far more institutionalized politically than the one his father inherited in 1953. There is still room for political evolution, reform, and development. But the kingdom now has a diversified bureaucracy, strong internal security forces, and the entrenched rule of tribal society, which while constantly evolving is a source of legitimacy and strength bequeathed by King Hussein and the region's history. The challenges facing 'Abdullah include the economy, the legacy of more than 2 million Palestinian refugees living in Jordan, and holding off insecure neighbors such as Iraq and Syria.

The biggest challenge will clearly be to improve Jordan's ailing economy. His tour of the Gulf states and the world's capital cities following his coronation secured the most favorable terms possible for repayment of Jordan's $8.5 billion national debt, and a new intellectual property law and lower import duties fostered admission to the World Trade Organization.[25] However, the failure of the Israeli-Palestinian peace process and continued UN Security Council economic sanctions against Iraq have closed the two markets most accessible to the Jordanian economy. Payments on the debt, long-standing commitments to a large bureaucracy, as well as a population that is fast outgrowing his kingdom's meager economy are challenges facing the new king. In an effort to improve the political climate within Jordan, King 'Abdullah appointed a new government in June 2000, shifting from a conservative prime minister, 'Abdel-Raouf Rawabdeh, to the more western-oriented 'Ali Abu Ragheb. The new cabinet includes representatives from a broad spectrum of Jordanian society, including Islamists and Palestinians. With nine of the thirty-seven ministers of Palestinian origin, the June 2000 cabinet contained more Palestinians than any since the decision to divest Jordan of the West Bank in 1988. 'Abdullah is the first of a group of new leaders in the region, and he may well play a role in stabilizing his generation as his father came to stabilize the previous one.

CHAPTER 9

The State of Israel

*T*he history of the state of Israel is rooted in the ideology of Zionism. Modern Zionism is a sociopolitical and nationalistic movement with one of its main goals the ingathering of the Jews as a nation in Palestine. Some of the more radical Zionist factions advocate an expansionist settler-colonizer objective in the Middle East and the expulsion of the indigenous Arab population. In the words of a prominent Israeli writer, Amos Elon, "The political imagination, like the imagination of the explorer, often invents its own geography. The early Zionists suffered from the common Eurocentric illusion that territories outside Europe were in a state of political vacuum."[1] Zionism derives its inspiration from a particular interpretation of the Judaic religion, viewing the covenant established by God with Abraham, Isaac, and Jacob as assigning the land of Canaan to the Hebrews "for an everlasting possession." It also bases its claim on Palestine on the fact that the Hebrews once inhabited that area. Zionism makes us aware of certain symbolic elements in Judaism that deal with ancient glories of the Jewish nation, as well as religious festivals that commemorate events in this history, and Jewish liturgy is permeated with prayers for a return to Zion. In the late nineteenth century, the spiritual belief in the return to Zion as a result of divine intervention (the coming of the Messiah) was politicized and made secular by the growing Jewish nationalist movement, whose main goal was to create a modern state as a homeland for the Jewish people, preferably located in the lands of their ancestors.

Zionism developed as a viable political movement in the late nineteenth century as a result of anti-Semitism in Europe, particularly between the East European and Russian Jews who suffered from widespread discrimination and frequent persecutions. One of the manifestations of political Zionism at the time was Leo Pinsker's pamphlet

Auto-Emancipation, published in 1882. Pinsker made the argument that legal emancipation was useless because it did not carry with it social emancipation, and that in order to achieve social emancipation, the Jews must establish their own state. In the same year, Pinsker helped establish the organization of Hovevei Zion (Lovers of Zion), which founded the first Zionist settlements in Palestine supported by funds from abroad, followed by other settlements that were mostly inhabited by East European and Russian Jews. The movement, however, remained a religious-philanthropic undertaking until Theodor Herzl transformed Zionism into an organized political movement. The anti-Semitism he witnessed while covering the Dreyfus trial in Paris troubled Herzl, a Hungarian Jew acting as a correspondent for a Viennese newspaper. In 1895, he published *Der Judenstaat* (The Jewish State), arguing that the Jewish problem could not be solved merely by migrations from one country to another, because Jewish minorities would eventually be persecuted wherever they existed. Herzl believed that a "Society of Jews" might acquire a national territory in either Argentina or Palestine and organize Jews in the Diaspora for migration to their new home. For him, the venue was not an issue.

In 1897, Herzl organized the first World Zionist Congress in Basel, Switzerland, attended by over 200 delegates. This congress established the World Zionist Organization, the "Society of Jews" prescribed by Herzl in *Der Judenstaat,* and formulated the Basel Program, which stated that "the aim of Zionism is to create for the Jewish people a home in Palestine secured by public law." As leader of the World Zionist Organization, Herzl attempted through diplomatic channels to get one of the major powers to sponsor a Jewish home in Palestine. In Germany and Turkey he met with little success. The British, however, were more sympathetic. In 1903, they offered what is now Uganda as a site for a Jewish home. Zionist internal opposition to this offer was so strong that Herzl, who initially favored acceptance, supported Uganda only as a temporary home. The Seventh Congress of the World Zionist Organization rejected the offer completely after an acrimonious debate. From that time on, the Zionist organization became unalterably committed to establishing the national home for the Jews only in Palestine.

During this period of diplomacy by the World Zionist Organization, other Zionist organizations were established to facilitate Jewish immigration to Palestine. The Jewish Colonial Trust was established in 1899, and the Jewish National Fund was established in 1901.[2] Both organizations purchased land in Palestine for settlement by European Jews.[3] The Zionist movement, however, was not without opposition from within the Jewish communities. The ultraorthodox Jews opposed the military and political ambitions of the Zionists on religious grounds. They believed that the return could occur only through divine intervention. Even stronger opposition came from the Reform Jews, who viewed Judaism as a religion and not as a nationality. Their views primarily represented the assimilationist tendencies of the Jews in western Europe, England, and North America, who feared that Jewish nationalism would legally and morally compromise their positions as citizens of their respective states. Thus, a split developed among the Jewish people over the problem of nationhood.

At the outbreak of World War I, the Ottoman government clamped down on Palestine and declared the Zionist movement a subversive element. During the war, Jewish leaders gave their support to the Allied governments in an effort to gain Allied sympathy for a Jewish state. Of greater importance toward that end, however, were the contributions of Dr. Chaim Weizmann, a chemistry lecturer at Manchester University and a Zionist leader. During the war, he gained influence in England by developing a process for producing acetone, an ingredient of the explosive cordite used in artillery shells. Dr. Weizmann used his influence to gain the support of British leaders for the Zionist cause, while U.S. Supreme Court Justice Louis Brandeis and Rabbi Stephen Wise convinced President Woodrow Wilson that he should support the now favorable British position on Zionism. The British position had been fully expressed in the Balfour Declaration of 1917, which stated: "His Majesty's government views with favour the establishment in Palestine of a national home for the Jewish people, and will use their best endeavours to facilitate the achievement of this object, it being clearly understood that nothing shall be done which may prejudice the civil and religious rights of *existing non-Jewish communities in Palestine* or the rights and political status enjoyed by Jews in any other country" (emphasis added). At the time of the declaration, Arabs constituted 92 percent of the total population of Palestine.

In 1918, Palestine was freed from Ottoman control, but the Allied powers had made several conflicting agreements and promises regarding the disposition of the freed territories: the Balfour Declaration; the Sykes-Picot Agreement, dividing the Middle East into spheres of influence for the Allied powers; and the Hussein-McMahon correspondence, promising the Arabs an independent state in the Arab lands of the Middle East. Out of these antithetical agreements and declarations arose the bitter struggle between Jewish (Zionist) and Arab nationalisms. The Arabs, no less than the Zionists, have a religious and historical attachment to Palestine. According to Muslim belief, Jerusalem is a sacred city. Perhaps even greater in importance to the Arab is the fact that a primarily Arab population has inhabited Palestine since A.D. 640. Furthermore, at the close of World War I, Palestine was inhabited by 620,000 Arabs (of whom 550,000 were Muslims and 70,000 Christians) and only 50,000 Jews. The Arabs feared that unlimited Jewish immigration would displace the Arab population and eventually make the Arabs a minority in a wholly Jewish state. The Zionists, on the other hand, considered the Balfour Declaration the equivalent of a British *promise* of a Jewish state in the whole of Palestine.[4]

The fate of Palestine thus remained undecided until 1922, when the League of Nations placed the territory under a British mandate, giving the British the "full powers of legislation and of administration, save as they were limited by the terms of this Mandate" and instructing them to work with "an appropriate Jewish agency" on matters affecting the establishment of a Jewish national home. The Zionist Organization was recognized as that agency, and the Jews set up a quasi-state within the mandated area. But the mandate was also "a sacred trust of civilization" expressly given the mandatory power for the "welfare" and development of the inhabitants of the mandated territories. The advent of World War II sharply curtailed the Zionist activities aimed at independence. Hitler's persecution of the European Jews caused both the Zionist Organization and the non-Zionist Jews of Palestine to expend most of their energy in support of the Allied war effort. Over 100,000 Palestinian Jews volunteered their services to the Allies, while those who stayed at home committed the agricultural and industrial resources they possessed to the war effort.

The Zionists also put considerable effort into pursuing the illegal immigration of European Jewish refugees from Hitler's persecutions. This effort led to increased friction among the Jews, the Arabs, and the British. The indigenous Palestinian-Arabs, inflamed by swelling Jewish immigration and the fear that Palestine would become a Jewish state rather than an Arab one, demonstrated and rioted against the Jewish population and British occupation. To quell the unrest, the British attempted to restrict Jewish immigration, and their naval patrols intercepted many refugee ships and sent the occupants to British colonies. In retaliation for the British measures, and to oppose the detachment of Transjordan from the Palestinian mandate—thereby closing it to Jewish colonization—the Irgun, Stern gang (Lehi), and Hagannah stepped up their terror campaign against the British.

The discovery of the Nazi death camps at the end of World War II caused world opinion to swing in support of the Zionists. Inspired by the same horror, the Jews themselves concentrated all of their efforts on the immediate illegal immigration of European Jews to Palestine. British attempts to limit immigration led to open clashes with the Jews. Many Jews were arrested. Meanwhile, some efforts were initiated to control Zionist activities. By this time, Palestine was becoming an unbearable administrative and financial burden to the British. After President Harry Truman announced in 1948 that he supported the immediate immigration of 100,000 Jews into Palestine, Great Britain declared that Jewish disarmament must precede any large-scale immigration.[5] The Zionists' military organizations—the Hagannah, the Irgun, and the Stern gang—responded to British demands with a military campaign.

Anxious to be rid of its burden, Britain placed the problem of Palestine before the United Nations. A UN investigating committee, sent to Palestine to study the situation, recognized that Arab-Jewish cooperation was unlikely. Consequently, in 1947, the UN, without the consultation and consent of the indigenous Palestinian-Arab population, and without the consultation of the International Court of Justice in The Hague about the legality of such a decision, voted to partition Palestine into an Arab state, a Jewish state, and an international zone in and around Jerusalem. The brewing conflict between Arabs and Jews broke out immediately following the partition recommendation. The Zionist forces moved to carry out Plan D, which consisted of attacking and securing strategic Palestinian villages under Zionist control, many of which were outside the partition lines. In the midst of this strife, on 14 May 1948, David Ben-Gurion, head of the Jewish Agency, announced the establishment of the state of Israel. Thus, the Society of Jews that Theodor Herzl had envisaged in 1895 was achieved within fifty-three years, but only at the cost of an irreversible alienation of the non-Jewish population of Palestine.[6]

The series of events that led to the foundation of the state of Israel in 1948 made refugees of between 700,000 and 800,000 Palestinians and led the Middle East into an era of tension, instability, and war. Thus far, five major wars have characterized the conflict: (1) the first all-out war of 1948–1949; (2) the 1956 Suez crisis, when Britain, France, and Israel invaded Egypt; (3) the 1967 Six-Day War, when Israel launched a major offensive against Egypt, Syria, and Jordan; (4) the October 1973 war when Egypt and Syria attempted to regain their lost territories from Israel; and (5) the 1982 Israeli invasion of Lebanon.

The utopian idealism associated with Israel's creation has since given way to self-criticism, doubt, and increasing polarization. Zionism today is much different than the Zionism of Herzl and Pinsker, to the extent that Israel has witnessed the rise of extremist nationalists, unhappy with the status quo, who seek a radical solution to the Palestinian problem—if necessary through violence and terror—by removing the Palestinians

from Israel's political landscape. For the past and present proponents of
extremism, such as Meir Kahane, Ariel Sharon, and Rafael Eitan,
Israel's difficulties originated in its inability to deal effectively with
the Palestinians within Israel and the occupied territories. To them, the
Palestinians are an obstacle and a hindrance to the realization of the
Zionist goals, and they need to be removed from Israel by forced mass
deportations to other Arab states or by other means. At the other end of
the political spectrum is the Israeli Left, which advocates the exchange
of land in the occupied territories for peace. For the proponents of
peace, Israel's difficulties lie in the intransigence of Israeli policy vis-à-
vis the Palestine National Authority. Concerned with the erosion of traditional Jewish values attendant upon the role of occupier, the liberal
intelligentsia that makes up the principal constituency of the peace
movement advocates some accommodation to Palestinian aspirations to
end the violence endemic in military occupation.

Creation of the Israeli State

The decision to partition Palestine plunged the whole region into turmoil. Whereas the Zionists were elated by the prospects of fulfilling
their dream of statehood, the Arabs were enraged. Tension between the
two communities escalated, and the country drifted into a civil war. In
a bid to make their exit as simple as possible, the British refused to get
involved in the implementation of the UN partition. This assertion is
problematic in light of the historical record of British collusion with the
Zionists. The British mandatory power, which had allowed the emergence of Zionist political and military infrastructures while suppressing
the Palestinian revolts (1936–39) and disarming their leadership,
claimed to play a neutral role. Their attempt at neutrality during the
final days of the mandate was a case of too little too late.

In the midst of the chaos, the state of Israel was proclaimed on
14 May 1948, coinciding with the termination of the British mandate.
The declaration of statehood, in a museum on the Tel Aviv waterfront,
was read out by David Ben-Gurion on behalf of the newly formed
Provisional Council, a group comprising the executives of the National
Council and Jewish Agency and delegates of Jewish groups not represented in the two bodies. The People's Council, established in March
1948, was transformed into the new Provisional Council of State on the
day that independence was declared. An executive committee of
thirteen, called the People's Directorate, earlier elected by the People's
Council, became the provisional government. The Jews, supposedly
in line with the UN partition requirements, unilaterally took the forma-

tions of these institutions. The British were concerned with pulling out, and the Arabs watched powerlessly as the Zionists were implementing their plans for takeover. The independence declaration formed the basic principles of the constitutional system. It was decided that if the country had no written constitution, like Britain it would not require one. Instead, the declaration of independence and a set of "basic laws" would fill its place. The decision was taken so as to sideline differences among Jews over some issues, especially religion, and to avoid dealing with the borders issues.

Immediately, the state of Israel was recognized by the United States and the Soviet Union, while its Arab neighbors belatedly and incompetently intervened to save the portions of Palestine that had not yet fallen to the advancing Zionist armies. Thus began the first major war to be fought between Israel and the Arab states. Between the adoption of the UN partition plan and the end of the British mandate, the Palestinian Arabs built armed groups which, after the proclamation of the state of Israel, were joined in their struggle by the armies of Egypt, Jordan, Syria, Iraq, and Lebanon. The joint Arab force was poorly coordinated, and the Israelis exploited their inferior lines of communications. When armistice agreements were signed in 1949, about 80 percent of the territory of Mandatory Palestine was under Israeli control, the area to the east of Jordan River was controlled by Jordan, and the Gaza Strip was ruled by Egypt.

Development of Political Institutions

The institutional development of the Israeli state can be traced back before 1948. During the British mandate, over a quarter of a century (1922–1948), the Jewish community in Palestine and the institutions it set up developed gradually but steadily. On the basis of these institutions and the system of governance laid down during that time, the postindependence political makeup of the country was established, as explained by David Zohar: "The coalition governments that have always governed Israel are a legacy of the pre-state era as much as the country's major parties."[7] It is therefore appropriate to have a short review of the institutions that were formed before 1948.

When the British mandate was imposed over Palestine, the Ottoman millet (community) system of administration continued. This system gave much autonomy to religiously defined communities to manage their own affairs. Failure by the mandatory authorities to create common and unified governing institutions for all the communities resulted in the evolution of separate and distinct institutions for the antagonistic

Jewish and Arab communities in Palestine. Before the imposition of the British mandate, the Jews had tried to form their own representative body. It did not succeed due to Ottoman objections. It was only in 1918 that a preparatory committee of party and community leaders made any headway. The success of the work of this committee led to the election of a quasi-legislature, the Assembly of Delegates, on 19 April 1920. This elected body chose the members of the National Council, which became the effective political leadership of the Yishuv (Jewish community) from 1920 to 1948. It became a practice for the National Council to meet several times a year to adopt decisions, which had the impact of progressively assuming the legislative functions of the Assembly. To implement its decisions, the National Council formed the National Council Executive from among its members. The members of the executive organ headed functional departments such as politics, local affairs, and rabbinical affairs. Local committees were elected for towns and settlements. To give a legal basis to these institutions, the British promulgated an ordinance entitled "Regulations for the Organization of the Jewish Community in Palestine" on 1 January 1928.

Although the elected assembly represented the Jews in Palestine, other Jewish institutions also played important roles during this time. The Jewish community in Palestine was still treated as a junior partner of the World Zionist Organization (WZO). The Zionist Congress, which convened inside and outside Palestine, was perceived as the parliament of the "state in embryo" rather than the elected assembly.[8] The executive of the Jewish Agency, which represented the WZO and other Jewish organizations of the Diaspora, also exercised immense political influence. Orthodox Jewish opposition to the participation of women marred the election to the first assembly. A mechanism was worked out by which a special arrangement was made for Orthodox Jews who had barred their women from voting, their votes being given double weight. When the demand to deny women the vote was turned down by the elected assembly, Orthodox members withdrew their participation, and that seemed to be a positive contribution to the development of secular democracy in the future state.

The first elected assembly met in Jerusalem on 25 October 1920. In all, four assemblies were elected by the community, the last of which was symbolically dissolved in February 1949 on the eve of the calling of the first constituent assembly of the state of Israel. The strong links between the last elected assembly of the pre-state era and the first of the postindependence time were evident in the fact that of the 171 members of the former, at least 55 joined the latter.[9] Even the Labour Party, which proved predominant in the elections before independence, maintained its dominance after independence for some time.

Legislative powers in the postindependence era have been vested in the Knesset, a successor of the Provisional State Council. Its 120 members were elected for four-year terms. The electoral system formed its salient features in the pre-state era. Since independence, the Basic Law provides the legal framework for the election system: Knesset, as well as other election laws and modifications. All citizens of Israel who have attained the age of eighteen may vote in Knesset elections, and they can stand for election at the age of twenty-one. The entire state of Israel is taken as a single constituency, and representation is proportional. A rigid system of candidate lists, decided by party leaders, is employed. A party is required to have received at least 5 percent of the national vote to be represented in the assembly. The party with the most seats in the Knesset forms the government. The president of the country, whose post is largely ceremonial, asks the prime minister, who is elected directly, to form the government. Because of the nature of the political landscape, no party has ever obtained an absolute majority in a national vote, and coalition governments have been the norm in Israel.

Party System

Among the few in the Middle East with a functioning representative system of government, Israel is a multiparty democracy. As mentioned earlier, the foundation of the system was laid down during the pre-state era. In spite of a turbulent history, the country has managed to nurture a vibrant democracy. Broadly speaking, there are four main political movements, namely, the socialists, nonsocialists (nationalists), religious parties, and the civil circles or progressives. Since the 1980s, there has also been a strong showing by radical nationalist groups.

The Socialists

The paramount socialist political force in Israel is the Labour Party dominated by the former MAPAI. MAPAI was founded in 1930 by the fusion of two older socialist movements, Achdut Ha'avodah and Hapoel Hatzair. Most of the founding fathers of the state of Israel were members of the MAPAI. This party managed to maintain its organizational unity until 1965, when it became the victim of a rift between the restive younger generation of leaders led by Levi Eshkol and Golda Meir, who then controlled its apparatus, and former prime minister David Ben-Gurion, who was supported by a group of new rising politicians such as Moshe Dayan and Shimon Peres. The latter formed a new political party and named it Reshimat Poalei Israel (Rafee). By 1968, however, most of its senior members had rejoined the old political group where they, together with other members, proceeded to form an allied Israeli

Labour Party. In 1969, the MAPAM, a Marxist-Zionist party formed in 1948, joined the Labour alliance to form the Labour alignment, which ran a single unified list of candidates in the elections held in the same year. However, MAPAM withdrew from the alliance after the 1984 elections in protest over the unity government that included the Likud bloc. The Labour alignment held power in Israel until 1977, when the Likud bloc defeated it. However, the party regained power in 1992 and held it until 1996, although it sometimes shared power with Likud in the interval periods.

Nonsocialists or Nationalists

The other major political movements, as mentioned earlier, are the nonsocialist (nationalists) and the civil circles, represented by the Likud bloc. Like the Labour alignment, the nonsocialist movement has never been entirely cohesive. The Likud bloc, formed in 1973, is a successor to an earlier bloc formed by the Herut (Freedom) and Liberal Parties in 1965 under the name Gush Herut Liberalim (Gahal). Menachem Begin formed Gahal's core component, the Herut Party, in 1948. Its doctrinal roots lay in the Zionist Revisionist movement set up by Vladimir Zeev Jabotinsky during the 1920s. Begin, like Jabotinsky, was a militant nationalist and a strong believer in Jewish activism. Unlike the limited retaliatory attacks of the main armed group, the Hagannah, the armed wing of the Revisionist network, the Irgun Zvai Leumi (IZL), later commanded by Begin, conducted aggressive military operations against the British and Arabs. After independence, when Ben-Gurion's government dissolved all armed factions, Begin transformed the militant IZL into the Herut political party.

Several nationalist and right-of-center groups joined the Gahal, forming the Likud (unity) coalition, which had a single list in the eighth Knesset election of 1973. This bloc was headed by Begin and, beside the parties that made up Gahal, it included the Free Center, the Liberal Party, and the Land of Israel Movement. The bond holding the coalition together was the adoption of the Land of Israel or Greater Israel Movement program of annexing territories acquired in the 1967 war.[10] The hard-line stance of the coalition attracted several radical anti-Arab and Zionist groups, which drifted away after the Camp David accord of 1978.

Religious Movements

A third force in the Israeli political system consists of a constantly changing constellation of religious political parties. These parties carry political clout far beyond what their numerical electoral strength may suggest. The reason is that the Labour alignment and the Likud bloc have never succeeded in winning a parliamentary majority, nor have any of their constituent members. Consequently, any leader before 1996 entrusted by the president with the task of forming a cabinet became dependent on the support of some, or all, of the religious political parties. This coveted support always carried with it a very high political and financial cost, including the appointment of members of these parties as cabinet ministers.

In the elections of the first Knesset, the religious parties presented a common list and acted in uniformity in the Knesset. In 1956, a few religious parties and factions formed the National Religious Party. Also represented were the ultraorthodox Agudat Israel (Community of Israel) and Poali Agudat Israel (Workers of the Community of Israel). The Agudat movement endorsed the establishment of the state of Israel but dissociated itself from the Zionist movement and its principles. The exception was the religious faction known in Israel as Neturei Karta (Guardians of the Gate), whose members refused to acknowledge the secular authority and government of the state of Israel because they believe that only God can govern Israel. Other marginal groups have recently appeared. These include the Gush Emunim, Shas, and Rabbi Kahane's Kach. After the May 1996 elections, religious parties formed the third largest bloc in the Knesset, and continued to sustain their political power and influence within a coalition government headed by the Likud bloc.

Emergence of the Radical Right

The radical right of the Israeli political spectrum consists of a small number of groups, many of which are characterized by religious extremism, extreme nationalism, and aggressive anti-Palestinian sentiments. Since 27 September 1978, the day Menachem Begin concluded the famous peace accord with Egypt, these groups have gained momentum and membership. According to Ehud Sprinzak, "The Israeli radical right is presently a great deal more than the movements that are directly associated with it. It is a general climate and a syndrome of political behavior. It crosses party lines, economic strata, and education. In my estimation, it pertains to 20–25 percent of the Jewish citizens of Israel and is felt everywhere, in schools, military camps, the markets, and the synagogues."[11]

Because of this trend, these groups have penetrated the center of political power, mostly at the expense of the center-right. The election of Rabbi Meir Kahane of the Kach Party to the Knesset in 1984 was a testimony to the growth of the radical right. Even more significant was the appointment by Prime Minister Yitzhak Shamir of Rehavam Ze'evi to the cabinet. Like Kahane, Ze'evi advocates the expulsion of the Palestinians from the Holy Land.

Although the radical right started crystallizing in 1978, most of its constituent members had begun surfacing and acting earlier. The most influential among them, an offspring of the Six-Day War, was the Land of Israel Movement (LIM). This movement succeeded in assembling a combination of religious fundamentalists, military hard-liners, and settlement fanatics, all of whom held a deep suspicion of Palestinian and Arab intentions and a strong belief in the military invincibility of the Israeli state. Their guiding political principle was that Israel should only trade "peace for peace," unlike a significant segment of the mainstream who were willing, in principle, to trade land for peace.

In the 1970s, two other groups joined the ranks of the radicals, Gush Emunim and Kach. Formed in 1974, the Gush following was made up of young and inexperienced people closely associated with the LIM. In fact, some of their mentors were the founding fathers of LIM. These young people were committed to the settlement of the West Bank to which they refer only with the biblical label of Judea and Samaria, which they viewed not only as a political act but as "a religious and metaphysical commandment."[12] The pioneering spirit of the group soon won the respect of the Labour veterans from the kibbutzim and moshavim (collective and cooperative villages). Rabbi Meir Kahane founded the Kach, which is known for its extremism against Palestinians and for its incitement of street demonstrations and disturbances. In 1973 and 1977, Kahane attempted, unsuccessfully, to get elected to a seat in the Knesset.

Although the radical groups operated independently of each other, they were united in their admiration of Menachem Begin. But they were stunned and outraged when Begin signed the peace accord with Egypt, which entailed an Israeli withdrawal from the Sinai. The radical right had orchestrated public street demonstrations and other actions, but they had failed to influence Begin, and the accord was signed 29 March 1978. The only legitimate recourse remaining was to take their cause to the Israeli voters. Consequently, the Tehiya Party was established in June 1979 to oppose the Camp David accord. In the 1981 elections, Tehiya won three seats in the Knesset. This was a significant success considering the disproportionate political power of small parties in multiparty coalition systems. After the debacle of the invasion of Lebanon in 1982, and in spite of sharp disagreement over the Camp David accord, Tehiya members decided to throw their weight behind Likud and join Begin's government. Likud was still perceived by Tehiya to be the mainstay of the Israeli nationalists and, as such, should be defended against the Left.

Toward the end of 1983, a retired army chief of staff, Rafael (Raful) Eitan, founded another radical political party, Tsomet. This catered to the Labour pioneering groups who espoused the maximalist position on the territories. Eitan subscribed to the view that, if necessary, as many as 1 million Palestinians should be deported from the West Bank. Another secular rightist who joined these extremists was Rehavam Ze'evi. Before the outbreak of the massive unrest among the Palestinians, the *intifada*, he advocated transferring Palestinians from the territories as the only solution to the Arab problem. In the elections of 1988, Ze'evi won two seats in the Knesset supporting the banner "Them or Us." Although the combined support of the radical parties in 1988 was only 6 percent of the vote and returned only seven members to the Knesset, when taken together with the hawkish wing of the Likud, observers estimated that the radical right could count on the support of 25 percent of the Israeli public.[13] Both the Tehiya and Tsomet joined the narrow right-wing government of Yitzhak Shamir in 1990.

A willingness of the members of the radical right to pursue their goals by all means, including extralegal, encouraged violent actions against Palestinians and Jews alike, and culminated in the 1995 assassination of Prime Minister Yitzhak Rabin, gunned down by a young man who claimed he was protecting the sacred land of Israel from being handed over to its enemies. This act was undoubtedly stimulated by the pronouncements of some radical rabbis and the hostile propaganda of the nationalist right. Immediately after Rabin's death, the right was thrown onto the defensive, facing attacks from a broad spectrum of groups in Israeli society who held the radical right responsible. The leader of the opposition hurriedly disassociated himself from the circumstances that led to the crime. The assassination of Rabin raised what is probably the most dreaded specter in the Israeli national consciousness—namely, civil war. The ensuing general feeling that civil war could break out because of internal Israeli opposition to the peace process was enough in itself to put a damper on the process and turn a substantial number of Israelis against it.

Shimon Peres believed he could take advantage of the opportunity presented by Rabin's assassination, and he moved rapidly to call an election to the Knesset for May 1996. His intentions, while being reasonable, did not take into account the intentions and actions of militant Palestinians. Two Palestinian militant groups, Hamas and Islamic Jihad, who vehemently opposed the ongoing peace talks, carried out a series of unprecedented suicide bomb attacks in the heartland of Israel, affecting the chances of a Labour reelection victory. A fourth bomb attack on 4 March raised the death toll of Israelis to 55 in just eight days of carnage. The tide of outraged public opinion reversed its course, and Peres saw what he had considered a certain electoral victory slip away. Likud leader Benjamin Netanyahu gained enough votes to form the new coalition government. It is not surprising that Netanyahu's victory contributed significantly to the collapse of the Middle East peace process and the stalling of any meaningful negotiations between Israel and the governing authorities of the Palestinians. These were among the most important short-term objectives of the Israeli radical right, as well as Hamas and other Palestinian extremists. The 1999 electoral victory of Labour's Ehud Barak gave rise to hopes that the peace process could regain lost momentum, but little had been accomplished by the end of 2000.

Economy

Israel's economy is small and open. The total area of the country, excluding the West Bank and the Gaza Strip, is approximately 22,000 square kilometers, and most of it is poor in natural resources. This situation is exacerbated by insufficient fresh water resources. This has created serious diplomatic tension and caused armed conflict between Israel and its Arab neighbors, who control much of the fresh water flowing from their territory into Israel. The population of Israel is estimated to be approximately 6 million, excluding the Palestinians living in its midst.

The main structures of the economy were laid down in the pre-state period. Until the early 1970s, Israel experienced unprecedented economic growth. From 1948 to 1972, real growth was 9 percent annually, and inflation was held at a single digit.[14] Although this was a time of massive immigration, economic expansion exceeded population growth, leading to the attainment of high per capita incomes. According to Arnold Blumberg: "In the course of half a century, per capita GNP rose from just 15 percent of the U.S. per capita GNP in 1922, to over half of the corresponding U.S. figure for 1973, or three-quarters of the average per capita GNP prevailing in western Europe, a feat surpassed at that time only by Japan."[15] Israel's development strategy has been based on industrial-led growth, with a large and growing high-tech component. Agricultural development, based on the kibbutz and moshav, was very successful. Exports from these two economic sectors are mainly destined for markets in Europe. Neighboring markets are very limited as a result of the Arab boycott against Israeli products, imposed for approximately forty-five years. After the 1973 war, the Israeli economy slumped. Growth plummeted to 2.5 percent, then slipped to 1.5 percent in 1982. In 1984, the economy was on the brink of disaster. Inflation was running at 450 percent, and the government's budget deficit was 17 percent of the GNP. The country managed to carry on by relying on massive foreign aid. A Labour-Likud coalition government, formed in part to implement the tough economic measures required to stabilize and revive the economy without fear of electoral backlash, adopted a package of stabilization measures that reduced inflation to 20 percent by December 1986 and 16 percent by December 1987. The currency was stabilized, subsidies were reduced, and wage hikes were restrained. In the late 1980s, the economy slowly began to recover. Also, Amos Elon notes, "As a colonial enterprise, the occupation was economically highly profitable for Israel. In one stroke it had enlarged the domestic market by almost 25 percent. With the tacit connivance of the Israeli trade unions, it provided industry and agriculture with a supply of cheap labor. The military administration of the territories curtailed all industrial development. The West Bank and Gaza were opened to all Israeli products. But West Bank agricultural and industrial goods were allowed into Israel proper only when they did not compete with Israeli produce."[16]

Israel established economic ties with most of its Arab neighbors in the early and mid-1990s and regained a high level of economic optimism. This was attributable mostly to the Israeli signing of the 1993 Oslo Agreement with the Palestinians on self-government arrangements in the West Bank and Gaza.

However, the reduction in government spending, also required for the revival of the economy, could not be achieved easily because of ongoing government financial commitments to the defense and security needs of the country. To sustain these needs, maintain a reasonably high standard of living, and service an ever-mounting debt load were extremely onerous tasks, especially when it was also necessary to pay the costs of four major military campaigns (1948, 1967, 1973, and the 1982 invasion of Lebanon). The absence of a genuine reconciliation with almost all of its large Arab neighbors has continuously imposed economic pressure. For instance, after the 1973 war, the country spent $16.6 billion on security and defense, surpassing by far the $6 billion allocated for defense in the 1973/1974 budgets.[17] In general, about 30 percent of the Israeli budget has been used for defense.

The immigration of Soviet Jews, beginning in the 1970s and rising to torrential levels following the collapse of the Soviet Union, has put Israel on a more stable long-term economic path, as most of these immigrants were skilled and well educated. They also, at least initially, favored centrist, secular politics and had been interested in economic issues. At the same time, however, many Soviet immigrants hate the Arabs and they advocate using a "Stalinist" iron fist policy against them. A case in point is Nathan Sharansky and his new Yisrael B'Aliyah political party, made up primarily of Russian immigrants who joined the right wing of Netanyahu's Likud government.

According to some Israeli analysts, however, these Soviet immigrants, like ultraorthodox Jews, are far less willing to sacrifice a good economy or risk a new war in order to keep the occupied territories or the newly created settlements.[18] The issue of the massive economic aid that Israel receives from the United States is a contentious one. The Netanyahu government, elected in 1996, promised to reduce this influence. However, when the government fell in April 1999 the reduction in aid remained unaccomplished, because Israeli society is unwilling to suffer the considerable economic hardship and a slowdown in its improving standard of living.

Foreign Relations: Ties to the West

Israel is a close ally of the West. It has good political and economic ties with western Europe, and the European Union is its largest trading partner. More significantly, ties with the United States are extensive, going back to the 1964 Eshkol-Johnson meeting. Annually, Israel receives U.S.$5 billion in economic and military aid, the highest U.S. foreign assistance commitment. It is this relationship which has ensured that Israel can maintain its military preponderance in the region, a relationship which was first developed with western Europe, predominantly France, during Israel's early years. Now, however, with a major domestic armaments industry and steady economic growth, Israel may find that this binding tie constricts more than it supports in the twenty-first century. The benefit to the Americans is that the country is a strategic ally in a volatile region, particularly important during the cold war. Perhaps partly for this reason, along with sociocultural proximity and religious traditions, the relationship has enjoyed a broader consensus of American public opinion than other foreign commitments.[19] Another factor sustaining the relationship is the highly efficient efforts of "friends of Israel" lobbies in the United States. The efforts are based on the solid support of Israel among American Jews, whose full participation in American society has been enhanced by the emergence of Israel and its demonstrated capacity to act as a strong military outpost of the West.

While the Americans were deeply involved in strengthening Israel during the cold war, the Soviets were supporting the Arab camp.

Ironically, the Soviet Union played a crucial role in creating the Israeli state, a support that ended after the 1967 war when ties were severed. In October 1991, just before the Soviet Union collapsed, diplomatic relations were resumed, and approximately 800,000 Soviet Jews emigrated to Israel. In the mid-1990s, Israel found itself in the position of an undisputed regional power. It no longer required the constant support of the United States, as the Arab states no longer had their Soviet backers. Ties with Western Europe are commercial in nature, as European states have difficulty supporting the more militaristic aspects of Israeli foreign policy. In dealings with Europe, and to a lesser extent the United States, Israel faces possible difficulties. Israel is now a commercial competitor in high-technology fields, especially armaments. Israel also faces criticism for its human rights record and its undeclared possession of nuclear weapons. Europe's commercial interests in Iran are at least as great as its interests in Israel, providing no audience for Israel's anti-Iran rhetoric. The European Union has adopted an explicit pro-Arab stance on the peace process, indicating its strong support for the principle of "land for peace," which the Likud government, elected in May 1996, abandoned. Israel's strongest ally, Bill Clinton, was reelected in 1996, and he appointed well-known pro-Israeli activists (for example, Martin M. Indyk and Dennis Ross) to key administrative positions.

Whether Israel would have anything to gain from remaining a client is another question. Israel's military superiority over its neighbors is unquestionable and can be sustained without U.S. technical support. Israel's relations with many Arab states, especially the rich oil states of the Gulf and the moderate regimes of the Maghrib, are improving drastically due to mutual economic benefit. Iraq has been removed as a regional player for the foreseeable future, and Syria will have to join in the peace process or join Iran in isolation. Israel is looking at other regional alliances. Israel and Turkey began signing military agreements in 1996, most notably a military cooperation agreement that included provisions for joint exercises, staff exchanges, technology transfers, and the use of bases for exercises. This is a geostrategic alliance that would greatly increase Israel's status as a regional superpower.

Interregional Ties and the Peace Process

The Middle East has been the site of several major conflicts between Israel and some, or all, of its Arab neighbors. In 1973 Israel confronted Arab forces who were determined to regain what they saw as land usurped by the enemy. Israel's overall military superiority, developed with U.S. support and now including nuclear weapons, is a fact of regional relations. This creates a quandary for Arab states, who do not have recourse to military action against Israel unless they are willing to accept apocalyptic consequences. Strategic territory captured from Syria on the Golan Heights in 1967 forms one of the major stumbling blocks to any reconciliation between Israel and its Arab neighbors. Nineteen sixty-seven was a major defeat for the Arabs because large sections of territory and more than 1 million Palestinian residents (most of them already refugees) came under the direct control of the Israeli military authorities. In addition, both during and after the 1967 Arab-Israeli War, the number of Palestinians who had already been dispersed out of the borders of the former Mandate of Palestine has largely increased. According to Meron Benvenisti, "About 250,000 of the refugees from 1948 who resided in refugee camps in the [nonoccupied] territories, where they had lived for twenty years, left of their own volition. At the end of the 1967 war, there were attempts to implement a forced population transfer. Residents of cities and villages in areas near the cease-fire line were expelled from their homes and their communities destroyed; the Israeli authorities offered financial 'incentives' and free transportation to Palestinians willing to leave; and [some] refugees from the Gaza area were transferred to camps on the Jordan Valley."[20] In Amos Elon's view, "The 1967 war was the great turning point in Israel's view of itself, and in its relationship with its neighbors. It had given them [the Israelis] more secure borders. It had also given them the bargaining chips they had lacked before. For the first time since independence in 1948, Israel could have traded land for peace. This opportunity, we now know, was missed."[21]

In 1982, Israel was involved in another war, but this time its forces invaded Lebanon—purportedly to bolster its security. The incursion into Lebanon failed to achieve this goal. Islamic fundamentalist groups based in the country continued to present security problems to Israel, in spite of the Israeli-imposed "security zone" set up along the Israeli-Lebanese border until Israeli withdrawal in June 2000. Within the Palestinian areas held by the Israeli military, popular opposition to the occupation came to a climax in 1987, in the form of the Palestinian *intifada*. Israeli measures to curb the uprising never solved the problem. Instead, its brutal actions against stone throwers and hecklers, some of them very young, discredited the claim that the country is democratic and respects human rights. International human rights organizations reported the high incidence of detentions, violent interrogations, and beatings perpetrated by Israeli security forces against Palestinians, including children as young as eleven years old. Israel also makes extensive use of "administrative laws," passed to restrict the movements and activities of groups and individuals and placing the latter under virtual arrest, without actually charging them with an offense.

Realizing that armed conflict with Israel does not serve their political interest well, some of the Arab countries and their leaders turned their attention to the negotiation process. To make this possible, the Americans used their power and influence in the region. The American role in the process is indeed dominant. After all, without the active participation of the Americans, the 1974 and 1975 disengagement agreements between Israel and Egypt would have been difficult to reach. Under the auspices of the Americans, Israel and Egypt signed a peace agreement in 1979, following the 1978 Camp David accord, negotiated by Begin and Anwar Sadat with the Americans acting as intermediaries. This agreement restored Egyptian sovereignty over most territories captured by Israel in 1967, and ended the state of belligerency between the two countries, establishing full diplomatic relations; however, the long-lasting bitterness between their peoples has continued. The fact that Egypt was keen to regain its pivotal place in the Arab world and the persistence of the Palestinian issue have jointly acted to retard the development of close formal and informal relations, as well as a genuine reconciliation.

After a few years, an opportunity to bring together Israel and its enemies arose during the Gulf war. The United States and its Arab allies emerged from this war with enhanced reputation, credibility, and political power. On the other hand, the opponents to the war against Iraq, such as the leaders of Libya, the Palestinians, Jordan, Yemen, and Sudan, found themselves isolated. Another important factor was the softening of the stance of the Soviets toward the West in the face of its internal difficulties. Seizing on this favorable climate, the Americans pressed for a Middle East peace conference, which opened in Madrid in late October 1991. The conference was formally sponsored by the United States and Soviet Union and attended by Israel, Syria, Lebanon, Egypt, and the Jordanian-Palestinian joint delegation. The framework of negotiations called for bilateral discussions between Israel and Syria, Israel and Lebanon, and Israel and a joint Jordanian-Palestinian delegation. By the end of 1992, eight bilateral sessions had taken place, but little progress was made for two reasons. First, the hard-line policies of the Shamir government would have made progress difficult under most circumstances. Second, the delegates from the Arab countries and the Palestinians realized that with an upcoming general election in Israel, they might stand a better chance negotiating with a Labour government if Labour won the elections. This is what actually happened, and a more positive environment was created by the change in government in Israel in 1992. Prime Minister Rabin won the June 1992 elections on the platform that he would conclude a peace deal with the Arabs.

While world attention was focused on the Madrid peace initiative, Israel and the Palestinians signed a peace deal. The Norwegians hosted secret negotiations that led to the Oslo Agreement. The 13 September 1993 agreement set out the Declaration of Principles of peace between the two parties. It entailed the establishment of an interim elected government in the occupied territories pending the discussion of final status for 1996. The Oslo II Agreement, signed in September 1995 in Washington, elaborated on the political arrangements for the interim period but did not provide any common ground for the final status negotiations. However, the Palestinians' situation did not significantly improve. A year after Oslo I was signed, Israel's control of West Bank land rose by 10 percent, and government funding for Jewish settlements increased by 70 percent.[22] As the reputed Israeli analyst Meron Benvenisti noted, "It goes without saying that cooperation, based on the current power relationship, is no more than permanent Israeli domination in disguise, and that Palestinian self-rule is merely a euphemism for Bantustanization."[23]

In fact, what the Palestinians did get in the Oslo II Agreement was far less than what the apartheid regime in the former white Republic of South Africa was willing to offer to the then widely condemned Bantustans. For instance:

1. The South African government forcibly removed white residents from the Bantustans, who angrily charged that they had been "sold down the river." In contrast, the Israelis kept and even expanded their settlements in the Palestinian enclaves.[24]
2. South Africa's apartheid regime, after withdrawing and recognizing the Bantustans' independence, continued to cover more than half the Bantustan budgets through grants. In contrast, the Israelis provided no financial assistance to the peace process whatsoever.[25]

In spite of numerous delays in the implementation of the agreement, there are also some tangible achievements. Israeli forces withdrew from 3 percent of the West Bank,[26] pending the last pullout, scheduled for 28 March 1996 from the town of Hebron, which was delayed by the Israelis. An elected council, with its leader Yasser Arafat, has been in place since elections in 1995.

The immediate development in the aftermath of the Oslo Agreement was the signing of a peace treaty between Israel and Jordan in October 1994. Jordan has proved to be the closest thing to an ally that Israel can claim in the peace process since late 1995, mainly for geographic and demographic reasons, as well as because the two countries share fresh water resources. Jordan's economic centers are located within 100 kilometers of Israel's economic centers. Israel can also provide Jordanians with commercial access to the Mediterranean coast. On the Syrian track, progress has essentially stalled as first the Likud government and then that of Ehud Barak seem to favor a hard-line approach with Syria, claiming that maintenance of Israeli sovereignty on the Golan will be the basis of any accord with Damascus. Success on this track was believed necessary for a solution to the occupation of southern Lebanon, until Israeli intransigence to withdraw from their self-declared security zone gave way under a unilateral withdrawal in June 2000.

Late in 1995, serious problems threatened to put a halt to the whole process as the rising number of acts of violence by Jewish and Islamic fundamentalists became an impediment to progress in the peace negotiations. The assassination of Rabin by Yigal Amir, an Israeli citizen of the Jewish faith, on 4 November 1995, provided a further blow to the peace process. Although the more moderate Peres assumed leadership, he did not command the level of trust that the Israeli public placed in their fallen leader as far as security was concerned—a situation Peres attempted to remedy in early 1996. Peres sped up the peace process and brought forward the date of the Israel general elections to May 1996, in the hope of benefiting from the tarnished image of the opposition in the wake of Rabin's death. His position was badly weakened by the four Hamas bombings in the heart of Israel, resulting in the loss of some fifty-five lives, further raising questions about the commitment of all sides to the peace process.

In an effort to project a tough political image, Peres took advantage of the opportunity presented when violence between Israeli military forces in the security zone of southern Lebanon and guerrillas from the Islamic Hizbullah movement intensified in March 1996. Hizbullah forces began rocket attacks on Israeli towns and villages in northern Israel. Peres responded with a massive military operation, hitting Palestinian refugee camps. A strike on Qana refugee camp killed over 100 Lebanese civilians and four Fijian soldiers serving as UN peacekeepers. Israel then agreed to a cease-fire.

In the closest election in Israeli history, Peres lost to Likud challenger Benjamin Netanyahu by less than 30,000 votes out of almost 4 million. Peres gained the support of many Israeli Arabs, despite low Arab-Israeli voter turnout, but Likud gained over 90 percent of the Orthodox Jewish vote. Knesset elections resulted in one of the most divided houses in Israeli history, resulting in massive losses for Netanyahu's Likud party—

from forty-three to thirty-three seats, and Labour, which fell from fifty-six to forty-three seats. Religious parties jumped from sixteen to twenty-four seats, becoming the critical allies in Netanyahu's coalition arrangement. Arab parties, however, controlled nine seats and allied themselves with Labour. Other centrist groupings, most notably parties representing recent Russian and Soviet émigrés, managed to gain eleven seats. The largest of these parties also joined the Likud coalition government.

One of Netanyahu's campaign planks, probably his strongest, was that he would continue the peace process but would never allow the establishment of an actual Palestinian state. He made it clear that Israel would only negotiate from a position of strength, dictating terms to the Palestinians and other Arab states rather than accepting any compromise. Netanyahu said that he would not even meet with Arafat unless it was vital to Israel's security. These hard-line views were increasingly pursued further by the need of the Likud government to maintain the support of the religious parties in the Knesset. As Amos Elon wrote for the Associated Press in June 1996, "The most he seems ready to grant the Palestinians is a form of very limited local autonomy in some two or three dozen Bantustan-style enclaves, on less than 10 percent of occupied territory, surrounded by ever-growing Israeli settlements established on expropriated Palestinian land."[27]

One of the most difficult issues obstructing the Middle East peace process is undoubtedly the establishment and maintenance of Jewish settlements in the occupied territories. These settlements are claimed to be very important to religious hard-liners and Zionist extremists who view them as the first step toward consolidating Jewish rule over all the land they believe was promised to them by God and in Zionist fervor. The Israeli government has justified these settlements on grounds of strategic necessity. As Elon writes, "The settlements, in the opinions of most military experts, did not increase Israel's security. On the contrary, during the Yom Kippur War the Golan Heights settlements imposed an additional burden that was very costly in human lives. But today, some 300,000 settlers in the former West Bank and Gaza Strip and in East Jerusalem make up a powerful parliamentary lobby that fights any possible territorial concessions in exchange for peace."[28] Be that as it may, to Palestinians and other Arab observers, the settlements are proof that Israel has no intention of ever giving up any land to the Palestinians or allowing them to form a real "nation-state." Among the provisions of the Oslo Accords was the removal of Israeli soldiers who had been placed in settlement areas, nominally to protect settlers from possible Palestinian actions. However, settlers tend to be religious and Zionist extremists, and they have proven to be at least as prone to violence as the surrounding Palestinian populations. There have been killings and acts of violence on both sides in settlement areas. The Likud government appointed Ariel Sharon as a minister responsible for infrastructure, which does not include jurisdiction over settlements but does include road building and management of fresh water resources. Sharon was known for his extreme stance on the expansion of Jewish settlement and his hard-line approach to negotiations with the Arab states. Without water, the Palestinian areas will remain impoverished and marginal.

Israel and Palestinians are the key, obviously, to opening a new era for greater peace in the Middle East. As Amos Elon noted, "The end of the Cold War had improved Israel's strategic position in the regional power game. The collapse of the Soviet Union had deprived Israel's adversaries of the war arsenals and political support of a superpower."[29] Today Israel still possesses a military and economic superiority and an alliance with the United States, which provides it with the ability to predominate the peace process, at least in the short term. In this position, Israel has chosen to press for more in the peace negotiations. In the long term, however, it still remains to be seen whether Israel can get more from the Palestinians, who actually do not have much to give.

The agreement on Hebron, which was long delayed and finally reached mainly because of the direct U.S. involvement on 15 January 1997, may be indicative of possible future directions of development. On the one hand, the agreement is an obvious expression of a heavy-handed Israeli superiority and Palestinian weakness. In order to protect 400 Israeli settlers living among Hebron's 120,000 Palestinians, Israeli troops would continue to control a central area of the city that includes 30,000 Palestinians and the Tomb of Patriarchs, holy to both Muslims and Jews as the burial place of Abraham and his family.[30] In addition, a joint force of the Israeli army and Palestinian police will patrol the heights overlooking the settler enclaves, and in areas close to them, Palestinian police will be allowed to carry only pistols. The PA also promised to "fight terrorism, complete the process of revoking sections of the PLO charter calling for the destruction of Israel, and consider Israeli requests to extradite Palestinian suspects who carried out attacks in Israel." On the other hand, by agreeing to withdraw from most of Hebron and from some rural areas of the West Bank by mid-1998, Israeli prime minister Netanyahu seemed to accept the principle that a final settlement must be based on a "land for peace" formula. The final outcome of what might be seen as a Palestinian autonomous entity can hardly be described as a state. Even Netanyahu, who stated that "the issue isn't independence itself, but what type of powers a Palestinian country would have," admitted that the level of Palestinian autonomy was the central issue. According to Netanyahu, possible models could be provided by Andorra and Puerto Rico, and it would imply Israeli political, economic, military, and security control over the future Palestinian micro-state. Such an outcome would be a logical consequence of the Oslo Agreements and in effect would implement the Israeli policy of encirclement of the indigenous population. Although such a solution would probably be acceptable to most Israelis and their international sponsors, its real and lasting acceptance by most Palestinians might be a matter of serious doubt.[31]

The 1999 Israeli Elections

Netanyahu's failure to secure peace with the Palestinians, or his unwillingness to move the process forward, led to a contentious election with Labour leader Ehud Barak. Barak's landslide victory led to increased pressure for progress in the Middle East peace process in general and the Oslo Agreements in particular. Within days of being sworn into office with his coalition government, Barak moved quickly with statements, meetings, and foreign trips to reinvigorate peace talks. In the coming negotiations, neither side will attain all its goals, but both sides will have to obtain the core objectives that are required by their people: security and genuine acceptance in the region for the Israelis, sovereign statehood and a reconstituted communal and national integrity for the Palestinians.

The past, however, is often a useful guide to the future and the lessons, fruits, and failures of the six years of peacemaking, since the signing of the Oslo agreement's Declaration of Principles in September 1993 gives the new momentum little time for concrete results. Today's odd mixture of simultaneous hope and despair, among Arabs and Israelis alike, is emblematic of the failure of the process thus far. The optimism that accompanied the election of Barak was a refreshing and heartening expression of hope after the years of deceit and gloom under the Netanyahu administration. The strategy of the peacemaking process is more clouded as the words and actions of Barak, in particular, have thus far reflected the built-in contradictions of having to respond to the needs and wishes of several constituencies. Arab nations in conflict with Israel had mixed reactions to Barak's words of peace, with Syria promising to "meet every step with a similar one" and Lebanon criticizing Barak for failing to refer to UN resolutions. In his inauguration speech, Barak asked Middle Eastern leaders to work with him to "forge a peace of the brave." But it will take more than speeches, because Israel's peace talks with Syria and Lebanon have been stalled since early 1996, and

Palestinian-Israeli negotiations failed to progress during Netanyahu's term. In Lebanon, the response was even more cautious. Prime Minister Salim Hoss pointed out that Barak did not say Israel would resume negotiations from where they were suspended in 1996. "He also did not mention UN resolution 425, which calls for unconditional Israeli withdrawal. . . . He instead spoke about guaranteeing security on Israel's northern border." Lebanon and Syria had pledged to stick together in future negotiations with Israel, and both demanded complete Israeli withdrawal from southern Lebanon and the Golan as part of any peace treaty.[32] The June 2000 Israeli unilateral withdrawal from Lebanon removed the pressure being applied through Hizbullah action and left the Golan still securely in Israeli hands.

In 1998 Netanyahu's government accepted Resolution 425, twenty years after it was adopted by the UN Security Council, tagging on demands for security guarantees to prevent any guerrilla cross-border attacks on northern Israel, despite Lebanon's refusal to give such guarantees. The largest disagreement between Palestinians and Israelis appears to be over the future of Jerusalem. Whether the 200,000 Palestinians living in Jerusalem should have national rights that will be discussed in negotiations of final status, or the eastern part of the city should become the capital of a future Palestinian state, will prove to be the most contentious point of long negotiations.[33]

Thus, for Barak to "freeze" any new Israeli settlements, as he promised to do, was a clear act of strategy—more meaningful than the niceties of style that allow for the process to be resumed, but less definitive than the hard decisions that will have to be made on final status issues, such as Jerusalem and the right of return for the dispersed Palestinian refugees. The freeze will not constrict the "natural growth" of preexisting settlements,[34] for while the freeze means that no new settlements will be built and no existing settlements will be evacuated for the time being, it is not an alteration of how the Israelis view the settlements themselves. The Israelis refer to the Jewish communities in Judea, Samaria, and Gaza not as illegal colonies or settlements in defiance of the Fourth Geneva Convention's Article 49 prohibition against an occupying military power transferring its population into the occupied territories, but rather as part of Israel proper. The continued Palestinian desire to convene a United Nations conference on enforcement of the Fourth Geneva Convention's application in Palestine is "strategy" of the highest order and explains why the Israelis are so irritated by such a suggestion.

The most difficult dimension of the negotiations is the substance of the final status agreements to be reached after the October 1998

Wye River Accord has been implemented. Most statements are sincere declarations of political desire, but they are not realistic or firm determinants of the final compromise positions that will be accepted. The Israeli insistence on not evacuating settlements and on maintaining a perpetual Israeli military occupation of the Jordan River and Golan Heights as a vital "security" requirement will need to be replaced by a more realistic way of ensuring the the security of Israel and the sovereignty and national dignity of the Palestinians and Arab neighbors. The parties to a permanent and just peace accord will have to redefine concepts of security, sovereignty, and territoriality in a manner that ensures all parties' national rights without perpetuating military occupation. The recurring periods of negotiations and nonnegotiations since 1993 allowed the Israeli government of Ehud Barak to engage in a negotiating style, in an effort to formulate an effective and flexible strategy raising expectations by the Palestinian and international community that could generate feasible interim compromises and meaningful gains for both sides and realistic final status agreements on the substantive issues at the heart of the modern conflict between Zionism and Arab national rights.

The Israeli Withdrawal from Lebanon

On 23 May 2000 the IDF withdrew from southern Lebanon. The move, a campaign promise of Ehud Barak, had been planned for 7 July. It was forced on Israeli authorities by the negotiations surrounding the peace process, by the change within Israeli society which called for an end to the needless occupation—best exemplified by the Four Mothers pro-withdrawal movement—and most directly by the long-standing guerrilla campaign conducted by the Lebanese Islamic militia's Hizbullah and Jihad. The withdrawal occurred without IDF casualties. Hizbullah, which took control of most of south Lebanon, refrained from any attacks against the retreating IDF and controlled retribution against those members of the SLA who decided to remain in Lebanon.

IDF soldiers, once back inside Israeli territory, received new open-fire regulations, in which soldiers would not open fire on armed men on the other side of the border unless they were fired on first—altering a long-standing policy of engaging any observed armed force while the IDF had occupied Lebanon. Israel also promised that it would not impinge on Lebanese sovereignty unless Israeli territory was attacked, meaning that IDF planes, ships, and ground forces would no longer routinely cross the international border.

"The Lebanese tragedy has ended," Barak declared triumphantly. However, he quickly added that Israel saw Lebanon and Syria as jointly responsible for ensuring peace in south Lebanon and that any attacks on Israeli soldiers or civilians would be seen as acts of war "that would mandate an appropriate response." To stress his point, he conveyed the warning to Syria via UN Secretary-General Kofi Annan. Syria responded that there would be no peace until Israel left all occupied Arab lands. The state-owned newspaper *Tishreen* wrote that the pullback was due to the Syrian-Lebanese armed struggle and that it "provides a good reason for Syria and the Palestinians to continue their struggles."

Analysts proposed that unilateral withdrawal was an Israeli effort to undermine the position of Syrian negotiators. However, unlike the prevailing conventional wisdom, it is not clear that the Clinton-Assad meeting in Geneva on 26 March 2000 put an end to the Syrian-Israeli peace process. It did perhaps reflect another Syrian attempt at forcing Israel to waive its demand for sovereignty over a 200–300-meter strip of land along the northeastern edge of Lake Kinneret, on the Syrian side of the 1923 international border, which appeared to be the stumbling block to full Israeli withdrawal from the Golan Heights. It is also possible that in Geneva, Assad did not receive a clear commitment from Clinton regarding western development and aid packages as he had expected. Syria had been pursuing beneficial financial packages from American, European, and Japanese aid agencies and NGOs as well as private investors. Furthermore, through either a comprehensive agreement or unilateral withdrawal by Israel, Syria would preserve its strategic and economic interests in Lebanon without endangering its relationship with members of the international community. A unilateral Israeli withdrawal may have removed the leverage gained by the prolonged guerrilla war along the Lebanese border, but it still left Syria in virtual control of Lebanon with the option of initiating such a conflict through the sponsorship of Palestinian groups.

Indeed, Hizbullah, which as the principal instrument of the guerrilla war against the IDF occupation appeared the victor in southern Lebanon, now intended to turn its energies to Lebanese domestic politics. Hizbullah Secretary-General Hassan Nasrallah conceded that while the guerrilla organization hadn't finished its fight against Israel, the Lebanese government, and not Hizbullah, would be responsible for security in south Lebanon. Nasrallah stated that without a withdrawal from the Shaba'a farms area on the western flanks of the Golan Heights, which they consider part of Lebanon, and the release of Hizbullah prisoners still held in Israeli jails, Hizbullah would continue to attack Israeli interests. In an effort to make conciliatory moves toward building a stronger Lebanon, he emphasized that the authority in south Lebanon would be the Lebanese government, and he noted that while Hizbullah was first into south Lebanon after the collapse of the SLA, the troops from the Israeli-backed militia who gave up their arms and surrendered to the Hizbullah were handed over to Lebanese authorities. Indeed, as the withdrawal was primarily a domestic Israeli decision, and as the future of the SLA membership was not addressed by Israeli planners, their fate was left to the Hizbullah, which presented the SLA with three options: surrender to the Lebanese authorities, withdraw along with the IDF, or stay and fight.

Both Hizbullah and the Lebanese government made it clear that they would not allow the SLA to hold positions inside Lebanon once the IDF retreated. To allow the continued existence of an independent militia, which could threaten Lebanon's delicate balance, was anathema to the rebuilding efforts well under way since the Ta'if Accord. SLA commanders continued in their attempts to negotiate a handover of heavy weapons to the central government, believing that negotiations— unlike over a decade of conflict—could keep Hizbullah at bay. However, the collapse of SLA positions during the earliest phases of the IDF retreat, as well as mass desertions to Hizbullah by Shiite conscripts of the SLA,[35] undermined their bargaining position, drastically reducing the SLA's ability to present the Lebanese government with a coherent list of demands or to threaten Hizbullah.

The collapse forced an expedited IDF withdrawal from the security zone in southern Lebanon, completely undermining the SLA's attempts to negotiate. The collapse of SLA Battalion 70 and the nearly unopposed takeover of villages in the central sector of the security zone by Hizbullah began when Battalion 70, which was predominantly Shiite, broke apart. Some of its men gave themselves up to Hizbullah or sought refuge in Israel. In less than twenty-four hours, Hizbullah took control of the central part of the security zone and large parts of the western zone, mostly without firing a shot. Flags of the Shiite organization began to appear within meters of northern Israeli villages. The advance triggered a hectic flight of SLA officers and men and their families who arrived at border crossings and sought asylum in Israel.

On paper, the IDF withdrawal plan had been convincing. The IDF would gradually withdraw from less important outposts in the security zone and the SLA would take over those positions. The outposts chosen for evacuation, such as Taibeh and Rotem, are situated near large Lebanese villages in which many of the SLA and their families lived. According to the plan, the SLA would protect its villages, at least until the Israeli withdrawal, which would be easier to accomplish because the IDF would hold fewer and fewer positions in southern Lebanon. As the retreat began, the IDF chief of staff, Lt. Gen. Shaul Mofaz, proudly announced, "The IDF is not running away. . . . When we leave, we shall do it from a position of strength." But Hizbullah exploited a significant weakness in the IDF's plan. With the tacit agreement of the United Nations Interim Force in Lebanon (UNIFIL), hundreds of Shiite refugees returned to their villages. The UN soldiers pushed the civilian columns to move south, as the numbers of returning Lebanese refugees overwhelmed them, even after it became clear that there were Hizbullah organizers and fighters among their ranks. As a result, Hizbullah was able to take over five villages, and the SLA—now surrounded and fearing for their families' safety—abandoned the Taibeh outpost without resistance only one week after taking it over from the IDF. The predominantly Shiite SLA Battalion 70 disintegrated as most of the men of the battalion hid their weapons and uniforms and went home; others, mostly officers, sought refuge in Israel.

At al-Khayam prison, in the occupied zone where human rights groups had long accused the SLA of torturing prisoners it seized in its battle against Hizbullah, SLA guards simply drove away as nearby villagers and relatives stormed the prison, freeing some 150 prisoners. The Red Cross treated all released prisoners, including many who had been incarcerated for more than a decade. Symbolic of the drama was the crowded Fatma crossing near Metulla. For years, the crossing had been reserved for Lebanese workers entering Israel for day jobs. With the SLA's collapse it became the scene of long lines of panic-stricken former SLA soldiers and their families who were forced to abandon hundreds of BMWs at the crossing as they attempted to get into Israel before Hizbullah arrived. In all, some 6,500 SLA refugees entered Israel.

About 1,000 refugees were given political asylum abroad, leaving Israel for new lives, after Israel agreed to finance the resettlement. Israeli officials negotiated on their behalf with countries in Europe and in North and South America who agreed to accept the former SLA soldiers and their families on humanitarian grounds. An Israeli government survey showed 47 percent of the refugees preferred resettlement abroad, while 32 percent said they would prefer to stay in Israel. Eight percent said they wanted to return to Lebanon, and 12 percent have yet to make up their minds. While those who returned faced trial for collaboration, none of the returnees is known to have been harmed upon return. Of the 6,500 refugees who entered Israel, 78 percent were Christian.

The Israeli government promised temporary permits to those wishing to use Israel as a transit point on their way to another country, while those who chose to stay in Israel were promised work permits and expedited citizenship. The Lebanese government announced that 1,488 SLA soldiers out of 2,600 surrendered to government authorities; 200 were quickly assigned to military courts for trial. The United Nations warned the Lebanese and Syrian governments that they considered Beirut responsible for the safety of SLA members following Israel's withdrawal. The United Nations also accepted Israel's request to deploy UNIFIL forces in southern Lebanon in order to prevent a power vacuum from forming in the area before the arrival of Lebanese army units.

While compassion for the families and most SLA soldiers abandoned by their officers and former IDF employers is understandable, as is the UN's desire to prevent atrocities, the motives of Israeli authorities are questionable. Their concern for the plight of victims of conflict was not evident when international agencies voiced concern for the nearly 1,000 Palestinians killed during the *intifada*,[36] or for the killing of 100 civilians in the Lebanese village of Kfar Kana, during the IDF's 1997 Operation Grapes of Wrath, or for the 2,200 Lebanese homes destroyed by Israel during the twenty-two-year occupation. Instead, it is the treatment of SLA soldiers that concerns Israeli authorities, not previously known for their great sympathy with Arab suffering. However, Israel's new refugees are not innocent victims but retired mercenaries. Lebanese who enlisted in the SLA consciously chose to sever themselves from their own country and join forces with its enemy. They couldn't have reasonably expected that the Lebanese government would forgive them for their betrayal. Most important, betrayal of their homeland is not the most serious act with which many are charged. Scattered among the SLA refugees are some who could be put on trial in front of an international tribunal for war crimes. Voluminous evidence of their wrongdoing is now available, collected by human rights agencies throughout the years of the Israeli occupation. Israeli authorities primarily decided the policies adopted in the occupation, but daily execution was carried out by the SLA. Human rights groups reported evidence of systematic torture and abuse from the liberated al-Khayam prison, including electric wires used to torture inmates during interrogation, a whipping-post, boards to which prisoners were tied, and letters that were never distributed. The acts of abomination at al-Khayam took place under Israel's supervision and perhaps with its encouragement, but SLA men carried them out.

With the IDF back within Israeli territorial limits and the SLA collapse, the United Nations was charged with establishing the actual location of the international border and confirming Israeli compliance with Security Council Resolutions 425 and 426, which had called for their evacuation. To avoid conflict, the Israeli government ordered the

IDF to pull out of Astra, one of its three outposts in the Har Dov area on the western foothills of the Golan Heights. Israel would not accede to Lebanese and Hizbullah demands to withdraw from the area both claim as the Lebanese Shabaʿa farms, since it was conquered from the Syrians in 1967 and not the Lebanese. Lebanon argued that the territory had been ceded to it from Syria in 1984, a claim which the Syrians confirmed but neither party could substantiate with documentation. The United Nations backed the Israeli claim that the Har Dov area was part of the Golan Heights captured from Syria during the Six-Day War in 1967 and was thus unrelated to the implementation of Resolution 425. According to the UN's decision, the dividing line between UN forces in Lebanon (UNIFIL) and the Golan Heights (UNDOF) would be considered the international border that Israel is obliged to honor, leaving most of the Har Dov area on the Syrian side of the border. Israeli forces could then remain in the area without violating the terms of Resolution 425; however, UN sources say that it is likely that Lebanon will agree to this "practical solution." Hizbullah or Palestinian groups adopting similar tactics will undoubtedly continue the struggle against Israeli occupation until the evacuation of all communities believed to belong to Arabs is complete. Villages such as the northern Israeli community of Kiryat Shmona—built on the lands of the Arab village of Halsa—will serve as motivation until a comprehensive peace treaty is consummated.

With the Israeli retreat complete and the peace process with Syria stalled upon the death of Hafez al-Assad, the legacy of Israel's invasion and twenty-two-year occupation is yet to be determined. Menachem Begin, who launched Israeli forces into the Lebanese civil war and made the defense of the Christians in Lebanon into a sweeping Israeli commitment, undermined the balance of forces within Lebanon and prompted Syrian involvement. Until Begin, the Israeli-Lebanese border was relatively quiet, with only sporadic Palestinian attacks against northern Israeli settlements. In establishing his covenant with the Phalanges, Begin compelled Syrian intervention and an escalation of the Lebanese conflict. International mediation efforts, such as those of U.S. diplomat Philip Habib, were either rejected out of hand or clouded by a refusal to be content with security arrangements under the umbrella of UN Security Council Resolution 425.[37] Instead, there was an insistence on the withdrawal of Syrian forces, which got Israel stuck in a standoff that destroyed Lebanon. The growth of Hizbullah and the internal divisions within Israeli society, which brought about the political pressure to withdraw, will continue as long as Israeli communities exist on lands to which the Lebanese or the Palestinians claim ownership. To continue to deny Arab rights to the benefit of a minority of fundamentalist Jewish settlers will only prolong civil strife and conflict.

The instability of the Oslo process, brinkmanship diplomacy by U.S. president Bill Clinton, the Israeli and Palestinian right to return, and sovereignty over Jerusalem, as well as the popular Palestinian rejection of continued Israeli settlement, led to increased tensions throughout the occupied territories. The visit of hawkish Likud party leader Ariel Sharon to the Haram al-Sharif/Temple Mount on 28 September 2000 outraged Muslims the world over and instigated the outbreak of a second *intifada*. Palestinians once again took to the streets to demand an end to the Israeli occupation in what came to be known as the Al-Aqsa *intifada*. Attacks on Israeli settlers, the lynching of two Israeli soldiers, and daily protests were overshadowed by the immense number of deaths and casualties suffered, the overwhelming majority of whom were civilian Palestinians at the hands of Israeli soldiers, police, and vigilante settlers. The increased settler violence and the use of indiscriminate and disproportionate force by the IDF led to international condemnation of Israel—including UN Security Council Resolution 1322 (2000)—and the fall of Ehud Barak's coalition government.

The February 2001 Israeli Election

Seventy-two-year-old Ariel Sharon, heading a newly reinvigorated right wing, rode a wave of Israeli apprehension with the Oslo process to an overwhelming electoral victory, becoming Israel's fifth prime minister in just over five years. Concluding a campaign held against a backdrop of the worst Israeli-Palestinian violence since the 1987–1990 *intifada*, Sharon defeated Prime Minister Ehud Barak by a stunning 62.5 to 37.4 percent of the vote. The margin is unprecedented in Israeli electoral history, as was the low voter turnout following expressions of disaffection with the candidates and the political system. Only 62 percent of Israelis went to the polls, compared with 80 percent in 1999. A resounding majority of the Israeli-Arab community, in particular, sat out the race to express their profound alienation from the political establishment of Israel. Barak's defeat followed just twenty-one months after he was elected by a then-record majority on a mandate to make peace with Israel's neighbors.

Sharon's call for "our Palestinian neighbors to cast off the path of violence and return to the path of dialogue and solving the conflicts between us by peaceful means" rings hollow in view of the use of preponderant Israeli military and vigilante force during the occupation and Al-Aqsa *intifada*, as well as his own military record in Lebanon.

Sharon is remembered as the party who was found responsible for the massacres at the Sabra and Chatila Palestinian refugee camps in West Beirut. In 1982 Sharon was the Israeli Defense Minister, presiding over the Israeli invasion and occupation of Lebanon. After encircling Beirut, the IDF allowed their Christian Phalange allies to enter the refugee camps, where they murdered hundreds of defenseless women, children, and elderly Palestinian refugees. An Israeli commission of inquiry—the Kahan commission—found that Sharon bore "personal responsibility" and recommended his removal from office. Sharon resigned, apparently ending his political career on the altar of a war crime. However, he remained on the Israeli political scene, becoming useful as a conduit between the Israeli government and the large number of Russian émigrés who entered the country after the fall of the Soviet Union. His ability to speak Russian and his championing of the émigrés' cause saw him serve as Minister of Construction and Housing from 1990–1992. His ability to build homes for some 70,000 émigrés a month saw him dubbed "the bulldozer" in a convenient amalgam of public policy and Zionist ideology. The homes he "found" for the Russian émigrés were predominantly inside the "green line," vastly increasing the number of both settlements and settlers in the West Bank. Sharon himself maintains a large encamped residence in Arab East Jerusalem. Chosen as the caretaker leader of Likud following the defeat of Benjamin Netanyahu, he again was thought to have committed a fatal political mistake when he made a heavily guarded visit to the plaza outside the Al-Aqsa mosque in Jerusalem in 2000. After his visit, the Israeli-Palestinian violence erupted and many world leaders accused Sharon of a reckless provocation at a sensitive moment. The Al-Aqsa *intifada*—as the uprising came to be known—spread, and hundreds of Palestinians were killed in escalating violence, leading to a general rejection of the peace process by many Palestinians and Israelis.

Thus, Sharon's call for a return to dialogue with the Palestinians following the February 2001 elections was met with great skepticism inside Israel, internationally, and particularly throughout the Arab world and weighed heavily upon Palestinian negotiators attempting to pursue a settlement.

CHAPTER 10

The Gulf Cooperation
Council Countries

*T*he GCC countries of Saudi Arabia, Kuwait, Oman, Bahrain, Qatar, and the United Arab Emirates, which are referred to here as the Arab Gulf states, are addressed together because their patterns of politics and government are sufficiently similar to justify collective treatment. Furthermore, the same forces of history, geography, and economics shape their patterns of political behavior. The region contains the largest concentration of conservative, nonconstitutional monarchies remaining in the world, and controlling over 60 percent of the world's proven oil reserves, they manifest a political tribalism that allows for a highly hierarchical society and unrepresentative governmental system.

The "age of oil" and the politics that it has produced began in the 1930s, although the rentier state did not come into being until after the Second World War.[1] The majority of all oil discoveries occurred in the 1930s when western multinational corporations explored the region.[2] Joint projects with Iraqi, Saudi, and Bahraini oil companies saw the first production and exportation of crude petroleum through new sea terminals and pipelines across Syria and Palestine. With the outbreak of war in 1939, oil exploration and production were interrupted and in some areas halted altogether. The huge increase in oil production and the increased income to the region mostly came in the form of rentier taxes, paid by the international oil companies to the ruling families. (See table 10.1, which outlines the largest reserves in the world.) Almost like a foreign subsidy, the income from oil was organized in such a fashion that it altered the power structures within each state and in the region by firmly entrenching those royal dynasties which were in place when the international cartels arrived, permanently freezing them in the form in which they were found, and providing their rulers with the apparatus of the modern state with which to entrench their authority.[3]

TABLE 10.1
Estimated Proved World Crude Oil Reserves
for Twenty Leading Nations, 1999
(thousands of barrels)

1.	Saudi Arabia	259,000,000
2.	Iraq	112,500,000
3.	United Arab Emirates	97,700,000
4.	Kuwait	94,000,000
5.	Iran	93,000,000
6.	Venezuela	71,688,879
7.	Former Soviet Union	57,000,000
8.	Mexico	40,000,000
9.	Libya	29,500,000
10.	China	24,000,000
11.	United States	22,017,000
12.	Nigeria	16,786,000
13.	Norway	10,422,215
14.	Algeria	9,200,000
15.	Angola	5,412,000
16.	Oman	5,238,000
17.	United Kingdom	5,002,795
18.	Neutral Zone	5,000,000
19.	Indonesia	4,979,710
20.	Canada	4,839,189
	Total World	1,019,545,664

Source: API Basic Data Book 2000, sec. 2, table 4.
Washington: American Petroleum Institute.

Khaldoun al-Naqeeb, a distinguished Kuwaiti sociologist, sees the prime feature resulting from the development of the "rentier state" as being "that the national economy of this kind of state does not depend directly on oil but indirectly on the state expenditure arising from oil concessions. Public spending becomes the primary channel through which oil revenues are distributed to society in the Gulf monarchies. Here the central role of the state becomes evident . . . in the social and economic life of the population. The state possesses a great deal of surplus capital . . . which leads to heavy interference in the economy through a monopoly on financing which sees the monarchies, in the guise of the state, initiate and guarantee the majority, if not all, of commercial and industrial projects" in the region.[4] The most dynamic sectors of the economy, export/import and construction, also depend heavily on the state's ability to guarantee bids for such ventures. This role of the state as both customer and guarantor is clear—and, by extension, the role of the royal families and traditional elites, frozen by the colonial-imperial protectorate treaties. The royal families are cast as the central authority for state control, with a monopoly over the economy. Al-Naqeeb explains, "For this reason the ruling families appear as if they are political associations who own the state [by birthright], rather than having ascended to authority through popular election or choice. The relationship with imperial powers [and the business elites of the western world] meant the adoption and adaptation of the modern capitalist state to the requirements of sectarian tribal demands and the necessity of the traditional conservative ruling elite to protect the traditional relations within the framework of the modern political system and new economic conditions [which had been adopted from the West]."[5]

All of these adaptations have resulted in a ruling regime that safeguards the existing political conditions, as they have existed since the beginning of the "oil age." The immense wealth that oil has brought to the region has not upset the traditional balances of society's social and economic class structure. In fact, this wealth has created a vast array of welfare programs, as money and social well-being trickled down to the population. As a result, citizens have begun to lose the desire to acquire the skills necessary for genuine employment, deeply altering societal views on work. This new division of labor has encouraged Gulf citizens to attempt political change, and governments to give a high priority to the instruments of oppression, in order to further secure and guarantee their place at the apex of a hierarchical society. The further adoption of such oppressive measures increases these governments' dependence, not only for external security but also against internal dissent.[6]

Civil Society in the Gulf

Active political organizations, especially political parties, are banned in all GCC countries, although political activities do find some expression in nongovernmental organizations such as clubs, professional associations, women's societies, and philanthropic organizations. Voluntary organizations are embryonic, only having begun to take legal and administrative shape between the late 1950s and the early 1970s. However, soon after the First World War, the traditional aristocracy initiated the formation of associations for commercial elites.

In Bahrain (1919) and in Kuwait (1922), literary clubs began to appear. These clubs played a major role in introducing the political thoughts prevalent at that time in Egypt, Syria, and Iraq. The British authorities tried to shut down the clubs, for fear of political subversion to British colonial rule. However, in the late 1930s, a new generation of social groupings, including merchants, teachers, government employees, students, and oil workers, formed new clubs.[7] Religious associations have been better organized and more powerful dimensions of Gulf civil society. Usually less receptive to change, they have been highly influenced by specific traditional religious hierarchies, especially those aligned with the ruling elites. However, with the advent of modern political Islam, some of these associations began to be more visible and active. The Muslim Brotherhood activists, who had emigrated to escape Nasser's oppression in the 1960s and moved to the Gulf emirates, were politically dormant, due to the repression experienced in Egypt and the political sensitivities of the Gulf monarchies. Nevertheless, they came to permeate many professions during the oil boom, and it was around this core group that the majority of Sunni Muslim activists gravitated.

The first of these religious associations appeared in Bahrain in 1941 under the name of Nadi al-Talaba (Students' Club). It later became Nadi al-Islah (Reform Club), under the influence of Bahraini students who had been exposed to the Muslim Brotherhood while studying Islamic and common law in Egypt. Twenty-two years later, in 1963, the Jameiat al-Islah al-Ijtimie (Society of Social Reform) was established in Kuwait, and in 1984 the Jameiat al-Islah wa Altawjih al-Ijtimie (Society for Reform and Social Instruction) was founded in the United Arab Emirates (UAE). These associations communicated and coordinated their activities throughout the Gulf and recruited in every Gulf state. The most notable Shi'a religious association was al Jameiat al-Thaqfah al-Ijtimaiyah (Society of Social Education). During this period, Shi'a religious associations were less politically active, focusing more on religious education. However, they became much more politicized and active in Kuwait during the Iranian Revolution.

Professional associations have not been viewed favorably by the states of the Gulf. Despite their exclusivity, their members' skills are a prerequisite for state maintenance, and foreign nationals performing such tasks were denied admission. These associations were formed in Kuwait in the 1960s, Bahrain in the 1970s, and the UAE in the 1980s. In the Gulf region, there were only about forty professional associations in the 1990s, sixteen in Kuwait, and ten each in Bahrain and the UAE. Labor unions were discouraged if not banned altogether.

Women's associations, which first appeared in Bahrain in 1955, were often social clubs and not politicized. Their early members were drawn mainly from the foreign community, predominantly the British colonial administration and the upper-class Bahrainis. However, by the early 1970s, these associations began to demand recognition and political rights for women. In the early 1960s, women's associations began to emerge in Kuwait, and by the mid-1970s a more activist, politically aware group from the upper classes established Nadi al-Fatat (Young Women's Club). This club represented the more educated young Kuwaitis returning from universities around the world, although they were religiously oriented and traditional. Only after the expulsion of Iraqi forces from Kuwait in 1991 did Kuwaiti women begin agitating for political equality, including the right to vote. In Saudi Arabia, women's associations did not begin forming until 1983. Drawn from the upper classes, they soon fell under the tutelage of the religious hierarchy of the Saudi state. In Oman and the UAE, women's groups did not appear until the early 1970s.

The Saudi special relationship with the Gulf resulted in a Saudi hegemony in the region and the imposition of the Saudi-Wahabi doctrine on religious thinking. Wahabism does not tolerate other religious interpretations, such as Shiʻism, and it considers their mere existence in the Arabian Peninsula a great challenge according to their Puritan Salafi doctrine. Also, the Wahabi doctrine completely rejects modern revolutionary political Islam, whether it is Shiʻi or Sunni in orientation, and combats this throughout the Gulf. The religious establishment and the political leadership became partners in the Saudi state and the Salafi movement, beginning as a limited partnership between the Saudi royal family and the Wahabi leadership. Muhammad Ibn ʻAbdul Wahab enlarged the partnership to include the "religious establishment, as represented by the leading Ullamah and the Saudi throne."[8]

A marriage of convenience emerged and, according to Anwar ʻAbdullah, the Saudi king "in the eyes of the ʻUllamah, was seen as the enforcer of the Shariʻah, thus he is not a legislator. In this way the Shariʻah is the foundation and the king is the defender . . . the throne then appears a part of the Wahabi religious establishment . . . the king then is required to appear as the supreme religious symbol for both the regime and the religious establishment. The king is the Imam who occupies the tip of the pyramid in that religious establishment. As a consequence he is surrounded and watched by a phalanx of important ʻUlama."[9] In the Gulf, all the traditional Sunni Islamic movements are, in one way or another, allies of the Saudi establishment, rejecting modern revolutionary political Islam. Various associations have become an extension of the Wahabi-Saudi establishment, basically because their overall political aims proved similar. Financial aid has flowed from Saudi Arabia to these associations and political support from the Gulf states, in addition to the protection by the Saudi state, gave these associations a free hand in society. Finally, under the guise of a return to Islam, more restrictions were placed on women and liberal political ideas, posing an obstacle to the development of democratization and civil society.

Gulf History and Political Culture

The GCC countries lie along some of the world's most ancient sea routes and have been centers of business and trade for centuries. Pearling, fishing, and boat building were the main industries of the Gulf region before the discovery of oil. In the desert climate, agriculture, if it existed at all, was necessarily limited. Settled populations lived along the coast and near oases, and nomads inhabited the desert interior of the Gulf region. The Gulf has played a significant role in the West's domination of the Orient since the age of imperialism. The hegemony of the British East India Company over India by the end of the seventeenth century initiated Britain's increasing effort to dominate the Gulf in order to protect and expand its imperial interests. Between 1820 and 1899, Britain achieved colonial control over the entire Gulf through a series of treaties with local leaders (1820 with Omani Coast, 1891 with Muscat, 1892 with Bahrain, and 1899 with Kuwait) under the guise of combating piracy. In 1915, Britain signed the Treaty of Darea with 'Abd al-'Aziz Ibn Sa'ud, in which Britain would provide protection for his expanding territory and pay him £5,000 sterling monthly in return for his refraining from attacking British interests and treaty partners in Kuwait and the southern Gulf.[10]

In the Treaty of al-'Aqeer in 1922, Britain drew new boundaries between Kuwait, Iraq, and Nejd, for the first time demarcating the Arabian Peninsula. The borders were established to control the movement of the nomadic peoples of the interior and to keep them from changing political loyalties from the leaders now established as the heads of the newly created states. Bedouin society had always been based on sociopolitical relationships, which focused on interpersonal relationships rather than geographic constraints. As such the treaty limited political movement, tying the people of the region, through tribal elites, to western-sponsored rulers.

Between 1915 and 1927, Ibn Sa'ud conquered the area of what is known today as Saudi Arabia. In 1927, in the Jeddah Treaty, Britain lifted its protectorate status and recognized Saudi Arabian independence. Now incorporating both the Hejaz and Nejd, the Jeddah Treaty altered the borders of both Iraq and Kuwait. The political motive behind such treaties was to use the ambition of Ibn Sa'ud as a counterbalance to the British promises to Sharif Hussein of Mecca. By the early twentieth century, the Gulf and the Arabian Peninsula were politically and economically part of the British Empire.[11]

Rather than administering the region directly as a colonial possession, Britain institutionalized its control of the Gulf by exploiting the historical tribal relations that had existed in the region for centuries. Within the framework of these tribal relations, government and politics were largely undifferentiated from the institution of kinship. Rulers (sheikhs), while holding authority, had no fixed lines of succession within the ruling families. Britain accomplished this subversion by aiding and abetting the transformation of the Gulf's ruling families into royal dynasties. This was achieved by concentrating economic and political power in the hands of one ruler, favorable to Britain, who readily exchanged authority based on community consensus for power based on British support. Succession was then limited to direct lines of descent from this ruler. The British guaranteed a royal family's rule against internal and external challenges in return for its support and loyalty.

Britain secured the consolidation of internal power in the hands of rulers committed to British policies in the region and took over direct control of all foreign relations for the Gulf states. By protecting the authority of the ruling families against claims of covetous neighbors and dissident social movements, Britain directly tied the geopolitical fate of the Gulf states to western strategic interests generally and British interests specifically. This structure remained in effect even after the British had formally withdrawn from the Gulf in 1971.

As the British hegemony waned and the cold war rivalry set in, American involvement increased. The need to protect the oil resources of the Gulf states from the control of hostile forces became an important consideration, particularly for the United States. With the end of the cold war, the threats to oil supplies have continued. The rich but militarily weak sheikhdoms straddle powerful and envious neighbors—Iran and Iraq. Being under the umbrella of the defense apparatus of the only remaining superpower has been reassuring to these royal families in the face of vocal demands for democratization.

The Gulf Cooperation Council

The power relations of Egypt and Iran have historically affected the geopolitics of the Arabian Peninsula because the peninsula has been a bridge between the Egyptian and Iranian cultures. When the power of one of the two civilizations weakens, Iraq often emerges as a regional power affecting the political dynamics of the peninsula.[12] In 1979, both Egypt and Iran were out of the regional power game—Egypt as a result of the Camp David accord, and Iran by virtue of the turmoil that accompanied the Islamic Revolution. The National Declaration on 8 February 1980 heralded a change of the Iraqi sphere of interest away from the Fertile Crescent and Greater Syria to the Gulf area. At the time, Iraqi aspirations for political hegemony in the Gulf, derived from its relative stability and military power, were further fueled by details passed to it about the near collapse of the Iranian state. This led Iraq to declare war on Iran in September 1980 to regain what it considered earlier concessions it had made in the Algiers Treaty of 1975 and thus to assert its leadership in the Gulf.

The Gulf Cooperation Council (GCC) was formed in March 1981 when Saudi Arabia, Kuwait, Oman, the United Arab Emirates, Qatar, and Bahrain signed an incorporation charter. At their first summit in April, they declared that their goal was self-protection from foreign interference. They emphasized that the GCC "comprises only states that are homogeneous in their political, economic and social orientations," which made it a sort of club to the exclusion of Iraq and Yemen.[13] As such, the GCC is a closed subterritorial organization whose strategic orientation is based on a fear of domination by regional neighbors, particularly Iraq and Iran and to some extent Egypt. The establishment of the GCC was not without serious problems. It lacked the founding parameters of concerted military plans, integrated economies, stable boundaries, and approved modalities for resolving conflicts.

The military failure of the GCC was dismally manifest when Iraq invaded Kuwait in August 1990. When Kuwait requested military assistance from the GCC according to the charter, no GCC member responded with force, nor did any member call for a military action in defense of Kuwait.[14] The reason was, and still is, that each state has been relying on foreign military protection rather than collective defense because they lack any strategic military conception of collective defense and they do not agree on any concrete criteria regarding what constitutes an enemy. For example, during the Iran-Iraq war, Saudi Arabia and Kuwait severed relations with Iran; yet the United Arab Emirates and the Sultanate of Oman maintained relations with Tehran. After the war, the GCC restored relations with Iran despite persistent Shi'i-phobia throughout the Gulf monarchies. Following the expulsion of Iraqi forces from Kuwait in January–March 1991, cracks in the GCC alliance appeared, with Oman never officially severing relations with the regime in Baghdad. In December 1992, Qatar restored diplomatic relations with Baghdad, to the consternation of Saudi Arabia and Kuwait.[15]

The same inconsistencies have prevailed on the continuation of UN Security Council economic sanctions against Iraq as Qatar, Oman,

Bahrain, and the UAE have championed their removal in the face of Saudi and Kuwaiti intransigence. More directly, border disputes have increased tension between GCC members, tension which was evident in December 1995 when the Qatari foreign minister announced that Qatar was "reviewing" its membership in the GCC. While several of the border disputes have been put before the International Court of Justice for resolution, divisions remain despite the dual "threats" from the northern Gulf. The December 2000 GCC meeting declared the formation of a joint defense force, although large technical obstacles remain due to multiple armament systems, the lack of a cohesive joint command, and agreement on mutual strategic goals.

After almost two decades, economic integration of the member states of the GCC is still little more than a dream because economic policies tend to be competitive, not complementary, and the economy of the GCC is based on oil, whose export ratio to the GDP is about 80 percent, a fact that makes the Gulf economy highly incorporated into the world markets. The situation is complicated further by disagreements over production quotas; this practically leaves each state to produce according to its discretion and consequently weakens a unified economic front. Third, the low level of diversification and the small domestic markets of the GCC make interdependence and integration almost unachievable. This has become most evident in light of the fact that the GCC has failed, since 1982, to unify its customs tariff, which is conceived to be instrumental in bringing about a necessary commonality for a possible common market and the founding of a unified front in negotiating economic agreements with the European Union.[16]

In December 1998, the GCC held its nineteenth summit to discuss three main issues: declining oil prices, relations with Iraq, and relations with Iran. The summit approved a plan for unifying customs tariffs by March 2001, and reiterated its routinely proclaimed position that the Iraqi regime was responsible for the crisis in the region. In addition, the summit urged Iran to end its occupation of UAE islands in order to improve relations with the GCC.[17] Despite declining oil revenues, GCC members have seen defense expenditures spiral dramatically since the Gulf war of 1991, with the purchase of billions of dollars worth of tanks, warships, training, and advanced fighter aircraft. However, the devastation of Iraq and the apparent alteration of Iran's foreign policy designs northwards leaves many in the GCC believing they no longer face any obvious or immediate threat, and in spite of the billions invested they cannot defend themselves without western support.[18] Also, the overtures of Saudi Arabia and Iran in 2000 increased anxieties for the UAE and, to some degree, Bahrain.

The GCC, since its establishment in 1981, has been fraught with disputes over territorial boundaries: Saudi Arabia versus Oman; Saudi
Arabia versus Bahrain; Saudi Arabia, UAE, and Oman over the area of
Buraimi; Saudi Arabia and Kuwait over the neutral zone; and Kuwait
versus Iraq. Almost all these disputes were resolved by 1995 except for
the two most rancorous: that between Qatar and Bahrain, and that
between Qatar and Saudi Arabia. The importance of these two problems
is that they have endured despite efforts at reconciliation or third-party
mediation, as in the case of Egypt mediating the Saudi-Qatari conflict
and Saudi Arabian efforts to conciliate territorial/boundary disputes
between Qatar and Bahrain.[19]

The Oil Economy

The economy of the region is entirely dependent on oil exports, individual states have accumulated vast wealth as a result of oil sales, and
each state has invested according to its own development plans. A
legacy of British imperialism is that control over oil is vested entirely in
the rulers' hands. Until recently there was little distinction between
state budgets and the private purse of the rulers. State and ruler are,
after all, indistinguishable.[20]

The economies of the Gulf are all narrowly centered around the production of oil and management of the resulting financial capital, which
is far greater than their absorptive capacities can accommodate. Until
the Gulf war in 1990–91, the net result was high consumption in both
public and private spheres and service-oriented economies based on
consumption rather than production. The indigenous population of the
Arab Gulf states constitutes a pampered leisure class, with labor predominantly performed by migrant workers. Indeed, the high number of
foreign workers in the region only increases the population's dependence, as they are not participating in the maintenance of their own
societies and instead rely on the foreign workers for both manual labor
and technical expertise; such dependence may well lead to political
instability. The numbers of foreign workers are staggering, estimated to
be 80 percent of the labor force in Kuwait, prior to Iraq's invasion in
1990. Only 20 percent of the UAE's 1.8 million population are citizens.
In the private sector the foreigners are almost the entire workforce,
reaching 98.6 percent in Kuwait and 99 percent in the UAE. Dominated
by construction and services, the private sector also employs foreign
labor in agriculture and industry, especially in the intermediate and
lower-level positions, while Gulf citizens maintain control of upper
management positions. In Saudi Arabia foreign workers constitute

some 55 percent, and in Qatar it reaches 90 percent. Most foreign workers come from Asia, estimated at 65 percent of the total with the majority coming from India and Pakistan. Twenty-five percent are fellow Arabs, mostly from Egypt, Syria, Jordan (Palestinians have been excluded due to their support of Saddam Hussein's invasion of Kuwait), and the Sudan. Five percent are from Europe.[21]

The economies of the Arab Gulf states are integrated into the global economy as high-powered consumer economies—high-powered not because of the size of the market but because of the size of the bankroll. They are economically independent of one another, and this increases their need for the unnecessary duplication of infrastructure technologies. With such wealth at their disposal, governments in the region have been able to achieve a great change in the socioeconomic situation of the GCC countries, keeping political opposition tranquil. Oil revenue also provides the greatest aid in controlling the royal purse; the ruler's share of oil sales amounts to several billion dollars annually, even in the case of Qatar. As Saed Abu Rich, the author of the book *House of Saud,* notes, "The figure in Saudi Arabia may be up to $7 billion a year out of estimated oil revenues of up to $50 billion a year." In other states, such as Abu Dhabi of the UAE, the proportion taken by the royal families is thought to be around 10 or 12 percent, while in Qatar it is thought to be 25 percent.[22] Clearly these tremendous financial resources allow the rulers of the Gulf states to run their economies essentially as private fiefdoms. Although the GCC countries remain an affluent group, since the 1980s sharp declines in the price of crude oil have had a negative effect on their economies. The GCC's annual earnings declined from a high of $180 billion in 1981 to a low of $70 billion eight years later.[23]

The 1991 Gulf war added to the economic problems facing the GCC countries. While the conclusion of the war was a victory for the GCC, in particular Kuwait, footing the bills was a major financial burden to the states closely involved. For example, the Saudi contribution, estimated at $60 billion, worsened the endemic budgetary difficulties already facing the country. The cost of the war was especially difficult for Kuwait, since its oil exports had been halted. Because the government had utilized income surpluses to build up investments abroad throughout the 1970s, it was able to meet financial obligations during and after the occupation. Still, the requirements were daunting. The unfavorable economic environment saw Gulf governments borrowing from the international market to tackle their financial strains. Saudi Arabia, for the first time in its modern history, was obliged to borrow from the international markets in May 1991.[24] Similarly, Kuwait began borrowing to meet reconstruction expenses in 1992.

Conscious of the drawbacks of overreliance on one source of income, the GCC states are gradually developing other sources. In the forefront of this endeavor are the member countries that are faced with the prospect of early depletion of their oil reserves. Bahrain, with a burgeoning population, has been trying, rather unsuccessfully, to shift its economy to financial services. Efforts to promote Bahrain as the commercial center of the Gulf were frustrated by the Iran-Iraq war, and in the mid-1990s industrialization through foreign investment was pursued. The UAE has been more successful in transforming its economy. The non-oil domain constitutes an increasing source of revenue for the federation, and it is expanding faster than the oil sector. Nevertheless, the UAE federal budget depends heavily on Abu Dhabi's oil revenues, as they contribute 60–75 percent of the total federal budget, and Dubai contributes 15–20 percent. The rest comes from federal revenues such as taxes. Dubai, one of the wealthiest emirates, is becoming the principal gateway for the entry of business and trade to the Gulf region.[25] Qatar, with limited oil revenues, is developing into a major player in the world liquefied natural gas market.

Deficit problems experienced by the GCC countries have called into question the government's role in the economy. It has been suggested that a reduction in government spending and reactivation of the private sector offer long-term solutions to the problem of deficits and balance of payments. Saudi Arabia adopted a series of reforms in its 1995 budget aimed at cutting spending by 6 percent with a goal of 20 percent in the near future.[26] Likewise, Oman slashed its 1994 budget by 10 percent in a drive to come to grips with the deficit problem.[27] The retrenchment policy is implemented cautiously to avoid social unrest, given a decline in the high standard of living.

Speculations on the seriousness of the Gulf states' debt problems vary. While the total GCC budget debts were over $22 billion, or 11 percent of GDP, in 1994, Saudi Arabia has pursued a massive program of government cost cutting, which has gained the confidence of investors. It is also worth noting that the revenues of the GCC states, especially Saudi Arabia, make their deficit crises pale in comparison with those faced by most western states.[28] However, the GCC states' public sectors are still inefficient, and the dependence on uncertain oil prices is potentially crippling.[29]

In Kuwait, the government has been cautious about cutting the public sector, which despite its inefficiency employs 150,000 of 188,000 Kuwaiti nationals for whom private-sector positions are not available. Kuwaiti culture has also been criticized, and it has been claimed, even in Kuwait, that the vast majority of Kuwaitis would refuse to hold private-sector jobs where productivity and efficiency might be required.[30] Fur-

TABLE 10.2
Trends in Military Expenditures (in current $ million)

	Saudi Arabia	Kuwait	Bahrain	UAE	Oman
1991	28,433	12,801	251	1905	1675
1992	15,369	6,341	268	1815	2008
1993	17,360	3070	259	1729	1889
1994	14,997	3338	263	1663	2001
1995	13,218	3685	273	1642	2018
1996	13,204	3140	289	1589	1915
1997	17,926	2395	287	1522	1812
1998	16,409	2298	294	1476	1828
1999	14,523	2259	n/a	1420	1614

Source: SIPRI Yearbook 2000 and the SIPRI data on military expenditure found at www.projects.sipri.se/milex/mex_data_index.

thermore, arms expenditures continue to be a major drain on oil revenues and have increased tremendously since the Gulf war (as shown in table 10.2).

To boost economic liberalization, the governments in the region are keen to attract foreign capital. However, industrialization is impossible in the absence of appropriate technology and labor and with western reluctance to make available the required technology. To answer concerns of prospective investors, some countries are introducing legal and administrative reforms to ease the business climate. Bahrain has relaxed ownership rules to allow foreign investors a 100 percent stake in any business, instead of insisting on 51 percent ownership by Bahrainis, and Oman has publicized its own series of incentives to attract capital.

Domestic Affairs and Civil Associations

The discovery of oil brought a social revolution to the Sunni nomad tribes of the region. The tiny uneducated populations of the Gulf states were unable to meet the technological and skill needs of the oil industry. Workers from Lebanon, Egypt, Palestine, India, Pakistan, and East Asia were called in. These expatriates have come to dominate the labor forces in all Gulf states since independence. The only significant sector of indigenous laborers is found in government, the second largest economic sector in the region, and this has become possible only recently as the educational levels of Gulf citizens have risen dramatically.

The influx of expatriates during the boom years did much to enhance what little economic diversification there was, by tremendously increasing the demand for consumer goods and housing that would not have existed through natural population growth alone. At the same time, expatriates put pressure on economic and social infrastructures: schools and hospitals had to be built quickly to handle the growing population, to keep them productive, and to ensure that their children would be accommodated. All this growth was handled relatively easily during the 1970s when oil revenues made the Gulf states among the richest in the world. With the decline in oil prices during the 1980s, the rapid growth in the expatriate population came to a halt. The housing market stalled, and the demand for domestically produced consumer goods fell dramatically. Nevertheless, tens of thousands of expatriates remain and constitute the majority of the population in several countries.

The overwhelming numbers of migrant workers in the GCC countries remain problematic to the rulers of the GCC states. The economic slowdown, resulting from low oil prices, and the political problems of large foreign populations have compelled some of the states to reduce their reliance on migrant labor. Also, some countries—Bahrain and Oman—have rapidly growing indigenous populations, raising the specter of significant unemployment. The Gulf war totally distorted labor and population flows in the region, creating untold suffering to individuals and disrupting the economies of poorer GCC nations. To some countries, it was a welcome opportunity to effect drastic demographic changes. Kuwait openly expressed its desire to reduce its total population. Before the occupation, the non-Kuwaitis made up 73 percent of the population and 86 percent of the workforce, and the government had made no secret of its plan to increase the proportion of Kuwaiti nationals in the workforce to at least 40 percent by 2015. The Iraqi occupation caused two-thirds of Kuwaiti nationals and 90 percent of nonnationals to flee. With liberation the government-in-exile began discussing the possibility of reducing the population to half of its prewar level. This plan was considered unrealistic, since reconstruction would push up labor demands. Also, the expulsion of 800,000 Yemenis from Saudi Arabia at the start of the Gulf crisis had a notable impact on the demographic profile of the concerned countries. This action led to a 6 percent decrease in the total population of Saudi Arabia and a 7 percent increase in that of Yemen.[31] The loss of remittances to the economy of Yemen was put at about 20 percent of GDP. On the other hand, the Saudis are in no haste to fill the vacuum created by the expelled Yemenis, for the Yemeni community was economically self-contained.

The Aftermath of the 1990–1991 Gulf War

The expulsion of the Yemenis from Saudi Arabia and the maltreatment of Palestinians in Kuwait at the end of the war were politically motivated, but the fallout of the war extended far beyond this human dimension.

The domestic politics of the Gulf states have been permanently altered by the war, with citizens becoming more critical of the manner in which they are ruled. The gradual loss of faith in the leadership of the Gulf states as well as other states in the Arab Middle East began before the Gulf war. However, the crisis only hastened this process. Increasingly, people have been calling for more participation in politics and for a more accountable leadership. So disturbing has this trend become that some leaders have begun to introduce some form of liberalization of the political life of their countries. As Ghassan Salame puts it, "Kuwait has been oscillating between a tribal authoritarianism and oligarchy republicanism. Under clear pressure, the ruling family has reluctantly submitted to several demands from the opposition."[32]

In the GCC states, agitation by democratic forces has been rewarded by increased citizen participation in governance, although the record of progress varies among countries. Kuwait has proceeded the furthest. In 1992, the ruling family honored the pledge, which it made while in exile, to return the country to the 1962 constitution. Some 81,000 Kuwaitis, out of a population of 650,000, went to the polls on 5 October 1992 to select fifty representatives out of 278 candidates from the emirate's twenty-five districts. Only males over the age of twenty-one whose family background could be traced to pre-1920 Kuwait were eligible to vote. Extension of suffrage to women and naturalized citizens, an issue greatly debated during the campaign, has yet to occur.

Resistance to the Iraqi invasion was founded on an active and involved civil society that existed before the war. More than fifty associations, including professional and political groups and trade unions, were registered in the country before the occupation.[33] These associations and nongovernment groups played pivotal roles in organizing service provision and civil disobedience during the war. The nonassociational groups, particularly the *diwanniya*—a private room where men meet to socialize and exchange views—were greatly relied upon when the formal associations could not function effectively due to Iraqi restrictions. This role of Kuwaiti society, rather than state, in organizing resistance to the Iraqis, has created a foundation for change in the relation between state and society in postwar Kuwait.

Kuwaiti women played an important role during and after the war. At the height of the anti-occupation campaign, women staged several demonstrations in which lives were lost. However, this loyalty was not translated into an increase in legal and human rights, as many of their aspirations and expectations have not been met since 1991. The law bars women from voting, although women have increased their participation in the political life of the Kuwaiti nation, and the traditional role of women has been questioned. They are better off than in other GCC countries like Saudi Arabia, where women are denied basic personal rights including the right to drive a car. Male literacy rates continue to surpass those of females, while urban females continue to be more educated than their rural counterparts. In law, women's rights to education and employment are the same; in practice, however, traditions and social norms determine a woman's access.

The parliamentary tradition in Kuwait is embedded in the sociopolitical life, which can be traced back to 1752 when Al-Sabah, the present ruling family, migrated to Kuwait from al-Zubara, adjacent to the coast of Qatar. There emerged an alliance between the merchants and the notables, and the Al-Sabah rule was based on consultation with members of their society. The pattern continued undisturbed until 1896, when Sheikh Mubarak Al-Sabah came to power and turned the political process into the tribal domination of the Mubark descendants. In 1921, a reform movement demanded the restitution of the consultation process, including the right of the community to select a ruler. This movement failed, however, owing to the intransigence of Sheikh Ahmad al-Jabir, then the ruler of the country, and his support by the British colonial authorities. Following the Palestinian uprising of 1936, and influenced by King Ghazy of Iraq, the reform movement again called for a constitutional regime, the building of a modern society, and processes whereby the Kuwaitis would have direct access to their ruler. In 1938, a people's legislative council was founded and promulgated the Document of the Basic Law, but six months later, al-Jabir dissolved the legislative council. Its supporters were suppressed, and its leaders were either jailed or exiled.[34]

The declaration of the Kuwaiti constitution of 1962 was a compromise of a tribal regime in the face of the Iraqi claims for the territory of Kuwait in June 1961. It was also the culmination of the political demands of the 1938 movement, which, according to Kuwaiti political scientist Abdullah Fahd al-Nafisi, was an effort to shift opposition attention away from the Al-Sabah royal family, making "the parliamentary experiment in Kuwait an instrument to protect British interests in that country."[35] The essence of the constitution is the Kuwaiti people's allegiance to the ruling family in return for complete allegiance of the ruler to the constitution. Further, during the two ensuing decades, the ruling family and the government showed little tolerance for free expression and majority criticism, and in 1982, the Kuwaiti ruler revoked the parliament and suspended popular political participation on the pretext of the Iran-Iraq War, governing once more as a tribal chieftain.[36]

The return to parliamentary life in 1992 was mainly due to western pressure, especially from the United States, and the fact that the Kuwaiti people, alone, had endured the struggle against the Iraqi invasion, earning them the right to greater participation. Yet the fact remains that the elections of 1992 and 1996 did not change the old pattern of "compromise politics" that has long been characteristic of Kuwaiti political life.[37] In this pattern, which is the modern form of traditional tribal politics, policy formulation is not so much an input of majority demand as it is the result of manipulation by the ruling regime, which ends in compromise between the parliament and the government and leads to factionalization in the opposition that serves the purposes of the executive and the royal family. The 1992 elections for the national assembly, widely reported to be fair, gave the opposition a clear victory. Opposition deputies (what is referred to as the opposition is an assortment of factions and independents professing differing views) captured thirty-five of the fifty seats. The new assembly moved fast to assert its authority by passing legislation aimed at promoting more openness and accountability in the government and widening citizen participation in running the country. The assembly adopted legislation allowing the sons of naturalized Kuwaitis to vote in the next election. However, the record of performance of the opposition-dominated assembly has not pleased many. Kuwaitis have been exasperated by the theoretical debates in the assembly, particularly between Islamists, secularists, liberals, and conservatives, while the practical concerns of the electorate are ignored.[38] Such debates are pleasing to government officials because the waning fortunes of their staunchest opponents in the assembly, the Islamists, allow their power to continue. The defeat of the Islamists on a number of fronts was witnessed in 1994 when, in April, a government reshuffle reduced their strength in the government, followed by another setback in November when Islamists lost elections to the assembly's select committees. Furthermore, a bill they supported to segregate male and female students in Kuwait University failed to pass.

In Saudi Arabia, the war never seriously threatened the dominance of the royal family. Nevertheless, the family had to contend with a rising tide of dissent and opposition, even from within the Wahabi establishment, due to increased western influence within the kingdom. The weakness of the ruling family and its dependence on the West was revealed as the crisis. Underwriting the cost of the war as well as subsequent military purchases have claimed a sizable proportion of Gulf wealth, including Saudi wealth, which worsened its deficit difficulties. Tackling the debt problem had political ramifications, since public discontent was likely to arise if the extensive welfare system was reduced in order to meet defense expenditures.

The Saudi regime is founded on the bipolar authorities of the Wahabi religious establishment and the ruling family of Saʿud. Their historical bond and relationship is manifested in the former's complete control over all socialization institutions (which include schools, presses, religious foundations, and all cultural establishments) and absolute hegemony in shaping sociocultural norms. The Wahabi establishment is a collective hierarchical organization, with tens of thousands of members, and it exercises power over the populace comparable in magnitude and effect to the Vatican in the Middle Ages. The fact that the Wahabi organization is the source of the religious legitimization of the regime bestows on them powers of self-autonomy and self-regulation. During the Second World War, President Roosevelt asked King 'Abd al-'Aziz of Saudi Arabia to deploy some American troops to the kingdom; the king declined to oblige the request owing to the pressure of the Wahabi establishment, whose religious zealousness and parochialism sees foreigners as equivalent to infidels.[39]

Political planning, policy formulation, and maintaining Saudi rule are the domain of the ruler without interference from Wahabism, which in terms of social control is independent of the political regime. However, there are a few issues that must be bilaterally concluded. These include opening dialogues with non-Muslim entities, setting public information policy, and declaring emergency law (as in the case of the uprising of Juhayman al-Otaybi, a leading Wahabi, who in 1979 along with a number of followers occupied the K'aba). This also includes the declaration of war, because, for Wahabism, war means *jihad* or holy war, which is the prerogative of the Wahabi leadership.[40]

It was the 1990–91 Gulf war that exposed the diversity within the Wahabi establishment and the conflicting views of different generations within Saudi society. The leader of Wahabism, Ibn Baz, and his high-ranking entourage supported the foreign coalition by issuing religious edicts. As soon as the war began, voices of opposition grew from within Wahabism. The opposition included Mohammed 'Abdullah al-Mas'ary, former president of the Grievance Board, 'Abdullah Bin Janrin, a member in the Edict Authority, and 'Abdullah Bin Ku'ad, a member in the Supreme 'Ulama Council. Immediately after the war, the religious opposition submitted a petition, signed by 400 members, demanding a number of changes including the reform of the military, a challenge given the fact that the royal family dominates the army and the air force. A year later, the same group publicly submitted what was called a Petition of Counseling to King Fahd, signed by forty-seven prominent Wahabi figures and university professors. The publicity of the opposition, the break in the traditions of secret counsel with the king, and the religious hard-line of the splinter Wahabi group posed a threat to both the Wahabi organization and the Saudi throne. The threat was compounded by the fact that the American embassy in Saudi Arabia had close communications with the religious hard-line splinter group after the western media focused on Saudi abuses of human rights. The contact polished the image of the religious opposition and allowed it to acquire political support and western exposure, resulting in the opening of offices in Britain and the United States. In response to such unusual western pressure, the Saudi regime commenced what was termed the "liberalization process" in the form of a consultative council in March 1992.[41]

In Saudi Arabia, underground opposition groups have surfaced occasionally in open protests and demonstrations that have been met with punitive measures. A series of demonstrations involved militant Muslims demanding the release of jailed opposition figures, including some younger members of the Wahabi movement; a number of protesters were jailed.[42] In its 1994 annual report, Amnesty International announced it had "received reports of numerous cases of possible extra-judicial executions or other unjustified killings of Iraqi refugees resulting from excessive use of force at the hands of the Saudi Arabian armed forces. On August 1991, at least two, and possibly as many as five, refugees were killed in the Artawiyya camp." The detained Wahabi dissidents had issued a petition to the king criticizing the deviation of the country from pure Islam. This underlines the fragmented nature of the Saudi opposition. It is divided between Islamist and liberal factions.[43] Although this wave of opposition does not constitute a major problem, it cannot be ignored. As Martin Wooacot points out, "The real weight of al-Massari [the leader of the religious opposition residing in London] . . . is hard to measure. But what he has demonstrated is that there is a front on which the regime is open to challenge."[44]

The establishment of the long-awaited Majlis al-Shura (consultative council) changed nothing, with its appointed members. It simply provided a better public relations image in the West while legitimating the system of consultation already in place.[45] The consultation involves regular public hearings by senior Saudis at which any citizen, in theory, may air his views and grievances. After a further period of waiting, King Fahd inaugurated the sixty-member Majlis on 29 December 1994. He used the occasion, however, to caution that pluralism, democracy, and other alien ideas were not for Saudi Arabia. The delay in forming the council may have been due to the rise in Islamic activism with the king keen to balance the influence of religious and secular elements in society.[46]

A similar pressure to liberalize the government filtered down to the rest of the Gulf states, and other countries of the GCC established their own consultative councils. Oman's Majlis al-Shura, whose next four-year term was scheduled to begin in January 1995, expanded its membership from fifty-nine to eighty, and women were finally allowed to participate. This represents the first political role for women as members of a consultative council, an unprecedented move in a Gulf Arab state that could produce the region's first female member of parliament. The process of filling the eighty seats in the Majlis involved the selection of elders, prominent businessmen, and intellectuals in each of the fifty-nine provinces to vote for two or four nominees according to the population of the provinces out of a pool of 160 nominees, from which the sultan selects the required number. The council has consultative powers but no say in foreign, defense, or security affairs.[47] Likewise, Bahrain set up a consultative council with limited powers in November 1992, a move that fell far short of the elected assembly dissolved in August 1975. This move has never quelled demands for the restoration of the liberal constitution adopted after independence. Instead, the opposition has intensified its activities. Since December 1994, clashes with police have left a number of protesters dead and others detained, forcing human rights groups to express concern over abuse. The root of Bahrain's difficulties is "the fact that the 65 percent Shi'a Muslim majority is ruled by a Sunni ruling family that is subservient to Saudi security policy and is intolerant of Shi'ism. Shi'a discontent has been exacerbated by high unemployment and rules keeping Shi'as out of the armed forces and sensitive administration posts."[48] The news media are severely restricted in all of the Gulf states except Qatar, with controls the harshest in Saudi Arabia and more relaxed in the UAE. In early 1996, the Saudi government banned even the previously approved BBC local service from broadcasting in the country due to its coverage of the activities of the Saudi opposition in Britain.

GCC Security Affairs

Western, particularly American, intervention during the Gulf war, while restoring Kuwaiti independence, did not answer long-term security concerns in the Gulf states. Instead of strengthening the position of the ruling families, it seriously undermined their legitimacy. Reliance on a western security umbrella is not popular with many in Gulf societies, especially Islamic activists. Saudi opposition to the presence of foreign troops on its soil after the war points to the gravity of the problem. Some western analysts have raised doubts not only about rivalries within the House of Sa'ud but also about a regime that is under challenge. "Among its problems are the growth of an Islamist opposition movement; a middle class seeking to break the princely monopoly on decision-making; cuts in the vast welfare system; high-level corruption and foreign policies seen as subservient to the economic and political interests of the United States."[49]

Although Iraq is subdued, other perceived threats to the GCC countries are cause for concern. Iran is often portrayed as a threat, but the real issues are far more complex. The Saudi and Iranian regimes are inherently incompatible for political, economic, and ideological reasons. The Saudis are clients of Iran's greatest enemy, the United States, both states are massively dependent on oil exports, and the Wahabists and Shiites regard one another as heretics. However, it would not be in the Saudis' interest to see the fundamentalist regime toppled, as a western-leaning Iran would quickly replace the Gulf states as the leading American client in the region. Washington, however, has no appetite for any thaw in its relations with the Iranian Islamic regime. Hostile ideological and political movements are on the rise, and internal differences among the GCC countries could flare up into open hostilities at any time. The eighth summit of the Islamic Conference Organization was held in Tehran in December 1997. Considered to be the most important diplomatic gathering hosted by Iran since its revolution over two decades ago, the summit paved the way for a warming of relations between Saudi Arabia and Iran as well as the rest of the Gulf states. This alarmed the UAE, which has its own territorial disputes with Iran. "For Iran, the priority is the cementing of warmer relationship with Saudi Arabia and the Arab Gulf states."[50] Outside the Gulf, Yemen poses a threat to both Saudi Arabia and Oman. Bolstering defenses to counter these challenges has become a main preoccupation of the GCC countries.

Individually these countries lack any capacity to build military forces capable of defeating an Iranian or Iraqi challenge, and they are forced to look for other ways to guarantee their security. In the aftermath of the Gulf war, a mutual defense pact between Egypt, Syria, and the GCC was signed in Damascus in March 1991. It envisaged the provision of a permanent force of between 100,000 and 150,000 troops by Syria and Egypt to support the defense forces of the GCC countries, with finances shouldered by the GCC. By the end of 1991, the pact had run into difficulties and was essentially shelved. In mid-2000 Egypt and Syria tried in vain to revive it, in spite of an explicit GCC preference for western protection. A series of defense pacts with western and other powers followed the Gulf war; Kuwait signed a ten-year defense pact with the United States in 1991, followed by other agreements with the remaining western permanent members of the Security Council.

On another front, fresh efforts have been devoted to revitalizing defense cooperation among the GCC. The pooling of resources presents the only hope of establishing a credible defense umbrella for the region. Oman has advanced a proposal for creating a force of 100,000 men, clearly intending that most of it would be Omani, but this proposal has met with little enthusiasm. Saudi Arabia responded by proposing a gradual expansion of the peninsula shield force that would be based on its territory, but this was similarly rejected. Thus, lack of consensus on a concrete course of action to be pursued continued to undermine hope for a unified defense among the GCC countries. Unresolved border disputes and national pride remain divisive factors that thwart the attainment of meaningful indigenous defense integration. Even when some form of cooperation has been achieved, difficulties often crop up. In the course of joint military exercises in 1992, planned maneuvers had to be put off because of the refusal of Omani forces to take orders from Saudi commanders. Likewise, Kuwaitis have been reluctant in the past to take commands from Omanis. This emphasis on national pride has extended to the acquisition of military equipment. Except for a few systems, each country has gone to some length to purchase hardware on its own as radically different from their neighbors as possible.[51] Indeed, this diminishes the hope of building a joint defense force in the near future.

Individually, these countries have invested much in enhancing their defense capabilities. Immediately after the cessation of hostilities, a panic buying of military equipment ensued. Saudi Arabia made large orders of arms to strengthen its ground forces as well as its air defense and also rapidly expanded its manpower from 40,000 at the time of the war to nearly double that figure by the end of 1993. Similarly, Kuwait began building an army. However, it will be difficult for these countries to realize all their plans, for economic reality forbids unlimited spending. Since the war, Saudi Arabia has been forced to suspend an order of 150 M-1A2 tanks from the United States because of cash flow problems. In addition to restrictions on spending, Kuwait had to contend with constant questions from the opposition-dominated national assembly and curtail its social services, and personal income tax laws were introduced in 2000.

The UAE is better off as far as the question of liquidity is concerned and may end up spending more on defense than all the other countries combined. Whether the spending is based on any semblance of rationality is another matter entirely. The UAE operates fourteen kinds of armored vehicles for a federal army of 65,000 troops, due to the rather whimsical procurement policies of different officials. In the mid-1990s, the emirates offered contracts for purchasing eighty multirole strike aircraft, with the British-built Tornado as the leading choice, bringing the value of the deal to $10 billion. However, the UAE already had ninety-seven modern aircraft, many of dubious utility as they lack the ground facilities and associated infrastructure required for modern air operations. While the UAE does not answer such questions, it is not a secret that most of its air force consists of foreign mercenaries. Saudi Arabia, especially, has strengthened its relations with the energy-hungry industrial nations of Southeast Asia. It is estimated that China alone will quadruple its energy requirements between 1995 and 2015, and the PRC has been very active in trying to establish an active diplomatic relationship with states in the Gulf.

The Kingdom of Saudi Arabia

Saudi Arabia is the largest member of the GCC at some 1,226,480 square kilometers, most of which is desert. The two most extensive parts of the desert are al-Rub'a al-Khali, about 647,000 square kilometers, and al-Nofud, about 56,580 square kilometers. The population, according to the 1998 UN census, is 20.2 million, and the harsh geography has had a strong impact on the sociodemographic structure of the country. It is mainly nomadic pastoralist along with a portion of nomads who settled in oases. Indeed, the intertribal relations composed much of peninsular politics until 1930, when with the production of oil and the incorporation of Bedouins into the oil industry there was a visible decline of pure nomadic Bedouins. The change witnessed their decline to only 14–16 percent of the population in the late 1960s, and by 1989, pure Bedouins had completely disappeared. Until the discovery of oil and the accumulation of wealth, the economy was based on pasture, limited agriculture around oases, and the pilgrimage trade. Between the fall of the Umayyad in about 750 and the first appearance of Wahabism (1792–1818), the peninsula never witnessed any central authority and was characteristically in a state of fragmentation in which tribal traditions and way of life dominated.[52]

The al-Sa'ud family has dominated the history of the Arabian Peninsula for the last two centuries. The family skillfully employed religion and oil to build a state from Bedouin tribes that had little in common. The founder of the modern state of Saudi Arabia was 'Abd al-'Aziz Ibn 'Abdul Rahman Ibn Sa'ud, known as Ibn Sa'ud. However, to understand fully how he managed to create this kingdom, it is appropriate to look at the Saudi dynasties that preceded it.

The first recorded ancestor of Ibn Sa'ud, Mani al-Muraidi, moved from the Qatif area to Wadi Hanifa, near Riyadh, around A.D. 1446. The al-Sa'ud used the town of Dir'iyya as their capital until its destruction by Egyptian artillery in 1818, after which Riyadh became the capital. The

Nejd homeland of the al-Sa'ud in central Arabia has been isolated for centuries by its difficult geography. Crucial to the consolidation of the rule of the al-Sa'ud in, and extension beyond, Nejd was the role played by Imam Muhammad Ibn 'Abdul Wahab, founder of the Wahabi movement.

Born in 1703 in Nejd to a family deeply rooted in Islamic law, Ibn 'Abdul Wahab received a religious education in several cities. He was dismayed by what he considered deviations from the Islamic faith, and he decided to advocate a return to the true faith and strict application of its laws. His preaching, however, never sat well with his people, and soon he was expelled. In 1744, he took refuge in Dir'iyya under the protection of Muhammad Ibn Sa'ud. Ibn 'Abdul Wahab's ideas led his protector to establish a theocratic state, namely, the Kingdom of Saudi Arabia. However, they also gave rise to the rapid military expansion of Saudi authority beyond the borders of Nejd and provided the moral basis for the unity of the various tribes in the Arabian Peninsula under al-Sa'ud.[53] The influence of tribal affinity within each clan, often a source of disunity between clans, was curtailed. Mecca and Medina were occupied, the Shi'a holy places of Nejf and Kerbela in Iraq were attacked, and taxes were collected as far as Aleppo in northern Syria. This expansion soon incurred the wrath of the Ottoman sultan, who acted through his viceroy in Cairo, Muhammad 'Ali, who was sent to put an end to the Wahabi state. A military campaign, from 1811 to 1818, ended in the destruction of Dir'iyya and the capture and execution in Constantinople of the ruler of the state, 'Abdullah, ending the first Saudi-Wahabi state.[54]

Nevertheless, in spite of this defeat, the al-Sa'ud family retained political control over central Arabia. 'Abdullah's uncle organized his forces, established Riyadh as his capital, and extended his control over the whole of Nejd and the eastern province. The Egyptians were forced to withdraw to Hejaz. Faisal al-Sa'ud succeeded his father, Turki, in 1834 and ruled until 1838, when Muhammad 'Ali defeated the al-Sa'ud house once again and imprisoned Faisal in Egypt. Khalid Ibn Sa'ud, a rival claimant to Saudi leadership, who himself was in custody in Egypt following the defeat of 'Abdullah, was installed as the new ruler under the guidance of the Egyptian forces. Later, Muhammad 'Ali withdrew his overextended Egyptian forces following the declaration of Egyptian autonomy from Ottoman rule.

In 1843 Faisal escaped from jail in Egypt and regained control of Nejd, ushering in his second reign, which lasted from 1843 to 1865 and was known as "the golden age of the second realm." His death in 1865 was followed by a long civil war between his sons, and the ensuing instability provided the Turks with the opportunity to occupy the eastern region in 1871. The growing power of a rival house, the al-Rasheeds, which had been put in power by the al-Sa'ud in Jabal Shammar, became a looming threat to future Saudi expansion. Muhammad Ibn Rasheed, the tribal leader of the Shammar tribe, extended his control over the whole of Nejd. The battle of Mulaida, in 1891, between Muhammad Ibn Rasheed's forces and the Saudis under the command of Faisal's youngest son, 'Abdul Rahman, was the final blow to the second Saudi-Wahabi state. 'Abdul Rahman and his family escaped to Kuwait.

Witnessing this defeat and also fleeing to Kuwait was 'Abdul Rahman's fifteen-year-old son, 'Abd al-'Aziz al-Sa'ud (Ibn Sa'ud), who later would establish the Kingdom of Saudi Arabia. In exile, the defeated father prepared his son for a remarkable future that would restore the glory of the family. 'Abd al-'Aziz had a strict religious education and thorough tutelage in military skills under his father. In the course of attending Sheikh Mubarak, the ruler of Kuwait's Majlis, he learned first-hand about governance.

In 1902, leading a small force of between forty and sixty relatives and retainers, Ibn Sa'ud attacked Riyadh, killing nearly all members of the garrison, including the governor of the town, 'Ajlan al-Shimari. The news of Ibn Sa'ud's success pleased Sheikh Mubarak, who immediately dispatched warriors to reinforce his position. 'Abd al-'Aziz Ibn Rasheed was furious and vowed revenge. To consolidate his hold over the town, Ibn Sa'ud raided the neighboring Bedouin tribes. When he felt strong enough, he called his father to join him, and on 11 May 1902, 'Abdul Rahman left Kuwait. Confrontations between Ibn Sa'ud and Ibn al-Rasheed continued with many losses being inflicted on al-Rasheed's forces. For the al-Sa'ud, the main factor motivating the struggle, particularly up to the time of Rasheed's death, was the desire to avenge family honor.[55] However, this factor would soon prove insufficient to build a kingdom.

In time, al-Rasheed lost territory and was forced to seek military support from the Ottomans. In July and August 1904, the Turks came to his aid primarily because of the relationship between Ibn Sa'ud and Sheikh Mubarak, who was a friend of the British and thus a concern to the Turks. The joint force of the Turks and Ibn al-Rasheed was defeated. Ibn al-Rasheed was killed near Burayda.

His successor, Mit'ab Ibn Abdul Aziz Ibn al-Rasheed, realized that loyalty to his leadership alone was insufficient to hold his followers together. On many occasions, the Bedouins, whose allegiance to their tribes remained strong, melted away at first sight of battle. Hence there was need to develop loyalty not only to Ibn Sa'ud but also to an ideal. Such an ideal presented itself in 1913 when a zealous religious group, the Ikhwan (brethren), revived Wahabism under the leadership of Faisal al-Dawish.[56] The Ikhwam called for a return to pure Islam as it existed in the early Islamic period. After initially clashing with them, Ibn Sa'ud was able to incorporate the Ikhwan, unify the peninsula under his leadership, and spread the doctrine of Wahabism.

Ibn Sa'ud assumed the title of imam. He sent Wahabi missionaries into the desert to preach the word of Wahabi Islam to the Bedouins. The zealous missionaries transformed the Bedouins into the Ikhwan, a formidable army that spread their puritanical brand of Islam.[57] By 1916, most of the Bedouin were part of the Ikhwan, and the sheikhs of the tribe were required to attend Islamic schools of law in the mosque in Riyadh.[58]

This element transformed the struggle into a truly religious one. Militarily, the Ikhwan enabled Ibn Sa'ud to easily subdue the al-Ahsa region of Arabia on 9 May 1913, after which its surviving Turkish defenders were allowed safe passage to Bahrain. In what amounted to international recognition, Ibn Sa'ud concluded the Darea Treaty with the British in 1915, in which Nejd, al-Ahsa, al-Qatif, al-Jubayl, and their dependencies and territories were recognized as being under his suzerainty.[59] Ibn Sa'ud was given a subsidy to encourage him to fight Ibn al-Rasheed and the Turks, while discouraging him from starting a war with Hussein Ibn Ali, who had also been enlisted to the allied side against the Ottomans during the First World War. However, the actions of both the Hashemites and their British patron soon jeopardized the truce. Hussein declared himself king of all Arabs, after receiving an arms consignment on 5 June 1916, and in 1919 he was bold enough to attack Wahabi territory, where his forces suffered great losses.

Meanwhile, after a three-month siege, the defenders of Ibn al-Rasheed's headquarters of Hail surrendered, bringing to an end the house of al-Rasheed as a rival for peninsular rule. Hussein continued to suffer a series of defeats in battles attempting to secure his territory, and in December 1925, Jeddah, the last town to fall in Hejaz, came under Ibn Sa'ud's control. By 1927, Ibn Sa'ud was being referred to as the king of Hejaz and the sultan of Nejd.

The government and educational system of Hejaz were more modern than those of Nejd. However, "purifying" the Hejaz became a serious issue of disagreement between the Ikhwan and Ibn Sa'ud. The overzealous Ikhwan were determined to apply their brand of Wahabi principles, but they were not allowed a free hand to do so. It was the insistence of the Ikhwan on equating Wahabism with a simple lifestyle that was the core of the disagreement between the Ikhwan and the townspeople.[60] Also, the telephone, telegraph, and radio were considered works of the devil by the Ikhwan, who called for their destruction. In time, the

Ikhwan began to undermine Ibn Sa'ud's leadership, and they sought ways of provoking an open conflict. By 1928, Faisal al-Dawish of Mutayr and other prominent emirs, sultans, and sheikhs were aligned against Ibn Sa'ud and his loyalist forces. Secretly, they had agreed to carve up Saudi territory among themselves, and following a series of clashes, the final battle was fought on 9 September 1929.

Faisal al-Dawish died in jail on 30 October 1931 after being extradited from Kuwait to Riyadh by the British. From then on, matters regarding religion would be referred to the 'ulama. The Ikhwan were converted into the army of Ibn Sa'ud. On 18 September 1932, a decree was issued changing the name of the realm to the Kingdom of Saudi Arabia, and six years later, petroleum was discovered in large quantities, immediately leading to the formation of the Arabian American Oil Company. From this point on, Saudi Arabia's future revolved around the production of oil, with commercial production beginning two decades later.

King 'Abd al-'Aziz Ibn Sa'ud died on 9 November 1953. His successor, King Sa'ud, lacked the leadership qualities of his father and was unable to arrest the social and moral disintegration that befell Saudi society, despite colossal oil profits. To lessen discontent, in 1958 the royal family and the Wahabi leaders transferred executive powers to his brother Crown Prince Faisal. King Sa'ud recovered power temporarily in 1960, only to be deposed in 1964. King Faisal restored Saudi political legitimacy, and in March 1965 he named his half-brother, Khalid ibn 'Abd al-'Aziz, crown prince, while indulging in a regional power struggle with Nasserism. Faisal shrewdly used Islam to counterbalance nationalism and established the Organization of Islamic Countries. On 25 March 1975, King Faisal was assassinated by one of his nephews, and the crown prince ascended to the throne. King Khalid died suddenly on 13 June 1982, and his younger brother, Fahd, took power. Fahd's half-brother, 'Abdullah bin 'Abd al-'Aziz, became crown prince and first deputy prime minister.

Fahd turned out to be a shrewd political operator who was capable of balancing conflicting secular and clerical interests and maintaining at least the appearance of independence from Saudi Arabia's American patrons. In early 1996, after a long bout of failing health, Fahd suffered a stroke and surrendered some of his powers, but he did not abdicate in favor of 'Abdullah. The heir is viewed as more of a traditional conservative than Fahd, and according to the *Guardian Weekly*, 'Abdullah is known to favor less blatantly pro-American policies and more Arab self-reliance.[61] However, there has been no apparent change in Saudi foreign policy. Fahd's health has improved, and 'Abdullah's position might be more properly considered a co-regency. The succession, in theory, passes next to the princes of the Sa'ud family, of whom there are some 6,000, and uncertainty over the secession is rife, if discreetly hidden. Adding to the confusion, many of the princes maintain small armed forces of their own supporters and clansmen.

Politics and Government

Saudi society is traditional, and Islam is strictly observed in a Wahabi guise. Traditional social networks, such as the tribe and extended family, as well as other sectarian connections are bound into the state.[62] These relationships form the core of overall societal cohesion and shape the political culture of the kingdom. The extended family is the central unit of the community, within which the different sexes are assigned separate roles. The male plays a dominant part in the life of the community, while women are subjected to unnecessarily onerous restrictions. Women are barred from public office, never allowed to travel unaccompanied without the written permission of a spouse or father, barred from driving, and required to wear a veil and long black robe when in public. Protesting their treatment, some veiled women attempted to defy the ban on driving, and drove themselves around central Riyadh during the Gulf crisis. This drew a swift response from the government, while garnering the attention of the international media. The customary ban was quickly transformed into a civil law. To cope with this stifling environment, women are compelled to devise some survival strategies and other methods of expression and communication. Access to information sources is entwined with the kingdom's efforts to modernize while maintaining traditional social values, and Saudi women have proven resourceful in their efforts to access information through any means possible, including the Internet.[63] In addition, women are successfully turning to business and the professions. Today some 40 percent of private wealth in Saudi Arabia is in the hands of women, and women now outnumber men in some of the science and medical fields.[64] However, the road to full female emancipation will be fraught with institutional hurdles.

Maintaining a conservative stance over women's affairs is only one aspect of the overall societal desire to retain its traditional values in changing times. The political challenge for the ruling family to sustain the conservative outlook of Saudi society, while at the same time modernizing, is indeed an immense one. This is particularly so due to the recent assertiveness of the Islamic fundamentalist domain. Saudi Arabia operates under the principles of shari'ah, or Islamic law as interpreted by Wahabism. Some aspects of this law provide very harsh penalties for certain acts. Amputation is still a punishment for theft, and the kingdom regularly beheads drug traffickers, political dissidents, and those accused of terrorist acts under a 1987 law. Amnesty International, which opposes all capital punishment, has charged that "the prisoners facing it in Saudi Arabia are denied due process,"[65] and in March 2000 Amnesty challenged the Saudi authorities by launching the first campaign on an individual country by an international human rights organization, arousing the ire of the Saudi government.

In its annual report for 2000, Amnesty International pointed out that the international community's indifference in the face of proven human rights abuses could be chalked up to Saudi Arabia's strategic position and economic might. Magnifying the arbitrary nature of arrest procedures and lack of judicial independence was the kingdom's increasing use of capital punishment, including beheadings, mutilations, and lashings.[66] Amnesty International counted more than 100 confirmed executions in 1999, which demonstrated a dramatic increase over the total of 29 in 1998. Death sentences were imposed for murder, rape, drug trafficking, armed robbery, and terrorism. Four Wahabists were beheaded in May 1996 for their role in the bombing of the U.S. embassy in Riyadh in 1995, which killed four Americans and two Indians. The Wahabists were Saudis who had volunteered with the *mujahadeen* in Afghanistan against the Soviet invasion in the 1980s and were agitating for the withdrawal of all U.S. troops from Saudi territory. Other militants warned that if the four were executed, further attacks against U.S. interests would follow. On 25 June 1998, a truck bomb outside a U.S. Air Force barracks in Dhahran killed nineteen American military personnel and injured over 100 others, apparently revealing the level of dissidence within the country.

Despite massive spending on armaments, Saudi Arabia does not maintain a large armed force by regional standards. This has been suggested as a way of ensuring that the army never becomes a factor in the internal power struggles of a dynastic regime. Perhaps for this reason, a national guard is maintained, nearly as large and well equipped as the regular army, consisting entirely of Bedouin with strong tribal and religious affiliation with the Saudi royal family.

The distribution of power and wealth in the kingdom is skewed in favor of the ruling family. In 1989, *Fortune* estimated the personal wealth of King Fahd to be $18 billion, making him the second richest man in the world after the sultan of Brunei. But after the Gulf war, and as a result of devaluation, this personal wealth declined to $10 billion, leaving him the sixth richest man. Since the founding of the kingdom, up to the time oil revenues started flowing into Saudi coffers, the affairs of the kingdom were managed just like those of a household. Ibn Saʿud had a tight grip on the running of the country, including the management of its income. He dispensed funds according to his whim, mainly to win the support of others. However, with the oil bonanza and the accompanying affluence, a proliferation of institutions and complexity in responsibilities gradually emerged. The need arose for an administrative capability to handle the government machinery and organizations, and the management of the oil economy required new administrative and management skills. Initially, foreigners met this demand. However, as education of Saudi nationals progressed, they assumed an increasing role in the administration of the kingdom.

In a token response to demands for change, a consultative council, which had no real authority, by the name Majlis al-Shura was established in 1991. Within five years, the Majlis al-Shura was enlarged from sixty-one members to ninety. Before its formation, the king managed public affairs singlehandedly with little input from the public. "It is the executive arm of the King, and, subject to the King's approval, it has the exclusive jurisdiction to pass laws, initiate policies, and oversee their implementation."[67] Further, members of the royal family hold most of the crucial positions on the council.

Saudi Arabia has attempted to play the role of a regional leader following the Gulf war, especially when the Middle East peace process began to collapse in late 1995. An Arab leader by default because of its tremendous wealth, Saudi Arabia has joined Israel and Egypt in jockeying for position as the chief American deputy in the region. While Saudi Arabia has the closest involvement in the pivotal American interest in the region—oil—it also faces a difficult succession and accompanying instability. Also, Saudi Arabia may be less than willing to act as a base for American troops, as the appearance of Saudi impotence and clientship at being forced to have U.S. troops on its soil following the Gulf war has deeply affected the support of the ruling regime.

Kuwait

Kuwait today is a far cry from its beginnings as a trading and fishing center in the eighteenth century. Oil revenues have turned it into one of the wealthiest states in the Gulf, if not the entire world. The beginning of the oil boom following the Second World War transformed Kuwait into a welfare state with a rapidly expanding economy. Welfarism has not been without its drawbacks, as dependence on oil has placed Kuwait in a vulnerable position. Geographically, it is also vulnerable given its proximity to Iran, Iraq, and Saudi Arabia, all of which have had dramatic effects on Kuwaiti development.

Kuwait entered the international arena as an independent state in June 1961, upon terminating its treaty ties with Great Britain. According to ʿAbdullah Fahd al-Nafisi, a respected Kuwaiti political scientist, "Kuwait hasn't achieved yet the full and complete transformation from tribalism into the state," although Kuwait insists on emphasizing the formality of its statehood. In Kuwait political parties are banned and no true opposition exists. "Kuwait is living in an unusual and extraordinary condition as after the liberation from the Iraqi invasion it has experienced administrative decay, social chaos, corruption, cultural and intellectual confusion and increased foreign domination."[68]

In June 1961, the Kassem regime in Iraq renewed historical Iraqi claims to Kuwait, as it had fallen under the jurisdiction of Basra during the long period of Ottoman rule. To retain sovereignty, the Kuwaitis received support from the British and the Arab League. Twenty months later, Kassem was overthrown and Iraq relinquished its claim to Kuwait. In 1968, when the Baʿath regime in Iraq came to power, the threat from Iraq was based on ideological challenges more than on historical territorial claims. Despite its attempts at governmental reform, however, Kuwait remained a conservative monarchy that was the antithesis to Baʿath ideology. Ideological hostility was diluted somewhat by the facade of Kuwait's adoption of an Arab nationalist stance in regional issues such as the Arab-Israeli conflict. Kuwait was one of the first Arab states to sever diplomatic relations with West Germany after Bonn initiated relations with Israel. Further, it sent troops to Egypt during the 1967 Arab-Israeli war, and it endorsed the Palestinian cause until the PLO supported the Iraqi invasion of Kuwait in 1990.

Surprisingly, despite its small population base and lack of overall capabilities, Kuwait has been an important player in the Arab world because of the Kuwait General Fund and the Kuwait Fund for Arab Economic Development, made possible by the excess wealth generated from oil revenues. Financial aid is distributed throughout the developing world by an arm of the Kuwaiti foreign ministry. In the Arab world, the fund has assisted states right across the ideological spectrum, but there have been instances when the Kuwaitis have withdrawn their support from those with whom they disagree, such as when funds were withdrawn from Egypt after the Camp David accord.

Although the Iran-Iraq war of 1980–88 never really threatened Kuwaiti territory (save for Iraqi mining of Kuwaiti waters in 1987), it did affect its ability to secure access routes into and out of the Gulf for its exports. Also, Iran attacked a number of Kuwaiti oil tankers, and the pressure was such that the Kuwaitis could not be sure how much longer tankers would have access to its oil export installations. As a remedy, Kuwait approached the Soviet Union and the United States for help in keeping the export routes open through the Gulf. The Soviets responded by lending the Kuwaitis a small number of vessels and agreeing to provide naval protection for Kuwaiti ships. The United States replied in kind and even reflagged a number of Kuwaiti tankers. Kuwait thus managed to ensure the safety of its oil exports out of the Gulf.

Kuwait has a longer and deeper history of political involvement than any other Gulf state, save Bahrain, and it has the honor of being home to the longest running national assembly in the Gulf. Early Kuwait was ruled by an oligarchy of noble families, all of whom were Sunni Arabs, who selected a political leader from among themselves. One of the leaders was Sabah al-Jabir, whose family, the Al-Sabah, has ruled Kuwait since 1896. The process demanded that the man chosen was to rule in accordance with the endorsement of the leaders of the other families. There was a high degree of consultation until the turn of the twentieth century, when Sheikh Mubarak Al-Sabah, who came to power in 1896, and his son, Salim, abandoned these informal lines of communications and sought to limit the sheikhdom strictly to his direct descendants. These attempts were met with considerable opposition. There were calls for a more formalized consultative body from other leading families as well as from the merchant class.

Sheikh Salim proved to be highly unpopular because of disputes with Ibn Sa'ud that negatively affected Kuwait's relationship with Arabia. The decline in trade with Arabia and the resulting economic decline mobilized the merchant class to pressure the Al-Sabah family to establish some kind of formal consultative body after Salim's death in 1921. The family agreed, and the initial council was formed with twelve representatives of the merchant class; however, it proved to be ineffectual and inefficient. By 1928, the council no longer existed, but demands for more democratic institutions continued to challenge the ruling family.

Sheikh Ahmad (who had succeeded Salim) was equally unpopular in Kuwait, and his family's rule was challenged by elements in Iraq. In addition, a Saudi blockade of Kuwait, initiated in 1923, the absence of any kind of development plan, and charges of financial incompetence led to a great deal of public dissatisfaction with Sheikh Ahmad's rule. Though political parties were banned, Kuwaiti exiles in Iraq formed the al-Shabiba and the national bloc, and other groups of all ideological persuasions began to spring up both outside and within the country. Discontent and dissatisfaction grew to include important notables, which in turn aroused the suspicions of the British. The pressure was such that Sheikh Ahmad was forced to agree to form the Majlis al-Ummah al-Tashri'i (the People's Legislative Council).

Members of the council came from a list of eligible voters from 150 Kuwaiti families, who elected the fourteen-member council. The council was very active during its six-month existence: it drafted an interim constitution, fought to reform the economy, and attempted to check the power of Sheikh Ahmad. It was opposed by the conservative elements of society, who were still quite powerful, and the council was replaced by a new twenty-member council (chosen from an electorate of 400), but with a new mandate: It was no longer a legislative council, as the previous council had been. Now it would to be an advisory council. In the interim, Sheikh Ahmad rewrote the constitution and gave himself veto rights. The new council opposed this change and refused to meet until its original status was restored. Sheikh Ahmad rejected its demand and dissolved the council four months later.

The democratic movement remained underground until the 1950s when, after a number of ineffectual councils, political opposition once again proliferated. Egyptian expatriates began a Kuwaiti branch of the Muslim Brotherhood in 1951, which later gave rise to the Social Reform Society. Movements such as the Teachers Club, the Pan-Arabist Cultural Club, and the Graduate Club later emerged. Syrian and Palestinian workers imported Ba'athist ideology, and Iraqi and Iranian Communists were instrumental in starting the Kuwait Democratic Youth. However, it was only after independence in June 1961 that an assembly of any worth was established, although it was still limited in its power.

The decision to create an elected constituent assembly was largely the product of Emir 'Abdullah al-Salim, who replaced Sheikh Ahmad in 1950. The new assembly had twenty elected members and eleven cabinet ministers, and its principal role was to draft the country's permanent constitution. This constitution, adopted in 1963, declared Kuwait a hereditary monarchy under the Al-Sabah family, whose ruler was to be a direct descendant of Emir Mubarak the Great. It placed restrictions on the ruler's authority and guaranteed personal liberties, the right to social and economic welfare, and freedom of the press, residence, and communications. Through a separation of powers, executive power rested in the hands of the emir and the National Assembly. The National Assembly was to consist of fifty secretly selected members, in addition to nonelected cabinet officers who served four-year terms. The assembly could question a minister, and ministers were subject to votes of no confidence, though only the emir was allowed to call for the resignation of the entire cabinet.

Theoretically, the constitution is a contract between the ruler and the people, represented by the national assembly, and the emir must swear an oath to respect the constitution. The National Assembly has been suspended on three occasions after severely criticizing government policies and the integrity of its ministers. The criticism was such that the emir considered the existence of the assembly to be contrary to the interests of both his government and the country. It was suspended for the first time in 1975. It remained suspended until 1981—four years after the emir's death, and his replacement by Sheikh Jabir al-Ahmad, who was more open to the concept of the national assembly, which remained popular throughout its suspension. The fifth National Assembly (1985) was accompanied by changes in the electoral laws that created more electoral districts. These changes served the sheikh's personal interests by bringing more representation from Kuwait's conservative Bedouin elements, at the expense of Shi'a representation of the cities. Charges of gerrymandering were common, and the electoral results seemed to bear out these charges: Bedouins gained twenty-seven seats, which were more than half of the total, while the Shi'as and nationalists were virtually shut out of the assembly.

The same types of results were obtained in the 1985 election, when the pro-government National Center Group (composed of Bedouins and conservatives) maintained control of the sixth assembly by winning nineteen seats. Combined with the seventeen cabinet members, pro-government forces controlled thirty-six of the sixty-five seats in the assembly. Both the fifth and sixth assemblies were forced to deal with the difficult economic situation in which Kuwait found itself in the 1980s. The sixth assembly proved to be more vigorous in its examination of the governmental and bureaucratic systems and succeeded in forcing the resignation of Justice Minister Sheikh Salman al-Duayj Al-Sabah and almost forcing that of the oil minister, Sheikh 'Ali al-Khalifa Al-Sabah, for financial mismanagement and impropriety. The assembly was so successful in its attacks on the government that it was suspended on 1 July 1986. Public demand for the restoration of democracy forced the ruler to announce the formation of a national assembly with consultative powers as an interim step to the resumption of parliamentary democracy. On 10 June 1990, elections for the assembly again took place with the assembly now consisting of seventy-five members, of whom fifty were elected by secret ballot and twenty-five were appointed. Twenty-seven members of the 1985 parliament boycotted the election, as did a number of political groups.

'Abdullah Fahd al-Nafisi explains this trend by placing it within its historical context, attributing the creation of the parliamentary system in Kuwait to British pressure rather than to any indigenous democratic instinct. The parliamentary experiment was to divert the population's attention away from any problems incurred by the ruling Al-Sabah family, tribal elites, and the governments appointed at their behest, to protect their rule and British and American interests. Thus, it was not invested with any political power of its own. It accomplished little parliamentary reform, and as an institution it could not alter government policy or the nation's structure of government. He went on to state, "Parliament is like a retail shop. . . . The government can close it at any time."[69]

Immediately following the liberation of the country from Iraqi occupation, the seventh national assembly was elected in 1992. Its Finance and Economic Committee identified nine key policy areas, all of which pushed for the extension of parliamentary control and public debate of policy matters, especially when they related to oil and investment policies that previously had been the prerogative of the ruling family. It was the debt settlement issue that provided the first showdown between the assembly and the Al-Sabah family. A sizable amount of bad debts, which dated back to the stock market collapse in 1982, had given rise to a crisis within the financial sector of Kuwaiti society. Many of the major debtors come from the highest echelons of Kuwaiti commercial society, including members of the royal family, and this gave the issue an explicit political overtone. It is widely believed that these well-to-do Kuwaitis are quite able to pay what they owe, but prefer to keep funds hidden abroad. In regard to foreign investments, the attention during discussion in the assembly was drawn "to the fact that most embezzlements in the past decade were committed in the wake of the dissolution of the 1985 national assembly. Key players in the emerging KIO scandal were Sheikh Fahd Mohammed Al-Sabah and Sheikh 'Ali al-Khalifa Al-Sabah, cousins of the Emir." In early 1993, during one of the assembly sessions, an opposition MP, 'Abdullah al-Nibari, shouted: "Those entrusted with our overseas investments acted on the assumption that Kuwait will not be liberated from Iraqi occupation. Had the occupation lasted longer, nothing would have remained of our money."[70]

The disbanding of Parliament, at the order of the rulers, has occurred three times: in 1976 and 1986 during constitutional crisis, and in 1999 to avoid the increasingly embarrassing probe Parliament was conducting into graft and the enormous amount of the state's overseas assets and investments, which had gone missing during the Iraqi invasion. The value of those investments, which had fallen to less than U.S.$25 billion in 1992, was approximately one-quarter of the reported U.S.$100 billion that had existed before the Iraqi invasion. The arbitrary dismissal of the assembly resulted in a new composition of members from the 1999 elections. The lack of Parliament's formal power to oversee the government, beyond the questioning of appointed ministers, which the royal family views as an infringement on its prerogative to appoint the government, has resulted in a gain for liberal reformers at the expense of both Islamic and "service" candidates (those who support the government).[71]

Two major political trends have appeared in Kuwaiti electoral campaigns, and though coalescing in and around some structure, they cannot be interpreted as parties in the western sense. The first is an Islamic trend, though not the same as the Islamist activist trend prevalent in the rest of the region, as Gulf Islamists are often more accurately described as "Gulfists first" due to their deep commitment to the Gulf and its way of life as opposed to emphasizing Muslim society the world over. Islamists may be broken down into three subgroupings. First is the Islamic Constitutional Movement, which is the closest to resembling a true political party, whose beginnings go back to the Egyptian Muslim Brotherhood of the 1950s. The second popular Islamic grouping is the Salafi movement, which began in the 1970s and looks to Mecca for guidance following the orientations of the Saudi Wahabi. Third is the National Islamic coalition, which is predominantly Shi'a and associated ideologically with Iran. Though more liberal than their conservative Iranian neighbors, they have been represented in Parliament since the Gulf war. The second trend contains more liberal and secular political groupings. The first is the Democratic Forum (al-minbr al-dimoqrati), which is progressive and somewhat secular. The second are the national Democratic Groupings (al-tajemu' al-watani al-dimoqrati), which largely are made up of moderates from the commercial and academic strata of Kuwaiti society.

It is important to note, however, that "all these groupings have never controlled more than one-third of the Parliament with the other two-thirds of representatives being tribal members who epitomize and protect the interests of the ruling elites."[72] It should also be noted that the Assembly is not truly representative of Kuwaiti society, as women do not have the vote, and the franchise is not even extended to all adult men. Furthermore, only 10 percent of those eligible to vote take advantage of their franchise.[73] Clearly there is no real commitment to democracy, as the ruling elites are not interested in sharing power with anyone outside of the hierarchical Bedouin society.

Kuwait and the Iran-Iraq War

The first Gulf war between Iran and Iraq (1980–1988) and Iran's initial successes in driving toward Basra and occupying the Fao Peninsula alarmed the Kuwaitis because of the proximity of the Fao to Kuwait's borders. Kuwait had reversed its suspicions of the Ba'ath regime in Iraq by fully supporting and financing its war effort against the Islamic revolutionary regime in Iran. Iran had made it clear that it would not stand for such support, and it began to vilify the Kuwaiti ruling family for its treatment of its Shi'a citizens. An Iranian victory over Iraq, or simply in the Fao, would have spelled disaster for Kuwait. In late 1983, Iran began to subvert the regime by sponsoring attacks against Kuwaiti oil installations and other targets. A pro-Iranian group bombed the U.S. and French embassies in Kuwait, and while members of the group captured proved to be Shi'as from Iraq and Lebanon, they were supported and sponsored by Iran. This caused the Kuwaiti regime to accuse Iran of terrorism. Tehran began to mine Kuwaiti waters and fired a number of missiles into Kuwaiti territory. In 1985 Iran became bolder: An attempt was made on the emir's life, and the attacks against oil installations and other targets of Kuwait's economic infrastructure intensified.

The situation changed dramatically in 1986 and 1987, when Iran stepped up its offensive against Kuwaiti shipping. At the same time, the oil installation at Kuwait's key port of al-Ahmadi, which held the country's main refineries, was bombed. Those responsible for these and other acts against the state were found to be Kuwaiti Shi'as opposed to Al-Sabah rule. Also involved was a Kuwaiti army officer and an employee of the Kuwait Petroleum Company, as well as other important members of Kuwaiti society. The acts occurred not only because the Shi'as were opposed to the ruling family but also because they were opposed to the ill-treatment they had received in Kuwait during the Iran-Iraq war. The results of these discoveries were swift. Attacks on Shi'as occurred in the press, tens of thousands of Shi'as from other Islamic states were deported, and Shi'as were removed from sensitive positions in the oil industry.

Iraqi Occupation and Liberation

On 2 August 1990, Iraqi forces invaded Kuwait. The emir fled to Saudi Arabia, where he set up a government in exile, while the Iraqis deployed over 100,000 troops in the neutral border area between Saudi Arabia and occupied Kuwait. UN Security Council Resolution 660 was consequently adopted, condemning the assault, and the major powers also censured the action. President George Bush ordered the deployment of U.S. forces on the pretext of defending Saudi Arabia on 6 August 1990. A few days later, France and Britain began augmenting the American forces in the Gulf region, and soon Arab countries including Syria and Egypt sent forces to participate in the campaign. The buildup of forces against Iraq continued, while diplomatic options were pursued. A coalition of twenty-eight nations under U.S. leadership had formed by the end of the year. On 29 November 1990, UN Security Council Resolution 678 was adopted, authorizing the use of force to repel the Iraqi aggression against Kuwait, if the 15 January deadline for withdrawal was not heeded. January 16 marked the onset of the war to liberate Kuwait, with the ground offensive coming toward the end of February. On 28 February 1991, Kuwait was freed after two short days of fighting, and Iraqi leader Saddam Hussein was forced to accept all twelve relevant Security Council resolutions.

In war-ravaged Kuwait, some 600 oil wells were set ablaze, ruining the oil-dependent economy until reconstruction efforts could clean up and repair the damage. On the return of the crown prince and premier, Saad al-Abdullah Al-Sabah, reconstruction began in earnest and proved to be a resounding success. However, reform and the construction of a more representative governmental structure has not progressed at a similar pace.

After the Iraqi invasion of 1990, reforms were promised to allow Kuwaitis more participation in the political process and decision making within their own state. The first elections in 1992 saw the liberal and nationalist Democratic Forum weakened and the Islamic trend become predominant within opposition politics, a preponderance that was maintained in the 1996 elections. However, in May 1998, Islamist parliamentarians forced the resignation of the minister of information, even though he was a member of the royal family, for circulating books they viewed as blasphemous to Islam. When in March 1999 a version of the Qur'an was published with several typographical errors, Parliament's attacks against the minister of religious affairs appeared to be following a similar pattern, and the emir disbanded the Parliament in an effort to avoid close scrutiny of the government's actions.[74]

In the 1999 summer election, the Sunni Islamist representation fell in Parliament while its Shi'a counterpart increased. The Islamist trend in Kuwait is unique, in that it is not predominantly fundamentalist but rather appears more traditionalist in character, capitalizing on those dissatisfied members of Kuwaiti society who oppose both the modernist trend and the hierarchical tribal power structure.[75] Islamists appear to be taking on the role of the previous liberal and leftist reformers in advocating social justice while the traditional tribal leadership maintains its support of government policy.[76] Islamic MPs and groups now face a conundrum in which they will be forced to choose between supporting women's inclusion, which Islam has no actual basis in opposing, and continuing to garner the conservative support of traditionalists who would be alienated by an increased role for women.[77] The liberal reform trend did gain some seats, but not the large increase that the international media had expected. Indeed, the election of the new parliament with eighteen independent MPs, fifteen selected by the government, and thirty-five opposition MPs—divided almost equally between liberal-reform and Islamist members—appears to have resulted in no clear victor and not to have dramatically altered the makeup of the Kuwaiti opposition.

The election seems to reinforce the historical reality of Kuwaiti society, whereby ideological leanings are overcome by sociological differences such as urban versus Bedouin society, and support for most political trends is based on tribal affinity. The parliament is stratified along two distinct lines, the first being one of urban society, dominated by business groups and intellectual elites, and the second based on the tribal or Bedouin society, which is divided along geographical north-south lines. Both strata stress an individual's background association, rather than current political, ideological, or issue-specific leanings. In addition, the nature of the welfare state, with its constitutional guarantees for housing, education, and public health, strengthens such an orientation. The cost, size, and location of public housing, not to mention the backlog of available new homes, makes the government appear weak and inefficient. This notion is further compounded by the government's exclusivity of membership and its unrepresentative nature. For example, Kuwait's cabinets—all eighteen of them—have had 43 percent of their membership come from the wealthiest strata of society, with a further 25 percent coming from the royal family.[78]

These impediments to an efficient government will create difficulties as the new government tackles three of its most pressing issues: the future role of the welfare state, the orientation of the economy, and the inclusion of women in the political process. The constitution, under article 25, guarantees compensation to Kuwaitis when they are injured by "acts of God" such as a war or a natural disaster destroying their home or business. After the incalculable costs of reconstruction following the 1990 Iraqi occupation, and with the burgeoning costs of the social aspects of the welfare state by the middle of the year 2000, the government introduced personal taxation to raise funds as well as to reduce the cost of social services. Opposition groups, however, propose that taxes should only apply to corporations and to the capital gains of the wealthiest within Kuwaiti society. Also, the government, under pressure from the World Bank and International Monetary Fund, as well as its close allies in Washington and western Europe, is being forced to open the economy. This only increases the prospect for more foreign influence and will allow for less control by the ruling elite. Finally, the inclusion of women within the political process appears to be divisive even in opposition groupings, as it would please the modernists while alienating the traditionalist and Islamist groups. Indeed, the participation of new political actors may well undermine stability.

Bahrain

Bahrain is unlike any other Gulf state. It is a group of small islands twenty miles offshore Saudi Arabia and Qatar, and its geographic position has greatly affected its political and economic development, as has the composition of its society. Moreover, Iran has historically laid claim to Bahraini islands for both strategic and nationalistic reasons. In addition, the emergent Arab nationalist movement of the 1950s and 1960s was a greater threat to the Bahraini monarchy than it was to the monarchies of the lower Gulf states. Thus, Bahraini development has taken place in an atmosphere of hostility toward outside powers and in an atmosphere of challenge from ideologies that disputed the position of the ruling family. In 1994, the U.S. Department of State Human Rights Committee issued an important report summarizing the various concerns surrounding Bahrain's repressive practices. The report also specifies: "Civil liberties . . . remain circumscribed in Bahrain. The main human rights concerns continue to include the denial of the right of citizens to change their government; the occasional practice of arbitrary and incommunicado detention, the absence of impartial inspection of detention and prison facilities; restrictions on the right to a fair public trial, especially in the Security Court, and restrictions on freedom of speech and press, freedom of assembly and association, women's rights and working rights."[79]

Bahrain has faced internal challenges as well. Bahraini society consists of three principal groups. First are members of the traditional aristocracy, centered on the ruling Al-Khalifa family, who are Arab Sunni Muslims. Second are the Hawala, who are also Sunni but who came to Bahrain from Persia over the last several centuries and who constitute the bulk of the upper classes of Bahraini society, including members of the ruling family, the aristocracy, and the commercial classes. Third are the lower classes,

Shi'a Muslims, who make up 55–70 percent of the population. The lower classes are divided further into Baharna (Bahraini) and 'Ajam (Persian) Shi'as; the 'Ajam migrated to Bahrain in significant numbers only in the last century, while the Baharnas, who are more numerous, are the native descendants of the original inhabitants of Bahrain, the majority of whom live in Bahrain's rural areas. Though constitutionally equal to their Sunni countrymen, Bahraini Shi'as have long complained about the political, economic, and social inequality between the sects that has seen them dominated by the Sunni minority.

The Al-Khalifa family, who migrated from central Arabia (Al-Zubara, a village in today's Qatar) in 1783, seized control of Bahrain after the collapse of Persian influence there, ruling the country since that time. From the outset they imposed Sunni control over the majority Shi'a population and were able to extend their influence throughout the islands.

The modern Bahraini national movement began before the First World War, and it has been influenced by the conflicting sectarian relationships that were exploited by the British and the Al-Khalifa, further dividing the nascent movement. Early in the twentieth century there were no formal governmental structures. The emir, with his own personal guards, kept order, while *Qadhis* (religious judges), appointed by the emir, applied Shari'ah law. Around 1905 two informal structures were established by Emir 'Isa al-Khalifa: the Majlis al-'Urf (Council of Custom), whose basic function was to mediate disputes between merchants, and the *Salfah* (money lending court), which handled pearling disputes. The British residents wanted more order and better organization, especially to deal with the jurisdictions of the British political agent over foreigners. Thus, in 1913 a British Order-in-Council was promulgated, though it was not applied until the end of the First World War, in which the political agent now had complete jurisdiction over foreigners. He also would appoint half of the Majlis al-'Urf while the emir appointed the rest. *Qadhis* were to be appointed in consultation with the political agent, in effect giving the political agent control over the entire judicial system. Consequently, the following years saw a futile attempt by the emir to regain control in which he attempted to elicit the support of tribes and the conservative element in his confrontation with the political agent, who eventually forced him to concede some of his power to his son, Hamed. Eventually, on 26 May 1923, 'Isa was forced to abdicate in favor of Hamed, who was more amenable to British influence. From then on, the British were in complete control over the affairs of Bahrain, and the emir was reduced to a mere figurehead.

During this period the Shi'a community, which was the most discriminated against, particularly as they carried the burden of taxation, benefited from the British administrative reforms, which imposed taxation equally on both religious communities. Some enlightened Bahrainis supported the reforms but argued that these changes should have come from Bahrainis and that a representative council of all Bahrainis should be convened. On 26 October 1923, a meeting of twelve notable and progressive Bahrainis resulted in the formation of the Bahrain National Council. It called for the restoration of 'Isa and granted him the prerogative of abdicating in favor of his son if he chose. They maintained that the Shari'ah and the 'Urf should be the basis of the Bahraini administration rather than only secular civil laws. They also called for the creation of a consultative council for the maintenance of the country's affairs, in which both Shi'as and Sunnis would be represented, and asked that the British should refrain from interference in the internal affairs of the country. They presented these requests to the British agent, who invited their leaders to the headquarters of the British Agency less than two weeks later. He detained the two most important Bahraini activists and banished them to India that same night.[80] Although this represented only one class of Sunnis, mainly prominent merchants and religious leadership, their demands had been mild as they laid the foundations of future political activism in the Bahrain National Movement.

A number of protests took place between 1926 and 1932, mainly by pearl divers. Although they were the economic backbone of the country, pearl divers were the most exploited and lowest-paid workers in a very dangerous occupation. Their problems were exacerbated by the global economic depression of 1929, so much so that in 1932, when they rioted, the emir himself led the police to crack down harshly on the divers, resulting in arrests and many deaths. This was considered to be the first genuine class uprising in Bahraini history.[81]

In 1934–35 the Shi'a community had mass protests, mainly calling for improvements in the legal system and fairness to their community. On 20 December 1934, eight leading Shi'as of Manama, the capital, presented a petition to the emir and the British political resident, Belgrave, asking for a reform of the courts in which legal procedures were to be strictly followed and the specific section of the law cited when people were charged with an offense. Next, since they had limited representation in the municipal councils and Majlis al-'Urf, set up by the emir and the British administration, they should have a proportional representation with the Sunnis, and finally, they should have the right to their own board of education. Belgrave was firmly against conceding to the demands, and eventually he rejected them outright on 29 January 1935. As a result, they decided to carry their petition to the British political agent, Lt. Col. G. Loch, but he refused to alter Belgrave's decision and referred the issue to the emir. The emir viewed this Shi'i demand as a surprising challenge to his authority, because the Shi'is were always passive and supportive of his rule. At the same time, the Shi'i leaders considered their requests to be moderate, legitimate, and not confrontational. Mohamed Rumaihi notes, "It was from this time that [the Shi'as] began to cast about in a search for new allies who shared their aspirations. It was this disappointment which later helped close the gap between Sunnis and Shi'is as they joined forces to lend weight to their political demands."[82]

Thus by mid-1938 there was growing unrest among Bahrainis, regardless of their religious affiliations, often responded to violently by the emir's personal guards and police, who were supported by British administrators. For the first time, a Shi'a-Sunni coalition of some sort began to emerge with clear political demands in which the leaders of both communities got together to discuss the conditions of the country and called for a legislative council that was to be composed of equal Shi'a and Sunni membership chosen in a free election, with the ruler having the right to appoint its speaker. They also called for the replacement of Indian government officials by Bahrainis and, if needed, by Iraqis; the establishment of a modern government bound by law that would be responsible both to the ruler and to the population; transparency in the financial affairs of the administration; the right of the people to examine the emirate's budget; the formation of a Bahraini police force to replace foreigners; the creation of a modern educational system and governmental support for overseas education for Bahrainis; a political newspaper that would encourage free expression and criticize the government; and communication with other political organizations in the Arab world, including exposure to their literature and ideas. Led by notables and merchants, the movement was not confrontational; their call was a mild appeal rather than an intransigent set of demands. However, both the emir and the British resident, Belgrave, rejected the appeals.

On the social level, the second half of the 1930s saw an improvement in the economic conditions of Bahrainis as a result of successful oil exploration in 1932 and the establishment of the Bahrain Petroleum Company. This resulted in an influx of foreign employees, more communication between Bahrain and the rest of the world, and exposure to new ideas. In this climate of change and political turmoil, the first oil workers' strike in the Gulf took place in 1938. At the same time, the reformist events in Dubai and Kuwait filtered through to the politically aware population. Soon open political activism subsided and the intelligentsia moved toward civil society organizations such as clubs and associations.

In 1938 Nadi al-Bahrain was established. While it emphasized sports, its political agenda was clearly anti-British and reformist. A year later al-Nadi al-Ahli (People's Club) was established by the rich Sunni merchants of Manama, who sympathetically followed news of the Egyptian struggle against British control in the 1930s. While this club had no declared political aspirations, it distributed the literature written by Egyptian activists, among which was the literature of the Muslim Brotherhood. In the same year a number of wealthy Shi'a and Sunni merchants, with the support of some of the upper echelon of Bahraini government employees, established the Nadi al-Uroba (Arabism Club), whose basic aim was "the unification of people and the combating of sectarianism in accordance with the principles of Arab nationalism."[83]

The Second World War witnessed a British military buildup in Bahrain, leading to a reduction of political activism due to increased British control and police vigilance to curb club activities, whose basic orientation was the creation of political consciousness, which was translated in this period to mean "the rejection of sectarianism, imperial domination, tribal control and the support of worker's rights."[84] The press and radio became the vehicle for this increased political consciousness, and a number of newspapers and journals were published with this purpose in mind.

In 1953 and 1954, sectarian conflicts began to appear. At the same time, a very well established network of communication among secular activists formed, especially with the increase of educated Bahrainis. In the face of this sectarianism, activists tried to remain neutral by mediating between Shi'as and Sunnis. This gave them the opportunity to put into practice their political ideology, which they had been propagating through their clubs and publications, especially the journal *Sawt al-Bahrain* (Voice of Bahrain). Their leaders were 'Abd al-'Aziz al-Shamlan, the founding president of the Arabism Club, 'Abd al-Rahman al-Bakir, Hassan al-Jashi, 'Ali al-Tajir, and Mahmoud al-Mardi, who were from both sects but had a secular outlook, giving them credibility within both communities. Like the outcast Shi'a, many of the leaders did not come from the traditional Sunni aristocracy, which led the ruling Sunni families to both suspect and resent the newcomers. Thus, some sort of rapprochement between the new reformist Sunnis and the Shi'a community began to appear, bonded further by their fellow Shi'a reformist activists.

The emir and the British both looked unfavorably upon those activities. In September 1954, the Network of the Five held a number of underground meetings, then embarked upon a campaign to create Bahraini consciousness and reject sectarianism. They further established a registry of a hundred people, identified as committed activists, which made this group an organizational cell within a larger network. The authorities responded angrily and threatened action against the upstart group. They called for public meetings in Shi'a mosques, and on October 6, they called for the formation of a unified political front whose aim would be to call for political reforms, elections to follow up these decisions, and the mobilization of popular groups. A week later, another meeting was held in which 120 people were selected to make up a General Assembly, which would elect an eight-member Higher Executive Committee (HEC). The General Assembly was then given the responsibility of becoming the liaison between the HEC and the rest of the population. The HEC was composed of equal numbers of Shi'as and Sunnis and was publicly endorsed at meetings held in mosques of both Sunni and Shi'a sects. Soon the HEC, with its increased public exposure and support, became bolder, calling on the ruler with the following clear set of political demands: the convening of a parliament elected by the people as its only voice in the country, the enactment of a unified penal and civil code for Bahrain, and the creation of a court of appeals whose membership must be from practicing lawyers. Finally, they called for the licensing of professional and workers' unions. They chose a prominent, nonsectarian delegation of leading Sunnis and Shi'as to present these demands to the rulers, who refused to even meet with them.[85]

British intransigence did nothing to quell demands for reform. The combination of the fermenting political demands of the Shi'as for political equality and the agitation of the Sunni merchant class for greater political participation made the political situation volatile. In this atmosphere, a great number of Bahraini students returned home from abroad, where they had been exposed to progressive and Pan-Arabist ideologies. The British were particularly resented because of the Arab-Israeli conflict and their unwillingness to bring about reform; in response, British interests became the subject of strikes by Bahraini workers. The pressure exerted by the striking workers and the growing politicization of society forced the government to act, and so it established a number of committees to study the demands of the opposition. The result was the formation of three councils (health, education, and municipal) that were to be half elected and half appointed. To the government's embarrassment, members of the Higher Executive Committee, formed by 'Abd al-Rahman al-Bakir, a student activist, swept the voting for the Health and Education Council, forcing the government to suspend voting for municipal councils, as they were opposed to the HEC. The councils proved to be unworkable because of conflicts with the government. Al-Bakir was forced to leave the country, and the HEC changed its name after police crackdowns were caused by an HEC-led general strike in protest of the political stalemate. The HEC was replaced by the Committee for National Unity, with 'Abd al-'Aziz al-Shamlan as secretary-general at the end of the general strike. The stalemate between the government and the reform movement remained, and throughout 1955 and 1956 the reform movement tried to force change through a further series of general strikes. These culminated in the return of al-Bakir to Bahrain. He, al-Shamlan, and others were arrested, and their movement was declared illegal.

Political opposition was driven underground by the regime's repression. Despite the repression, there is evidence that numerous Ba'ath, Marxist, and Arab nationalist cells were able to operate in Bahrain at that time. These cells grew, and there emerged radical groups such as the National Liberation Front of Bahrain and the Bahraini branch of the Popular Front for the Liberation of Oman and the Arabian Gulf, in addition to branches of Pan-Arab political groups who permeated society with secret cells. These cells were, nevertheless, small and unable to bring about an end to either British rule or the rule of the Al-Khalifa.

The end of British rule in 1971, with their withdrawal from the Gulf and the formal independence of Bahrain, finally brought about the reform of government structures. Bahrain, upon independence, intended to join the British-originated federation of the Gulf's nine emirates, but it subsequently decided to go it alone. Despite the creation of an administrative council during the turmoil of the 1950s, the executive power of the Al-Khalifa remained supreme. A number of ministries were added to the government, and the Administrative Council was renamed the Council of State. The council became the cabinet, and members were appointed by the sheikh to represent his interests. Local officials, chosen by the sheikh, administered outlying Shi'a areas. Also accompanying independence was the formation of a Constituent Assembly that had as its primary duty the ratification of a new constitution. The assembly consisted of twenty-two members, appointed by the sheikh, and the twelve members of the cabinet. Ten were reformers or nationalists, and fourteen were Shi'as. The members appointed by the sheikh ensured government control over the assembly and the passing of the Al-Khalifa–authored constitution. In the constitution, which was modeled after Kuwait's, Bahrain was described as a hereditary monarchy whose ruler was to be declared on the basis of its forefathers. Bahrain is a monarchy with no democratically elected institutions or political parties. The Al-Khalifa extended family has ruled Bahrain since the late eighteenth century and dominates its society and government. While there is a separation of executive, judicial, and legislative powers, the emir and the National

Assembly are to share legislative functions. The emir can veto any bill passed by the assembly and has the right to appoint cabinet members. He can ratify laws, while those he vetoes are sent to the National Assembly for further review. The thirty-member assembly has the right to question any minister, and ministers are responsible to the assembly. Individual assembly members may initiate legislation, and the assembly, as a whole, must ratify the annual budget. The assembly—except for the concept of hereditary rule—may also challenge any principle of the constitution if a two-thirds majority supports the amendment.

The initial National Assembly included a bloc of populist candidates (including Baʻath, Marxist, socialist, and Arab nationalist elements) whose goal was to broaden the institutions which, they hoped, would eventually lead to Bahraini democracy and involve Bahrain more deeply in Arab affairs. Opposing it was a bloc of conservative and religious leaders and independent members who supported the policies of the emir. The National Assembly was suspended in 1975 because of continuing labor unrest and government fear that the situation might lapse into turmoil similar to that of the 1950s. The government bypassed the assembly and unilaterally imposed a security law to deal with the unrest. In 1975, the assembly was dissolved, and the constitutional principle requiring new elections was suspended. The National Assembly remains suspended and has never reconvened. The emir has never shown a great affinity toward government accountability and seems quite willing to keep governing the country without any popular input into government policies. After the 1990–91 Gulf war, a consultative council was formed, but this move has not eased the strong political tide working for the reinstatement of the assembly.

Bahrain faces an internal challenge from its dispossessed Shiʻa majority. The Shiʻa live mainly in rural villages and are separated from the prosperity that marks the rest of Bahraini society. Beginning in late 1994, isolated acts of violence became more frequent. The Bahraini regime accused Iran of fomenting unrest among the Shiʻa and began arresting leading Shiʻa figures and charging them with dissidence. As one astute observer of Gulf politics analyzed the situation:

> Soon after Bahrain independence in 1971, the Saudis began treating that island . . . as if it was part of its eastern district and soon after, the Iranian revolution of 11 February 1979, Saudi Arabia was concerned with the Shiʻa Islamic tide represented by the revolution . . . in Tehran and began pressing the Bahraini regime—whose Shiʻites make up a huge percentage of its 350,000 population, to isolate the Shiʻites from the political and economic life of the country and exclude them from participating in senior government positions, fearing their sympathy with Iran. In this

unwise action, they pushed the Shiʿas in Bahrain into the lap of Iran. . . . Saudi Wahabism is a social doctrine antagonistic to anything that is not Wahabi and one of the most important features of Wahabism is to regard Shiʿism as totally heretical . . . but instigating the Bahraini Sunni regime . . . and inciting it against the majority Shiʿa population is contrary to the historic class evolution to the intimate Bahraini society . . . the Shiʿas in Bahrain participated in the nationalist movement against Britain during the colonial period. Through this Saudi policy, the social fabric of Bahrain was torn and the Bahraini government, after 26 years of independence, followed a new policy of exiling or expelling its Shiʿa citizens outside the country.[86]

According to Amnesty International's *Annual Report 2000,* the human rights situation in Bahrain has remained grave since the outbreak of mass protests in December 1994, which called for the restoration of democratic rights. Between 1,000 to 1,500 political detainees and prisoners are currently being held, most of them without charge or trial. Torture and ill-treatment, including women and children, remain rife. More than 150 people were convicted after unfair trials before the State Security Court since March 1996, three of whom were sentenced to death.

The threat posed to Bahrain by Iranian attempts to extend influence in the Gulf is unclear. While this is well within the realm of possibility, given the Shiʿa connection and the geopolitical advantage Iran would enjoy by having a puppet state in Bahrain, this scenario is seemingly exploited as part of the division and dissatisfaction that exists in Bahraini society, and serves as a cover for continued oppression. It also provides more ammunition for the American and American-influenced portrayal of Iran, as Bahrain has become a key Gulf ally of the United States and the headquarters of the American Fifth Fleet.

Sheikh ʿIsa Ibn Salman al-Khalifa, the emir of Bahrain, died of a heart attack on 6 March 1999. The emir had ruled the Gulf state since 1961, when he succeeded his father, Sheikh Salman, to the throne, having served as crown prince for three years. Sheikh ʿIsa took the title emir in August 1971, assuming full power when Bahrain achieved independence from Britain that year.[87] Sheikh Hamad bin ʿIsa al-Khalifa, a career soldier, has pledged to continue pro-western policies and work to maintain the stability his father established. Sheikh ʿIsa was renowned for his close links to Britain, whereas Sheikh Hamad, who commanded Bahrain's armed forces, is known to be closer to the princes of Saudi Arabia. Since taking power, Sheikh Hamad has made overtures to Bahrain's Shiʿa population, increasing optimism that a restoration to democracy may well come about under his reign.[88]

Qatar

Like the other Gulf states, Qatar's political development since indepen-dence has focused on the actions of its ruling family, and its economic expansion has resulted from oil wealth. Its development, however, has followed a slightly different path than that of its neighbors, Kuwait and Bahrain, because of differences in social and cultural homogeneity. These differences have resulted in Qatar's political development being marked by greater stability and a general lack of political activity among Qataris. Qatar also "enjoys reasonable relations with Tehran, mainly because it fears Iran could make trouble for the huge North Dome gas field."[89] Qatari society is marked by tremendous homogeneity—the indigenous population is entirely Sunni—and it is bound together by centuries-old social networks that combine with the powerful influence of Wahabism to make it politically and socially stable. Unlike other Gulf states, Qatari society has not emerged from a commercial tradition cen-tered on coastal trade; rather, it has grown out of a Bedouin tradition with its center of influence in the interior.

The tribes migrated to Qatar from the Arabian Peninsula, and among them was the Maadhid, to which the current ruling family—the al-Thanis—belong. First emerging as a powerful force during the intro-duction of Wahabism, the al-Thanis succeeded by tying themselves to the interests of foreign and regional powers who were shaping the region's development. Since the late 1800s, when Kassim al-Thani man-aged to defeat a superior Ottoman force sent to overthrow him, the fam-ily's position has remained unchallenged.

At various times in its history, Qatar has been tied by the al-Thanis to the interests of the Ottoman Empire, the British, and, finally, the Saudis. These linkages resulted from two factors. The first is that Qatar is small, devoid of natural defenses, and lacking the basic capabilities necessary for defending its territorial integrity. Historical enmity between Qatar and its neighbor, Bahrain, caused Qatar to turn to outside powers for protection against al-Khalifa claims. Ultimately, the interplay between the foreign and regional powers prompted the al-Thanis to agree to for-malize their relationship with the British in 1916, making Qatar a British protectorate.

The second reason why the al-Thanis aligned themselves with foreign powers was to cement their influence in Qatar. Indeed, by the time the treaty with Britain was signed, the family's position was secure. They had managed to play off foreign powers against one another to gain the best possible deal for Qatar and, in the process, begun to construct the infrastructure through which they would rule the country into the twenty-first century. When the British government announced it would withdraw from the Gulf in 1971, Qatar did not opt to join the other Gulf emirates in the proposed UAE. This necessitated the formation of some kind of governmental structure, but the structure chosen was in reality no different than the one that had existed under the British. A provisional constitution was drawn up in 1970 and was subsequently amended in 1972 after the succession of Sheikh Khalifa to power. Although it was to be purely a transitional document, it still remains in force. In it, Qatar is described as a democratic Islamic Arab state that derives its laws from the shari'ah. Executive and legislative power lies in the hands of the emir. The constitution, however, provides for the creation of a council of ministers and an advisory council, which are both designed to discuss issues and make recommendations to the emir on legislative matters. Constitutionally, the advisory council should consist of twenty appointed members in addition to the cabinet, but membership was expanded to thirty in 1975. There has never been an election for the council; there has only been one council since the constitution came into effect, and it is regularly extended by emiri decree. The council elects its own president, vice president, and standing committee.

Sheikh Khalifa has been careful to use the composition of the council as a means of extending his personal and familial influence. Members of the merchant community and important tribes hold seventeen of the thirty seats and thereby constitute a majority. The most important constituencies in the state are well represented in the council, and it appears from all accounts that its members are respected and would likely be elected were a free election ever held. The council's reputation speaks well for al-Khalifa's political acumen and evidences popular disinterest in reform in Qatar.

Events in Qatar took a surprising turn in June 1995 when the emir's son, Hamad, apparently with the promise of a U.S.$2.5–5 billion "buyout," deposed the ruling sheikh peacefully. Hamad has moved further along a path to reform than his father, and in 1999, direct elections for the Central Municipality Council took place. Hamad promised a permanent constitution and a freely elected Shura Council; he also enfranchised women who not only voted in the 1999 civic elections but also ran as candidates. The twenty-nine-member Central Municipality Council is responsible for municipal affairs, agriculture, infrastructure, and public health. An estimated 22,000 people registered to vote for the 227 candidates who ran for office. Hamad appears willing to continue Qatar's role as the black sheep of the GCC, by opening even closer ties with Iran and also, surprisingly, with Israel, including a U.S.$5.5 billion natural gas endeavor with an Israeli consortium. Qatar was the first member-state of the GCC to restore diplomatic relations with Iraq, and it has championed an end to UN-sponsored economic sanctions. As a vocal leader in the condemnation of the sanctions and their dramatic effects upon the Iraqi people, Qatar has used both mass media and its diplomatic offices to consistently maintain pressure, even within GCC councils. Qatar has a vocal position supporting the plight of the Iraqi people. Another example of the new trend of liberal political orientations in Qatar is the freedom accorded to media outlets, which occurred after the emir abolished newspaper censorship laws on 9 October 1995. In May 1996 when the ministry of culture was abolished, government radio and television facilities were privatized. One outlet to take advantage of the new freedoms is the successor to the Arabic–BBC *al-Jazirah*, which began broadcasting in Arabic with no government censorship, earning it more credibility as complex and controversial political issues were freely examined. The change allowed for the development of increased freedom of expression in the public sphere of Qatari and Arab political life, but also earned Qatar the wrath of many Arab regimes, including the alienation of many of its friends in the GCC. In November 1997, a number of Arab governments, including Saudi Arabia and Egypt, "boycotted a United States backed business conference in Qatar designed to cement the ailing Middle East peace process."[90] The deposed sheikh has been an honored guest in GCC capitals, and the Saudis, in particular, have spoken of the need to bring the new sheikh "in line." However, no action appears to have been taken, and the steps that Hamad has taken in Qatar's foreign relations appear to be more cautiously followed by the rest of the GCC states, who cannot afford to isolate themselves from the Middle East's two economic giants. He appeared to be breaking new ground once again when on 8 August 1999 he became the first GCC head of state to visit the Palestinian territories. A rapprochement between the Palestinians and the Gulf states, which became angry with the Palestinians for supporting Iraq during the 1991 Gulf war, would again reintegrate the Arab world.

Oman

The Sultanate of Oman stretches over some of the most strategic territory in the Middle East. At the entrance to the Gulf, the Strait of Hormuz lie just off the tip of Oman's Ras Musandam. The harsh climate and geography of the region have determined much of Oman's history, and its development has been constrained by both sea and desert. Historically, Oman was not a wealthy state, because of its hostile climate and accompanying lack of resources as well as its poor and often corrupt rulers. Throughout much of their history, Omanis had been led by an elected imam. Most Omanis belong to the Ibadhi sect of Islam, whose leader (the imam) heads the state. The present dynasty (the Al Bu Sa'ids) dates back to 1744, when the family managed to expel Persian influence. Trying to extend the influence of the family to the interior and southern reaches of Oman proved to be difficult—a fact that has colored much of Oman's political history. The family has managed to retain control, despite opposition from within and from early Wahabi interference from Saudi Arabia, and despite the separation of the functions of the imamate and the sultanate, which occurred in 1783. The sultanate, the seat of real political power in Oman, has remained in the hands of the Al Bu Sa'ids, while the imamate is in the hands of the Hinawi tribe.

This arrangement, brought about largely through British influence in the 1800s, has had real and dramatic effects on Oman's politics. The sultanate had to fight very hard to extend its influence inland and into the southern reaches of the state while trying to prove itself the real leadership of Oman at the expense of the imamate. The Hinawi have, until recently, resisted Al Bu Sa'id attempts at control of Oman—even going so far as to apply for Arab League recognition for the interior of Oman in 1954. Although the movement was defeated and the sultanate managed to increase its influence among outlying tribes, the opposition to the sultanate from the imamate has not ceased.

As with other Gulf states, the discovery of oil marked a turning point in Omani history. The rapid influx of oil revenues, after oil was discovered in 1962, led to societal demands for modernization. By 1968, oil revenues were such that Sultan Sa'id Ibn Teimour began to put together a development and planning program. He was, however, a conservative man, determined that whatever progress was made should be undertaken slowly. At the time, Oman was one of the most underdeveloped areas in the Gulf: it lacked hospitals (it had one hospital plus a number of dispensaries), schools (it had three schools with 100 students), and doctors, and its infant mortality rate was among the highest in the world. Not only was the sultan conservative; he was authoritarian as well. His inability to meet the needs of Omanis resulted in the formation of the Dhufar Liberation Movement in 1964, whose goal was to free southern Oman from the rest of the sultanate. Though the rebellion in Dhufar lasted well into the 1970s, the political situation changed with the overthrow of the sultan in July 1970 by his son Qabus Ibn Sa'id, who had been under house arrest since returning from school in England. Upon his assumption of power, Qabus pledged to modernize government structures and the economy and to liberalize society. While liberalization and modernization proceeded in fits and starts through the 1970s, Qabus managed to increase his personal influence within the ruling family and within Oman itself. By the end of the Dhufar rebellion in 1975, he had managed to extend the power of the sultanate throughout the entire state—an accomplishment never achieved by his father. While Sultan Qabus was also autocratic and ruled without any sort of consultative body, he was more open than his father had been. He ruled on the basis of personal and tribal relationships that had developed before he came to power and which he continued to foster after coming to power. As a result, during the 1970s, he succeeded in introducing reforms of the basic economic and social infrastructures of Oman.

The situation changed in 1981 when the Sultanate of Oman's State Consultative Council (SCC) was established after Sultan Qabus formed a small ministerial committee to report on the feasibility of introducing a formalized consultative body. Initially, the SCC had forty-three appointed members, although that number was expanded to fifty-five in 1983. The original SCC committee selected members, and names were then forwarded to the sultan, who has accepted every nomination forwarded to him. The SCC president is the only SCC member directly chosen by the sultan and has always been a member of the cabinet. Of the fifty-five members, nineteen are members of the government, and the Chamber of Commerce elects a further nineteen. The remainder represent each of Oman's seven geographic regions, and their numbers vary according to the population of the region.

The SCC has developed into a government watchdog, and its members are encouraged to criticize government policy at every opportunity. Ministers, chosen by the sultan and tending to represent all regions of Oman, are held responsible to the SCC and are expected to appear before it when called. The government cannot be subject to a vote of no confidence, and no one can question the ultimate rule of the sultan. The success of the SCC in fostering unity among the population of Oman has encouraged the government to further the people's participation in politics. On 18 November 1990, Sultan Qabus announced the formation of a Majlis al-Shura. This announcement came at a time of increased Islamic activism. The *New York Times* called Sultan Qabus "America's most reliable ally in the Persian Gulf."[91] Thus the creation of the Omani Consultative Council attempted to curry favor with the sultan's foreign ally, the United States, and undermine activists by increasing the appearance of political participation in the country.[92] The invasion of Kuwait and the Gulf war led GCC leaders to seek more extensive domestic support and stronger external alliances. This necessity made it attractive to Gulf leaders to increase political participation to varying degrees. Although the most recent institution of political participation in the Gulf, coming after the Kuwaiti national assembly (1963) and the Bahraini national assembly (1973–75), it has been the first to incorporate women into its membership, when the sultan appointed two women as regional representatives in 1994.

While balancing this need, GCC leaders must avoid radical changes that do not correspond with religious practices and traditional culture, and look to the councils in an incremental fashion, which still allows for the stability of governments in the region.[93] The new constitution of November 1997 paved the way for the creation of an appointed state council, which when combined with the Majlis al-Shura would form a new supreme consultative council entitled the Council of Oman. Oman conducted advisory council elections in September 2000, becoming the second Gulf state to allow its citizens to vote for councilors following Qatar—albeit only to advisory positions. In the September 2000 election, the number of women voters trebled, and in the 2002 council elections, citizens will be allowed to nominate their own candidates, as opposed to voting for sanctioned candidates, which will lead to a more legitimate opposition. A substantive program to reform the economy has accompanied political reforms, and over the past twenty-five years the sultanate has been able to transform its economy from traditional to modern through the development of its petroleum resources. Oil has come to generate 37 percent of Oman's GNP, 75 percent of the state's revenues, and 76 percent of the sultanate's total exports. In an effort to diversify its economy and reduce its dependence on oil, the sultanate has invested in a developmental infrastructure to take advantage of its large reserves of natural gas. Exports began in 2000, and Oman has estimated proven reserves of 16 trillion cubic meters. The concentration upon economic development has led Oman to focus its foreign policy on economic contacts with other nations around the globe, manifested in its championing for the establishment of the Indian Ocean Group for Economic Cooperation. Initially advocated by Mauritania, this economic bloc would increase cooperation and stimulate growth between economies as diverse as South Africa, Singapore, Kenya, Australia, New Zealand, Indonesia, Malaysia, Sri Lanka, Mozambique, Madagascar, Yemen, and India.[94]

United Arab Emirates

The UAE was formed as a federation of the Omani coast emirates on 2 December 1971. These emirates and others had previously attempted to unify under British auspices but failed. However, when the British government announced in 1968 its intention of ending its control in the Gulf by 1972, the rulers of Abu Dhabi and Dubai announced their intention to unite. Soon other lower Gulf leaders expressed their desire to join the union, and by December 1971, Abu Dhabi, Dubai, Sharjah, 'Ajman, Umm al-Qaywayn, and Fujairah had joined to form the United Arab Emirates. Finally, Ras al-Khaymah joined the federation on 10 February 1972. A provisional constitution was promulgated for the UAE in 1971 and was declared permanent on 20 May 1996. Abu Dhabi was also declared the official permanent capital of the UAE.

Despite the ethnic and social ties that bind the people of the UAE together, the emirates differ vastly in size, wealth, and economic capabilities. Historically, Abu Dhabi (the richest of the emirates) and Dubai (the most populated) have dominated the union. Abu Dhabi's Sheikh Zayid Ibn Sultan al Nahyan has served as the UAE's only president and is considered one of the most powerful and respected leaders in the Gulf region. Dubai's ruler, Sheikh Rashid Ibn Sa'id al Maktum, was the UAE's vice president, and from 1979 until his death in 1991 he also held the post of prime minister. His son, Sheikh Maktum, assumed all of his father's posts. The smaller emirates are plagued by their limited size and population and insufficient economic bases, which limit their ability to influence the direction of the UAE's policy.

Theoretically, there is a separation of powers in the UAE. The executive consists of the Supreme Council, the presidency, and the Council of Ministers. The Federal Supreme Council, composed of the sheikhs of each emirate, is the highest executive body in the federation and is chaired by the president. Each sheikh has one vote on issues before the council; a simple majority suffices on ordinary matters, but five of the seven members must approve substantial matters, and two of those votes must come from Abu Dhabi and Dubai. Therefore, although the power of Abu Dhabi and Dubai has been constitutionally balanced to some extent, they remain in a position to dominate the union. They dominate also because of the tremendous power vested in the president. He signs laws, convenes sessions of the Supreme Council, appoints the prime minister, deputy prime minister, and cabinet, can end the term of any and all ministers, and can veto all motions brought before him. Sheikh Zayid's reelection at the end of each five-year term and the powers vested in the presidency reflect both his role and Abu Dhabi's position as the most powerful of the seven member states. This concentration of power has not gone unopposed; one of the reasons Ras al-Khaymah did not join initially was because of the veto power that would be possessed by Zayid and Rashid. Sheikh Saqr, ruler of Ras al-Khaymah, has been outspoken on this and other issues concerning the dominance of the two largest emirates, but, on the whole, the sheikhs of the smaller members seem to have accepted the dominance of Abu Dhabi and Dubai.

Differences do exist among the sheikhs, however. The UAE is a federal state, and the constitution gives the federal government exclusive jurisdiction over defense, finance, foreign affairs, the use of the armed forces (both externally and internally), and other areas. Defense policy was not unified until 1978, and despite the unification, Dubai's forces are not fully integrated with the federal defenses. All powers not included in the constitution are controlled by the emirates, which have, through this arrangement, retained many of the political and economic institutions that existed prior to union. Although the powers of the federal government are explicitly stated, this did not prevent it from trying to expand its areas of jurisdiction.

The leaders of the smaller emirates must carefully balance their federal commitments with their local ones. The sheikhs are hereditary rulers who must rely on tribal support to stay in power. They must satisfy local needs in order to secure a local base of support, a difficult feat in a federal setting where federal policies often infringe on local interests. Such was the case in Sharjah in November 1972 when Sheikh Sultan took a move to merge all his local institutions to the federal institutions.

Sheikh Khalid was killed in a coup d'état on 25 January 1972.[95] The federal government proved its willingness to interfere in the internal affairs of the emirates when, on 17 June 1987, Sheikh 'Abdul 'Aziz al-Qassimi moved to depose his younger brother, Sheikh Sultan, as ruler of Sharjah because of financial profligacy and Sharjah's $1 billion debt. The Supreme Council of the UAE rejected the move and refused to recognize 'Abdul 'Aziz's rule of Sharjah. The crisis ended when Sheikh Sultan agreed to reorganize Sharjah's administrative structure.

The federal national council is a consultative body of forty members who are proportionately distributed among the emirates. Abu Dhabi and Dubai have eight representatives, Sharjah and Ras al-Khaymah have six each, and the remaining emirates each have four. A ruler is allowed to choose the members from his emirate. The majority are representatives of the commercial classes, and many from Dubai, Sharjah, and Ras al-Khaymah come from prominent merchant families. Members from the other emirates tend to represent the dominant tribes of the emirate.

The UAE's main foreign concern is its defense. Iran claims significant portions of UAE territory, especially several strategic Gulf islands— Tunb and Abu Musa—which Iran actually occupied on 30 November 1971. The UAE makes no secret of its willingness to allow large numbers of U.S. and British troops on its soil in the event of possible conflict with a more powerful neighbor.

CHAPTER 11

The Republic of Yemen

On 22 May 1990, the Yemen Arab Republic (YAR, or North Yemen) and the People's Democratic Republic of Yemen (PDRY, or South Yemen) declared a union of their two states in order to form the Republic of Yemen. Translating this act into lasting stability has been difficult due to differences over power-sharing arrangements that have surfaced between the former leaders of the two states and subsequent escalation to internecine violence and even civil war. Only force of arms brought about unity, and although the victorious leaders of the north have introduced measures to placate the south, apprehension is still apparent. Cognizant of the fact that for over 150 years the two regions developed along separate paths, expression here will be given to the uniqueness of each.

The Republic of Yemen occupies the southwest corner of the Arabian Peninsula. It is bordered by Saudi Arabia to the north, Oman to the east, the Gulf of Aden to the south, and the Red Sea to the west. Excluding the empty desert quarter (Rub al-Khali), its land area is 555,000 square kilometers, although large portions of the country's borders have only recently been demarcated. Agreements between Yemen and Oman and Yemen and Saudi Arabia have enabled the Yemeni government to settle border disputes. The country's climate and geography vary widely. Along the Red Sea coast are the Tihama lowlands, where the terrain is sandy with generally sparse vegetation. The central highlands rise abruptly from the coastal desert area, serrated by mountain ranges rising to 10,000 feet above sea level, including the highest mountains in the Arabian Peninsula, Jebel Sha'ib around Sana'a and Samara in Ta'z. The valleys of the rugged mountain ranges are fertile and covered with dense vegetation. Along the Red Sea, the climate is arid, moderating toward the central highlands where temperate conditions and high precipitation are found. The climatic diversity has favored a variety of crops, ranging from tropical fruits to temperate nuts. Agriculture is the main occupation in the country, and most Yemenis live in the terraced fields along the mountains of the central highlands, although pastoral nomadism and fishing villages also exist.

In the settled agricultural highlands, society is tribal, with tribes forming important social, cultural, and political entities closely linked to definitive territories. They are hierarchically organized, with the highest structure being the confederation or association of tribes. There are three major confederations of Yemeni tribes in the Viz highland region: the Hamdan federations (Hashid and Bakil in the northern and central parts of Yemen) and the Madhhif federation in the southern part. These social blocks constitute important bases of common societal interaction. In Yemen, like many other tribal societies, tribalism is conceived in terms of honor (Sharaf, 'ardh, wajh), and action is called for when tribal honor is undermined, such as when territorial integrity is threatened. This possibility of mobilizing large groups of people has special political significance, which political leaders in the country and other foreign forces have exploited for their own ends. Although the tribes command the allegiance of many people, the communities in the urban centers and along the coast, descending from generations of officials, traders, craftsmen, and slaves, are mainly detribalized.

The arrival of Islam in Yemen, as in much of the region, had a profound impact. Except for a few Jews, Christians, and Hindus, all Yemenis are Muslims. The Zaydis, one of the three main branches of Shi'as, have been the politically dominant group, a fact viewed with uneasiness by the more numerous Shafi'is of the Sunni sect. Also, there is a less prominent group, the Isma'ilis, from a different branch of the Shi'as—small in number but politically powerful. Another important consequence of religious division is the group of Sayyids, who are descendants of the Prophet. The Sayyids enjoy special privileges and status, in both social and economic terms, and as a consequence they have played a key role in the politics and administration of the country.

The southern Arabian Peninsula has been home to a number of kingdoms, the last of which was the Himyar, during the pre-Islamic period. These kingdoms prospered because of the caravan trade in luxury commodities for which southern Arabia became famous during the Greek and Roman eras. Before these kingdoms collapsed, as a result of the discovery of an alternative route to the Orient, they bestowed some enduring cultural hallmarks on Yemeni society, such as its system of terraced agriculture. The Islamic faith readily won converts in Yemen, to the joy of the Prophet, who chose to send his cousin and son-in-law, 'Ali ibn

Abi Talib, and other close companions to proselytize in the region. The message of Islam soon provided a sort of cultural unity among the Yemenis, but it also introduced new factionalism following the death of the Prophet when the Islamic world was divided over the question of the succession. The division gave rise to the two main Islamic sects, Sunni and Shi'a (including its several minority factions). The implication of this development for Yemen was the rise of the Zaydi and the Isma'ili (or Fatimid) version of Shi'a as contenders for power against the Sunni Umayyad and Abbasid caliphs. More significantly, the Islamization of Yemen led to the emergence of the Zaydi imamate.

In the sixteenth century, the port city of Aden became a focal point of imperialist competition due to its strategic location on the Red Sea. The Ottoman Turks, warding off the Portuguese and other European intruders, captured Aden from its sultan in 1538. Almost three centuries later, Napoleon's military campaign in Egypt (1798) rekindled European interest in Aden. By 1802, the British government had signed a friendship treaty with the sultan of Lahej, and in 1839, Aden was incorporated into the British Empire under the administration of the colonial government in India. The increasing maritime traffic, driven by trade and improvements in navigation and the opening of the Suez Canal in 1869, made Aden even more vital, and the British, spurred by a vision of further conquests and riches, began to consolidate their position in South Yemen. Aden was declared a crown colony in 1937, bringing the city and its hinterland under the supervision of the Colonial Office in London.

By the turn of the twentieth century, the Zaydi imams in the central highlands confronted the Ottomans with resistance to their central authority. In June 1904, a new Zaydi imam, Yahya ibn Muhammad Hamid al-Din al-Rassi, received the bay'a (oath of allegiance) from the Zaydi leaders. This accession had an immense influence on highland Yemen. Initially, the sway of the imamate was limited, since Yemen remained nominally part of the Ottoman Empire. In 1918, however, this changed when Imam Yahya declared the country a sovereign and independent kingdom following the defeat of Turkey by the Allies in the First World War. With the declaration of independence, Yahya extended his claim to other areas that had previously been outside his control, including British Aden and its surrounding areas (South Yemen). The imam refused to recognize the territorial agreements between Britain, Turkey, and local Arab chiefs, particularly the Anglo-Turkish boundary agreement of 1905, which formally delineated the frontier between the south and the north. Yahya attempted to evict the British by force, but failed in his bid, and after a concentrated bombardment of towns by

British planes, the imam was compelled to withdraw his forces to the 1905 boundary. His government was highly autocratic, and he survived several challenges to his position by playing various tribal factions against one another and by isolating the country from the outside world.

Yahya's autocratic rule and persistence in isolating Yemen earned him the resentment of many, especially those who had studied in Iraq and Egypt. Soon the discontented gathered in Aden, where a subversive political organization—the Free Yemenis—was born in 1944. The number of plotters against Yahya increased until, on 17 February 1948, the imam was shot to death while traveling in a car a few miles outside Sana'a. 'Abdullah al-Wazir, the mastermind of the assassination, was then declared imam with the support of the Free Yemenis. However, Crown Prince Ahmad, with the help of several tribal leaders, attacked and overran Sana'a, and barely four weeks after the death of his father, Ahmad was proclaimed imam. Ahmad then wreaked vengeance on his opponents. 'Abdullah al-Wazir was publicly beheaded, as were a score of others who had supported the coup.[1]

In administering the imamate, Ahmad generally followed in his father's footsteps. He ruled until he passed away after several days' illness on 18 September 1962. His son, Crown Prince Mohammed al-Badr, succeeded him at a time when resentment against the regime had escalated greatly. The Free Yemenis had never given their support to Ahmad, and they continued to oppose his regime. On 26 September 1962, a military revolt was staged, led by a clandestine organization formed ten months earlier. It was modeled after the Egyptian Free Officers' Movement, which had taken over royalist Egypt a decade earlier. The commander of the Royal Guard, Col. 'Abdullah al-Sallal, headed the coup and declared a republic. He became its first president and allied the new regime with that of the United Arab Republic as a vanguard of Arab nationalism, espousing an ideology of modernization against the reactionism and monarchy of the royal regime. The supporters of the royalist regime turned to Saudi Arabia, and the Arab cold war came to dominate Yemeni politics as the republican regime, whose survival was completely dependent on Egyptian forces, engulfed Yemen in a bloody five-year civil war.

The Republican Era in North Yemen

The opposing parties in the civil war received backing from foreign governments. Egypt supported the republicans and had troops in Yemen until 1970, while Saudi Arabia, many Gulf monarchies, and Jordan supported the royalists out of the fear that republican movements might spread to their own states. The British, who still held South Yemen, also supported the imam. In the midst of the civil war, it was virtually impossible for President al-Sallal to build a viable modern infrastructure; his influence was limited to towns, villages, and some territory in the southern part of the Yemen Arab Republic. In the wake of the Egyptian defeat, in the June 1967 war with Israel, and at the Khartoum Arab Summit Conference of August and September 1967, Egypt and Saudi Arabia agreed to withdraw their troops from Yemen.[2] The withdrawal of Egyptian forces led to the collapse of al-Sallal's presidency on 4 November 1967. A power struggle ensued between moderates and radicals represented by the National Democratic Front. The moderates, mainly Zaydis, emerged victorious, which enhanced the process of reconciliation with the royalists, who were also primarily Zaydis. The radicals, on the other hand, were Shafi'is, and this rapprochement among the Zaydis returned Yemeni politics to the traditional Zaydi versus Shafi'i politics of earlier eras.

A republican council replaced the president, with Abd al-Rahman al-Iryani emerging as the most prominent leader. However, the council was still unable to exert effective control over the countryside, as various sheikhs continued to hold sway over the tribalized army as well as the central government. Nonetheless, al-Iryani was able to bring significant changes to the state building process in Yemen. Some institutions hastily set up by the Egyptians were strengthened, and new ones were founded, such as the Central Bank and the Central Planning Organization. The inability of the regime to deal with many problems facing the country began to tax the people's faith in the republican council, and on 13 June 1974, a bloodless coup ended the regime and inaugurated an era of military involvement in politics.

The coup was led by Col. Ibrahim al-Hamdi, who had served previous governments in both military and civilian capacities. By virtue of his traditional training as a Qadhi or religious judge, and his military training as an officer, al-Hamdi's predisposition was to support a strong state. Consequently, his move to extend the central government's power brought him into conflict with the sheikhs. He improved relations with the south, which angered the Saudis and their tribal allies. To compensate for the resulting loss of support, he maneuvered to incorporate the modernist radicals. However, these attempts to stabilize Yemen were cut short by al-Hamdi's assassination in 1977.

Col. Ahmad Hussein al-Ghashmi, who succeeded al-Hamdi, quickly overturned the rapprochement with the south and purged those loyal to the previous regime. Among the changes he introduced was the appointment of a ninety-nine-member People's Constituent Assembly

(PCA) in February 1978, an institution dominated by urban elements. Then, on 20 June 1978, al-Ghashmi was assassinated by a briefcase bomb. A four-person Republican Council was created, paving the way for 'Ali 'Abdullah Saleh to emerge as president, a position he has held ever since.

Although many doubted the new leader's ability to tackle the problems facing the country, Saleh has proved the pessimists wrong. Over time, he has enhanced the state's capacity both in the center and in the countryside. The government has also extended its authority into the traditional strongholds of the large semiautonomous tribes, occasionally through harsh crackdowns on tribal challenges and protests. Further, the armed forces have been reformed, enlarged, and reequipped with Soviet and American support.

Stark evidence of Saleh's strength can be found in his elimination of the threat posed by the leftist National Democratic Front (NDF). Throughout the 1970s, this movement increasingly challenged the government in Sana'a, until open conflict broke out in early 1980; Saleh's forces were unable to quell the revolt until 1982.

Independence in South Yemen

Although British rule gave much leeway to traditional Yemeni administration, it failed to solicit the cooperation of all tribes. A number of revolts occurred between 1936 and 1959, but the British were successful in crushing all dissent. Discontent with the status quo was then channeled into an anticolonialist movement that ultimately drove the British from South Yemen and toppled the power of the traditional tribal elite. Popular resistance to the constitutional route to South Yemeni independence envisaged by the British government—leaving intact the power of the largely pro-British traditional elite—was stronger than in many other British colonies for three reasons: first, the indelible association between British colonialism and the traditional Yemeni rule led to strong feelings of resentment toward London; second, British involvement in the creation of the state of Israel in 1948 and in the Suez crisis of 1956 did much to discredit its power and authority; and third, the growing popularity of Arab nationalism—personified by Gamal Abdel Nasser—finally provided a unity previously lacking in the South Yemeni anticolonial struggle.

In an attempt to appease growing pressures in the region, particularly those of Arab nationalism, the British initiated a series of discussions in 1954 with sheikhs and sultans interested in forming a federation of Arab emirates of the South. This autonomous entity would have been tied to Britain by treaty, governed by a Yemeni legislative council (albeit in name only), and protected by the British army. A mass boycott of legislative council elections in 1956 and again in 1964 led to constitutional talks concerning the incorporation of Aden into an enlarged South Arabian Federation. Despite British efforts, nationalist demands for immediate independence grew louder and more organized; political efforts were often led by the Aden Trade Union Congress (ATUC) and military efforts by the nascent National Front for the Liberation of Occupied South Yemen. The nationalists won international support for independence in the United Nations in 1963 and again in 1965. British efforts in the summer of 1965 failed to co-opt the accommodationist forces within the national movement, and conditions continued to deteriorate until May 1967 when Aden's new high commissioner, Sir Humphrey Trevelyan, announced that Britain would grant South Yemen independence on 9 January 1968. With independence at hand, nationalist forces—the NF and the Front for the Liberation of Occupied South Yemen—began to compete for supremacy. The ensuing civil war resulted in the triumph of the NF, a Marxist-oriented socialist movement, which entered into final negotiations with the departing British. On 30 November 1967, the independent People's Republic of South Yemen was established. The National Front and its successors—the United Political Organization of the National Front (1975–78) and the Yemeni Socialist Party (YSP, 1978)—retained tight control over the apparatus of power in the newly independent country. Only two other organized political forces were tolerated (both having ideologies consistent with those of the NF): the Popular Vanguard Party (a Ba'athist party) and the Popular Democratic Union (a Communist party). Both were subsequently co-opted within the ruling structure, joining the National Front–dominated United Political Organization in October 1975 and remaining with the organization when it became the Yemeni Socialist Party three years later.

The National Front was a coalition of Arab nationalists and trade unionists who had support from both urban and rural Yemenis, though not among the tribal elites. It was anti-British and also anti-traditional elites, and many within it favored the union of all of Yemen. Divisions in the NF began to show as early as 1965. One group, heavily influenced by Nasserism and upholding social-democratic Arab nationalist ideals, successfully came to dominate the party. A second group emerged consisting primarily of NF cadres fighting inside the country whose ideological outlook had been radicalized by the experience of the armed struggle and whose position had grown increasingly distant from the formal leadership of the NF. These divisions were brought to a head in

1966, when Egyptian pressure led to the merger of the NF with another Yemeni and Egyptian-influenced nationalist group, the Organization for the Liberation of the Occupied South Yemen (OLOS), forming the Front for the Liberation of Occupied South Yemen (FLOSY). The second, more radical wing was against unity, opposing the program and the composition of FLOSY, particularly its inclusion of sultans, princes, sheikhs, and members of the Adeni elite. Amid strong party discord, NF leaders signed the merger in 1966. Continued internal opposition to what was called foreign interference in Yemeni affairs led to a reshuffle of NF leadership, resulting in eventual domination by the radical forces. These forces succeeded in defeating FLOSY in a civil war that accompanied the withdrawal of the British so that, upon independence, the leftist version of the NF established itself as the sole governing power in South Yemen.

Despite its success in achieving independence, the NF continued to be plagued by internal dissension over the means of alleviating the economic and political problems facing the nascent country. The army, in particular, opposed not only the land reform policies of the leftists but also their notion of militia formation, which would have challenged the army's privileged position. Less than two weeks after the Fourth Congress of the National Front in March 1968, where leftist leaders shored up their political strength, the army launched a coup, claiming it was saving the country from communism. Qahtan al-Sha'abi, who had been appointed president in 1967 for a two-year term by the NF General Command, was reinstated as leader. However, tribal dissension within army factions soon led to a second coup, only two months later, which forced al-Sha'abi to resign. This period in South Yemeni history has become known as the Corrective Step of 22 June 1969. Although the party and state apparatuses were now firmly in the control of the leftist wing of the NF, the party had not yet developed the ideology, organization, and trained cadres necessary for the transformation of South Yemeni society. Nor had it yet solved the problems associated with tribalism, underdevelopment, hostile neighbors, and stability.

In the decade following the Corrective Step, the NF underwent a structural transformation of its own, with the aim of rendering the organization ready and able to act as the socialist leader of the Yemeni masses. In March 1972, at the party's Fifth Congress, several bylaws were adopted, including scientific socialism (which has in practice meant a sort of eclectic Marxism); the struggle against imperialism, Zionism, and reaction; democratic centralism, collective leadership, and the purging of counterrevolutionary and decadent forces; and a new centralist structure based on the communist model. In other words, the measures adopted at the Fifth Congress were meant to signify the NF's readiness to embark on a "national democratic stage of the revolution," within which the political preconditions for South Yemen's continued progress would be established, and the NF would become prepared for final evolution into a bona fide vanguard party. The transition of the United Political Organization–National Front continued for three years until, in October 1978, the Yemeni Socialist Party transcended the NF.

Upon independence, South Yemen was left virtually devoid of an organized civil service through which government policies could be enacted. The British and Indian colonial officials who had occupied most middle- and upper-ranking government administrative positions left the country upon independence, and others followed after the Corrective Step. These changes, and the general lack of educated cadres in the country, left South Yemen with few civil servants who were not either corrupt, from elite backgrounds, or otherwise politically unreliable due to service with the prior colonial administration. The service was thoroughly purged, and a new system of hiring by qualification and promotion by merit was adopted. These and other measures proved effective in building a relatively large and efficient government bureaucracy.

Theoretically, the Yemeni Socialist Party (YSP) formulated revolutionary policy and ensured that the state implemented it. This relationship was enshrined in the constitution; there was an overlap of party/state membership; the state bureaucracy was monitored and controlled by the party bureaucracy; and mass organizations served to integrate party and state. Although South Yemeni party and state leadership were theoretically two parts of a single system, tensions between party and state leadership constituted a source of political instability. In addition to party-state tensions, problems of an internal nature plagued the YSP, despite the rhetoric of party unity since the Corrective Step of 1969. Notable among these were the execution of the former president, Salem Rubayi' 'Ali, in June 1978; the sustained power struggle between three liberation-era figures—'Ali Nasser Muhammad, 'Abd al-Fatah Isma'il (exiled 1980–84), and 'Ali Antar—that followed Rubayi' 'Ali's overthrow and continued until January 1986; and the January 1986 civil war, which saw Muhammad deposed, Isma'il and Antar dead, and the emergence of new party and government leadership.

Political instability within the PDRY could be traced to five main causes. One was ideological differences: what the goals and tactics of the revolution should or should not be. A second involved tension between the ideology of the party leadership and pragmatism of day-to-day executive officers. A third involved the persistence of tribal and other subnational loyalties, which were often manipulated to engender political support. Fourth, regional and international involvement in PDRY affairs—whether Soviet, Cuban, or Saudi—fomented disputes. Finally, personal conflicts within the PDRY led to dissension, and sometimes violent repression, within the ranks of the party.

The Tortuous Road to Unity

Although Yemeni unity was supported by the YAR and the PDRY, and despite North Yemen's support for South Yemen's liberation struggle, the gap between the two countries widened following South Yemen's independence. Reasons for this include the north's harboring of the remnants of FLOSY and other defeated groups as well as dissident splinters of the NF. This fact, combined with the ongoing disputes concerning their shared border and control of Kamaran Island, led to a Saudi-fomented war in 1972. A cease-fire was soon agreed on, but rapprochement between the two Yemens was stalled by the profound differences in ideological orientation. The 1977 assassination of the north's pro-unity president, Col. Ibrahim al-Hamdi, only worsened the situation, and the 1979 assassination of the north's pro-Saudi president, Ahmad Hussein al-Ghashmi, prompted a full-scale war. In February 1979, National Democratic Front guerrillas, in opposition to the YAR and supported by the South Yemeni regime, advanced into North Yemen. Fighting lasted only a short time, and a new unity agreement, reached through negotiations, was announced in March 1979.

In 1981, a draft constitution for unity was declared, though ideological differences proved insurmountable. The 1988 war in South Yemen virtually wiped out all of the ideological hard-liners remaining in the south; thereafter, South Yemen adopted a more pragmatic position on the unity question. In May 1988, an agreement for joint oil exploration in the Ma'areb (north) and Shabua (south) border zones defused potential conflict over the border oil deposits. On 30 November 1989, North Yemen's president, Col. 'Ali 'Abdullah Saleh, visited Aden and negotiated an agreement to merge the two states within six months of the approval of the 1981 draft constitution by both parliaments. Preparing the ground for unification on 22 January 1989, Saleh visited the United States and was able to convince George Bush that unity would bring about an end to terrorism. Saleh said, "I guarantee that all kinds of terrorism from the regime in the south will cease with unification; however, if division were to continue I could not guarantee that terrorism would no longer be with us. . . . I told King Fahd in February that we will end the border controversies between us with unification."[3] With fears allayed, unification took place on 22 May 1990.

Political System Laid Down
by the First Constitution of United Yemen

Sana'a is the capital of the new republic, and the first constitution of the Republic of Yemen established a presidential council as well as a parliament, which would serve as the highest legislative body. The presidential council had five members who were elected by the parliament through secret ballot to five-year terms, and the council would then elect the president from its membership. Parliament was to be elected for four-year terms by all citizens eighteen years and older. The council of ministers was the highest executive and administrative organ of the state; it was composed of the prime minister and his deputies and ministers who were appointed by the prime minister in consultation with the presidential council and approved by parliament. The constitution guaranteed fundamental human rights declared in the UN Charter, including political freedom and equality for all citizens. The first cabinet of the new republic, headed by Haidar Abu-Bakr al-Attas (the last president of the PDRY) had thirty-nine members, twenty-two from the south and seventeen from the north. The presidential council, headed by 'Ali 'Abdullah Saleh (formerly the president of the YAR), had two members from the north and two from the south. The parliament of the new republic had 301 members, 159 from the north, 111 from the south, and 31 elected at large. Article 39 of the constitution guarantees a multiparty system, and article 3 of the "political parties code" of 1991 reaffirmed civil rights for Yemeni citizens, including the freedom of association.

Before unification, the south had been a one-party state, and political parties were banned altogether in the north. Only the GNP movement, which formed under Saleh in August 1982, was an organized entity at the time of unification. Created as an umbrella organization for all activist groups, it included the Muslim Brotherhood, liberal reformers, and Ba'athists in its ranks. The Muslim Brotherhood became the Islah Party with the move toward unification and political freedoms. A well-known analyst of Yemeni political affairs, Riad Najib el-Rayyes, described the decision to lift the ban on political parties in Yemen and the uncertainty and inexperience of the process within the state:

> Lifting the constitutional ban on political parties did not result in the citizens exercising "this right" or the political parties practicing "this role" actively and sufficiently. The development of a Yemeni multiparty political system has faced a number of obstacles. The major stumbling block has been the social stratification within Yemeni society, whether it is sectarian or tribally based. Some of the obstacles are connected to the ability

[or lack thereof] of the parties due to their limited political experience, their structural formations, as well as the often oppressive setting of the Yemeni political scene. This oppressive setting controls most active politicians and allows for the minor dictators who have emerged on the Yemeni stage since the [1962] revolution. After a quarter of a century there has been no experimentation with democracy, in either the north or the south.[4]

Yemeni society, in el-Rayyes's view, was not ready for such a dynamic political culture after thirty years of civil strife. Such oppressive measures were directed against vestiges of partisanship, which really meant that partisanship, so necessary in a democracy, became synonymous with fragmentation and division. In addition to the internal bickering, partisanship allowed for any citizen to be seen as an agent for foreign powers. Added to this threat of being partisan is that most parties are ideologically based, whether nationalist, Marxist, or Islamist in nature, and are often a product of dictatorial systems that will not allow for democratic reforms. Thus, "political parties do not always experience the necessary voluntary interaction between interested parties and in turn recognize the role individuals play in propagating political principles . . . expected as part of the dialogue between partisans."[5]

The 1993 Multiparty Elections

Based on a constitution negotiated by the leaders of the former separate states, which was ratified by a popular referendum in May 1991, the Yemeni people went to the polls on 27 April 1993 to elect the members of a new legislature. The exercise in democracy was unique in the region and a source of uneasiness to the Gulf fiefdoms to the north, as it challenged not only autocracy but also patrimonialism when female candidates were allowed to run for office. Campaigning for the votes of 2.7 million were 2,500 candidates (including 200 women) representing more than forty political parties with some independent candidates. The elections were held in a free atmosphere, with more than 100 journalists covering a wide range of issues. The major parties fielding candidates were the General People's Congress (GPC), led by the president, 'Ali 'Abdullah Saleh; the Yemeni Socialist Party (YSP), led by the vice president, Ali Salim al-Baid; Yemeni Islah Party (YIP), led by Sheikh 'Abdullah bin Hussein al-Ahmar; and the Ba'ath (Renaissance) Party, headed by Mujahid Abu Shuarib. Of the 301 seats in the parliament contested, the GPC garnered 123, the YIP 62, YSP 56, and the Ba'ath 7, with several minor parties and independents winning the rest of the seats.

Following the elections, a coalition government involving the three largest parties was constituted. The GPC and YSP took two seats each on the presidential council, and the remaining seat went to the YIP. The leader of the GPC retained the post of president, and that of the YSP was appointed vice president, while the YIP leader became the Speaker of the House of Representatives. Similarly, cabinet positions were distributed among the coalition partners, with the prime ministership going to Haidar Abu-Bakr al-Attas. However, the distribution of power between the ruling parties of the formerly separate states soon turned into a source of discord. In spite of the demographic disparity, in 1986 the population of the north was 9 million and that of the south only 2 million; the southern leadership, based on an informal understanding, believed that power would be shared equally between it and the northern leadership in the new arrangement.[6] As the differences between the south and the north deepened, in August 1993 'Ali Salim al-Baid went into seclusion in Aden and refused to join the new government in Sana'a; instead, the YSP published a program containing eighteen points that amounted to conditions for their return to the government. Although steps were taken to overcome the differences, peaceful resolution of the impasse proved illusive.

The Yemeni Civil War

Unity of the Yemeni state has been a popular slogan in both South and North Yemen, but its realization has remained elusive because of differences among the political leaders. These differences are a product of the long periods of divergent paths of political development, which led to radically different political cultures and perceptions of interest. A relation between the two Yemens has oscillated between conflict and agreement for unification. Two border wars were waged, in 1972 and 1979, both culminating in unfulfilled pledges for unity. It is not surprising that conflict arose in the course of implementing the unity agreement, as with the demise of the former Soviet Union the PDRY was deprived of its main backer, making it vulnerable to a military onslaught from the north, whose position was bolstered by its demographic numerical superiority.

Aware of its precarious position, the YSP, the governing party in the south, sought allies in the north among groups marginalized by 'Abdullah Saleh's leadership. These were not in short supply, for power in the north was held narrowly by a group that included the president and his clansmen from Sanhan, an area just south of Sana'a. The regime's broader support derived from the Hashid, one of the two main tribal federations in the former North Yemen. For his part, being an astute manipulator, Saleh courted the neo-Islamic right, disaffected tribes, and dissident former factions of the party exiled by the YSP leadership. Finally, in addition to the south's fear of economic domination by the north, the secular-minded southerners opposed the alliance of the tribal-based regime in Sana'a and Saleh's newfound Islamic fundamentalist allies.

When war flared up between the forces of the south and those of the north on 4 May 1993, the southern leadership failed to solicit the active support of its allies in the north. In frustration, it announced the secession of the south after a month of fighting, stressing that it still wished for unity but could not accept it under the present conditions. Meanwhile, the northern leadership trumpeted the secessionist drive of the southern leaders as an indication of the YSP's desire to keep Yemen divided. Indeed, the unity issue has long been a valuable arsenal for mobilizing popular support and discrediting opponents. The military conflict went badly for the south, although the northern forces never got the easy victory they anticipated. After seventy days, the whole sad affair was over, with the defeated southern rebels fleeing abroad. The remaining 500,000 inhabitants of Aden were left dangerously short of even potable water supplies.[7]

Contributing to the defeat of the south was its failure to gain recognition of its new independent status from other Arab countries. Diplomatically the Arab countries were supportive of the cause of the south, although they would not go beyond that. This support was essentially the result of lobbying by the Saudis, who were wary of a united Yemen and resentful of Saleh for his support of Iraq during the 1991 Gulf war.

The forcible unification of Yemen presented other complications for Saleh's leadership. The regime was caught in the dilemma of enhancing its legitimacy, especially in quarters loyal to the defeated YSP, and agreeing to the demands of conservative Islah, its partner in government. When a group of 2,000 armed fundamentalists descended on Aden in September 1994 to destroy its religious sites, Saleh used force to disperse them, leaving fifty people dead.[8] To counter the new threat and mollify the YSP, Saleh offered amnesty to all except the top sixteen members of the secessionist leadership. However, the YSP was excluded from the new government. After the cessation of hostilities, the House of Representatives adopted a new constitution founded on Islamic law on 28 September 1994. The former five-member presidential council was abolished, and Saleh was elected president by the parliament for a five-year term on 1 October 1994. A new government was formed, with Lt. Gen. Abd Al-Aziz Al-Ghani (of GPC) as its prime minister.

The Aftermath of the War

With the conclusion of the war, the YSP's defeated leaders—who had fled into exile—remained discredited and the party's fifty deputies in the 301-seat parliament failed to exert any influence, creating a leadership vacuum in the south. Moreover, the victorious northerners did not bother to take significant steps toward genuine reconciliation with the south; instead, they continued to use the Socialists as scapegoats for economic failures. The relationship between the remaining two coalition partners, Islah and the GPC, in the government was not without conflict as differences over a number of issues, particularly economic policy, emerged with Islah voicing strong opposition to the austerity measures introduced by the government, which were in line with International Monetary Fund dictates. Removal of subsidies and implementation of other policies to cut public spending were unpopular with the Yemeni people, and street demonstrations protesting these measures resulted in arrests, leading to the detention of some YSP members in March 1995 as they protested against hikes in the prices of staple goods, gasoline, and public services.

Politically, the government was forced to contend with a rising tide of opposition, which was increasingly better organized. In October 1994, the National Front for the Opposition (MOG) was launched, bringing together a number of political leaders who, at one time or another, had been banished from the country. The group, under the leadership of Abdul Rahman Ali al-Jifri, vice president in the short-lived Democratic Republic of Yemen, included other prominent figures such as Salem Saleh Mohammed, a member of Yemen's presidential council, Abdullah al-Asnag, a former foreign minister, and Haidar Abu-Bakr al-Attas, the last president of the PDRY.[9] In response to the deepening disillusionment of the population and the increase in political opposition, the government acted resolutely against its opponents, detaining a number of opposition figures, raising the concerns of human rights organizations, and damaging its credibility in the international community. In August 1996, Mubarak Salih al Zaydi, Sheikh Mohammed al Zaydi, and others were reportedly arrested for being followers of the MOG, and it was reported that a trial—in absentia—of members of the organization in exile had been ordered by President Saleh.[10]

When the parliamentary election of April 1997 took place, the YSP boycotted it on the grounds that they had not been permitted to promote their platform and that the state had hindered their activities. They also charged the government with corruption and interference in the election process. The result of the election was that the ruling GPC gained control of 220 of the 301 seats with Islah winning 60, virtually giving Saleh carte blanche in running the state. The GPC—already victorious in the civil war and having destroyed its main antagonist, the YSP—no longer needed the Islah Party. Although it has continued to give the position of Speaker of the House to Islah leader Abdullah al-Ahmr, the GPC has significantly reduced Islah numbers in the cabinet and also minimized Islah's control of administrative positions in key ministries. The presidential election of September 1999 virtually guaranteed Saleh the presidency for another term, as the opposition was not able to nominate a candidate who, according to the constitution, would need the endorsement of thirty members of parliament in order to get on the ballot. This was impossible by virtue of the fact that 280 of the 301 members of parliament were members of the GPC or Islah—neither of whom were prepared to support an opposition candidate. In order to give the election the semblance of legitimacy, a well-known southerner, the son of the first president of the PDRY from the GPC, ran as a presidential candidate to oppose Saleh. The lack of opposition within the official electoral process makes the cost and trouble of an election seem unnecessary, as the results are a foregone conclusion. Oppositional groups, such as the SYP, were left on the sidelines, unable to oppose Saleh openly by boycotting the election or to participate with a viable candidate.[11]

Yemen's economy was shattered after the civil war, with foreign debt standing at U.S.$8 billion, inflation officially at 65 percent, and oil production a paltry 380,000 barrels per day—far below what is needed to provide for the country's 15.8 million inhabitants. In addition, 10 percent of the poorest in the population earn less than 1.5 percent of gross national income while the top 10 percent earn 50 percent of gross national income.[12] The economic downturn has been caused essentially by the loss of remittance income from abroad and the severance of financial support from traditional donors during the Gulf war and Yemen's civil war. Long before unification, Yemenis were sustained economically by the foreign currency sent home by Yemenis working abroad, especially in the Gulf region. A slump in the price of oil, which started in the early 1980s, began to curtail this source of income, and it stopped altogether in 1990 when Saudi Arabia expelled 800,000 Yemenis in retaliation for Yemen's support of Saddam Hussein's invasion of Kuwait. On top of the loss of remittance income, Yemen had to reabsorb the returnees, something its economy could ill afford.

The decision to ally with Iraq cost the country dearly in another respect: Direct financial subsidies from traditional donors in the Gulf were immediately lost as Saudi Arabia's substantial financial commitments to the former North Yemen evaporated. Furthermore, Yemen could no longer count on support from the international community, since its image was now tainted. Other factors that have contributed to the gloomy economy are alleged government corruption, a bloated bureaucracy, and increased spending on the military. The Islah has been vocal in denouncing corruption, but tackling this ill is politically sensitive, since key backers of the government could be alienated, while at the same time Islah has been critical of any plans to reform the bureaucracy as some of its supporters might be affected. More frustrating of any hope of securing meaningful development for Yemen is the government's massive plans to rebuild its military under the auspices of a growing U.S. presence since 1995. The news weekly *Al-Wasat* sees the relationship between the United States and Yemen as a barter with "Washington supporting Yemeni unity, democratic and [economic] reform in addition to support in normalising its relationship with international organizations . . . as well as providing financial aid . . . in return for Yemen's acceptance of American equilibrium in the region in the areas of peace, regional security, combating terrorism as well as the provision of logistical support especially in Aden and Ukla."[13] It has been reported that the government signed contracts valued at $300 million to purchase thirty MIG-29 fighters; Saleh then raised military salaries by 30–50 percent and authorized the purchase of spare parts for F-5 fighters, seventy M113A armored personnel carriers, and fifty M60A1 main battle tanks.[14]

The discovery of oil reserves in the country allowed for the hope of improving the troubled economy, but this venture has fallen drastically short of expectations. The Hunt Oil Company found the first oil in commercial quantities in 1984, and production has taken place ever since. Other companies, including French oil giant Total, Canadian Occidental Petroleum, and the U.S. Occidental Petroleum Company, have joined forces in prospecting for further reserves, with some success. In the first ten months of 1992, government exports of crude oil totaled 9.8 million barrels, which would have yielded revenues of about $200 million, far short of the bonanza many Yemenis had hoped for.[15] Exports have grown since then, but are still insufficient to solve the country's economic predicament. It was estimated that oil revenues would exceed $1.5 billion in 1999, an increase of 51 percent over 1998. Oil revenues accounted for 58 percent of the state budget for 2000.[16]

In response, Yemen has adopted an adjustment program under the tutelage of the IMF. The plan includes the removal of consumer subsidies on petroleum products, electricity, and basic imported food staples, besides the devaluation of the currency, all too familiar measures for many countries in the region. Expectedly, the measures have been met with social unrest, which has combined with the economic malaise to trigger public riots in 1991, 1992, and 1995, causing the death and injury of many Yemenis at the hands of state security personnel.[17] Any long-term plans for economic recovery will depend on a restoration of good relations with the Gulf countries, especially Saudi Arabia.

Foreign policy concerns of the newly united country center on its relationship with Saudi Arabia, which has been involved in the political affairs of the peninsula for almost a century. The motivation for this interference is the threat that Saudi Arabia perceives as emerging from a strong Yemen, with a liberal ideology at variance to its own. A united Yemen is demographically larger and, coupled with the prospect of a Yemeni oil boom, has the potential of challenging the dominance of the Saudi regime on the Arabian Peninsula. Yemen has fought territorial wars with Saudi Arabia for over seven decades in which some parts of its territory were lost, and until June 2000 it had not officially renounced any claims to some or all parts of the lost territories.

Yemeni unification as a secular republic and accompanying free elections brought uneasiness to many Gulf states. Before the elections, Saudi Arabia was known to be channeling funds to the fundamentalist Islah while fomenting northern tribal leaders to resist central control.[18] Saudi displeasure with Yemen also stemmed from Yemeni support of the Iraqi 1990 invasion of Kuwait. Until the June 2000 border agreement, relations were far from normalized, at times deteriorating into armed hostility. The source of the conflict had been centered on the undemarcated border between the two countries, within or close to which petroleum reserves have been found. The problem came to a head when the 1934 Treaty of Ta'if, which had settled the border dispute between the two countries, expired in 1996. That agreement had only temporarily delineated part of the border, while 1,000 miles or so remained in contention. However, with outside mediation, the hostilities were brought to an end and a memorandum of understanding was signed in February 1995. Saleh made a visit to Jeddah four months later, during which he stated that the expired treaty would be renewed without alteration— something that his Saudi hosts were pleased to hear. This signaled the thawing of the tense relationship between the two neighbors and presented an opening for a normalization of relations, which was capitalized on in June 2000 with the borderline agreement. The agreement, signed on 12 June 2000, will be implemented by joint committees from the Interior Ministries of both countries, who—along with an independent outside body—will demarcate the borders. The agreement will go beyond the Ta'if mandate and include the entire border, including the eastern frontier, which was left open while Yemen was divided into two countries. With the border secure and the cessation of any possibility of internal hostilities, Yemen will now be able to pursue development of its petroleum reserves in the border region. Yemen also is expected to attempt to join the Gulf Cooperation Council while improving its political alliances in the Gulf region.[19]

CHAPTER 12

The Arab Republic of Egypt

*E*gyptian civilization is largely a product of the Nile River, whose rich silt deposits have enabled settlement along its banks dating back more than 5,000 years. At that time a civilization emerged whose main feature of social formation was peasant-tributary, from which the rulers could appropriate an enormous surplus. The tributary system evolved into a highly centralized form of government. It was under the pharaohs that the first Egyptian advances in architecture and science occurred and Egypt evolved into a highly sophisticated culture. During the Hellenistic, Byzantine, and Arab Empires, Egypt was reduced to a province whose agricultural surplus, which had once supplied the pharaonic ruling class, was now appropriated by foreign courts. Between the tenth and sixteenth centuries, and during the Tulunid, Fatimid, Ayubid, and Mamluk dynasties, Egypt once again benefited from the profits that accrued from the southern trade route through the Red Sea, which supplemented the revenue from the countryside and supported the emerging urban centers and Egyptian agriculture. In towns, wage labor and various forms of mercantilism developed, along with an increasing number of artisan guilds. Arabic literature flourished. With the Ottoman conquest in 1517, Egypt lost its economic and literary prominence, and with this the countryside became impoverished and the peasants were increasingly exploited.[1]

Emergence of Modern Egypt

Napoleon invaded the Ottoman province of Egypt in 1798, intending to use that territory as a base from which to threaten the British Empire by attacking India. His plan was unsuccessful, and Napoleon departed, leaving behind an occupying French army. In 1801, this force was compelled to withdraw by the collaborating Turkish and British armies.

When the British departed in 1803, Muhammad 'Ali, an Albanian junior officer, was left in control of several thousand Albanian and Bosnian troops. He ruled Egypt between 1805 and 1849 and is credited with founding modern Egypt. He competed for power with four groups: the Ulema, which he was able to co-opt; the Turkish garrison, which he was successful in controlling; the Ottoman governor, whom he deposed with the help of the Ulema; and various factions of warring Mamluks, whom he eliminated. Having thus neutralized all opposition to modernization, Muhammad 'Ali, now the pasha of Egypt, was forced to wrestle with the fact that the socioeconomic structure was incapable of undertaking a comprehensive reformation that would combine European sciences and technology with a revived Arab-Egyptian heritage. Under these circumstances, Muhammad 'Ali launched a state-driven program in which his primary objectives were modern industrialization, economic diversification, a strong national army, and the creation of a bureaucracy. Resources were drawn from assessed taxation on the peasantry, made up of small landholding families, and the surplus was used to finance factories, irrigation, and the expansion of agriculture, transportation, education, and the army. In the political arena, he set up three-tiered political councils to be elected without religious or racial discrimination.[2] It is indeed astonishing how this unlettered officer was able to modernize Egypt to the point where state workshops and factories employed tens of thousands of workers who produced steam engines, cannons, iron, and more cotton goods than most European countries. All of this was achieved through the adoption of foreign technology, which was assimilated by Egyptian managers.[3]

Muhammad 'Ali's vision of a modern, powerful, and independent Egypt included a sphere of influence that the Egyptian army carried out in the campaign in the Arabian Peninsula against the Wahabis in 1828 and in Greater Syria in 1836. This expansion of the Egyptian domain into these regions was seen as posing a serious threat to Britain's trade arrangement and regional hegemony, and this revived in Britain a sense of urgency, which Bonaparte's earlier invasion of Egypt had initially awakened.[4]

Some political economists, particularly Samir Amin, argue that given time, Egypt could conceivably have become an autocentric capitalist power because the characteristics of Muhammad 'Ali's modern reforms were much the same as those of both the Meiji in Japan and Peter the Great of Russia, which took place at about the same time.[5] The failure of the Egyptian awakening can be traced to a set of causes that Japan did not face. The first set was the proximity of Egypt to Europe and the threat that Egypt was felt to pose to Britain's strategic and economic interests. This culminated in the Anglo-Ottoman military campaign of 1840, which put an end to Egyptian ambitions and subjected the country to the terms of the Ottoman capitulations, flooded the country with foreign imported goods, and bestowed on foreigners extrajudicial privileges. The second cause was the fact that the local social conditions did not sufficiently mature. Muhammad 'Ali's successors (1849–82) were much less capable, and they abandoned his self-reliant economic policy in the hope of Europeanizing Egypt with European capital. This, however, ultimately turned the country into a cotton plantation for Lancashire, integrated it into the world markets through extroverted, lopsided development,[6] and plunged the country into ruinous debts that resulted in the imposition of the European Debt Commission, known as the Dual Control, in 1876. The Commission acquired such financial and economic powers that it was described as "veiled colonial administration."[7] In this context, the ruling class, with the help of the state, seized land and transformed itself into a class of agrarian capitalists—landowners whose prosperity was now dependent on global markets.

Egypt was thus polarized between the landed aristocracy and the urban Third Estate, which consisted of clerks, artisans, traditional merchants, administrators, and intellectuals, along with the rural equivalent of village notables. Together, they formed the mainstay of a rekindled renaissance seen in an adaptation to cultural and technical innovation and a renewal of a general critical spirit, which together, in the environment of imperial economic domination and the expansion of a modern education system, awakened a spirit of nationalism and patriotism, which came to be symbolized by the 1880s movement led by Col. Ahmed Urabi. However, the Third Estate failed to develop sufficiently along capitalist lines and remained shackled by a precapitalist mentality, clinging desperately to tradition in an attempt to preserve its personality.[8]

Urabi was an army officer from a peasant background, and he represented the Egyptian discontent with increasing European domination of his country. Accordingly, in May 1880, he presented a petition to the government in an attempt to redress several grievances. He was immediately arrested, then freed by an army revolt that installed him as a minister of war. Urabi's followers gained control of parliament as the National Party and were powerful enough to force Ismail's successor, Tewfik, to ensure a constitution. The party then called a national assembly, and in 1881 drew up a moderate reform program. In 1882, however, Britain and France protested the formation of a constitutional government. They felt that Egypt's nascent nationalism would free it from European control and jeopardize their financial interests. The British government claimed that "no satisfactory or durable arrangement of the Egyptian crisis was possible without the removal of Urabi." It systematically denounced his regime as an example of military despotism and foretold dire consequences for Egypt. Subsequently, Britain presented two ultimatums to the Egyptian government. When both were rejected, the British invaded Egypt and on 11 July 1882 defeated Urabi's forces and the nationalist movement in the battle of Tel el-Kabir, north of Cairo. Declaring that they had no intention of staying longer than necessary to restore financial stability and good government, the British installed themselves as the true power in Egypt and imposed their rule for seventy-two years.[9]

It is worth noting that Britain never declared Egypt as one of its colonies, even at the outbreak of the First World War, when it declared Egypt a protectorate. However, the slogans of the Egyptian national movement were still expressed in anti-British terms, such as "evacuation of the British" and "Egypt for the Egyptians." The slogans reflected an uncompromising national spirit and a rejection of the British foreign presence.[10] Urabi's revolt had been one of the most significant events in the development of Egyptian nationalism. It was a social revolution as well as a political movement because the peasantry and the new middle class, a Third Estate, were for the first time expressing themselves as a political force. They were signifying their dislike of both foreign intervention in Egyptian affairs and the collaboration of their own rulers with foreign powers.

British Occupation

British rule in Egypt was strict. For seventy-two years, political power was a tug-of-war between the king, the British proconsul (or high commissioner), and Egyptian politicians. As a general rule, the British opposed national demands and only grudgingly gave way under pressure, as was seen in the case of the third British proconsul, Lord Kitchener, in 1913. The Egyptians were allowed a legislative council, but real power was held by the British administration under the British proconsul. The British began to organize Egypt's administration and reduce its debt, but these improvements were made at a cost. Social and political problems as well as education were almost entirely ignored. The British refusal to allow an increase in self-government led much of the nationalist movement to develop independently. This was especially true after Khedive Tewfik was succeeded by Abbas Hilmi II, who allied himself with the nationalist forces against the British. Eventually he was deposed, and the eldest member of the line, Hussein Kamel, was appointed sultan. In 1914, Britain declared Egypt a protectorate, and institutional amelioration was frozen.

Between 1900 and the outbreak of the First World War, the Third Estate was systematically eliminated, both politically and economically, and replaced with petty bureaucrats who unquestioningly accepted foreign domination. The landed aristocracy gradually became agrocapitalists and then, from 1919 onward, a commercial and industrial business elite. The working class barely existed, and the rest were forced to struggle for even basic survival. The reaction of the intelligentsia, represented by Mustafa Kamel and Mohammad Farid, who established the National Party, was not a resort to revolution but an explanation of the Egyptian case by appealing to European public opinion through their elites. When the whole nation rose in revolt in 1919, the National Party withered away. The emerging rural landowning middle class, represented by the Ummah Party, was ideologically conservative; it supported the British administration and shared the aristocracy's fear of the landless peasantry.[11]

During the First World War, the country was used as a military base. Labor was conscripted, a large number of British forces (whose arrogance and ethnocentrism antagonized the native population) were brought into Egypt, and rampant inflation took place because of British ability to pay higher prices for commodities. Restrictions on the production of cotton were imposed, and confiscated crops were sold at huge profits. Thus, all levels of Egyptian society grew embittered toward the British. However, nationalist leaders were determined to hold their forces in check while the war lasted. Two days after the armistice, Sa'ad Zaghlul (a prominent nationalist) and his followers formed the Egyptian delegation (Wafd) to present a demand for independence to the British proconsul, Sir Reginald Wingate. Although Wingate urged his government to allow Zaghlul to proceed to London, permission to hear the Egyptian demands was refused. This gave rise to a popular revolution in 1919 throughout Egypt. In response, the British authorities were forced to allow the Egyptians to attend the Paris Peace Conference, but Zaghlul's delegation failed to secure Egyptian independence, as the protectorate status was recognized by the attending nations.

Independent Egypt

Despite Zaghlul's failure in Paris, the British decided to take steps to ameliorate Anglo-Egyptian antagonisms. They drew up a treaty of alliance with Egypt in 1920 to replace the protectorate. Both Zaghlul and the Egyptian people rejected the treaty, fearing a disguised continuation of British occupation. Realizing that Zaghlul would agitate against any treaty, the British deported him and unilaterally terminated the protectorate in March 1922, reserving for themselves security of communications, the defense of Egypt, and the protection of foreign nationals in Egypt and the Sudan. Egypt immediately became a monarchy under King Ahmad Fouad I, but Britain continued to hold power.

During the 1920s and 1930s, three agricultural crises culminated in the Great Depression of 1929–32. The slump in the demand for Egyptian cotton, with dire financial consequences for the Egyptian economy, awakened the national movement to the importance of industrialization as a component of independence. Independent intellectuals like Salama Mussa and the Misr al-Fatat Party called for Egyptianizing the economy by establishing Egyptian economic parallels to the existing foreign ones.[12] New industries and companies began to appear, symbolized by the establishment of Banque Misr, which was envisioned by the Misr Group as an industrial and banking base independent of the landed aristocratic bourgeoisie and foreigners.[13] The real success of the bank was shown by the fact that there was an indigenous entrepreneurial group capable of breaking the monopoly of foreign investors and forcing the government into a tariff reform that increased the duty on imports in 1930 in order to protect local industries.[14]

In many industries, such as sugar refining, tobacco and shoe manufacturing, cement, soap, and furniture production, the Banque Misr achieved 90 percent self-sufficiency. Between 1919 and 1935, there were twenty governments and eight rounds of negotiations in which the Egyptians tried to reduce British control. In 1936, Britain, fearing the Italian threat from Libya and Ethiopia and the looming war in Europe, compromised in what became the Anglo-Egyptian Treaty, which was intended to be valid for twenty years. The treaty granted Egypt a greater degree of independence, while Britain retained control of the Suez Canal, as well as the right to station troops there.[15]

At the beginning of the Second World War, Egypt was once again turned into a British base of operations. Although the upper echelon of Egyptian society prospered as a result of 200–300 percent appreciation in the value of land and buildings, the masses suffered severe deprivation analogous to their experiences in the First World War, due to a 330 percent increase in wholesale commodity prices between 1939 and 1944. The British took drastic measures to keep Egypt neutral. Axis sympathizers were purged from the government, the palace was barricaded, and Fouad's successor, Farouk, was forced to hand over the reins of government to Mustafa al-Nahas, leader of the Wafd Party, who was perceived as a representative of the people, able to handle a turbulent national situation during the war.

The conditions of the war helped strengthen the burgeoning Egyptian capitalist class. During the war, 375 companies with a paid capital of Egyptian £78 million were established, and the production value increased by 350 percent between 1938 and 1945. A corollary to the increase in industrial projects was a significant increase in labor employment and the Wafd Party's promulgation of the right to form labor unions in 1942. In January 1946, there were some 530 labor unions, but layoffs, especially from war-related facilities, were estimated to be around 100,000—almost a quarter of the active workforce. The unemployment problem turned into a serious social and political crisis as the laid-off workers had no social insurance protection, which was exacerbated by the rise in the cost of living by 600–700 percent. In addition, unemployment affected the employment prospects of about 10,000 recent university graduates. The worsening socioeconomic conditions, and the instability caused by political multicenter power relations that involved the Palace, rival political parties, and Imperial Britain, bridged the gap between various socioeconomic and political formations, such as the labor force, intellectuals, the petite bourgeoisie, entrepreneurs, lawyers, teachers, students, and the progressive or democratic wings of political parties.[16]

Despite the severe disparity in landownership (0.5 percent of the population owned 34 percent of the land while 94 percent owned only 35 percent of land, with an additional 11 million landless), the rural masses did not rise up, nor did their urban counterparts, against the British and their collaborators. During the war, rural labor wages had increased more than twofold and most of the landed aristocracy were Egyptians, some of them even active members and leaders in the Wafd Party, which came to enjoy widespread popular support. Also, the small landowners, as well as the landless peasantry, were somewhat removed from the effects of foreign domination.[17]

The end of the war saw the Wafd ousted from power, beginning a long period of domestic instability and anxiety that culminated in Egyptian demands for a revision of the Anglo-Egyptian Treaty of 1936 in response to the recalcitrance and procrastination of Britain. Coupled with the creation of the state of Israel in 1948, these events substantially altered Egypt's perception of Britain. In 1948, Egypt joined the Palestine war. The poor performance of its army against Zionist forces and corrupt government practices humiliated the Egyptian people, particularly junior army officers. Egypt considered Britain, above all, to be responsible for the establishment of Israel. Against this tense background, the Wafd Party regained power in 1950, and on 8 October 1951 it unilaterally abrogated the 1936 Anglo-Egyptian Treaty. It also declared Farouk king of Egypt and Sudan, thereby laying claim to a unity with the Sudan, which technically was jointly ruled by both Britain and Egypt at the time.

The political significance of the abrogation of the treaty cannot be overestimated. The political institutions of the regime rested on a delicate balance between the coalescence of the British and the Palace vis-à-vis the national popular movement, which the Wafd Party represented. The British presence in the Suez Canal was legal by the terms of the treaty, which the Wafd had earlier signed. The document of abrogation, signed by the Wafd and the king, not only exposed British presence as an aggression but also broke the alliance between the king and Britain. The Wafd, which historically had adopted a tactic of peaceful struggle toward genuine independence and democracy, transcended itself into opening the door to popular armed struggle without new instruments for mass mobilization appropriate for the new phase, which it was successful in bringing in. This explains why, after declaring the abrogation of the Anglo-Egyptian Treaty in the Parliament, Mustafa al-Nahas said to the press, when asked about the next move, "The government has done its duty; the decision is now for the people."[18] Hostilities broke out between Egyptians and the British authorities on 13 October 1951. On 25 January 1952, forty-three Egyptian policemen were killed during a British attack on the police barracks of Ismailia. Riots erupted in Cairo on Black Saturday, 26 January 1952, and most of the foreign quarter was burned.

Between October 1951 and Black Saturday, all socioeconomic strata, political organizations, professional societies, and segments of the rural centers joined together in a popular uprising, employing methods of boycotting, sabotage, and constant street demonstrations. For example, on 14 November 1951, demonstrators were estimated to number 1 million, some relying on Fedayeen (guerrilla warfare), for which training camps had been opened. The Socialist, Communist, and Wafd Party press launched daily attacks on the Palace and British imperialism, urging people to bring down the regime.[19] Spontaneous attempts to organize a national front that would include national political movements, such as the Wafd, the National Party, the Socialist Party, the Muslim Brotherhood, the Muslim Youth, etc., were undertaken as early as 20 October 1951.[20] The period from late 1951 to the launch of the coup d'état on 23 July 1952 reflected the militarization and radicalization of society in the face of monarchical despotism and the British use of naked force, which had paralyzed the political process. On 27 January 1952, the king removed the Wafd from office and asked the pro-Palace

Ali Maher to form a new government. This failed.[21] Another government followed, led by Najib al-Hilali, who suspended the constitution, censored the press, and exercised extrajudicial powers. However, he was forced to resign in late June 1952.[22] The paralysis continued for four days while tensions mounted. The king then appointed one of his most trusted aides, Hussien Serry, to form a pro-Palace government on 2 July 1952. This government, too, was met with popular scorn.[23] The Palace attempted to impose its will on a politicized and vociferous population utilizing the only remaining force at its disposal: the army and state security police.

Professionals were organized into associations: lawyers in 1912; journalists in 1940; physicians and pharmacists in 1942; engineers in 1946; and teachers in 1951. In 1919, the Wafd was built on workers' support; in 1922, the Socialist Party espoused workers' interests; in 1929, the Society of Artisans allied itself with the Communist Party; in 1934, the Labor Federation coalesced with the Wafd.[24] By December 1951 there were 490 labor unions, and these were about to merge into a General Labor Union whose groundwork and preparations were the design of the Egyptian Communist movement, Al-Haraka al-Democratiyya lil-Taharur al-Watani (or the Democratic Movement for National Liberation, DMNL). The declaration of martial law after Black Saturday stalled the formation of the Najib al-Hilali government but did not succeed in stopping it. The influence of the movement extended among students and the intellectuals who orchestrated strikes and espoused a socioeconomic agenda for reform and development. Perhaps the reason for the movement's success was its ability to reach the isolated rural peasants. By 1952, the movement had established branches in about 100 villages where it propagated its program of land reform and the abolition of large land holdings.[25]

By the end of the 1940s, it was evident that Egypt had already become a self-mobilizing society with a civil apparatus that expressed national interests contrary to those of the king and his allies among the aristocracy and foreign powers. During that phase of politicization, there had been attempts and negotiations to form a national front composed of the DMNL, the Socialist and National Parties, and the Muslim Brotherhood in support of a popular platform for comprehensive reform. Needless to say, the negotiations included the young Wafdist democratic generation.[26]

In sum, the character of the popular opposition after the Second World War was, first, open organizations supported by large segments of society; second, articulated ideological-based platforms; and third, political participation of the large, mobile middle class. Both the salaried and self-employed of this group had benefited politically from the earlier introduction of the educational system and the expansion of the mass media. (In 1950, there were 22 daily newspapers, 203 weekly magazines, and 18 bimonthly, 82 monthly, and 15 miscellaneous journals.)[27] The same period witnessed changes at the international level, which had repercussions on the Egyptian scene. As a result of the Second World War, Britain had become financially exhausted; the world was ideologically polarized between the USSR and the United States, which were filling the vacuum created by French and British decline in the region. The United States strived to contain the rising Soviet influence and to consolidate its position as the new leader of the free world. It was the era of Pax Americana and an era of reinforcement of the earlier incorporation of the Middle East into western capitalist markets.

As early as January 1951, the Egyptian daily *Al-Gomhour al-Misri* reported that the American embassy in Cairo had informed the U.S. State Department of anti-American demonstrations staged by Communist groups. The paper also reported that there was a plan to create an anti-Communist office staffed by Anglo-Americans and Egyptians, and that the press section in the American embassy had requested extra appropriations to co-opt and recruit influential figures, including journalists, to counterbalance the anti-American spirit.[28] After the abrogation of the 1936 treaty, national mass movements systematically employed anti-American (as well as anti-British) slogans and urged a treaty of cooperation with the USSR. Indonesia also supported this Egyptian political stance.

Egypt in Revolution

On the night of 22 July 1952, a group of young Egyptian army officers led a successful coup against the monarchy. King Farouk abdicated on 26 July in favor of his son and went into exile. The Egyptian monarchy came to a formal end on 18 June 1953 when a republic was proclaimed.

The causes that led to the Free Officers' Movement were numerous. Egypt's socioeconomic problems had become extreme by 1952 and the existing political structure had rendered them insolvable. Its economic problem was twofold: overpopulation and poverty. At the time of Muhammad 'Ali's suzerainty over Egypt, the country had a population of 3 million. By 1952, 150 years later, it had grown to about 20 million. This tremendous increase had severe economic and social consequences. No attempt at modernization had led to the expected trickle-down effects. Income inequalities increased, thereby exacerbating poverty, which led to high population growth. Egypt remained a desperately poor and underdeveloped nation whose masses were thoroughly and hopelessly impoverished.

Poverty was further compounded by the concentration of landownership in the hands of the few. At the time of the revolution, less than half of 1 percent of the proprietors owned 37 percent of the arable land. These landowners were concentrated in the cities and were out of touch with conditions in the countryside where 80 percent of the population lived. This minority invariably shaped Egypt's political, social, and economic life. The political landscape was as stagnant as the economic scene. The monarchy had lost all remnants of popular support, and the nationalist movement—symbolized by the Wafd—had lost its dynamism and credibility. The conservative old guard was not prepared to undertake the necessary economic or political reforms. All these factors, combined with dissatisfaction with British actions in Palestine, and their refusal to withdraw their forces from the Sudan or the Canal Zone, paved the way for the army takeover.

The Free Officers' Committee was primarily a group of lower- and middle-rank army officers who had attended military college together. The acknowledged head of the secret organization was Lt. Col. Gamal Abdel Nasser, the son of a post office clerk. In order to obtain wider support, the group had chosen as their symbolic leader a respected officer and distinguished soldier, Gen. Mohammed Naguib. The leading group consisted of about twenty officers, four of them descended from the upper class (major landowners, merchants, and bureaucrats), and about sixteen from the petite bourgeoisie and the salaried strata.[29]

Scholars have raised serious questions about the timing and context of the coup, connecting it to the appointment of Jefferson Cafry, a CIA counterinsurgency expert in the American embassy in Cairo about the time of the coup. The question has also been raised regarding the increasing frequency of military coups in the region that coincided with the emergence of Pax Americana and the assistance it represented on the part of the United States (three coups in Syria alone in 1949). What, for example, were the grounds for the original suppression of Marxist activities by the junta when Marxist socioeconomic programs for reform and democracy were later propagated and adopted by the Revolutionary Command Council itself? Why did the junta cooperate with the Muslim Brotherhood, who lacked any clear program for reform, only to suppress them later? And why was Dr. Ahmed Hussein chosen as a member in the first government after the coup, in 1952, and later appointed the Egyptian ambassador to Washington by Nasser, when he had close ties to the United States, he had been a cabinet minister in the last Wafd government, and he was an active member in the party that the military coup had dissolved on the grounds of corruption?[30]

Perhaps the most pertinent question pertains to the personnel who led the coup. With the exception of Khaled Muhie al-Din and Yousef Seddiq, who were briefly members of the DMNL, those who led the coup on 23 July 1952 were not affiliated with any civil or political organization. This nonaffiliation accounted for the name "Free Officers." Recruitment into the movement was strictly on the basis of a personal relationship, mutual trust, and similarity of outlook. The movement operated on a cell structure in the armed forces, was limited to a small number of young army officers, and had no grassroots support or any connection to civil society. That is why, immediately after the success of the coup, all ranks above lieutenant colonel were debarred from any command until the whole army had been brought under the control of the junta. This was achieved either by retirement or by reassignment to civil posts. Nasser later commented, "It took us five years to disengage the army from any involvement in politics."[31]

The question, then, naturally arises as to the odds of success of a movement whose clandestine structure prevented it from gaining any popular support. Further, how were the coup leaders able to ensure that the 80,000 British troops stationed in the Canal Zone did not attempt to suppress the coup?[32]

Some political analysts go so far as to suggest that there was some understanding between the coup leaders and the American embassy in Cairo, according to which the United States persuaded Britain not to interfere in return for the junta's suppression of leftist groups and the continuation of good relations with the West. This should not imply, however, that the Free Officers were dupes of the United States; rather, it simply indicates that in their desire for power, their interests coincided in a marriage of convenience with American and British positions in the region at the time, which were directed at preempting any leftist populist movements that might lead to a drift toward the USSR.[33]

In the first months after the July coup d'état, under the leadership of their thirteen-man executive committee, the Revolutionary Command Council (RCC), the Free Officers attempted to reorganize the political system and restore order to Egyptian life. Politically, this meant controlling the political environment enough to make the economic and social goals of the revolution come about more quickly. Within months of the revolution, the political parties of prerevolutionary Egypt were dissolved and a new constitution was proclaimed. Resistance to the revolution remained, of course, such as that from the Muslim Brotherhood (the only remaining substantial political organization to survive the dissolution of the parties), though on a limited scale, but nonetheless important enough to prevent the RCC from consolidating the revolution as quickly as it would have liked.

However, all was not well with Naguib, who was replaced by Nasser in April 1954 after a short power struggle. Naguib was placed under house arrest in October after an attempt on Nasser's life, an attempt sponsored by the Muslim Brotherhood, whose involvement gave Nasser the excuse to disband the organization forcibly. Thus by late 1954, Nasser had reached the pinnacle of power, a position that was consolidated by revoking the Anglo-Egyptian condominium over the Sudan and the evacuation of British troops from the Canal Zone in 1956 after years of negotiations. In June 1956, a national plebiscite endorsed Nasser's presidency with the support of 99.9 percent of the electorate, thus formalizing his power and laying the ground for the political ideology of Nasserism.

Nasserism

Practical considerations colored Nasser's initial approach to politics. The concerns of building a viable political order and maintaining the position of the Revolutionary Command Council were paramount. His main concern before the Suez crisis was the domestic security of his regime of moderate revolution. Even positive neutralism and the Suez situation were pragmatic responses to threatening circumstances, although they were an important tenet of his ideology.

The notion of stability and order dominated the thinking of the RCC. For Nasser and his close associates, political instability was generated by the system of plurality—the different orientations of the parties and other civic organizations, whose discourses created a state of sociopolitical chaos. The remedy was to dissolve all such organizations. It followed that freedom of expression, free election, majority rule, constitutional guarantees, and the rule of law were all compromised, and all social forces that refer to such groups as large landowners, big merchants or the private industrial sector, top executives, unionized labor, religious organizations, the intelligentsia and the intellectuals, students, unions, peasants' societies, and even ethnosectarian associations that had access to power were to be controlled. This led to a civil "vacuum" to be filled by the regime. However, the political instability that focused on frequent formation and dissolution of governments during the monarchical period endured well into Nasser's regime. Between 1924 and 1946, there were twenty-one governments (an average of nine and a half months for each government). Between 1952 and 1972, there were twenty-three.[34]

"Nasserism" is usually construed at the level of national discourse and theory, as opposed to the level of praxis. The theory of Nasserism refers to a historical epoch that commenced after 1956 when the magnetic personality of Nasser, and his Arab nationalist and antiwestern nationalist slogans in favor of independence and a resistance to pacts and foreign alliances, personified popular feelings in the Arab world. The very nature of the discourse engendered a quest for a national dynamic identity and a common culture that would transcend conflictual interests, reduce the misery of the oppressed groups, and bring about a collective bond and solidarity. It was articulated as a discourse of grand principles, and it fostered fervent national pride during a time of revolutionary intensity that reached its zenith in the mid-1960s, with the measures of nationalization and the five-year economic plan that showcased Egyptian economic independence.[35]

Praxis, the other side of Nasserism, involved domestic, economic, and foreign policy. Nasser's domestic policy was founded on a systematic acquisition of organizational power, numerical power, and capital-resources power. The phases of monopolizing the sources tended to overlap, but a rough scheme may be as follows:

1. The RCC was a parallel body to the state organs whose top decision-making positions, ranging from ministries to executive posts in organs of local government, the bureaucracy, and the press, were immediately filled by army officers. All decisions were made within the RCC, which acted as a military corporatist structure.

2. The use of the oppressive power of the state apparatus intensified to eliminate all forms of opposition that emanated from organizations such as parties and civic associations perceived to be a threat and culminated in the annulment of the 1923 constitution in January 1953, despite the Free Officers' earlier slogan that "We are for the Constitution" and the detention of political leaders of all stripes (except the Muslim Brotherhood, whose turn came in 1954). A transitional phase of three years was declared in which the regime enforced martial law and exercised legislative, executive, and quasi-judiciary functions. The regime transformed itself into a body with unlimited sociopolitical power and attempted to establish a reserve mass organization, the Liberation Rally, under Nasser's direction in 1953, when the struggle with General

Naguib was fomenting.[36] In 1956 it was superseded by a more elaborate body, the National Union, for mass mobilization and indoctrination.

3. Prior to the new constitution, which was promulgated on 16 January 1956, the military had already controlled the numerical sources of power: labor, student unions, civil associations such as the Muslim Youth Society, and professional organizations. By monopolizing the information media and recruiting a large segment of the intelligentsia who became the regime's ideologues, the state was able to assume control.

4. Concurrent with the above phases, Nasser had deprived the traditional groupings and classes of their power base: ownership of large economic assets in both land and capital. A number of sweeping new laws, initiated by the Land Reform Act, were promulgated in 1952 and followed by a series of nationalization measures in 1961. In reality, such measures transferred the financial, industrial, agrarian, and service sectors to state control.

A closer look at the first land reform law of 1952 reveals that, despite slogans of social justice, the reform was politically motivated to liquidate the power of the landed aristocracy. It targeted ninety-three persons and confiscated 118,748 feddans (1 feddan = 1.038 acres).[37] Yet those who owned less than five feddans (the small owners) and who constituted 94.3 percent of the farming population were not affected, though there was an increase in the total area of ownership, which rose from 35.3 percent to 46.6 percent. Between 1961 and 1965, with further confiscations and an increase in the gross cultivatable area, the percentage of landowners remained the same, while the percentage of area farmed increased to 57.1 percent. Distribution of confiscated and reclaimed land (the latter was 478,000 feddans) for small peasant ownership did not entail legal proprietorship, but only the right of usufruct as the land was regarded as state property. In effect, the state decided what was to be produced, at what price the crop should be bought, and at what price it should be sold. Most peasants became subjugated to the state. Further, the rural middle stratum, owners of 20–50 feddans, increased both in number and area ownership for the same period, from 22,000 owners to 30,000, and from 654,000 feddans to 818,000 feddans. The importance of this stratum was that it had historically represented rural notables who, in addition to their own interests, had been a linkage between the state apparatus and the peasant masses. The political position of that group was strengthened by the land reform and their connection to the state thus increased.[38] Indeed, the land reform may have worked in the interests of some of the peasantry, but it was not universally beneficial to all of that class.

On 16 January 1956, a new constitution was promulgated, and Nasser was elected president of the Republic of Egypt. Accordingly, a legislative assembly was created in 1957. However, article 192 of the constitution stipulated that anyone running for parliament was to be vetted by the National Union, established in 1956. Article 8 gave a mandate to the National Union to arrange and approve the list of candidates. The Mission Statement of the National Union read: "The National Union is not a government. It is an organization of the rulers and the people, which makes possible the mutual cooperation to solve domestic problems within the framework of the Socialist Democratic Cooperative society. It is the instrument of proper democracy which makes people feel that they govern themselves." It was the National Union that ultimately rejected 1,188 out of 2,058 candidates who put themselves forward for the National Assembly (the legislature) in 1957. As a consequence, loyalists, regime cronies, and officers filled the Assembly seats. The National Union was a device for controlling the legislature. Despite the enormity of control, Nasser was intolerant of an emergent modicum of criticism in the Assembly, which he suspended after the union with Syria in 1958, on the grounds of reorganizing a more relevant legislature in 1960. However, that did not take place because of the breakup of the union in September 1961, partly in response to Nasser's attempt at large-scale nationalization measures.[39]

In November 1961, Nasser appointed the Preparatory Council to organize a Congress of the Popular Forces to draft the National Charter for Egypt and create the Arab Socialist Union (ASU) to replace the defunct National Union, along with preparation for the election of a 350-member National Assembly.[40] The deliberations of the council were broadcast live on radio and television. The structure of the ASU was developed in fourteen months, between 1963 and 1964, and membership, except for the police and the army, was open to all people including women who were not politically disenfranchised. Membership in the ASU became a prerequisite for running for the National Assembly and even for promotion to top positions in the public sector companies or the bureaucracy. Although the ASU claimed to represent the interests of the active popular forces, and peasants and workers were assigned half of the seats in the National Assembly, the criteria as to who was a peasant or a worker were never clearly defined; as a consequence, only the rural notables were allowed into the ASU and the

Assembly. Further, during the lifetime of the ASU, no one represented the workers and peasants on the ASU's Supreme Committee.[41]

The pyramidal structure of the ASU lacked a defined role and a coherent ideology, and its relationship with the other institutions, such as professional labor unions and the army, was never stated. In fact, the attempt to use the ASU to control all civilian life led some to infer that the objective role of the ASU for Nasser was really to check the increasing power and popularity of Marshal 'Abdul Hakim 'Amer, Nasser's vice president, who enjoyed the complete loyalty of the army.[42] This inference is supported by the fact that after the debacle of the Egyptian army in June 1967 and the suicide of Amer, which gave control of the army back to Nasser, the ASU was practically irrelevant.

Nasser's Economic Policy

The initial economic success between 1957 and 1965 coincided with a favorable international cold war environment for Egypt. After the Second World War, the region became the focus of American investment and trade. This resulted in a loosening of the dominating grip on the Third World, including Egypt, by the ex-colonial powers.[43] Nasser conceived that political independence was inseparable from economic autonomy, a conception that materialized in large-scale industrialization projects. Economic strategy was based on import substitution, the commonly accepted economic paradigm of the time. However, Nasser's policy of centralizing power deprived him of the socioeconomic infrastructure necessary for the success of these projects, even though this policy availed to him the necessary capital base for his visionary economic program.

Between 1961 and 1966, sequestration and nationalization contributed to the state possession of £E33 million in cash, 7,000 properties, and 293 enterprises.[44] In addition to these funds, Egypt received, from western countries and other financial institutions, $50 million from 1955 to 1960; $200 million from 1961 to 1966; and $16 million from 1967 to 1969.[45] The development strategy of import substitution, however, has its inherent contradictions. First, it relies on the developed world economy, in its present state, without corresponding developmental stage or infrastructure. Second, it favors allocation of scarce resources to the production of capital goods, to the detriment of the production of basic consumer goods, such as subsistence agriculture, which stagnated relative to the increase in total population and its high rural proportion. Third, it does not create a sufficient technological and research base; this, in effect, creates a technological dependence (the deeper the capital-intensive industrialization, the greater the dependence).[46]

The economic policies of Nasser's regime can be understood in terms of etatism and dirigisme. The first refers to centralized administration and economic management; the second refers to the state as an essentially interventionist agent of economic transformation.[47] We shall refer to the combined effect of these two instruments, henceforth, as state-planned capitalism (SPC). Nasser employed two main engines for what he called economic self-sufficiency and social justice: overexpansion in the civil service (or the bureaucracy) and the establishment of a huge public sector that was in charge of 91 percent of total investment between 1961 and 1966 and in control of 83 percent of all production tools: finance, insurance, extractive and processing industries, and all import and export activities.[48]

There were four layers within the civil service and the public sector. At the top of the bureaucracy, whether in the city or the rural areas, were the loyal military personnel and members of the original 1952 coup. The middle and lower management of the public sector were filled with the prerevolutionary private sector socioeconomic groups whose business expertise was required. This second layer, the traditional bourgeoisie, acted as intermediaries between the military at the top and the third layer, the technocrats (professors, technicians, and professionals) who were necessary for the socioeconomic transformation. The fourth layer was the rural notables who controlled the local governments and village councils and who transformed themselves into powerful pressure groups whose interests were not dissimilar to the other layers.[49]

Within ten years, state employees, with special privileges (thirty-seven expense accounts) increased by 400 percent, and between 1961 and 1965 expanded by another 150 percent.[50] The expansion of the bureaucracy and the public sector created its own complex array of bureaucratic checks, discretionary procedures, and rules that allowed the emergence of what Gunnar Myrdal called "the norm of corruption," which becomes the prevalent pattern of mores concerned with the attainment of personal gain in the sphere of public power and responsibility. This corruption ranged from large-scale grafts by politicians and high-ranking army officers as well as higher technobureaucrats, to petty bribery to settle a deal at the lower levels.[51]

Thus, Nasser's state-planned capitalism generated a corporatist salaried stratum (which might be called a bureaucratic bourgeoisie) whose interest was to exploit the power of the state apparatus for personal gain. In the mid-1960s, this group had become so powerful that some observers called it a "counter-developmental stratum."[52] Despite initial financial success, state-planned capitalism could not generate and satisfy basic material needs: sufficient food, clothing, shelter, mobility, quality education, and health insurance. In the process of building his new society, Nasser did not protect human rights or provide equal opportunities for a positive contribution to the decision-making process because, for all his good intentions, popular participation was extremely limited.[53] The military defeat, in June 1967, put an end to the SPC and coincided with European economic reinvigoration and a growing interest in the Third World markets as important outlets for Euro-American products and a transfer of capital for project developments. This is particularly true of American transnationals, which were facing the triple problem of significant wage increases, scarcity of some raw materials, and legal constraints on environmental and industrial pollution at home.[54]

Foreign Policy

Nasser's foreign policy revolved around three axes: the Palestinian-Israeli conflict, the international cold war, and the macro-political dynamics of the region. As a result of the Palestine debacle, throughout the Arab world Israel is regarded as a western creation of a powerful avant-garde of western imperialism that acted to the detriment of the Arab people.[55] By making Israel a foe whom all Arabs could reject, Nasser could expand the conception of the Egyptian identity and give it a regional dimension in what would also be called Nasserism: a brand of Arab nationalism, the epithet of Arab unity. The rallying point was the Palestine problem, which generated a sense of "Arabness" and solidified an antiwestern sentiment. The solution to the Palestine problem, as Nasser conceived of it until the defeat of 1967, was based on the UN Partition Resolution of 1947.[56] Palestine, therefore, was a political tool of Nasserism and tangential to Egyptian foreign policy.

The international dimension of Nasser's foreign policy is usually pinpointed at the tripartite aggression of Britain, France, and Israel in 1956. In fact, it had taken shape in 1955, when Israel's raid on Gaza revealed Egypt's military weakness. This was exacerbated by the American refusal to sell arms to Egypt, which forced Nasser to distance himself from the United States and seek military assistance from the Socialists, first through Czechoslovakia, while being careful not to be too closely identified with the USSR. These developments coincided with the heyday of the nonaligned movement, symbolized by the Bandung Congress of April 1955, and created the Afro-Asian Solidarity Movement.[57]

In the early sixties, Egypt was accepted as an equal partner by the leaders of China, India, Yugoslavia, and Indonesia, in the nonaligned movement. This allowed Nasser to balance great power blocs against each other to maximize Egypt's foreign policy goals. Under the umbrella of the Afro-Asian Solidarity Movement, he lent moral and material support to Third World liberation movements, particularly in Africa. Nasser's nationalization of the Suez Canal in 1956, and the failure of the 1956 Anglo-French-Israeli invasion affected Nasser's (and Egypt's) political stature. However, these early foreign policy successes made any accommodation with western interests politically dangerous.[58]

The intertwining of the Palestine problem, which Nasser helped bring to the fore, with his anti-imperialist foreign policy was an integral part of his regional politics. Nasser's commitment to Arab unity even justified his direct involvement and intervention in regional politics. He dominated politics and diplomacy in the region. However, the Israeli attack on Egypt and the occupation of the Sinai in the June 1967 war now involved Egyptian sovereignty and challenged the credibility of the regime at home. The Palestine problem, in effect, had now merged with, but was subordinate to, the issues of Egyptian sovereignty. Liberation became the solution, and Palestine maintained the sense of unity and "Arabness" in the face of the external foe, Israel. The weakness in this context was the extrinsic character of "Arabness" that derived from a taboo relating to an enemy, as change in the perceived relations to that enemy would necessarily involve corresponding change in the self-image of the Arabs.

Nasserism as a discourse and theory did not die with the Egyptian military defeat in June 1967 and the Israeli occupation of the Sinai. The defeat brought the Arab world to the rallying call of Arabism. However, the main goals of Nasserism, especially Arab unity, proved to be unachievable because of international, regional, and Egyptian political realities. Externally, the international system is founded on asymmetrical power relations that allow the powerful to impose, to various degrees, their strategic interests on the weak; such a feature, given the asymmetry of power, may be viewed as legitimate within the international context. The sustained confrontation between the dominant western powers and the Middle East is unmatched in the history of colonialism, and on the regional level the incorporation of the Arab states into the world capitalist system, in terms of power relations, has rendered the regional political system very open to penetration.

On the local level, Nasser's regime was founded on intelligence institutions that checked on each other. He ruled through intelligence reporting without disseminating an ideology that could exercise a totalizing hegemony on the individual and the group and relate the ruler to the ruled. Public political participation was marginalized by the systematic creation of doctrinaire political organizations that ultimately alienated any direct popular input into the political process. The state, though in control, stood remote from the psyche of the masses.

The Sadat Regime

Sadat's accession to office, after Nasser's death in September 1970, was the work of chance rather than worthiness. Between September 1970 and May 1971, he promised to pursue Nasser's policy in form and content. A power struggle erupted, and Sadat ensured his position by appointing a loyal army chief of staff as commander of the presidential guard. In early May, Sadat rounded up more than ninety members of the old Nasser regime and initiated an about-face against Nasserism.[59]

In many western works, Sadat is credited with making peace with Israel and liberalizing Egypt. As early as 1971, Sadat declared the permanent constitution, which created a legislature (the People's Assembly) through election but gave to the office of the president much power over any other institution, including the ability to make laws and dissolve the People's Assembly. The constitution maintained the single-party nature of the Arab Socialist Union of Nasser, and continued to lack a definition of "peasant and worker" whose ratio in the People's Assembly was stipulated to be 50 percent. The ASU was then reorganized into three forums: the Right, the Center, and the Left, which in 1977 were transformed into parties. As early as 1973, and according to Yahia al-Gamal, a professor of law and a Sadat cabinet minister, the only political reality in the political decision-making process was the person of the president. All others were simply the cast for the political backdrop.[60]

The general framework of Sadat's policy was based mainly on whim rather than strategy.[61] He did not have a clear plan for dealing with the Palestinian dimension of the Arab-Israeli conflict, although he viewed Palestine as an aspect of the inter-Arab rivalry for leadership.[62] In the first few months during his rule (1970–81), he opened communication with Washington through his friend Kamal Adham, the Saudi director of intelligence. First, he was seeking a nonmilitary accommodation with Israel, something which he believed only the United States could bring about; second, he entertained the idea that with such a peaceful solution, Egypt's position would be even stronger. To this end, Sadat committed himself in writing to President Nixon, offering to make peace with Israel under American auspices, after an initial phase of Israeli withdrawal.[63]

Eager to win American support and to show his change of direction, he ordered the expulsion of the Soviet military personnel in July 1972,

and by the end of August, all 7,725 of the Soviets were forced out.
However, American support never eventuated because Sadat's diplomatic demarche did not correspond with American interests in the
region at the time, which was replacing the USSR to become the only
superpower in the area, an American dream ever since the Eisenhower
doctrine fifteen years earlier.[64] Frustrated by American procrastination
and Israeli intransigence (Israel was wreaking havoc in Syria and
Lebanon in September 1972), Sadat decided to launch a limited war,
conceived by the military during the Nasser era, to break the diplomatic
deadlock and steer the superpowers, particularly the United States,
toward a peaceful settlement.

The October War

On 6 October 1973, Egypt and Syria launched a war that was essentially
a diplomatic gambit. The Egyptian strategy was founded on crossing the
Suez Canal, advancing for only about 15 kilometers so as to remain
within the protective umbrella of the surface-to-air missiles installed on
the western side of the canal, and thus minimizing the risk from the
Israeli Air Force. From 5 to 15 October, Israel was forced to fall back
and its counteroffensive was halted. Sadat, without any real military
experience at the front, decided at this point to change the strategy and
send the army into the open desert despite strong objections from
Egyptian army commanders. The result was a military setback for
Sadat's army, with Israel pinning down the Egyptian Third Army on the
canal's eastern bank. Because of this, the initial victory turned into a
stalemate. The demilitarization of the Sinai and Sadat's consistent mismanagement of the war prompted the Egyptian general chief of staff,
Saʿad al-Shazli, to file a court case with the prosecutor general against
the president, accusing him of treason, in July 1979.[65]

The political outcome of the war and the consequent Egyptian-Israeli
peace in what came to be known as the Camp David accord involved the
intertwining of the domestic, regional, and international political levels.
Domestically, the Sinai became demilitarized, and Egypt became indefi-
nitely bound by the terms of an American memorandum, attached to
the accord, which stated the U.S. determination, in the event of
Egyptian violation of the treaty, to take "such remedial measures as it
deemed appropriate, which may include diplomatic, economic and military measures."[66] Thus, Egypt became unable to engage in any active
role in Arab regional politics lest it be construed as a violation of the
terms of the accord, a case in point being the Israeli invasion of southern Lebanon in 1982. Regionally, as the Egyptian negotiators sat face-to-

face with their Israeli counterparts, the mental taboo, which had given birth to their sense of Arabness, began to break down and ultimately diminish with the conclusion of the Camp David negotiations. Further, the separation between the "framework for peace" and the bilateral Egyptian-Israeli agreement left the problem of Palestine to be negotiated between concerned parties. In effect, the Palestine problem was postponed and, because of Sadat's political management, Egypt was banished from the Arab League in 1979.

At an international level, Sadat helped in dislodging the USSR from the peace process and, for that matter, from the Middle East and gave up Egypt's capacity to balance the interests of one superpower against those of the other. Sadat's Egypt became obsequious to U.S. policy and the second largest recipient of American financial assistance. The Egyptian-Israeli peace began cold amid passionate pronouncements of optimism and has remained cold ever since. However, the same Arab leaders who voted to expel Egypt from their midst in 1988 urged Egypt's return to the Arab camp, under the slogan "Mubarak is not Sadat," leading one analyst to call the move "Arab political hypocrisy."[67]

Egyptian Economic Policy

Between 1971 and 1975, the commodity sector percentage of GDP slid from 55.6 to 51.3 percent, and the service sector rose from 44.4 to 48.7 percent. The government relied on short-term commercial loans, which by 1974 represented 36 percent of the current operating account in order to compensate for the reduced domestic private savings that had gone down from 12.7 to 4.5 percent. The same period witnessed a deficit in the current operating account of 21 percent of the GDP.[68] The net outcome was a sharp increase in inflation and a reduced ability to supply basic needs. Between 1973 and 1976, Egypt received from the Arab oil-rich countries soft loans totaling U.S.$4.4 billion.[69] In 1976, Egypt concluded an agreement with the International Monetary Fund (IMF) for a stabilization program, which required a reduction of the deficit by controlling wages and cutting state subsidies to basic staples and goods. The social cost was so high that riots broke out in 1977, though most of those arrested were released by the court which in its ruling found the causes of the riot justifiable. Ironically, Sadat described the people's riot as a "thugs action."

By 1974, the government moved toward liberalizing the economy through measures that came to be called the "economic open door policy," or *infitah,* and issued the Investment Law 43/1974 for Arab and Foreign Capital, which was amended by Law 32/1977. The goal of the two laws was to give privileges and legal protection to the operation of Arab and foreign capital. The pre-1952 revolution bourgeoisie reemerged in alliance with the bureau technocrats and the military, constituting a new indigenous socioeconomic stratum whose prime motivation was the establishment of import agencies and speculating in brokerage and in the financial sector. By 1982, there were more than 1,800 import agencies, which constituted a pressure group powerful enough to incorporate the Egyptian economy fully into world capitalist markets.[70]

Because the constituents of the neo-economic elite originally came from state institutions, they already enjoyed enough power to have established, ex officio, a wide network of relationships that were further augmented by intermarriage and the reciprocity of favors. This economic stratum included top decision makers who ranged from managing directors to ministers, members of parliament, and influential journalists (also including President Sadat himself), many of whom were in partnership with people accused or indicted of smuggling, fraud, and embezzlement.[71] The fact that the neo-stratum pursued a self-serving policy and interlocked with foreign capital, without being a part of a comprehensive economic development plan, has resulted not only in unbalanced sectored development and debt accumulation but also in increasing the gap between the poor and the rich and reinforcing the mores of corruption.[72]

Between 1975 and 1981, the annual average growth in agriculture was 1.8 percent; in mining and industry 6.2 percent; in transportation and storage 7.6 percent; in government civil services 9.9 percent; and in the finance sector 17 percent.[73] Between 1970 and 1975, the average annual growth of wages was 33.1 percent; the average increase in the urban food basket (amount available) was 46.6 percent; and in clothing 34.7 percent.[74] Further, the open-door policy did not inject new capital; most investment funds came from the public sector or groups of individuals. In 1980, public external debt was U.S.$19.1 billion, and debt service was 13.4 percent of exports of GDP. Between 1981 and 1990, rural poverty rose from 16.1 to 28.6 percent and urban poverty rose from 18.2 to 20.3 percent. If we consider the expenditure deciles, the bottom 80 percent fared worse than previously, while the top 20 percent was better off.[75]

Between 1984 and 1988, external debt increased progressively from U.S.$37.8 to $45.7 billion; the debt service from the U.S. sources alone was U.S.$2.4 to $3.4 billion while the export value of goods and services dropped from U.S.$3.4 to $2.7 billion. The obvious conclusion of this is that the Egyptian economy was not even able to pay the necessary debt service amount.[76] The liberalization of the economy impoverished the majority while it enriched and empowered the few who had taken refuge in a linkage with the foreign capital and the regime, while depleting economic resources without any indication that the neo-stratum was capable of transforming itself into a genuine national bourgeoisie that would undertake the comprehensive project of economic development and political reform.[77]

Political Liberalization

Although the notion of political plurality cannot be assumed to be the same in all times or places, an Egyptian scholar argues that it normally embodies three main principles: freedom of expression and tolerance for differences of opinion, commitment to a peaceful transfer of power in accordance with majority voting, and the supremacy of law.[78] In 1974, concomitant with the "open-door policy," Sadat presented, in what he called the October Document, some vague and undefined proposals for the creation of a political plurality. He proposed to divide the ASU into three forums within the body: one for the political Right, a second to represent the Center, and a third for the Left—all this in contravention to his constitution, which stipulated that the ASU was the only recognized party. After the 1976 general election, Sadat decreed the final transformation of the forums into independent political parties. In 1977, the Political Parties Law no. 40 was issued and succeeded by a series of amendments (Laws 36/1979, 144/1980, 30/1981, 156/1981) the main motivation of which was to control and limit the efficacy and power of any political party.[79] Thus the Liberal-Socialist Party, representing the Right, and the Progressive Unionist Party, representing the Left, were licensed, and the rest of the ASU was transformed into the National Democratic Party (NDP), which was the party of the ruling elite and headed by Sadat himself. The constitution was amended only in 1981 to abolish the ASU and permit, among other things, political plurality, the reelection of the president for an indefinite number of terms, and the establishment of the Supreme Council of the Press in order to covertly control, regulate, and organize it. In 1978, as a result of the Parties Law, a new political party was licensed, the New Wafd, whose leaders were the old prerevolutionary Wafd elite.

It is germane to emphasize that by reviewing the laws that saw to the founding of the parties and the procedures that regulated their activities, Sadat's plurality was no more than a safety valve for the political pressure that had been mounting with each act of regimentation and suppression. The organized political participation of popular forces was not considered, and even a modicum of expressed opposition was not tolerated, as was seen in September 1981 when Sadat rounded up all the leading political figures in the country (reported to number 1,519 from all walks of life) and detained them in prison where they remained until his assassination in October 1981.

After 1956, as events in Egypt began to impinge upon the politics of other states, there developed a more deliberate construction of ideological tenets and the application of these tenets to both domestic and foreign affairs. Thus the term *Nasserism* came into general use to explain the relationship between Nasser's ideas and Egypt's internal and external politics. Nasser's thought was, to a large degree, typical of Middle Eastern political thought, and his role was simply that of the first effective articulator of policy with this general set of attitudes. The term *Nasserism* is misleading because the movement was neither originally nor exclusively Nasser's. Yet the force of Nasserism, with the principles and the movement it designated, spread throughout the Arab world as a new nationalism to upset the status quo and threaten the balance of power—not only in the immediate area but in the world as well.

Mubarak: Continuity and Change

As soon as Hosni Mubarak came to power in 1981, following the assassination of Sadat, he made several statements that emphasized his concern with continuity and stability despite the fact that his regime has operated under martial law ever since. One of his earliest steps was to deal with the acute economic problem facing the country as a result of the open-door policy. Accordingly, he called for a meeting of a broad section of Egyptian economists in order to examine and offer suggestions on solving Egypt's economic difficulties. Mubarak also stressed the fact that the open-door policy should concentrate on productive projects. The economic situation has worsened, rather than improved, because of the lack of will on the part of the political leadership to implement these recommendations. As a result, housing, transportation, and inflation problems were exacerbated, and the foreign debt continued to rise. Under Mubarak, the Egyptian economy has maintained its mixed character, and the basic tenets of the open-door policy are still operative. The process of privatization was evaluated.

On the political level, Mubarak attempted to expand the democratic process by immediately releasing political prisoners and rehabilitating opposition forces. He also declared a policy of open discussion with everyone and respect for the opposition, which during Sadat's time was severely attacked and slandered. The Wafd Party returned, and the Islamic-oriented Ummah Party was established in 1983. Despite such efforts, however, several forces failed to be represented in the political system, such as the Nasserites, the leftists, and the religious groups, a fact which deprived the party system of its essence and continued to aid Mubarak's hold on power. Despite these setbacks to widening political representation, he succeeded in opening up to the Arab world and reintegrating Egypt in the Arab order.

Egyptian Domestic Politics

In 1993, Egypt was torn between two elements: the nomination of Mubarak to a third six-year term as president with extravagant propaganda and celebrations to cover the event, and the rise of terrorist activities of the Jihad group to an unprecedented level. In that year, a secularist writer, Farag Fouda, who reiterated the government's position on Islamic activism on a weekly television show, was assassinated and attempts were made to assassinate the information minister, the interior minister, and the prime minister. Although the latter attempts failed, they nevertheless caused the death of innocent people. That turbulent scene raised several questions and uncertainties with regard to the future of Egypt. Is the country heading to an Islamic overthrow of the regime? Will it be a prolonged civil war like Algeria? Or will the regime crush its militant opponents at the expense of respect for democracy and human rights?

So far, it is the third alternative that seems more on its way. In 1994, Mubarak initiated a national dialogue, involving the government and opposition parties, in an attempt to get the acting political forces' agreement on basic issues facing the nation and in order to mobilize their support against Islamic militants. This dialogue proved fruitless, especially as the government refused to discuss issues like constitutional and political reform, which had been a basic demand of the opposition groups. Thus, what began as a sign of furthering democracy ended in confirming the public view that the government was not ready to recognize any political opposition.

This coincided with other steps taken by the government to consolidate its power and eliminate any political threat from Islamic and oppositional forces, even the moderate ones. A new unified law for professional syndicates was passed in 1993 that gave the judiciary the authority to supervise elections rather than have each syndicate be totally responsible for the electoral process. The government used this law to curb the increasing Islamic influence within professional syndicates. It was opposed not only by the Islamists but also by the professional technocrats, including members of the ruling National Democratic Party (e.g., Hamdi al-Sayed).

Moreover, the confusion created by the new law had a negative impact on the performance of syndicates.

Another law with the same objective stipulated that deans of colleges are to be appointed by the government rather than elected by faculty members, thus undermining the relative independence of academic institutions from the government. Finally, in 1994, the government banned the activities of the society of the Muslim Brotherhood, accusing it of illegally supporting the terrorist Islamic groups, thus alienating even the moderate elements within the Islamist movement. Officially, the Brotherhood had been banned since 1948, but its existence had been openly tolerated.

The legal inhibitions were matched at the security level. In late 1993 the government began to pursue a more aggressive policy against Islamic opposition groups leading to a sharp drop in terrorist attacks, at the expense of respect for human rights. Prominent journalist and writer Mohammad Heikal claimed that in 1994 an average of fifty Egyptians were detained daily, five private citizens were killed every week, whether by the government or by the Islamic groups, and three Egyptians were hanged by the government every month, whether they had pleaded guilty or not. Heikal commented that while Islam cannot be preached by murder, so the law cannot also be implemented by having the police announce its killing of a group suspected of being Islamic fanatics. Even the pro-government *Arab Strategic Report,* in a rare admission, warned that the problem of "thousands of detainees" can be a future threat to the society, although it may seem necessary at present to counter terrorism.[80] While the Egyptian government tightens its control over society, it tries to present an image of fostering democracy and mass participation by claiming to encourage the establishment of non-governmental organizations (NGOs). Civil society, a novel concept for Egypt, became popular around 1992 and suddenly attracted enormous intellectual attention and political propaganda. In June 1995, Egypt's First Lady, Suzanne Mubarak, sponsored the first conference of NGOs at the national level.

According to political scientist Ahmed Abdallah, although Egypt has 15,000 NGOs that are active in many fields and could form a solid basis for a sound civil society, the rules regulating these organizations curb their activities. First, a single department in the Ministry of Social Affairs supervises all of these organizations, and all are regarded equally despite the differences that exist in terms of nature and objective. Second, they are regulated by Law 32 of 1964, a law promulgated during Egypt's single-party era and thus setting all activities of the civil society under the control of the central authorities. Third, the government has been manipulating these organizations as a counter to real opposition groups. Finally, these organizations have proved to be in the hands of a small elite that monopolizes influence and power and pays little attention to involving the average citizen. All these factors work to undermine mass participation in the system and make *civil society* a term with no meaning in Egypt.

Parliamentary Elections

The 1984 parliamentary elections were controversial, and the results were challenged. The opposition made charges of violence and forgery. Results showed that the National Democratic Party won the majority of votes while the Wafd emerged as the only opposition party to garner enough votes to be admitted into the People's Assembly. In February 1987, Mubarak decided to dissolve the parliament and hold elections in April on the basis of the Supreme Constitutional Court's decision to declare illegal the state's electoral laws forbidding independents to run for election. The elections resulted in better representation of the opposition parties, with the National Democratic Party still retaining a wide majority. The trilateral alliance of the Labor Party, the Liberal Party, and the Muslim Brotherhood enabled them to win sixty seats (twenty-two for Labor, thirty-four for the Brotherhood, and four for Liberal) and thus become the prime opposition force in the parliament. The Wafd won only twelve seats.

The true state of democracy in Egypt was revealed in the general election of November 1995. Opposition to the government centered on the outlawed Muslim Brotherhood, which was participating in the election despite its illegal status. Mubarak responded by ordering a massive detention of its membership and trial by military court. One Brotherhood candidate was arrested twice at his own campaign rallies, despite a court order allowing him to campaign freely. Pre-election violence at rallies between opposition supporters and security forces claimed twelve lives, and over 1,000 people were arrested. Fifty-four Brotherhood leaders were found guilty of sedition and sentenced to hard labor in the week before the election. The results of the poll were predictable: Of 444 parliamentary seats, Mubarak's supporters claimed over 400. Egyptian election monitors claimed that state security officers intimidated voters at polling stations, that officials cast hundreds of votes on behalf of the dead and children, that electoral registers were rigged, and that ballot boxes were set on fire, damaged, or stuffed.

Eberhard Kienle, perhaps the only foreigner who closely followed the 1995 election, reported, "The election was one of the most conspicuous illustrations of the erosion of positive liberties so far, combining direct interference by the regime, fraud by the NDP candidates, and impunity for them at unprecedented levels."[81] Following the election, in which NDP candidates won 95 percent of the races, the court ruled on about 950 cases and invalidated the election results in about 100 electoral constituencies involving over 200 deputies out of a total of 444. However, the government refused to abide by the ruling and appealed to a higher court.[82] By December 1996, the court had invalidated the election results of 250 deputies. However, the Assembly refused to accept this ruling on the grounds that it alone was the supreme authority in adjudicating the legalities of the election results.[83]

According to a semiofficial report, throughout 1997, the deputies lost credibility in the eyes of the people as they had virtually relinquished their constitutional obligation to monitor government performance in order not to antagonize the regime, which had been instrumental in giving them their positions. Very few independent voices in the Assembly protested the regime's thwarting of the deputies' role, and the Assembly was unable to enact a law to prosecute ministers for abuse of their office.

The regime's lack of commitment to true democracy and the overriding power of the executive branch have resulted in the enactment of unconstitutional laws. By 1997, the Supreme Constitutional Court had invalidated 121 laws. Six had been proclaimed before the 1952 revolution, 27 in Nasser's regime, 38 in Sadat's regime, and 50 under Mubarak's government. Thirty-two of these laws had been enacted in 1996–97. Despite the apparent seriousness of such a situation, it must be emphasized that not all unconstitutional laws are challenged in court.[84]

In July 2000 the Higher Constitutional Court invalidated the election of the 1990 parliament on the grounds that a clause in the law which governed its election was unconstitutional. The ruling, although specifically aimed at the 1990 parliament, meant that the parliament currently in session was also invalid, since it was elected by the same law. President Mubarak stepped in and issued two decrees: The first one introduced amendments to the law on practicing political rights, and the second summoned parliament from its summer recess to accept or reject the changes. The changes, contained in Decree 167/2000, were unanimously endorsed by parliament, during an extraordinary session on July 16, and the constitutional crisis was averted. They met a key opposition demand, validated by the court's decision, that elections at all the main and branch polling stations should be supervised by judges rather than public sector officials. The changes further oblige the government to stagger elections over three weeks instead of holding them all on one day.[85]

Observers have claimed that the real danger of Mubarak's crackdown is that it will increase the radicalization, especially that of the Islamic opposition, by denying it any role in the legitimate political life of the country. The Brotherhood and its splinter groups are very well connected, especially in the academic and professional spheres, as well as in small and medium-sized business. It has tremendous support with thousands of Egyptians abroad, many of whom donate financial support. Like most Islamist groups, the Brotherhood is more than a political organization. It ran schools, medical facilities, and media outlets, and it had strong connections with groups monitoring human rights abuses. Many of its operations were crippled by the government crackdown in the run-up to the 1995 elections. Brotherhood leaders have had their cases transferred to military courts despite the protests of human rights groups and the Egyptian civil judiciary itself, which in 1996 found it necessary to declare that confessions or testimony extracted under torture would not be admitted in court. Amnesty International claims that Brotherhood supporters or activists are regularly rounded up and detained, without charge or on false charges. While detained they are often beaten, electrocuted, or threatened with the rape or abuse of their female relatives.

Both government and opposition groups raise the specter of Algeria. Mubarak claims that the Brotherhood welcomes violent terrorists like the FIS, while Islamists reply that the FIS was not a violent organization until it was driven underground and denied a political voice. Almost 1,000 people have been killed in clashes between the government and Islamists since 1992, including both Egyptians and foreign tourists. Amnesty International reports that twenty-five people were executed in Egypt in the first four months of 1996. While the Brotherhood enjoys broad support among both the lower and middle classes, it poses significant problems for Mubarak's view of Egypt's future. It does not accept the peace with Israel, and it has been linked with Hamas and other groups, though its denunciation of violence has been very public and backed by its actions. It has also proved to be a staunch foe of the corruption that permeates the Egyptian regime and provides much grease to the wheels of Egypt's developing big business interests and foreign commercial operations.

Mubarak and his supporters won the 1995 elections with over 94 percent of the popular vote. However, voting irregularities have led to approximately one-third of those elected having their seats challenged, and as of June 1998 the appeal court had nullified some 170 members of the Assembly.[86] However, the People's Assembly was still decidedly in the NDP's grip when it nominated Mubarak for a fourth six-year term as president. Despite Mubarak's landslide electoral victory, his government still faces large credibility problems.[87] According to the *Arab Strategic Report 1998,* with the beginning of the parliamentary session in 1998 Egypt's government was faced with a credibility crisis. Because of the large number of members losing their seats due to electoral irregularities and a high level of absenteeism in the People's Assembly, new elections were needed to reestablish legitimacy. The Assembly had seemingly abdicated its legislative role to the executive, limiting itself to rubber stamping government programs without any serious review. This was evident in the sporadic activity conducted by the 51st Assembly during its third session, in 1997. A paltry eleven laws were passed with practically no discussion, while the Assembly enacted twenty-nine pieces of legislation giving the government emergency powers, despite a decline in religious terrorism.

The focus that regional governments have placed on combating terrorism and religious fundamentalism as a political opposition has demonstrably allowed organized (and even petty) crime to flourish. Violent crime, burglary, and theft have increased dramatically in rural areas. "While religious terrorism is declining, social and political dissatisfaction has become prevalent and it is natural that this will produce social terrorism despite its lack of intellectual framework which has justified its religious fundamentalist cousin."[88] In February 1999, legislation was hastily enacted to curb such social violence, especially its spread in high schools and universities, where youth violence had doubled since 1991.[89] The general level of corruption, the lack of a governmental presence in the social sphere of the population, and the government's constant preoccupation with religiously based opposition groups and terrorism has allowed for a further erosion of both civil society and governmental legitimacy.

The 2000 Egyptian General Elections

The 2000 Egyptian general elections evidenced a significant shift in Egyptian politics. Increasingly throughout the 1990s, the judiciary replaced the opposition in a number of political tasks, such as the promotion of democracy and political liberalization. In fact, a number of the political parties who gained support and seats in the Egyptian People's Assembly in 2000 acquired their legality only by means of court orders. With the substantial electoral abuses, which saw a large number of results overturned from the 1995 national election, the judiciary was appointed—by the Egyptian Supreme Court—to oversee the 2000 voting process. Prior to the judiciary's involvement there were accusations of government manipulation of candidate lists and voter registration. The 2000 elections were conducted to the satisfaction of many in the opposition as well as international observers. Accusations of violations of the electoral process by government security forces were reported, such as keeping voters away from polling stations and losing ballots, but it appears that the results will not face court challenges as in 1995. Egyptian commitment to both democracy and plurality must be further guaranteed, and such a continued active role by the judiciary and the concomitant promotion and enshrinement of the rule of law can only encourage such a path. However, the government's campaign against Gama' al-Islamiyya will be the litmus test of Egyptian political progress.

Results indicated gains for a number of opposition parties and a dramatic ouster of incumbent NDP Assembly deputies. Of the 442 contested seats only 132 deputies managed to return to office. The breakdown of seats again favored the ruling NDP with 388 deputies, but this number was down from 410 in the last election. Some 256 independent candidates won seats with 218 joining the NDP, swelling the government's majority. Opposition members rose to 35, an increase of 21 seats from the previous Assembly with the major parties represented as follows: Muslim Brotherhood (17), Wafd (7), Tagammu (6), Nasserists (2), Liberal party (1), and two opposition members remaining independent. The government's clampdown on the Muslim Brotherhood is seen as one of the principal reasons for its success. The jailing and high levels of harassment exacted upon Brotherhood members and supporters created empathy for their policies, and allowed them to run a slate of young and unknown candidates more immune to government scrutiny after longstanding and highly visible party candidates had been arrested. The increasing representation of opposition candidates was evident not only in the ranking of party deputies but also in the composition of the candidates themselves. Fifty-seven Christian candidates ran for office, with seven winning election to the Assembly (six Copts and one Roman Catholic). Gender disparity, long a criticism of the Assembly's composition since the 1979 abrogation of the law imposing mandatory representation for women, saw a record 120 women candidates run for office. With five winning election, and a further six women appointed by President Mubarak—out of the ten members he is constitutionally required to select—it is the highest level of female representation since 1979. Further growth in plurality in the general elections of 2005 could well cement a laudable legacy for the Mubarak administration.

Structural Adjustment

One factor that has led to the rise of Islamic militancy in Egypt and the delegitimization of the regime is the rapidly increasing gap between rich and poor in Egyptian society. In fiscal year 1993–94, Egypt ended the first stage of its structural adjustment program, initiated in 1991 as a result of two agreements with the IMF and the World Bank in which

Egypt pledged to launch immediate policies to stabilize the economy by minimizing inflation, budget deficit, and balance of payment deficit. Meanwhile, it would implement structural reform policies to increase the efficiency of the public sector, followed by a planned period of privatization. Handing successful enterprises over to the private sector is supposed to lead to future economic development.

Although the structural adjustment program had some success at the macro level, by reducing the budget deficit as compared with GNP from 17 percent in 1989 to 3.5 percent in 1993, and reducing inflation from 21.2 to 11.1 percent in the same period, austerity measures taken by the government involved a high social cost on the standard of living for the middle and lower classes in Egypt. According to a World Bank Report, average individual income in Egypt has fallen from U.S.$670 per year in the early 1960s to U.S.$610 per year in the early 1990s. At the same time, the Egyptian government was following World Bank instructions in minimizing the social subsidies that offered the poor minimum levels of food, clothing, health, education, etc., and increased prices by almost 300 percent, excluding new taxes. New economic policies also led to a high unemployment rate, estimated in 1994 by the World Bank at 17.5 percent and by other sources as high as 20 percent. Unlike the rich countries, unemployment in Egypt is not covered by social insurance or social welfare.

At the other extreme of Egyptian society, corruption, arms sales commissions, widespread bribery, and commercial services have led to the concentration of huge wealth in the hands of the neo-stratum that accumulates wealth while not contributing to the country's economic development. These elites invest their gains outside Egypt and, of course, avoid paying taxes. According to a study by Mohammad Hassanein Heikal, in Egypt there are 50 individuals whose wealth amounts to or exceeds U.S.$100–200 million, 100 whose wealth falls between U.S.$80 and $100 million, 150 whose wealth falls between U.S.$50 and $80 million, 220 whose wealth falls between U.S.$30 and $50 million, 350 whose wealth falls between U.S.$15 and $30 million, 2,800 whose wealth falls between U.S.$10 and $15 million, and 70,000 whose wealth falls between U.S.$5 and $10 million. Heikal adds that these figures are probably lower than the actual numbers. If we consider only the first five groups, we can see that over the last twenty years almost 1,000 individuals have accumulated over U.S.$50 billion, more than the foreign debt of Egypt, and all of these individuals have accumulated this wealth from within the country, either in the form of estates, through monopolies of essential goods, or as agents of international companies.[90]

Foreign Policy Orientations

In the Egyptian-Israeli sphere, Mubarak attempted to minimize interactions between the two governments, especially after the Israeli invasion of Lebanon and Israel's reluctance to relinquish the Taba Strip to Egypt. These developments prompted the opposition forces to call for severing relations with Israel and terminating, or at least suspending, the Camp David accord. Mubarak's reaction was to emphasize the centrality of the Palestinian issue and his commitment to any treaties Egypt had signed. In response to Israel's action in Lebanon, he recalled the Egyptian ambassador to Israel and called for an Arab summit to examine the new developments. Mubarak also declared that the Egyptian ambassador would not return to Israel until Taba was returned and Israel withdrew its forces from Lebanon. By early 1985, however, Egyptian-Israeli relations showed signs of improvement as official visits were exchanged and Israel participated in the Cairo Book Fair.

Since that time, relations have continued, although Egypt is careful not to appear to be too close to the Israelis. Mubarak has kept relations formal and sporadic. By the late 1980s, the relationship focused on the issue of elections in the occupied territories. Although the issue is at its root competitive (with both states trying to push their proposals on the Palestinians, and on the international community), there is a degree of cooperation as well. However, with minimal contacts between the governments and their formal nature, it is highly unlikely that this cooperation will deepen and give Egyptian-Israeli relations a dynamic of their own.

Mubarak also moved to enhance bilateral relations with the Arab countries. In an interview published in all the daily newspapers he stated, "Egypt is an Arab country. We are neither Westerners nor Easterners," further emphasizing the fact that Egypt's return to the Arab fold was only natural. Mubarak ordered the cessation of any propaganda attacks against other Arab regimes, even if they attacked the Egyptian regime. Officially, Mubarak believed that any restoration of relations with Arab states should be based on an Arab initiative, since they were the ones who broke off the relations initially. Behind the scenes, the story was different, as Egyptian diplomats and Mubarak worked feverishly to regain Egypt's credibility. As a result, Egyptian troops on the Libyan border were relocated, and Mubarak cultivated ties with Oman and Jordan. He also stressed the historic links between Egypt and the Sudan, which transcended personal leadership.

Finally, Egypt regained its dominant role in the Arab and Islamic world. In 1984, five years after it was dismissed, Egypt restored its membership in the Islamic Conference Organization. At the same time, bilateral relations between Egypt, Arab, and Muslim countries began to improve. It was in late 1987 that the Arab League decided to give Arab countries the right to restore bilateral relations with Egypt—although it was a mere formality, as bilateral relations had never completely ceased. In February 1989, Egypt, Iraq, Jordan, and North Yemen established the Arab Cooperation Council, and by 1990 Egypt had restored formal diplomatic relations with all its Arab neighbors. In order to exhibit some measure of independence, Mubarak renewed diplomatic relations with the Soviet Union in July 1983. By 1987, Egyptian-Soviet cooperation had gained momentum in several fields. The Egyptian-Soviet Friendship Society was reestablished, and the Soviets agreed to upgrade a number of existing projects. A satisfactory settlement was reached with regard to Egypt's military debt to the USSR, and Soviet Foreign Minister Eduard Shevardnadze arrived in Cairo in February 1989 to discuss Middle Eastern issues and ensure a Soviet role in establishing a comprehensive peace settlement. During the visit, he urged a greater Egyptian role in bringing about peace in the Middle East, making it once again appear that the Russians had come to terms with Egypt's importance to Russian interests in the region.

Mubarak participated in the conference of nonaligned countries, which convened in New Delhi in late 1984. He also tried to illustrate the importance of national independence by calling on the United States to be more flexible regarding economic assistance to Egypt and by criticizing the American attitude and position on the Israeli invasion of Lebanon. But he did not embark on any fundamental change in policy that would reduce Egypt's dependence on the United States. After almost twenty years of rule, Mubarak had achieved great success through his foreign policy initiatives. He had returned Egypt to the Arab League and the Islamic Conference Organization and had made Egypt active in developing world forums, especially in the Organization of African Unity, which Mubarak headed in 1989. At the same time, Mubarak was trying to maintain the delicate balance between Egypt's new commitments toward the peace process and the United States, on the one hand, and the regional commitments toward Arab states and Egypt's national sovereignty, on the other. Mubarak seems to have achieved some success in this balancing of policy and has emerged as one of the region's leading statesmen. Egypt appears to be once again assuming a leading role in tackling the region's most important issues, although its achievements have been somewhat diminished by continuing economic difficulties—largely related to debt—and its domestic instability.

In the second half of the 1980s, the budget deficit was 15 percent of GDP, inflation was 20 percent, exports were a fraction of imports (U.S.$2.7: $10.1 billion, respectively), and the balance of the current account was negative. Real growth in GDP stood at 2.7 percent between 1985 and 1990 and fell to 0.3 percent in 1991–92, while annual population increase remained as high as ever at 2.7 percent. Annual per capita growth of GNP was at 2 percent in 1990, 1 percent in 1991–93, and 1 percent in 1994. Real wages fell between 1985 and 1995 by about 40 percent, and total unemployment rose from 8.6 percent in 1990 to 11.3 percent in 1995. In terms of basic needs, for 1995–96, 23.2 percent of the Egyptian people were considered desperately poor. If we include the category of the moderately poor for the same period, the ratio would rise to 50.2 percent in the rural areas and 45 percent in the urban centers.[91]

Egypt after the Gulf War

With the liberation of Kuwait and the initiation of the Middle East peace process, Egypt's political leadership pursued a more aggressive foreign policy, especially at the regional level, and took an active role in bilateral negotiations in the Arab-Israeli peace process. Egypt also became an active partner in international peacekeeping operations both inside and outside the region. Mubarak has attempted to solidify regional political blocs, detach Egypt from some U.S. policies, and present it as an independent country acting in the interest of the Egyptian people and Arab nations rather than as an ally of the United States.

The Madrid peace process, initiated by the United States after the 1991 Gulf war, allowed Egyptian representation only in the multilateral negotiations, which discussed general regional issues, and not in the bilateral negotiations, which were to establish peace between the two hostile parties. Egypt insisted on carving a vital role for itself in the bilateral talks, as it was the only Arab party that had good relations with Israel and the Arab countries involved in the process. In doing so, its role was something between a mediator and a partner in the negotiations. In some instances it acted as a third party, trying to simply mediate between the Israelis and Palestinians or between Israelis and Syrians, and in other instances it acted as a partner by adopting the Arab stand and thus abandoning the "neutrality" assumed previously. In this context, Mubarak himself had occasionally met with Yitzhak Rabin, Hafez al-Assad, and Yasser Arafat whenever there was a deadlock in negotiations. It is also reported that Egypt decided not to interfere in the

Israeli-Palestinian Oslo negotiations when it learned of them. It was Mubarak, upon Arafat's request, who persuaded Rabin to add part of the West Bank to the self-rule area so that Arafat would not be accused of trading the West Bank for Gaza; thus Jericho was also included under Palestinian control. Later on, Cairo hosted the Israeli-Palestinian negotiations for the implementation of the Declaration of Principles and was involved in last-minute negotiations to get the implementation agreement signed on 4 May 1994.

Egypt had been consulting closely with Syria as well. On 1 December 1994, Mubarak visited Syria to discuss the peace process with Assad. The Israeli reaction suggested Egypt should take a stand for peace, not a stand for Syria, illuminating Egypt's significance. Later that month, Egypt hosted a trilateral summit with Syria and Saudi Arabia following the Casablanca Summit, which was to foster economic cooperation between Israel and the Arabs. The aim of the trilateral summit was to slow down the normalization process with Israel until a comprehensive peace was achieved. Assad was concerned that the Arab states would end their economic boycott of Israel before Israel agreed to withdraw from the Golan Heights, thus leaving Syria out in the diplomatic cold in its peace negotiations. Other theories claim that Mubarak hosted this summit because he feared that other Arab states would conclude economic deals with Israel in the absence of Egyptian leadership. This would have been ironic, as it was Egypt which originally opened the door for normalization with Israel at Camp David and paid dearly with almost ten years of isolation from the rest of the Arab world. Egypt pursued its active involvement in the peace process to convince the western world, especially the United States, that it, and not Israel, was the key to the region in the time of peace as it had been in the time of war. Thus, it should not be excluded from reaping the economic benefits of peace or ignored when the alliances and interests are revised.

In the upsurge of violence that followed the assassination of Rabin in November 1995 and the Palestinian elections in January 1996, Egypt again seized the chance to act as a regional leader. It hosted the March 1996 Summit of the Peacemakers in the Red Sea town of Sharm-al-Sheikh, with U.S. president Bill Clinton, Russian president Boris Yeltsin, and Israeli prime minister Shimon Peres, as well as King Hussein of Jordan and Yasser Arafat. While the leaders presented a united front in condemning terrorism, deep divisions were evident. Egypt took the opportunity to advance itself at Israel's expense by blaming the spate of Hamas suicide bombings on Israeli intransigence in the occupied territories, and successfully isolated Israel in its failed attempts to gain a united condemnation of Iran for its role in supporting terrorism. Syria boycotted the conference, as did Lebanon. Both are key players on the Arab side of the Palestinian issue. For Egypt, the hosting of the conference was an end in itself, and the Egyptian press and government trumpeted the return of Egypt to prominence in regional affairs. Mubarak seized the opportunity to make further gains following the May 1996 election of Benjamin Netanyahu and the Likud government in Israel. In response to Arab concerns about the direction of the new hard-line regime in Tel Aviv, Mubarak, King Hussein, and King Fahd of Saudi Arabia called for an Arab summit to be held in Cairo in late June. This summit strengthened Egypt's position, as have its continued efforts to maintain communication with Israel without expressing any support for the new Likud interpretation of the peace process.

Peacekeeping Operations

In order to assert its role as a regional power and an active advocate for peace, Egypt was keen to play an effective role in assisting the United Nations. In 1992, Mubarak announced that Egypt would be ready to participate in a UN Rapid Deployment Force, if one were formed. The idea was to assist in asserting the independence of the UN from the great powers. In 1994, Egypt participated in UN operations in Somalia, Liberia, Rwanda, the Western Sahara, Mozambique, and Bosnia. Because of Egypt's emphasis on its regional role, five of these operations were in Africa. The only one outside of the continent, in Bosnia, was highlighted because of the religious dimension. In those six countries, Egypt had 2,095 soldiers, 66 observers, and 51 policemen.

Regional Blocs

After Iraq invaded Kuwait in 1990 and the Arab Cooperation Council disintegrated, Egypt became involved in yet another attempt at an Arab bloc. The Damascus Declaration, announced in March 1991, was to engage the six Gulf states, Egypt, and Syria in a security and economic pact with the aim of establishing an Arab regional security system. However, the Declaration never materialized, because Kuwait and the other Gulf states sought to conclude bilateral security arrangements with the United States and Britain and replace Egyptian and Syrian troops with troops from those countries. In 1994, there was an attempt to revive the Damascus Declaration. Foreign ministers of the eight countries involved met in January, July, and October, but nothing materialized. By the Fifth Summit for the Gulf Cooperation Council, in Bahrain in December 1994, the Declaration was ignored altogether.

Another attempt to revive the Damascus Declaration arrangement was made in 1998 by the eight countries involved—once again with no substantive results.

Egyptian policymakers made a surprise move in November 1994 by requesting permanent observer status and possible membership in the Arab Maghrib Union (AMU), a security and economic bloc encompassing Mauritania, Morocco, Algeria, Tunisia, and Libya. Previously, Egypt had intensified its cooperation with the Maghrib countries to counter Islamic militancy. Analysts have observed that the failure of the Damascus Declaration and Egypt's concern about its future role after the peace process may be the reason for its willingness to join the AMU. However, official statements as to the real motive appear contradictory. A councillor in the Egyptian Ministry of Foreign Affairs noted that "Egypt's membership in the AMU would constitute a bridge between North Africa and the eastern end of the Mediterranean." Another Egyptian diplomat has said that "Egypt's membership is a political message with economic consequences, and that Egypt does not only relate to the Arab East." A third diplomat has stated that "Egypt, at present, does not expect concrete results from the membership, but there is a global trend toward forming large blocs." It seems at the moment that Egypt is trying to find a new political compass and is searching for a role in regional Arab politics.[92]

Relations with the United States

Although still maintaining its special relations with the United States and being its second largest aid recipient in the region, the Egyptian government has demonstrated a desire to be emancipated from its American patron. Trouble began in early November 1994, when the American press criticized Mubarak for violating UN sanctions against Libya. An American report on human rights in Egypt then accused the government of human rights abuses. In both these instances, Egyptian press and intellectuals attacked the Americans for distorting Egypt's image and adopting double standards. At the political level, the government was upset at U.S. interference in domestic politics and denied the allegations. Part of the reason given for U.S. media attacks was to get at Egypt for its position concerning the extension of the Nuclear Non-Proliferation Treaty.

This treaty, signed in 1970, was due for renewal in April 1995. Egypt declared that it would not approve any extension of the treaty unless Israel joined, adding that Israel had its justifications to keep its nuclear arsenal when it was at war with the Arab states, but that as the region now approached an era of peace there was no reason why it should not join the treaty. When the United States expressed its intention to have a collective vote for the indefinite extension of the treaty, Egypt tried to rally the Arab states, and the Third World in general, behind its cause. But the American policy succeeded, and the treaty was renewed for an indefinite period. During the debate, Mubarak was portrayed by the Egyptian press as a nationalist leader who was ready to stand up to the only superpower for the sake of the national interests of his country and his people.

The United States, however, found itself increasingly dependent on Egypt in the complex difficulties that sprung up in the path of the U.S.–sponsored peace process in late 1995 and early 1996. Egypt has been the regional chairman, hosting first the Summit of the Peacemakers and then the June 1996 Arab summit. As the Israeli government and public appeared less than committed to any lasting settlement of the Palestinian issue, western-aligned Arab states took up the cause, with Egypt at the head. Mubarak has placed Egypt in a position of some influence with the United States, as there is considerable American political capital tied up in the peace process. There is also domestic concern in the United States about the continued cost and dubious benefit of U.S.$3 billion per year in foreign aid to Israel (most of it military assistance), especially if the peace process collapses and a more militant Israel emerges. Egypt is now the United States' best contact in the Middle East and must be carefully supported if moderate Arab states are not to simply abandon the peace process in the face of Israeli obstruction. Egypt's only competition in this role is Saudi Arabia, which has also attempted to act as an Arab leader. To appeal to the United States, Saudi Arabia has the advantage of its oil reserves, but in the Egyptian case, it is the United States that needs the support of the Egyptian regime because there is no guarantee that a future leader would show the same degree of support for the peace process while the American administration's double standard continues to cause the Egyptian regime much embarrassment.[93]

Appendix A

Social Groups, Languages, and Religions

*T*his listing approximates the situation of distinctive social categories in the Arab world, with an emphasis on those set off by language (L) or by religion (R). Some but not all are minorities in the sociological sense of the term. The percentages indicate an order of magnitude more than an exact count; where none are given the numbers are small. Arabic-speaking Sunni Muslims are generally but not always the majority.

Algeria	L: Berbers, including Amazigh (25%) R: Ibadhites
Bahrain	R: Shi'a (70%), Sunni (30%)
Comoros	L: Comorian, Swahili (majority)
Djibouti	L: Somali (47%), Afar (37%)
Egypt	R: Christians (7%) L: Nubians; Beja; Berber (<1%)
Iraq	L: Kurds (20%), Turkmen, etc. R: Shi'a (55%), Sunni Arab + Kurd (40%); Christians (3%)
Jordan	R: Christians (8%) Social Groups: Circassians
Kuwait	R: Shi'a (20%), Sunni (80%)
Lebanon	R: Christians (Maronites; Greek Orthodox; Greek Catholics; Armenians) (25–30%) Muslims (Shi'a; Sunni; Druze; Alawites) (70–75%)
Libya	L: Berber (5–10%)
Mauritania	L: speakers of African languages (Wolof, Tukulor, Soninke, etc.) (30%)
Morocco	L: Berber languages (33%)
Oman	R: Ibadhites (75%), Sunni (25%) L: South Arabian languages
Qatar	-
Saudi Arabia	R: Shi'a (5%)
Somalia	L: Somali (90%), Bantu languages
Sudan	L: Various African languages (60%) R: Christians (5%) and pagans (18%); Muslims (70%)
Syria	R: Christians, incl. Armenians (10%); Alawites + Druze (16%); Sunni (74%)
Tunisia	L: Berber (<1%) R: Ibadhites (<1%)
UAE	-
Yemen	R: Sunni (53%); Shi'a (46%); Isma'ili

Historically the major concentrations of Jews in the Arab world were in North Africa (Morocco, Algeria, Tunisia, and Libya), in Iraq, and in Yemen. There were also proportionately smaller Jewish communities in Syria, Lebanon, Palestine, and Egypt. Only small groups remain. There are recent migrants with distinctive backgrounds in the Gulf countries. Many are from the Indian subcontinent, and include Hindus and Christians as well as Muslims. There are also ethnic Persians, Baluches, Filipinos, etc. There are Arab minorities in Turkey, Iran, Israel (16%), Chad, and Mali. In addition, there is an Arab diaspora that covers much of Europe, the Americas, and Australia.

Source: Nicholas S. Hopkins and Saad Eddin Ibrahim, eds., *Arab Society: Class, Gender, Power, and Development* (Cairo: American University in Cairo Press, 1997), xv.

Appendix B

Population and Health in the Middle East

Country	Population (in millions)	Under 15 Yrs. %	Urban %	Growth Rate %	Literacy Men %	Literacy Women %	Access to Safe Water %	Access to Health Services %	Population per Doctor
Algeria	30.2	44	56	2.4	74	49	78	98	1,064
Bahrain	0.6	31	88	2.0	89	79	-	-	775
Egypt	65.5	39	43	2.2	64	39	87	99	-
Iraq	21.8	43	70	2.8	71	45	78	93	1,667
Iran	64.1	40	61	1.4	79	69	95	80	1,200
Israel	6.0	30	90	1.5	97	93	-	-	-
Jordan	4.6	41	78	2.5	93	79	98	97	649
Lebanon	4.1	34	87	1.6	95	90	94	95	413
Libya	5.3	-	-	-	-	-	-	-	-
Mauritania	2.5	43	54	2.5	50	26	74	63	16,667
Morocco	27.7	36	52	1.8	57	31	65	70	-
Palestine	2.9	47	-	3.9	-	-	-	-	-
Sudan	28.5	43	27	2.1	58	35	50	70	-
Syria	15.6	45	51	2.8	86	56	86	90	1,220
Tunisia	9.5	35	61	1.9	79	55	98	90	1,852
Turkey	64.5	31	59	2.2	89	72	-	-	1,934
Yemen	15.8	47	25	3.3	53	26	61	38	4,348
UK	59.1	19	90	0.2	99	99	-	-	-
USA	270.2	22	75	0.6	99	99	100	100	24

Source: United Nations Population Information Network (*POPIN*), UN Population Division Department of Economic and Social Affairs with support from the UN Population Fund (UNFPA) (*www.undp.org/popin*).

Appendix C

Size, Income, and Diversity of the Middle Eastern Nations

Country	Land Area (sq. km)	GNP per capita	Languages	Ethnic Groups	Religions
Algeria	2,381,740	US$1,520	Arabic (official) Berber French	Arab (majority) Berber Tuareg	Islam
Bahrain	680	US$	Arabic	Arab Iranian Indian Pakistani	Islam (Sunni) Islam (Shi'ite)
Egypt	1,001,450	US$1,080	Arabic (official) English (business) French (business) Nubian Oromo	Arabs (Hashemite origin) African origin East Asia origin	Muslim Coptic Christian
Iran	438,320	n/a	Arabic (official) Kurdish	Arab (majority) Kurd	Islam (Shi'ite) Islam (Sunni)
Iraq		US$3			
Israel	20,770	US$15,870	Hebrew (official) Arabic (official)	Jewish (majority) Arab	Judaism (majority) Muslim Christian
Jordan	89,210	US$1,650	Arabic (official) English	Palestinian (majority) Circassian	Muslim (Sunni)

Country	Number	GDP	Ethnic Groups	Religion
Lebanon	10,400	US$2,970	Arab Armenian (minority) European (minority) Syrian (minority) Kurdish (minority)	Muslim (Sunni) Muslim (Shi'ite) Muslim (Druze) Christian (Maronite)
Mauritania	1,025,520	US$470	Arabic French (official)	Moors descendants (majority) African descendants (Peul) African descendants (Soninke)	Muslim (official and predominant)
Morocco	710,850	US$1,290	Arabic (official) French Spanish Berber dialects	Arab (majority) Berber	Muslim Christian (minority) Jewish (minority)
Palestine			Arabic (official) Hebrew	Arab	Muslim (majority) Christian
Sudan	2,505,813		Arabic (official) Local dialects	Arabs Nubians and 570 other minorities	Sunni Muslim (majority) Traditional African Christian
Syria	185,180	US$1,160	Arabic (official) Minority languages	Arabs (majority) Kurds Turks Armenians	Muslim (Sunni) Muslim (Alamite) Muslim (Shi'ite) Muslim (Ismai'lites)
Tunisia	163,610	US$1,930	Arabic (official) French Berber	Arab Berber (minority) European (minority)	Islam (Sunni) Jewish Catholic

(continues)

Appendix C (*continued*)

Country	Land Area (sq. km)	GNP per capita	Languages	Ethnic Groups	Religions
Turkey	527,970	US$380	Arab (official and predominant)	Arab Persian (minority)	Muslim (Shi'ite) Muslim (Sunni)
Yemen	779,452		Turkik Arabic Kurdish (minority)	Turks (majority) Arabs (minority) Kurds (minority)	Muslim (Sunni) Muslim (Shi'ite) Christian (minority)
United Kingdom	244,880	US$19,600	English (official) Welsh Gaelic	English Scots Welsh Irish Pakistani (minority) Indian (minority) Afro-Caribbean (minority)	Christian Catholic Anglican Presbyterian Methodist Baptist Muslim Sikh Hindu Jewish
United States	9,372,610	US$28,020	English (official) Spanish	German ancestry Irish ancestry African origin (minority) Latin American origin (minority) Asian origin (minority) Indigenous Americans (minority)	Protestant (majority) Catholic Jewish Muslim

Source: United Nations Population Information Network (*POPIN*), UN Population Division Department of Economic and Social Affairs with support from the UN Population Fund (UNFPA) (*www.undp.org/popin*).

Notes

1. The Burden of History: From Empire to Nation-States

1. Fromkin, *The Way of the World*, 28–37.
2. Ibid., 29–30.
3. For a survey of general history of the Middle East, see B. Lewis, *The Arabs in History*; Gibb, *The Arab-Conquests in Central Asia*; Hitti, *The Arabs*; Mansfield, *The Arabs*; Fisher, *The Middle East*; Hourani, *A History of the Arab Peoples*; Inalcik, *An Economic and Social History of the Ottoman Empire, 1300–1914*; and Cleveland, *A History of the Modern Middle East*.
4. For further information on the Arabian conquest, see Lapidus, *A History of Islamic Societies*, 37–45.
5. Hourani, *A History of the Arab Peoples*, 25–26, 28.
6. The language spoken in Persia and modern-day Iran is Farsi.
7. Uzuncarsili, *Osmanli Tarihi*, 1:123–24.
8. Inalcik, *The Ottoman Empire: The Classical Age, 1300–1600*, 309–16.
9. For Timur's policies see ibid., 326–28.
10. Ibid., 328–45.
11. Inalcik, *An Economic and Social History of the Ottoman Empire, 1300–1914*, 11.
12. Wheatcroft, *The Ottomans*, 195, 259.
13. Uzuncarsili, *Osmanli Tarihi*, 501–6.
14. Inalcik, *An Economic and Social History of the Ottoman Empire, 1300–1914*, 21.
15. Ibid., 510–13.
16. Ibid., 363–90.
17. T. Ismael, *The International Relations of the Contemporary Middle East*.
18. Fisher, *The Middle East: A History*, 282.
19. Hourani, *A History of the Arab Peoples*, 232.
20. Mansfield, *The Arabs*, 75–82.
21. Ibid., 174.
22. Fisher, *The Middle East: A History*, 109, 282.
23. Fromkin, *A Peace to End All Peace*, 17.
24. Fisher, *The Middle East: A History*, 282, 445.
25. Hourani, *A History of the Arab Peoples*, 319–20.
26. Fisher, *The Middle East: A History*, 282, 293–94.
27. Mansfield, *The Arabs*, 65–67.
28. I gratefully acknowledge my indebtedness in this section to Dr. Adel Safty, who has provided a more complete and critical analysis in his important book, *From Camp David to the Gulf* (University of Toronto Press, 1992, 1996).
29. Beckman, *World Politics*, 16.
30. Sid-Ahmed, "Ambitieux et risqué, le choix de l'Egypte."

31. Simons, *Iraq*; Jentleson, *With Friends like These*; Timmerman, *The Death Lobby*; Darwish and Alexander, *Unholy Babylon*.
32. Klare, "Dissuasion selective et vieilles recettes."
33. T. Ismael and J. Ismael, *The Gulf War and the New World Order*.
34. *New York Times*, 7 February 1990.
35. Milton Viorst, "A Reporter at Large: The House of Hashem," *New Yorker*, 7 January 1991.
36. *Al-Ahram* (Cairo), 25 January 1991.
37. *Manchester Guardian Weekly*, 23 September 1990.
38. *New York Times*, 19 September 1990.
39. *Ahkbar al-Yum* (Cairo), 9 February 1991.
40. *Al-Ahram* (Cairo), 25 January 1991.
41. *New Yorker*, 7 January 1991.
42. *New York Times Magazine*, 27 January 1991.
43. *New Yorker*, 7 January 1991.
44. Thomas L. Friedman, "When War Is Over: Planning for Peace and U.S. Role in Enforcing It," *International Herald Tribune*, 21 January 1991.
45. Heikal, *Azamat al-'Arab wa Mustaqblahim*, 25.

2. The Political Heritage of Islam: Continuity and Change

Portions of the section entitled "The Muslim Brotherhood and Islamic Activism" were adapted from T. Ismael and J. Ismael, *Government and Politics in Islam*, 59–79.

1. el-Rayes, "Al-Nadhriyyat al-Siasiyya al-Islamiyya," 117–20.
2. Tamadonfar, *The Islamic Polity and Political Leadership*, examines the life of the Prophet of Islam.
3. Ibn Qutaiba, *Al-Imamah wa al-Asiyasah*, 9–22.
4. Ibid., 23–31, 74–188; Subhi, *Nadhariyat al-Imamah lada al-Shi'ah al-Ithnay 'Ashriyah*, 101.
5. Subhi, *Nadhariyat al-Imamah*, 101–2.
6. Arnold, *The Caliphate*, 17.
7. See the views of Abu al-Hassan al-Ash'ari in Yusaf Ibish, *Nusus al-fikr al-siyasi al-Islami*, 19–26.
8. Subhi, *Nadhariyat al-Imamah*, 24.
9. Saleh, *Al-Yamin wa-Yasar fi al-islam*, 51–87.
10. See al-Baqilani's views in Ibish, *Nusus al-fikr al-siyasi al-Islami*, 31–118.
11. Sherwani, *Studies in Muslim Political Thought and Administration*, 49.
12. Ibid., 71.
13. Ibid., 73.
14. Ibid., 80–84.
15. Ibid., 77–79.
16. Ibid., 148.
17. Ibid., 165.
18. Ibish, *Nusus al-fikr al-siyasi al-Islami*, 172.
19. Sherwani, *Studies in Muslim Political Thought*, 167–74.
20. Ibid., 176–80.
21. Ibid., 107–8.
22. al-Mulk, *The Book of Government*, 60.

23. Sherwani, *Studies in Muslim Political Thought and Administration*, 169–84.
24. Hassan, *Islam: A Religious, Political, Social, and Economic Study*, 161.
25. Quoted in ibid.; Subhi, *Nadhariyat al-Imamah*, 69.
26. 'Abd al-Razeq, *Al-Islam wa usul al-Hukm* (Islam and the principles of government), 92–93.
27. Ibid., 93.
28. Ibid., 129.
29. Ibid., 136.
30. These are the views of al-Hilii in Sherwani, *Studies in Muslim Political Thought and Administration*, 172; see also al-lmam al-Rida in Subhi, *Nadhariyat al-Imamah*, 25.
31. Brown, *International Politics and the Middle East*, 22–27.
32. Fisher, *The Middle East*, 102–22.
33. Ingram, "It Was Islam That Did It," 18–20; Hourani, *A History of the Arab Peoples*, 78, 172–74, 175, 179–80, 183, 198, 202.
34. Fisher, *The Middle East*, 123–27.
35. Wheatcroft, *The Ottomans*, 167, 183.
36. The 1980s witnessed the formation of several regional organizations: the Gulf Cooperation Council, Arab Cooperative Council, and the Arab Maghrib Union.
37. Cordovez and Harrison, *Out of Afghanistan*, 163, 371.
38. For an excellent source on the Al-Da'wa Party, see al-Kharsan, *Hizb al-Da'wa al-Islamia*.
39. Al-Ahram, "Al-Taqrir al-Istratiji al-'Arabi" (1994), 315–18.
40. R. Mitchell, *The Society of the Muslim Brothers*, 261.
41. Military Order No. 63, 8 December 1948, quoted in al-Husaini, *The Moslem Brethren*.
42. Hamroush, *Qisat Thawrat 23 Yolyo*, 299; Radhwan, *Asrar Hikomat Yolyo*, 145–49; and Ramadhan, *Abd al-Nasir wa Azmat Mars 1954*, 107–10.
43. Hamroush, *Qisat Thawrat 23 Yolyo*, 132.
44. T. Ismael and J. Ismael, *Government and Politics in Islam*, 75, as taken from *Al-Ahram*, Cairo, 15 January 1954.
45. Ramadhan, *Abd al-Nasir wa Azmat Mars 1954*, 127–45.
46. The movement aimed at reviving the practices and thoughts of the early generations of pious Muslims, from *salaf*, meaning the predecessors.
47. Abu-Amr, *Islamic Fundamentalism in the West Bank and Gaza*, 66–67.
48. Ibid., 79–80.
49. Ibid., 23–52.

3. The Oppressive State and Civil Society

This chapter was coauthored with Jacqueline S. Ismael, professor of social work, University of Calgary.

1. For a succinct discussion of this distinction between Marxist and liberal conceptions of civil society, see Swift, *Civil Society in Question*.
2. Tibawi, *Arabic and Islamic Themes*, 101.
3. *An Economic History of the Middle East and North Africa*, 9–11.
4. Owen, *State, Power, and Politics*, 13–14.
5. Ayubi, *Over-stating the Arab State*, 90–91.
6. Owen, *State, Power and Politics*, 14–16.
7. T. Mitchell, *Colonizing Egypt*, 179.

8. Halliday, *Islam and the Myth of Confrontation*, 29.
9. Goldberg, "Khatima Nadhariya wa-Tarikhiya," 384.
10. Hassan, *Islam*, 462–67.
11. al-Dury, *Muqadima fi al-Tarihk al-Iqtasadi al-'Arabi*, 69–70.
12. Hassan, *Islam*, 472.
13. al-Dury, *Muqadima fi al-Tarihk al-Iqtasadi al-'Arabi*, 66, 67–68.
14. Hassan, *Islam*, 472.
15. Goldberg, "Khatima Nadhariya wa-Tarikhiya," 386, 365.
16. al-Dury, *Muqadima fi al-Tarihk al-Iqtasadi al-'Arabi*, 68.
17. Ibid., 69–70
18. Ibid., 91–92.
19. Fuller and Lesser, *A Sense of Siege*, 30.
20. al-Dury, *Muqadima fi al-Tarihk al-Iqtasadi al-'Arabi*, 99.
21. Ibid., 100–101, 104–11.
22. Inalcik, *An Economic and Social History of the Ottoman Empire, 1300–1914.*
23. Ismael and El-Sa'id, *The Communist Movement in Egypt;* see also Mustapha al-Sayyid, "A Civil Society in Egypt?" in Jillian Schwedler, *Toward Civil Society in the Middle East?* 46–48.
24. J. Ismael and S. Ismael, "Gender and State in Iraq," in Suad Joseph, *Citizenship and Gender in the Middle East;* see also Zuhair Humadi, "Civil Society under the Ba'ath in Iraq," in Schwedler, *Toward Civil Society in the Middle East?* 50–53.
25. J. Ismael, *Kuwait;* see also Crystal, *Oil and Politics in the Gulf;* Neil Hicks and Ghanim al-Najjar, "Civil Society in Kuwait"; and Jill Crystal, "Civil Society in the Arab Gulf States," in Schwedler, *Toward Civil Society in the Middle East?* 59–61, 61–63.
26. Muhammad Muslih, "Palestinian Civil Society," and Sara Roy, "Civil Society in the Gaza Strip," in Schwedler, *Toward Civil Society in the Middle East?* 65–69.
27. Tanör, Boratav, and Aksin, *Türkiye tarihi.*
28. Ibrahim, "Civil Society and Prospects," 39–44.
29. See *Turkiye Ekonomik ve Toplumsal Tarih Vakfi*, 3.
30. J. Ismael and S. Ismael, "The International Humanitarian Response to the Turkish Earthquakes."
31. Norton, *Civil Society in the Middle East*, 1–25.
32. Ibn Khaldun Center for Developmental Studies, *Files of the Arab Data Unit (ADU).*
33. "Al-Haraka al-Arabiyya li Hoquq al-Insan," in al-Ahram, "Al-Taqrir al-Istrateji al-'Arabi" (1995), 327–28.
34. Human Rights Watch, "Middle East and North Africa Overview," *World Report 1999.*
35. Buergenthal, *International Human Rights in a Nutshell*, 1.
36. Amnesty International, *Middle East and North Africa, State Injustice.*
37. Human Rights Watch, "Middle East and North Africa Overview," *World Report 1999.*
38. Human Rights Watch, *World Report 1999: Algeria.*
39. Human Rights Watch, "Middle East and North Africa Overview."
40. Human Rights Watch, *World Report 1999: Bahrain.*
41. Amnesty International, *Middle East and North Africa, State Injustice.*
42. *Al-Ahram*, 12 April 2000.
43. "Iran's Elections: The People against the Mullahs," *Economist*, 19 February 2000, 26–28.

44. Amnesty International, *Fear Flight and Forcible Exile: Refugees in the Middle East.*

45. While notorious, its actions are consistent with the performance of other states in the region whose violations of human rights have not received the same level of world attention. In other words, the government of Iraq has not done anything that was not already done with impunity by some other state in the region.

46. al-Khalil, *Republic of Fear.*

47. J. Ismael and S. Ismael, "Gender and State in Iraq."

48. T. Ismael and J. Ismael, "Cowboy Warfare," 16–24.

49. T. Ismael and J. Ismael, "The UN in Iraq."

50. Falk, "International Law versus Indiscriminate Sanctions."

51. *Economist,* 19 February 2000, 47.

52. Quoted in Human Rights Watch, *World Report 1999.*

53. These violations are well documented in human rights reports. See Amnesty International and Human Rights Watch annual and special reports for details.

54. 'Ali Mahfadha, "Al-Ardun . . . ila Ayn?" 27–28.

55. Quoted in Amnesty International, *Jordan: Human Rights Reforms: Achievements and Obstacles.*

56. Amnesty International, *Jordan: An Absence of Safeguards.*

57. Human Rights Watch, *Jordan: A Death Knell for Free Expression?*

58. Human Rights Watch, *HRW to Jordanian Deputies: Oppose Tight State Grip on Newspapers, Journals, and Books,* press release, New York, 25 June 1998.

59. Human Rights Watch, *Academic Leaders and Scholars Advocates Critique Proposed Jordanian Press Law,* press release, New York, 13 July 1998.

60. Human Rights Watch, letter of Jordanian prime minister, 9 August 1999.

61. Human Rights Watch, *National Jordanian Campaign to Eliminate the So-called Crimes of Honor.*

62. Human Rights Watch, *A Victory Turned Sour: Human Rights in Kuwait since Liberation.*

63. J. Ismael, *Kuwait,* 161–86.

64. Human Rights Watch, *The Bedoons of Kuwait: Citizens without Citizenship,* 1995.

65. Amnesty International, *Annual Report 1997: Kuwait.*

66. Quoted in Amnesty International, *Annual Report 1998: Middle East and North Africa* (regional country index, Kuwait).

67. Amnesty International, *Annual Report 2000: Kuwait.*

68. Human Rights Watch, *Civilian Expulsions from South Lebanon Continuing,* press release, November 1999.

69. Human Rights Watch, *HRW Condemns Israel's Detention of Twenty-one Lebanese for Years without Charge,* press release, 14 October 1997.

70. Human Rights Watch, *South Lebanon: Rights Crisis Looms,* press release, 23 May 2000; and Human Rights Watch, *Israel's Withdrawal from South Lebanon: The Human Rights Dimensions,* May 2000.

71. Human Rights Watch, *Operation Grapes of Wrath* 9, no. 8(E) (September 1997).

72. Amnesty International, *Lebanon: Human Rights Developments and Violations.*

73. Ibid.

74. Human Rights Watch, *Israel's Withdrawal from South Lebanon: The Human Rights Dimensions,* May 2000.

75. Amnesty International, *Annual Report 2000.*

76. European Union, Presidency Statement [Bulletin EU 4–1999].
77. Amnesty International, *Annual Report 1997.*
78. Amnesty International, *Annual Report 1998.*
79. Amnesty International, *Annual Report 1999.*
80. Amnesty International, *Annual Report 2000.*
81. Amnesty International, *Annual Report 1999.*
82. Amnesty International, *Annual Report 1998.*
83. Amnesty International, *Annual Report 2000.*
84. Amnesty International, *Annual Report 1998.*
85. Amnesty International, *Annual Report 2000;* see also United Nations, *Committee against Torture Concludes Twenty-second Session,* press release, 14 May 1999.
86. Amnesty International, *Annual Report 2000.*
87. Human Rights Watch, *Prison Conditions in the Middle East and North Africa.*
88. Amnesty International, *Annual Report 1997.*
89. Amnesty International, *Annual Report 1999.*
90. Amnesty International, *Annual Report 1998.*
91. Amnesty International, *Annual Report 1997.*
92. Amnesty International, *Annual Report 1998.*
93. Amnesty International, *Annual Report 2000.*
94. Human Rights Watch, *World Report 1999: Middle East;* see also Amnesty International, *Annual Report 1999.*
95. Human Rights Watch, *Western Sahara* and *Human Rights in Morocco.*
96. Amnesty International, *Annual Report 2000.*
97. Amnesty International, *Annual Report 1999.*
98. Amnesty International, *Annual Report 2000.*
99. Human Rights Watch, *World Report 1999: Middle East.*
100. Amnesty International, *Annual Report 1999.*
101. Amnesty International, *Israel/Occupied Territories and the Palestinian Authority: Five Years after the Oslo Agreement—Human Rights Sacrificed for "Security,"* 15, 16.
102. Human Rights Watch, *Palestinian Arrests Condemned,* press release, New York, 2 December 1999.
103. Amnesty International, *Palestinian Authority Defying the Rule of Law: Political Detainees.*
104. Amnesty International, *Annual Report 2000: Palestinian Authority.*
105. Amnesty International, *Annual Report 1999.*
106. Amnesty International, *Annual Report 2000.*
107. Human Rights Watch, *World Report 2000: Saudi Arabia.*
108. Amnesty International, *Annual Report 2000: Saudi Arabia.*
109. Human Rights Watch, *World Report 1999: Middle East.*
110. Human Rights Watch, *World Report 2000: Saudi Arabia.*
111. Human Rights Watch, *World Report 1999: Middle East.*
112. Amnesty International, *Annual Report 2000: Saudi Arabia.*
113. Human Rights Watch, *World Report 2000: Saudi Arabia.*
114. Human Rights Watch, *World Report 1999: Middle East.*
115. Human Rights Watch, *World Report 2000: Saudi Arabia.*
116. Ibid.
117. Human Rights Watch, *World Report 1999: Middle East.* See also Amnesty International, *Syria: Double Injustice—Prisoners of Conscience Held beyond the*

Expiry of Their Sentences, and Amnesty International, *Syria: Caught in a Regional Conflict—Lebanese, Palestinian, and Jordanian Political Detainees in Syria.*

118. Human Rights Watch, *World Report 1999: Middle East.*
119. Amnesty International, *2000 Annual Report 2000: Syria.*
120. Amnesty International, *Annual Report 2000: Tunisia.*
121. Human Rights Watch, *World Report 1999: Middle East.*
122. Human Rights Watch, *World Report 2000: Tunisia.*
123. Human Rights Watch, *World Report 1999: Middle East.*
124. Human Rights Watch, *World Report 2000: Tunisia.*
125. Amnesty International, *Annual Report 2000: Tunisia.*
126. Human Rights Watch, *World Report 1999: Middle East.*
127. Human Rights Watch, *World Report 2000: Tunisia.*
128. Amnesty International, *Annual Report 2000: Tunisia.*
129. Human Rights Watch, *World Report 2000: Turkey.*
130. Amnesty International, *Annual Report 2000: Turkey;* see also Amnesty International, *Turkey: Creating a Silent Society—Turkish Government Prepares to Imprison Leading Human Rights Defender.*
131. Amnesty International, *Annual Report 2000: Turkey.*
132. Ibid. See also Amnesty International, *Turkey: The Duty to Supervise, Investigate, and Prosecute.*
133. Amnesty International, *Annual Report 2000: United Arab Emirates.*
134. Human Rights Watch, *World Report 2000: Yemen.*
135. Ibid.
136. Amnesty International, *Annual Report 2000: Yemen.*
137. Human Rights Watch, *World Report 2000: Yemen.*
138. Ibid.
139. Amnesty International, *Annual Report 2000: Yemen.* See also Amnesty International, *Yemen: Empty Promises—Government Commitments and the State of Human Rights in Yemen.*
140. Human Rights Watch, *World Report 1999: Middle East.*
141. Amnesty International, *Annual Report 2000: Yemen.*
142. Human Rights Watch, *World Report 2000: Yemen.*
143. Human Rights Watch, *World Report 1999: Middle East.*
144. Human Rights Watch, *World Report 2000: Yemen.*
145. Ibid. See also Amnesty International, *Yemen: Empty Promises.*

4. The Islamic Republic of Iran

1. Although the historicity of Zoroaster appears to be beyond question, the actual age of the religion is hard to judge. Some of its texts appear to date from at least the twelfth century B.C.E. The most basic influence of Zoroastrianism on these religions is the concept of a Shaitan, Satan, or Devil figure, which allows for an ongoing and conscious conflict between good and evil, and a Hell, or a place of eternal punishment, concepts which are mostly lacking in rabbinical Judaism.
2. Kamrava, *The Political History of Modern Iran*, 21.
3. Ibid., 29.
4. Avery, *Modern Iran*, 292.
5. Diba, *Mohammed Mossadegh: A Political Biography.*
6. Kamrava, *Revolution in Iran*, 25.
7. Ibid., 22.

8. Milani, *The Making of Iran's Revolution*, 85.
9. Ibid., 99.
10. Ibid., 149.
11. Kamrava, *Revolution in Iran*, 66.
12. Rohallah al-Khomeini, *Al-Hukuma al-Islamiyah*, 9.
13. Ibid., 53.
14. Ibid., 70–71.
15. Ibid., 43, 47.
16. Ibid., 107–8.
17. Ibid., 70–72.
18. Ibid., 38.
19. Wright, *The Last Great Revolution*.
20. "Female Medical Pupils Go on Strike in Iran," *Globe and Mail* (Toronto), 14 January 2000.
21. "Iran: Time Matures," *Economist*, 15 May 1999, 50.
22. Jonathan Lyons [Reuters], "Hard-liners Set for Showdown with Protestors," *Globe and Mail*, 14 July 1999, A7.
23. "Political Law," *Economist*, 18 September 1999, 51.
24. "Iran's Zealots Fight to Curb 'Tehran Spring,'" *Times* (London), 28 June 1999.
25. "Conservative Courts Muzzle Iranian Reformers," *Turkish Daily News*, 28 November 1999, A1.
26. "Booting Out the Better-Known," *Economist*, 15–21 January 2000, 46–47.
27. "Iran's Reformist Victory," *Economist*, 26 February–3 March 2000.
28. Amuzegar, *The Dynamics of the Iranian Revolution*, 414.
29. Ibid., 416.
30. Sick and Potter, *The Persian Gulf at the Millennium*, 158.
31. *Middle East Economic Digest*, 26 January 1996.
32. Ibid.
33. Rushdie has, however, continued to publish, and has made some very public statements including an onstage appearance with Irish rock group U2 in front of 70,000 people in 1994. He is protected by elements of the British security apparatus.
34. Iran's entire military budget is approximately one-third that of Canada's, a country with half the population.
35. For country-specific analysis of Islamic activism today, see Abu-Amr, *Islamic Fundamentalism in the West Bank and Gaza*; Ibrahim, *Egypt, Islam, and Democracy*.
36. Shipler, *Arab and Jew*.

5. The Republic of Turkey

1. Mango, *Turkey*, 17–18.
2. Heper, *The State Tradition in Turkey*, 22.
3. G. Lewis, *Modern Turkey*, 31.
4. Ibid., 37.
5. Berberoglu, *Turkey in Crisis*, 4.
6. Fisher, *The Middle East: A History*, 274–76.
7. Inalcik, *The Ottoman Empire*, 53–56.
8. William Campbell, trans., *Atatürk* by Jorge Blanco Villalta (Ankara: Türk Tarih Kurumu Basimevi, 1979), 25.

9. Heper, *The State Tradition in Turkey*, 46.

10. Berberoglu, *Turkey in Crisis*, 5.

11. G. Lewis, *Modern Turkey*, 31, 65.

12. Davison, *Reform in the Ottoman Empire*.

13. Gökalp, *Turkish Nationalism and Western Civilization*.

14. Campbell, *Atatürk*, 278.

15. Tachau, *Turkey*, 18.

16. Tachau, *Political Elites and Political Development*, 554.

17. Dodd, *Democracy and Development in Turkey*, 136.

18. Tachau, *Turkey*, 22.

19. J. White, "Islam and Democracy," 1.

20. Ibid., 7.

21. Salt, "Nationalism and the Rise of Muslim Sentiment in Turkey," 19.

22. J. White, "Islam and Democracy," 10.

23. Doxey, "Turkey: Post-election Uncertainty Continues," 14.

24. A small party led by Cindoruk that was established by the MPs who had resigned from the DYP over their dissatisfaction with the insistence of Tansu Çiller in continuing the RP-DYP coalition.

25. "February 28 Decisions Bring About End of Political Islam," *Turkish Probe*, 5 March 2000, 1, 5.

26. Ibid.

27. *New York Times*, 17 January 1998.

28. *New York Times*, 23 February 1998.

29. *Turkish Daily News* (Ankara), 12–30 November 1998.

30. "Rebirth of the Gray Wolves," *Turkish Daily News*, 20 April 1999, A1.

31. "Islamists Defeated in Parliamentary Polls, Successful in Local Elections," *Turkish Daily News*, 20 April 1999, A1.

32. "Official Tally Out, Parliament to Convene Sunday," *Turkish Daily News*, 28 April 1999, A1.

33. "CHP's Baykal, the Bitter Loser," *Turkish Daily News*, 20 April 1999, A1.

34. "Parliament Breaks Record," *Turkish Daily News*, 31 December 1999, A3.

35. "A Century-long Journey from a Closed Farm Economy to a Troubled, Semi-liberal System," *Turkish Probe*, 2 January 2000, 1.

36. "The Apo Reports," *Turkish Daily News*, 5 January 2000, B4.

37. "Mixed Signals from Turkey to Europe," *Turkish Daily News*, 7 January 2000, A3.

38. "Overwhelming Support for the President-Elect," *Turkish Daily News*, 8 May 2000, 1–2; "Sezer: Democratic, secular republic," *Turkish Daily News*, 17 May 2000, 1, 9; "A New Era: President Sezer," *Turkish Probe*, 8 May 2000, 1, 4.

39. "President Sezer's Rule of Law Pledge," *Turkish Probe*, 22 May 2000, 3.

40. "President Sezer Receives Full Support from Politicians of Kurdish Descent," *Turkish Daily News*, 22 May 2000, 5.

41. Gunter, "The Kurdish Problem in Turkey," 395.

42. *Turkish Daily News*, 5 October 1998.

43. "Ocalan Caught in Italy: Nowhere to Run," *Turkish Probe*, 15 November 1998, issue 305, 9.

44. "Human Rights Diary," *Turkish Probe*, 14 March 1999, issue 322, 4.

45. "Turkey and Abdullah Ocalan: Both on Trial," *Economist*, 5 July 1999, 36.

46. Ibid., 16.

47. "Demirel Backs Abolishing Courts with Military Judges," *Turkish Probe*, 14 March 1999, issue 322, 4.

48. "Addressing Human Rights Problems Awaits Government Will," *Turkish Daily News*, 1 May 2000, 1; "Renewed Claims of Torture," *Turkish Daily News*, 10 May 2000, 3; "Parliamentary Human Rights Initiatives Documented," *Turkish Daily News*, 27 May 2000, 5.

49. "Military Gives Cautious Support to Civilianization of the MGK," *Turkish Daily News*, 8 May 2000, 1–2.

50. *Turkish Daily News*, 6 April 2000, 16; and 29 March 2000, 4.

51. Hale, *The Political and Economic Development of Modern Turkey*, 55.

52. Ibid., 132.

53. *Economist*, 19 November 1994, 23.

54. Ibid., 24.

55. Ibid., 23.

56. Rouleau, "The Challenges to Turkey," 116.

57. "Main Opposition leader Recai Kutan speaks out: We cannot get into European Union with a prohibitive constitution," *Turkish Daily News*, 19 November 1999, Special Section: Turkey at the OSCE Summit, 1.

58. "Times Are Changing, but All for the Better," *Turkish Daily News*, 19 November 1999, Special Section: Turkey at the OSCE Summit, 1.

59. "Language: To Go for 'National Unity' or Integration with Europe?" *Turkish Probe*, 7 November 1999, 3.

60. "Ecevit: Yes to EU, but Not at All Costs," *Turkish Daily News*, 30 November 1999, A3.

61. "Oil: United States Diplomacy Prevails," *Turkish Daily News*, 21 November 1999, 5.

62. *Middle East Times*, 21–27 April 1996, 6; and *Turkish Daily News*, 25 May 1998.

63. Gresh, "Turkish-Israeli-Syrian Relations," 190–91.

64. "Sharing Mesopotamia's Water," *Economist*, 13 November 1999, 45–46.

65. Douglas Frantz, "Military Bestrides Turkey's Path to the European Union," *New York Times*, 14 January 2001.

66. Eric Rouleau, "Turkey's Dream of Democracy," *Foreign Affairs* (November–December 2000), 100–114.

6. The Republic of Iraq

1. Hopkins and Ibrahim, *Arab Society*, xv.

2. Roux, *Ancient Iraq*, 122, 151–57.

3. See Khairi, *Mulahadaat awaliyah an al-islah al-manshod fi al-'Iraq*, 11–44; al-Zubaidi, *Thawarat 14 Tamouz 1958 fi al-Iraq*, 32–37.

4. The Fabian Society was established in 1884 in London and proposed the permeation of English political and social institutions by socialists in an effort to alter society without the resort to revolutionary tactics. The society concentrated on practical issues, such as public services and a leveling of society through abandonment of laissez-faire and the adoption of egalitarianism and the elimination of poverty. The acceptance of existing constitutional arrangements and commitment to not violently overthrowing the government brought respectability to English socialists and allowed them a voice in parliamentary politics. See "Fabianism," in Bullock and Trombley, eds., *The Fontana Dictionary of Modern Thought*, 305.

5. Khadduri, *Republican Iraq*, 8–10. See also *Khairi Mulahadaat awaligah an al-islah al-manshod fi al-Iraq*, 43, and al-Zubaidi, *Thawarat 14 Tamouz 1958 fi al-Iraq*, 31–33.
6. Ovendale, *Britain, the United States, and the Transfer of Power in the Middle East, 1945–1962*, 216.
7. For more details on the tribalization of Iraq, see Baram, "Neo-Tribalism in Iraq," 1–31.
8. Ovendale, *Britain, the United States, and the Transfer of Power in the Middle East, 1945–1962*, 231–35.
9. Hazelton, *Iraq since the Gulf War*, 32–38.
10. Ibid., 40–41.
11. Jabbar, Shikara, and Sakai, *From Storm to Thunder*, 17–22.
12. Baram, "The Ruling Political Elite in Ba'thi Iraq, 1968–1986," 466.
13. Ibid.
14. Hazelton, *Iraq since the Gulf War*, 465.
15. Ibid., 25.
16. Amnesty International, *Annual Report 1989*, 258.
17. See Baram, "The Ruling Political Elite in Ba'thi Iraq, 1968–1986," 447–93.
18. *New York Times*, 9 December 1999.
19. Timmerman, *The Death Lobby: How the West Armed Iraq*.
20. Hiro, *The Longest War*, 250–51.
21. Simons, *Iraq*, 283.
22. Alnasrawi, *The Economy of Iraq*, 80.
23. Ibid., 79.
24. Ibid., 9, 89.
25. Ibid., 91–94, 100.
26. Ibid., 91–94.
27. Simons, *Iraq*, 283–84.
28. Timmerman, *The Death Lobby*.
29. Aronson, *The Politics and Strategy of Nuclear Weapons in the Middle East*, 169–84; Timmerman, *The Death Lobby*, 96–97; Simons, *Iraq*, 303; Hilsman, *George Bush vs. Saddam Hussein*, 41, 179.
30. Hilsman, *George Bush vs. Saddam Hussein*, 80.
31. "Iraq: Banking on Credit," *Economist*, 30 September 1989, 39.
32. Alnasrawi, *The Economy of Iraq*, 109.
33. "Stopping Saddam Hussein," *Economist*, 11 August 1990, 22.
34. Alnasrawi, *The Economy of Iraq*, 84, 113.
35. "OPEC: Getting That Sinking Feeling," Middle East Economic Digest, 13 July 1990, 4.
36. Alnasrawi, *The Economy of Iraq*, 75, 103, 117–18.
37. "Iraq's Opposition Purged," *Economist*, 1 September 1990, 36.
38. Bradsher, "War Damages and Old Debts Could Exhaust Iraq's Assets."
39. Simons, *Imposing Economic Sanctions*, 173; see also Haselkorn, *The Continuing Storm*.
40. Hazelton, *Iraq since the Gulf War*, 80.
41. "Iraqis Count the Cost of Sanctions," *Economist*, 19 February 1994, 46.
42. Simons, *The Scourging of Iraq*, 50.
43. al-Nasarwi, *Middle East Studies Association Bulletin* 33, no. 1 (summer 1999): 132.
44. Simons, *The Scourging of Iraq*, 148.

45. Charges have emerged from former U.S. Attorney-General Ramsey Clark and U.S. Congressman Henry Gonzalez and are amply portrayed in Geoff Simons, *The Scourging of Iraq*. Furthermore, Denis Halliday, who had been the UN official placed in charge of humanitarian operations in Iraq under the oil-for-food program, has repeatedly accused the United Nations and the Western powers of Great Britain and the United States as war criminals for their continued maintenance of the sanctions regime. See "Death for Oil," *Al-Ahram Weekly*, Online edition, 13–19 July 2000, issue 490 [*http://www.ahram.org.eg/weekly/2000/490/ intrvw.htm*].

46. 'Abdullah Mutawi', "Sanctions on Iraq: Illegal and Indefensible," *Middle East International*, 10 April 1998.

47. Simons, *The Scourging of Iraq*, 227.

48. Ritter, *Endgame*, 8.

49. "Iraq's Opposition Purged," *Economist*, 1 September 1990, 36, 37.

50. *Jordan Times*, 5 July 1999, 1.

51. Warren A. J. Hamerman, International Progress Organization, presentation to the UN Organization Sub-Commission on Prevention of Discrimination and Protection of Minorities, 43d session, 13 August 1991; as quoted in Simons, *Imposing Economic Sanctions*, 169.

52. Ibid., 174–78.

53. Mueller and Mueller, "Sanctions of Mass Destruction," 51.

54. See "Death for Oil," *Al-Ahram Weekly*, Online edition, 13–19 July 2000, issue 490.

55. See *Al-thakafa Al-jadidah* 8, no. 14 (January/February 1960): 130–36, for program of the KDP.

56. "Old Enemies Come Together against the Common Foe," *Economist*, 16 March 1991, 37.

57. "Northern Iraq: A New Page in Foreign Policy," *Turkish Probe*, 15 November 1998, 10.

58. "Barzani: Cooperation with Turkey Will Help Peace and Stability," *Turkish Daily News*, 8 November 1998, 1.

59. "The Washington Agreement: The Most Serious Mistake Washington Has Ever Made?" *Turkish Probe*, 8 November 1998, 10, 12.

60. *Turkish Daily News*, 29 March 2000.

7. Syria and Lebanon

1. Fromkin, *A Peace to End All Peace*.

2. Seale, *The Struggle for Syria*, 25.

3. The Hashemite Emirate of Transjordan was reconstituted as the Hashemite Kingdom of Jordan through self-proclamation in 1946. It maintained control of the Western Bank of the Jordan River until King Hussein's abdication of responsibility in 1991 during the Madrid portion of the peace process, which allowed the Palestinians to negotiate on their own behalf with Israel in pursuit of self-determination.

4. Yorke, *Domestic Politics and Regional Security*, 101.

5. Haddad, *Revolutions and Military Rule in the Middle East*.

6. Seale, *The Struggle for Syria*, 310–11.

7. Seale, *Assad*, 67.

8. Roberts, *The Ba'ath and the Creation of Modern Syria*, 55; see also Van Dam, *The Struggle for Power in Syria*.

9. Seale, *Assad*, 85.
10. Dickey, "Assad and His Allies," 59; see also Knudson, "United States–Syrian Diplomatic Relations," 55–77.
11. Drysdale and Hinnebusch, *Syria and the Middle East Peace Process*, 34.
12. Abu Khalil, *Lubnan wa-Suriya: mashaqqat al-ukhuwwah*, 84.
13. Abu Khalil, *Lan ansa: mudhakkirat*, 85.
14. Radio Monte Carlo, 8 June 2000.
15. *Middle East Economic Digest*, 18 November 1994, 10.
16. Ibid.
17. Pertues, "Incremental Change in Syria," 25.
18. Ma'oz, *Syria and Israel*, 245–46; see also Rabinovich, *On the Brink of Peace*, 170.
19. Other perennial members of this list include Iran and Libya, and more recently, Sudan. Iraq, once a staunch U.S. ally, joined this club following the 1990–91 Gulf war.
20. Rabinovich, *On the Brink of Peace*, 129.
21. Ibid., 147–48.
22. Ibid., 220–24.
23. Gordon, *The Republic of Lebanon*, 30.
24. Ibid., 38.
25. *Middle East*, January 1996, 17.
26. Gilmour, *Dispossessed*, 27.
27. Khoury, *Syria and the French Mandate*, 20.
28. Gilmour, *Dispossessed*, 34.
29. Khoury, *Syria and the French Mandate*, 15.
30. Ibid., 16.
31. Gilmour, *Dispossessed*, 41.
32. Khalidi, *Conflict and Violence in Lebanon*, 51.
33. Avi-Ran, *The Syrian Involvement in Lebanon since 1975*, 27.
34. Khalidi, *Conflict and Violence in Lebanon*, 64.
35. Gilmour, *Dispossessed*, 142.
36. Avi-Ran, *The Syrian Involvement in Lebanon since 1975*, 151.
37. Cobban, *The Making of Modern Lebanon*.
38. Gordon, qtd. in Norton, *External Intervention and the Politics of Lebanon*, 464.
39. Ibid., 466.
40. *Time*, 15 January 1996, 17.
41. *Middle East Economic Digest*, 17 June 1994, 10.
42. *Time*, 15 January 1996, 18.

8. The Hashemite Kingdom of Jordan

1. Salibi, *The Modern History of Jordan*, 87.
2. Ibid., 94.
3. Sinai and Pollack, *The Middle East Confrontation States*, 38.
4. Ibid., 27.
5. Gubser, *Jordan: Crossroads*, 12.
6. Abu-Odeh, *Jordanians, Palestinians, and the Hashemite Kingdom in the Middle East Peace Process*.
7. Salibi, *The Modern History of Jordan*, 180.
8. Ibid., 213.
9. Abu-Odeh, *Jordanians*, 101–17, 214.

10. See T. Ismael, *The Arab Left*, 62–77, 92–125.
11. Abu-Odeh, *Jordanians*, 221–23.
12. Cantori, "Democratization in the Middle East," 21.
13. Ibid., 23.
14. *Al-Mithaq al-Watani al-Urduni.*
15. Gubser, *Jordan: Crossroads*, 51.
16. Abu Jaber, "The Economy of Jordan: A Current Assessment."
17. "Business Booms as Peace Dividend Flows," *Middle East Economic Digest*, 30 September 1994, 3.
18. Zunes, "The Israeli-Jordanian Agreement," 58.
19. "Business Booms as Peace Dividend Flows," *Middle East Economic Digest*, 30 September 1994, 2.
20. "Moving the Middle East Closer to Peace," *Middle East Economic Digest*, 4 November 1994, 2.
21. "Jordan: Adjusting to More Sober Expectations," *Middle East Economic Digest*, 21 April 1995, 9.
22. "Unseemly Haste," *Middle East*, April 1995, 5.
23. Baram, "Ba'athi Iraq and Hashimite Jordan," 57.
24. "Unseemly Haste," *Middle East*, April 1995, 5.
25. "Jordan's Warrior King," *Economist*, 8–14 July 2000, 41–42.

9. The State of Israel

1. Elon, "Israel and the End of Zionism," 22.
2. Tessler, *A History of the Israeli-Palestinian Conflict*, 53, 54.
3. O'Brien, *The Siege: The Saga of Israel and Zionism.*
4. Caplan, *Futile Diplomacy: Early Arab-Zionist Negotiation Attempts, 1913–1931.*
5. Halperin, *The Political World of American Zionists.*
6. Khalidi, *From Haven to Conquest: Readings in Zionism and the Palestine Problem until 1948.*
7. Zohar, *Political Parties in Israel*, 15.
8. Ibid., 18.
9. Ibid., 15.
10. Peretz, *The Government and Politics of Israel*, 112.
11. Sprinzak, "The Emergence of the Israeli Radical Right," 173.
12. Shindler, "Them or Us," 23.
13. Ibid.
14. Blumberg, *The History of Israel*, 195.
15. Ibid., 23.
16. Elon, "Israel and the End of Zionism," 27.
17. Wolffsohn, *Israel: Polity, Society, Economy, 1882–1986*, 219.
18. Sprinzak, "Netanyahu's Safety Belt," 28.
19. Bergus, "'Forty Years On': Israel's Quest for Security," 203.
20. Benvenisti, *Intimate Enemies: Jews and Arabs in a Shared Land*, 190–91.
21. Elon, qtd. in Bergus, "'Forty Years On,'" 202.
22. Finkelstein, "Whither the Peace Process?" 144–48.
23. Benvenisti, *Intimate Enemies*, 232.
24. Southall, *South Africa's Transkei*, 149.
25. Butler, Rotberg, and Adams, *The Black Homelands of South Africa*, 143.
26. Farsoun and Zacharia, *Palestine and the Palestinians*, 266.

27. Elon, "Israel and the End of Zionism," 26.
28. Ibid.
29. Ibid., 27.
30. *Globe and Mail*, 15 January 1997, A11.
31. *Globe and Mail*, 16 January 1997, A1, A10.
32. "Arabs Condemn Israeli Attacks against Lebanon," *Jordan Times*, 26 June 1999.
33. "Israel's Choice," *Economist*, 15–21 May 1999, 15.
34. "Clinton-Arafat-Barak Peace Summit in December—Palestinian Official," *Jordan Times*, 18 June 1999, 1A.
35. Amnesty International, *Annual Report 1998*.
36. See *New York Times*, 5 December 1989; and Tessler, *A History of the Israeli-Palestinian Conflict*, 701n. 66.
37. Options included the absorption of Saad Haddad's militia, the predecessor of the South Lebanese Army, into the southern division of the Lebanese army.

10. The Gulf Cooperation Council Countries

1. al-Naqeeb, *Al-mujtma' wa al-dawlah fi al-khlij wa al-Gazira al-'Arabiya*, 119–20.
2. Sampson, *The Seven Sisters*, 56–136; and Yergin, *The Prize*, 134–302.
3. al-Naqeeb, *Al-mujtma' wa al-dawlah fi al-khlij wa al-Gazira al-'Arabiya*, 120–25.
4. Ibid, 123–25.
5. Ibid., 125.
6. Ibid.
7. al-Najar, "Al-Mujtama' al-Madani fi al-Khalij wa al-Jazira al-'Arabiyya," 566–68; see also Sirhan, *Waqie' al-Harka al-Fikriya fi al-Bahrain, 1940–1990*, 135–55; and Musa, *Al-Bahrain: al-Nidhal al-Watani wa al-Dimoqrati, 1920–1981*, 17–18.
8. 'Abdullah, *Al-'Ulama wa al-'Arish*, 51, 119.
9. Ibid., 255.
10. Aburish, *The Rise, Corruption, and Coming Fall of the House of Saud*, 20, 152.
11. al-Naqeeb, *Al-mujtma' wa al-dawlah fi al-khlij wa al-Gazira al-'Arabiya*, 112–14.
12. el-Rayyes, *Riyah al-Samoom*, 46–47.
13. Ibid., 58–59.
14. Ibid., 61.
15. Ibid., 309–10.
16. al-Ahram, "Al-Taqrir al-Istratiji al-'Arabi" (1996), 193.
17. *Al-Wasat*, 14 December 1998, 10–11.
18. "The Gulf: Won't You Buy?" *Economist*, 20 March 1999, 50.
19. al-Ahram, "Al-Taqrir al-Istratiji al-'Arabi" (1996), 285–96.
20. Kathy Evans, "A Sour Taste at the Gulf Sheik's Feast of Enrichment," *Guardian Weekly*, 24 September 1995.
21. *Al-Wasat*, 8–14 January 1996, 13–19.
22. Evans, "A Sour Taste."
23. *Middle East Times*, 30 April–6 May 1995.
24. *Middle East Economic Digest*, 8 November 1991, 4.
25. *Middle East*, December 1994, 17.
26. *Middle East*, February 1995, 19.
27. *Middle East*, November 1994, 18.
28. *Le Monde*, 4 December 1994.
29. *Jordan Times*, 12 March 1996.
30. *Middle East Times*, 26 February 1995.

31. *Middle East Economic Digest,* 4 October 1991, 5, 6.
32. Salame, in Aart, "The Limits of Political Tribalism."
33. Ghabra, "Voluntary Associations in Kuwait: The Foundation of a New System?" 200.
34. J. Ismael, *Kuwait,* 69–77.
35. Interview with Abdullah al-Nafisi, on al-Jazira Television, Qatar (JSC), 22 June 1999.
36. el-Rayyes, *Riyah al-Samoom,* 265–69.
37. Ibrahim, *Al-Mujtam'a al-Madani wa al-Tahawul al-Dimocrati fi al-Watan al-'Arabi,* 179–88.
38. al-Ahram, "Al-Taqrir al-Istratiji al-Arabi" (1996), 252–53.; *Middle East Economic Digest,* 24 February 1995, 10.
39. 'Abdullah, *Al-'Ulama wa al-'Arish,* 373–75, 381.
40. Ibid., 284–386.
41. Ibid., 390–406. See also Dekmejian, "Saudi Arabia's Consultative Council," 217.
42. *New York Times,* 8 October 1994, 41.
43. *Le Monde,* 4 December 1994.
44. *Guardian Weekly,* 14 January 1996.
45. *Economist,* 17 November 1990, 53.
46. *Middle East Economic Digest,* 3 December 1993, 26.
47. *Middle East,* November 1994, 24.
48. *Times,* 13 April 1995, 13.
49. David Hirst, "Ailing Saudi King Hands Reins to Heir," *Guardian Weekly,* 7 January 1996.
50. Kathy Evans, "Islamic Conference Helps Polish Iran's Image," *Guardian Weekly,* 14 December 1997.
51. *Middle East Economic Digest,* 10 December 1993, 12.
52. 'Abdullah, "Al-Betrol wa al-Akhliq," 18–24.
53. McLoughlin, *Middle East Economic Digest,* August 1993, 8.
54. Lebkicher, Rentz, and Steineke, *The Arabia of Ibn Saud,* 28.
55. Goldrup, "Saudi Arabia, 1902–1932," 37.
56. Dickson, *Kuwait and Her Neighbours,* 151.
57. 'Abdullah, *Al-'Ulama wa al-'Arish,* 30–32.
58. Rashid, *Industrialization in Oil-based Economies,* 25; see also al-Qahtani, *Zilzal Juhaiman fi Maka,* 36–37.
59. Goldrup, "Saudi Arabia, 1902–1932," 106–61.
60. Ibid., 395.
61. David Hirst, "Ailing Saudi King," *Guardian Weekly,* 7 January 1996.
62. Ayubi, *Over-stating the Arab State,* 133.
63. Mariam Sami, "Saudi Women Surf the Net in Quest for Knowledge," *National Post,* 16 August 1999, A13.
64. *Economist,* 4 February 1995, 41.
65. William Branigin, "Turks Angered by Saudi Beheadings," *Guardian Weekly,* 27 August 1995.
66. Human Rights Watch, *World Report 1999: Middle East.*
67. Subramaniam, *Public Administration in the Third World,* 190.
68. Interview with Abdullah Fahd al-Nafisi on al-Jazira Television, Qatar (JSC), 22 June 1999.
69. Ibid.

70. Aart, "The Limits of Political Tribalism."
71. "A Bolder Kuwait," *Economist*, 10–16 July 1999, 39.
72. Ibid.
73. al-Naqeeb, *Sira' al-qabaliyah wa al-dimocratiyah, Halat al-Kuwait*, 167.
74. "Kuwait: An Unholy Row," *Economist*, 8 May 1999, 49.
75. Faisal Jalul, *Al-Wasat*, 12 July 1999, 24–26.
76. "Peace Allows Kuwaitis to Tackle Domestic Concerns," *Globe and Mail*, 3 July 1999, A15.
77. "Kuwaiti Elections Could Lead to Women's Vote," *Calgary Herald*, 5 July 1999, A16.
78. Faisal Jalul, *Al-Wasat*, 12 July 1999, 25.
79. Aart, "The Limits of Political Tribalism."
80. Rumaihi, *Bahrain*, 263.
81. Musa, *Al-Bahrain*.
82. Rumaihi, *Bahrain*, 263.
83. al-Khuri, *Al-Qabilah wa al-Dawlah fi al-Bahrain*, 265–69.
84. Ibid., 300; see also Sirhan, *Waqie' al-Harka al-Fikriyah fi al-Bahrain*, 187–90.
85. al-Khuri, *Al-Qabilah wa al-Dawlah fi al-Bahrain*, 296–308.
86. el-Rayyes, *Riyah al-Shamal*, 251–53.
87. "Bahrain: Emir Dead of Heart Attack; Son, Sheik Hamad Assumes Power," *Turkish Daily News*, 7 March 1999, A2.
88. "Suddenly, It's Time for Charm," *Economist*, 17 July 1999, 41–42.
89. Ian Black, "Iran Call the Shots in the Gulf Region," *Guardian Weekly*, 17 March 1996.
90. Evans, "Islamic Conference Helps Polish Iran's Image."
91. *Guardian Weekly*, 28 March 1993, quoting the *New York Times*.
92. *Al-Wasat*, no. 205, January 1996, 14.
93. al-Haj, "The Politics of Participation in the Gulf Cooperation Council States."
94. *Al-Wasat*, no. 283, 27 June–3 July 1997, 12.
95. Ibrahim, *Al-Mujtam'a al-Madani wa al-Tahawul al-Dimocrati fi al-Watan al-'Arabi*, 179–88.

11. The Republic of Yemen

1. Douglas, *The Free Yemeni Movement*.
2. Stookey, *The Politics of the Yemen Arab Republic*, 251–60.
3. el-Rayyes, *Riyah al-Janub: al-Yemen wa Dawruhu fi al-Jazira al-'Arabiyya, 1990–1997*, 92.
4. Ibid, 358.
5. Ibid, 359.
6. Schmitz, "Civil War in Yemen: The Price of Unity?" 34.
7. "Yemen: The End?" *Economist*, 9 July 1994.
8. Schmitz, "Civil War in Yemen," 36.
9. Watkins, "Yemen: Saleh Cracks Down on the Opposition," *Middle East*, October 1995, 16.
10. Ibid., 17; see also Al-Ahram, "Al-Taqrir al-Istratiji al-'Arabi" (1997), 145.
11. *Al-Wasat*, 16 August 1999, 26–27.
12. "Reconciliation Proves Elusive a Year after Yemen's Civil War," *Jordan Times*, 6–7 July 1995.

13. Faisel Jalul, "America Supports Unity . . . and Yemen Combats Terrorism," *Al-Wasat*, 3 July 2000, 24.
14. Scott, "Yemen: Arms and the Man," *Middle East*, July/August 1995, 6.
15. "Yemen Goes to the Polls," *Middle East Economic Digest*, 19 March 1993.
16. *Al-Wasat*, 29 November 1999, 47.
17. Scott, "Yemen: Arms and the Man," 7.
18. Killion, "Saudi Meddlers in Yemen," *New York Times*, 30 July 1994, 19.
19. Nasser Arrabyee, "Borderline Agreement," *Al-Ahram Weekly*, Online edition, 22–28 June 2000.

12. The Arab Republic of Egypt

1. S. Amin, *The Arab Nation*, 18–20.
2. S. Amin, *Unequal Development*, 302.
3. S. Amin, *The Arab Nation*, 30.
4. al-Naqeeb, *Al-mujtma' wa al-dawlah fi al-khlij wa al-Gazira al-'Arabiya*, 105–6.
5. S. Amin, *The Arab Nation*, 31.
6. S. Amin, *Unequal Development*, 302–4.
7. Hopwood, *Egypt: Politics and Society, 1945–1981*, 11.
8. S. Amin, *The Arab Nation*, 31–32.
9. Hopwood, *Egypt: Politics and Society, 1945–1981*, 11–12.
10. al-Bishri, *Al-Harakah al-Siyassiya fi Misr*, 7–8.
11. S. Amin, *The Arab Nation*, 35–36.
12. al-Bishri, *Al-Harakah al-Siyassiya fi Misr*, p. 10.
13. S. Amin, *The Arab Nation*, 35.
14. Hopwood, *Egypt: Politics and Society, 1945–1981*, 18.
15. G. Amin, *Al-Mashreq al-'Arabi wa al-Gharb*, 16, 35.
16. al-Bishri, *Al-Harakah al-Siyassiya fi Misr*, 11–13.
17. Ibid., 13–14.
18. Ibid., 481–85.
19. Ibid., 488–508.
20. Ibid., 492.
21. Ibid., 559–63.
22. Ibid., 567–77.
23. Ibid., 578–79.
24. al-Naqeeb, *Al-Dawlah al-Tasalutiyyah fi al-Mashreq al-'Arabi*, 90–91.
25. al-Bishri, *Al-Harakah al-Siyassiya fi Misr*, 422–26.
26. Ibid., 434–38.
27. al-Naqeeb, *Al-Dawlah al-Tasalutiyyah*, 90–96.
28. al-Bishri, *Al-Harakah al-Siyassiya fi Misr*, 417.
29. al-Naqeeb, *Al-Dawlah al-Tasalutiyyah*, 133–35.
30. Keshk, *Thawrat yulio al-Amrikiyya*, 176, 208.
31. al-Bishri, *Al-Harakah al-Siyassiya fi Misr*, 467, 472, 474; Hamroush, *Al-Inquelabat al-'Askariyya*, 21, 55–56, 58–59 (Hamroush was a member of the Free Officers).
32. Ovendale, *Britain, the United States, and the Transfer of Power in the Middle East*, 74–76.
33. Keshk, *Thawrat yulio al-Amrikiyya*, 23, 28.
34. al-Naqeeb, *Al-Dawlah al-Tasalutiyyah*, 66, 80, 124–26.
35. Ibid., 149–50.

36. Ibid., 140; see also Hamroush, *Al-Inquelabat al-'Askariyya*, 80; and Owen, *State, Power, and Politics*, 267.
37. al-Naqeeb, *Al-Dawlah al-Tasalutiyyah*, 102.
38. 'Abd al-Fadhiel, *Al-Tashkilat al-Igtema'iyya wa al-Taqwimat al-Tabaqiyya fi al-Watan al-'Arabi*, 84–85, 87.
39. Hamroush, *Al-Inquelabat al-'Askariyya*, 82–83.
40. Owen, *State, Power, and Politics*, 267.
41. Hamroush, *Al-Inquelabat al-'Askariyya*, 84–86.
42. Owen, *State, Power, and Politics*, 268.
43. G. Amin, *Al-Mashreq al-'Arabi wa al-Gharb*, 48–49.
44. Imam, *Man Yamluk Misr*, 57, 86.
45. G. Amin, *Al-Mashreq al-'Arabi wa al-Gharb*, 74.
46. S. Amin, "Classes and Nations," 137–39.
47. Ayubi, *Over-stating the Arab State*, 13.
48. Imam, *Man Yamluk Misr*, 83–84.
49. Ibid., 87–93.
50. Ibid., 97, 92.
51. Myrdal, *The Challenge of World Poverty*, 233–34. For examples of corruption, see Imam, *Man Yamluk Misr*, 90–91, 97.
52. Imam, *Man Yamluk Misr*, 99.
53. G. Amin, *Al-Mashreq al-'Arabi wa al-Gharb*, 54.
54. Ibid., 57–60.
55. Heikal, *Secret Channels*, 29–49.
56. Ibid., 132.
57. Ibid., 106–9.
58. Brown, *International Politics and the Middle East*, 166–67.
59. Heikal, *Secret Channels*, 168.
60. al-Gamal, "Al-Ta'adudiyya al-Hizbiyya fi Misr," 220.
61. Rabinovich, "Egypt and the Palestine Question," 336.
62. Heikal, *Secret Channels*, 306.
63. Ibid., 161–71.
64. al-Shazli, "Harb October," 164.
65. Ibid., 304–5.
66. Heikal, *Secret Channels*, 286.
67. G. Amin, *Al-'Arab wa Naqbat al-Kuwait*, 11–12.
68. G. Amin. "Al-Mashreq al-'Arabi wa al-Gharb," 84–86.
69. Ibid., 99.
70. Imam, *Man Yamluk Misr*, 59.
71. Ibid., 106–16, 142–43, 212.
72. Ibid., 129–35, 138–39.
73. Ibid., 192.
74. G. Amin, *Al-'Arab wa Naqbat al-Kuwait*, 145.
75. Kienle, "More than a Response to Islamism," 231–32.
76. G. Amin, *Al-'Arab wa Naqbat al-Kuwait*, 65.
77. Imam, *Man Yamluk Misr*, 230.
78. al-Gamal, "Al-Ta'adudiyya al-Hizbiyya fi Misr," 215.
79. Murad, "Tagrubat al-Ta'adudiyya al-Hizbiyya fi Misr," 200–205.
80. Heikal, *Bab Misr ila al-qarn al-Wahid wa al-'ushroun*, 28.
81. Kienle, "More than a Response to Islamism," 225.

82. al-Ahram, "Al-Taqrir al-Istratiji al-'Arabi" (1995), 33–34.

83. Ibid. (1996), 290–91.

84. Ibid. (1997), 269, 271, 277.

85. "Mubarak Rescues Illegal Parliament," *Middle East Times,* Online edition, 21 July 2000.

86. al-Ahram, "Al-Taqrir al-Istratiji al-'Arabi" (1999), 295–98.

87. "Mubarak Wins 94 Percent in Plebiscite," *Globe and Mail,* 28 September 1999, A15.

88. al-Ahram, "Al-Taqrir al-Istratiji al-'Arabi" (1999), 342.

89. Ibid., 337–40.

90. al-Ahram, "Al-Taqrir al-Istratiji al-'Arabi" (1997), 20; Heikal, *Bab Misr ila al-qarn al-Wahid wa al-'ushroun,* 20.

91. Kienle, "More than a Response to Islamism"; see also Heikal, *Bab Misr ila al-qarn al-Wahid wa al-'ushroun,* 231–33; and G. Amin, *Al-'Arab wa Naqbat al-Kuwait,* 65.

92. el-Rayyes, *Riyah al-Shamal,* 390–91.

93. Ibid., 401, 403–4.

Bibliography

Aart, Paul. "The Limits of Political Tribalism: Post War Kuwait and the Process of Democratisation." *Civil Society* 4, no. 37 (January 1995).

'Abdullah, Anwar. "Al-Betrol wa al-Akhliq." *Dar al-Dhuha,* 1990.

———. *Al-'Ulama wa al-'Arish.* London: Mosasat al-Rafid, 1995.

Abu-Amr, Ziad. *Islamic Fundamentalism in the West Bank and Gaza: Muslim Brotherhood and Islamic Jihad.* Bloomington: Indiana University Press, 1994.

Abu Jaber, Kamel. "The Economy of Jordan: A Current Assessment." *American-Arab Affairs,* no. 9 (summer 1984).

Abu Khalil, Juzif. *Lan ansa: mudhakkirat.* Beirut: Dar al-Farabi, 1996.

———. *Lubnan wa-Suriya: mashaqqat al-ukhuwwah.* Beirut: Sharikat al-Matbu'at lil-Tawzi' wa al-Nashr, 1991.

Abu-Lughod, Janet. "The Demographic Transformation of Palestine." In Abu-Lughod, ed., *The Transformation of Palestine.* Evanston, Ill.: Northwestern University Press, 1971.

Abu-Odeh, Adnan. *Jordanians, Palestinians, and the Hashemite Kingdom in the Middle East Peace Process.* Washington, D.C.: U.S. Institute of Peace Press, 1999.

Aburish, Said K. *The Rise, Corruption, and Coming Fall of the House of Saud.* New York: St. Martin's Press, 1996.

al-Ahram. "Al-Taqrir al-Istratiji al-'Arabi." Cairo: al-Ahram Center for Political and Strategic Studies, 1994, 1995, 1996, 1997, 1999.

Ali, Z. Ben. "Co-Development between the Maghrib and the European Community." *Mediterranean Quarterly* 5, no. 1 (winter 1994).

Alnasrawi, Abbas. *The Economy of Iraq: Oil, Wars, Destruction of Development, and Prospects, 1950–2010.* Westport, Conn.: Greenwood Press, 1994.

———. Review, "The Scourging of Iraq: Sanctions, Law and Natural Justice, by Geoff Simons." *Middle East Studies Association Bulletin* 33, no. 1 (summer 1999): 132.

Amin, Galal. *Al-'Arab wa Naqbat al-Kuwait.* Cairo: Madbouli Bookshop, 1991.

———. *Al-Mashreq al-'Arabi wa al-Gharb.* Beirut: Markaz Derasat al-wahdah al-'Arabiyya, 1979.

Amin, Samir. *The Arab Nation.* London: Zed Press, 1978.

———. *Classes and Nations, Historically and in the Current Crisis.* London: Monthly Review Press, 1980.

———. *Unequal Development.* London: Monthly Review Press, 1976.

Amnesty International. *Annual Report 1989.* (*www.amnesty.org*).

———. *Annual Report 1997.* (*www.amnesty.org*).

———. *Annual Report 1997: Kuwait* (*www.amnesty.org*).

———. *Annual Report 1998.* (*www.amnesty.org*).

———. *Annual Report 1998: Middle East and North Africa* (regional country index, Kuwait). (*www.amnesty.org*).

———. *Annual Report 1999.* (*www.amnesty.org*).

———. *Annual Report 2000.* (*web.amnesty.org*).

————. *Annual Report 2000: Kuwait (web.amnesty.org).*

————. *Annual Report 2000: Palestinian Authority (web.amnesty.org).*

————. *2000 Annual Report: Saudia Arabia.*

————. *2000 Annual Report: Syria. (web.amnesty.org).*

————. *Annual Report 2000: Tunisia. (web.amnesty.org).*

————. *Annual Report 2000: Turkey. (web.amnesty.org).*

————. *Annual Report 2000: United Arab Emirates. (web.amnesty.org).*

————. *Annual Report 2000: Yemen. (web.amnesty.org).*

————. *Fear Flight and Forcible Exile: Refugees in the Middle East.* AI Index: MDE 01/01/97, August 1997. (*www.amnesty.org*).

————. *Israel/Occupied Territories and the Palestinian Authority: Five Years after the Oslo Agreement—Human Rights Sacrificed for "Security."* MDE 02/04/98, 9 September 1998. (*www.amnesty.org*).

————. *Jordan: An Absence of Safeguards.* AI Index: MDE 16/11/98, November 1998.

————. *Jordan: Human Rights Reforms: Achievements and Obstacles.* AI Index: MDE 16/02/94. (*www.amnesty.org*).

————. *Lebanon: Human Rights Developments and Violations.* AI Index: MDE 18/19/97, October 1997. (*www.amnesty.org*).

————. *Middle East and North Africa, State Injustice: Unfair Trials in the Middle East and North Africa.* April 1998. (*www.amnesty.org*).

————. *Palestinian Authority Defying the Rule of Law: Political Detainees.* MDE 21/03/99, April 1999. (*www.amnesty.org*).

————. *Syria: Caught in a Regional Conflict— Lebanese, Palestinian, and Jordanian Political Detainees in Syria.* AI Index: MDE 24/001/99.

————. *Syria: Double Injustice—Prisoners of Conscience Held beyond the Expiry of Their Sentences.* AI Index: MDE 24/010/99.

————. *Turkey: Creating a Silent Society—Turkish Government Prepares to Imprison Leading Human Rights Defender.* AI Index: EUR 44/005/99.

————. *Turkey: The Duty to Supervise, Investigate, and Prosecute.* AI Index: EUR 44/024/99.

————. *Yemen: Empty Promises—Government Commitments and the State of Human Rights in Yemen.* AI Index: MDE 31/004/99.

Amuzegar, Jahangir. *The Dynamics of the Iranian Revolution: The Pahlavis' Triumph and Tragedy.* Albany: State University of New York Press, 1991.

Arnold, Thomas. *The Caliphate.* London: Routledge and Kegan Paul, 1965.

Aronson, Shlomo. *The Politics and Strategy of Nuclear Weapons in the Middle East: Opacity, Theory, and Reality, 1960–1991: An Israeli Perspective.* Albany: State University of New York Press, 1992.

Avery, Peter. *Modern Iran.* London: Ernest Benn, 1965.

Avi-Ran, Reuven. *The Syrian Involvement in Lebanon since 1975.* Trans. David Maisel. Boulder, Colo.: Westview Press, 1991.

Ayubi, Nazih N. *Over-stating the Arab State: Politics and Society in the Middle East.* London: I. B. Tauris, 1995.

Baram, Amatzia. "Ba'athi Iraq and Hashimite Jordan: From Hostility to Alignment." *Middle East Journal* 45, no. 1 (winter 1991): 51–70.

————. "Neo-Tribalism in Iraq: Saddam Hussein's Tribal Policies 1991–96." *International Journal of Middle East Studies* 29 (1997): 1–31.

————. "The Ruling Political Elite in Ba'thi Iraq, 1968–1986: The Changing Features of a Collective Profile." *International Journal of Middle East Studies* 21 (1989): 447–93.

Beckman, Peter R. *World Politics in the Twentieth Century*. Englewood Cliffs, N.J.: Prentice Hall, 1984.

Benvenisti, Meron. *Intimate Enemies: Jews and Arabs in a Shared Land*. Berkeley: University of California Press, 1995.

Berberoglu, Berch. *Turkey in Crisis: From State Capitalism to Neo-Colonialism*. London: Zed Books, 1982.

Bergus, Donald C. "'Forty Years On': Israel's Quest for Security." *Middle East Journal* 42, no. 2 (spring 1988): 202–8.

al-Bishri, Tarek. *Al-Harakah al-Siyassiya fi Misr, 1945–1952*. Cairo: al-Haya'h al-Misriyya al-'Ammah lil-Kitab, 1972.

Blumberg, Arnold. *The History of Israel*. Westport, Conn.: Greenwood Press, 1998.

Brown, L. Carl. *International Politics and the Middle East: Old Rules, Dangerous Games*. Princeton: Princeton University Press, 1984.

Buergenthal, Thomas. *International Human Rights in a Nutshell*. 2d ed. Nutshell Series. St. Paul, Minn.: West Publishing, 1995.

Bullock, Alan, and Stephen Trombley, eds. *The Fontana Dictionary of Modern Thought*. New York: Fontana Press, 1988.

Butler, Jeffrey, Robert I. Rotberg, and John Adams. *The Black Homelands of South Africa*. Berkeley: University of California Press, 1977.

Cantori, Louis J. "Democratization in the Middle East." *American-Arab Affairs*, no. 36 (winter 1991).

Caplan, Neil. *Futile Diplomacy: Early Arab-Zionist Negotiation Attempts, 1913–1931*. London: Frank Cass, 1983.

Cleveland, William L. *A History of the Modern Middle East*. Boulder, Colo.: Westview Press, 1994.

Cobban, Helena. *The Making of Modern Lebanon*. Boulder, Colo.: Westview Press, 1985.

Cordovez, Diego, and Selig S. Harrison. *Out of Afghanistan: The Inside Story of the Soviet Withdrawal*. New York: Oxford University Press, 1995.

Crystal, Jill. *Oil and Politics in the Gulf: Rulers and Merchants in Kuwait and Qatar*. New York: Cambridge University Press, 1994.

Darwish, Adel, and Gregory Alexander. *Unholy Babylon: The Secret History of Saddam's War*. London: Victor Gollancz, 1991.

Davison, Roderic H. *Reform in the Ottoman Empire, 1865–1876*. Princeton: Princeton University Press, 1963.

Dekmejian, Hrair. "Saudi Arabia's Consultative Council." *Middle East Journal* 52, no. 2 (spring 1998).

Diba, Farhad. *Mohammed Mossadegh: A Political Biography*. London: Croom Helm, 1986.

Dickey, Christopher. "Assad and His Allies: Irreconcilable Differences." *Foreign Affairs* 66, no. 1 (fall 1987): 58–76.

Dodd, C. H. *Democracy and Development in Turkey*. Beverley, U.K.: Eothen Press, 1979.

Douglas, J. Leigh. *The Free Yemeni Movement*. Beirut: American University of Beirut Press, 1987.

Doxey, John. "Turkey: Post-Election Uncertainty Continues." *Middle East*, March 1996.

Drysdale, Alasdair, and Raymond A. Hinnebusch. *Syria and the Middle East Peace Process*. New York: Council on Foreign Relations, 1991.

al-Dury, 'Abd al-'Aziz. *Muqadima fi al-Tarihk al-Iqtasadi al-'Arabi*. Beirut: Dar al-Tali'a, 1969.

Elon, Amos. "Israel and the End of Zionism." *New York Review of Books* 43, no. 20 (1996): 22–31.

European Union. Presidency Statement [Bulletin EU 4–1999]. (*www.europa.eu.int/abc/ doc/off/bull/en/9904/p104009*).

'Abd al-Fadhiel, Mahmoud. *Al-Tashkilat al-Igtema'iyya wa al-Taqwimat al-Tabaqiyya fi al-Watan al-'Arabi*. Beirut: Markaz Derasat al-Wahadah al-'Arabiyya, 1988.

Falk, Richard. "International Law versus Indiscriminate Sanctions: The Case of Iraq." Dr. Irma M. Parhad Lecture, University of Calgary, 4 March 1999.

Farsoun, Samih, and Christina E. Zacharia. *Palestine and the Palestinians*. Boulder, Colo.: Westview Press, 1997.

Feld, Werner J., and Gavin Boyd. "The Comparative Study of International Regions." In Feld and Boyd, eds., *Comparative Regional Systems: West and East Europe, North America, the Middle East, and Developing Countries*. New York: Pergamon Press, 1980.

Financial Times: Oil and Gas International Yearbook. London: Longman, 1995.

Finkelstein, Norman G. "Whither the Peace Process?" *New Left Review* (July–August 1996): 144–48.

Fisher, Sydney Nettleton. *The Middle East: A History*. New York: Alfred A. Knopf, 1979.

Friedman, Thomas L. "When War Is Over: Planning for Peace and U.S. Role in Enforcing It." *International Herald Tribune*, 21 January 1991.

Fromkin, David. *A Peace to End All Peace: The Fall of the Ottoman Empire and the Creation of the Modern Middle East*. New York: Avon Books, 1989.

————. *The Way of the World: From the Dawn of Civilizations to the Eve of the Twenty-first Century*. New York: Alfred A. Knopf, 1999.

Fuller, Graham E., and Ian O. Lesser. *A Sense of Siege*. Boulder, Colo.: Westview Press, 1995.

al-Gamal, Yahia. "Al-Ta'adudiyya al-Hizbiyya fi Misr." In Sa'ad al-Ibrahim, ed., *Al-Ta'adudiyya al-Siyassia wa al-Democratiyya fi al-Watan al-'Arabi*. Jordan: Arab Thought Forum, 1989.

Ghabra, Shafeeq. "Voluntary Associations in Kuwait: The Foundation of a New System?" *Middle East Journal* 45, no. 2 (spring 1991): 199–215.

Ghanem, As'ad. "State and Minorities in Israel: The Case of Ethnic State and the Predicament of Its Minority." *Ethnic and Racial Studies* 21, no. 3 (May 1998).

Gibb, Hamilton R. *The Arab-Conquests in Central Asia*. London, 1923.

Gilmour, David. *Dispossessed: The Ordeal of the Palestinians, 1917–1980*. London: Sidgwick and Jackson, 1980.

Gökalp, Ziya. *Turkish Nationalism and Western Civilization*. Trans. Niyazi Berkis. New York: Columbia University Press, 1959.

Goldberg, Ellis. "Khatima Nadhariya wa-Tarikhiya: al-Mujtama' al-Madani." In Ahmed 'Abdulla, ed., *Al-Dimuqratiya fi al-sharq al-Aswat*. Cairo: Markaz al-Geil, 1995.

Goldrup, Lawrence. "Saudi Arabia, 1902–1932: The Development of a Wahhabi Society." Thesis, University of California, Los Angeles, 1971.

Gordon, David C. *The Republic of Lebanon: Nation in Jeopardy*. Boulder, Colo.: Westview Press, 1983.

Gresh, Alain. "Turkish-Israeli-Syrian Relations and Their Impact on the Middle East." *Middle East Journal* 52, no. 2 (spring 1998).

Gubser, Peter. *Jordan: Crossroads of Middle Eastern Events*. Boulder, Colo.: Westview Press, 1983.

Gunter, Michael M. "The Kurdish Problem in Turkey." *Middle East Journal* 42, no. 3 (summer 1988).

Haddad, George. *Revolutions and Military Rule in the Middle East*. Vol. 2. New York: Robert Speller.

al-Haj, Abdullah Juma. "The Politics of Participation in the Gulf Cooperation Council States: The Omani Consultative Council." *Middle East Journal* 50, no. 4 (autumn 1996): 559–72.

Hale, William. *The Political and Economic Development of Modern Turkey*. London: Croom Helm, 1981.

Halliday, Fred. *Islam and the Myth of Confrontation*. London: I. B. Tauris, 1996.

Halperin, Samuel. *The Political World of American Zionists*. Detroit: Wayne State University Press, 1961.

Hamroush, Ahmed. *Al-Inquelabat al-'Askariyya*. Beirut: Dar Ibn Khaldun, 1980.

———. *Qisat Thawrat 23 Yolyo*. 2d ed. Vol. 1. Beirut: al-Mu'asasah al-'Arabiyah lil Dirasat was al-Nashir, 1977.

Haselkorn, Avigdor. *The Continuing Storm: Iraq, Poisonous Weapons, and Deterrence*. New Haven: Yale University Press, 1999.

Hassan, Hassan I. *Islam: A Religious, Political, Social, and Economic History*. Baghdad: Times, 1967.

Hazelton, Fran, ed. *Iraq since the Gulf War: Prospects for Democracy*. London: Zed Books, 1994.

Heikal, Mohammad H. *Azamat al-'Arab wa Mustaqblahim*. 3d ed. Cairo: Dar al-Shuruq, 1997.

———. *Bab Misr ila al-qarn al-Wahid wa al-'ushroun*. Cairo: Dar al-Shuruq, 1995.

———. *Secret Channels*. London: HarperCollins, 1996.

Heper, Metin. *The State Tradition in Turkey*. Beverley, U.K.: Eothen Press, 1985.

Hilsman, Roger. *George Bush vs. Saddam Hussein: Military Success! Political Failure!* Novato, Calif.: Lyford Books, 1992.

Hiro, Dilip. *The Longest War: The Iran-Iraq Military Conflict*. London: Paladin Press, 1990.

———. *Sharing the Promised Land: An Interwoven Tale of Israelis and Palestinians*. London: Hodder and Stoughton, 1996.

Hitti, Philip K. *The Arabs: A Short History*. Princeton: Princeton University Press, 1949.

Hopkins, Nicholas S., and Saad Eddin Ibrahim, eds. *Arab Society: Class, Gender, Power, and Development*. Cairo: American University in Cairo Press, 1997.

Hopwood, Derek. *Egypt: Politics and Society, 1945–1981*. London: Allen and Unwin, 1982.

Hourani, Albert. *A History of the Arab Peoples*. New York: Warner Books, 1991.

Human Rights Watch. *Academic Leaders and Scholars Advocates Critique Proposed Jordanian Press Law*. Press release, New York, 13 July 1998. (www.hrw.org).

———. *The Bedoons of Kuwait: Citizens without Citizenship*. 1995. (*www.hrw.org*).

———. *Civilian Expulsions from South Lebanon Continuing*. Press release, November 1999. (*www.hrw.org*).

———. *HRW Condemns Israel's Detention of Twenty-one Lebanese for Years without Charge*. Press release, 14 October 1997. (*www.hrw.org*).

———. *HRW to Jordanian Deputies: Oppose Tight State Grip on Newspapers, Journals, and Books*. Press release, New York, 25 June 1998. (*www.hrw.org*).

———. *Human Rights in Morocco*. (*www.hrw.org*).

———. *Israel's Withdrawal from South Lebanon: The Human Rights Dimensions*. May 2000. (*www.hrw.org*).

———. *Jordan: A Death Knell for Free Expression?* June 1997. (*www.hrw.org*).

———. Letter of Jordanian prime minister. 9 August 1999. (*www.hrw.org*).

———. "Middle East and North Africa Overview." *World Report 1999*. (*www.hrw.org*).

———. *National Jordanian Campaign to Eliminate the So-called Crimes of Honor*. (*www.hrw.org*).

———. *Operation Grapes of Wrath* 9, no. 8(E) (September 1997). (*www.hrw.org*).

———. *Palestinian Arrests Condemned*. Press release, New York, 2 December 1999. (*www.hrw.org*).

———. *Prison Conditions in the Middle East and North Africa*. (*www.hrw.org*).

———. *South Lebanon: Rights Crisis Looms*. Press release, 23 May 2000. (*www.hrw.org*).

———. *A Victory Turned Sour: Human Rights in Kuwait since Liberation*. (*www.hrw.org*).

———. *Western Sahara: Keeping It Secret: The United Nations Operation in Western Sahara*. (*www.hrw.org*).

———. *World Report 1999: Algeria*. (*www.hrw.org*).

———. *World Report 1999: Bahrain*. (*www.hrw.org*).

———. *World Report 1999: Middle East*. (*www.hrw.org*).

———. *World Report 2000: Saudi Arabia*. (*www.hrw.org*).

———. *World Report 2000: Tunisia*. (*www.hrw.org*).

———. *World Report 2000: Yemen*. (*www.hrw.org*).

al-Husaini, Ishak Musa. *The Moslem Brethren*. Lebanon: Khayat's College Book Cooperative, 1956.

Ibish, Yusaf. *Nusus al-fikr al-siyasi al-Islami*. Beirut: Dar al-Tali'a, 1966.

Ibn Khaldun Center for Developmental Studies. *Files of the Arab Data Unit (ADU)*. Cairo: Ibn Khaldun Center for Developmental Studies.

Ibn Qutaiba. *Al-Imamah wa al-Asiyasah*. Vol. 1. Cairo: Al-Halabi and Co. Institute for Publishing and Distribution, 1967.

Ibrahim, Sa'd al-Din. *Al-Mujtam'a al-Madani wa al-Tahawul al-Dimocrati fi al-Watan al-'Arabi*. Cairo: Markaz Ibn Khaldoun, 1996.

Ibrahim, Saad Eddin. "Civil Society and Prospects for Democratization in the Arab World." In Augustus Richard Norton, ed., *Civil Society in the Middle East*. New York: E. J. Brill, 1995.

———. *Egypt, Islam, and Democracy: Twelve Critical Essays*. Cairo: American University in Cairo Press, 1996.

Imam, Samya Sa'id. *Man Yamluk Misr, 1974–1980*. Cairo: Dar al-Mustaqbal al-'Arabi, 1986.

Inalcik, Halil. *The Ottoman Empire: The Classical Age, 1300–1600*. Trans. Norman Itzkowitz and Colin Imber. New York: Praeger, 1973.

———, ed. *An Economic and Social History of the Ottoman Empire, 1300–1914*. New York: Cambridge University Press, 1994.

Ingram, Edward. "It Was Islam That Did It." *Philosophy Now: A Magazine of Ideas* 23 (spring 1999).

Ismael, Jacqueline S. *Kuwait: Dependency and Class in a Rentier State*. Gainesville: University Press of Florida, 1993.

Ismael, Jacqueline S., and Shereen T. Ismael. "Gender and State in Iraq." In Suad Joseph, ed., *Citizenship and Gender in the Middle East*. Syracuse: Syracuse University Press, 2000.

———. "The International Humanitarian Response to the Turkish Earthquakes," a paper presented at the Third International Conference of the International Center for Contemporary Middle Eastern Studies, "Turkey in the Twenty-first Century: Changing Role in World Politics?" held at Eastern Mediterranean University, 26–28 April 2000.

Ismael, Tareq Y. *The Arab Left*. Syracuse: Syracuse University Press, 1976.

———. *The International Relations of the Contemporary Middle East: A Study in World Politics*. Syracuse: Syracuse University Press, 1986.

———. *The International Relations of the Middle East in the Twenty-first Century: Patterns of Continuity and Change*. London: Ashgate, 2000.

————. *The Middle East in World Politics: A Study in Contemporary International Relations.* Syracuse: Syracuse University Press, 1974.

Ismael, Tareq Y., and Rifa'at El-Sa'id. *The Communist Movement in Egypt.* Syracuse: Syracuse University Press, 1990.

Ismael, Tareq Y., and Jacqueline S. Ismael. "Cowboy Warfare, Biological Diplomacy: Disarming Metaphors as Weapons of Mass Destruction." *Politics and the Life Sciences* 18, no. 1 (March 1999).

————. *Government and Politics in Islam.* London: Frances Pinter, 1985.

————. *The Gulf War and the New World Order.* Gainesville: University Press of Florida, 1994.

————. "The UN in Iraq: Disarmament in Theory, Genocide in Practice." International Conference on Globalization: Political, Social, and Economic Perspectives. Eastern Mediterranean University, TRNC, November 1998.

Issawi, Charles. *An Economic History of the Middle East and North Africa.* New York: Columbia University Press, 1982.

Jabbar, Faleh A., Ahmad Shikara, and Keiko Sakai. *From Storm to Thunder: Unfinished Showdown between Iraq and U.S.* IDE Spot Survey. Tokyo: Institute of Developing Economies, 1998.

Jabber, Fuad. "The Palestinian Resistance and Inter-Arab Politics." In William B. Quandt, Fuad Jabber, and Ann Mosely Lesch, eds., *The Politics of Palestinian Nationalism.* Berkeley: University of California Press, 1973.

Jentleson, Bruce W. *With Friends like These: Reagan, Bush, and Saddam, 1982–1990.* New York: W. W. Norton, 1994.

Jiryis, Sabri. *The Arabs in Israel.* New York: Monthly Review Press, 1976.

Kalkas, Barbara. "The Revolt of 1936: A Chronicle of Events." In Janet Abu-Lughod, ed., *The Transformation of Palestine.* Evanston, Ill.: Northwestern University Press, 1971.

Kamrava, Mehran. *The Political History of Modern Iran: From Tribalism to Theocracy.* Westport, Conn.: Praeger, 1992.

————. *Revolution in Iran: The Roots of Turmoil.* London: Routledge, 1990.

Keshk, Mohammad G. *Thawrat yulio al-Amrikiyya.* 2d ed. Cairo: al-Zahr'a lil-I'alam wa al-Nashr, 1988.

Khadduri, Majid. *Republican Iraq: A Study in Iraqi Politics since the Revolution of 1958.* London, 1969.

Khairi, Zaki. *Mulahadaat awaliyah an al-islah al-manshod fi al-Iraq.* Baghdad: Al-Sha'ab Press, 1974.

Khalidi, Walid. *Conflict and Violence in Lebanon: Confrontation in the Middle East.* Cambridge: Harvard University Press, 1981.

————, ed. *From Haven to Conquest: Readings in Zionism and the Palestine Problem until 1948.* Beirut: Mu'assasat al-Dirasat al-Filastiniyah, 1971.

al-Khalil, Samir. *Republic of Fear: The Politics of Modern Iraq.* Berkeley: University of California Press, 1989.

al-Kharsan, Salah. *Hizb al-Da'wa al-Islamia: Haqaiqn wa Wathaieq.* Damascus: al-Mo'asasa al-'Arabiya lil dirsat wa al-Buhuth al-Istratijiya, 1999.

al-Khomeini, Rohallah. *Al-Hukuma al-Islamiyah.* 2d ed. Beirut: Dar al-Tali'a, 1979.

Khoury, P. S. *Syria and the French Mandate: The Politics of Arab Nationalism, 1920–1945.* Princeton: Princeton University Press, 1987.

al-Khuri, Fuad Isaq. *Al-Qabilah wa al-Dawlah fi al-Bahrain.* Beirut: Arab Development Institute, 1983.

Kienle, Eberhard. *Ba'th v. Ba'th: The Conflict between Syria and Iraq, 1968–1989.* New York: St. Martin's Press, 1990.

———. *Contemporary Syria: Liberalization between Cold War and Peace.* New York: St. Martin's Press, 1996.

———. "More than a Response to Islamism: The Political Deliberalization of Egypt in the 1990s." *Middle East Journal* 52, no. 2 (spring 1998).

Killion, David. "Saudi Meddlers in Yemen." *New York Times,* 30 July 1994, 19.

Klare, Michael. "Dissuasion selective et vieilles recettes." *Le Monde Diplomatique,* May 1988.

Knapp, Wilfrid. *North Africa: A Political and Economic Survey.* London: Oxford University Press, 1977.

Knudson, Erik L. "United States–Syrian Diplomatic Relations: The Downward Spiral of Mutual Political Hostility (1970–1994)." *Journal of South Asian and Middle Eastern Studies* 19, no. 4 (summer 1996).

Krammer, Arnold. "Arms for Independence: When the Soviet Bloc Supported Israeli." In Walid Khalidi, ed., *From Haven to Conquest.* Beirut: Mu'assasat al-Dirasat al-Filastiniyah, 1971.

Kretzmer, David. *The Legal Status of Arabs in Israel.* Boulder, Colo.: Westview Press, 1990.

Kumaraswamy, P. R. "Special Majority for Golan: Democratic Dilemma of the Rabin-Peres Governments." *Journal of South Asian and Middle Eastern Studies* 22, no. 3 (spring 1999).

Lapidus, Ira M. *A History of Islamic Societies.* New York: Cambridge University Press, 1991.

Layachi, Azzedine. "Political Economies and the Algerian Crisis of Transition." Draft paper presented at MESA, Providence, R.I., 21–24 November 1996.

———. *The United States and North Africa: A Cognitive Approach to Foreign Policy.* New York: Praeger, 1990.

Lebkicher, Roy, George Rentz, and Max Steineke. *The Arabia of Ibn Saud.* New York: Russell F. Moore, 1952.

Lesch, Ann Mosley. "Sudan." In Jay A. Sigler, ed., *International Handbook of Race and Race Relations.* Westport, Conn.: Greenwood Press, 1987.

Lewis, Bernard. *The Arabs in History.* 6th ed. Oxford: Oxford University Press, 1993.

Lewis, Geoffrey. *Modern Turkey.* 4th ed. New York: Praeger, 1974.

Lustick, Jan. *Arabs in the Jewish State: Israel's Control of a National Minority.* Austin: University of Texas Press, 1980.

MacDonald, Robert W. *The League of Arab States.* Princeton: Princeton University Press, 1965.

Mahfadha, 'Ali. "Al-Ardun . . . ila Ayn?" In *Al-Mustaqbal al-Arabi,* June 2000, 22–34.

Manai, A. Supplice Tunisien le jardin secret du général Ben Ali. Paris: La Découverte, 1995.

Mandel, Neville J. *The Arabs and Zionism before World War I.* Berkeley: University of California Press, 1976.

Mango, Andrew. *Turkey.* New York: Thames and Hudson, 1968.

Ma'oz, Moshe. *Syria and Israel: From War to Peacemaking.* Oxford: Clarendon Press, 1995.

Mansfield, Peter. *The Arabs.* 3d ed. Harmondsworth: Penguin, 1992.

Matar, Jamil, and 'Ali E. Hillal. *Al-Nidham al-Iqlimi al-'Arabi: Dirsatun fi al-'Alaqat al-Siyasiyah al-'Arabiyah.* 4th ed. Cairo: Dar al-Mustaqbal al-'Arabi, 1983.

Milani, Moshe M. *The Making of Iran's Revolution: From Monarchy to Islamic Republic.* Boulder, Colo.: Westview Press, 1988.

Mitchell, Richard P. *The Society of the Muslim Brothers.* London: Oxford University Press, 1969.

Mitchell, Timothy. *Colonizing Egypt.* New York: Cambridge University Press, 1988.

Al-Mithaq al-Watani al-Urduni. Amman: Military Presses, 1991.

Momen, Moojan. *An Introduction to Shi'i Islam.* New Haven: Yale University Press, 1985.

Moore, John Norton, ed. *The Arab-Israeli Conflict.* Vol. 3: *Documents.* Princeton: Princeton University Press, 1974.

Morrison, Godfrey. "The King's Gambit." *Africa Report,* November–December 1984.

Mortimer, Robert. "Algeria: The Dialectic of Elections and Violence." *Current History,* May 1997.

———. "Islam and the Multiparty Politics in Algeria." *Middle East Journal* 45, no. 4 (autumn 1994).

———. "Islamists, Soldiers, and Democrats: The Second Algerian War." *Middle East Journal* 50, no. 1 (winter 1996).

Mueller, John, and Karl Mueller. "Sanctions of Mass Destruction." *Foreign Affairs* 78 (May–June 1999).

al-Mulk, Nizam. *The Book of Government; or, Rules for Kings: Siyar al-Mulok or Siyasatnama.* Trans. Hubert Drake. London: Routledge and Kegan Paul, 1978.

Murad, Mohammad Helmy. "Tagrubat al-Ta'adudiyya al-Hizbiyya fi Misr." In Sa'ad al Din Ibrahim, ed., *Al-ta'adudiyya al-Siyassiya wa al-Democratiyya fi al-watan al-'Arabi.* Oman, Jordan: Arab Thought Forum, 1989.

Musa, Hussein. *Al-Bahrain: al-Nidhal al-Watani wa al-Dimoqrati, 1920–1981.* London: al-Haqiqa Press, 1987.

Mutawi', 'Abdullah. "Sanctions on Iraq: Illegal and Indefensible." *Middle East International,* 10 April 1998.

Myrdal, Gunnar. *The Challenge of World Poverty.* New York: Random House, 1970.

al-Nafisi, 'Abdullah Fahd. *Kuwait: al-Ray al-Akhar.* London: Taha Advertising, 1978.

al-Najar, Baqir Ghanim. "Al-Mujtama' al-Madani fi al-Khalij wa al-Jazira al-'Arabiyya." In *Al-Mujtama' al-Madani fi al-Watan al-'Arabi.* Beirut: Center for Arab Unity, September 1992.

al-Naqeeb, Khaldoun H. *Al-Dawlah al-Tasalutiyyah fi al-Mashreq al-'Arabi.* Beirut: Markaz Derasat al-wahdah al-'Arabiyya, 1991.

———. *Al-mujtma' wa al-dawlah fi al-khlij wa al-Gazira al-'Arabiya.* Beirut: Center for Arab Unity, 1987.

———. *Sira' al-qabaliyah wa al-dimocratiyah, Halat al-Kuwait.* London: Dar al-Saqi, 1996.

al-Nashar, 'Ali. *Nasha'at al-Fikr al-Falsafi fi al-Islam.* 4th ed. Cairo: Dar al-Ma'arif, 1969.

Niblock, Tim. *Class and Power in Sudan: The Dynamic of Sudanese Politics, 1898–1985.* New York: State University of New York Press, 1987.

Norton, Augustus Richard. *External Intervention and the Politics of Lebanon.* New York: Foreign Policy Association, 1991.

———, ed. *Civil Society in the Middle East.* New York: E. J. Brill, 1995.

Nyrop, Richard F. *Area Handbook of Algeria.* Washington, D.C.: Government Printing Office, 1972.

O'Brien, Conor Cruise. *The Siege: The Saga of Israel and Zionism.* New York: Simon and Schuster, 1986.

Offe, Claus, and Volker Ronge. "Theses on Theory of the State." In Anthony Giddens and David Held, eds., *Classes, Power, and Conflict.* Berkeley: University of California Press, 1982.

Orr, Akiva. *The Un-Jewish State: The Politics of Jewish Identity in Israel.* London: Ithaca Press, 1983.

Ovendale, Ritchie. *Britain, the United States, and the Transfer of Power in the Middle East, 1945–1962.* New York: Leicester University Press, 1996.

Owen, Roger. *State, Power, and Politics in the Making of the Modern Middle East*. London: Routledge, 1992.

Peretz, Don. *The Government and Politics of Israel*. Boulder, Colo.: Westview Press, 1979.

Pertues, Volker. "Incremental Change in Syria." *Current History*, January 1993.

Piscatori, James, and R. K. Ramanzani. "The Middle East." In Werner I. Feld and Gavin Boyd, eds., *Comparative Regional Systems: West and East Europe, North America, the Middle East, and Developing Countries*. New York: Pergamon Press, 1980.

Poirer, Robert A., and Stephen Wright. "The Political Economy of Tourism in Tunisia." *Journal of Modern African Studies* 31, no. 1 (1993).

al-Qahtani, Fahd. *Zilzal Juhaiman fi Maka*. London: Organization of Islamic Revolution and the Arabian Peninsula, 1987.

Rabinovich, Itimar. "Egypt and the Palestine Question before and after the Revolution." In Shimon Sahmir, ed., *Egypt from Monarchy to Republic*. Boulder, Colo.: Westview Press, 1995.

———. *On the Brink of Peace: The Israeli-Syrian Negotiations*. Princeton: Princeton University Press, 1998.

Radhwan, Fathi. *Asrar Hikomat Yolyo*. Cairo: Madboli, n.d.

Ramadhan, 'Abd al-'Adhim. *Abd al-Nasir wa Azmat Mars 1954*. Cairo: Rose al-Yusuf, 1977.

Rashid, Masood. *Industrialization in Oil-based Economies: A Case Study of Saudi Arabia*. Delhi: ABC, 1984.

el-Rayes, Mohammed D. "Al-Nadhriyyat al-Siasiyya al-Islamiyya." *Dar al-Turath*. 7th ed. Cairo, 1977.

el-Rayyes, Riad Najib. *Riyah al-Janub: al-Yemen wa Dawruhu fi al-Jazira al-'Arabiyya, 1990–1997*. London: Riad el-Rayyes Books, 1998.

———. *Riyah al-Samoom*. Beirut: Riad el-Rayyes Books, 1994.

———. *Riyah al-Shamal*. London: Riad el-Rayyes Books, 1997.

'Abd al-Razeq, Ali. *Al-Islam wa usul al-Hukm*. Beirut: Al-Mu'assassah al-'Arabiyah Li al-Dirasat wa al-Nashr, 1972.

Ritter, Scott. *Endgame: Solving the Iraqi Problem—Once and for All*. New York: Simon and Schuster, 1999.

Roberts, David. *The Ba'ath and the Creation of Modern Syria*. New York: St. Martin's Press, 1987.

Robinson, Glenn E. *Building a Palestinian State: The Incomplete Revolution*. Bloomington: Indiana University Press, 1997.

Rosenhek, Zeev. "The Exclusionary Logic of the Welfare State: Palestinian Citizens in the Israeli Welfare State." *International Sociology* 14, no. 2 (June 1999).

Rouhana, Nadim N. *Palestinian Citizens in an Ethnic Jewish State: Identities in Conflict*. New Haven: Yale University Press, 1997.

Rouleau, Eric. "The Challenges to Turkey." *Foreign Affairs* 72, no. 5 (November–December 1993): 110–26.

———. "Turkey's Dream of Democracy." *Foreign Affairs* 79, no. 6 (November–December 2000): 100–114.

Roux, Georges. *Ancient Iraq*. 3d ed. New York: Penguin Books, 1992.

Rumaihi, Mohamed G. *Bahrain: Social and Political Change since the First World War*. Kuwait City: University of Kuwait Press, 1975.

Safty, Adel. *From Camp David to the Gulf*. Toronto: University of Toronto Press, 1996.

Said, Edward W. *The Politics of Dispossession: The Struggle for Palestinian Self-Determination, 1969–1994*. New York: Random House, 1995.

Saleh, Ahmad Abbas. *Al-Yamin wa al-Yasar fi al-islam.* 2d ed. Beirut: Al-Mo'assasa al-'Arabiyah Leal-Dirasat Wa al-Nashr, 1973.

Salibi, Kamal. *The Modern History of Jordan.* London: I. B. Tauris, 1993.

Salt, Jeremy. "Nationalism and the Rise of Muslim Sentiment in Turkey." *Middle Eastern Studies* 31, no. 1 (January 1995): 13–27.

Sampson, Anthony. *The Seven Sisters: The 100-Year Battle for the World's Oil Supply.* 4th ed. New York: Bantam Books, 1991.

Schissel, Howard. "Tunisia: Facing a Future without Bourguiba." *Africa Report,* November–December 1984.

Schmitz, Chuck. "Civil War in Yemen: The Price of Unity?" *Current History* 94, no. 588 (January 1995): 33–36.

Schwedler, Jillian, ed. *Toward Civil Society in the Middle East? A Primer.* Boulder, Colo.: Lynne-Rienner, 1995.

Scott, Roddy. "Yemen: Arms and the Man." *Middle East,* July–August 1995.

Seale, Patrick. *Assad: The Struggle for the Middle East.* Berkeley: University of California Press, 1988.

———. *The Struggle for Syria: A Study of Post-War Arab Politics, 1945–1958.* London: Oxford University Press, 1965.

al-Shazli, Sa'ad al-Din. *Harb October: Mothakrat.* London: n.p., 1988.

Sherwani, Haroon Khan. *Studies in Muslim Political Thought and Administration.* Philadelphia: Porcupine, 1977.

Shindler, Colin. "Them or Us: How the Israeli Far Right Has Penetrated to the Center of Power." *New Statesman and Society,* 1 March 1991, 23.

Shipler, David. *Arab and Jew: Wounded Spirits in a Promised Land.* New York: Penguin, 1987.

Sick, Gary, and Lawrence G. Potter, eds. *The Persian Gulf at the Millennium: Essays in Politics, Economy, Security, and Religion.* New York: St. Martin's Press, 1997.

Sid-Ahmed, Mohmed. "Ambitieux et risqué, le choix de l'Egypte." *Le Monde Diplomatique,* January 1991.

Simons, Geoff. *Imposing Economic Sanctions: Legal Remedy or Genocidal Tool?* London: Pluto Press, 1999.

———. *Iraq: From Sumer to Saddam.* 2d ed. London: Macmillan, 1996.

———. *The Scourging of Iraq: Sanctions, Law, and Natural Justice.* 2d ed. New York: St. Martin's Press, 1998.

Sinai, Anne, and Allen Pollack, eds. *The Middle East Confrontation States: The Hashemite Kingdom of Jordan and the West Bank.* New York: American Academic Association for Peace in the Middle East, 1977.

Sinora, Hanna. "How the Palestinians Became Refugees: Denial of Basic Human Rights." *First United Nations Seminar on the Question of Palestine.* New York: United Nations, 1980.

Sirhan, Mansur Mohammed. *Waqie' al-Harka al-Fikriya fi al-Bahrain, 1940–1990.* Manama, Bahrain: Makatbat Fakhrawi, 1993.

Southall, Roger. *South Africa's Transkei.* New York: Heinemann, 1982.

Spencer, Claire. "Algeria in Crisis." *Survival* 36, no. 2 (1994).

Sprinzak, Ehud. "The Emergence of the Israeli Radical Right." *Comparative Politics* 21 (January 1989): 171–92.

———. "Netanyahu's Safety Belt." *Foreign Affairs* 77 (July–August 1998): 18–28.

Stookey, Robert W. *The Politics of the Yemen Arab Republic.* Boulder, Colo.: Westview Press, 1978.

Subhi, Ahmad Mahmoud. *Nadhariyat al-Imamah lada al-Shi'ah al-Ithnay 'Ashriyah.* Cairo: Dar al-Ma'arif, 1969.

Subramaniam, Venkateswarier. *Public Administration in the Third World: An International Handbook.* Westport, Conn.: Greenwood Press, 1990.

Swift, Jamie. *Civil Society in Question.* Toronto: Between the Lines, 1999.

Tachau, Frank. *Political Elites and Political Development in the Middle East.* Cambridge, Mass.: Shenkman, 1975.

———. *Turkey: The Politics of Authority, Democracy, and Development.* New York: Praeger, 1984.

Tamadonfar, Mehran. *The Islamic Polity and Political Leadership: Fundamentalism, Sectarianism, and Pragmatism.* Boulder, Colo.: Westview Press, 1989.

Tanör, Bulent, Korkut Boratav, and Sina Aksin. *Türkiye tarihi: Yayin yönetmeni.* Vol. 5. Istanbul: Cem Yayinevi, 1987.

Tessler, Mark. *A History of the Israeli-Palestinian Conflict.* Bloomington: Indiana University Press, 1994.

Al-thakafa Al-jadidah 8, no. 14 (January–February 1960): 130–36.

Tibawi, A. L. *Arabic and Islamic Themes: Historical, Educational, and Literary Studies.* London: Luzac, 1976.

Timmerman, Kenneth R. *The Death Lobby: How the West Armed Iraq.* Boston: Houghton Mifflin, 1991.

Turkiye Ekonomik ve Toplumsal Tarih Vakfi. Uc Sempozyumi Sivil Toplum Kuruluslari. Istanbul: Numune Matbaacilik, March 1998.

United Nations. *Committee against Torture Concludes Twenty-second Session.* Press release, 14 May 1999.

Uzuncarsili, Ismail Hakki. *Osmanli Tarihi.* 6th ed. Vol. 1. Ankara: Turk Tarihi Kurumu Basimevi, 1994.

Van Dam, Nikolas. *The Struggle for Power in Syria.* New York: St. Martin's Press, 1979.

Viorst, Milton. "A Reporter at Large: The House of Hashem." *New Yorker,* 7 January 1991.

Watkins, Eric. "Yemen: Saleh Cracks Down on the Opposition." *Middle East,* October 1995.

Wheatcroft, Andrew. *The Ottomans.* New York: Viking, 1993.

White, Jenny B. "Islam and Democracy: The Turkish Experience." *Current History,* January 1995.

Wolffsohn, Michael. *Israel: Polity, Society, Economy, 1882–1986.* Atlantic Highlands, N.J.: Humanities Press, 1987.

Wright, Robin. *The Last Great Revolution.* New York: Knopf, 1999.

Yergin, Daniel. *The Prize: The Epic Quest for Oil, Money, and Power.* New York: Simon and Schuster, 1991.

Yorke, Valerie. *Domestic Politics and Regional Security: Jordan, Syria, and Israel; The End of an Era?* Aldershot, Hampshire: Ashgate, 1988.

Zeine, Zeine N. *The Emergence of Arab Nationalism.* New York: Caravan Books, 1973.

Zohar, David M. *Political Parties in Israel: The Evolution of Israeli Democracy.* New York: Praeger, 1974.

al-Zubaidi, Layth Abdul Hussan. *Thawarat 14 Tamouz 1958 fi al-'Iraq.* Baghdad: Dar al-Rashid, 1979.

Zunes, Stephen. "The Israeli-Jordanian Agreement: Peace or Pax Americana?" *Middle East Policy* 3, no. 4 (April 1995): 57–68.

Index

Note: Italicized page numbers indicate tables.

TAREQ Y. ISMAEL is professor of political science at the University of Calgary and President of the International Center for Contemporary Middle East Studies at Eastern Mediterranean University (TRNC). His publications include *International Relations of the Contemporary Middle East* (1986); *Middle East Studies: International Perspectives on the State of the Art* (1990); *The Communist Movement in Egypt* (1990); *Politics and Government in the Middle East and North Africa* (1991); *The Gulf War and the New World Order: International Relations of the Middle East* (1994); *Canada and the Middle East: The Foreign Policy of a Client State* (1994); *Civil and Political Rights in the Arab World* (1995); *Social Policy in the Arab World* (1995); *The Communist Movement in Syria and Lebanon* (1997); and *The International Relations of the Middle East in the 21st Century: Patterns of Continuity and Change*.